# THE AMERICAN COLONIES

## IN THE

## EIGHTEENTH CENTURY

**COLUMBIA UNIVERSITY PRESS**
Columbia University
New York

———

**SALES AGENTS**
London
**HUMPHREY MILFORD**
Amen Corner, E.C.

Shanghai
**EDWARD EVANS & SONS, Ltd.**
30 North Szechuen Road

# THE AMERICAN COLONIES

## IN THE

# EIGHTEENTH CENTURY

BY

HERBERT L. OSGOOD, Ph.D., LL.D.

PROFESSOR OF HISTORY IN COLUMBIA UNIVERSITY

VOLUME I

New York

COLUMBIA UNIVERSITY PRESS

1924

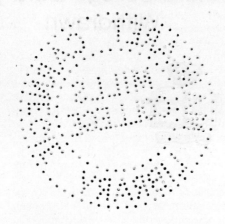
PRINTED BY
THE PLIMPTON PRESS
NORWOOD · MASS · U·S·A

# NOTE

The manuscript of *The American Colonies in the Eighteenth Century* was left nearly complete at the time of the author's death, September 11, 1918. He intended to write a chapter on slavery as it stood before the law in the colonies and affected government with respect to land, defence, finance and other matters, and another chapter in which he would compare institutional tendencies in the continental colonies with those of Ireland and the West India islands, discussions — especially the latter — where his power of generalization would have had full play. His final chapter lacks some paragraphs that he had planned upon the Peace of Paris. He intended also to write an essay briefly summing up conclusions from the four volumes, whose value, if he could have had the opportunity to finish it, might be guessed by reference to those which he inserted at the close of volumes two and three in his earlier work.

His last illness came without much preliminary warning, and there was no time for going over his manuscript with the strict revision that he doubtless would have given it. Consequently there fell to the unready hands of the undersigned many matters of detail, filling in blanks, checking references and developing some notes that had been roughly indicated, working out an analytical table of contents, *et cetera*. The author's handwriting was small, somewhat cramped and difficult to copy, and without doubt there are errors in the text as it is presented to the reader which his practiced eye would have immediately detected. Cordial thanks are due to Dr. Austin Baxter Keep for his very generous cooperation in reading proofs.

Quite unexpectedly the problem of publication turned out to be difficult, and for a long time, indeed, seemed insoluble. Though there was universal esteem for the author and his work, commercial publishers believed that the volumes could not be sold in sufficient numbers to pay for their production. The resources of endowed presses were found to be inadequate for such an enterprise. Finally the publication by the Columbia University Press was made possible through a substantial donation from Mr. Dwight W. Morrow, once a student of Professor Osgood in the School of Political Science at Columbia.

DIXON RYAN FOX

# PREFACE

THE present volumes are a continuation of " The American Colonies in the Seventeenth Century," the last installment of which was published by the author in 1907. In that work the history of the colonies was brought down to the English Revolution, though in the case of some of the provinces, which were founded subsequent to the Restoration, it was necessary to follow their development to later dates. But in the present work the account of every colony and of every subject is resumed at the point where it was left in the preceding volumes.

Though the point of view and the method of treatment in the present work are substantially the same as in its predecessor, some variations will be noticeable. I have not attempted to continue the history of such subjects as the land system, the judiciary, finance and the systems of defence in the different types of colonies, which were so necessary in the account of the earlier period. One reason for this is that in such matters the changes of the eighteenth century occurred only in minor details and with them it is useless further to cumber the pages of the work. New and really significant developments in these lines are referred to in the text, in connection with more general movements of which they formed a part.

The classification of the colonies, which was illustrated from all points of view in the earlier volumes, has of course been adhered to in this; but with a difference. When treating of colonial beginnings in the seventeenth century, it was necessary to make types of colonial government the basis upon which the material in the work as a whole was classified. But when the narrative reaches the eighteenth century, a different set of conditions must be met. From that time on the controlling fact of the situation was the gradual coalescing of the colonies into one system, under the control of the British government. Though the two types of chartered colonies — the feudal elements in the system — continued to exist, their number steadily diminished and about those which survived were thrown restrictive regulations and various lines of administrative control. This fact has made it necessary in the present volumes to consider the colonies together and as a whole. Therefore the material contained in them could not be classified on the basis merely of chartered colonies and provinces or imperial control, but the development of the colonies as a whole, in their internal growth, their interrelations and their connection with Great Britain, must be traced chronologically. Their growth into one system, or into a part of a somewhat larger system, should thus be made to appear. There is no doubt whatever but that the group of continental colonies, in most essential particulars, and especially in their capacity for growth, constituted by far the most important part of the British Empire as it then existed. The dominions of Spain vastly surpassed them in extent, but it has not yet been shown that they contained within themselves a potentiality of growth in the elements of political and social power which equalled this group of thirteen British colonies. In the present volumes an effort has been made to trace their development during a period of seventy years, — from 1690 to 1763.

Under the conditions which existed in this period, the arrangement and organization of material has been more difficult than was the corresponding task for the seventeenth century. Viewing the subject, as I have done, from the political standpoint, it has been absolutely necessary to bring out, through the entire period, the growth and individuality of the colonies. They were the political structures of the time and no sectional grouping of them, except to an extent in the case of New England, was possible. To give such individual treatment in the case of thirteen colonies, without sacrificing unity and clearness, has not been an easy task. At the same time imperial relations have demanded adequate attention, so that the position of the colonies as a part of the British Empire might be made clear. Certain general subjects, like the colonial wars, immigration, Indian affairs and ecclesiastical relations, possessed intercolonial significance and have been treated as distinct wholes.

tainly has no right to employ. Self-satisfied indifference probably accounts for her neglect while, year after year, students who have the boldness to inquire into her history subsequent to the fall of the Puritan Commonwealth are forced, with pen and pencil, to grope their way laboriously through the manuscript volumes of perhaps the most valuable body of state archives on this continent. How long, in these days of widely diffused interest in history and of the cheap printing press, will this condition of things be permitted to continue?

Such being the scope and difficulties of the subject, it is apparent that, if a single and unaided hand were to attempt the collection and organization of the material for the present work, and in addition should write it, the better part of a lifetime would be needed. But the labor which has been necessary to bring the task to its present stage of completion has been performed in about a decade, and that too while the author, during nearly all the time, has discharged his regular academic duties. This means that much assistance has been rendered by others in the collection of material, though the planning, organization and writing is all his own. In this sense the work is a cooperative one, and due acknowledgment for the assistance received is made to the many by whom it has been rendered.

First of all thanks are due to Columbia University for the opportunities for teaching and research which it has offered, during a period of nearly thirty years, to the author of these volumes. Some welcome financial aid has been given by the University, but chiefly is the author indebted to her for the sympathy of colleagues on the Faculty and for the inspiration and help which have come from a generation of students who have passed through his classrooms. But notwithstanding this, had it not been for a grant from the Carnegie Institution, continued for a number of years, it would have been impossible to collect the material upon which the work is based. For this sincere thanks are due. To the help and sympathy of friends, both in my immediate family and outside, much is also due and is gratefully acknowledged. To the able and faithful work of three of my former students, Drs. George A. Wood, Newton D. Mereness and Elmer B.

Efforts toward colonial union occupy much the same position. The economic side of events also has not been neglected, but appears in abundant references, not only in connection with individual colonies but with the evolution of British policy. Though not in any wise denying the great importance of economic history, the point of view which I have chosen for this work is the politico-economic, with the emphasis on the first part of the compound. Others, of course, will put the emphasis on the last part, but that the two never can be and never ought to be separated, is perfectly evident.

The history of any nation, at any stage of its development, is a subject of great complexity, far too great to be thrown upon the canvas of a single historical work. He who essays to write such a history, at the present stage of knowledge, must choose from among a number of points of view, without denying the equal validity of others, and adhere consistently to his chosen path throughout. In the volumes of the present work already published, and in those which are now in process of completion, a persistent effort has been made to fulfill this condition. Criticism, it is believed, should be directed to the measure of success attained under this limitation.

The plan which has been adopted, in order to avoid confusion and to overcome as many as possible of the difficulties of the subject, is the following one. As the colonial wars were a very prominent series of events in this period, and those which fundamentally distinguished it from the periods which preceded and followed, they have been thrown into the foreground and made in a sense the basis upon which the material has been classified. The work has been divided into parts according to the succession of wars and intervals of peace in the prolonged struggle between the British and French. In connection with these, though not in unnecessary subordination to them, have been traced the varied and successive phases of British imperial policy, the development of those general aspects of colonial life above referred to, and the growth and characteristics of the individual colonies.

The greatest difficulties have been those connected with the treatment of the colonies as distinct political structures. They, of course, were institutionally and socially unlike in many particulars and yet were grouped together and subject to a certain uniform pressure and many similar influences. The problem has been to bring out their peculiarities and their uniformities, the characteristics which each possessed in distinction from all the rest and also the place which each was coming to occupy in relation to its immediate neighbors and to the group and empire as a whole. As the process has gone on, these colonies have assumed, in the mind of the author, some of the aspects of personality, and he has treated them as a group of companions, being equally interested in doing justice to the characteristics and ambitions of every member of the group. This has been the effort and the ideal, though doubtless it has been only imperfectly realized. The problem is analogous to the more difficult one of writing, for example, a genuine international history of Europe — something which has never yet been really attempted, but toward which the efforts of the future should be directed. It should be something other than a bundle of national histories, but rather should deal with the continent and its adjacent islands as a unit and in outline exhibit, in their slow evolution through centuries, the position, characteristics, relations and ideals of every nationality which has had a decisive influence upon the world and upon the European section of the human race. Books likewise have been written upon the subject of which I am now treating which are only a bundle of colonial histories. In others the subject has been so chopped and divided that the reader finds it difficult, if not impossible, to perceive either unity or development. In the present volumes and their predecessors an effort has been made to avoid these faults and so to present the history of the colonies, on its political and institutional side, as to show that there was in their development both unity and diversity, and also to show to a limited extent in what these respectively consisted.

In the comparative treatment of the colonies themselves New York has been brought into a position of considerable prominence. It is not the intention to base upon this any undue claims to leadership on the part of that province. But, of course, in all military relations in which Canada was involved New York was the strategic centre of the colonial

territory. In a period of wars, therefore, it necessarily [held?] a prominent place, while in all that pertained to In[dian] relations its position was a leading one. As the period [pro]gressed, New York also became increasingly prominent [as a] centre of trade. In the mixture of national stocks w[hich] contributed to its population, New York, and the m[iddle] colonies as a group, differed widely both from New Eng[land] and from the colonies further south. In this respect [it] foreshadowed more accurately the nation which was t[o be] than did the colonies of more purely English descent. [The] location of the colonies which lay between the Great L[akes] and the Potomac gave them a predominant influence in [all] that related to the frontier, colonial union and westw[ard] expansion. It is therefore proper that they should be giv[en a] corresponding place in the treatment of the period, and [that] attention should early be called to the peculiar condit[ions] which were to give rise to sectionalism in the extreme no[rth]east and the extreme south.

In addition to the difficulties inherent in the natur[e of] the subject, the investigator of this period is also compe[lled] to face equally great obstacles of another sort. These a[rise] from the condition of the source material of the per[iod.] Not only is it varied in character and scattered among [the] archives of all the thirteen original states, with the m[ost] important part of it still procurable only in London, but m[uch] more than one-half of it still exists only in manuscr[ipt.] Among the unprinted material are to be found by far [the] most important sources which relate to the British [and] imperial side of the subject. At present there is no likeli[hood] that even the Journal of the Board of Trade, a source [of] prime importance, will be printed for many years to co[me.] Efforts which were formerly made by the states to proc[ure] and publish the materials which relate to their own hist[ory] in the eighteenth century have apparently come nearly [to] a standstill. Small undertakings are still possible, but [the] future offers little immediate prospect for large enterpri[ses] of this nature. Meantime, Massachusetts and South Ca[ro]lina stand shoulder to shoulder as the most backward sta[tes] in this regard, the latter using as an excuse for its indiffere[nce] the plea of poverty, an argument which Massachusetts c[an]

Russell, who have assisted me in collecting material and otherwise perfecting the work, I am most deeply indebted. The Reports upon the material in the British Archives which relates to America, prepared by Professor Charles M. Andrews for the Carnegie Institution, have saved much labor and, in my case, have well served the purpose for which they were intended. To the officials of the Public Record Office and the British Museum thanks are due for their courtesy during many months when heavy drafts were made upon them to meet the demands of this work. Similar thanks are also due to the keepers of the archives of nearly all the thirteen original states of this Union, as well as to the officials of most of the State Historical Societies, and to those of certain of our largest public and private libraries, for the readiness with which they have put at my disposal the rarities of their collections, both in print and manuscript.

In submitting this history of the American Colonies during the Eighteenth Century to the public, one final word should be said. Though many have already written upon certain aspects of the period, and some have attempted to cover it as a whole, it has yet been accurately characterized as the " unknown period " of American history. This is due to the almost total neglect, on the part of the more ambitious writers concerning it, of the British or imperial side of the subject. Moreover, no one has previously attempted so thoroughly to investigate the individual colonies as to show what they were in themselves, or how they were related to one another and to the British government. This may be attributed in part to the inaccessibility of the sources, but more to a failure to study the colonies as institutions of government and to examine the structure and policy of the old British empire as a whole. This has now been attempted for the first time, and much of the material which is here presented has never before been used. In scope and plan, as in much of its material, this is a pioneer work. It suffers from the imperfections of such an effort, and no claim is made that it exhausts any line of inquiry. May it be accepted as an attempt to explore a region which hitherto has been to a large extent uncharted, and to view the main features of a period which many, both in America and in Great Britain, have been disposed to ignore as too remote, petty or uninteresting to deserve special attention. A period of history in which the beginnings of both the American nation and the British empire may be traced is certainly not unworthy of study.

# CONTENTS

## VOLUME I

### PART ONE

*THE COLONIES DURING THE FIRST TWO INTERCOLONIAL WARS,* 1690–1714

#### CHAPTER I

## CHAPTER II

### The Wars of the Eighteenth Century in General

## CHAPTER III

### The First Intercolonial War, 1689–1697

## CHAPTER IV

COLONIAL ADMINISTRATION DURING THE EARLY YEARS OF THE WAR. ORIGIN OF THE BOARD OF TRADE

## CHAPTER V

### COMMERCIAL RELATIONS BEFORE AND AFTER THE ACT OF TRADE OF 1696

## CHAPTER VI

ADMINISTRATIVE CHANGES CONSEQUENT TO THE TRADE ACT OF 1696.
POLICY TOWARD THE CHARTERED COLONIES

## CHAPTER VII

### WAR, FACTION AND FINANCE IN NEW YORK UNDER SLOUGHTER AND FLETCHER, 1691–1697

CHAPTER VIII

COLONIAL UNION: THE ADMINISTRATION OF THE EARL OF
BELLOMONT IN NEW YORK AND NEW ENGLAND,
1697–1701

## CHAPTER IX

### Massachusetts at the Beginning of the Colonial Wars

## CHAPTER X

### VIRGINIA DURING THE FIRST INTERCOLONIAL WAR

## CHAPTER XI

### Maryland as a Royal Province. The Administration of Copley and Nicholson, 1691–1698

## CHAPTER XII

### SURRENDER OF PROPRIETARY GOVERNMENT IN NEW JERSEY, 1702

## CHAPTER XIII

### The Second Intercolonial War, 1702–1713

## CHAPTER XIV

### Indian Relations during the Early Eighteenth Century. Development of the Western Frontier

## CHAPTER XV

### THE POLICY OF THE BRITISH GOVERNMENT IN REFERENCE TO THE PRODUCTION OF NAVAL STORES

## CHAPTER XVI

### Piracy during the Early Colonial Wars

# PART ONE

## THE COLONIES DURING THE FIRST TWO INTERCOLONIAL WARS, 1690–1714

# CHAPTER I

GREAT BRITAIN AT THE BEGINNING OF THE EIGHTEENTH
CENTURY. THE ADMINISTRATIVE FRAMEWORK
OF THE EMPIRE

IN American as well as in English history the year 1690
marks approximately the transition from the seventeenth to
the eighteenth century. This was the date of the second
English Revolution, and it was the time when events
assumed the form which were to be characteristic of the
coming century. If we look at the fall of James and the
accession of William from the standpoint of domestic relations and of the British constitution, we can hardly call this
event a revolution at all. It simply confirmed the supremacy
of parliament and gave to this condition, which had long
existed in fact, a more precise statement in written law.

But in the domain of international relations the Revolution was an event of the greatest importance,[1] for it broke
the alliance which had existed for twenty years between
France and Great Britain and ushered in a period of conflict between those two powers which was to continue until
1815. In the person of William III the great European opponent of Louis XIV was brought to the British throne. A
system of alliances against France was founded which was to
continue without decisive change for more than half a century. The unrest in Great Britain itself, which had been
occasioned by the alliance between the Stuarts and France,
was gradually brought to an end. A barrier to the ambitious
plans of the French monarchy was set up which in the end
was to prove insuperable. Thus a system of relations, both
internal and external, was evolved which was deemed natural
and permanent, which Burke was later to glorify by his
eloquence as a great and most abiding achievement in government. It was the period of the rule of the British aris-

[1] Seeley, Growth of British Policy.

tocracy, through a parliament both houses of which it controlled and ultimately with a royal family which was virtually its instrument. For the principles of a dynastic policy, which had previously received crushing blows in England, was substituted one based on national interests in which trade and oversea expansion held a leading place. In this the spirit of the island kingdom found its natural expression.

In the course of the three decades which preceded this Revolution the naval supremacy of the Dutch in the waters of northern Europe had been broken, as well as their control over the carrying trade of the world. To this certain faults in the system of government of the United Provinces as well as the hostility of France had contributed; but the result was chiefly due to the influence of the British acts of trade, to the vigorous exercise by the British of the practice of search and seizure in the Channel, and to a series of great naval victories. A gain of great importance to England which was incidental to this was, that plans to close the Sound to her trade were defeated and her access to the Baltic countries, from which came her supply of naval stores, was kept open. In the Triple Alliance of 1667 Sir William Temple had helped to foreshadow a combination of sea powers of northwestern Europe under the lead of England. With the restoration of the House of Orange in the Netherlands and the marriage of William III with Mary of England, the possibility on the dynastic side of consummating this alliance was secured. The policy of unlimited territorial and military aggression, combined with the Revocation of the Edict of Nantes, which was pursued by Louvois and Louis XIV during the years following 1680, helped powerfully to convince both the English and Dutch that a rival combination was necessary. The reckless measures of James II in England effectually broke the hold of the Stuarts upon that country and revealed to all Protestants more clearly than ever the danger which their pro-Catholic and French alliance involved. The elaborate preparations of the French for the annexation of territories of indefinite extent along the Rhine prepared the leading states of the Empire to enter an alliance of which the Sea Powers would be the nucleus. Spain, meantime, was being drawn away from its Hapsburg connection, which had continued since the time of Charles V, and was falling into the wake of France. This was the European background of the Revolution, the alignment of the powers which made William's expedition and his winning of the throne of England a necessity and a masterstroke of policy. It cemented the alliance of the Sea Powers, brought the Dutch permanently into a position subordinate to England and opened the way for infinite combinations with German and Scandinavian states beyond, and even with Russia. Since the Thirty Years War, with so much besides which it had wrecked in Germany, had destroyed the power of the Hanseatic League, no dangerous competitor of Great Britain in naval strength was left among the states about the Baltic and North Seas. So far as these states were concerned, she could continue to enjoy the advantages which the fortunate location of the British Isles gave her for the development of naval and commercial supremacy over the Narrow Seas and the ocean beyond. Provided her lead could be established, the mercantile system of policy was admirably contrived to enable her to maintain it.

Spain was far on her decline. France was left as the one rival which stood in the way of Great Britain; and a powerful one she was, in resources and position the leading nation of Europe. With a long and accessible coast line, on both the Atlantic and the Mediterranean, France was well situated for naval, commercial and colonizing enterprises in any quarter of the globe, though she had few and inadequate harbors. Her Norman and Breton fishermen, with much more than a century of experience behind them on the Newfoundland Banks, were among the best seamen in the world; but they scarcely equalled one-half of the number of seamen available in Great Britain.[1] France, after all, was predominantly agricultural and the wide extent of her interior provinces was destined long to keep her so. The French, however, already had possession of the Gulf and great waterway of the St. Lawrence, which led straight into the interior of the North American continent. Her explorers had dis-

---

[1] A seaman, said Sir William Petty, is a navigator, a merchant and a soldier, and so is more valuable than any one of these could be by himself alone.

covered the Mississippi, and the chance of occupying the interior of this continent and confining the English to the seaboard or actually forcing them into the sea was far from being an impossibility in 1680.  French interests were also established in the Caribbean and the way was open for their development in Africa and the Orient.  But in obedience to tradition, the chief efforts of France were turned by her government into the comparatively narrow fields of European exploitation.  Her armies were sent to the Rhine and the Netherlands frontier, and into Spain and Italy.  Her energies were exhausted in the vain task of attempting to dominate Europe.  For a few small territories on the Rhenish frontier she sacrificed the chance of ultimately securing a continent across seas.  After winning the battle of Beachey Head and losing the more important one of La Hogue, her navy sank into comparative neglect and land warfare absorbed the chief attention and resources of the nation.  Her other effort to invade the British Isles through Ireland was defeated in 1690 at the Boyne, and, with the exception of the weak attempt of 1715, the British remained undisturbed in what was virtually their impregnable island fortress until near the middle of the eighteenth century, their resources steadily increasing from commerce and the growth of manufacturing, while their rival was recovering from exhaustion and preparing for another series of continental wars.

In addition to this the Huguenots, when driven from their homes by ruthless persecution, were allowed to find a refuge under foreign flags and went to strengthen the rivals and enemies of France.  Had she chosen to liberalize ecclesiastical relations in Canada sufficiently to make existence for them tolerable there, or had she permitted the founding of a colony on the Mississippi for their exclusive use, she might in the end have dominated the American continent.  But her government was too strong and confident for that, and what the weakness of the early Stuarts made possible for England in the case of the Puritans was cast aside with disdain by Louis XIV.  This of itself was enough to carry the day against France in North America, and when this blunder is considered in connection with the other miscalculations which have been mentioned, it will appear that the struggle for colonial possessions was as good as decided before the first stage of the conflict was ended. But on the British side also natural resources at the beginning were not large, government at home lacked intelligence and energy, in the colonies unity of action on a large scale was quite impossible, and until the very last stage of the struggle was reached the decision was left almost wholly to the comparative growth of population and resources among the British and French colonists respectively. This explains the long continuance of a conflict in America between two parties who were extremely unequal in natural strength but between whom for more than half a century the chances of success seemed equally balanced. The course of events in America was conditioned throughout by the struggle in Europe, and that reached a provisional issue with the treaty of Utrecht. After a generation of comparative quiet the conflict was resumed, to reach another provisional issue at the treaty of Paris in 1763. But this event was decisive in the colonies, and since that date there has been no question of the leadership of Great Britain as a naval and colonizing power. Such is the background — chiefly European — of the period whose history, so far as the English upon the continent of North America were concerned, it will now be our duty to trace.

In explaining the development of British institutions in America we have reached the period of the predominance of royal provinces. Chartered colonies now were slowly but steadily diminishing in number and administrative restrictions were being thrown around those which were to be permanent. As royal provinces were governed directly by the crown, and as the attention paid by Great Britain to the colonies was for the time steadily increasing, it is necessary at the outset to describe, though only in outline, the framework of the British government so far as it was related to the colonies. We shall begin with parliament.

By the Revolution the long struggle between crown and parliament had been brought to an end through the final triumph of the latter. By the act of settlement, a decade later, a parliamentary title to the throne was definitely established. It was therefore inevitable not only that the ultimate control of affairs should be in the hands of parliament, but that this fact should be more and more frankly recognized. During the reigns of William and Anne there was hesitation in certain quarters upon this point, but with the accession of the Hanoverian line all doubt respecting it was laid to rest. After the Revolution the trend toward commerce and industry, which had been strengthening since the struggle with the Dutch had begun at the middle of the century, received a further impulse through the steady growth of the colonies and trading companies and the conflict which now began with France. Thenceforward trade ocupied a large part of the attention of the two houses, and especially of the lower house. Subjects of this kind were closely related to those of revenue and expenditure. The complicated system of customs duties and the important contribution which came from that source to the public revenues were an index of the value of the foreign and colonial trade of the nation. War vastly increased the importance of questions of this nature. Supply bills, with their contributory and related subjects, now held the chief place upon the calendars, especially of the house of commons. Attention must necessarily be given to them at every session. Problems of defence by sea and land, for which they furnished the sinews, demanded less continuous attention than did revenue bills, while in comparison the attention given to other subjects was desultory.

The trade of Great Britain, considered as a source of national wealth and even from the standpoint of public revenue, had by this time become an object of large and steadily increasing importance. With its protection and that of her American colonies and the various trading stations which her adventurers had established along the coasts of Africa and Asia, the navy was intimately concerned. Any one who reads comprehensively the British sources of the time, with whatever bodies or offices they may be concerned, must be impressed with the wide extension and manifold character which British interests had already attained outside of Europe. The impression made by reading the journals of parliament is no less strong than that which is afforded by the records of the various executive offices. We have now definitely reached the time when the merchants and their interests secured large and, in certain respects, controlling recognition in councils of state. As a class they formed a very important element in the membership of the house of commons. The parliament, including of course the king, stood at the centre of the political organism. Before it, especially before the lower house, came all the more serious questions of trade regulation and colonial interests throughout the British oversea possessions. Either as a whole or through their committees the houses called at their discretion upon the king and the various departments or executive boards for information bearing upon questions of trade and colonization. Testimony was received in written or oral form, was digested by committees and reported to the house where, after further debate, it might be embodied in statutes. Reports were or might be periodically required from administrative boards, in order that the houses might keep themselves informed upon the condition of trade and the colonies. If controversy, disturbance or a crisis had developed at any point or in any interest, the tables of the houses were likely soon to be loaded with papers relating to the questions at issue. Trade and other statistics were also regularly sought as the basis of finance legislation. Subjects and proposals in great number were considered by the houses which never found their way into statutes. But when the highest expression of authority was sought, whether by officials or by others, it was found in an act of parliament. And, subject to limitations of space and administrative efficiency, the force of such acts reached to all oversea dominions, however remote. In this broad and inclusive sense the dependencies were an extension of the realm and parliament was the centre of the entire imperial fabric. [1]

In the British system colonial administration has never been separated from the government of the realm. The securing of dependencies added new duties and subjects to those which previously occupied the attention of officials. A few additional organs of administration had to be provided, but no radical changes were made and the additional

[1] The confirmation of this may be obtained by collecting from any of the journals of parliament, especially after 1689, and from the statutes, the material relating to trade and the dominions.

business was done in accordance with the spirit and forms which had long been developing in the administration of the realm. When statutes were passed their purpose was to define or further extend recognized policies, the duty of enforcing which was imposed on the executive. It was the executive, as previously organized and with such additions as the task of securing dominions beyond seas necessitated, upon which rested the duty of administering the colonies and enforcing in detail the policies which itself and the nation through parliament prescribed. In my earlier work, as well as in many other accessible sources, the nature of the British executive, metaphorically called "the crown," has been described, and the changes through which it passed prior to 1690, so far as they affected the colonies, have been traced. This ground need not be traversed again, neither is it necessary for the purposes we have in view to go into the technicalities of this subject or treat it in detail. That belongs to the history of the British constitution. Preparatory to a discussion of the American colonies from the standpoint which has been chosen in this work, it is more important to know what was done in England and the probable motives therefor than painfully to follow in all cases the routine of action among the executive offices and boards with the help of which it was accomplished. In certain cases this may well be done by way of illustration, but generally the main results will be sought rather than all the steps by which they were reached.

But we are now fairly committed to the task of tracing the development of the British system of administration as illustrated in the history of the colonies upon the continent of North America. The earlier stages of that evolution, while the feudal relations which arose from the existence of so many chartered colonies were predominant, have already been described. We are entering upon a period when royal provinces were assuming more and more the leading place. As dependencies they were directly under royal administration; that was their essential characteristic. The position of parliament in the body politic as a whole has just been indicated. But contemporaneous with the events which are to be described certain changes were in progress in the British executive which it is necessary briefly to indicate, while in a properly balanced account of the system of royal provinces some further attention to the boards and officials in England that administered them is necessary.  The facts and changes to which we refer in some cases had their origin prior to 1690, but they came into full operation after that date.

At the centre of the British executive stood the monarch, surrounded by a group of officials and boards which were developing into the modern departments.  The king, though possessed of only limited powers, was the source of office and honor and the sovereign to whom allegiance was due. All governmental acts were done in his name.  His assent was necessary to every statute and to all important executive acts, while his influence upon measures of government was, or might be, very great.  But his acts were performed with the advice of a council or body of ministers and upon them rested more or less fully the responsibililty for the measures and policy adopted.  These were grouped, at the close of the seventeenth century, in and around the privy council, from which the treasury and admiralty were to an extent differentiated.  It was in the privy council and the cabinet, which was now developing out of it, that some of the most interesting changes were going on.  In part these were merely changes in routine, devised apparently in order to facilitate the prompt transaction of business in a body which was always too large for that purpose, and in part they were of great political importance. [1]

Changes of the first class have to do with the development of committees in the privy council.  During the three-quarters of a century which passed before the English Revolution the tendency to the creation of committees in the council was active and reference has already been made to some of the forms under which they appeared.  This practice was kept up during the period of the Restoration — some well known committees of great political importance being formed — and was continued, though with less fre-

[1] Register of the Privy Council, Acts of P. C., Colonial.  Andrews, British Committees, Commissions and Councils of Trade and Plantations, 1622–1675; J. H. U. Studies, XXVII, 1908;  E. R. Turner, Am. Hist. Rev., July and October, 1913, and July, 1914;  ibid., English Hist. Review, October, 1912, and later numbers to April, 1917;  H. W. Y. Temperley, Eng. Hist. Rev., October, 1912.

quency, into the eighteenth century. But under the later Stuarts the custom also began of " appointing all the members of the council to be on a committee," that is of transacting business through committees of the whole. After the Revolution this practice became much more common, continued until the latter part of the eighteenth century and, except for minor and formal affairs, largely supplanted the special committees which at an earlier time had been so numerous. These committees could be attended by any of the councillors who chose to come, but usually the attendance was not large. They were formed for business of all kinds and under a corresponding variety of names. It was also common for them not to confine themselves to the business which was indicated by their names. Prominent among the committees which had to do with oversea affairs were those for Jersey and Guernsey, or Jersey and Guernsey with the addition of one or more American colonies; the " committee for plantation affairs," with various changes in the phraseology of its title; the " committee for hearing appeals from the plantations." Apparently any combination of business which would naturally come before the council at a session might be assigned to one of these committees, and all committees were sometimes combined into a single committee of the whole. The conclusions reached by all these bodies had to be ratified by the council in regular session before they could carry its authority. The committees also met at the Cockpit within the enclosure of Whitehall, while the council usually met at one of the royal palaces. This shows that they were distinct bodies.

Gradually also, during the period from Charles II to the accession of the Hanoverian line, another committee of the whole council was developing, with which the sovereign often met. This was composed of high officers of state and trusted councillors of the king or queen. At its meetings affairs of the highest importance were considered and no formal minutes were kept. It was known as " the committee of the council," " the committee of lords," " certain lords of his Majesty's privy council." With the accession of George I, after which the monarchs ceased regularly to attend, the separation between this body and the council became to all intents complete and the term cabinet, which had long been coming into use, became the regular designation of this body. As time passed the cabinet also increased in size and tended to become unwieldy. Then an inner circle of ministers with special influence developed within it, and the participation of the king was secured largely through interviews of the secretaries of state or others with him in the closet. With the expansion of public business departments were increased and developed. These were bound together by the cabinet, in which the heads of departments, including especially the lord chancellor, held seats. In the departments — the treasury, admiralty, that of the secretaries of state — were carried out in administrative detail the policies which were decided upon by the king and the cabinet as being those for which the support of parliament could be secured. After about 1714 this was the process by which the really important business of the British government was carried on.

Meantime the power of the privy council was steadily declining. This process had long been going on and the Revolution and especially party and cabinet government, as it was fully installed under the Hanoverians, hastened the result. The development of the committee system within the council shows how ill adapted that body as a whole was to the needs of government, even in the early eighteenth century. The rise of the cabinet furnishes conclusive evidence of the same thing. As the Hanoverian period progressed only minor and routine business affecting the realm was brought before the council and its committees. After about 1730 business from this source which came before the council related to such matters as the calling and proroguing of parliament, the election of Scotch peers, the regulation of prices, the appointment of sheriffs, the improvement of turnpikes, inquiries respecting fees, establishment of charities, regulation of the statutes of colleges and universities, issue of charters to boroughs, and granting of pensions.[1]

But the changes which thus took place in the organs through which the business of the realm was administered were not clearly reflected in colonial administration.

[1] See entries in the Privy Council Register of 1732 and succeeding years.

Throughout our colonial period the privy council and its committees retained a large share in the administration of the colonies. The judicial powers which the council lost in the realm by the legislation of the Long Parliament it retained as a court of appeal over the dominions. It also, as we know, approved or disallowed colonial legislation, and in the sphere of general administration there was no subject upon which orders in council could not be issued with important, if not decisive, effect. These three functions the council regularly performed in colonial affairs, only one of which, and that in steadily diminishing degree, it discharged in the affairs of the realm during the eighteenth century. The work of the council in colonial affairs, as it was in the seventeenth century, has already been outlined.[1] As imperial control, beginning with the island colonies and extending to those on the American continent, became more systematic, the activities of the council in this domain underwent a corresponding development. The laws of an increasing number of colonies were submitted for its action. Applications were made for judicial and executive action on appeals. Were the orders in council collected which embodied its decisions upon these and other related affairs, and which are scattered through all classes of colonial papers, as well as in the Privy Council Register, they would go far toward a statement of the substance of British administrative law in colonial matters.

The acts of government which were regularly performed by the monarch were of great variety, but they were done under the advice of the cabinet or ministry, and upon this body rested the political responsibility for them. It is from this statement that the work of the secretary of state must be approached. That office in the eighteenth century was filled by two incumbents, one having charge of the so-called northern, and the other of the southern department. The latter included relations with France and the Romance states and nations of southern Europe, Turkey, the Barbary States, the Western Islands and the American colonies. Though the office was a unit and the two secretaries occasionally

[1] Osgood, Am. Colonies in the 17th Century, III, 16, and other references through the volume.

exchanged duties, until 1768 the head of the southern department was colonial secretary. In those days the secretaries had charge of relations with Scotland and Ireland and also of the duties of the modern home office, including the supervision of domestic trade, industry and police. A secretary's duties therefore were numerous and varied; probably no member of council or cabinet exceeded him in scope or degree of activity. These two officials stood at the centre of affairs and, if they were men of ability, none could exert more influence than they in parliament and over both the details and the main issues of policy.

As a rule, the secretaries of state were the ministers who had most regular access to the monarch. With him they intimately discussed affairs of government, and acted as intermediaries of prime importance between him and parliament, as well as with the nation and world outside. In reference to the colonies their control over appointments to office, over military and naval affairs, diplomacy and large questions of policy, was clear and continuous. The secretary was the keeper of the king's signet and sign manual. These were affixed to royal warrants and it was through them that the will of the king and secretary was most often expressed. In that department they correspond to the orders which were issued by the council.[1] When, for example, a colonial governor was to be appointed, a warrant was issued to the law officers or to the council of trade, or to both, to prepare a bill for the king's signature to pass the great seal. Commissions, as well as instructions, of governors were countersigned by secretaries of state. The same was true when a commission was revoked. Warrants were also issued for the drafting of colonial charters and for the preparation of seals for the colonies. In a similar way warrants were regularly issued for the appointment of colonial secretaries, councillors

---

[1] The Domestic and Colonial Papers are filled with the correspondence of secretaries of state. But the two series of volumes in which the record of their doings is most continuous are the S. P. Dom. Entry Books, Sec. of States' Letter Books, and the Plantations General Royal Letters, Grants and Warrants, both beginning about 1690. The private papers of statesmen who had served in this office, notably the vast collection of the Newcastle Papers, are a mine of information on the politics of the time. Unlike the privy council and other boards, no minutes were kept by the secretaries of state.

and all other patent officers, that is those who were designated by the king.[1] The issue of commissions for the adjustment of boundaries between colonies and for the settlement of other disputes was initiated in the same way. The appointment of special commissioners, like Larkin in 1701 to assist in executing the act for the suppression of piracy, and Nicholson in 1713 to inquire into financial and other conditions in the colonies, were made in similar fashion.

A large and probably the most important part of the correspondence which was carried on between the colonies and the crown passed through the office of the secretary of state who was charged with that jurisdiction. It probably never equalled in volume that which centered within the council or board of trade, but it related to matters which, outside the sphere of trade, were of more decisive importance. Appointments, defence by land and sea, and matters which had a diplomatic bearing were the peculiar concern of the king and secretary. The sources abound in letters which were interchanged between England and the colonies on those subjects. Indian relations were a closely related matter, as also was finance so far as it bore on defence, and they fell largely into the same current. Addresses which were sent from colonial legislatures or other bodies to the king regularly passed through the office of the secretary. The secretaries also were not restrained from writing on other subjects and their correspondence ranged widely over the field of colonial relations. From the intimate knowledge which the secretaries had of public affairs, it may be inferred that their letters, even to colonial officials, might afford unusual insight into policies and events. It also occasionally happened that relations of friendship existed between governors and secretaries of state and then a certain confidential flavor was sometimes given to their letters. Many of the orders of the British government were transmitted to governors and other officials through the medium of letters from the secretaries. Their letters were a constant support to the efforts of the governors in the royal provinces to uphold imperial claims.

[1] The Calendars of State Papers Colonial, our printed Colonial Records and the Mss. Series referred to above contain hundreds of instances of the issue of warrants and of the practice in general of the office of secretary of state.

The dualism which was introduced into the British executive by the development of the cabinet was not so long or so severely felt in the administration of the realm as it was in that of the plantations. This was due to the fact that the power of the council in the realm rapidly declined, but in relation to the plantations that body retained much of its authority during the eighteenth century. Subordinate to the council was the board of trade,[1] though in a less direct way it was also subordinate to the secretary of state. For this reason governors were always required to correspond both with the board of trade and with the secretaries. This caused confusion, for individuals knew not to which office to apply and were often referred from one to the other. Contradictory orders might be issued or the issue of any orders might be prevented. In 1752, as a consequence of the effort of the earl of Halifax, then president of the board, to increase its importance, an order of council was issued that the board of trade should propose the names of persons who were qualified for any or all offices except those in the customs service, and that what concerned governmental matters should be sent by the governors to it, except in the case of subjects which demanded immediate attention and these should be sent to the secretary.

But this was not in line with the natural course of development and the plan of Halifax failed of permanent acceptance. In 1761 that part of the order of 1752 which referred to the wide activity of the board of trade in connection with appointments was revoked. As a matter of fact also, during the war which was just closing, of necessity the most important correspondence had been with the secretary of state When the war was ended and the earl of Shelburne became for a short time president of the board of trade, he tried to secure a better definition of relations with the secretary's office. At this time, too, Thomas Pownall published his "Administration of the Colonies" and criticised the system of divided control at length.[2] In 1766, after Shelburne had become secretary of state in the Rockingham ministry, the

---

[1] The origin and powers of the board of trade will be explained in a later chapter.

[2] Pownall, p. 12 *et seq.*

order of 1752 was entirely revoked and governors were required to send all communications relating to government to the secretaries of state and duplicates thereof to the board for its information, and in the case of matters of a secret nature this even should not be done. Henceforth the inferior position of the board was fixed as that of a body whose advice was to be given only or chiefly in such matters as were submitted to it by the privy council or its committee or by the secretary of state.[1] The establishment, two years later, of the secretaryship for the colonies made no change in this particular.

Colonial finance, like that of the realm, was administered through the treasury. The modern treasury evolved from the mediaeval exchequer, by processes of change which it is not necessary here to outline, but which form an important part of English constitutional history.[2] In the reign of Elizabeth the king's treasurer, who had been simply the financial servant of the monarch, received the title of lord high treasurer. This was a change similar to the rise in the same reign of the queen's secretary to be a principal secretary of state. But yet he remained largely the administrative agent of the monarch, without real control over income or expenditure. The office, however, was a dignified one and in rank stood next to that of the lord chancellor.

In 1612, on the death of the first earl of Salisbury, the office was put in commission, that is a number of officials were appointed to perform the duties which previously had fallen to the lord treasurer. This was the origin of a treasury board, secretaries of state being sometimes among its members. After the Restoration office of the treasury was put permanently in commission and was separated from the exchequer proper, which was the department of account and receipt and where the treasure or funds were actually kept. The Cockpit was as-

[1] Hillsborough to Shelburne, Aug. 14, 1766. C. O. 5/216, Order of Council of Aug. 8, 1766. N. Y. Col. Docs., VII, 848; Fitzmaurice, Life of Shelburne, I, 269 et seq.; Hillsborough to Shelburne, Aug. 14, 1766.

[2] See Madox, History of the Exchequer; Thomas, The Ancient Exchequer; Thomas, History of the Public Departments; Gneist, Englische Verwaltungsrecht; H. Hall, The Customs Revenue of England; Atton and Holland, The King's Customs; Ed. Chamberlayne, Angliae Notitiae, or the State of England; Calendars of Treasury Papers; Andrews, Report on Materials in Pub. Rec. Office, II; Anson, Law and Custom of the Constitution, II.

signed for the use of the treasury, while the exchequer remained
at Westminster. In 1667 the minutes of the treasury board
as a regular series begin and from that time it may be regarded
as an organized department. Lord Godolphin and Robert
Harley, earl of Oxford, in the reign of Anne, were the last
to hold the office of lord high treasurer for any length of time.
In 1714 a board, consisting of the first lord of the treasury,
the chancellor of the exchequer and usually three junior lords,
became permanently the head of the department.[1] The first
of these was always a leading member of the cabinet and came
usually to be prime minister. The second has been more often
the parliamentary leader in the department of finance. The
board usually met on four days of each week and had as a
keeper of their records and helper in the business routine of
the office a secretary to the treasury.

Meantime, as a result of the Revolution of 1689, parliament
assumed control of finance, which originally had been in the
hands of the monarch, but over which the houses had been
contending with the executive for nearly a century. In 1694 the
Bank of England was established to act as financial agent of
the government, and although it was not made in a full sense
the depository of the public funds until 1834, the tendency was
for the exchequer to decline until it became an unimportant
office. Throughout the eighteenth century, however, the cum-
bersome " course of the exchequer " was continued and with it
many sinecure offices with large incomes which served as comfortable berths for political leaders and favorites. By the
" course of the exchequer " is meant the devices for receipt
and issue of funds contrived with the object of seeing that
" the king got his rights and did not pay more than was due
from him." [2] With the reign of Charles II appropriations,
except the king's hereditary revenue, were made in the form of
subsidies, for special purposes. All receipts were kept in separate funds and against these charges were made. Theoretically
payments from the exchequer could be made only on a royal
order, and for this purpose letters of privy seal in various
forms, or royal signs manual, were issued. Based upon these
in theory, but less and less in fact, were the treasury warrants

---

[1] It acted by patent under the great seal.
[2] Anson, *op. cit.*, 312–316, 8 & 9 Wm. III, c. 28.

countersigned by the treasury board, which conveyed the real authority for all payments of money. They were directed to the auditor of receipt and on his orders payments were made. Among the records of the treasury, warrants occupy as important a place as they do among the papers of the secretary of state. They begin with 1660, though the regular series begins with 1676,[1] and they relate to every variety of treasury payment. A separate series of books was also kept for the orders drawn by the auditor on receipt of the treasury warrants and returned to the board for verification and signature. These orders were entered in the treasury books and in the books of the office of the pells and then were forwarded to one of the tellers, who actually opened the chests and made the payments. The treasury board also kept minutes of its frequent meetings and carried on an extensive correspondence with other departments and with officials abroad and at home. Every form of revenue and variety of payment, in both realm and plantations, came directly or indirectly under the cognizance of this board, and therefore its acts and correspondence were of great importance. It prepared elaborate reports to parliament, the privy council and the board of trade, and considered subjects which were referred to it from these and other sources, coming in the form of petitions, memorials or addresses. No appointment could be made or act done which involved expenditure without the consent of the treasury. It was fully conscious of the power which came from its control of the purse and was often more imperious in its spirit than any other department. It was wont to criticise, and often harshly, proposals for additional expenditure and was slow to recognize their utility after they had once been decided upon.

Immediately subordinate to the treasury board, in a way similar to the relation which existed between the board of trade and the privy council, was the customs board or commissioners of the customs. This, in a rudimentary form for England, originated in 1671.[2] Wales was added to its jurisdiction in 1676, Scotland in 1723. In 1742 the commission was divided, nine serving for England and Wales and five for Scotland. The duty of this board was to collect the

---

[1] Andrews, *op. cit.*, 138.
[2] Andrews, *op. cit.*, 111 *et seq.*

customs revenue, nominate and approve the appointment of inferior officers in that department and enforce the performance of their duties. The power of appointment rested with the treasury board. The commissioners corresponded freely on the subject of revenue with other officials and boards in England and with officers in the colonies. They drafted general instructions for governors and special instructions for minor officials on the subject of collecting the revenue, and were concerned in the drafting of acts of trade. They prepared memorials and reports and acted in all respects as experts on the subject of trade as related to revenue.

Immediately subordinate to the customs board was the very large body of officials in the customs service of London and the out-ports of Great Britain, and also the collectors, searchers and surveyors of the imperial customs in the colonies. During the seventeenth and eighteenth centuries the body of legislation concerning the customs became exceedingly complicated and that branch of the revenue, for various reasons, important. With the growth in the intricacy of customs regulation and the increase of duties kept pace the temptation to illegal trading. It was under the act of trade of 1673 that custom houses were established at various colonial ports along the Atlantic coast. These were gradually increased and organized by districts, in most cases each colony constituting a district. The exceptions to this were that the Bahama Islands were joined with South Carolina and the entire coast from southern Rhode Island to the eastern extremity of Nova Scotia was included as the New England district. This was the arrangement in 1755.[1] In every district were one or more custom houses, each with one collector. In the great majority of cases he was the only officer. At Savannah and at Boston there were a collector, a controller, a surveyor and searcher; at New York, a collector and a controller. On the Delaware there were a collector at Lewes and a controller resident at Philadelphia who acted for the entire bay. At

[1] The development of custom houses and their officials can be traced as to location and personnel in the volumes of Edward Chamberlayne's "Angliae Notitiae or the State of England," an annual publication started in 1669 and continued by Chamberlayne and successors — though it was issued somewhat irregularly — until 1755. It was a statistical annual and was the most important predecessor of the Annual Register.

certain ports in Virginia only a surveyor was stationed, but it was intended to have a custom house on every important river.   Until about 1720 this entire coast was under the supervision of one surveyor general, but at about this date a second surveyor general was appointed and the coast and islands from Jamaica to Newfoundland was divided between them, the line of division being the Delaware river.   These officials were all paid from the exchequer of England and belonged to its civil list.   Their duties were the same as those of corresponding English officials, the customs service being strictly an extension of that of the realm.   It should also be borne in mind that each of the colonies had a somewhat developed customs system of its own, under its own officials, and the two coexisted though with an occasional conflict of jurisdiction.   The service, taken as a whole, was not adequate, upon such a length of coast and one with so many inlets and such long unsettled stretches, to the prevention of illegal trade.

By the act of trade of 1663 (15 Charles II) it was provided that in the plantation no vessel should be allowed to load or unload any commodities until its master had made known to the governor, or to an officer authorized or appointed by him, its arrival, name, the name of the master and had proved that she was an English-built ship and was navigated according to law.   As it was impossible for colonial governors to attend to details of this nature, the provision gave rise to the appointment of clerks of the naval office or naval officers.[1]   In Maryland the need of such an official was early recognized.   In 1682 naval officers were established by the colonial governments in both Massachusetts and Rhode Island; but after the establishment of the Dominion of New England Andros appointed a naval officer for that jurisdiction whose status was to be imperial and not merely local.   But, as usual in matters of this kind, events moved more rapidly in the island colonies.   In 1672 the governors of the more important of them were ordered to send to the lord treasurer lists of all bonds which they had taken and of the entries of vessels as required by the statute mentioned above.   Such naval office lists presently began to appear in the records of the treasury.

For a time it was uncertain whether the right to appoint

---

[1] Beer, Old Colonial System, I, 267 et seq.

naval officers belonged to the governors or to the crown. In 1676 a dispute over this subject arose between Henry Coventry, secretary of state, and one of the governors of Barbadoes, which resulted in a settlement of the question in favor of the claims of the crown. Coventry wrote at the time, " that it concerneth his Majesty to be a little better acquainted with those that bear offices in his Plantations than of late he hath been, for till some late Orders of the Councill, his Majesty hardly knew the Lawe or the men by which his Plantations were governed. The Governor was the only person known to him, but his Majesty was resolved to be better acquainted with them and let them know, they are not to govern themselves, but be governed by him." This very aptly described the attitude which the home government was assuming, especially toward the chartered colonies. In 1692 and again in 1698 laws of Massachusetts were disallowed in England because they specified powers and duties of naval officers in such a way as could be done only under the authority of English statutes. Therefore, as time progressed, the colonies limited themselves to determining the fees of these officials.

By the administrative act of 1696 naval officers and their appointment were distinctly mentioned. It was provided that within two months, or as soon thereafter as was convenient, they should give proper security to the custom board for the performance of their duty, the governors to be answerable for their neglect. The duty of the naval officer was to enter and clear vessels, whether they were bound for Great Britain, for foreign countries or islands or were engaged in the coastwise trade. He had to examine and record the certificates or coquets presented by the masters showing that bond had been given at the port of departure as required by the laws of trade, to give permit to land goods, to reload, to examine and record certificates of lading and the bond that the return voyage would be made in full conformity with the requirements of the trade acts. As the collector had also to examine these papers the one officer could check the other, provided the two were not acting in collusion.

The collection and regular payment of the revenue which was levied by the respective colonies was a matter of importance to the home government, for upon that depended the salaries of certain royal officials and the support of the provincial governments. Until late in the seventeenth century no effective steps to this end were taken. In 1663 an office with the title of receiver general of plantation revenues was created and bestowed on Thomas Ross and Thomas Chiffinch. The income from the office was fixed at £400 and it appears to have been sublet to George Povey. The grantees were interested only in the revenues of Barbadoes and the Leeward islands and made no attempt to inspect or regulate the revenues of the other colonies.[1] On the continent the quit rents of Virginia became early an object of attention and by patent in 1650 Colonel Henry Norwood was made treasurer and escheator of that province, an office which included responsibility for collection of the quit rents.[2] It is doubtful if Norwood performed these duties during the decade of the Commonwealth. But the Restoration found him in office and he continued to hold the position until 1669. But he neglected to account for his receipts and affairs drifted on at loose ends until 1680.

Meantime the office of auditor was created by the Virginia assembly, to be held only by members of the council, and Thomas Stegg, Jr., was appointed to it by royal patent. He held it till his death in 1670, when John Lightfoot received an appointment in England as Stegg's successor. But the former governor, Edward Diggs, had already been appointed by the farmers of the customs in England to execute in Virginia an order of council of 1668-9 for the better enforcement of the acts of trade.[3] Governor Berkeley also appointed Diggs to the vacant auditorship of Virginia before the date of Lightfoot's patent, and, as Diggs was a member of the council there and an old resident and Lightfoot was not, when it came to a contest between the two claimants, it was proved that Diggs had the superior qualifications and the king, at the close of 1671, ordered that Lightfoot should be suspended and Diggs continued in the possession of the office. He was succeeded by Giles Bland.

[1] Cal. St. P. Col. 1661–1668, pp. 35, 112, 128, 141, 142, 182, 482.

[2] Blathwayt, Journal.

[3] Cal. St. P. Col. 1669–1674, pp. 40, 68, 69, 297. As to Stegg and his connection with the Byrd family, which later rose to prominence, see Bassett, Reports of Am. Hist. Assoc., 1901, I, 556, *et seq.* Andrews, *op. cit.*, 143.

In 1679 a comprehensive investigation of the budgets of the royal provinces was made by the committee of the privy council [1] and it was decided to establish permanent revenues in Jamaica and Virginia. It was in connection with this general movement that the office of surveyor and auditor general of the king's revenues in America was created, and William Blathwayt was appointed as its first incumbent.[2] The purpose of this measure, as stated in Blathwayt's commission, was to secure a more orderly administration of the revenues in the royal provinces by means of audit and the systematic stating of accounts. The functions which were supposed to be performed by the auditor of the exchequer in England were to be extended to the colonies. Collectors and other local revenue officers there — including the auditor of Virginia who now became a deputy under Blathwayt — were to be kept better up to their duties through the pressure exerted upon them by this superior official. According to his commission, the accounts of such officials in reference to every branch of royal revenue in their provinces since the Restoration were to be submitted to Blathwayt and by him to be examined and stated, and this was to be done in accordance with directions which he should receive from the treasury, toward the perfecting of which he naturally would make suggestions. Under warrants from the treasury he was to appoint and remove deputies in the plantations, and in addition to their services he was also to receive the aid of all officials in the said colonies. His control extended over every form of hereditary and appropriated revenue which belonged to the king in the respective colonies, but not to the revenue which was collected under authority of acts of parliament. Over customs duties collected in England on colonial products he of course had no jurisdiction. He was entitled to audit receipts from all import and export and tonnage duties in the colonies, the four and one-half per cent duty in the West Indies, fines, forfeitures and escheats, prizes and prize goods, port and weigh-house dues, the king's thirds of vessels and cargoes seized for illegal trading, quit rents, license fees,

---

[1] Beer, Old Colonial System, I, 205 and references.

[2] Blathwayt's Journal, Treas. 64/88; Brit. Mus. Addit. Mss., 12429, 223571 (printed in Mass. Col. Recs., V, 521).

wrecks, treasure trove and droits of the crown not claimed by the admiralty, together with payments due from the crown under the terms of colonial charters.[1] Later instructions to governors, as well as the history of the office under Blathwayt, show that an effort was made to bring the entire colonial budgets, direct as well as indirect taxes and expenditures, under the purview of the auditor general and his deputies — the auditor in Virginia and deputy auditors in other provinces.[2]

Blathwayt's salary was fixed at £500 per annum, £100 of which should come from Virginia and the rest from the West Indies. Later this was nominally increased to about £600 by a levy of 5% on New York revenues. After 1730 each of the Carolinas was required to pay £100 and thus the salary of the office — then held by Horatio Walpole — was raised to £800, to which should be added certain fees. But payments on this amount were likely to be in arrears or totally lacking, this being specially true in the case of New York and the Carolinas.[3]

Like the treasury, the admiralty was of mediaeval origin. The office of admiral of the fleet and of admirals of local squadrons fitted out at different parts of the coast appear in the late thirteenth and early fourteenth centuries. The title of lord high admiral, together with his court in which maritime law came to be administered, originated in connection with the prevalence of piracy in the Channel before the opening of the Hundred Years War. It was in connection with conflicts in the Channel at this time, and the notable victory of Sluys, that England began to claim the sovereignty of the adjacent seas. The French had asserted that the admiral of their king was entitled to control of the Channel and that under his command the French had a right to seize English ships there. The English asserted that from time immemorial their admiral, and in his absence English mariners, had exercised jurisdiction over trespasses and other offences on the

---

[1] Andrews, 144.

[2] For some years, as we shall see, this office and that of receiver general in Virginia were united in the same hand.

[3] See a statement from the New York assembly on this subject in the chapter of the present work entitled "New York and New Jersey from 1716 to 1730."

English seas, and proctors who appeared before arbitrators appointed to settle disputes with France after 1303 defended this claim in the *Fasciculus de Superioritate Maris,* a part of which was printed by Selden and Coke centuries later.[1] The claim thus put forward seemed to the English to have been made good by the victory of Sluys, which destroyed the French fleet. But in order further to support the claim the jurisdiction of the admiral was extended and the beginnings of an admiralty court appear. Though in many early cases common law procedure was followed, by an act of 1354 it was provided that foreign merchants who had been despoiled might have restitution of goods without suit at common law, and there is a record three years later of a trial of a case before the admiral. In 1360 Sir John de Beauchamp was given command of the fleets of the north, south and west, with a grant of maritime jurisdiction. He was also given power to appoint a deputy, who was probably a judge. Patents to lords high admirals appear from this date, though later they became more elaborate in form. Civil cases, as well as those involving piracy and treason, soon after appeared before the admiralty court and other courts were excluded.

But as the jury was not employed, as early as 1371 complaints against the admiralty court and its procedure began to appear.[1] To meet these the statutes of 1389 and 1391 (13 and 15 Richard II) were passed, which confined the jurisdiction of the admiralty courts to the sea and its immediate coasts. They were prohibited from concerning themselves with contracts, pleas or quarrels which arose within the bodies of the counties; these, it was declared, should be remedied by the law of the land. It was at this time also that the admiralty courts were given jurisdiction over murders and maimings which were committed on shipboard in the main streams of large rivers below the first bridges and near the sea. Under Henry VIII, because conviction was often found difficult in the admiralty courts, owing to

---

[1] For opinions of Hedges and Penrice, early in the eighteenth century, on the extent of the British seas, see Marsden, Law and Custom of the Sea, II, 231, 256, in Pubs. of Navy Records Soc.

[2] Marsden, Select Pleas in the Court of Admiralty, I, Selden Soc.

the requirement that the accused must confess or his guilt be proved by actual witnesses, the rules of the common law were extended, as in the fourteenth century, to cases of treason, murder and felony which were committed at sea or below the bridges.[1] But commissions for the trial of these cases were addressed to the lord admiral, his deputies or lieutenants and three or four others, whom the lord chancellor should name. It was before commissions so organized that piracies were henceforth tried in the realm.

It is now necessary to turn to the admiralty in its connection with the administration of the navy and of naval affairs.[2] As early as the reign of John appeared an officer who was called " keeper of the king's ships." In the later middle age this same official was known as " clerk of the ships," or by some equivalent title. He had control, sometimes nominally, sometimes really, of naval organization until the formation of the navy board or navy office in 1546. Interest in the navy was then being revived. Trinity House was founded, the ordnance office improved and the docks at Deptford and Woolwich constructed. Induced largely by the increase of the navy and the necessity for long cruises, which required more administrative work, Henry VIII reduced the clerk of the ships to membership in a newly created navy board consisting of six members. This may have been modelled after the ordnance office, which Henry had recently reorganized. The lord admiral now ceased to be merely an official of dignity and occasional high command and came to devote himself more to regular administrative work. He probably was president of the navy board, received its advice and decided matters referred to him by it. It was through this board that naval affairs were administered during the rest of the sixteenth century and into the early Stuart period. In the later years of Elizabeth and under James I its efficiency declined. When, in 1618, the duke of Buckingham was made lord high admiral, a board of commissioners known as the " council of the sea " was appointed, but no improvement could develop under the system of favoritism which then existed.

---

[1] Chalmers, Opinions, 512, Opinion of Richard West, 1720. 28 Henry VIII. C. 15. 5 Eliz. C. 5.

[2] Oppenheim, History of the Navy; Andrews, *op. cit.*

After the death of the duke of Buckingham, in 1628, the office of lord admiral was administered for ten years by a board. It was then revived and during the Civil War was held by the earl of Warwick. At the Restoration the duke of York was appointed to the office. This he held until 1673, when the passage of the test act compelled him to resign. The office was then put in commission until 1684, when the duke, who had been absent from England much of the time since 1679, returned and assumed control which he continued informally to exercise as king. From the Revolution until 1701 the office was again in commission, when the earl of Pembroke and Prince George of Denmark held it successively until the death of the prince in 1708. It then was placed again in commission and has been continued in that form ever since, except for the year 1827, during which the duke of Clarence, afterwards William IV, was lord high admiral.

In executive and military affairs the admiralty board controlled the business of the department. It held frequent meetings and, generally under orders from the king and secretary of state, directed the movements of the navy. It corresponded with the officers who commanded it, made appointments, signed warrants, even to the lowest employees. It was especially concerned with the outfit of convoys, with imprests, transports and supplies. In performing these many duties it corresponded with subordinate boards connected with the admiralty and with paymasters, commissioners of prizes, Greenwich Hospital and all others who were connected with naval administration. It authorized the payments of all its subordinates and expenditures for the maintenance of the navy. It requested the bishop of London to name suitable chaplains for the fleet. It issued commissions for vice admiralty officials and kept in close touch with the High Court of Admiralty. It issued warrants for letters of marque, ordered the holding of courts martial and had supervision over mariners wherever they might be.

Subordinate to the admiralty board were the navy board, victualling board, navy pay office, office of treasurer of the navy, the board of transport service, prize office and a number of other offices and boards. Of these the most important

and general in its scope was the navy board. This body
had direct charge of the management of the navy. " It built,
equipped, and repaired the ships, fitted them for sea and paid
the bills; it reported on their general condition, prepared
estimates, hired extra boats, and had some control over the
impressment of seamen; it looked after the building of docks
and yards, took charge of prizes at the great stations, fitted
up hospital ships, reported on the personnel of those employed
in the land service, and had the care of lighters and tenders
and their equipment. In the main the board was held
accountable for the general condition of docks, yards, and
ships, for the conduct and efficiency of all seamen and employees, who were not ranked as fighting men, and for all
contracts connected with the building, repairing or stocking
the ships of the navy. On certain days the Navy Board
attended the Admiralty and took part in its proceedings; at
other times it submitted reports on questions referred to it,
and sent in representations on its own account. It had no
authority over the other subordinate boards; it could issue
requests or express desires, but it could not order or require.
To other departments, such as the Ordnance Office, with
which it had dealings, it generally expressed its wishes
through the Admiralty." [1]

Connected with the admiralty and navy boards was a
counsellor who acted as legal adviser in all prosecutions.
Later, as business increased, the navy board and victualling
board each had a counsellor of its own. Reports were also
called for from judges and advocates of the high court and
from the law offices of the crown. With other departments
and boards the admiralty had constant dealings. Though
at first it refused to communicate with the board of trade
except through the privy council, later the two boards came
to correspond on a relative equality. In reference to matters
of convoys, piracy, illegal trade and naval stores they had
common dealings on an extensive scale.

The war office during the eighteenth century was subordinate to that of the secretaries of state. The conduct of war
was directed by the one of the secretaries within whose territory it happened to be — if in northern Europe by the secre-

[1] Andrews, Guide to the Materials in the Public Record Office, II, 4.

tary for the northern department, if in southern Europe or the colonies by the secretary for the southern department. The militia was under the care of the southern department. Arms and ammunition were supplied by the ordnance board, which dealt directly with the king. Victualling and transport were managed by the treasury, while the paymaster general, to whom the troops looked for wages, was a treasury official.

A secretary at war appeared during the Civil War, and the post was held by William Clarke under Cromwell.[1] He was knighted and continued in the office by Charles II. On his death Matthew Lock, private secretary to the duke of Albermarle, was appointed. He held until succeeded by William Blathwayt in 1683. George Clarke, son of William Clarke, acted as his deputy during an absence on the continent. Blathwayt held the office until 1704, when he was succeeded by Henry St. John. He was followed by a list of secretaries which contained the distinguished names of Walpole, Wyndham, Pultney, Pelham, Henry Fox, Lord Barrington, and Charles Townshend before the close of the colonial period.

The army estimates were made up by the secretary, with the aid of the paymaster general, the master general of the ordnance and the treasurer of the navy. Recruiting and the duties connected with the raising of levies, with the inspection of regiments when full, fell directly under the care of the secretary. So did the billeting and quartering of soldiers and the giving of marching orders. As a member of the house of commons the secretary had to move the army estimates and, in conjunction with the judge advocate general, defend the conduct of his office and that of the commander-in-chief against the attacks of the opposition. The royal sign manual authorizing appointments of officers was countersigned by the secretary, and he looked after the issue of their commissions and the payment of fees. Payments of the troops were regularly made through the office of the paymaster general. During the Seven Years War the importance of the secretary's office rapidly increased and at its close it

---

[1] Firth, Cromwell's Army, 60. Captain O. Wheeler, The War Office Past and Present.

had reached the position virtually of a great department. Under Barrington, for example, extended correspondence was carried on with under officers in the field, with colonial governors and commanders-in-chief in America, and the manifold details connected with the transport, supplies, and money which related to the organization of the troops in service were attended to by his office. The care of artillery, the engineer corps, barracks and fortifications was in the hands of the ordnance office, over which the secretary at war had no control. Correspondence was carried on by the war office with other departments and offices concerned, as was customary in all similar cases. Plans of campaign, however, were formulated by the secretary of state and the commander-in-chief, though when there was no commander-in-chief in England, as sometimes happened, the secretary at war had considerable influence upon matters of policy. But this office had not yet reached cabinet rank and the constitutional responsibility of a fully developed department of state.[1]

Even the beginning of a British standing army was not made until after the Restoration. Throughout the eighteenth century it was small and in many ways poorly organized. It was an object of some jealousy and as an arm of national defence was far less valued than was the navy. During practically the entire century it was under civilian control, the secretaries at war being politicians whose interests centered in party conflicts in and out of parliament. The officers, who had obtained their rank largely by purchase, systematically increased their rewards by stoppages from the supplies, especially of clothing, which should have gone to the common soldiers. Peculation and favoritism, which were everywhere rife, affected the army most seriously. During parts of the reigns of William and Anne dishonesty, one of the chief centres of which was the office of the paymaster general of the forces, culminated in a scandal which led to the removal of the earl of Ranelagh, who was then its incumbent, but not to a serious effort to change or improve the system.[2]

[1] Andrews, Guide to the Materials in the Public Record Office, II, 271–273. Anson, Law and Custom of the Constitution, II, 358 et seq.

[2] Wheeler, op. cit. Fortescue, Hist. of the British Army, II.

With the exception of the bishop of London and the other agencies of the English Church that cared for the interests of the Establishment in the colonies, and whose work will be later described, this completes the circle of governmental bodies in England which were concerned in their administration. In matters of government exclusively the royal officials who were appointed for residence in America were the connecting links between the crown and the colonies. They were the arms and hands, so to speak, by which the king reached his subjects oversea and kept up his connection with them. In every colony there were two classes of officials : those who derived their authority directly and solely from the colony or its proprietors and those whose authority came directly from the crown. In writing of the seventeenth century the position and spirit of officials of the former class have been sufficiently described. In the royal provinces, where the official system was fully developed, the crown was directly represented by the governor, councillors, secretary, surveyor general, receiver general, attorney general and justices of the supreme court, or at least the chief justice, who were its own appointees. The appointments to the lower positions, however, were made very largely on the recommendation of the governors, with or without the advice of the councils. There were also the royal customs officials, the deputy auditor, and after a little the officials of the admiralty courts who were also direct representatives of the crown in secular affairs. The councillors formed the upper house of the provincial legislature, and they with the governor at their head were its permanent executive board. Chancery jurisdiction, if exercised at all, was in the governor's hand, and the council was usually well represented upon the higher judicial bench. This shows in brief how effectually, provided these appointees were faithful and loyal, the crown was brought into the province under the royal system, as compared with that which existed in the chartered colonies. The typical royal province, in which, unlike Massachusetts, the council was appointive and not elective, was heavily weighted on the side of the executive and therefore was well adapted to serve the ends of systematic imperial administration. Success in the prosecution of that policy depended not alone on energy and efficiency at home, but quite as much on the development of well organized royal provinces and the successful management of them in the colonies. The study of the political struggles which went on within them reveals a part of the history of imperial control and comes much nearer the heart of the subject than would exclusive attention to the doings of officials and governing boards in England. It was in the colonies, even under the old system, that the elements of strength or weakness existed which finally determined the chief points at issue.

Authority and directions as to its exercise were transmitted to the governors, and as well to officials of lower rank, by royal commissions and instructions. Of these the commissions to the governors were letters patent, having passed the great seal, and their instructions were letters close, having passed only the privy seal. In a certain sense the governors' commissions ranked with colonial charters, but commissions did not imply a contract and could be recalled or modified at any time without judicial action. This made them much less permanent and reliable, when viewed from the standpoint of the colonists and considered as embodying the elements of a constitution for the individual colony. The purpose of the commissions was to set forth the powers of the governors as the chief agents of the British government in the provinces and as the heads of the provincial executives and coordinate parts of the legislatures. The governors were endowed with vice-regal powers, analogous though inferior in degree to those of the monarch.[1] The instructions which were given to royal governors were much longer and more detailed than were the commissions. The purpose of their issue was to direct the governors in the details of their office and duties. While the commission was the authentic document to which a governor or others must look for the source and general definition of his powers, the instructions were intended for his guidance in particulars, so that the intent

---

[1] See Greene, Provincial Governor, Harvard Hist. Studies; Stokes, View of the Constitution of the British Colonies, London, 1783, p. 149 *et seq.* Various English law books refer to the same subject. Proprietary as well as royal commissions and instructions are discussed in Osgood's Am. Colonies in the 17th Century; consult indexes.

of the crown might be made clearer and the general statements of the commission more intelligible.   The instructions
lay within the domain of administrative law and implied
at every point that the governors to whom they were issued
were agents of the crown.   Two sets were regularly given,
one relating to duties under the acts of trade and the other
to miscellaneous duties outside that domain.   Before the
close of the seventeenth century both sets had become
voluminous and as to their general contents underwent little
further change.   Changes in detail, however, were made with
every issue, these being limited in many cases to the phraseology and in others extending to directions concerning new
questions of policy or modifications of action upon old issues.
Many details also were introduced which related only to a
single province and these also were subject to change with
every successive administration.[1]

The instructions, together with the support which was given
the governors and all other officials by the British government, in the form of letters of advice and exhortation, orders,
statutes, judicial proceedings, allowance or disallowance of
laws, and in all other known ways, embody the policy and
influence of the executive in the colonies, and especially in the
royal provinces.   Its pressure also was felt, though far less
effectively   and   continuously,   in   the   chartered   colonies.
Loyalty to the crown and to the interests of Great Britain was
its watchword.   This it sought to promote in every province
and in all lines of activity, by prohibitions and restrictions
as well as positive and affirmative measures.   It upheld regular   and   legal   proceedings,   custom   and   tradition,   British
forms and practices.   It guaranteed property rights and all
duly acquired private rights as well.   It opposed fraud,
irregularities, all tendencies toward anarchy, and was very
apt to brand mere innovations as acts which proceeded from
sinister intent.   It was conservative in all its instincts.   Its
acts and policies were imperialistic, and carried with them

---

[1] Commissions and instructions contain another large and important body
of colonial law.   Many have been printed in the various series of official publications of colonial records by our states and also in the collections of some
historical societies.   As an indication of their volume and of their whereabouts
among the British State Papers, see the valuable list published by Professor
Andrews, in the Report of the Am. Hist. Assoc., 1911, Vol. I.

that degree of subjection which the colonies inherited by birth and allegiance. It accompanied those who migrated to the colonies and into it were born the later generations which originated on colonial soil. It was as natural to them as was English dress or speech. The extent to which it limited their initiative and their choice in social and political action marked the degree to which the colonists lacked self-government.

At the opposite pole in the colonial constitution stood the assemblies, the embodiment of colonial self-government. In every case they had their origin in the action of patentees and not of the crown itself, though provision for calling them was made in the proprietary charters. They were a most characteristic expression of the British spirit and caused her colonies and their history to differ from those of other nations. Her executives were in spirit and traditions like those of France and Spain, and if they had not been checked by the assemblies would probably have been quite as autocratic. The principles for which assemblies in the royal provinces contended were common practices in the chartered colonies, and before 1680 a large body of precedents had been accumulated in the colonies, especially those of New England, upon which assemblies could base their claims in later times. When we consider the fate which, in the early seventeenth century, seemed likely to overtake parliaments in Europe, the flowering out of so many institutions of this kind in America, small and obscure though they might be, and the concerns with which they dealt often petty, must be regarded as an event of great significance. Within their walls popular liberty, sometimes factious, it is true, and never fully representative, found a refuge at a time when it seemed likely to perish from the earth. As a result of the two revolutions of the seventeenth century the ascendancy of parliament in the English constitution was secured. They also indirectly insured the permanence of assemblies in the American colonies, and when the period with which we are now concerned began no one considered their abolition to be among the possibilities of the future. Through the lower houses as representatives of the freeholders their spirit and desires found expression. In their demands the councils, or members thereof, sometimes joined. This formed the colonial opposition, and while it cooperated with the executive in many things, in many others there was disagreement and persistent conflict between the two. These conflicts fill the chief place in the political history of the colonies, their history as institutions of government, and as a result of them civil and political rights were established, executive discretion was limited and the constitution of the colonies was developed.

A fundamental point upon which there was disagreement, and one second in importance to no other, was that of the binding force of royal instructions. The crown, or at least the board of trade, always contended that they were law in the full sense of that term and were binding on assemblies and the people as well as on the governors. The assemblies, however, when questions of great importance came to a direct issue, refused to be bound by them. Their claim was that, while they were law to the governors, they could not bind the colonists or their assemblies except with their free consent. The power of the crown in the colonies never became sufficiently strong to override this claim, and therefore instructions must be considered to have been administrative regulations binding on the provincial executives but operative on the colonists and their assemblies only so far as the governors could make them effective by influence and political action. Many instructions were obeyed as a matter of course, but the statement just made applies to cases where a direct issue was raised and the principle which was worked out as the result of action in such cases.

In the American colonies, as well as in England, a certain balance of forces and permanence of institutions was reached with the Revolution of 1689. The plan of extreme centralization which had taken form in the Dominion of New England had to be abandoned. The colonies for the most part were restored to their original boundaries and their assemblies were recognized as permanent.[1] The process, however, by which the royal province was steadily to assume a more prominent place in the British colonial system was destined to go on. The chartered colony was to give way before it

[1] See Osgood, American Colonies in the 17th Century, Vol. III, Conclusion.

until, as a form of government, it sank into an inferior
position, though the spirit which had animated its founders
and guided its policy still remained strong in the breasts of
the majority of the colonists and formed the traditions which
guided their action. In this statement we may sum up in
briefest form the political and institutional history of the
American colonies during the first half of the eighteenth
century, or, in other words, during the period between the
English Revolution and the beginning of the controversy
which was to lead to the American Revolution.

In the colonies this was a period of slow and steady
development, with few dramatic episodes and no revolutionary changes. Emigration from Great Britain to America,
as we shall see, continued in a moderate and somewhat
irregular stream, it still being chiefly the result of war and
misgovernment. The victims came largely from Scotland
and Ireland. From the continent of Europe also came a
large number of German emigrants who settled chiefly in
New York and Pennsylvania. But the increase of population was chiefly of the American born, who passed their
lives wholly under colonial conditions. Open places along
the coast were gradually filled. Population crept up the
river valleys. The frontier was slowly extended on the
north toward Canada and on the south toward the modern
boundary of Florida. It advanced slowly toward the Alleghanies, but scarcely was a single weak outpost planted
beyond them.

The principles of British colonial administration were
steadily applied during this period and, as a result, they
were perfected in various details. One uniform system was
developed which, so far as possible, was applied to all the
colonies. Under its steady pressure the colonies gradually
emerged from their primitive and isolated state as settlements of trading companies or of proprietors, and became
a group of politico-economic structures, nearly all of which
were patterned, superficially at least, after the same model.
Upon each, however, its origin, location, make-up of population, grouping of religious sects and industrial classes, and
other causes, had stamped an individuality, so to speak,
which it shared with no other colony. Each colony was

unique, had its own peculiar problems and history, and contributed its part to the general blend or composite which we call the British colonial system. The slow evolution of this system during a period of seventy years it is the purpose of these volumes to describe. Attention will be chiefly devoted to the internal affairs and inter-relations of the colonies themselves, but due reference will also be made throughout to their connection with the British government and its influence and policy, so far as these bore upon them. No effort will be made to deal with any but the thirteen colonies which finally revolted and formed the United States of America. For this reason the British-American colonial system as a whole will not come within our view, and the organs of the British government which were concerned with the colonies and with their officials will not be discussed separately and in such detail as would be the case if distinctly English history were our object.

Under the old British colonial system the empire, in theory and to an extent in practice, was relatively consolidated and autocratic, with the ultimate authority lodged in crown and parliament. Considered in that connection, its history furnishes an illustration of the workings of government from a remote centre, with the delays and the ignorance and indifference toward conditions among the governed which necessarily attend such experiments. Like the present one all studies of so-called expansion, unless it is followed by confederation, are expositions of phenomena of this kind. But we have seen that the British continental colonies, in the process of their settlement and the main tendencies of their early history, pursued a course which was inconsistent with this. Their drift toward self-government was so strong as to suggest a federation rather than an empire of the Roman or autocratic type. This was checked with considerable violence during the last decade of Stuart rule. But on the outbreak of the Revolution of 1689 the colonies reverted for the most part to their former condition and the preference of their inhabitants for a large degree of self-government was most clearly shown. During the period of the French wars, upon which we are now entering, we shall find the two tendencies actively asserting themselves

in conflict with one another. At the close of the period the
outcome was still in doubt, and it is clear that at any period
along the way the structure which had developed was of a
mixed character. It was neither an autocratic empire nor a
federation, but something between the two with characteristics of both and therefore beset with inconsistencies, complicated in structure and not easy to understand. A large
number of colonies had been allowed to develop, many of
them small and originating largely from accident or caprice
and formed without regard to the interests of the group as a
whole or to any union larger than their own. Free rein at
the outset had been given to the individualism and the
spirit of localism which inhere in frontier conditions. Could
these colonies have been permanently combined into two or
three dominions or larger unions, a marked gain in strength
and efficiency would have followed. But government at
home was too weak and disturbed to effect this and a succession of compromises or half-measures followed, none of which
was prosecuted with special vigor or carried through to
complete success.

In studying this group of colonies as parts of an empire
which was still in the experimental stage of its growth,
either of two points of observation may be chosen. The
observer may station himself in London and view everything from the British standpoint, noting the uniformities
and emphasing the successes of imperial policy, but viewing
from a distance the obstacles which beset the execution of
that policy. The evolution as a whole will then appear to
be a branch of British history, in a literal sense an expansion of England. The observer may also take his position
in the colonies, but in such wise that, as well as he is
able, he may keep in touch with the people as their desires
are voiced through their representative assemblies, the press
or in other ways, and also with the officials who owed their
appointment to the crown and somewhat more remotely with
administrative boards and officials in England. The difficulties of this method of procedure are surely much greater
than those of the former. But that it must be chosen, if one
is to face the real conditions of the problem, is evidenced
by the fact that in the colonies, that is in America, were

located both the land and the people — the people in their natural environment — and these are the two fundamental elements of the state. To the observer at this point the variety of colonial life and hence the clash of interests between the colonists and those to whom were entrusted the enforcement of imperial policies will be ever present and likely to receive due emphasis. But this position must be a movable one. For the observer must shift his point of view from colony to colony so as to bring out the individuality of each, to view the system from the particular angle of each colony and to note what it contributed to the general composite. The resultant will be not British history, nor simply the expansion of England. Nor will it be simply American history in a narrow and exclusive sense of the term. But it will be more American than British and that in increasing measure with every decade that passed. This means that, though a subtratum of British law and precedent lay at the foundation of our colonial system, at the same time physical, social and political conditions in America from the first differed to such an extent from those in Great Britain as to lead to the early development of a distinct type of society and government. Before the middle of the eighteenth century, as the result of struggles carried on upon this side of the ocean, by precedents distinct from those of England though analogous with them, a system of American liberty and institutions was developed which should not be confounded with that of England. These institutions and principles of liberty are to be found today in the states of the American Union. They are the survivors, with such changes as were necessitated by independence, of the British-American colonies. A consideration of this fact alone, to say nothing of the many details which enforce and illustrate it, will show the extent to which in matters of government the British system was weighted upon the American side.

# CHAPTER II

## THE WARS OF THE EIGHTEENTH CENTURY
## IN GENERAL

IF one were to trace fully the antecedents of these conflicts, one would have to follow the record back through the religious wars of the sixteenth century to the struggles between the papacy and the empire and between the nobles, the cities and the crown during the middle age, back to the wars of Rome and Greece and of the Asiatic monarchies, to the cave dwellers in the stone age and even to the fierce conflicts which were waged in prehistoric jungles before the advent of man. Unfortunately the spirit which has expressed itself in this hideous and gory record still survives among men as among beasts, and the curious inquirer could still find in the present or not remote past, in the jungles and on the battle fields of various continents, elegant examples of every kind of armed conflict or battle with tooth and claw which has occurred in the past. Religion, industry, commerce, art, science, diplomacy, government, every form of human activity which was nominally intended for the improvement of man, has been so perversely manipulated as to contribute by means of wars to his wholesale destruction. And yet the perversity of this course is not revealed except in the light of a morality which has been evolved by and for the best of human kind. The great masses of mankind, of whatever race, color or social condition, have always been and still are largely animal in their natures, subject to primitive reactions of all kinds, and physical conflict has always been with them a favorite and ready method of settling questions which were in dispute. They have also sought to dignify and idealize war by throwing about it a mantle of grand ideas, of honor, courage, glory, liberty. These when illustrated by the history of a nation and enshrined in one's native language and inherited institutions, give rise to the sentiment of patriotism, which may easily assume a bel-

ligerent form.  But an appeal to physical force for the decision
of questions which are susceptible of elucidation by argument
is essentially a childish and stupid procedure, characteristic of
the lower animals.  It is human only in the lower and animal
sense, but it is inhuman in the light of every higher and
idealistic consideration.  But in a blundering and questionable
way such appeals, in our imperfect human condition, are sometimes unavoidable and have wrought good, though always with
large attendant evils.  They can never be neglected by the
historian, because important political and social changes have
been caused by them, though to these rather than to their
external events attention should be directed.

The European wars of the early modern period were an
inheritance from the middle age.  Society was intensely aristocratic and the idea of human rights, with the corresponding
enthusiasm for the well-being and progress of humanity in
general had not developed.  Europe was filled with the conflicts of the feudal age, in which cruelty toward enemies and
oppression of the lower orders of society everywhere prevailed.
The feuds of nobles and princes brought war and its sufferings home to every class and every locality.  The church and
chivalry did little and that ineffectually to relieve the universal evil.  In addition to the wars of nobles and princes the
ideal of the empire survived and wars undertaken for the
purpose of its revival added to the alleged glory, but the real
confusion, of the time.  This ideal assumed an ecclesiastical
as well as a temporal form, and from this arose the age-long
conflict between papacy and empire.  This prevented the attainment of a tolerable degree of unity both in Italy and
Germany and thus helped greatly to increase and perpetuate
the conflicts and confusion of the mediaeval period.  While
in this weakened condition Europe was compelled to face the
assaults of the infidel from the east and the south and had to
yield large areas to his sway.

Meanwhile out of general chaos the nationalities of France,
Spain and England began to emerge and, under kingships
wholly or nearly absolute, were able to curb the nobility and
to gain the mastery to an extent over the internal tendencies
toward dissolution which beset them.  Italy and Germany,
though also clearly distinct nationalities, owing to the diver-

sion of their energies into the seductive paths of imperial politics, remained disunited and a prey to the ambitions of the papacy and of every neighboring state. It was among the struggling states of the Italian peninsula that the ideas of a balance of power and of diplomacy developed, Machiavelli giving classic expression to the methods of statecraft which were to spread thence throughout Europe. Though the rise of the nationalities set limits to the assertion of the imperialistic ideal, in the person of Charles V, of Burgundy, this ideal suddenly revived and as speedily declined, though his descendants, the Spanish Hapsburgs, supported by the papacy, continued during the latter half of the sixteenth century to provoke the opposition of the rest of Europe by the ambitions which they cherished in this direction. But the speedy decline of Spain after Philip II and the almost total wreck of political power, as well as of social well-being, in Germany by the Thirty Years War, put an end to efforts for the revival of the empire in that quarter. This left central Europe, that part of the continent which upon its wide stretches of territory should naturally develop a population and resources which would insure the stability of the entire system, weak and divided. The condition of permanence or of a stable equilibrium based on the unquestioned superiority of a single state, as in North America, was lost and has never since been recovered. Instead we have had struggles between rival nationalities and their groups of allies for the balance of power, with the result thus far that peace and stability have been sought in vain.

Out of these conflicts and strengthened by territory which she wrested from all the surrounding states, France under the Bourbons rose to the chief place in Europe. The *grand dessein* of Henry IV was far surpassed by the suppression of religious and other forms of internal opposition under Richelieu and Louis XIV, accompanied by a continuous series of wars of conquest against all the surrounding states and their dependencies. Treaties were systematically disregarded and weaker neighbors were ruthlessly attacked — as a rule without warning — when the French monarch and his ministers felt themselves prepared and the occasion opportune for the seizure of adjacent territories the possession of which would help to extend the natural frontiers toward the ideal limits of the ocean, the Rhine, the Alps and the Pyrenees. Then it was that France, the most perfect example of absolutism in modern times, domineered over Europe for half a century and threatened the revival of the empire in a more oppressive form than ever. The crisis reached its climax with the establishment of a Bourbon on the throne of Spain. But the exhaustion of the resources of France as the result of her efforts had already begun to be apparent. A thirty years' truce, interrupted by several minor though related wars, followed the treaty of Utrecht.

When, toward the middle of the eighteenth century, the struggle was renewed over the Austrian Succession, an imitator of the French, so far as their method of beginning wars was concerned, appeared in the person of Frederick II, of Prussia. But he surpassed their best achievements in generalship, as, following the example of his father, he also did in the completeness of the organization of his small state as a fighting machine. The Silesian Wars and the great Seven Years War permanently changed the system of Europe by creating a dualism in the Holy Roman Empire and raising Prussia from the status of a principality to a position where she might claim a place among the great powers. At the same time Russia had made her advent into European politics, while Austria had been compensated for losses in central Europe by the establishment of her control over northern Italy. The decline of Spain as well as the weakening of France had removed for the time the danger of Bourbon predominance and Europe breathed again. By the treaties of Paris and Hubertusburg an equilibrium seemed to have been reached. But had not the hoped-for equilibrium been reached many times in the past, especially by the treaties of Westphalia and Utrecht? War had succeeded war and treaty had succeeded treaty for centuries in the vain or pretended effort to secure a permanent equilibrium. The equilibrium, however, had proved to be a perpetually shifting quantity, a balance which was only established in order to be speedily upset and readjusted. So the game went on and still continues in our own day. And it was a game, for the monarchs, cabinets and diplomats of those centuries lived and throve upon the playing of this game and were interested in seeing that it should never cease. The populations of their respective countries were their pawns and Europe their chess board. Exchanges of peoples and territories were made with the zest or, indifference of gamesters. Louis the XIV's policy of *réunion* as applied in western Germany, the treatment by the various powers of the Pragmatic Sanction which was intended to regulate the Austrian Succession, and the Partitions of Poland are the classical examples on a large scale of the results of this policy. The claims of humanity received not the slightest attention. Reasons of state, the attainment of political power were the dominating considerations with all governments. Populations, speaking different languages, cherishing rival faiths and forms of culture, were left in ignorance of one another. Feelings of contempt or hate toward foreign peoples were nourished, instead of a desire for mutual understanding and cooperation. Intense rivalry in varied lines of activity was stimulated, instead of the generous feelings which should accompany a sense of common humanity. Ruses, spies, deceit, a cynical diplomacy often descending to bribery and lies in order to gain an advantage over a rival, and all frequently culminating in atrocious wars, this was the system which was perpetuated in Europe as the accepted and customary form of international relations under the so-called old régime. It was the result of a self-interested nationalism of a specially brutal type, and in those days, as was true later in the time of Napoleon, France was the chief offender, or to put it differently, the chief instructor of Europe. As the lives and memories of nations are measured by centuries and not by years or decades, as in the case with individuals, this fact should be borne in mind by those who would rightly estimate later events. Those who sow the wind at least put themselves in the way of reaping the whirlwind.

But for our purpose it is specially necessary to define the relation in which Great Britain stood to this European system. In certain respects she was deeply involved in it and was part and parcel of it; in certain other respects she stood to an extent outside of it. Her insular position protected her to a large degree from the turmoil of the continent, while it gave her free access to the ocean and the world outside and also assured to her, especially in time of war, a large degree of control over the seas and coasts of northern Europe. Her comparative isolation delayed for centuries her complete entry into the European political system, but it also assured to her a comparatively peaceful growth toward national unity and the attainment at her maturity of institutions which avoided the extremes of absolutism on the one hand and of feudal anarchy and consequent political weakness on the other. After her mediaeval experiment in foreign conquest and dynastic politics during the Hundred Years War had failed and been abandoned, England developed a pronounced and consistent nationalist policy according to the type which was then common. She became a regular participant in the system of alliances which were intended to maintain the balance of power in Europe, opposing first the ambitious plans of the Spanish Hapsburgs and later the more dangerous policy of the Bourbons. Her natural place was therefore among the smaller states and those in whom unity had not been attained, in opposition to more consolidated states and combinations which threatened to dominate Europe. She fully and rather decisively entered upon the stage of general European politics in the latter half of the seventeenth century and especially after the Revolution of 1689. It was that event and William III that drew her more completely than before from her isolation.

As a participant in the conflict which immediately preceded and followed the Revolution Great Britain contributed armies of only moderate size to the assistance of her allies on land. Though her government and people had the reputation of being as arrogant as any and her internal peace was disturbed by not a few actual or threatened revolutions, she was not a distinctively military power. Her exemption from invasions, which permitted the uninterrupted development of commerce and industry, enabled her to grow steadily in wealth. This in turn enabled her to subsidize her allies and greatly to increase her own armies with hired troops. Therefore she fought more effectively with money than with steel. She also had the support of states on the continent which felt the need of her assistance against the common foe, or which had become commercially dependent upon her and so fell under the control of her navy. Such was the origin of the alliance of the Sea Powers, expressly set forth in the plan of Sir William Temple and, as was stated in the previous chapter, put fully into effect during the reigns of William III and Anne. Great Britain and the Dutch Republic formed the main strength of this league, with Denmark as an occasional addition. The anti-German interests of Sweden drew her usually to the side of France. The objects of the Sea Powers were to prevent France from conquering the Low Countries and by their fleets to control the Channel and North Sea and defeat the efforts of France, or of France and Spain, to rival or surpass them on the ocean. The campaigns of William and those of Marlborough, with the exception of the one which ended in the victory at Blenheim, were fought in what is now Belgium, which was then held as a dependency by one group of powers or the other and was always sure to be one of the chief battlefields of Europe. The smaller German states, unless coerced by France, ranged themselves in the alliances which were formed by the Empire and Great Britain. The armies which were commanded year after year by William and Marlborough were composed more largely of Dutch and German contingents than they were of British troops. In the War of the Austrian Succession and later Great Britain became in some respects even more deeply involved in German politics owing to her connection with Hanover. At the opening of the Seven Years War the situation was further changed by the reversal of alliances caused by the animosity of Austria toward Prussia and the consequent alliance of the former with France. The advent of Russia also further modified the alignment and Prussia in that struggle found her support in an alliance with the Sea Powers.

Such was one of the buttresses — the chief one — of British power in Europe. Upon it rested British influence throughout Germany and its extension eastward to Vienna and St. Petersburg. A permanent partnership thus existed and by virtue of it Great Britain shared in all the crises of both central and western Europe. Her naval and trade connections, furthered by chartered companies, were extended along all the coasts of the inland waters of northern Europe and these, together with the alliances, found mutual support the one from the other. The British Isles themselves, large

enough to sustain a considerable population but not of sufficient extent to compete at least in potential resources with
the large stretches of the continent, lay at the portal of those
seas with the possibility of controlling the exits and entrances
of them.  In this essential fact of European geography will
be found the origin of very much that is peculiar to Great
Britain and to her part in history.

Another point at which Great Britain became closely involved with the continent and its affairs was at the strait
of Gibraltar, in connection with the Spanish peninsula and
the control of the Mediterranean Sea.  The Channel opened
out in this direction also, but the objective was somewhat
more remote and its full significance did not begin to be ap-
preciated till somewhat late.  Though hostilities with Spain
had been in progress much of the time for a century and a
half, the decisive steps which determined future relations were
not taken until the War of the Spanish Succession.  They
were the conclusion of the Methuen treaty with Portugal,
which brought that country permanently into the wake of
Great Britain, and the occupation of Gibraltar and Minorca,
accompanied by the stationing of a squadron permanently in
the Mediterranean.[1]  This move had been preceded by the
temporary occupation of Tangier, for which the need of
restraining the Barbary corsairs had furnished an occasion.
But the seating of a Bourbon on the Spanish throne, followed
by the later Family Compacts, led to the far more decisive
steps just referred to.  This enabled Great Britain to watch
Toulon, the chief naval station of the French, very seriously to
hamper if not to prevent the cooperation of that part of the
French fleet which was at any time stationed in the Mediterranean with that part which was operating from Atlantic
ports, and to thwart French operations in general in the
Mediterranean.  For purposes of naval strategy France was
then pretty effectually encircled.  Gibraltar is the original and
classic example of naval stations or bases as they have been
occupied and utilized on a large scale by Great Britain in
the development of her maritime empire.  As a violation of
the territorial integrity of a neighboring nation its seizure is
comparable with the policy of *réunion* to which Louis XIV

[1] Corbett, England in the Mediterranean.

had just resorted in his dealings with Germany. It survives as a reminder of the high-handed policy of the old régime, controlled by reasons of state and considerations of military or naval strategy. By repeating the tactics pursued at Gibraltar, Great Britain extended her centres of influence till she came to control the Mediterranean, while by the contemporary extension of her trading posts down the west coast of Africa and the operations of the East India Company in the Orient new and remoter termini of her influence were established which, when duly connected up at intervening points, were destined to complete the encircling of the world with British naval stations, trading factories, spheres of influence, vassal or dependent states and colonies or dominions. These gains, though made at sea and at points more or less remote from the continent of Europe, and which therefore did not so much disturb settled and civilized populations, were the equivalent in the development of a maritime empire of the proceedings of the rival conquerors within Europe itself. Like the development of the Roman Empire, this was not the result of an original and settled purpose of conquest, but complications resulting from one step of advance led almost necessarily to the next and so on indefinitely. Trade was the lure in the case of England, but domination was the final result, and any view which ignores that fact is incomplete and misleading. While the British Empire was being built up and until the nineteenth century was well advanced this dominion was exclusive commercially as well as in other respects.

It is needless to say that the commercial and naval development to which this brief reference has been made and which began to assume definite form as the result in part of the struggle with France, is the most characteristic feature of British history as related to Europe and the world in general. This maritime empire, as it slowly took shape, rested upon Great Britain as its centre and upon her as a part of the Europe of the old régime. Nearly all the continental states with which she was brought into connection, whether of friendship or hostility, also had their navies and oversea dependencies. Portugal, Spain, France, Holland, even Sweden and Denmark, had them, — all except the nationalities of Germany and Italy which had not attained political unity.

Great Britain in the end was destined to surpass them all and to create the one great maritime empire of history.   The reason for this is to be found largely in her fortunate location by which she was protected from invasion and was never tempted seriously to exhaust her resources in the struggles of the continent.   While her more dangerous rivals were sacrificing their navies to their armies and using up their resources in schemes of conquest which were exclusively European, Great Britain was picking up the choice sites outside, operating in real estate in the suburbs out of sight, beyond the visible horizon, and preparing to wait, if necessary, until the expansion of the civilized nations should make these investments valuable.   Great Britain has always been in a special sense amphibious, a sea power and a land power, partly European and partly non-European, and by relying upon both has profited greatly, her gains, when compared with the small territories upon the European continent which were won at so much cost, showing to an extent the character of an unearned increment.

The feeling of security and possession, with the resultant sense of comfort so prominent in English life, was never better expressed than it was by Edmund Waller in a panegyric addressed to Cromwell as lord protector, written in or about 1654, when the development to which we are referring was in its earlier stages.

> Lords of the world's great waste, the ocean, we
> Whole forests send to reign upon the sea,
> And every coast may trouble, or relieve;
> But none can visit us without your leave.
>
> Angels and we have this prerogative,
> That none can at our happy seats arrive; [1]
> While we descend at pleasure, to invade
> The bad with vengeance, and the good to aid.
>
> Our little world, the image of the great,
> Like that, amidst the boundless ocean set,
> Of her own growth hath all that Nature craves,
> And all that's rare, as tribute from the waves.

[1] Montesquieu wrote, "L'empire de la mer a toujours donné aux Peuples qui l'ont possédé une fierté naturelle; parceque, se sentant capables d'insulter par tout, ils croient que leur pouvoir n'a pas plus de bornes que l'Océan." Esprit des lois, livre XIX, c. XXVII.

As Egypt does not on the clouds rely,
But to the Nile owes more than to the sky;
So what our earth, and what our heaven denies,
Our ever constant friend, the sea, supplies.

The taste of hot Arabia's spice we know,
Free from the scorching sun that makes it grow;
Without the worm, in Persian silks we shine;
And, without planting, drink of every wine.

To dig for wealth we weary not our limbs;
Gold, though the heaviest metal, hither swims;
Ours is the harvest where the Indians mow;
We plough the deep, and reap what others sow.

Things of the noblest kind our own soil breeds;
Stout are our men, and warlike are our steeds;
Rome, though her eagle through the world had flown,
Could never make this island all her own.

A similar glorification of sea power appeared anonymously in 1703,[1] which may be quoted as typical of similar utterances in prose. " He that is master of the sea," writes the author, " may be said in some sort to be master of every country, for he is at liberty to begin and end war where, when and on what terms he pleaseth, and extend his conquests even to the Antipodes." This writer, like others of his class, quoted Selden and other authors in support of the doctrine of sovereignty over the British seas, with its control over the fisheries and the obligations to strike the flag and lower the topsail which were enforced as among its consequences. The navy of Great Britain was her *primum mobile,* without which it was impossible to secure her trade and sovereignty of the seas. It was in accordance with the plan of God that by means of trade, the profitable exchange of products operating like the philosopher's stone and all duly protected by sea power, a nation situated like Great Britain should rise to world power. These ideas for centuries were accompanied with their correlative, that France and Great Britain were natural enemies, and that it was only by securing and maintaining a clear ascendancy at sea that the rival power could be held in check.

[1] The Glory of Her Sacred Majesty Queen Anne in the Royal Navy and Her Absolute Sovereignty as Empress of the Sea, etc., 1703.

Upon the colonial policies and ambitions of each of the European states were stamped the characteristics of the parent nation. The rivalries and conflicts in which they had become involved in Europe were extended to their dominions and thus were spread over seas and to all the outlying continents. The new world in this way inherited the wars of the old and had stamped upon its politics from the first the evils of the old régime. The process began with the papal bull of 1493 and the events which immediately followed it, by which an attempt was made to divide all the islands and continents, discovered and to be discovered, to the east and to the west, between Spain and Portugal. This colossal assumption was the parent of all later claims to spheres of influence which governments have created as pretexts for expansion and for the quarrels incident thereto. Claims resulting from voyages of discovery were pushed to the utmost possible limits by the rival nations under whose flags they were made, one of the most conspicuous examples being the extension which was given by Great Britain to the voyages of the Cabots and the claims which were deduced therefrom by the British in all later negotiations over boundaries in North America.

The proximate cause of hostilities between the French and English in North America was a boundary dispute, an over-lapping of territorial claims which originated in the way just indicated. Behind it, of course, lay differences of culture and spirit, of language, religion and government. The original grants of both crowns included the entire coast from Labrador to Florida and extended indefinitely to the westward. Strictly interpreted these grants made the colonists of each nation interlopers in the eyes of the other. By the process of settlement the section of the vast original grants which each nation was to occupy was gradually defined, but the boundary controversy persisted, remaining acute, however, only with reference to certain adjacent territories, sections of the frontier which were considered specially valuable by the two parties. But the conflicting claims always involved the possibility of war and, when hostilities began, the further possibility arose of complete mastery by one contestant over the other and his removal from dominion over any part of the continent.

This permanent condition of actual or possible hostility

was reflected in Indian policy and relations. They were always closely connected with defence, this being necessitated not only by the war-like character of the aborigines but by the arts of diplomacy which both whites and Indians practiced toward one another in the effort to secure allies or to outwit foes. Those solemn and often farcical assemblies known as peace congresses in Europe had their counterparts at Albany and Onondaga, at Quebec and Montreal, and at many other places in the American wilderness or in her settled towns. Not only was the red man a past master in the noble craft of warfare, but he could often give points in the tricks of diplomacy, especially to the dull Englishmen and Dutchmen who were called upon to deal with him. The grunts and periods of sober silence with which the sachems usually received the bland but utterly deceptive offerings of French, British and Dutch officials, their hypocritical references to the glories and the benevolence (God save the mark!) of their royal fathers beyond the sea, were the counterpart among the savages of the deceptions and reticences, the maskings and masqueradings of European diplomacy. The red man was faithless and so was the European. The red man systematically aided the French while he was professing himself the friend and ally of the English and *vice versa.* And he was perfectly logical and clear sighted in doing so, for it was the custom under the old régime, while the Indian well knew that all Europeans, of whatever name or profession, were bent upon plundering him, upon reducing him to subjection or driving him from the face of the earth. And was not the Englishman continually trading with the enemy in time of war? Was he not all the time making laws and affirming beliefs only to violate them, professing loyalties which he did not feel? It was to a large extent a game of brutality and deception on the part of all the participants and in the end the booty went to the strongest. Such was the spirit of the old régime — and not so completely out of date but that we can still recognize its features — as it was when extended to America and exhibited on the frontier. It is with these accompaniments that the process of " civilizing " the " backward races " has gone on down to the present day.

Had the French and English colonists been left to themselves and not been subjected in this affair to the domination of Europe, a much longer time, at any rate, would have passed before they came to blows. There were physical obstacles, if no others, which would have prevented this, for it was not until near the close of our colonial period that their frontiers approached near enough to make possible such a result. Owing to the long distances which separated them and the total lack of means of communication except what nature had provided, during the first three intercolonial wars it was extremely difficult, in fact next to impossible, for the antagonists to get at one another. It was the Indians chiefly who were able to penetrate the recesses of that wilderness which lay between them. Small bodies of Frenchmen, guided by Indians, succeeded in this from time to time and in a futile way carried murder and rapine to the frontier farms and villages, chiefly of New England. But the British signally failed in their far more ambitious plans of invading the enemy's territory, showing that they never succeeded in mastering the art of frontier warfare. Had it not been for Europe and for a group of Jesuits and other religious fanatics on the French side, and of Puritan zealots, chiefly resident in New England, on the other side, when the combatants met they might easily have fraternized across the lines. What interest had the Dutch traders and land speculators of New York, or the Quakers and German pietists of New Jersey and Pennsylvania, or the Catholics of Maryland in fighting the French? And he will search in vain who looks for an exhibition of enthusiasm and spontaneity on the part of the people of the southern colonies in these conflicts. The same indifference prevailed among the French *habitants* of Canada. The officials on both sides were continually prodding the colonists and drafting them, under one form or another, into war. The clergy were adding their exhortations and benedictions and were assuming that their tribal god, on either side, was blessing their respective enterprises. But the rank and file, in the assemblies and outside, were always hanging back, protesting against the taxes and insisting that the wars should be carried on and the burdens borne by some other colony or section of colonies, in short by the other party. This was

intensely human, but it was not ardent patriotism. If it
had not been to an extent overcome by Europe and by official
and clerical influence, the French might never have been
driven from the North American continent and its wide
stretches opened to the exploitation of the Anglo-American,
the race of destiny.

And why should not the British and French — and the
Spanish as well — have dwelt together in peace and friendship
on this continent? Was it not spacious enough for all of
them, especially as the French and Spanish have never been
migratory peoples and were never likely to be represented by
large numbers of colonists? And the British, too, had it not
been for the conflicts, persecutions and general misgovernment
which made Great Britain and Ireland intolerable as a dwelling place for tens of thousands of the best of their subjects,
would have found great difficulty in peopling any very large
part of the American continent. Large bodies of Germans,
too, and important contingents from other nationalities, were
driven by the same causes to add their numbers to the general
body of colonists who owned allegiance to the king of Great
Britain. Had such a result as we have just mentioned been
worked out, American civilization would have been enriched
by the cultures of three great nationalities, working together
in friendly rivalry to develop each its peculiar genius and the
products to which their endowments naturally gave rise. Even
the German, too, might have been admitted, after he had
sufficiently recovered from the exhaustion of the Thirty Years
War to have strength for over-sea colonization. Instead, we
have had for a time a sordid fragment of Spain on the south,
and they still have in Canada an isolated remnant of the
French nationality which, under the control of a domineering
clergy, has fallen back, in the persons of large components of
it, into a state of more than mediaeval obscurantism. And
we have spread over the vast bulk of the continent a polyglot
Anglo-American type of civilization, developed with very little
competition from outside, and certainly suffering from lack
of depth, variety and beauty.

But such a result as has just been briefly sketched was
made impossible by the wars and the national jealousies and
hatreds of Europe. These were of varied origin, social, politi-

cal, economic, religious, and were inherited by the colonists. They were systematically promoted and kept alive in the colonies by officials, merchants and clergymen. Lawyers, too, would have given their aid, had they existed as a distinct class before the later colonial period and, as it was, their influence was exerted largely in common with the official class. The end also was attained without the aid of newspapers until about the time when the influence of lawyers began to make itself felt. But when public opinion did begin to find a voice through the newspaper press, slight though its influence was at that time, it certainly was not pacifist in type and did not tend to abate national prejudices or pugnacity.

In New York we have already seen the way preparing for the outbreak in the perplexing three-cornered relation between the French, the Iroquois and the British in the region of the Mohawk valley.[1] For a decade or more the French had been trying to keep missionaries among the Iroquois as a means of winning them over to peace and an alliance, and this directly threatened the ascendancy which the British claimed over them. Among the Abenakis in Maine analogous conditions existed. In both cases Indians who were converted under French influence were induced to remove to Canada where they could be better kept under the control of the priests and the government and employed against the English. To the territory in both these regions well defined English and French claims existed, of which the keen rivalry for control over the Indians was one of the expressions.

One of the stretches of territory the possession of which was violently disputed from the first was Acadia and the land extending to the westward of it at least as far as the Kennebec river. We have seen that the English had made many grants in that region and established some more or less temporary settlements.[2] The French had done the same. The frontier between the Kennebec and Hudson rivers had been so well defined by the planting of English towns and hamlets that it had to be accepted by the French as a fact, though the wilderness to the north lay open to their raids. The energy of French explorers, priests and traders

---

[1] Osgood, American Colonies in the 17th Century, III, 367 *et seq.*
[2] *Ibid.*, I, 122 *et seq.*

had meantime opened pathways along the Great Lakes and revealed the existence of the Ohio and Mississippi rivers. By means of this the sphere of relations between the French and the Indian tribes of the far West had been wonderfully broadened, their fur trade increased, and their prospect of dominion enlarged almost beyond their fondest dreams. At the time of which we are speaking plans of colonization and conquest which must necessarily result from such momentous discoveries were just beginning to be formed. These first of all directly affected the right to the control of Lake Ontario and to the territory of the Five Nations. This territory neither party had yet settled, but over it they were beginning to reach out eager hands. The Indians were still in full possession. They were the allies of the English and the bitter hereditary enemies of the French; really they were trying to balance between the two, and were open to such propositions from both as would enable them to maintain at least a nominal independence. The topography of the country and the claims of the French were such that, following the courses of the rivers, they might easily be extended to the Gulf of Mexico. If they were followed up by settlement, the English might easily find their entire western frontier threatened and themselves cut off from the interior of the continent. Against such a contingency as that their sea-to-sea charters would prove a very flimsy parchment defence.

This was the issue, in its broadest terms, which was just appearing above the horizon when Andros was imprisoned in Boston and Leisler seized the reins of government at New York. The few among the English who thus early began to understand it were forced to think of their frontier as a whole and of the colonies as having common interests which should unite them in joint measures of defence and in a common Indian policy. These measures they must adopt for defence against a common foe who would concede to them no right to American soil which they were not able to defend. They must think and act continentally. Upon the minds of the mass of English colonists these ideas had not dawned. It will be one purpose of these volumes to exhibit the slow and hesitating process by which, on the English side, this issue was met and the evolution of the political system which conditioned and accompanied it.  The drama opened simultaneously in the two storm centres, the country of the Abenakis in Maine and the country of the Iroquois in New York.

In the colonial wars only small bodies of troops were employed and they for the most part militia drawn from the farms and shops and almost destitute of military training. Their leaders were little better than the rank and file and terms of service were very short.  Discipline was weak and ineffective.  Military authority was often at the lowest ebb. The administrative arrangements also under which the forces were called out, trained, armed, paid, fed, clothed, and transported were of the simplest and crudest nature, and whole departments of activity as they had been developed in European armies, even of that time, were nearly or wholly lacking.  Therefore, according to modern standards, these wars were slight affairs and their effects correspondingly superficial.  But they involved considerable effort for the primitive semi-frontier conditions of that place and time and left corresponding effects.  The wars were the one new and important influence which, after 1689, was added to the forces that had previously been operating upon the life of the colonists.  They furnish a key to the understanding of much that is new in the period to come.  For evil and for good they ultimately produced widespread political effects and social changes.  In colonial relations they affected every department of administration.

So far as France and her allies were concerned, they occasioned the suspension of the acts of trade and substituted therefor in law an absolute prohibition of trade with the enemy.  Temporary embargoes were laid both by the British government and by the colonies and for various purposes.  It became necessary that trading vessels should go in fleets and under convoy, and elaborate regulations were made concerning these.  The effect of war upon finance, both in the colonies and in Great Britain, was immediate and great. Resources were strained, debts were incurred.  In the colonies the wars gave rise to paper money, with all its varied phenomena of depreciation, stay laws, partial or complete repudiation, fluctuation of exchange and general confusion in the relations between debtor and creditor. The currency in turn gave rise to some of the most difficult problems in colonial administration. Requisitions for men and money by the home government would scarcely have been needed had it not been for war. As expenditures and debts increased, abundant opportunities were given for the assemblies, already well assured of the power of the purse, further to limit the discretion of the colonial executives. War drew the colonies to an extent out of their isolation. It necessitated communication and cooperation in various forms, congresses, the despatch of messages and troops across colonial boundaries, the combining of forces and joint efforts to procure supplies of all kinds for their use. This spread geographical knowledge and information concerning the character of the people in the different colonies and revealed the necessity of better means of communication. The wars kept the need of colonial union in some form before the minds of officials and people and revealed the weakness which came from its absence. That war affected the numbers and distribution of population, that it extended the frontier at certain points and contracted it at others, is perfectly evident. It necessitated the strengthening of the navy in Europe and the building of vessels of force in the colonies, and this brought forward the important subject of naval stores. By promoting privateering and piracy, war occasioned an increase in the amount of illegal trading and so in the difficulty of enforcing the acts of trade.

War, of course, was one of the two chief instrumentalities by which the British maritime empire was built up and strengthened. By means of it power was tested and results attained. The navy grew as an incident of the struggle and naval strategy was developed. According to the mercantilist principles which were then predominant the island colonies were considered the most valuable which Great Britain possessed. Near by lay French and Spanish territories which were coveted by Great Britain and with which a profitable contraband trade was incessantly carried on. These conditions made the Caribbean Sea a cockpit of the nations. Expedition after expedition, naval and military combined, was sent thither by all the contending powers. The purpose of Great Britain was to protect Barbadoes, the Leeward Islands and Jamaica and to win territory, plunder and trade from the French and from both French and Spanish after the two nations had become allies under Bourbon rule. The principle was recognized and expressed that " all turns upon the mastery of the sea; if we have it our islands are safe; if the French have it, we cannot raise enough men in all the islands to hold one of them." For a long time these expeditions affected the northern colonies indirectly and remotely, but they lay in the background even of their relations and gave form to the conflict in general. Toward the middle of the century, however, as the scope of the struggle extended, the Gulf of St. Lawrence became a rival centre of naval and military activity and the northern colonies by that time were brought fully into the wars as they were being conducted on the largest scale. The French, too, had their grand schemes for great fleets and expeditions which should sweep the coasts and land forces which, in conjunction with troops from Canada, should lay waste town and country and force the English into submission. These never assumed very substantial form, but occasionally some such attack seemed imminent enough to awaken the fears of the British and stir them to a brief fever of activity.

Considerations such as those which have been briefly sketched reveal the essential unity of the period under review. Amid an almost infinite diversity, and a certain rugged incompleteness which attaches to all colonial and frontier life, such broad tendencies and movements show the general direction of events and give the inquirer his bearings. The wars of the period, though four in number, were only successive stages in one and the same series of events, interrupted by longer or shorter intervals of peace. The general characteristics of the struggle were the same throughout — it was a prolonged duel between France and England for supremacy and incidentally for the possession of North America. The names of the wars which have been widely used will be cast aside as meaningless and the successive stages of the struggle will be called simply the First, Second, Third and Fourth Intercolonial Wars.

War, Indian relations and the expansion of settlement make the frontier significant in American history. So far as it affected the continental colonies, the First Intercolonial War was confined to the northern frontier. The reasons for this were that Spain was a member of the League of Augsburg and an ally of Great Britain, and that the French had not yet extended their settlements into the Mississippi valley. Hence the powerful Indian tribes along the Ohio and those who lived to the southward in the Carolinas were not affected by this war and the western frontier of the colonies was not.disturbed. The operations in which Great Britain was directly concerned occurred in the West Indies and were mostly naval. Upon the colonies devolved the struggle with Canada, for Great Britain was so hard pressed by her enemies, foreign and domestic, in Europe as to have no energy to spare for the defence of any of her colonies except those upon which she directly depended for food supplies and raw materials and which were closely connected with her system of naval strategy.

Philip's War, the close of which had preceded the opening of the conflict with the French by only a decade, had extended along the entire New England frontier. The colonists of that section had carried it on unsupported by outside help. The introduction of Canada and the French brought New York at once into the intercolonial wars. Her frontier, so far as it was determined by settlements, did not as yet extend west of Schenectady, and reached only a few miles north of Albany. It consisted of a few weak posts connected with the body of the province to the south by the line of the Hudson. The river furnished the only means of communication and it took nearly a week to transport troops on board sailing craft from New York to Albany. From Hartford they could be marched overland in somewhat less time. Such stretches of wilderness lay between Albany and Boston that overland communication in either direction was almost impossible.

But although the New York frontier, as compared with that of New England, was small in extent, it was strategically very important. It was situated in the direct and easy line of communication between Canada and all the

colonies to the south. Adjacent to it lay the territory of the
Five Nations with whom the French and their allied Indians
had been in bloody conflict ever since the settlement of
Quebec and Montreal. Their expeditions had passed back
and forth through Lake St. Sacrement, Lake Champlain
and the Richelieu river, or further west across or around the
eastern end of Lake Ontario and down the St. Lawrence.
By the outbreak of war between France and England the
Dutch and English of New York were brought into this conflict as allies of the Five Nations. Albany and the adjacent settlements became outposts of defence for the entire
Iroquois country extending to and beyond the Genesee valley
on the west, for all the English colonies to the south, and to
an extent for New England as far east as the Connecticut
river. Viewed from one standpoint and in relation to
Philip's War, the New York frontier was an extension of
that of New England; but in its relation to the struggle
which was to follow it was much more than that.

It was central in location and imperial in the lines of
connection which radiated from it and along which the wars
for possession of North America were to be carried on.
Owing to the fact that these wars necessarily involved the
Indians, as well as the French and English, they necessarily
extended westward and southward toward the central valley
of the continent. The Mohawk valley and the Great Lakes
constituted the earliest and one of the most important
avenues of this approach, and the advance began from the
original New York frontier and resulted in its indefinite
extension westward and southward. At first only New England and New York were directly concerned. But gradually
Pennsylvania and Virginia, and the two protected colonies,
New Jersey and Maryland, were drawn in. Finally the
conflict extended to the Carolinas and thence to the Gulf,
and the territory along the entire stretch of the Alleghanies
became involved. All the colonies as far south as Virginia
then found it necessary to look for their protection to the
New York frontier, and chiefly so until near the middle of
the eighteenth century. This fact was finally realized by
the government of New York and by the officials and their
advisers in London, and became the leading idea behind the

efforts of the home government to secure united colonial action in the form of the contribution of quotas of men or money toward the defence of the New York frontier. Indian policy was also largely determined by the same consideration. In this way the location of New York gave to it and its frontier an importance far beyond that to which population or resources would have entitled them.

The Indian wars of the early seventeenth century, whether of the French or English, were local and sporadic, their character being determined wholly by colonial conditions. The wars of the eighteenth century were intercolonial and general by virtue of the fact that they were waged primarily between the French and English. All the colonies on both sides became finally involved in them, while the Indians were drawn in by virtue of their alliance with one side or the other. When this stage had been reached, the European combatants planned the operations of these wars and furnished the commanders and — especially on the English side — the most important part of the troops. The arms and supplies of food and the general equipment came also mostly from them. On the French side, from the first, the wars were conducted in general accordance with directions from home. On the English side this was less true, but yet the tendency toward it greatly increased toward the end of the struggle. But in all the wars, until the last, the Indians played an important and to some extent a determining part. The contest was waged in the wilderness and in the scattered settlements which bordered it; marches were made through the wilderness which covered the great expanses of territory that separated the combatants; and of the wilderness the Indians were the inhabitants, giving to it an essential part of its character as a scene of warfare. On the French side throughout the wars the Indians formed an important part of the fighting force. They always supplemented the strength of the French and often far exceeded them in numbers. On the English side this was much less true. The New Englanders received little aid from the natives in their part of the struggle. In New York the alliance with the Iroquois constituted a very important element throughout, and the influence of this was felt among all the colonies to the south and to an extent in western New England. But, as time advanced, the Indian allies of the English, except in the Carolinas and Georgia, formed a minor and a steadily decreasing part of the actual combatants, though their friendship was always considered of the greatest importance and something to be kept at all hazards. Indian methods of warfare were imitated by both sides, though less by the English than by the French. They were adapted to the forest and the clearing, and it was amid these natural surroundings that the fighting had to be done. It was these unavoidable natural and social conditions which made the wars in the colonies differ from those which were carried on at the same time in Europe and to a large extent unfitted Europeans for directing or sharing in them.

As we have seen, in point of resources and population, Canada was at a great disadvantage. But she found to a very large extent compensation for this in her political system, in the greater familarity of the French with the wilderness, their greater facility in dealing with the Indians, and in the geographical location of Canada. From Quebec or Montreal, by three or four well known routes, any of the settlements along the New England or New York frontier could be reached with almost equal facility. From the standpoint of the French the northern frontier was a unit, every part of which was almost equally accessible to them. Against this, or any point on it, they, as one colony, with a centralized autocratic government, could project their entire white and native force as they saw fit; or they could send war parties simultaneously against different points. With their force, trained as it was, this could be done better in winter than in summer, though it was quite possible at any season. To the English, with their loose political system, their frontiers appeared not as a unit, but as a series of disjointed sections, for the defence of which only the colonies immediately adjacent were responsible. Many of the colonies were so remote from the northern frontier that it was very difficult for them to send troops thither at all, and practically impossible to raise and dispatch them in time to meet a sudden emergency. So great were the distances that overland communication in those days between Albany and Virginia, Maryland, or even Pennsylvania, was almost impossible, and communication by water very slow and difficult. To send aid from these colonies to New England was never thought of as possible. Neither had New York the strength or inclination to do this. New England was therefore regarded as a section apart, which must depend chiefly upon her own resources for defence, except in cases where help could be procured from Europe. She, in turn, until the last war, was able to give little aid to the other colonies. These considerations, showing that the geography of the region was such as to enable the French to fight on the inner lines, explain in general how it was that they were able to assume the offensive at the beginning of the struggle and maintain it so long, and that in spite of their greatly inferior resources. They lived under geographical, social and political conditions which fitted them well for war. The English were sprung from a nation which had lost to an extent the militant spirit and certainly the militant form of organization. The social and political conditions under which the English colonies had been founded and grown emphasized that character. Hence, when war came upon them, they were naturally thrown upon the defensive, and even in that capacity they found it difficult to make headway against a very inferior enemy. In this connection it should also be borne in mind that the war began just as the Dominion of New England collapsed and the colonies which had composed it fell apart into even more than their usual isolation and weakness. As an accompaniment of this, New York was distracted by the revolt of Leisler, from which the Dutch of Albany long held aloof.

From the conditions which have just been described it followed that the campaigns of the intercolonial wars were of two varieties, or, in other words, that they consisted of two kinds of operations. The one was the ordinary raid, such as occurred during Philip's War and the other a local struggle with the natives. Their character has already been described [1] and will receive much further illustration in what follows. Taken together, they constituted what the French aptly called *la petite guerre,* war on a small scale, approxi-

---

[1] Osgood, American Colonies in the 17th Century, I, 546.

mately what we know as guerilla warfare. This was war of the purely local or colonial type, and the larger part of the operations of the first three intercolonial wars was of this character. Conquest was not their object but simply the infliction in a brief time of the utmost possible damage on the enemy and his country. This shows at a glance how essentially American these conflicts were — so far at least as the continental colonies were concerned — and how remotely they were affected by European conditions. It also shows to how important an extent the methods used in the fourth war differed in the main from those which had preceded.

The second form of campaign consisted of expeditions on a large scale, having as their object the invasion and conquest of the enemy's territory. These were resorted to by both the French and the English, though far oftener and on a larger scale by the latter, especially as the struggle advanced through its later stages. In *la petite guerre* the French most often assumed the offensive and provoked the English simply to measures of defence and retaliation. But when it came to operations of the larger kind, the English usually took the initiative. To these they were naturally led by a consciousness of their superior resources and of their ability, if these could be properly utilized, to conquer Canada and expel the French from the continent. These efforts usually took the form of plans for joint expeditions by sea and land against Canada, the land force to proceed from New York by the Lake Champlain route against Montreal, and the naval force — also carrying troops — to sail from the New England coast against Acadia or Cape Breton and ultimately, by way of the Gulf of St. Lawrence, to Quebec. For colonies situated as those of England were at the time, these, so far as they passed beyond the initial stages, were gigantic efforts. The distances to be covered were vast. The perils of the sea were great, especially for the sailing craft of those times, and the St. Lawrence and its adjacent waters were very little known to colonial seamen. By land the obstacles to the transportation of men and to the procuring of supplies for them while on the march were well nigh insuperable. For any considerable body of men they could hardly be overcome by colonial resources

and methods.    Communication between the force on the march
and the base of supplies was difficult to maintain.    Exposure
and suffering in their extremest forms were usually the lot of
the soldier on the march.    Nothing was more common than for
a force to be crippled by disease caught and spread by the
infection of unhealthy camps.    Between the land and naval
contingents of such an expedition the maintenance of effective
communication was impossible.    Each had to go its independent way, trusting to fortune to carry it through to a successful meeting at the Canadian capital.    When we take into
account all the difficulties which were involved, it is not
strange that such a junction was not effected until after many
futile efforts prolonged through a period of seventy years.
Both Great Britain and her colonies had to grow to a stature
in some way commensurate with such a result before the triumph could be won.    The process involved a slow accumulation of experience in the art of cooperation between the
colonies looking toward some form of colonial union.    The
methods used were very crude and the results disappointing,
but one of the most valuable lessons to be drawn from the
experience as a whole is that which bears on the subject of
colonial union.

# CHAPTER III

THE FIRST INTERCOLONIAL WAR

1689–1697

HOSTILITIES on the Maine frontier were in part occasioned by the measures which Governors Andros and Dongan had taken to establish English control over Cornwall, the territory which had been granted to the duke of York, east of the Kennebec river. Within that region, on the Penobscot, St. Castin, a French adventurer, had established a small settlement. Three times, in successive years between 1686 and 1688, his fort was plundered by the English. On the last occasion Andros appeared there in person, with the "Rose" frigate, and took everything in the house except a small altar with the pictures and ornaments about it. St. Castin was informed that his property would be restored to him if he would become a British subject, a condition to which he never conformed.

On the French side Jesuit priests were active among the Indians, rousing them again to attacks upon the English. In the fall of 1688 Indians who were said to have come mostly from mission villages near Quebec began seizing cattle and committing other outrages to such an extent in the neighborhood of Falmouth (now Portland, Maine), that soldiers were sent from Boston for the protection of the inhabitants. The people began to take refuge in garrisons and a number of Indians were captured and sent to Boston. On the arrival of Andros from New York he ordered the Indians set free and issued a proclamation requiring them to surrender their captives. On this proving ineffectual he made his winter expedition to the eastward with a force of about 700 men. He advanced as far as Pemaquid distributing nearly 600 of his men in garrisons at the various frontier settlements. At Falmouth he left 60 and at Pemaquid twice that number.[1] In thus providing for the defence of the frontier, though without any more hostile move against the Indians, Andros was

[1] See Andros' account of this in N. Y. Col. Docs. III, 723.

occupied about four months, and had just returned to Boston when he found the preparations far advanced which led to his overthrow.[1]

These events for the most part occurred before the outbreak of war in Europe. Had the Dominion of New England continued and the peace been broken only by local hostilities with the Indians, the New York system of administration would have been permanently established in Cornwall, and it may be supposed that Pemaquid would have become an outpost for defence, Indian trade and negotiation in that region similar to what Albany was on the upper Hudson. The chain of frontier posts in Maine was already better developed than were the corresponding defences in New York. But with the collapse of the Dominion of New England, the attempt to solve the problem of Indian relations along the entire northern frontier through the executive of a great royal province, and under generally peaceful relations with the French, came suddenly to an end. Whether in time of war anything effective could have been accomplished under that system would have depended largely on the personality of the executive. So great was the unpopularity of Andros and such his lack of originality and initiative, that probably little could have been achieved by him. Pressure would soon have restored the assemblies, at least one at Boston and one at New York, for in what other way could a war revenue have been raised? The result of that would have been to re-establish the two centres of government, and from each of these two the war must have been managed. No natural obstacles to cooperation would have been removed and the only political gain would have come from the joint efforts of a governor and a lieutenant governor rather than from those of two cooperating governors. In those days natural, as well as political, conditions kept New York and New England apart.

But with the fall of Andros New York was at once restored to its former status and the New England colonies to theirs. The New England frontier seemed foreign to New Yorkers and the New York frontier the same to people of eastern New

---

[1] For details respecting conditions on the Maine frontier at this time, see 3 Mass. Hist. Colls. I, 85: The Andros Tracts, III: Williamson, History of Maine, I, 586; Parkman, Frontenac.

England, though not to quite the same degree to inhabitants of the Connecticut valley. The former governments were resumed in the three southern colonies of New England. The first measure of the restored governor in Massachusetts was to reduce the garrisons which Andros had established along the frontier and to recall officers who were suspected of being Catholics. Lieutenant Weems was left in command at Pemaquid. Wait Winthrop was appointed sergeant-major-general of the Massachusetts forces, and a garrison of 50 soldiers was placed in the Castle at Boston.[1] It was also ordered that the commissions of all officers in the militia which were standing in May, 1686, the holders still living and not incapacitated or removed from their towns, should be restored and continued until further steps could be taken. Vacancies should be filled by election and approval by the aged governor, Simon Bradstreet, and the council. All laws under the old charter, so far as they were not repugnant to those of England, were declared to be in force, this implying the continuance of the existing militia system, and of the former methods of raising revenue for the support of the war.[2]

On June 28, 1689, while some steps were being taken for the dispatch of 60 men to the eastward and for the raising of volunteers for the protectoin of the towns on the Massachusetts frontier, a body of Indians surprised Dover, New Hampshire, captured three of its five garrison houses, destroyed other houses and mills, killed 23 of the inhabitants and carried off 29 as captives.[3] Major Richard Waldron, the leading inhabitant of the place, was tortured and slain in his house and his family carried into captivity. The immediate motive for this assault was the desire to avenge upon the person and family of Waldron the outrage which he had committed thirteen years before by sending 200 Indians away to be sold as slaves.

The measures which were taken after this dramatic event were typical of all those to which Massachusetts resorted during this and the succeeding wars for the punishment of

[1] Ms. Recs. of Gen. Court, VI, 39 *et seq.*
[2] Osgood, Am. Colonies in 17th Century, I, p. 468 to the end of the volume.
[3] N. H. Prov. Papers II, 49, Journal of Rev. J. Pike, *ibid.*, 55, 56. Belknap, Hist. of New Hampshire, I.

such attacks and the defence of the adjacent frontier. On the fall of Andros the New Hampshire towns had been left without a governor or a general court. Massachusetts had no authority to govern them and declined to undertake the task. But they constituted a part of her frontier and she was now compelled to do what she could for their protection along with that of the other towns to the eastward. This of course helped to revive the condition of dependence in which they had always stood toward Massachusetts.

On receiving information of the attack upon Dover, volunteers under Majors Pike and Appleton at once started for its relief from a number of the towns of northern Massachusetts.[1] They marched a distance into the woods beyond Dover, but were unable to find the enemy. The Massachusetts government also ordered 240 men to be impressed for pursuit, and that drums should be beaten in Boston and elsewhere for volunteers. John Stanton, of Connecticut, was asked to raise, if possible, one hundred Mohegan Indians, and Captain Benjamin Church to bring one hundred Indians from Plymouth. A bounty of £8 was offered for scalps and it was agreed that Indian plunder should belong to the captors. As a result of consultations between the regimental commanders and the captains of troops, it was to be decided how troopers could be used as scouts outside the towns. The committees of militia in the several towns were instructed to order their foot companies and troops to be well furnished with arms and ammunition according to law, and to give necessary assistance to neighboring towns, if attacked. Three hundred additional men were drafted from specified regiments, and from those in active service detachments were stationed at Chelmsford, Dunstable and Lancaster for the protection of the northern frontier.

Preparations were hastened by the news that, on August 2, Pemaquid had surrendered.[2] The reduction of the number of its garrison, together with the temporary absence of fourteen men, of which the Indians learned, led them to appear before the place. After a brief resistance it was surrendered by

[1] N. H. Papers, II, 54.
[2] Parkman, Frontenac, 225; Johnston, History of Bristol, Bremen and Pemaquid.

Weems on the promise of the life and security of all its residents; but, as was so often the case, these terms were violated, part of the English being killed and the rest carried into captivity. This event was at once followed by the abandonment of all English settlements east of Falmouth, a most serious contraction of the frontier on the northeast.

The general court was now called at Boston and a committee for war, consisting of three members, was appointed to act under orders from the general court and council in providing the soldiery with food, ammunition and other necessaries, and to assist in all other possible ways.[1] But the legality of the existing government was questioned by many, and occasionally impressment[2] and orders for the collection of taxes had been resisted. The evident purpose for all this activity was to strengthen the hands of the executive and to quicken action by placing directly behind it the authority of the general court. A consciousness that the government was weak appears also in another resolve calling on the selectmen of the towns to procure subscriptions for the war. A general call was also issued to persons of estate in the colony to advance money and other necessaries, the public faith being pledged that they should be paid out of the first rates which should be collected.

On August 20 the decisive order was issued by the general court for the despatch to the eastward of a force of 600 horse and foot.[3] These were to be drafted from the town militia by means of orders from the majors to the town committees. The local committees, on receipt of these warrants, were to meet and direct the press master of each town to impress the persons named on a list which should be given them. The committee of war and the colony treasurer were to see that food and other supplies were provided for the expedition and lodged at Casco and other convenient places on the route. In the Maine settlements, President Danforth appointed a committee to cooperate in the preparations and the general work of defence.[4] Captain Jeremiah Swaine, one of the

[1] Gen. Court Records, Ms.
[2] Palfrey, History of New England, IV, 28.
[3] Gen. Court Records.
[4] Williamson, *op. cit.*, I, 613, 614.

executive council, was appointed commander, and near the close of August his force rendezvoused at Newickwannock (the modern Berwick) and thence marched eastward.

Appeals were also made to the neighboring colonies for aid. To Plymouth, which was again enjoying a brief period of separate existence, Bradstreet appealed for cooperation in procuring the help of friendly Indians[1] and suggested a future meeting of commissioners of the colonies concerned. Thomas Danforth and Elisha Cooke were appointed to act in this capacity. The general court of Plymouth was called and Governor Thomas Hinckley and John Walley were appointed commissioners to cooperate with Massachusetts and act as a special council of war for Plymouth.[2] Various other regulations were issued, and Captain Church was appointed to command the Plymouth force.[3] From Massachusetts he received authority to take two of her companies under his command when he should reach Casco. The appeal of Massachusetts also resulted in the meeting of the general court of Connecticut,[4] at which Samuel Mason and William Pitkin were appointed to go as commissioners to Boston. Connecticut, contemplating the possibility of sending forces of her own, instructed her commissioners that the troops she might raise must remain under the immediate command of her own officers and that she should not be bound to furnish or pay more than 200 English and Indians. Thus quickly and for the moment did the shadow of the New England Confederacy reappear and with it the particularistic spirit of Connecticut.

But aid from Connecticut was not required for this expedition. Swaine and his men accomplished nothing. Church drove back a body of Indians in a skirmish near Falmouth, and then visited neighboring garrisons, going as far east as the Kennebec river and Pemaquid and leaving officers where they were needed.[5] The ordnance at Pemaquid was brought back to Boston lest the French might use it, and was subsequently restored to New York. This was an early sign of what soon appeared to be the settled opinion of Massachusetts,

[1] Hinckley Papers, 4 Mass. Hist. Colls. V, 203.
[2] Plym. Recs. VI, 212–216.
[3] Church, Eastern Expeditions, Dexter's edition, 4 et seq.
[4] Conn. Recs., III, 468; IV, 3 et seq.
[5] Church, passim.

that Pemaquid was too remote to be of value as a fortified outpost and should be abandoned. On the approach of cold weather, the forces of Massachusetts and Plymouth returned home. The settlers begged for permanent protection, and Church urged the Massachusetts government to permit it, but without result. The elaborate preparations had resulted in nothing more than an ineffective raid, at the close of which the border settlements were left as completely exposed to assault as ever. The commissioners of the three colonies had also separated never to meet in that capacity again,[1] though the delegates from Connecticut had signed a statement that their colony would maintain in service during the war a force proportional to its estate as compared with the estate of Massachusetts and Plymouth.

In addition to her other solicitations for outside help, Massachusetts had sent John Pynchon, Thomas Savage and Andrew Belcher as envoys to obtain, if possible, the aid of the Iroquois.[2] Jonathan Bull from Connecticut had accompanied them. A conference was held and several assurances of friendship and cooperation were given, but nothing more. Instead, the magistrates of Albany sent an urgent call for one hundred soldiers from New England for the defence of the New York frontier, and gave as their reason for this that help from the Leisler faction, in control in the southern part of the province, had been refused.[3] The magistrates of Massachusetts thought that such aid should be sent, but as the distance from Boston was so great, they suggested to Connecticut that it should send a company under Captain Bull. Connecticut fell in with this proposal and sent Bull to Albany with eighty men, and he remained there through the winter. The condition which was at first prescribed by Connecticut for this service was that the commissioned officers should be paid by the Albany Convention. To this the Convention agreed, but required in turn that the troops should obey its orders. Justice Kiliaen Van Rensselaer and Captain Gerrit Teunissen were sent to Hartford to thank Connecticut and

[1] Hinckley Papers, 212, 218. Acts and Res. of Mass. VII, 464.
[2] Conn. Recs. IV, 7; Doc. Hist. of N. Y. II, 89; N. Y. Col. Docs. III, 625; Brodhead, II, 584; Colden, History of the Five Nations, I, 106; Smith, History of New York, I, 99.
[3] Doc. Hist. II, 96.

arrange final terms.[1]  These were that Albany should furnish
the Connecticut men sufficient ammunition, food and lodging
and should pay to their three officers together eight shillings
per day.  If any of the men should be sick or wounded, the
cost of medicine and attendance should be borne by Albany.
The terms were approved by the Convention at Albany.

Until March, 1690, when they made submission to Leisler,
Schuyler and his Albany Convention made themselves responsible for the defence of the New York frontier.  It was not
a perfectly legal government, and in the matter of troops and
money suffered more from that defect than did Massachusetts.
While Massachusetts stood as a unit, Albany had to face
strong opposition from Leisler.  Certain of the regulars and
militia [2] declined to obey unless their pay was definitely assured.  When subscriptions were solicited from the burghers
and farmers toward raising one hundred men, not half enough
was subscribed.[3]  Robert Livingston was repeatedly called
upon to advance money upon their majesties' account to meet
necessary charges.  In order to induce him to continue this
after the close of September, seven members of the Convention, with Schuyler and Wessels at their head, pledged themselves in writing to see him reimbursed, and if this should not
be done within six months after the arrival of a royal governor, they agreed to pay him and to rely on the public rates
for their reimbursement.[4]

It was after Milborne had paid his first visit to Albany
and failed in his attempt to bring it into submission that Bull
arrived with his men from Connecticut.  Lieutenant Talmage
with 24 Connecticut men, was sent to garrison Schenectady.[5]
This was part of a plan which the Convention desired to
execute for reinforcing the neighboring outposts — Schenectady, Half Moon and Canastagione.  Lieutenant Staats, who
had been left in Albany in command of a company of Milborne's men and their sympathizers, was called upon to detach

[1] Doc. Hist. II, 99, 119.
[2] Ibid., 105.
[3] Ibid., 96, 103 et seq.
[4] N. Y. Col. Docs. III, 699, 710.  In a letter to Andros Livingston states
that he and "brother Cortlandt" had maintained the king's regular soldiers
at Albany until March 12, 1690.
[5] Doc. Hist. II, 135.

a part of his force for this purpose. But he made several
excuses, and finally acknowledged that, though he had been
left in the city nominally under the control of the Convention
he was still subject to orders other than those he received
from them. As no other troops could be spared, Schenectady
was the only outpost for which any provision was made. Bull
continued to act in full harmony with the Convention and
both he and Connecticut refused to recognize the claims of
Leisler. This was the situation when Count Frontenac, who
had recently entered upon his second term as governor general
of Canada, sent out his three war parties, one of which destroyed Schenectady, February 9, 1689-90.

Upon the history of the origin of these raids it is not my
purpose to enter in any detail. The events themselves are
well known and the space at command is too limited to permit
an adequate explanation of the complicated doings and relations involved. It will be sufficient to state that since the previous administration of Count Frontenac Canada had fallen
on evil times. Through the weakness of one governor general
and the lack of decisive success on the part of another, she
had been exposed to the contempt of the Iroquois. Affairs
had fallen into confusion and by the cunning of a Huron
chief a plan for peace with the Iroquois had been thwarted
and they were provoked to commit the terrible massacre at
La Chine, early in August, 1688.[1] More than two hundred
of its inhabitants were killed with horrible barbarities, and
six hundred captured, the savages suffering scarcely at all.
In the despair of the time an order was issued for the abandonment of Fort Frontenac (Cataraqui), the advance French
post on Lake Ontario, and it was carried out even to the
partial demolition of the fortress itself. For months the
Iroquois roamed at large through the open country, the
French finding safety only in their fortified towns.

It was to this scene of humiliation and despair that
Frontenac was recalled. His purpose was to restore courage
by assuming the offensive and it was only on his arrival
that the French began again to take an active and open
share in the war. An ambitious plan for the immediate

---

[1] The damage here inflicted was greater than that suffered by any single
English town at the hands of the French and Indians.

conquest of New York had to be abandoned. An effort was then made to draw the Iroquois chiefs into a peace conference at the ruined Cataraqui, but they proudly replied that all Indian prisoners must be restored by the French before peace could even be discussed. Meantime Frontenac organized his three war parties, consisting of French and Indians, one to start from Montreal, another from Three Rivers and the third from Quebec. The first was to strike at Albany, the second at the border settlements of New Hampshire, the third at those of Maine. The first accomplished the total destruction of Schenectady, sixty of the inhabitants being slain and between eighty and ninety captured. This was effected by surprise, which was made possible through the gross neglect of the inhabitants. More than a month later, Sieur d'Hertel and his party from Three Rivers destroyed the village of Salmon Falls, New Hampshire, slaughtering twenty-seven and carrying away more than fifty as captives. When Hertel, on his return, reached the Kennebec river, he met Portneuf and the party from Quebec. The united force, numbering between 500 and 600 men, then laid siege to Fort Loyal, at Falmouth, Maine, the strongest post which yet remained on that coast. Captain Sylvanus Davis, at the head of its inhabitants and a small garrison, bravely defended it till the enemy had approached dangerously near, when, learning that he was dealing with Frenchmen and not wholly with savages, he surrendered, on the solemn promise that the lives of all should be spared and they should be taken to the nearest English town. But the agreement was grossly violated. All the prisoners were given over to the Indians, who murdered part of them and carried off the rest as captives.

These attacks not only restored the spirits of the French, but spread terror throughout the English settlements. Their effect, however, did not end with this. Like the barbarities of La Chine, they in turn aroused the English to action, and in their case this took the form of plans for a joint expedition from the colonies against the French possessions. But if this was to be successfully engineered, the hostile relations between Albany and New York must be improved and that province enabled to act as a unit. Upon this also to an extent depended the possibility of cooperation on the part of Connecticut, for that colony had hitherto sided with Albany and viewed Leisler with a degree of suspicion which might easily develop into open hostility. As soon as Leisler heard of the disaster at Schenectady he sent envoys to Connecticut with power to conclude what might be needful in the crisis.[1] What they first desired was to bring the Connecticut troops at Albany under the control of orders which should be agreed upon between the government of Connecticut and that at Manhattan. Then it was desired that they should consider what measures were necessary for the joint defence of Albany and whether Massachusetts should not be consulted. Connecticut gave these reasonable proposals a cool reception. She advised Leisler to come to terms as soon as he could with the Albanians, to send them reinforcements and to disturb their Indian policy as little as possible. This cold answer kindled the ire of Leisler and his council and they charged the magistrates of Connecticut, especially Allyn, with encouraging rebellion in New York. This Allyn, writing on behalf of the governor and council, denied, and showed that the troops had been sent to Albany in order to protect the frontier, and also that they had advised the Albanians to come to terms with Leisler.

But the fall of Schenectady was surely effecting what negotiation seemed powerless to bring about. As the Albanians looked about for help they saw that little reliance could be placed upon the Indians, while Esopus, because of local " distractions," could send them no aid. Livingston and his former associates were again sent to New England, but at best appeals in that quarter offered only a remote prospect of help. Leisler sent to Connecticut and Massachusetts a warrant for the arrest of the envoys on the charge of rebellion.[2] But Massachusetts flatly refused to arrest Livingston and Connecticut promised to do so only on condition that security was given to prosecute the complaint and pay all damages if the charge was not proved to be true. No one appeared as prosecutor and Livingston was not molested. But when, under these conditions, Milborne again appeared

[1] Doc. Hist. II. 68, 75 et seq.    [2] Ibid., 179, 186.

at Albany, submission was made to him, as the only course
which seemed to offer a chance of protection, especially as
Connecticut now recalled Bull and his men.

Affairs, however, were not long allowed to remain in this
condition. Livingston and his associates in a series of forcible memorials described to the governments of Connecticut
and Massachusetts the perilous situation at Albany and the
need of a joint effort not only for its protection but for an
attack upon Canada itself with a view to its conquest.[1]
Leisler was already working in the same direction. Massachusetts urged Connecticut not to abandon Albany. The
immediate result was that, on April 11, the Connecticut
assembly voted to raise 135 whites and 80 Indians for the
relief of Albany and adopted other suitable measures of
defence. Massachusetts was prevented from taking similar
action by the destruction of Salmon Falls and Fort Loyal and
by a plan which was already under consideration for the
conquest of Acadia. As a consequence of those events New
Hampshire was formally taken under the protection of Massachusetts.[2]

But already the idea of a colonial congress was in the air.
On March 19, whether or not it was due to the persuasions
of Livingston, the general court of Massachusetts issued a
call for such a meeting to be held in New York the last
Monday in April.[3] This was directed to the governors, who
were desired to appoint commissioners to " advise and conclude on suitable methods in assisting each other for the
safety of the whole land." The governor of New York was
desired to inform Maryland, Virginia and the parts adjacent of
this plan. In some way, which the sources do not clearly
reveal, Connecticut understood, as late as April 11, that the
conference was to be held at Newport, Rhode Island.[4] But
the decisive step was taken by Leisler when he issued a call
for a congress to meet at New York, April 24, and sent it not
only through New England but to the colonies as far south as
Virginia.[5]

---

[1] This correspondence will be found in N. Y. Col. Docs. III, 692–731;
Mass. Arch. (Ms.) vol. 35; Conn. Recs. IV, 15; Doc. Hist. of N. Y., II, 232.
[2] Mass. Arch. (Ms.) vol. 35, Order of March 19, 1689/90.
[3] *Ibid.*      [4] Conn. Recs. IV, 15.      [5] Doc. Hist. II, 211.

The congress met at New York on the first of May.[1]  It
was attended by William Stoughton and Samuel Sewall of
Massachusetts, by John Walley of Plymouth, by Nathaniel
Gold and William Pitkin of Connecticut, and by Jacob Leisler
and Peter De la Noy of New York.  Because there was not
sufficient time for calling its assembly, Rhode Island sent no
delegates, but undertook to raise £300 for the common enterprise.[2]  Maryland expressed the intention of sending one
hundred armed men.  President Bacon of Virginia replied
that the proposal would require the action of the assembly
and nothing could be done until the new governor arrived.[3]
The delegates from Massachusetts and Connecticut were
appointed and instructed by the general courts, both colonies leaving to them considerable discretion.  Massachusetts
desired that the cost of garrisons on the frontiers and of the
expedition to Nova Scotia be made a common charge.  She
also said that she could not join in an expedition against
Canada unless the other governments supplied two or three
ships and stores of ammunition.  It also might be necessary
that suitable vessels be made ready at Boston, Rhode Island
and New York to guard the coast against attacks by privateers and pirates.  If delegates should appear from all or
most of the colonies north of Virginia, Massachusetts felt
inclined to bear one-fourth of the common levy; otherwise
the quota must be left to the discretion of the delegates,
as also the determination of the way in which the money
must be raised.  The delegates from Connecticut were
authorized to pledge the colony to that part of the common
expense which justly fell to its share, this to be determined
on the basis of population.  An expedition for the conquest
of Canada was the only enterprise which they contemplated,
and the troops which Connecticut might send must serve
under officers of its own appointment, except in the case
of the chief field officers.

Of the proceedings of the congress we know nothing.[4]  Its

[1] Doc. Hist. II, 239;  Mass. Arch.  vol. 36, April 15, 17, and 18.
[2] R. I. Recs. III, 273          [3] Doc. History of N. Y. II. 249.
[4] Samuel Sewall attended, but he thought it more important to set down
in his diary the number of the psalm which they sang at the Sunday service
in the Dutch Church than any statement whatever about the business of the
Congress.  5 Mass. Hist. Colls. V, 318.

final resolutions were to raise by quotas from the colonies which were represented 735 men. The number promised by Maryland was counted on to raise the total to 855 men. It was probably understood that the Massachusetts and Plymouth contingents — 220 men in all — should accompany the expedition by sea, and that the rest attack Canada by land. Of the land force it was provided that the governor of New York should appoint the commander and that the second in command should be designated by the other three colonies. Important questions that arose while the expedition was in progress should be decided by a council of war consisting of the commander and the commissioned officers. Troops who were sent out should not be employed on any other service without the further consent of the colonies. The influence of New England appeared conspicuously in the final provision, that the officers should be required to maintain good discipline, punish vice, and see that the Sabbath was kept and the worship of God observed.

The influence of war in developing the spirit of colonial union was never more evident than in the events of 1690. By them a vista of possibilities was opened to view. But the sequel will show how great were the obstacles to the success of such plans and how far short the hopes which were then cherished came of realization. Massachusetts had already committed herself to the conquest of Acadia and her expedition had sailed for Port Royal before the congress met at New York.[1] This enterprise was a revival, though on a larger scale and in time of war, of that kind of bucaneering expedition which in former days had been sent against D'Aunay.[2] The idea of it originated among the merchants of eastern Massachusetts, to whose trading and fishing enterprises the presence of French in Acadia was a menace. They appear in connection with it as "undertakers," ready,

---

[1] The most important sources of information for that enterprise are in the Mass. Arch. (Ms.), Vol. 35 and the Recs. of Gen. Court (Ms.) for the early months of 1690. See also a "Journal of the Expedition from Boston against Port Royal," with a summary of a muster roll appended to it. This is among the papers of Geo. Chalmers, in the Harvard College Library. It is referred to by Parkman, Frontenac, 236 and by Palfrey. See also the Memoire de Meneval au Ministre. Bowen, Life of Phips (Sparks, Am. Biography).

[2] Osgood, Am. Colonies in the 17th Century, I, 412.

that is, to meet its chief expense in view of the reward which would come to them in the form of plunder and in other ways. In January, 1690, they applied to the general court to give their plan its recognition and assistance. The court voted to allow them the use of the two sloops of war which belonged to the colony, with their ordnance and appurtenances, for three or four months, with all the profit they could make from the French, and all the trade of the places they should take, till further orders from the king. They were also to receive in the king's name from the governor of Massachusetts a commission for the expedition, provided they would not plunder those who should surrender peaceably, that honorable terms should be offered them and that the king should be informed of what had been done.

Prominent among the merchants and others who supported the enterprise were John Nelson, nephew and heir of Sir Thomas Temple, James Taylor, John Foster, Edward Bloomfield, Elias Heath and Joseph Appleton. A memorial of Nelson's to the governor, council and representatives, of the same date as the vote authorizing the expedition, shows what his ideas were.[1] After enlarging on the advantages to the fishery and on the influence over the Indians which would come from the conquest of Acadia, he stated that, as public charges were heavy, divers gentlemen had resolved to offer to provide for the attack on Port Royal at their own expense and in such a way as " by a committee from you joined with ourselves may be thought most convenient." To this end they applied to the general court to permit volunteers to be raised and commissions to be granted to all necessary officers and such rules and instructions prepared as should be agreed on and thought most fit for such an expedition.

After a favorable report by the joint committee of the two houses, on February 6 the general court passed the desired act. It made no appropriation, but gave permission for raising volunteers and provided for commissioning the officers. One sloop was to be lent gratis. As to plunder

---

[1] For some time after this Nelson appears as a leading advocate of the conquest of Canada. His views were similar to those of Robert Livingston and they may have discussed them together.

and rewards, it was provided that, if the artillery should be taken from the place, the Massachusetts government should have the first offer of it; the Indian trade and such plunder as might reasonably be made should belong to the undertakers, pending the king's settlement. In preparing for the expedition a committee of the two houses took charge of the transport of ammunition and stores and another committee was concerned with preparations in general. This committee was empowered to impress men and also vessels, if volunteers did not readily offer themselves. The offer of shares in the prospective plunder probably did not attract the requisite number of volunteers, and so in the end the expedition became a government enterprise.

Seven vessels in all were provided for the expedition, with 288 sailors and between 400 and 500 militia. Sir William Phips offered himself for the post of commander and was appointed. He was an energetic, self-confident ship-carpenter and sea captain from the Maine frontier. By enterprise, a fortunate marriage and his good luck in recovering a large treasure from a Spanish galleon which had sunk in the West Indian seas, he had risen to a place among the wealthy men of Boston and had won a baronetcy. He had recently returned from England and was now to make his advent as a public man in his native colony. Preparatory to that he had connected himself with the North Church of Boston, Cotton Mather's church, and thus had insured the support of that powerful interest and after his death the publication of a highly laudatory biography of himself. His experience as a commander had thus far been confined to a single vessel, though there he had shown the ability on two occasions to quell incipient mutiny among the crew. Though a novice in war, he had shown the energy and daring which recommended him to the leaders of this enterprise. As usual, a council of war was named in Phips' instructions, the advice of which he was ordered to take in all important emergencies. If the fort at Port Royal should hold out against his summons to surrender, he should attack and destroy both it and the shipping which might be there, and then seize other French settlements along the coast.

The expedition reached Port Royal on the eleventh of

May and took the French wholly by surprise. Meneval, the governor, had a garrison of only seventy men, and the fort was in poor repair. He therefore surrendered without attempting resistance. According to French accounts, Phips violated the terms of the surrender, by plundering merchants and desecrating the church. Phips' excuse for what occurred beyond what was authorized by his instructions was that the French carried off some of the booty and tried to conceal it in the woods. After demolishing the post and reducing a few places at the head of the bay of Fundy, the expedition returned to Boston, bringing its plunder and about sixty prisoners, including the governor. A president and six councillors, chosen from the inhabitants, were appointed by Phips to govern Acadia, and were told to expect support as long as they remained faithful to Massachusetts. Possession was also taken in the name of the king of the sea coast from Port Royal to the Penobscot river.

As soon as the expedition returned, the " undertakers," in conjunction with the governor and council, began to plan for the permanent occupation of the region and the exploitation of its advantages for trade. It was agreed that in return for mounting a garrison at Port Royal the " undertakers " should retain control of trade with Acadia for five years, or until the crown should issue orders for the settlement and trade of the entire region. An invitation apparently was issued for English settlers to remove eastward and in connection therewith the possibility was considered of reaching some understanding with St. Castin as to bounds and trade which would consist with the king's honor and the plan of the " undertakers " to supplant the French in trade with the Indians. A suitable vessel was to be maintained on the coast. In prosecuting this interesting experiment its supporters went so far as to appoint Edward Tyng, an officer and agent of the " undertakers," to be governor of Nova Scotia and Acadia.[1]

But the most important questions which had to be faced

---

[1] Mass. Arch. (Ms.) vols. 36 and 37. Sewall's Diary, I, 337, 339, contains references to a violent controversy between Phips and John Nelson about money of Meneval's which was kept by Phips. Cotton Mather defended Phips.

on the return of Phips were connected with the projected
expedition against Canada. In order to reveal the main
features of this enterprise in their true relation, it will be
necessary to attend first to the land expedition from New
York. It was with this that the congress had chiefly concerned itself. Massachusetts at first drafted 160 men and
ordered them to rendezvous at Sudbury and march thence
to Albany.[1] But when they were on their march toward
Springfield news came of the attack on Port Royal and this
necessitated their immediate recall. With that ended all
hope of assistance from Massachusetts to the expedition
against Montreal. From the colonies to the south of New
York came no aid whatever. Hence the force was limited
to the troops which could be furnished by Connecticut and
New York, and to such Indian contingents as might be procured. At the congress New York had promised 400 and
Connecticut 135 men. Connecticut lived up to its agreement,[2] but of the New York quota only 150 men had reached
Albany by the middle of July. Leisler also had hoped that
about 1800 Iroquois could be induced to join the expedition,[3]
but when the western tribes of the confederacy learned of
the outbreak of small pox at Albany, they said that the
great God had stopped their way.[4] Only a few Indians,
some of whom came from Connecticut, accompanied the
force.

At the outset a serious difficulty arose as to the appointment of the commander. It had been agreed that Leisler
should appoint him, and his friend Milborne was at once
selected.[5] This was unsatisfactory to both Connecticut and
Massachusetts. Before the appointment was made Connecticut expressed to Massachusetts the aversion felt towards
him by its troops and their desire that a man of some emi-
nence and one who was acceptable to the soldiers should be
chosen.[6] Fitz-John Winthrop, the eldest son of their distinguished governor, who as a young man had served under
General Monk and in recent years had been an honored

---

[1] Mass. Arch. (Ms.) vol. 36, dates of May 14 et seq; Doc. Hist. of N. Y
II, 259.  [2] Conn. Recs. IV, 26.  [3] Doc. Hist. II, 247.
[4] N. Y. Col. Docs. IV, 195.  [5] Doc. Hist. II, 240.
[6] Mass. Arch. Vol. 36, May 14.

citizen and official of Connecticut, was their choice. Secretary Allyn wrote the sentiments of Connecticut on this matter to Leisler, and he, after consulting his council, sent a blank commission for Winthrop, if he chose to accept it, which he did.[1]

This honorable action on the part of Leisler was accompanied with great vigor and energy in preparing for the expedition. It is in his measures for defence that Leisler, though autocratic, appears at the greatest advantage. He used his power of impressment to the full extent in order to secure an adequate supply of provisions. But the amount available he found insufficient, and had to call upon Connecticut to supplement it. In an effort to avoid the scourge of small pox, he resolved to enlist no man who had not had the disease. But the small pox had already broken out in Albany and some of the Indians had died of it.[2] It was also reported that half of the Connecticut soldiers there were sick from disorders attributed to the eating of bad pork. These were among the obstacles which were to wreck the expedition. When Winthrop arrived to take command the prospect was already most discouraging.[3] " I found the design against Canada," he wrote, " poorly contrived and little prosecuted, all things confused and in no readiness or posture for marching the forces toward Canada, yet every one disorderly projecting something about it "; a good description of what must have been true of many colonial enterprises.

On the first of August the march northward began, though the small pox was already spreading rapidly among the soldiers. Schuyler had gone ahead to have canoes prepared for transportation. On August fourth it was found that the supply of pork was " scarce eatable," and that the bread was fast giving out. As a result especially of the vigorous labors of the Dutch soldiers, they reached Wood Creek. Word was then sent back for more provisions, but the reply was returned that no more were to be had. Soon after it was learned that, owing to the lateness of the season, the bark would not peel and so no more canoes could be built,

[1] Doc. Hist. II, 253, 265.     [2] Doc. Hist. II, 255.
See his Journal, in N. Y. Col. Docs. IV, 193 *et seq.*

though the supply they had was not enough to transport half
the Christians. Among the victims of small pox was Lieutenant Hubbell, one of the best of the officers. There therefore seemed no choice left but to return.[1]  Having detached
Captain John Schuyler, brother of Peter Schuyler, with forty
English and one hundred Indians to make a raid toward La
Prairie de Madeleine, opposite Montreal, the order was given
to return. On August 20, three weeks after their departure,
the troops, sick and demoralized, reached Greenbush opposite
Albany.

French scouts, sent out by Frontenac, presently discovered
some English on Lake Champlain and reported the fact at
Montreal. Frontenac at the time was there in conference
with the western Indians. Some precautions were taken
against surprise or attack, but Schuyler's men pounced on
a group of French farmers who had come out of the fort
at La Prairie to cut grain, captured nineteen and killed six.
Their cattle were also killed and barns destroyed. The
English then retired with their prisoners and reached Albany
the last of August.[2]

Leisler, on Winthrop's return, had put him under arrest
for alleged neglect and cowardice in ordering the retreat.[3]
This provoked the anger of the Connecticut soldiers and the
Mohawks at Greenbush and also, when the news reached it,
of the Connecticut government. Leisler was reminded in
no uncertain terms that the army was a confederate body,
over which he had not individual control, and that a prison
was not the proper remedy for the evils from which they
suffered. Leisler attempted to defend his act, but was so
threatened with uprisings in the southern part of the province
that he could not afford to make additional enemies, and so
Winthrop was at once released. Thus ended in hopeless
failure the first attempt to send a land force through the
wilderness to Canada as part of an expedition which should
embody the joint forces of all the northern frontier colonies.

Meantime Massachusetts and Plymouth had resolved to
attack Quebec by sea and were pushing forward preparations
for their part of the joint enterprise. They first sent an

---

[1] Winthrop Papers, 6 Mass. Hist. Colls. III, 13.
[2] See Schuyler's Journal, Doc. Hist. II, 285.    [3] Doc. Hist. II, 288 et seq.

application to the British government for a grant of arms and ammunition,[1] and delayed the start for some time in hope of a favorable response; but they received none. An embargo was laid on vessels which should enter at Boston between the middle of June and the tenth of September. Bounties were offered for the capture or destruction of the enemy and for the release and return of English captives. The families of those who enlisted should, if necessary, be relieved by the selectmen of their towns on the credit of their wages. As in the previous expedition, volunteers were first solicited and then a draft was ordered to complete the number needed. Five ships and about 34 trading vessels, great and small, were ordered impressed for the expedition.[2] The largest of these was the " Six Friends," which had been in the West Indies trade and now carried 44 small cannon. From New York came a frigate of 24 guns, a brigantine and a sloop.[3] The crews and officers of the vessels in most cases went with them, and the owners who subscribed to the expenditure were to share in the booty equally with the government.[4] The privateering element in this expedition, however, was small as compared with that in the raid on Port Royal. A force of about 2300 effective men sailed on this expedition, and the whole was placed under the command of Sir William Phips and Major John Walley, of Barnstable. The success of Phips at Port Royal made him appear to be the natural and providential leader, and he received instructions almost identical with those which had been given him for the previous expedition. The force sailed from Nantasket,[5] August 9,[6] with provisions for four months,

---

[1] Mass. Arch. (Ms.) vol. 36; Mayrand, Phips devant Quebec, 175, 182.

[2] Cotton Mather's Life of Phips, in Magnalia, Book II. Mayrand, Phips devant Quebec, 195 et seq.    [3] Letter of Leisler to governor of Barbadoes, Doc. Hist. II, 245.    [4] Mayrand, 177.

[5] Governor Bradstreet, in a letter to Governor Treat of Connecticut, states that the departure was delayed by the presence of privateers on the coast. He adds, "The burden of the sea expedition lies exceeding heavy upon this colony . . . It was always expected we should have had your assistance therein, and that soldiers from your parts would have appeared to make up the number proposed.   What you have done at Albany is very inconsiderable to bear a proportion with this in which we are so far engaged and have been at so vast expense." In a letter a month later Bradstreet deplores the failure of the expedition from Albany, which had been planned to reach Canada just in time to prevent the relief of Quebec.    [6] Conn. Mss. War, I, 112 et seq.

insufficient ammunition and no pilot for the St. Lawrence. Though Phips reached his destination, to call his expedition foolhardy, starting as it did so late in the season and upon so long a voyage, is to speak with moderation. Moreover, while he was starting, near the close of the summer, on a voyage of 1500 miles over dangerous and mostly unknown waters, the force which was intended to cooperate with him in the reduction of Canada was returning to Albany disabled and without striking a blow. If Canada was to be conquered, it must now be by the dash and courage of the New Englanders alone. If they had stopped to count the chances, they would never have faced the risks which lay ahead. But they did not know of the failure in New York, they had the confidence of zeal and inexperience and were under a leader whose successes, in small enterprises, had been won by good luck. Fortunately they had good weather, and their small craft without serious accident reached the Isle of Orleans, below Quebec, on the 15th of October. They had consumed two months on the voyage, and the leisurely way in which they had proceeded up the St. Lawrence, with repeated sessions of the council of war, was to continue to the end.

But now that they had reached Quebec, the New Englanders had no reasonable chance of capturing the town unless they could attack it before Frontenac was able to complete its defences and to rouse the country for its protection.[1] In this they failed, for they had arrived too late. During the early summer the fortifications of the city had been considerably strengthened, and this work was completed and batteries placed at important points during the ten days which passed between the arrival of news of the approach of the English and their appearance before the town. In that interval also Frontenac himself had come from Montreal, where, as we have seen, he had been holding a great

---

[1] The various accounts of the siege are printed by Mayrand, with the sources whence they were taken. Two other accounts have since been printed in 2 Mass. Hist. Soc. Proc. XV, 281. One of these is by the Rev. John Wise, of Ipswich, who had led in the resistance to taxation by Andros. He went as a chaplain on the expedition and severely criticises the conduct of Walley. The events of the siege have been many times described and the purpose of the text is simply to indicate the main features.

Indian conference, followed by all the troops who could be spared from its garrison. The militia of the surrounding country also was called to arms. In this way, before the English were ready to begin their assault, a force had been collected in the capital which was superior in numbers to the men Phips had brought with him. Under a leader like Frontenac, in a town by nature so nearly impregnable as Quebec, a force of such strength made the prospects of Phips hopeless from the first.

Phips made no attempt to pass the town and attack it from above, thus cutting off, if possible, reinforcements from the interior of the colony. He arrived too late for that, and such a plan would scarcely have been possible for him. A direct frontal attack, accompanied by an assault on the part of the land troops from the Beauport shore and across the St. Charles river, was the only course left and it was that which he followed. Two days were spent in preliminaries, including the spectacular challenge and reply which passed between the two commanders. On the third the troops were landed on the south shore, to make the assault under the lead of Major Walley. They were met by the French in repeated skirmishes in a rough country, but made headway toward the St. Charles, above which rose the fortified heights of Ste. Genevieve, the north-eastern approach to the city. It is possible that the courage of the English would have been equal to an assault, and their condition suitable for it, if it could have been made the day after the landing; but even then it would have been necessary to ford the shallow river, unsupported by an artillery fire, and to have scaled the height in the face of cannon and of defenders at least equal in number to their assailants. But the supply of ammunition among the English was very inadequate, and their rations were scanty. During the nights, which were bitterly cold, they had to lie unprotected on the ground. Something therefore must be done at once or, under such conditions, men would become unfit for duty. Meantime Phips, who never left his vessels, wasted his ammunition in a futile bombardment of the Lower Town and the face of the Rock, and when it came to the pinch Walley's courage failed him. He had not the resolution to attempt the assault, which of course

he would be expected to conduct in person. During the
preliminary skirmishes even he was seen to keep himself
carefully out of the firing line.

After two nights on shore, Walley sought an interview
with Phips on board the latter's vessel, and it was resolved
to withdraw the troops. This was done the following night
(October 11th) under fire from the enemy, Walley being
among the first to leave the shore. His men were left to
find their way on board the boats as best they could. All
hope of capturing Quebec was now practically abandoned,
and after a brief delay, for repairs and exchange of prisoners,
the fleet withdrew down the river and entered on its long
homeward journey. The speedy approach of winter necessitated haste on this voyage if disaster was to be avoided.
As it was, the fleet became separated, one of the vessels
being wrecked on Anticosti and others not reaching Boston
till the following February. Three or four of the vessels
never returned.

The failure of this expedition was a serious blow to
Massachusetts. Its outfit, taken in connection with the other
expenses of the war, had drawn heavily upon her resources.
Had the venture proved a success the advantage she would
have considered cheaply purchased; but, as it was, her
treasure and hundreds of lives had been lost. The heretic
and the savage were now as well able to assail her frontier
as ever they had been, while Massachusetts was plunged
into debt and had to resort to the issue of paper currency,
from the depreciation of which she did not escape for nearly
two generations.

In February, 1690–91,[1] just after his return to the colonies, Joseph Dudley wrote to Blathwayt that they were
then raising twenty rates in Massachusetts, making thirty-
seven rates since the Revolution, and all were too little
to pay for the last expedition against Canada. The blame
for it, he said, was divided between Phips and the field
officers. Three months had passed since the return of the
expedition, and still there was no news of five vessels, which
had not a month's provision on board. If they were lost,
it was feared that about one thousand men had been lost on

[1] Cal. St. P. Col. 1689–92, pp. 387, 409.

this expedition, and nothing accomplished. The country was in a bad state and should be no longer neglected. Laurence Hammond and others were also writing home to the same effect, and the severe criticism of the Massachusetts government may in part have been inspired by Dudley.

Though Phips went at once to England to procure assistance for a second attempt on Quebec the following year, all that he obtained was the governorship of Massachusetts. No force was sent to the northern colonies, and their joint efforts on a large scale against Canada during the first Intercolonial War ceased with 1690. The operations in New York as well as in New England during its remaining years consisted of minor raids organized in response to similar attacks of the enemy or to unfounded alarms caused by rumors of their approach.

Throughout 1690 there were many alarms and much activity on the New England frontier. Reports of losses and threatened attacks on Saco and Wells, in Maine, were followed by the calling out of three small detachments in the course of the summer. Finally, Major Church and his Indians and Indian fighters were again summoned.[1] His failure to get his pay for the last raid made him wary of the Massachusetts council. But his objections were overcome and he undertook to muster the men at Plymouth and sail thence to the Piscataqua. Many irritating delays occurred while the transports were being fitted out, during which Church had to quiet the clamors of his recruits with rum. Some 200 whites and Indians went with Church, and Massachusetts sent, or called out from the eastern garrisons, about 300 of her militia. Major Robert Pike, of Salisbury, was placed in command. Captain Converse, of Wells, one of the best Indian fighters of the day, accompanied the force. From Piscataqua they went to Pejepscot, near the modern town of Brunswick, and thence to Winter Harbor. On the way they had several skirmishes with the Indians, destroyed some of their corn and released a few English captives. When they returned to the settlements, the men were in a pretty sorry plight. Various reports unfavorable to Church had also got abroad, to which he had to reply. But his

[1] Church, *op. cit.*, 67.

doings helped to incline the Indians to a brief truce, which some of them agreed to at Wells in November. On the strength of this, orders were issued for the recall and disbanding of all troops on the eastern frontier which were in Massachusetts pay.[1]  Church denounced this policy, but this is to be accounted for in part by the discouragement and exhaustion which resulted from the failure at Quebec. Fortunately, in this case, no harm resulted, for the enemy remained quiet during the winter.

Under the conditions of alarm which then existed, towns like Saco and Wells were literally outposts, garrisons, holding the frontier. Their inhabitants were so constantly exposed to attack that they raised little food for themselves, and to a large extent were dependent on other towns or the province at large for support. Earlier in the year a committee of the general court had reported in favor of a more systematic treatment of the frontier as a whole.[2]  It proposed that the court should designate certain places, situated like those just mentioned, as frontier towns. Possibly there would be twelve of them, and they should be maintained as such. A garrison should be kept in each, proportional in size to the number of inhabitants. In such towns also one-half of the males of proper age, with such officers as were necessary, should be kept under continuous orders, so that on notice of any part of the frontier being attacked the men of the three nearest towns might go to its relief. It was estimated that about 500 men would be necessary for this service, while from 250 to 300 others should be organized as a flying force or scouts. Had this plan been adopted, it would have proved an anticipation of the " minute men " of the Revolution.

The hopes which had been entertained that peace might be concluded with the Indians in the spring of 1691 were disappointed, and attacks on the frontier near Wells and York were renewed.[3]  The inhabitants, therefore, renewed their appeals for protection. It was said that some of the

---

[1] Mass. Arch. Vol. 36, contains many orders and much correspondence relating to this expedition.

[2] Mass. Arch. Vol. 35.

[3] Mass. Arch. Vol. 37; Gen. Court Recs. Sess. of April, 1691.

garrison houses had been abandoned because of lack of men. The people did not dare to go into the fields for planting and one settlement could not go to the defence of another. These reports made the necessity for another expedition evident. In preparation for this, at the close of June, the governor and council sent a letter to certain gentlemen in Suffolk, Middlesex and Essex counties, requesting them to visit the towns and talk with the leading men there about the financial straits of the colony, and see if £1000 could not be at once raised as a part of the rates already voted, those who advanced anything to have it put to their credit in the assessment. The proceeds were to be used for ammunition, provisions and clothing for the troops. How this plan succeeded we do not know, but early in July another expedition, under Captains March and King, went to the eastward.

A letter from these officers, dated Portsmouth, July 11, throws some light on the endurance of recruits. On a march of one day through the woods from Haverhill to Exeter, 14 men had given out, but with the aid of horses had been carried into town. On the short march from Exeter to Portsmouth they had to leave a number of men, " the quality of whom," say the writers, " besides the badness of their arms, makes them very unfit for the service." When they reached the frontier, with the men from York and those who had been transported on a sloop, they had but 108 men, not above 60 of whom were fit for any but garrison service. Their ranks must be filled up or they could not attempt an advance against the enemy. After consulting with Vaughan and others of the New Hampshire council, they asked for authority to impress fifty or sixty men at Portsmouth, with vessels for transportation by sea to Saco, where Indian fishing places were and where it was hoped the savages might be surprised. The governor and council of Massachusetts approved this suggestion and wrote to Vaughan to further it. It seems also that some of the militia officers in Massachusetts had failed to draft their full quotas for the expedition and strict inquiry was to be made into this.

March and King also found difficulty in securing a surgeon. Surgeons about Portsmouth could not be hired because, they said, they had served their country more than any others in the profession and had been paid for none of their expenditures. They therefore were not able to furnish themselves for the expedition. A messenger was now sent back to Boston to inform the authorities of the straits to which the force was reduced. He returned with an additional supply of medicines, a surgeon, a promise of reinforcements and orders to press on. They reached Pejepscot,[1] where Church had been the year before, and after meeting with a sharp attack from the Indians returned without accomplishing anything decisive. Vaughan reported at the middle of August, that about eighty men had come back shattered and unfit for any but garrison duty, so that they were distributed among the frontier towns. Later communications show that these soldiers were almost destitute of clothing and that they must receive a supply before winter. In October Buckley, the commissary, wrote from Portsmouth, a centre for distribution, that he knew of no clothing available for soldiers' use, " without which I conclude it impossible for the most of them to subsist." · A month later Vaughan wrote that all the soldiers were in such want of clothing that they were unfit for service. This brought an order from the governor and council to the majors of the several Massachusetts regiments to collect clothing and provisions for the troops. Contributions were solicited in Connecticut, and Rhode Island was also applied to, but she met it with her usual *non possumus*, her plea[2] this year being that, because of disloyal and discontented people, the colony was unable to levy a tax. A call for provisions was also made necessary by the fact that so many cattle had been killed on the frontier that meat, as well as bread, was exceedingly scarce. A vessel loaded with supplies was sent from Massachusetts to the northern settlements.[3]

During the winter of 1691–2 the terrors of the frontier were increased by an attack on York, Maine, in which 48 were killed, among whom was the minister, and about 70 were made captive. This was followed by the appointment

---

[1] Niles, Hist. of the Indian and French Wars, 227.
[2] Mass. Arch.; Cal. St. P. Col. 1689–1692, p. 477.
[3] Mass. Arch.; Niles, 228.

of Elisha Hutchinson to the command of forces in the east. Captain Converse now returned to service after a year's absence, and was finally stationed at Wells. There, in the following June, his capacity as an Indian fighter was conspicuously proven by the brave defence of that place against the prolonged attacks of 500 French and Indians under Portneuf. The conduct of Converse, Storer, and the handful of men they had, bravely aided by the women, was exceeded in heroism by nothing in the annals of Indian warfare.[1] Converse was soon after promoted to the rank of major and put in command in the eastern settlements. While he held this office he scoured the woods extensively and caused a fort to be built at Saco. Such was the stage which had been reached in the long struggle which was to test the endurance of the English and the Indians, when Massachusetts received her charter and a royal governor in the person of William Phips.

On the English side the conditions of the conflict along the frontiers had not yet differed essentially from those of Philip's War. It had consisted of a series of brief expeditions, mostly defensive in character and sent out after the enemy had inflicted his worst injuries. The colonists had shown themselves capable of much activity and of great sacrifices, but strategy had been impossible and they had shown little foresight or capacity for forming and executing general plans. Commissary arrangements were defective or totally lacking. When the troops were transported by sea to or near the scene of action, they arrived in fair condition, but long marches through the woods disabled all but the most fit. No baggage trains accompanied them and when they camped, whether in heat or cold or storm, it was in the open without any covering except what they carried on their backs.

It required hardened farmers, woodsmen, sailors and artisans to stand such trying experiences, and it was of these classes that the troops chiefly consisted. In the region where they were fighting, the wilderness, a few miles back from the coast, was unbroken. The streams, except in their lower courses, were difficult to navigate. The natives had no large towns or great storehouses of corn, like those of the

---

[1] Parkman; Bourne, Wells and Kennebunk, 212; Niles, 228.

Five Nations, and such settlements as they had were so far inland as to be nearly inaccessible to the English. It was therefore not possible to destroy them by a single expedition, but they must be slowly worn away by the destruction of their food supply and the gradual diminution of their numbers. That was the result which, if any, was to be expected from *la petite guerre*.[1]

In the fall of 1692 the British government entered upon the policy of demanding requisitions from the neighboring colonies on the east and south for the defence of the New York frontier. Under an order of council circular letters were sent to the governors of New England and of the other colonies as far south as Virginia requiring them to give assistance in men and money on application from the governor of New York. Letters accordingly were sent, it being left on this occasion to the colonies to determine the quotas which they should contribute.[2] In the following February similar letters were again sent to Connecticut and Rhode Island and a commission was ordered prepared bestowing on the governor of New York the command over the militia of Connecticut. It was characteristic of British policy that, though Massachusetts was bearing the brunt of the conflict, the aid was to be given to New York. Moreover, if Phips was to have the enlarged powers mentioned below, the absurdity of making New York the object of requisitions from New England is apparent. No result followed this action. In the autumn of 1693 Governor Fletcher of New York sent to the lords of trade an estimate of the annual cost of the defence of the Albany frontier and also of the quotas of men which, in proportion to their population, the colonies from Massachusetts to Virginia might furnish.[3] If this plan were executed in full, a force, including the New York levy, of 600 men would be raised, at an annual cost of about £21,000.

---

[1] From the correspondence and other sources of the time it would be possible to trace the progress of the struggle and to illustrate its character vividly and in detail. So far as external events are concerned that has already been done by other writers, though the administrative features of the conflict and the type of warfare, as illustrative of social conditions then existing, have hitherto received scant attention.

[2] Cal. St. P. Col., 1689–1692, pp. 717–719.

[3] *Ibid.*, 1693–1696, pp. 26, 173.

In the summer of 1694 orders to furnish quotas were actually sent to all the colonies, with the exception of the Jerseys, from Massachusetts to Virginia, but the numbers mentioned were quite different from those which appeared in Fletcher's estimate.[1] It is sufficient here to say that all the colonies involved excused themselves upon one pretext or another, though special conditions which led to these refusals and the extent to which appeals that came directly from New York influenced the final result will be indicated elsewhere.[2]

Closely connected with these initial efforts to establish the policy of requisitions was that of securing greater unity of action in military affairs within New England. The principle upon which the crown acted in these cases had been stated, as against the claims of the Long Parliament, in the preambles of two of the earliest statutes of the Restoration.[3] It was that in all the king's realms and dominions the sole and supreme command and disposition of the militia and of all forces by sea and land ever was in the king and could not be pretended to by either or both houses of parliament. The same principle of course applied to the assemblies in the colonies. Now that a stable royal government existed in New York, and in 1692 William Phips was installed as royal governor of Massachusetts, it appeared possible to apply this principle especially to the militia of Rhode Island and Connecticut. In Phips' commission it was provided that he should command not only the militia of his own province but that of the two colonies just mentioned and of New Hampshire as well.

As New Hampshire during the administration of Phips was organized under Samuel Allen, as proprietor and governor, and his son-in-law, John Usher, as lieutenant governor, that province fell nominally into the same class with Rhode Island and Connecticut. But owing to its exposed situation on the frontier and to the long period during which it had willingly submitted to the government of Massachusetts, its position was really very different from theirs. It also lacked their corporate consciousness and to a degree their social

[1] N. Y. Col. Docs. IV, 108, 109, 111.
[2] Cal. St. P. Col. 1695–1696, pp. 315, 316, 335, 593, 713 (index).
[3] 13 Car. II, c. 6, and 13; and 14 Car. II, c. 3.

and political opposition to Massachusetts. Its inhabitants were too few to defend themselves and therefore welcomed the continuance of military control by Massachusetts, a condition to which they had long been accustomed. It was now continued in much the same form as before, Massachusetts keeping a company of soldiers in New Hampshire for several months during the latter part of 1692 and beginning of 1693. It fully realized its need of protection and addresses on this subject were sent to England. This was also one of the burdens of Usher's correspondence, and the provision that the militia of New Hampshire should be under the command of the Massachusetts governor was a step toward the revival of the Dominion of New England, which on the whole Usher welcomed.[1] But the political and social affiliations of Phips were with the party of Vaughan and Waldron, the opponents of Usher, and that led the lieutenant governor and Allen to fear that this might be a prelude to the extinction of the proprietorship and the full incorporation of New Hampshire with Massachusetts. For this reason, and because of the value of its forests, Usher urged somewhat later the interposition of the crown and the sending of an independent company from England to garrison the fort at the mouth of the Piscataqua. But these were vain ambitions and had no real effect upon events. The conduct of the war and of negotiations with the enemy along the entire northeastern frontier continued essentially under the control of Massachusetts, New Hampshire contributing such men and such sums of money as its exposed and ravaged condition permitted.[2]

The entire history and the present condition of Rhode Island clamored against submission to the powers of Phips in any decisive form. Jealousy of Massachusetts and fear that the members of the Atherton Company were using this as a means of promoting their claim were at once used as adverse arguments. So too was the stock argument that Rhode Island was exposed toward the sea more than other colonies and would be especially imperilled if her men were drawn away to distant points. The military rights granted to the

---

[1] Cal. St. P. Col. 1693–1696, pp. 64, 96, 106.

[2] Ibid., 75, 88, 121, 129, 168, 192, 235. N. H. Prov. Papers, II, 74, 102, 104–5, 110; III, 3, 7, 9.

colony by its charter furnished the legal backing for these objections. The general assembly was called in special session to consider the question, and two of its members were sent to Boston to ascertain what powers over their militia had been granted to Phips. But they were not allowed to see his commission and received no satisfactory reply to their inquiries. They were informed, however, that Phips had sent into their colony several military commissions the object of which was to displace most of the officers who were already in command. The assembly met this with the order that none of the commissioned officers, chosen at the last election, should lay down their offices without its permission and that in the meantime they should keep their companies in a suitable posture of defence. Addresses were sent to the crown, setting forth the rights which existed under the charter and asking that, because of this affair and of the disputes about boundaries, the charter might be confirmed. Christopher Almy was sent to England as agent.[1]

The plea of Rhode Island was referred to the attorney general, and he rendered an opinion that the powers over the militia given in the charter were in force and he thought that the chartered rights of the colony might be confirmed. The committee of trade reported to the same general effect, but with the qualification that the crown might appoint a commander-in-chief who should always have authority to command such parts of the force of any colony as were deemed fit, and in times of invasion to take charge of the rest of its forces for the preservation of those colonies most in need, provided a force sufficient for defence was left at home.[2]

When Phips informed Connecticut of the authority which had been given him over its militia and desired full information as to the state of its defences, Governor Treat called the assembly together in June, 1692.[3] A letter, which received its approval, was sent to Phips expressing surprise at the power which had been conferred on him, as it was well

---

[1] R. I. Recs. III, 285–300. Cal. St. P. Col. 1693–1696, pp. 161, 191, 216. We hear of French privateers occasionally visiting the Rhode Island coast and of one being driven off by the frigate "Nonesuch."

[2] Ibid., 151, 216, 277, 282.

[3] Conn. Recs. IV, 77.

known that by charter the colony had the full government of its militia and had always used it faithfully. They were ready to contribute aid, but they should adhere to their charter. Correspondence followed in reference to the sending of aid, but it does not appear that Phips repeated his demand for full command over the Connecticut militia.

In the winter of 1692/3 Phips asked Connecticut for a quota of whites and Indians to serve on the northeastern frontier. This implied no unusual authority and the general court at first voted to meet the desire of Massachusetts in part. But in the end the feeling that their men were all needed for the defence of the Connecticut valley prevailed and no relief was sent. Instead, an empty promise was made for the next year that £400 should be granted in provisions and pay at Connecticut rates. This angered Phips and drew from him a sharp reply. " It is their Majesties' just expectation," he wrote, " and you will find it accordingly directed, that their several governments do bear an equal proportion of the common charges of the war, both of men and money, and pursuant to their commands unto myself referring unto your colony, I expect it accordingly." But this demand elicited no response.[1]

Pressure upon Connecticut was next brought to bear by the home government through New York. In May, 1693, that part of Phips' commission which related to Connecticut was revoked and the command of its militia was bestowed on Governor Fletcher. The natural aversion of the Puritan colony to being ruled from New York as a centre was thus aroused. A few months before, this feeling had been awakened afresh by correspondence with Fletcher in which he had expressed sympathy with a small group of malcontents, under the leadership of Gershom Bulkeley and others, and had warned the governor and council at Hartford to treat these people with greater justice, as well as to increase their activity in the war. The argument of Bulkeley was to the effect that since the overthrow of Andros and the resumption of government under the charter affairs had been on an uncon-

---

[1] There was correspondence at the same time in reference to the defence of Deerfield and an alleged outrage by certain Mohawks. Goodell, Acts and Resolves of Mass, VII, 377–382.

stitutional basis in Connecticut [1] and that the charter could never legally be revived by action of the colony alone. Fletcher doubtless thought that by identifying himself with this group of loyalists he could secure a foothold in the colony. But he was doomed to disappointment.

Early in October, 1693, a French privateer named Reaux was arrested in New York and he reported that 700 recruits had recently arrived in Canada from France. This stirred Fletcher to the resolve to publish his commission relating to Connecticut, while he was at the same time considering the advisability of taking up his residence for the winter in Albany. The council advised him to go to Albany by way of Connecticut and take troops with him from that colony, adding that others would be dispatched up the Hudson for his support, if necessary. Such were the preliminary steps which led to the visit of Fletcher to Hartford.[2]

The magistrates of Connecticut were not unaware of what was coming and early in the previous September had appointed Fitz-John Winthrop as agent to England to obtain, if possible, a confirmation of their privileges under the charter.[3] He carried with him a letter of credence and a long exposition and defence of the services of Connecticut men in Philip's War and the present struggle. As soon as he arrived in England Winthrop began to labor for the revocation of the power which had been granted to Fletcher over the militia of the colony, with what success will appear in the sequel.[4]

About the middle of October Fletcher, taking Bayard and Clarkson and a small train of attendants, repaired by sea to Connecticut to publish and enforce his commission. The general court was then in session at Hartford and awaited the New York governor's arrival. On October 24th, after having

[1] "Some objections against the pretended government of Connecticut" abstracted in Cal. St. P. Col. 1689–1692, p. 705. Bulkeley's "Will and Doom," Colls. of Ct. Hist. Soc. Bulkeley's views will be referred to at greater length in a subsequent chapter.

[2] N. Y. Ex. C. Min. Oct. 10, 1693, and Cal. St. P. Col. 1693–6, p. 172. Conn. Ms. Recs. War, I, 170, 172.

[3] Conn. Recs. IV, 102. Conn. Ms. Recs. Foreign Corresp. I, 42 et seq.; ibid., War, I, 79.

[4] Cal. St. P. Col. 1693–1696, p. 193 et seq. Winthrop Papers, 6 Mass. Hist. Colls., III, 22 et seq.

received a call from Governor Treat, and Allyn and Pitkin of the council, Fletcher announced his arrival to the general court and asked that his commission be read. Governor Treat told him instead that they were ready to hear what he had to say. Fletcher then ordered Secretary Clarkson to read the commission. This was done, many of the people trying to force their way in to hear it. Treat then suggested that Fletcher hear the Connecticut charter read, and on the latter protesting that he had no concern with their charter or their civil affairs, one of the members cried out, " Let the charter be read, that all the people may hear it."

That public feeling in and about Hartford was deeply stirred, was made evident in this and other ways. When, therefore, Fletcher insisted on a prompt compliance with his demands, both Governor Treat and the general court urged that further action be postponed until they could learn from their agent what the home government was going to do. Messages daily passed back and forth, Fletcher becoming more irritated and imperious in his demands as the delay continued. The general court informed him that it found in his commission no express superseding of the authority over the militia which they found in their charter, nor any order to surrender it, and finding in the commission several things which required explanation they would await further orders. Fletcher was by this time in a blustering mood and declared that they had no right to their militia and required their obedience or they would answer the consequences. Bayard also was repeatedly sent with insistent messages to the court. But it could not be moved. Its final reply was that, as Fletcher had said, the military power was in the king, but " it has been settled on us " and enjoyed during the last two reigns as well as the present. Fletcher also tried to secure recruits directly from among the people and possibly, with the aid of Bulkeley [1] and other loyalists, induced a few to accept the king's commission. But the general attitude was one of determined opposition and, after Fletcher had been in Hartford a week, armed men were seen prowling about his lodgings and threats were made to shoot him if he tried to

---

[1] Conn. Mss. 197, 206. Palmer, Trowbridge and the two Rosewells are mentioned.

publish his proclamation in the streets. Bulkeley also wrote to Fletcher that he and his friends were in danger of attack and were suffering great damage both to person and property. Finding it to be dangerous to proclaim his commission himself and impossible to induce the Connecticut authorities to proclaim it, Fletcher returned to New York to await further orders from England. To Blathwayt and the lords of trade he sent a full account of his reception, and declared that Albany would be lost if Connecticut were not forced to submit. A report had also come to his ears that the towns at the eastern end of Long Island had instructed Winthrop to secure in England, if possible, an order for their separation from New York. Later, in order to stop misrepresentations, Fletcher had his commission relating to Connecticut printed and circulated among the people of that colony.[1]

In April, 1694, this matter came up before the authorities in England.[2] As Rhode Island and the Jerseys were in somewhat the same situation as Connecticut, Mr. Almy appeared with Winthrop on behalf of the former colony and Dr. Coxe for the latter. Connecticut pleaded its charter and asked that Fletcher's commission be explained and restricted, so that they might continue in quiet and prosperity and his majesty's interests be furthered. The law officers, Ward and Trevor, were called upon for their opinion and their reply was, " We are of the opinion that the charters of Connecticut, Rhode Island and East and West New Jersey do give the ordinary powers of the militia to the respective governors thereof, but do also conceive that their majesties may constitute a chief commander, who may have authority at all times to command or order such proportion of the forces of each colony as their majesties shall think fit; and further, in times of invasion and approach of the enemy, with the advice of the governors of the colonies, to conduct and command the rest of the forces for the preservation and defence of those colonies which shall most stand in need thereof, not leaving the rest unprovided of a competent force for their defence and safety; but in time of peace, when the danger is over, the militia within each of the said provinces ought . . . to be under the govern-

---

[1] Ex. C. Minutes (N. Y.), Jan. 8, 1693/4.
[2] N. Y. Docs. IV, 102–108.

ment and disposition of the respective governors of the said colonies." The agents of Connecticut and Rhode Island promised to provide their respective quotas. The committee of trade recommended that these terms be accepted, and it was so ordered by council.[1] Fletcher was instructed to receive a quota of 120 men from Connecticut in time of war only and to call out no larger number unless quotas from the colonies were proportionately increased. The rest of the forces of Connecticut were to be commanded by Fletcher " with the advice " of the governor of that colony. The general conclusion reached after a full hearing of the case was that, while the ordinary power over the militia was in the colonies mentioned, the crown might appoint a commander for general purposes of defence against an enemy who was common to all or several of the colonies, this to be done with the advice and aid of the governors involved.[2] Thus, owing to the failure of the law officers to find legal justification for the plan of the administration in the unqualified form in which it was first stated, another interesting experiment of the imperialists came to naught. It is true that the government bestowed upon Bellomont and Dudley the same authority over the militia of neighboring colonies as had been given to their predecessors, but there was even less prospect of its being enforced in the second war than there was in the first.

The only naval expedition sent out by England during the war which reached or was intended to reach the continental colonies was that of Sir Francis Wheeler. He was sent to the West Indies in the winter of 1692–3, with a squadron of twelve men-of-war, and two regiments.[3] It was the plan that in the spring he should sail to New England, there refit and proceed to attack the French in Canada. Governor Phips was ordered to prepare ships, men and provisions for the expedition and Fletcher was instructed to consult with Phips

[1] This was Aug. 2, 1694; R. I. Recs. III, 299; Cal. St. P. Col. 1693–1696, p. 316. By this Phips' commission, so far as it affected Rhode Island, was virtually annulled.

[2] No one was appointed to what was really such chief command until Braddock, while it was natural at the time of Fletcher that Connecticut should suspect his errand to be a step toward subordinating it to New York or even toward annexation.

[3] Cal. St. P. Col. 1693–96, pp. 31, 124, 128, 133, 156, 165. Acts and Res. of Mass. VII, 384; Sewall's Diary, I, 380.

as to the share of New York in the enterprise. Sickness broke out after Wheeler's squadron reached the tropics and carried off from a half to two-thirds of the men. The consequence was that he did not reach Boston until July. Phips stated that instructions concerning the expedition had failed to reach him and therefore no preparations had been made. The season was now so far advanced and Wheeler's strength was so reduced that, in the opinion of Phips, an attempt to ascend the St. Lawrence that year was not to be thought of. When Wheeler prepared to attack Placentia, in Newfoundland, the Massachusetts governor discouraged him by the statement that he was forbidden to send the militia outside Massachusetts without the consent of the assembly and that it had just adjourned. The Indian war nearer home was also absorbing the energies of the province, while the men were unwilling to go on board the vessels of the squadron from fear of catching the contagion, which had not entirely ceased.

The news of the coming of Wheeler gave rise to large plans for defense in New York.[1] For many sessions during the summer the governor and council were busied with projects for collecting a land force at New York, building batteries on either side of the Narrows and a battery on the point of rocks just at the end of Manhattan Island, the building of a new stockade about Albany, the laying of an embargo and a plan for spreading the alarm by means of beacons through the province, when cattle should be driven into the woods and all should repair to their colors, and those of the militia who lived south of Ulster and Dutchess counties should march to New York. The Jerseys and Connecticut were called on for troops and Maryland for money. Much attention also was paid to the providing of funds at home, in which Robert Livingston bore a prominent part. The imagination of Fletcher in planning quickly rose far beyond the capacity of the province, especially as it was stimulated by a letter from Wheeler and by a rumor that the Five Nations were inclining toward peace with the French.

The council of New York had meantime resolved to send one of its number to Boston to welcome Wheeler, ascertain his designs and find if there was still time to prepare for his

[1] Cal. St. P. Col. 1693–96, pp. 131, 148, 151, **157**.

assistance. Under directions from home a circular letter was also ordered to be sent to the neighboring colonies asking them to send commissioners to New York on the first Wednesday of October to deliberate as to quotas to be furnished for the relief of the guards on the frontier. This proposal looked directly toward joint action for the defence of New York and under its lead, though, if carried out, it would revive the methods of the hated Leisler.

As to the other part of the plan Chidley Brooke, the collector and receiver of New York, was sent to Boston to interview Wheeler and Phips. Phips' anger against Fletcher and New York was still hot, as Brooke was soon to find. After four futile attempts he secured an interview with the governor. The conversation, as reported by Brooke, did not refer at all to Wheeler's plans — which now had apparently been abandoned — but to the defence of New York and to the share which it was hoped Massachusetts would take in the proposed conference. When Brooke came to demand two hundred men, fully equipped and paid by Massachusetts, as its proper quota for the defence of New York, Phips' anger broke forth in loud and confused speech. As soon as he could articulate, he was understood to declare that he woud not send a farthing and that the proposal was monstrous. Brooke coolly replied that it was the thought and plan of the queen. When Brooke asked that commissioners be sent to the proposed October meeting, Phips again roared, " If they have no other business, no commissioners shall come from me." " I found his reason drowned in passion," adds Brooke, " and the storm increasing, so thought it high time to leave him." Some of the Massachusetts councillors who were present were naturally ashamed of Phips and, with some of the representatives, they gave the New York agent a very unflattering account of the governor.[1] In August Brooke reported to Fletcher and his council in New York the reception he had met with at the hands of Phips, and it was decided to send an account to England of his refusal to furnish aid or even to send a commissioner to the projected conference in October.

After 1690 the military operations in New York, so far as they affected the English, were insignificant. Alarms were

[1] N. Y. Col. Docs. IV, 58.

frequent, caused chiefly by raids of the French which were directed primarily against the Five Nations. These awakened fears at Albany and her calls for help were reechoed through the province and the neighboring colonies. Forces were hastily gathered and sent northward from New York City only to arrive after the French and Indians had done their work and started on their retreat toward Canada. If any execution was done at all on the enemy, it was by troops sent out from Albany immediately after the alarms. Such an episode as this occurred in February, 1692/3, when Fletcher made a quick passage, in three days, from New York to Albany, and Schuyler with his Albany force pursued the retreating French as far as the upper Hudson on their toilsome march back to Canada. In the summer of 1696, owing to an ineffective invasion of the Iroquois country by Frontenac, the province was much alarmed, but no attack was made upon the English. A little later in the same year came rumors that a French squadron would soon appear on the coast. The alarm was renewed, but it proved to be a false one. On such occasions Connecticut was called on to send reinforcements to Albany and she usually responded favorably and with reasonable promptness. These matters did not appreciably affect the course of the war, for it resolved itself into a struggle over the New England frontier and a continuation of the conflict between the French and the Iroquois. The English of New York directly had little to do with the result, and what did happen will best be told when we speak particularly of that province. Various exhortations to united action will then come under review, which were a direct outgrowth of New York conditions and looked toward a time when the chief centre of war would be the western frontier.

But indirectly, as a result of the alarms in New York, the Connecticut valley and western frontier of Massachusetts were affected. After 1692 the valley became an important centre of the war, and conditions similar to those which existed there in Philip's War returned. The problem of securing the co-operation of Connecticut with the valley towns again arose. As to the previous war Colonel John Pynchon,[1] of Springfield,

---

[1] There is much interesting correspondence of Pynchon in the Mass. Arch. See also Burt, Hist. of Springfield; Sheldon, Hist. of Deerfield; Goodell, Acts and Resolves of Massachusetts, VII, 460, *etc.*

commander of the Hampshire county regiment, was a central figure. Pynchon was again the medium of communication between militia committees and officers of that region and the seat of government in Boston. Through him also much of the negotiation with Connecticut was carried on. He frequently applied to the authorities at Hartford for men to do scout duty in Deerfield and other valley towns. Reports of Indians and their outrages in all western Massachusetts came at once to him and he saw to it that parties were formed for pursuit. During the winter of 1692 Deerfield and adjacent towns were much worried by an encampment of Mohawks on the adjacent hills. They were there to hunt, but it was feared that they meant to attack some settlement. Much correspondence resulted and the garrison at Deerfield was strengthened, but the winter passed quietly.

It was Pynchon who informed Phips of the attack of the French on the Mohawks in February, 1692/3, and precautionary measures against an attack were adopted, though they again proved unnecessary. In the summer of 1693 an attack on Brookfield caused Pynchon to organize a party for pursuit, which overtook the retreating Indians and recovered most of their captives. Under a warrant from Pynchon Deerfield was fortified and so strict a watch was kept there that the French did not succeed in surprising it. After the repulse of an attack on Deerfield in September, 1694, much unprofitable correspondence passed between Massachusetts and Connecticut about the garrisoning of that place, as well as the furnishing of part of a crew and equipment for a galley for the defence of the Rhode Island coast. Connecticut gave little help and that rather grudgingly, while Massachusetts was sure that the burden of war was very oppressive upon her. Pynchon kept well informed concerning local politics in the towns of the valley, for these had a bearing on the kind of militia officers who were chosen. His letters contain more than one amusing reference to contests in town elections and many shrewd estimates of the men who were nominated to the governor for militia officers.

Though alarms and conflicts continued in the neighborhood of Wells and Kittery, the effect of the appearance of Phips as royal governor of Massachusetts was to move the scene of events somewhat to the eastward. This was due to an order which he brought from the home government to rebuild the fort at Pemaquid. This was essentially a resumption of the policy which had led to the grant of Cornwall to the duke of York and the efforts of Andros and Dongan to establish English influence in that region. Since the fall of Pemaquid the English frontier had greatly contracted, and it was the purpose of this order to restore it, as a means, if nothing more, of maintaining the claim of England to the disputed region between the Kennebec river and Nova Scotia. Had the raid of Phips against Port Royal been a genuine act of conquest, it should have been supported by the rebuilding of Pemaquid and the assertion of control over all the intervening coast. This was considered necessary as a defence against the French and pirates.

The stone fort built by Phips at Pemaquid in 1692 was quadrangular in form, 737 feet in circumference around the outer wall; the south wall, fronting the sea, was 22 feet high, and more than 6 feet thick at the port holes, which were 8 feet above the ground. The wall on the east line was 12 feet high, on the north 10, on the west 18 feet. A round tower, or flanker, at the southwest corner was 20 feet high. The fort stood twenty rods from high-water mark and had 18 guns mounted, 6 being 18 pounders. It was garrisoned with 60 and sometimes with 100 men and was named William Henry. It was one of the largest and strongest forts built by the English during the colonial period. As the expense of it was burdensome to Massachusetts and it was remote, the policy of building and maintaining it was never popular there. Church expressed to Phips the opinion of the average Indian fighter and colonist concerning such structures, when he said that " he had never any value for them, being only nests for destruction." [1]

As an accompaniment of the rebuilding of Pemaquid, an unusually large expedition was sent to the eastward. An embargo was also laid by Massachusetts, and a committee of war was appointed to provide a supply of clothing and other stores.[2] Eight hundred men in all were sent out for two

[1] Church, Eastern Expeds. edited by Dexter, p. 86; Thornton, Me. Hist. Colls. V, 282.  [2] Mass. Archives.

months, and the expedition was to go by sea. At Phips' request, Church raised as many as possible of his old soldiers and Indians and led a raid to the islands and coasts about the mouth of the Penobscot river, destroying some of the corn of the Indians and capturing some of their peltry. He then went up the Kennebec and destroyed more corn and also the Indian fort at Teconnet, — the site of the later Fort Halifax, opposite Waterville. Church then returned to Pemaquid, where his men worked for a time on the fort.

Provoked by a renewal of Indian outrages, in the spring of 1693 Major Converse, at the head of about three hundred men, scoured the frontier from Piscataqua to the Kennebec river. This was followed by the appearance of Indians at Pemaquid, with a proposal for the cessation of hostilities. A truce was agreed to be operative until August 10, when they promised to return with more sachems and treat. Phips went to Pemaquid at the appointed time and concluded what was expected to be an enduring peace with them.[1] The Indians agreed to abandon the French, to cease hostilities and submit to the English crown. For the performance of all this they gave hostages. This gave a brief respite to the frontier and was followed, according to English practice, by the immediate reduction of the number of soldiers posted there. The efforts of the French priests — Bigot on the Kennebec and Thury on the Penobscot — with their supporters, to break the peace were incessant. They were bent on destroying the heretic and on maintaining the connection between Canada and Acadia. In the following year they were successful in reopening hostilities. About midsummer 1694, Oyster River, now Durham, in New Hampshire, was attacked with the usual disastrous results, and ten days later a less successful descent was made on Groton, in Massachusetts. This spread alarm again along the entire New England frontier.

The rebuilding of Pemaquid should have been followed by the permanent occupation of the adjoining coast and, if possible, by the strengthening of English hold on Acadia. But that was not to be. The resources of Massachusetts, and particularly the abilities of Phips and his successor, were inadequate to this task. Since 1690 no steps had been taken

[1] Mather, Magnalia.

to follow up the occupation of Port Royal. No force had been kept there which was able to make headway against the French. Villebon was now established at St. John, and thence privateers were sent out, as formerly, to prey on English shipping. So burdened was Massachusetts by the war, that the expediency of trying longer to keep Port Royal was questioned. The English government was asked to take both it and Pemaquid under its immediate charge, but that called forth no response.

Such were the evils suffered from the French privateers that, in the spring of 1696, preparations on a considerable scale were made for an expedition against St. John.[1] Connecticut and Rhode Island were applied to for help, but without result. Church was again called out and a body of men advanced to Portsmouth and the settlements of western Maine. Then came news that, in the Bay of Fundy, the French had captured the frigate "Newport," which had been relied on to co-operate with the land force. This was followed by the descent of a French force under Le Moyne d'Iberville on Pemaquid. He brought with him the Baron St. Castin and a body of Indians. Captain Pasco Chubb, who commanded the fort, had 95 well armed men, 15 cannon and abundance of ammunition and provisions. But as soon as bombardment began and he was told, on a second summons by St. Castin, that if an assault was made he must expect no quarter, he at once surrendered. Even as it was, some of the English were massacred, though most of them were rescued by the French. The fort was partially destroyed and the cannon carried off. Chubb was tried for high treason, though not convicted, and soon after perished in an attack of the Indians on Andover.[2]

In retaliation for this blow Church was at once sent on what was, for this war, his most extended raid. He went as far as the Bay of Fundy and up Chignecto bay, in which region he destroyed much property and captured a few Frenchmen. Thence he returned to St. John, where he plundered a new fort, but did not attempt to capture the town. On his way back Church met a force under Colonel John Hathorne,

[1] Goodell, Acts and Res. of Mass., VII, 505, 513. Mass. Arch.
[2] Acts and Res. of Mass., VII, 590.

who had been sent out to supersede him and to lead the combined troops against Villebon at St. John. Church quietly submitted, and they returned to the neighborhood of St. John, but accomplished nothing. Hathorne had said, when appointed, that he felt too inexperienced for such a task. These two expeditions have well been called a reconnaissance in force, with the result of ascertaining that the enemy had temporarily deserted their old haunts along the coast and retired into the country. The next year the New England settlements were thoroughly alarmed by reports that the French would send a squadron to complete the conquest of Newfoundland and thence, in cooperation with the Abenakis and 1500 troops from Canada, sweep the coast from Penobscot southward. Active preparations on the part of Massachusetts and Connecticut for joint defence were occasioned by this, but the French never came and with this episode the war came to an end in that region.[1]

So far as the immediate purpose of the belligerents was concerned, this war in the colonies was wholly without result. The French had caused much suffering in certain New England villages and had filled the minds of women and children with terror throughout the colonies on the northern frontier. But they had gained no territory from the English and had made no progress toward conquering them. The same was true of the English as the result of their raids and futile expeditions against the French. The English had not even done enough to inspire their enemies with fear. No territory had permanently changed hands. With the reoccupation of Port Royal by the French the colonies, so far as territory was concerned, were restored to substantially the situation in which they were at the beginning. The lines of the frontiers on either side had not appreciably changed. The Canadians had apparently not suffered at all, while the contractions of the frontier which had occurred on the British side could easily be obliterated by the extension of settlements during a few years of peace. The Indians, who did most of the fighting on the French side, showed as yet no sign of exhaustion.

---

[1] Cal. St. P. Col. 1699, p. 478. Acts and Res. of Mass. VII, 536, 548. Hutchinson, Hist. of Mass. II, 97 *et seq.* It was estimated that the war cost Mass. and N. H. £150,000 and the loss of 1000 families.

So far, therefore as the settling of the issues between the French and the British in North America was concerned, the efforts and sacrifices which had been made were vain. At the end the contestants were substantially where they had been at the beginning and the war might as well never have been fought. In Europe also the immediate results of this struggle were not very apparent, though the separation of England from the alliance with France was an important event, and through the formation of the alliance of which William III was the leading spirit, a combination had been brought into existence which Louis XIV had not yet been able to overpower. The resources of France alone, or of France in combination with such allies as she might gain on the continent, were not likely to prove sufficient to enable her to triumph over the Sea Powers and their allies within the Empire. At Ryswick a truce under the name of a treaty of peace was concluded, which gave Louis time to seat a Bourbon on the Spanish throne and thus bring Spain fully within the circle of his influence.

But certain indirect consequences, which were of some importance, had followed from the war in the colonies. These had chiefly to do with the promotion of intercourse between the colonies, a limited exchange of ideas and feeble efforts toward cooperation in military enterprises. But this affected only officials and the small forces which crossed intercolonial boundaries. Governmental action and also industry in furnishing supplies for the troops were quickened by the war. The people within the colonies which shared actively in the raids and expeditions were somewhat stirred from their accustomed ways and thoughts. The better part of them had to bestir themselves, in council house, legislature, town meeting, and in their offices, shops and houses to procure the men and means for carrying on the war. Some new administrative devices were tried and old ones were put to new and severer tests. But this war and all which were like it — the conflicts of the old régime — were limited in their means and scope and directly or deeply affected only a small part of the people. The great mass were left by them as immobile as ever. The scope of government was only slightly or transiently enlarged; occupations and social groups were not changed. Taken altogether the effects of this war were slight and superficial.

# CHAPTER IV

## COLONIAL ADMINISTRATION DURING THE EARLY YEARS OF THE WAR.  ORIGIN OF THE BOARD OF TRADE

It was by means of a temporary union of forty leaders that William and Mary were brought to the throne, the parliament and church saved, and the alliance with France broken. The so-called Revolution was a compromise, and William, cold, far-seeing, experienced, a foreigner in England, knew the weakness of his position and the degree of diplomatic skill which was necessary to secure it. He regarded himself as the instrument for accomplishing great things, rather than as the founder of a dynasty or an end and object in himself. His views also were European rather than specifically English, and the immediate prospect of war absorbed his chief energies, as well as those of the nation.

From the conservative character of the Revolution it naturally followed that no great or sudden change was made in the administration of the colonies. Since 1675 this had been in the hands of a committee of the privy council. The leading ministers of state were its most important members — the two secretaries of state, the lord treasurer, the president of the council and others — and the personnel changed with the shifting of parties and cabinets. A specially close connection had thus been maintained between the cabinet — particularly the offices of secretary of state, the treasury, and the admiralty — and colonial business. The leading statesmen of the time were sure to be on the board, and the council might sit in committee of the whole on colonial affairs. Experts in colonization, even such as later appeared, men, that is, who were called into such a body primarily because of their knowledge of trade and colonial affairs, do not appear on the committee. It was emphatically a political body, an adjunct of the government, depending largely on clerks, like Southwell and Blathwayt, to keep it informed of the routine of business.

116

The chief colonial appointments came, as always, from the king through the secretary of state. The committee of trade and plantations inquired into all colonial questions which were brought before it, by petition or otherwise, and reported to the privy council upon those whose importance demanded it. The council, of which the members of the committee constituted an important part, usually approved the reports and they were given effect through orders of council or some other form of executive action. In the discharge of its functions the committee kept in as close touch as possible with the treasury and admiralty and their subordinate offices, with the attorney and solicitor general, and, as occasion demanded, exchanged communications with any or all officials, lay or ecclesiastical, who were connected with the British government.[1] These other offices also, especially the treasury, admiralty and the law offices, were or might be themselves the originators of action, for aid in which they would call upon the council and its committee of trade and plantations. The relations, that is, were mutual.

With the accession of the new monarchs the personnel of the committee was changed. Among its members were now included some of the leading statesmen who had carried through the Revolution, both Tories and Whigs, men of great force and experience, some, too, who, at different times in the past, had served on the same committee. The earl of Danby[2] the lord president, the marquis of Halifax, the lord privy seal, the earls of Nottingham and Shrewsbury, secretaries of state, Viscount Mordaunt who was placed at the head of the treasury and Sir Henry Capel who was associated with him on that board; Sir Henry Powle, a distinguished lawyer and parliamentarian, who had long been prominent as an opponent of the Stuarts and who was now speaker of the Convention Parliament; the earls of Devonshire and Bath, Viscount Fauconbridge, Henry Compton, bishop of London, and Mr. Russell. The ministerial changes prior to the death of Mary occasioned a few shiftings in the personnel of the committee, but in relation to colonial affairs they are without traceable significance.

In the hands exclusively of notable men like these, planta-

[1] Acts of Privy Council, Colonial, 1613–1680, p. xv.
[2] Cal. St. P., Col., 1689–92, p. 6.

tion affairs remained until the creation of the council of trade, popularly known as the board of trade, in 1696. These men were deeply immersed in European affairs. They had neither leisure, equipment nor inclination for the consideration of colonial questions on their own merits. The point of view of the colonists, if they had any which was opposed to English interests, was a matter of indifference to them, or an occasion of irritation. It is not probable that they ever seriously attempted to investigate it or to weigh its merits. They had never visited America, had never felt the limitations of colonial life. To them the colonists stood on the level of the lower trading and agricultural classes at home, with the added depression in the perspective which was due to remoteness and to the fact that they lived in dependencies. The magistrates and clergymen of New England, the traders and landed proprietors of the middle colonies, the officials and planters of the south might lord it over their dependents and play the aristocrat in their little provincial capitals or on their estates, but in London they sank to the common level of colonials and all alike were objects of a more or less supercilious patronage. If the colonists were capable of feeling it, they would have been made to perceive that by the emigration of their fathers they had indeed been removed from beneath the shadow of antiquity, rank, culture and wealth and had camped upon a frontier clearing. Whatever the procedure of government and the regulation of customs duties might indicate, they were now not a part of Great Britain, but inhabitants of one of its plantations, one of its possessions. By conceiving the colonies so largely in terms of trade and industry, a type of policy had already been developed which implied that they were plantations and little more. Already preferences had set in favor of the tropical or semi-tropical colonies, and upon this was based the theory of trade. This view was emphasized as time went on, as the insistence upon the policy of enumerated commodities and the slave trade conclusively shows.

That the colonies should be regarded in this light among the aristocratic, mercantile and official classes in Great Britain at that time was natural and unavoidable. To these people they were satellites of England, means to an end far more than ends in themselves. A career of indifference or independence toward the metropolis they could not have; it was inconceivable. They must revolve around or follow in the wake of the central luminary. The planting and trading constituency in the colonies fell in with the dominant tendency or were able to develop no theory or consistent course of action which was opposed to it. In war and in other relations their affairs were managed as those of an appendage of England, as if they were an extension of it, though their inhabitants were socially inferior. This relationship was maintained in a spirit of easy, tolerant good nature, characteristic of much in the old régime, but it was the relation of a superior toward an inferior, and the petty colonial aristocrats whose eyes often turned so reverently toward the grandees of England were simply a grade in a loosely adjusted hierarchy of dignities which extended downward from the duke to the British peasant and the indentured servant of the colonies. In British history, as in that of other nations, the eighteenth century was intensely aristocratic, and the history of the colonies themselves at that time involves a study of certain phases of a kindred form of society.

Prior to the Revolution the committee of trade frequently presented to the council rather elaborate reports as the basis of their recommendations, and from these some general ideas of a colonial policy can be deduced. But until near the close of its post-revolutionary existence the committee's reports were few and brief and it indulged in no generalizations about colonial policy. This is to be accounted for chiefly by the pressure of war and of its attendant business. Before the committee passed in rapid succession a large volume of business [1] which related to the fitting out of expeditions — chiefly to the West Indies — to embargoes on trade and convoys for fleets of merchant vessels engaged in colonial trade. The privy council was drawn into this line of activity, as were all government officials and boards. Merchant vessels could no longer go singly, but, so far as possible, must combine into fleets and the times of their sailing and return — varying with the quarter of the globe to which they were bound —

[1] See Acts of Privy Council, Col., 1680–1720, and the Calendars of State Papers Colonial.

must be arranged in advance by agreement chiefly between the privy council and its committee and the admiralty. We have seen the origin of this system during the Dutch wars of the period of the Restoration, but now it was more fully developed and kept in operation during the prolonged struggle with France. There were exceptions to its enforcement, but in general it was required as a protection against commerce destroying. The embargo was one of the means of its enforcement, that being the more or less extended prohibition of the dispatch of vessels except at the time of the sailing of fleets under convoy. Whenever, too, a hostile fleet was especially threatening off adjacent European coasts, the sailing of merchant vessels was often totally prohibited for a time. Nothing better illustrates the influence of war on commerce than these regulations.

On April 15, 1689, the realm was laid under a complete embargo and the admiralty was instructed to issue orders accordingly.[1] While such embargo continued, vessels could sail only with passes specially granted and for reason approved by the admiralty under orders from the council. The reasons usually were that the vessels were carrying provisions, ammunition or other military supplies needed in the colonies or in other places to which they were bound. Embargoes applied to coastwise as well as outward bound traffic. Embargoes were often confined to certain parts of the coast only. Because of hostilities in Ireland, during the first war a stop was put to its trade with the colonies.[2] As the British West Indies procured much of their provisions thence and supplies for the production of sugar, they suffered from this cause and urged the despatch of supplies from England. This situation was favorable to the increase of trade between the colonies on the American continent and the West Indies.

The procedure in the matter of fleets and convoys is well illustrated by what was done in the autumn of 1690.[3] On the request of the plantation merchants, the king was pleased, notwithstanding the present embargo, to allow so many ships to go that year to Barbadoes, the Leeward Islands and Jamaica

[1] Acts of P. C., Col., 1680–1720, p. 117.
[2] Acts of P. C. Col., 1680–1720, pp. 86, 87, 118, 152, etc.,
[3] Ibid., p. 173, et seq. An especially full report for 1692 is on pp. 228–9.

as would be navigated by 1200 English seamen, and the like
number to Virginia and Maryland.  The treasury, through the
commissioners of the customs, was required to give directions
what ships should go to these several plantations and how
the men should be apportioned among the merchants at each
British port.  A fit distribution as between London and the
out ports must be made, regard being had to the customs paid
in those ports.  On October 1 the customs board reported that,
in making this same adjustment, they had found that many
ships, especially from Bristol, had already gone with more
than the complement of seamen intended for them.  But the
board submitted lists specifying the number of ships which
should go from London to each of the colonies named, and
these were sent to the admiralty, in order that it might give
directions for the necessary convoys.  The master of each
ship was required to give to the customs board a true list of
the mariners on board and give bond to sail only to the port
for which he cleared and to return with the convoy and hand
over the mariners to such person as the admiralty board should
appoint.  Three months were allowed, after arrival in Virginia, for loading and the return voyage.  Two months were
allowed for this in the West Indies.  When naval squadrons
were crossing the Atlantic at convenient times, men-of-war
from them were sometimes ordered detached for convoy service.  The demand for ships and seamen for the navy made
necessary these regulations as to their supply, and their addition to the requirements of the acts of trade determined the
rules under which trade was carried on in time of war.  Repeated efforts were made to induce parliament to suspend the
navigation act in part in order to substitute foreign seamen
for a proportion of those of British origin and thus release the
latter for service in the navy or on merchant ships; but except
in a few very special cases this was not done.  That there
were manifold violations of these rules in practice, going often
to the extent of wholesale trading with the enemy, we shall
see; but these were in keeping with a general ineffectiveness
of colonial administration in those days, which in all lines
caused the reality to fall considerably short of the ideal.

Into the office of the committee of trade and plantations,
during the first year or two of the war, came a long succes-

sion of letters, reports and memorials concerning the state of defence in the colonies, especially in those along the northern frontier. So far as New England was concerned, these came chiefly from the friends of Andros and his régime and the opponents of the governments which then existed in New England. So far as New York was concerned, these reports were in the main unfavorable to Leisler and strongly urged the full establishment of royal government in that region. That these statements contained much truth it would be useless to deny, but the partisan tone and coloring which were given to them all is evident in every line, and they share these qualities with very much that was written home about the colonies throughout the entire period.[1]

In the autumn of 1689 Randolph wrote twice to the lords of trade in reference to the war and also to alleged disorder and general inefficiency which had followed the overthrow of Andros. He told of the successes of the French and Indians in Maine, New Hampshire and northern Massachusetts, of the sufferings of the people and the widespread devastation of the country. The defences were now destroyed and the country abandoned for the protection of which Andros had so comfortably provided when he was in power. All this reminded Randolph of the straits to which he had found northern New England reduced when he first visited it during Philip's War, and the conclusion which he drew was that, unaided and in their divided condition, the colonists could never prevail over their enemies. They must be reduced to a firm dependence on the crown and troops sent from England to aid them or they would be overrun by the French. The republican spirit of Vane and Peters, he thought, was again triumphant; the rabble were in control in New York, and the name of Venner, of Fifth Monarchy fame, was used to suggest the anarchy with which the colonies were threatened under their renewed experiment in self-government.

Early in 1690 [2] several merchants who traded to New England called attention to the damage done to the lumber and fishing interests there and to the apparent loss, as the result of the war, of the region to which the government must look for its chief supply of masts for the navy. This account was

---

[1] Cal. St. P. Col., 1689–1692, pp. 140, 156.    [2] *Ibid.*, 217, 219, 220.

supported later by inhabitants of Great Island,[1] at the mouth of the Piscataqua river. These were of Anglican connection and they told how they had long been engaged in lumbering and fishing to the profit of the English nation, but were now beset by the French and Indians and were so neglected by the government that, do what they could — being only 40 or 50 men in number — they could not defend the fort. Their deplorable condition they attributed to the overthrow of the late government, the dismantling of the forts and disbanding of the soldiers by whom they were protected. They were not now to be considered as properly under the government of Massachusetts, and about the only help which it had given them was to send Major Church on an ineffective expedition in the fall of 1689, from which he was soon recalled. Benjamin Bullivant, ex-justice of the peace, also kept a journal of events in New England, filled with a running comment which was unfavorable to the existing government there, and this found its way to the office of the lords of trade. So also did the bitter attacks of Robert Livingston on Leisler's efforts at defence. Through 1690 and into the following year reports of sufferings on the northern frontier and of operations of French privateers [2] continued to come in, all reflecting more or less on the weakness of colonial defence by both sea and land. Governor Nicholson also added his accounts of alarm on the Virginia frontier. In the earlier stage of this business, Andros and his leading associates in the recent government of New England arrived in Europe and added their testimony to that of the other critics of the existing colonial régime.

On the other side, Increase Mather and his two associates, Cooke and Oakes, were in England engaged in negotiations concerning a charter for Massachusetts. Mather had been there several months and had been active far and wide, by speech and through the press, in spreading information concerning New England, all of which was most unfavorable to Andros, Randolph and their system of government. Sir Henry Ashurst, a wealthy Whig merchant, of Presbyterian connections, was actively enlisted in their cause as permanent agent for Massachusetts in England. Among the Whigs and supporters of the Revolution, lay and clerical, every effort was

---

[1] *Ibid.*,2 62, 263.          [2] *Ibid.*, 280, 297, 299, 308.

made to explain or defend the course which the colonies were taking. Twice during October, 1689, Simon Bradstreet, governor of Massachusetts under the restored charter, gave to the British authorities his account of what was occurring in New England. He had to acknowledge that the French and Indians were inflicting terrible blows upon the frontier settlements, and that the measures of defence were not wholly successful. The weakness of the government was revealed by his statement that the whole expense of the war was being borne by a few private persons, there being no public revenue and the stores of ammunition being very low. The officials and their sympathizers, who had been thrown out of power and employment by the revolution, were now malcontents, circulating false reports and seeking in various ways to weaken the hands of the government. They sought to lay the blame wholly on the men who were trying to revive the old corporate governments. Again, near the end of March, 1689/90, Bradstreet wrote of the disasters at Salmon Falls and Schenectady and he, with the council of Massachusetts, begged for a supply of arms and ammunition and for other favors.[1]

Not until January, 1689/90, did the lords of trade begin officially to consider the body of evidence which was thus accumulating before them.[2] Toward the end of February they reported to the king that the government in New England was weak and unsettled, that the people refused to pay rates and taxes, that the Indians were doing great damage and that the acts of trade were being daily violated. Nearly a month later,[3] as the result of further hearings, the lords reported more evidence of the same nature. During May [4] the board showed more activity in this matter than before, being attended by the agents of Massachusetts, hearing the report of Andros concerning the forces he had raised and the forts he had built on the eastern frontier and the reply of the agents to that report. The plan of Phips for an expedition to Quebec had also come to their notice, though not the report of his success at Port Royal. Sloughter was slowly making

[1] Cal. St. P. Col., 1689–1692, 240. See on following pages various private letters from New England.
[2] Ibid., 219, 220.
[3] Ibid., 224.
[4] Ibid., 272 et seq.

preparations to go to New York as governor. On June 12 the lords of trade reported in favor of hastening the convoy and the two companies which were to accompany him, sending a ship of war to America and a supply of ammunition to Massachusetts. Immediately an order in council was issued for the despatch of 500 fuzees, 200 barrels of powder and 12 tons of lead to New England; a long succession of orders was also issued relating to the preparations and departure of Sloughter, but he did not leave the English coast until almost the close of the year. As we know, he proved worse than a failure, and New York, the strategic centre of the northern frontier, was left practically to her own resources at least until another governor should appear.

From the meagre journal of the committee of trade which has been preserved no record appears of further hearings, even on the affairs of the northern frontier, until the spring of 1691. The attention of the board was then somewhat aroused by the accounts which came in of the wreck of several vessels of Phips' expedition, with the loss of all the men on board, when they were returning from Quebec. Sickness with great loss of life had also prevailed on others. The Rev. Samuel Myles of Boston and James Lloyd,[1] a Boston merchant, gave very depressing accounts of this and charged that the whole affair had been mismanaged. According to another exaggerated account eight vessels and 400 or 500 men were missing. John Usher was active in forwarding tales which were damaging to the government of Massachusetts and the Mathers, as well as to Phips and paper money. Dudley reported that the blame for the failure was divided between Phips and the field officers and that possibly five vessels with 1000 men had been lost. Governor Nicholson was in communication with several persons in New England and with masters of vessels. As we shall see, he also sent an agent there and the information which he thus obtained was sent to the lords of trade, with the desire that the affairs of all the northern colonies might be regulated. The cost of Phips' expedition, amounting to some £40,000, the increase of taxation and the first resort to paper money which it occasioned, all drew ex-

[1] *Ibid.*, 368, 376, 379, 383, 387, 408, 409.

clamations, almost of despair, from English sympathizers and loud demands for the interposition of the crown.

But in April, 1691, Phips presented to the lords of trade his own account of the expedition.[1] The agents of Massachusetts replied at length to various hostile addresses, showing that they contained errors, that they did not come from particularly authoritative sources, and that the destruction which had been wrought was confined chiefly to the remote settlements of the north and east and by no means equalled the havoc of Philip's War. What they desired was the restoration of their ancient liberties, for which their fathers had transported themselves into the wilderness and had since defended it against all enemies and with considerable advantage to England. The war in Europe and on the ocean was absorbing all energies. The king was soon to leave for his second continental campaign. Andros and Randolph were sent back to America for service wholly or chiefly in the colonies to the south. Attacks on Massachusetts gradually ceased and it was seen that England was in no position actively to defend her or to undertake a reconstruction of New England governments. Therefore the committees of trade settled down to the systematic drafting of what was to be the Massachusetts charter of 1691, and when it came to the appointment of a man to inaugurate government under it, the Mather interest prevailed and Sir William Phips, whose conduct of the expedition against Canada had been so recently attacked, was selected. This was the most important business affecting the continental colonies which was transacted before the plantation committee during 1691. As New Hampshire was not included within the enlarged province of Massachusetts, the committee, early in 1692, recommended its nominal proprietor, Samuel Allen, to be its governor and John Usher its lieutenant governor.[2] Benjamin Fletcher was soon after designated by the crown as governor of New York, Andros as governor of Virginia in the place of Lord Howard of Effingham, and Francis Nicholson as lieutenant governor of Maryland. The instructions of Allen, Andros and Fletcher were laid before the king together and all the appointees asked that arms and other military supplies be sent to their respective colonies, Fletcher request-

---

[1] *Ibid.*, 415 *et seq.*     [2] *Ibid.*, 589, 592, 597, 603, 606.

ing in addition that presents be sent for the Five Nations.[1]

For a time the main attention of the committee was diverted to New York and the colonies along the western frontier. The factional strife in New York, which had been made more bitter by the execution of Leisler and Milborne, called for measures which should remove the effects of this stupid blunder. Leisler's son petitioned in England for the restoration of their estates and was successful.[2] Also pardon was extended to six of Leisler's associates. The Leislerians got the ear of the committtee sufficiently [3] to draw from it a recommendation suggesting that a general pardon for so-called seditious or treasonable acts toward William and Mary might be granted in the plantations and the accused parties released from their recognizances. But the action already taken seems to have been considered sufficient to meet the existing need.

As the war progressed on the northern frontier the question of requisitions of men and money by quotas from the colonies as far south as Virginia in aid of New York became an important one, and it received a share of attention from the committee. So did the restoration of Penn to his rights of government in Pennsylvania, the quarrels in which Phips became involved in Massachusetts and his recall. Much time was given to the various applications of merchants for charters to enable them to procure naval stores in America, and some to the question of the Northern Neck in Virginia and to Baltimore's claim to revenue in Maryland. Charges of illegal trade in Rhode Island, Virginia and Maryland also received some attention. But, so far as available evidence [4] goes, the committee of trade was not particularly active in affairs which concerned the continental colonies. Its inactivity led gradually to complaints from the merchants and these to a threat of action on the part of parliament, which resulted in the creation of the board of trade.

By 1695 the losses which British trade had suffered during the war, from French privateers, from embargoes and in many other ways, had caused widespread discontent among

---

[1] *Ibid.*, 604, 610.

[2] *Ibid.*, 612, 619; Acts of P. C., Col., 1680–1720, p. 204.

[3] Cal. St. P. Col., 1689–93, p. 635.

[4] See Acts of the Privy Council, Col., as well as Calendars of State Papers.

the merchants. This was added to the other elements of opposition and peril to the king which now brought on the most serious crisis of the reign. It was said that the government was indifferent to trade, that it was playing into the hands of the Dutch and transferring commercial advantages to them.[1] In the fall, after the return of William from his annual campaign on the continent, the parliament was dissolved, and by the election which followed not a few Whigs were returned who were dissatisfied with the king and jealous of Dutch influence. Among the important questions which demanded attention and which were referred to in the king's speech were the condition of the coin and the better preservation of trade to the East Indies. Piracy was rife there and the Company was engaged in bitter conflict with interlopers who threatened its monopoly of trade beyond the Cape of Good Hope. The Royal African Company was facing a similar problem. For a number of years illegal trade between the American colonies and Scotland had been developing and, early in 1695, many facts concerning it had been aired in the house of commons.[2] The new Scotch trading company, which was to lead to the attempt to plant a colony on the isthmus of Darien was already being formed and as a result the prejudices of commercial England were deeply aroused.

In anonymous pamphlets of the time the profitableness of the war on the one hand and on the other its burdens and evils, including the weight with which it rested on the poor, had been set forth, but without approximating a conclusion upon the subject as a whole. In 1695 John Cary, the Bristol merchant, who was deeply engaged in the West India sugar trade, and was also one of the most prominent writers upon commercial subjects of his generation, put out his " Discourse concerning the Trade of Ireland and Scotland as they stand in Competition with the Trade of England." John Locke welcomed this as the best discourse he had ever read on the subject. As it would be difficult to exaggerate the rigid mercantilism of Cary's views, this helps to locate the position of Locke in reference to this question. Cary treated Ireland

[1] Burnet, Hist. of My Own Times, ed. of 1734, II, 162–163.
[2] Journal of Commons, XI, 252; Cobbett, Parl. Hist., V, 964–978; Dickerson, Am. Col. Govt., 20.

as a plantation and, because it had embarked on foreign trade and manufactures, he declared that to England it was the most injurious of all the plantations. Ireland should have devoted herself strictly to agriculture, he said, and should now be restrained by law so to order her economy as to serve the interests of England, since England must defend her. He therefore proceeded to argue in favor of prohibiting the exportation of Irish wool abroad and also the importation by her of tobacco direct from the American plantations.

But to us the immediate interest of this pamphlet is to be found in the parallelism which Cary saw between the position of New England and that of Ireland in the British trade system. The two, he said, had followed similar courses. New England had not cultivated so much land as other colonies had done, and with far less numbers. Instead, the New Englanders had tried to live by buying and selling, by fishing and ship building, by the profits and freights which accrued from trade. They smuggled much to foreign nations. The freedom which they were using should be curtailed by act of parliament and they should be made to confine their activities to the cultivation of the soil and other allied industries. A quarter of a century before, Roger Coke, in his " Discourse of Trade," though fundamentally a mercantilist, had argued in favor of freedom and of imitating in certain respects the example of the Dutch; but under the influence of Colbertism in France, of war and awakened imperialist ambitions, the current was now running strongly in the opposite direction. Coke was opposed to plantations, because it required so heavy a drain of people from Great Britain to settle them. In the same way he deprecated the wars and massacres in Ireland, because so many people must be sent thither to fill the gaps so created. But Coke had not thought the problem through; he was weak and sentimental and dwelt too much on people apart from commodities. To men of the Cary type the British Isles and oversea possessions presented themselves as susceptible of division into sections, to every one of which should be assigned its foreordained economic activities, and as a result of this grand scheme of inter-sectional division of labor the greatness of the empire, and especially of England, would be assured. Unfortunately for Ireland, she lay sufficiently near and, for reasons other than economic, was also sufficiently obnoxious, to be subjected to the crushing weight of this policy.

A few years earlier Sir William Petty, making a practical application of his theory that a dense population, like that of the Netherlands, and a consequent high rental of land, were proofs of national prosperity, had expressed much the same opinions as Cary. As to Ireland, he thought it would be better if the main part of its people were removed into England and if Ireland itself were made a cattle range. This was particularly Cromwellian and illustrates the close relationship between war and mercantilism. Like Cromwell also, he thought that the New Englanders could be better utilized in Ireland, whether as ranchmen or not he did not say.[1] Before Petty wrote, Sir Josiah Child, in his famous " New Discourse of Trade," had expressed a poor opinion of colonies unless they were bound to the mother kingdom by good laws strictly executed. People, he said, expressing a characteristic and widely held opinion of the time, were riches and they were lost to mother kingdoms unless their employment abroad furnished employment for as many more at home. As to New England, therefore, Child expressed himself with an emphasis which even Cary did not equal. He said that, notwithstanding the great excellence and strength of its people, it was to England the most prejudicial of its colonies, that what came from thence was of little value as compared with the staples produced in the plantation colonies farther south. The trade of New England, he thought, must surely be regulated, but the process would require " great tenderness and very serious Circumspection." Child, of course, was speaking largely from the standpoint of the East India Company and its interest, but if views concerning colonization so one-sided as those which have been quoted were to prevail, the planting of colonies outside the tropics or semi-tropical regions would come to be regarded as useless and that broad conception of colonization as nation building, which was held by some of the pioneers, would be lost to view.

[1] Petty's Political Arithmetic, written in 1671.

British merchants were now making their influence seriously felt.  Since the middle of the seventeenth century the
volume of opinion from this source had been steadily growing.  Naturally the attention of merchants was fixed on the
interests of their calling to the exclusion of about everything
else.  They had a cut and dried theory which they applied
to all situations.  It was made to fit their country to the
exclusion of all others.  It was simple and easy to expound.
Such statistics from the custom houses or elsewhere as
they had at command could easily be manipulated to suit
their purpose.  All the writers on economic subjects of the
time — and this was to be true for more than two generations to come — were on their side.  Like the Dutch and
to an extent the French, they interpreted national life, and
colonization as well, chiefly in terms of trade.[1]  That side
of things was now kept persistently in the foreground and it
corresponded quite as well with natural conditions and tendencies in England as it had done with those of the Netherlands.  Every effort was made to bend public policy to
this view and make administration its agent and hand-
maid.  The spirit in which it was advocated by its leading
apostles was as partisan and dogmatic as that exhibited in
their ecclesiastical sphere by the colonies of New England.
The type of mind from which the two systems proceeded was
much the same in each case.  Very likely New England
never heard of John Cary, perhaps not of Child; but if they
had ever come seriously in contact with her, she might have
had occasion to add their names to those of Andros and
Randolph as synonyms of all that seemed offensive in the
spheres of trade and government.

Cary and Child have been referred to at some length as
representative of the strong mercantilist and imperialist
trend under which the board of trade was established.  In
1695, in an anonymous pamphlet entitled "Considerations
requiring greater Care for Trade," the establishment by act
of parliament of a council of merchants, sitting in London
and vested with the power to improve domestic manufactures
and foreign trade, was urged.  The writer argued that par-

[1] F. K. Mann, Merscholl Vauban u. die Volkswirthschaftslehre des Ab-
solutismus.

liament was too large a body and too busy to debate and resolve particulars and the council he proposed would supply the lack. A few months later James Whiston, in a pamphlet frequently reprinted and entitled " Causes of our present Calamities etc," urged the formation independently of government of a society or committee of merchants for a similar purpose. The former of these two publications may have been inspired, for action closely corresponding with the proposal of its author was soon initiated.

Near the close of January, 1695/6, the house of commons went into committee of the whole on the state of the nation and a series of resolutions concerning trade were adopted, most of which were later approved by the house in regular session.[1] The main points in these as they finally stood were: that a council of trade should be established by act of parliament, with powers adequate to the more effectual promotion of the trade of the kingdom; that its members should be named by parliament and that members of parliament might have seats in the council; that it should inquire into the protection furnished for outgoing and incoming vessels and send its directions on this subject to the admiralty; that it should receive complaints respecting trade and the misbehavior of officers [2] and represent the same to the king and direct the admiralty as to the punishment of such offenders; that the board should consider plantation trade and all other trades, manufactures and fisheries and the best means of their improvement, as also the best methods for setting to work the poor of the kingdom. A bill embodying these ideas was ordered to be brought in.

In the house this policy was opposed on the ground that it was a dangerous encroachment on the executive and that

---

[1] Commons Journals, XI, 423 et seq.

[2] Various complaints had been made against the admiralty and the conduct of men-of-war. For example, it was said that when British ships had been recaptured from the enemy the former had been plundered of from 20 to 30 % of their cargoes. Owing to long detentions in the West Indies, it was said that seamen had died and ships had been forced to come home half-manned and so had fallen into the hands of the enemy. This, it was said, could have been avoided if squadrons had been ordered to cruise off headlands in the Channel and commissioners appointed in the respective ports to keep men-of-war to their duty. It was stated that since the war began more than 1,500 sail, valued at £3,000,000, had been lost. Commons Journal, X, 701.

it was not easy to see how far it would be carried.[1] If parliament should create the council and name its members, though at first only restricted powers were given them, these were likely to be enlarged every session till finally they might come to appoint convoys and cruisers and draw to themselves the powers of the admiralty and control over the expenditure of appropriations for the navy. The earl of Sunderland, through fear of the prevalent dissatisfaction, favored the measure, but the king was opposed to it and action was at once taken in the cabinet to frustrate the parliament by the creation on the part of the executive of a council of trade with powers similar to those which the legislature had in mind. Such was the motive which led to the issue of the commission of the council — commonly known as the board of trade. The bill, however, had passed its second reading before it was dropped, its abandonment probably being due to prompt action on the part of the executive,[2] though it was about contemporaneous with a threatened invasion of England and the discovery of a plot against the life of William.

On May 15, 1696, the commission for the board of trade passed the privy seal.[3] The ideas underlying it, of course were mercantilist and its provisions did not essentially differ from those expressed in the commissions which had been issued just after the Restoration. Unlike earlier commissions but resembling those to follow, domestic and foreign trade and the plantations were not separated, but were left under the control of one and the same board.[4] In the commission trades and industries were classified as beneficial and hurtful, and the board was ordered to deal with them accordingly; the former should be improved and extended and the latter rectified and discouraged. This furnishes the key to the policy which the board was expected to follow and to

[1] Burnet, II, 163.

[2] Burnet II, 164. Dickerson, p. 22. Lord Somers has been credited with suggesting a council of trade. See Pownall, Administration of the Colonies, p.20.

[3] N. Y. Col. Docs., III, xv; *ibid.*, IV, 147 *et seq.*; Dickerson, 22 *et seq.*; Macpherson, Annals of Commerce, II, 681–2.

[4] Kellogg, The American Col. Charter, 215; Dickerson, *op. cit.* 24 *et seq.*; Andrews, British Committees, Commissions and Councils of Trade and Plantations, J. H. U. Studies, XXVI; Osgood, Am. Colonies in 17th Century, III, 149, 280.

very much that it did. The protection and extension of the useful trade of the kingdom and the fostering and introduction of profitable manufactures was simply another form of stating the same principle. Joined with these duties was that of considering means by which the poor might be employed, so as to relieve the country to an extent from the burden of the poor rate.

In applying the policy thus laid down to the colonies, the board was to enquire into their limits, soil and products, what naval stores they could furnish, how the production of staples within them which the British had hitherto been obliged to import from foreign states might be encouraged. Hurtful industries and trades in this case were chiefly those which enabled the colonists to supply themselves with commodities which usually had been furnished from England. They should be diverted from such trades and from whatever else might turn to the hurt of the kingdom of England.

The powers of government which were bestowed in order to secure these objects included an examination of the instructions which had been given to the royal governors to see if they might in any way be improved, the taking yearly account of the administration of said governors and the submission of reports upon this to the king, and further the consideration of suitable candidates for the offices of governors, councillors, secretaries and counsellors-at-law in the plantations, in order to present their names to the king in council for appointment. The board was not actually to bestow the offices, but to share in the nomination to them. An analogous function it was to perform in reference to acts of the colonial assemblies. It was ordered to " examine into and weigh such acts of the assemblies of the plantations respectively as shall from time to time be sent or transmitted hither for our approbation and to set down and represent as aforesaid the usefulness or mischief thereof to our crown and to our said kingdom of England, or to the plantations themselves, in case the same should be established for laws; and also to consider what matters may be recommended as fit to be passed in the assemblies there; to hear complaints of oppressions and maladministrations in our plantations, in order to represent as aforesaid what you in your discretion shall think proper, and also to require an account of all monies given for public use by the assemblies in our plantations, and how the same are and have been expended and laid out." The purpose of the commission, therefore, was to create a board of information and report, while authority over trade as well as for the government of the colonies rested elsewhere, in the parliament, the king, the cabinet and the privy council, with the departments which were subordinate thereto. At the close of the commission was a blanket clause empowering the board to " execute and perform all other things necessary and proper for answering our royal intentions in the premises." It was to have the assistance, when necessary, of the law officers of the crown and other counsellors-at-law, and was empowered to send for persons and papers and examine on oath. The oath was very rarely resorted to. The board was made immediately subordinate to the privy council, to which its proceedings were to be reported.

As to the personnel of the board of trade, the leading ministers of the crown were to be *ex officio* members of it. This had been the case with earlier bodies of this nature. They attended at rare intervals, when some question which was considered of special political interest was before the board. By way of contrast, only one or at most two ministers had seats in the treasury or admiralty boards, the rest being members by virtue of what at least were supposed to be special qualifications. On the other hand, the arrangement in the board of trade was analogous to that of the privy council. Some eight non-official members of the board really did its work and were the experts in trade and plantation business. Among them were one or two lords, one of these being president of the board. The first set of appointees was made up of really able men, who possessed superior qualifications for the work in hand. They were the earls of Bridgewater and Tankerville, Sir Philip Meadows, William Blathwayt, John Pollexfen, John Locke, Abraham Hill and John Methuen.[1] Of the two noblemen, one

[1] Dickerson has sketched the personnel of the board, and anyone can read what is given about the careers of the members in the Dictionary of National Biography. Information concerning Locke is of course available in many other places, though no study of this phase of his activity has yet been made.

was an Egerton and the other a Grey and both were privy councillors.  The earl of Bridgewater was president of the board of trade and during his life held several high offices. He was undoubtedly a man of worth.  Grey had just been raised to the peerage, as well as to the privy council, and had had a very tumultuous career under the last two Stuarts. He did not remain long on the board and, if he had, that a man of his stamp would contribute anything very valuable to the deliberations of such a body is not probable.  To the commoners on the board we must therefore look for its chief strength.  They were certainly an able group of men.  The experience of Blathwayt in lines bearing directly on the work of the board was greater than that of all the others combined.  He held a variety of offices connected with the privy council, trade, finance and war, and from about 1680 until the death of Anne no man's name appears so frequently in connection with the management of colonial affairs in England as does his.  As auditor general of the plantations he instituted as careful a survey and inspection of the finances of the royal provinces as was easily practicable under conditions which then existed.[1]  In the correspondence of the time his influence over colonial appointments appears at almost every step.  Though acting more quietly and in a narrower field, his influence as a dispenser of patronage was comparable with that of the duke of Newcastle at a later time.  For a long time he was also a member of parliament and evidences of his work there are abundant.  He was an able and under the limitations of the time, so far as we can see, an honest official.  No man was better qualified to impart vigor and efficiency to the board of trade.

Next to Blathwayt, but far superior to him in grasp of the broader meaning of the office, one would naturally place Locke, because of his great mental powers and his connection with the earl of Shaftesbury at a time when the guiding principles of British colonial policy were being worked out.  But his great abilities and knowledge of principles were, for practical purposes, counterbalanced to an extent by age and poor health, though he attended meetings

[1] For proof of this see the papers brought together in the so-called Blathwayt's Journal.

quite regularly during the first four years of the board's existence.[1]

The "Discourse of Trade, Coyn and Paper Credit," published by Pollexfen in 1697, enables us to check up his ideas better than those of any other member of the board. We find that he thought very highly of the plantation trade and would have been glad to see it entirely confined to England, she re-exporting such of the colonial products as her people could not consume. As to Irish trade he held the ordinary ideas, while Holland seemed now so bound up politically and commercially with England that trade with her was analogous to that between one English county and another. Naturally his chief comments were reserved for the French and they show that he was greatly impressed with the progress which that nation had made in naval, commercial and industrial strength under the system of Colbert. Colbertism he greatly admired and bemoaned the fact that England by her heavy imports, especially of luxuries, had contributed so much to its success. Had the French also got possession of Flanders and control over the United Provinces, as they tried to do, and overmatched England at sea, they "would have brought us into an irrecoverable condition." The existing alliance was therefore formed, he continues, " and in point of trade it concerns us all that the French should never again reap such advantages as formerly, for it is that which enables them to carry on these designs, especially at sea." As all Europe is concerned to reduce them to their old limits by land, so is England especially to reduce their naval strength. This is not likely to be effected without solid counsel, a great charge and circumspection in matters of trade. " They have made war on us with much of our own money got by trade. As matters now stand, nothing can be more dangerous than to permit them, so far as we can help it, to obtain anything that may tend to increase their naval strength or diminish ours "; what they have already being such an impending evil and a Rod over us, by the advan-

---

[1] The Journal shows that Locke inquired specially into plans in vogue in Holland for settling differences between merchants by arbitration, and that he drafted a plan for the employment of the poor of England. Hill and Pollexfen also reported on the latter subject, October, 1697.

tage they have by their Ports in the Mediterranean Ocean and our Channel, as may require ever hereafter what may be called a standing Army of Seamen, as well as many Men of War, in a constant readiness to protect our Trade. . . ." Therefore, though peace had come, he would levy prohibitive duties on French trade and prevent smuggling by most vigorous measures and also reduce the consumption of French wines and brandies. In some of these sentences may be seen the point of view which was soon to lead to the Methuen treaty with Portugal and the stationing of a British squadron in the Mediterranean. As to the African and East Indian trades, Pollexfen was a strong opponent of joint stock monopoly and an advocate of regulated companies. In view of this statement and of the extent to which it agrees with programs later set forth by the board of trade, Pollexfen must be credited with large influence in its counsels.[1] As Locke, Pollexfen and Blathwayt had held office under the committee of trade and plantations, they helped to continue its traditions in the new board.

The interest of Meadows was chiefly in diplomacy, though that by no means unfitted him for service in a board where trade was to be treated as a branch of statecraft. Methuen was an actual attendant on the board for only a short time and it is likely that his influence there was not great. Hill is said to have had wide acquaintance with both science and business, but it is hardly probable that he was an aggressive member.[2] All of these men were Whigs and the board continued Whig until 1711, when, with the political overturn which then occurred, the Tories secured control. But this made little difference, for the questions which divided parties did not affect colonial policy. Upon that all were substantially agreed — they were mercantilists — and after the supremacy of parliament in the constitution had been estab-

[1] On October 12, 1697, Pollexfen told the board that he had been considering the Book of Rates, in order to secure such alterations as might be advisable. Later he presented his observations on this subject, carefully tabulated. On September 4, 1700, he reported on the state of justice in the colonies, especially in Barbadoes, and later an elaborate report on this was submitted to the house of commons.

[2] On August 19, 1696, Hill was desired by the board to inquire of Russia merchants about the constitution of that country and the humor of the people. See Journal.

lished, other things being equal, the colonists might have had more to fear from Whigs than from Tories. In 1699 another Grey, the earl of Stamford, became not only a member of the board but its president, holding that office with a brief interruption until 1711. He belonged to the same group of radical opponents of the later Stuarts and supporters of the Revolution as did Forde Grey, the earl of Tankerville. The diligent work of the board of trade during his presidency helps to confirm the impression of contemporaries that he was a man of ability. George Stepney and Matthew Prior, the latter of whom succeeded Locke in 1700, were representatives of the class of literary men who also went in for diplomacy and public business. The few years of Tory supremacy at the close of the reign of Anne brought the earl of Winchelsea and Arthur Moore into the board; but they did not remain long enough to have very traceable influence on its work, except that Moore, the able adviser of Bolingbroke, was very influential in determining the liberal character of the projected treaty of commerce with France in 1713. But the influence of the mercantilists, with policies such as Pollexfen had advocated, of the trade interests and of those who supported the Methuen treaty with Portugal, prevailed and the treaty with France failed in parliament.[1]

With the close of the reign of Anne the really original and productive period in the history of the board of trade came to an end. Blathwayt was a member for a full decade and Pollexfen nearly as long. The inference would be that their influence upon its work was greater than that of any other members prior to 1714, much credit of course being due to William Popple, its efficient secretary, and the members of his family who succeeded him. But it is impossible to tell in detail what individual members did, and though the record of attendance and their signatures attached to reports furnish some indication, the conclusion to be reached from it does not differ much from that already stated. On January

[1] Lecky, Hist. of England, Am. Ed., I, 154. A few letters of Moore to Bolingbroke, early in 1711, indicate Moore's activity in preparing for the expedition of that year against Canada. C. O. 5/1341. Letters to Secretary of State.

15, 1696/7, because of the volume of the papers from the plantations which it was necessary to examine, the board divided the work of preparing extracts from these to be submitted to it as follows: Meadows was given Virginia and Maryland; Blathwayt and, in his absence, Locke the island colonies; Pollexfen the chartered colonies and trade in general; Hill New York, New England and Newfoundland.[1] On the 27th of the following April Meadows presented a general estimate of the state of British trade, beginning with tobacco and reviewing sugar and the East India trade. His general conclusions were, that the East India and African companies should be supported by the authority of parliament, that the plantation trade should be protected by adequate convoys in both directions, the fisheries encouraged, naval stores procured from New England and the productions of the realm and plantations alike protected and their advantages not abandoned to the adversaries of England. This was a perfectly obvious policy, in harmony with the recommendations of the board in general and with the course actually pursued.

The object sought by the creation of the new board was to secure more vigilant attention to the commercial interests of Great Britain by separating their management to an extent from the general work of the cabinet and privy council and bringing to it a larger share of expert intelligence. After making all allowance for the superior abilities and knowledge in many lines of a few of the best men who served upon the board of trade, it must be said that experts in those days would not rank high in the eyes of the modern scientific man. So far in particular as the political and social sciences were concerned, it was a pre-scientific age. The best informed men of those days were not scientific students of such phenomena, and the literature which then existed was not based upon critical study of sources and wide and careful induction, nor did its writers in most cases reach conclusions which were intended to be of general application. By experts should be understood permanent officials

---

[1] C. O. 5/388, 6; B. T. Commercial, O. P. This was in the time of Randolph's voluminous correspondence and it was soon followed by the still more frequent letters of Lord Bellomont and others.

who for a period had devoted themselves to a single department of administration, and men whose business or professional life had given them a certain large acquaintance with one or more special subjects. In the domain of trade, merchants and writers upon that subject were especially prominent as experts and advisers. The board of trade was continually calling upon them.[1] But they were men of the street and their expertness lacked the objectivity of the scientist, for they viewed questions through the medium of class interest and sought to identify the public weal wholly with that. But these two are never exactly identical and they may diverge to any extent.

Though merchants in many cases might have visited the plantations or had means of securing first-hand information, officials in the central boards very rarely, if ever, visited the regions whose affairs they were called upon to administer. They simply absorbed the ordinary current ideas of the time, for example about the colonies and commercial policy, fortifying them by incomplete and loosely interpreted trade statistics and by some study of the course pursued by other nations. All their knowledge was grouped about Great Britain and its interests; it was refracted, so to speak, as it passed through that medium. The same was true of the French and of other nations. The standpoint from which trade and government were viewed was national, not universal or cosmopolitan. It was this type of culture and attitude of mind that gave rise to mercantilism, the characteristic of which was the laying of an excessive emphasis on material interests and the national point of view. During the period which we are considering this tendency was strengthened by war and the necessity of defence and in turn produced these phenomena, a condition which nationalism in trade and politics had made chronic. To this spirit and to ideas of this type the Whig party committed itself during the reigns of William and Anne. As the Whigs were the pronounced supporters of the Revolution and the war, it was natural that they should assume this attitude and apply their principles as best they were able, especially to relations with the national enemies, the French and Spanish.

[1] The Journal of the board is filled with entries of this kind.

Under these circumstances even the most intelligent members of the board of trade were largely dependent for their information and views upon specific conditions in America on the letters and memorials which they received from the colonies. Of these the most important were those which came from the governors; of less importance and frequency were the addresses from the provincial councils and assemblies and from minor colonial officials. With the development of the system of royal provinces, all colonial laws, the journals of both houses of their legislatures and their executive councils were required to be sent to the board of trade, and they were actually forwarded with considerable regularity. Testimony connected with appeals passed through the same channel. All these were more or less carefully examined by the board and its legal advisers in connection with the general work of administration and with decisions upon appeals and the approval or disapproval of colonial laws. During the first two colonial wars, which comprised most of the early period of its vigorous activity, it is clear that the members of the board studied this mass of evidence with measurable care. But it is not probable that the board read with great thoroughness the legislative journals or could have impartially interpreted much that was in them, if they had. The same was true of some of the colonial laws and of addresses from the lower houses of the legislatures, in cases where these dealt with matters outside the main trend of imperial policy. As colonial agents were multiplied and kept more permanently in London, and especially when such agents were appointed to represent exclusively the demands of the lower houses, they could state to the board somewhat more adequately the views of the people and reinforce their addresses. But as a rule the board and all other officials depended for their interpretation of events in the colonies on the letters of the governors and the utterances of the councils. These were official utterances and therefore always betray a certain bias, the nature and extent of which changed with every official or group of officials and with ever varying conditions of harmony or conflict. The governors were often strangers in their surroundings and embittered by the privations to which they were subjected. The tone of their correspondence was in the main adversely critical — sometimes highly so — of the intelligence, good faith and loyalty of the average colonist. Many natural tendencies of colonial life and policy they condemned and would gladly have seen changed. In many cases religious bias made them unsympathetic with the varied forms of dissent which prevailed among the colonists. Upon the rough and unsubdued country, the free and easy way of the colonists, the looseness which prevailed in business relations, the narrow and local views, the parsimony of legislative bodies, the financial vagaries of communities which were permanently in debt, and upon much besides, the royal officials looked with the prejudice born of admiration for the maturer European conditions from which they had come. Much just and true criticism is to be found in their letters, but it was too much attuned to the same key. It moved within a restricted circle of ideas and failed properly to take into account much that was inevitable in colonial life, which could be removed, if ever, only by the growth of generations.

By this correspondence, corrected to a certain extent by the agents, formal hearings and personal interviews, the board of trade was necessarily guided in the formation of its opinions. The so-called experts of the board, that is its members who were not at the same time active in cabinet and privy council, interpreted its meaning and this was incorporated in the representations and memorials to the king and the other boards or to the houses of parliament and in the letters to the governors in the colonies. It found permanent embodiment in the statutes of parliament, orders in council, instructions to the governors and in all which made up the law and tradition of British colonial administration. To this some important contributions were made by the treasury board and the commissioners of the customs, fewer by the admiralty board, while some emanated from the church. As to general principles all the boards and officials connected with the system were in substantial agreement. That was true before the establishment of the board of trade, and for a generation before that time they had been expressed in various practical but more or less informal ways. But the board, which was given little executive power of its own, was created primarily to collect information and report. Therefore, from all the sources of information which converged in its office it prepared from time to time detailed reports and representations on the state of the colonies in general or on certain aspects of their condition and phases of policy which should be followed toward them. In this way British policy in reference to trade and colonies became more definitely formulated and was then reflected to the colonists through the letters of the board and the various orders and instructions issued in harmony therewith. The cabinet and parliament, with which rested the ultimate authority in all matters of government, were in general agreement with these views, but oftentimes practical objections prevented action in harmony with them. The views of the governors and the board embodied in general the official ideal, legislative and executive action falling always some degree short of putting it into practice. If the board could have had its way and its principles have been carried into execution, the colonies would have found themselves under far more rigid control than any which they ever experienced. The ideal of the consolidated autocratic empire would in large measure have been realized. But manifold causes, natural, social and administrative, prevented this result. The task of the historian of the system of royal provinces is to trace the strivings on both sides, of colonists and officials, the resultant of which was the gradual formation of natural habits and the establishment of precedents.

The formal work of the board of trade may therefore be summed up under the following heads: It corresponded with the governors and to an extent with other patent officers in the colonies; it received memorials, reports and petitions from officials and others in the colonies and from merchants in Great Britain; it might have dealings with all the central administrative officials and boards in England and with some of them its relations were continuous; the superintendence which it exercised of the commercial interests of Great Britain at home and in all quarters of the globe brought it into close relations with the trading companies and with leading merchants of all groups and classes; it had also to make use of information from official and other sources in Ireland and Scotland and from diplomatists abroad, and on occasion the collection of masses of documents and the formulation of the British case in support of treaties of peace or commerce was imposed as a part of its duties. In these ways chiefly was business brought before the board, while the knowledge and ability of its secretaries were brought continuously into requisition in the preservation of its records and the preparation of materials and business to be considered by it. The journal of the board is one of the monuments of their labors. The reactions of the board to these approaches took the form of letters, references, memorials and above all reports and representations, the more important of the latter being directed to the king or the privy council, to the treasury or admiralty, and to one or both of the houses of parliament. It also granted hearings on complaints against officials and upon matters of trade and colonial policy.[1] Though the board itself did not possess the power of decisive action, the materials and arguments which it furnished to the individuals and bodies which possessed such power regularly led to action in many lines. The opinion which the board sought to convey in all these forms was the official opinion of the British government, the most extended and authoritative which we possess, on matters of trade and colonial policy. One of the main objects of this work will be to trace its development in part, and the volumes will abound in concrete examples of the action of the board and of all agencies with which it was connected in evolving this opinion and attempting to make it prevail. In one form or another this must occupy a prominent place in every work on British colonization in that period, if it is to meet the demands of the subject and explain events as they actually occurred.

As has been indicated, the period of the board's greatest activity and fruitfulness in ideas was that between its formation and 1714. With a very few exceptions all the prob-

[1] Instances of the work of the board in all of its forms may be found in great numbers in our printed colonial records and archives, while the manuscript British records can be used to complete the list.

lems to which it addressed itself or upon which it expressed opinions came under discussion during these two decades. Its opinions were then formulated and they underwent little subsequent change. But even during that period the board should not be credited with any unusual degree of orginality. Its ideas and policy were wholly confined within the circle of mercantilism and of those measures as to government which were intended to keep the colonies sufficiently loyal and dependent to satisfy the conditions of commercial and naval growth which British statesmen had set up as their highest ideal for the empire. The policy had been sketched out in the acts of trade, and under the committee of trade, the predecessor of the board, the bearing of this legislation upon the chartered colonies and other colonial interests had become pretty well known.

Certain of the early reports of the board [1] reveal with unusual clearness its fidelity to traditional British ideas in reference to the trade of the realm and the relative importance of its different branches. It spoke of woolen manufactures as " for centuries our staple, on which the strength of England rests." This deserved their first care. The rise and fall of a great part of the rents of England depended upon wool, and as labor constituted nine-tenths of its cost, upon the condition of the wool industry depended very largely the problems of unemployment and of poverty as they then were in England. The British had great advantages for the production of wool and the manufacture of woolens and for distributing them over the world. But the mistakes from which their difficulties arose were that they did not work up all their wool at home but sent part of it unwrought abroad. As French wool by itself was not fit for the higher forms of manufacture, they used all means in their power to secure the raw product from England and by mixing it with theirs to make a product by means of which they hoped to exclude English woolens largely from their market. Some Englishmen were not ashamed to engage in this " criminal trade," and to smuggle wool over, there-

[1] See a report to the Commons, October 31, 1696, in B. T. Miscel. C.O. 389, 36; and another, a report to the king, Dec. 23, 1697, in B. T. Commercial, C. O. 389, 36.

by encouraging the importation of French silks and other goods.

To the board of trade, as to all mercantilists, trade with certain countries was good and with others was bad, this depending on the balance, whether it was favorable or unfavorable to England, thus causing a flow of the precious metals into or out of the country. At that time the balance of trade with Sweden and the countries to the south of the Baltic was unfavorable, not only because of the excess of the imports thence, but because a large part of them was brought in foreign bottoms and under the restrictions of heavy duties on British goods when imported. Going back to about 1670 in the history of trade relations with the Scandinavian countries and France, the balance in trade with them all was shown to have been generally unfavorable to England. Trade with Hamburg, on the other hand, was advantageous. With the countries of southern Europe, Turkey, the Barbary States and Guinea the trade balance had been kept at least equal. They took large quantities of British manufactures, also commodities which were re-exported from England, and sent goods in return which could be improved by manufacture. The board considered, in both its general and its special reports, trade with all the different nations and recommended measures to change the unfavorable balances. The re-exportation of about one-half of the goods imported from India modified that unfavorable balance. The same was true in the case of British trade with the American colonies. The fact also that they furnished employment for so much shipping and that they were settled by Englishmen made their trade deserving of the greatest encouragement. The southern or plantation colonies were always regarded as the more valuable of the group, because they produced the staples, the enumerated commodities, and they should be plentifully supplied with slave labor at the cheapest rates. Hence the African trade, whether carried on in joint stock or by a regulated company, was considered one of the chief supports of the British commercial system.

The board had very clear notions, as did the mercantilists generally, about the position of Ireland [1] within this circle

[1] C. O. 389, 40. B. T. Commercial, Rept. of B. T., Aug. 31, 1697.

of relations. It also was determined largely by the interests
of the English woolen industry. Ireland had ventured to
compete in that field and had large natural advantages, of
a character similar to those of England, for carrying on the
industry. But it was held that the production of linen must
be substituted for that of wool and woolens in Ireland.
This must continue to be a cardinal principle of English
policy, and impositions, penalties and measures of all kinds
must be resorted to, if necessary, to prevent the export of
woolens to any places except England. The importation
into Ireland of oil and all utensils employed in the business
should be prevented. On the other hand, let everything be
done to encourage the linen industry. Let hemp seed be
imported free, let flax and hemp growing be tax and tithe
free, let the industry be heavily taxed in England, let the
export of products of linen of all kinds — not mixed with
wool — from Ireland be free, let spinning schools be established and workers in the industry be freed from office
holding and jury duty, let premiums be given for products
of the best quality. A fund should be raised for use in
positive encouragement of the industry and laws should be
passed to enforce the policy in detail. Some of the ideas
upon Irish trade which were set forth by the board it received
from a merchant, named William Culleford, others from
Crommelin, a French refugee, while John Methuen, when he
became lord chancellor of Ireland, interested himself
especially in this phase of national policy. During the earlier
years of the board's existence the houses of parliament annually called on it for reports[1] on the condition of trade and
the plantations, and in these comprehensive statements the
efforts which were making to develop the policy thus sketched
may be followed. Such was the background of ideas relating to commerce and industry in general from which the
board approached the more specific problems of colonial
administration.

To trace all the activity of the board relating to the colonies, as was said of the privy council, would be to write a
very important part of their history, so far as it was determined by imperial control. But reference in general terms

---

[1] Commons Journal, XIII, 298, 446, 502, 721, 876.

must be made to the important questions with which it was concerned and to the attitude which it took upon them. Attention will be confined in this place to the work of the board prior to 1714, though during that period all the questions, with few exceptions, which came up before 1763 received consideration.

The problems of illegal trade, piracy and defence were very prominent during the first two intercolonial wars. These were the subject of frequent and prolonged discussion and gave rise to many questions of closely related interest. In July, 1696, one or more presentations were received from the commissioners of the customs through the treasury board stating that the colonies, and especially the proprieties, were violating the acts of trade by sending goods direct to foreign countries. These statements were largely inspired by Randolph and were accompanied with suggestions that the governors of chartered colonies be properly qualified, by oaths and in other ways, for their posts. The establishment of admiralty courts was also urged. Randolph repeatedly attended the board and these subjects were thoroughly discussed with results which are elsewhere more fully described.[1] In the following March an address from the house of lords brought up the same subject again, and circular letters were sent out on the enforcement of the acts of trade. A report on pirates, made by the board in February, 1697/8, brought up again the conduct of the proprietors and led to the utterance of a threat that parliament would be called upon for an effectual remedy. Between 1696 and 1700 the board submitted many representations on the subject of pirates in the plantations and the East Indies and this also brought the discussion back to the chartered colonies, because they were considered, though probably with injustice, to be the chief offenders in this matter. Another administrative problem was the regulation of the coinage used in the plan-

---

[1] Plants. Gen., Original Papers, IV; *ibid.*, Ent. Books, 1696; B. T. Journal, IX, beginning with July 24, 1696. As the material under these and later dates is now in the printed Calendars, the general course of events can be followed without recourse to the originals. But if one wishes to follow in detail what was done, this material can be found in the B. T. Journal and the Plants. General Entry Books and Original Papers, C. O. 391, and C. O. 323, 324.

tations, and here again complaints were launched especially against the chartered colonies.

It will be noted that, though these discussions began upon the subject of trade, they led straight back to government, that is to administrative measures and changes in organization which were intended to correct the evils that were found to be existing. Trade, however, was the valuable asset which the administrative policy was intended to secure. It was not trade in general, carried on for the purpose of exploiting the resources of the globe for the benefit of humanity at large, but trade carried on in strict conformity with the rules laid down in the acts of trade and for the benefit, primarily if not exclusively, of the English-speaking people. The orthodox rules of procedure in this matter were as definitely prescribed as were the rules for reaching heaven by the clergy of the times, and psychologically the mental type of the mercantilist and the Calvinist, or the rigid Catholic, Anglican or Lutheran, was fundamentally the same. To the furthering of these principles of commercial policy the board of trade was pledged, by both the convictions of its members and the conditions of its establishment. They, together with the desire for territory which contained or would produce the raw materials of trade, had been powerful contributory causes of the wars with the Dutch and now with the French, as religion and greed for dominion had produced the wars of the previous century. Before the British government awoke to these ideas, her continental area had been thoughtlessly parcelled among proprietors and divided up into an absurdly large number of colonies. The operation of private initiative, or the principle of liberty, had led to this and since the Restoration, or a little later, British statesmen had been trying to correct the tendency. Colonial union under a vigorous executive was now their watchword, and it was certainly necessary if the accepted trade policy was to be executed and a successful offensive against the French prosecuted. The chartered colonies, of course, seemed to be the chief obstacles in the path to success, and without doubt they presented an obvious and convenient target for the shafts of mercantilist reformers. They might be gotten rid of, though still manifold natural and social obstacles, of which they were only one expression, would and did remain. For some fifteen years after the establishment of the board of trade and for a still longer period before it, a chief object of its agitation was the abolition of the chartered colonies, in order that thereby the interests of trade and defence might be better secured. Between 1696 and 1711 some forty reports on this subject were made by the board. The central ideas which they all contained have already been sufficiently indicated and more concerning the details and results of the policy will appear in other connections.

Next in importance to trade and to colonial union, which was its corollary in the domain of government, was the subject of defence. The first formal report of the board on this subject related to the northern colonies, under date of September 30, 1696.[1] This was based largely on letters from Governors Nicholson and Fletcher and a memoir by John Nelson. It dealt with the expense of maintaining standing forces and forts in the colonies and insisted that the resources of the dependencies were adequate to their defence, while England was already heavily burdened[2] by war. But united action was necessary, and with the number of separate and chartered colonies that existed, there was no way of uniting the colonial forces except by putting them under one military head or captain general. The board admitted that in time of peace the militia was subject to their respective governments, but in time of war the king had the right to appoint a chief commander and in time of invasion the entire militia of the colonies imperilled might be called out and placed under his orders. He should have the power of government of the royal provinces when he was present in them.[3] A certain control over Indian relations should also be in his hands. The board favored requisitions on neighboring colonies for the defence of New York[4] and all measures of colonial union which were consistent with a strong

[1] N. Y. Col. Docs., IV, 206–211, 227 *et seq.*

[2] It, however, favored sending ordnance stores, and in February, 1712, recommended that a fund be established for that purpose, as many colonies could no longer provide themselves with them. Plants. Gen. E. B. E., 38.

[3] See also B. T. Journal, Nov. 20, 1696, and March 16, 1696/7.

[4] *Ibid.*, Apr. 9, 1702, Feb. 11 and 16, 1704.

executive and royal control. It always took the lead in formulating the English case against the French in America, enlarging on the boundaries claimed by the English, the encroachments of the French, the claims of the latter in reference to the fisheries. In a representation of December 1, 1708, upon a memorial from Samuel Vetch, the board dwelt on the danger which arose from the French meddling with the Five Nations and also with the Indians of northeastern New England. For these reasons it always favored the expulsion of the French from North America. In an exhaustive representation to the queen, under date of June 2, 1709, the board enlarged not only upon the territorial claims of the English but upon the sovereignty which they claimed over the Five Nations and the necessity of this for the security of the northern colonies. The West Indies, though they as a section of the empire lie outside the sphere of our immediate attention as to both trade and government, were the pets of British officials and received much greater care than did the continental colonies.

Minor subjects which, during the period under review, engaged the attention of the board of trade were the salaries of governors, the encroachment of assemblies on the powers of the provincial executives, the establishment of courts and defects in the administration of justice throughout the colonies in general, absentee officials and the need of correcting the evils arising from this cause, the audit of accounts by officials of the crown and the retention in the hands of royal governors of the power to control the objects and amount of expenditures, and certain general restrictions on colonial legislation in the interest of the passage only of laws without limitation of time and in greater conformity with British precedents. These questions all related chiefly or exclusively to the royal provinces, and as that form of colony on the continent of America had not yet reached the prominence which it later attained, they were more persistently brought to attention after the accession of the Hanoverians.

In reference to nearly all of these subjects precedents which were favorable to colonial initiative, exercised largely or wholly through their assemblies and sanctioned by laws which they had passed, already existed. Throughout New

England the supremacy of the assemblies over all matters of government had been unquestioned. In New Jersey, Pennsylvania and the Carolinas it had hardly been less. In Maryland the extreme claims of the executive had been warmly contested, with the establishment of precedents which were inconsistent with several principles later embodied in the instructions of royal governors. In Virginia even it was only during a part of Berkeley's administration and the brief one of Lord Howard that the executive had some success in dominating affairs, and that at the cost of a notable rebellion and later of a continuous opposition to the unaccustomed exercise of executive discretion. Only in New York had the executive enjoyed a nearly unobstructed course, but even there as soon as a legislature was brought into existence it assumed to fill a sphere of influence similar to the others and to parliament, which was more or less the model of them all, and because of opposition before many decades began to equal or lead them all in the assertion of what may be called British-American rights.[1]

But the board of trade and the other British authorities sought to ignore these precedents and this course of development. They did not study it, but affected rather to treat it with contempt as too insignificant and remote — the practice of small proprietary communities — to be taken seriously. These practices also had resulted from pure assumption or had resulted from dealings with proprietors in which the crown had had no share. In the early colonies there had been no salaries of officials or they had existed in very rudimentary form. Fees were largely regulated by statute. They had established their own courts and developed such an administration of justice as was possible in communities which were almost destitute of trained lawyers. So small had been their revenue and expenditures that the necessity of auditing accounts had not been very apparent. In those days conflicts with the Indians had scarcely developed any of the problems of finance in war time. A modified system of barter existed nearly everywhere. And so it was throughout the circle of relations. Like frontier life in small agri-

[1] The development of the colonies in all these respects is the main subject of detailed exposition in the author's American Colonies in the 17th Century.

cultural communities, the institutions which existed were primitive and crude, and everything was on a small scale. But such ways and conditions were natural and had been quite spontaneously evolved. The task of training a people out of such habits into those adapted to wider relations is not an easy one and the British government undertook to effect the change without any sympathetic knowledge of and little respect for the customs which it proposed to modify. It launched against them certain laws and administrative orders, formulated under advice that was mostly partisan and given by lawyers and officials three thousand miles away. The practices which they sought to set aside they did not exactly pronounce illegal, neither did they acknowledge that they were legal. The administrative system of the chartered colonies was allowed to remain in a status of undefined *de facto* legality, but subject to a degree of change by acts of parliament and executive orders to which no limits were set. This was accompanied by no propaganda or system of teaching among the people in general, no effort so to broaden the culture or improve conditions of life in the colonies as to convince the people of the advantages of the new régime. Its advent was made known chiefly by the appearance of new officials, acting largely under private instructions and referring for their authority to acts of parliament and orders from the crown.

In this way the people who had grown up under the old conditions might find themselves gradually enveloped within wide-reaching imperial relations and subject to requirements of which they had previously had no idea. From this they shrank, ignoring it as long as they could and then opposing it with such means as they could command. This was the fundamental issue between the colonists and the British government, as the policy of imperialism developed, between localism and imperialism, between the lower houses which voiced the feelings of the people, so far as they found a voice, and the royal executives. This opposition or, more truly, this inertia the British government never succeeded in overcoming, for its measures were legal and administrative, and rather weak at that, rather than cultural. The mere establishment of royal provinces or abolition of chartered colonies was not adequate to the production of far-reaching social results. The spirit of the colonists remained substantially the same under royal officials as it had been while they lived in the feudal relation. The exhortations and protests and threats of officials were powerless to effect a fundamental change. The colonists were never converted to mercantilism. They were never in a position to become its disciples. They never even read the writings of its apostles or knew them by name. Only the officials and those who did business with them knew its requirements or understood anything of its principles. Moreover, most of those who carried on trade were ready to violate its principles, if profit lay in that direction. Not a war with the French passed during which a brisk trade in some quarter was not kept up with the enemy, though we may suppose that on the whole after the second war the acts of trade were fairly well obeyed; the details we shall never know. However, under the operation of the acts, taken in connection with other causes, Great Britain grew steadily rich, and that was the chief object of the policy.

The question of the salaries of royal governors, leading to the prohibition of their taking presents, meaning by that annual allowances the amounts of which were fixed by the assemblies, was first brought to the attention of the board in 1696 by an application from the governor of Barbadoes. In order to prepare a regulation on the subject, the board drew up a list of the standing allowances of all the governors. Nothing further appears until 1701, when a representation was signed.[1] A petition from Cornbury and another governor early in 1703 led to another general representation.[2] It was concluded that the salary of £2000 in Virginia was sufficient; that the £1200 granted from the export duty of 2s. per hogshead on tobacco in Maryland, with about £500 from the 3d. additional duty recently voted there, should be permanently secured; that £600 should be added from the revenue to the £600 already assured in New York; that the New Jersey assembly should settle a fit salary on Cornbury; that the queen should write to the council and

[1] B. T. Journal, IX, 311; XIV, 6, 8.
[2] Printed in full in Acts P. C. Col., 1680–1720, p. 427.

assembly of Massachusetts to settle a permanent and suitable salary on their governors, or else effectual remedies would be taken. Similar directions should be given to New Hampshire. As to the chartered colonies where the governors had mean salaries and hence connived at unlawful trade and other irregularities, the board could propose nothing.[1] These proposals were approved by the queen in council and letters to the governors were ordered drafted to prohibit their receiving presents. So far as the island colonies were concerned, orders were given to pay the salaries out of the revenue from the $4\frac{1}{2}\%$ export duty on sugar from those plantations. Instructions prohibiting the acceptance of presents were later given to all the governors, but did not become effective in Massachusetts, New Hampshire, New York or New Jersey. This was one of the questions which brought the so-called encroachments of the assemblies clearly to the attention of the British government, and its effects can properly be studied only in connection with the internal history of the provinces concerned. However important it may have been in the northern colonies, it never assumed such magnitude in the eyes of the British as to lead them to pay the salaries out of the royal exchequer. This would have been a serious blow to self-government, but from the standpoint of imperialism might have been one of the best of investments.

As a matter of course, the administration of justice in the colonies was of importance to the British government. It was the duty of the authorities to see that it was kept in reasonable conformity with the principles of the common law and the procedure of English courts. British merchants and officials had rights and claims to be prosecuted in the colonies and in them all there was a great dearth of trained lawyers. In 1700 Pollexfen, moved by difficulties in Barbadoes, presented to the board an elaborate memorial on this subject, showing that the governors, who exercised the equity power, were not lawyers.[2] As Pollexfen suggested, the most effective way to have secured these things was to have seen that the colonies were adequately supplied with

---

[1] Plants. Gen. E. B., Apr. 2, 1703.
[2] B. T. Journal, XIII, 173, Sept. 4, 1700. Plants. Gen. E. B.

trained lawyers to act as attorneys general and and judges of their higher courts. It was a reasonable request which, a little earlier, Bellomont made in this connection for New York, but what might briefly be called Blathwayt's theory of colonial appointments resulted in the sending over of two men to hold the office of chief justice under whom judicial administration, even in that province, probably touched its lowest point. These are extreme cases, but they show that even in direct royal appointments lay the liability to great evils. Complaints that in Virginia councillors were not subject to prosecution for the payment of their just debts led to the issue of new instructions on such points to its governor and some new instructions were also sent to Maryland. There were irregularities in New Hampshire, but with the chief complainant against them, Samuel Allen, the historian can have little sympathy.[1] The organization of the judicial systems in the colonies, the distribution of powers between general and local tribunals, the rates of fees and many other things in that connection were of very great importance to the colonies and after they had once been accustomed even to the partial regulation of them, it was certain that they would never willingly part with the power to establish and regulate their courts by statute. Pennsylvania had occasion to feel that even the power to disallow acts for the establishment of courts was one which might be very unwisely used in England. Over and over again the board of trade dogmatically asserted the right of the crown to establish such and so many courts in the plantations as it thought necessary, but except in the case of the chancery jurisdiction, which was exercised by the governor alone or in conjunction with the council, the courts continued to rest on a statutory basis.

An analogous situation existed in reference to the audit of accounts, and the defects of the British policy in reference to this were shown perhaps more clearly in New York than elsewhere. The system of audit for colonial expenditures provided by the crown through the deputy auditors and the auditor general in England, accompanied with the power of the governors to issue all warrants for expenditures, was proved

---

[1] Plants. Gen. E. B., April 19, 1701.

to be inadequate, even under Blathwayt, to prevent gross frauds.  Therefore the colonists for their own protection had to develop an auditing system of their own, if they had any, and officials in charge of their finances who were responsible to the assemblies were designated for this purpose.  Another remedy which they sought for the same evils was the making of appropriations specific, a practice which the board for good reason condemned.  But this development can best be studied as a part of the history of the provinces themselves.

Very many of the so-called colonial laws, especially those of New England, were more truly administrative orders intended to meet special and temporary needs.  Against legislation of this kind the board never ceased to protest. It opposed temporary laws, because it considered them a means of avoiding the exercise of the veto power of the crown, and also the reenacting of laws which had been once disapproved.  Legislative riders also were not permitted and private bills were not to be passed without due notice to all parties concerned.

In the autumn of 1697 the important question of the transportation of convicts and of disbanded soldiers to the colonies came up.[1]  The inquiry upon both these subjects came from the lords justices, and they desired to know what laws had been passed in the plantations against receiving convicts.  This had been suggested by a resolve of the government to send thither some fifty females from Newgate.  Because the colonists had complained of injury which would come to them therefrom, the board disapproved of the policy. Virginia and Maryland had passed laws against receiving them and Massachusetts had always expressed a similar feeling.  It was recognized that disbanded soldiers would be a valuable addition to the labor power of the colonies, but no action in reference to either of these matters seems to have been taken at this time.

Just at the close of the year a memorial from Lord Cutts, Sir John Pickering and Joseph Dudley suggested another subject which needed attention, and that was the supplying the colonies with a fractional coinage.  The petitioners asked for a patent for seven years to coin half-penny, penny and

[1] Plants. Gen. E. B., October and November, 1697.

two-penny pieces of a new composition for plantation use and of such value as not to encourage counterfeiting. Micajah Perry, that omnipresent merchant, who had a patent for a similar purpose, was asked if this would inter- fere with his rights.   He and his associates of course opposed the proposal and nothing was done by any one.  What is said of the board of trade in this as in many other connec- tions applies also to the privy council and to the British de- partments in general.  The board gave the most elaborate statements of what was substantially the policy of the crown, but the spirit of them all was fundamentally the same.

# CHAPTER V

## COMMERCIAL RELATIONS BEFORE AND AFTER THE ACT OF TRADE OF 1696

In 1696 the lines of commercial policy had already been laid down by parliament in the acts of trade. The special instructions embodying all the main provisions of these acts had been drawn and for several years had been regularly issued to the colonial governors. For twenty years administration under the acts had been in progress and the principles of that system, as applied to the colonies, were reaching the stage of administrative traditions and customs. The outbreak of the war, of course, affected and modified the trade system and its workings in important ways, as has been indicated in what has been said about convoys. Another way in which it was affected by the war, and which will also demand separate treatment, was through the increased attention which now had to be given to the development of a navy and hence to the procuring of a supply of naval stores, if possible, from the plantations. Privateering also was again brought in by the war and that was easily and often accompanied by illegal trade and degenerated into piracy — an evil which had been seriously on the increase for more than a decade. But apart from these special phases of the situation, trade and enterprise in general were active and demanded attention at this time because of the need of conserving the resources of the realm and dominions for war.

It was in these lines that Edward Randolph continued the activity which had been so characteristic of him for years before the Revolution. His complaints against trade irregularities in New England were continued after his arrival in England, with Andros and his other fellow prisoners from Boston. The attention of the privy council was called to this subject early in June, 1690, and such of the

160

commissioners of the customs as the treasury ordered were required to attend with information and proposals for checking illegal trade in New England.[1]  A summons was also issued to the agents of New England and merchants trading in those parts and others who were acquainted with that trade or had recently been employed in New York to attend with information.  Letters which had been received from Randolph and Robert Livingston on this subject were read and sent to the agents of New York, whose reply was duly returned and forwarded to Randolph.  His charges, as transmitted through the lords of trade,[2] were that his own imprisonment at Boston had been due to a determination on the part of Massachusetts merchants to regain for their vessels free trade to all European ports, to make Boston a free port of entry for European goods of all sorts, and as a means to this end to deter any one from thereafter accepting the post of collector there.  He stated that several New England vessels had gone direct to Scotland, Holland and the Straits and he doubted very much if the Massachusetts agents could show that copies of all the bonds required from masters who loaded with enumerated commodities had been sent to England. He declared that those people would continue openly to violate the acts unless a competent officer was sent to enforce them.

The agents did not attempt to ascertain what bonds had been returned to the customs officials,[3] but asserted that the Massachusetts government and people had always been ready to detect and punish offenders against the acts, and in support of that remarkable statement declared that Randolph's evidence in the cases he had brought to trial before 1689 had been so defective that the juries could not convict.  He desired himself to be the only informer and so prevent the execution of the Massachusetts act which required all officials to assist informers, in order to make the enforcement of the acts more impartial.  But his great offence — amounting to a crime — was his attack on the charter, for the destruction of which he was chiefly respon-

[1] Acts of Privy Council Colonial, II, 156.
[2] Cal. St. P. Col. 1689–93, p. 284.
[3] Ibid., p. 287.

sible. Next to that among his guilty acts were his efforts
to procure grants of land within the colony and to introduce
the system of quit rents. These afforded sufficient reasons
for Randolph's imprisonment, and the agents hoped that his
statements would not be believed, though it was difficult
for them at that distance to disprove what he said about
the various ships which were charged with illegal trading.

Nothing further on this subject appeared for a time, the
subjects of convoys and naval stores coming to the front.
But in 1691 Randolph was appointed surveyor general of
the customs in America, with the jurisdiction over the continent and a part of the islands. Of the existence of this office
under William Dyer and Patrick Mein previous to the
Revolution we have evidence, though it is not large in
amount. Judging, however, from later utterances of Randolph, Mein was a jolly, pleasure-loving Irishman, whose
hand would rest lightly on offenders. He was still employed
as surveyor general in Barbadoes.[1] But now officials and
traders were soon to feel the presence of the grim and asser-
tive Randolph, whom opposition and the advance of years
had made still more overbearing and determined. His
career now underwent a remarkable expansion, but his spirit
was not broadened or mellowed in the least. Yet during
the decade of his activity as surveyor general he was to
accomplish as much toward the development of institutions
which were needed for the enforcement of the acts of trade
as he had before 1690 in tearing down obstacles to the
assertion of royal rights in New England.

Randolph reached Virginia at the beginning of April, 1692,
and wrote home to his friend William Blathwayt an account
of his voyage and of the general good conduct of Nicholson
as governor.[2] But he deprecated the appointment of councillors as collectors of the customs, because most of them
lived far away from their custom houses and had other and
absorbing interests. Nicholson[3] had been writing home about
the looseness of government in Maryland and that therefore,
because of illegal trade, they had abundance of goods and
their tobacco sold well; he hoped for the speedy arrival there

---

[1] Writings of Edward Randolph (Prince Soc.), VII, 434.
[2] Ibid., VII, 347; Cal. St. P. Col. 1689–92, p. 622.    [3] Ibid., 602.

of Copley, the king's governor, that affairs might be settled
and offenders punished.  Tobacco was being taken from Virginia to Maryland without paying the duty required by the
act of 1673 and in other ways the king's interests in Virginia
were suffering.  Randolph came with an appointment as
deputy auditor of Maryland, holding thus two offices, and
aroused by such criticism of that province as the above, he
would easily be incited to his usual trenchant words and
acts.  One of his earliest requests was that he might be admitted to the councils of Virginia and Maryland, so that he
might better see the inside working of things and profit by
a councillor's fees or salary.[1]

In the session of 1691 the Virginia assembly had revived
an earlier law for the encouragement of manufactures and
had passed an elaborate act for the establishment of ports.[2]
They were sent to England and were reported on adversely
by the commissioners of the customs.  Their objections to the
former act were that it made debts payable in commodities
at the option of the debtor and that it exempted servants,
houses, and lands from being chargeable for debts.  These
regulations, it was held, would ruin the trade between Virginia
and England.  Even if practiced by the planters in transactions among themselves, such customs should be used with
great caution; but they should not be applied at all to the
debts of English merchants lest the credit of colonists with
them be entirely destroyed.  As to the other act, it was
desirable that there should be ports through which export
and import trade could be exclusively carried on, but many
of the places so designated in this act had no conveniences
for trade whatever.  Another part of the act provided for
an export duty on hides and furs equal to about 25% of
their value.  This, it was believed, would be prohibitive and
thus cut off the market for coarse English woolens, for which
the hides were exchanged.  The board therefore urged that
the act should not be approved, but that the governor be
instructed to have wharves and quays built and that, as
the object of the export duty was the support of the clergy,
a new act should be passed with a $7\frac{1}{2}\%$ duty, which the

[1] *Ibid.*, 381, 611.
[2] Hening, II, 506, III, 50, 53; B. T. Jour. Trade Papers, VII, pp. 63, 105.

trade would probably bear. In accordance with this report,[1] an order in council was issued that the act be returned for amendment as suggested, and also that the governor of Maryland be instructed to procure the passage of a similar port act in that province.

Another question which closely affected the interests of English merchants who were trading to Virginia and Maryland at that time was that of the exportation of tobacco in bulk.[2] A memorial in favor of the prohibition of this practice, signed by most of the merchants and masters who were engaged in that trade, was forwarded by the commissioners of the customs to the lords of trade with a request that the governors be instructed to recommend favorable action to their assemblies. The arguments against the export of tobacco in bulk were, that it facilitated fraud against the colonies which levied duties on its export, that it required more shipping and the services of more customs officials, and in general was inimical to fair and honest trade. This was a view to which the officials always adhered against what was clearly a loose practice,[3] and on this occasion the lords of trade agreed to recommend in the council that the governors of Virginia and Maryland be ordered to procure the passage of laws prohibiting the exportation of tobacco in bulk.[4] The orders were accordingly issued. In the Maryland house it was resolved that, since the tobacco exported in bulk was of such poor quality it would not be worth the freight if exported in cask and thus would not be worth purchasing for export, the planters should cease raising it, though it paid 5d. per pound duty in England and so brought in a large revenue. The governor and council concurred.[5] The opinion of the Virginia burgesses was to the same effect,[6] but the Virginia acts were based on the supposition that tobacco was to be exported wholly in casks. No law on the subject was at this

---

[1] Cal. St. P. Col. *loc. cit.*, 663    [2] *Ibid.*, 614.
[3] B. T. Jour. Trade Papers, VII, p. 105.
[4] Cal. *ibid.*, 675.
[5] Journal, Sept. 25, 1694.
[6] *Ibid.*, Oct. 30, 1694. A later letter of Nicholson shows that he was of the opinion that the export of a part of the crop in bulk was a necessity. See Cal. 1693–6, p. 512.

time passed in Virginia, but abstracts of proceedings relating to this subject and to ports were [1] sent to England and referred to the treasury.

Soon after his arrival Randolph went on a tour of inspection through Virginia, Maryland and the Delaware region, reporting the results of his observations in a long letter to the commissioners of the customs. [2] Evils, personal and administrative, in the customs service he found everywhere. He found that all the collectors in Virginia were members of the council and that their deputies had not been instructed or authorized to do their duty properly. In Virginia power almost inevitably gravitated into the hands of the councillors; they were appointed naval officers, and as a result of that, Randolph said, Scotchmen and others had been admitted to trade without regard to the qualifications of their ships or other legal requirements. Here he touched a point on which he was to ring the changes during the remainder of his life, the amount of illegal trade which went on with Scotland, its causes and its remedies. The Potomac river required careful watching, especially as a check on the irregularities which were common in Maryland. But Randolph found that Christopher Wormsly, who was collector for the Potomac district, lived fifty miles away and went thither only once or twice a year to receive his fees. His deputy lived nearer the river and from his books Randolph was able to tell how many hogsheads of tobacco the masters swore they had in their vessels, but whether or not their oaths conformed to the facts Randolph was apparently in doubt.

Another thing which he deplored was the fact that the customs offices in the colonies generally were not better manned, so that, as in Barbadoes, there should be at least a collector and surveyor for each office, the one acting as check on the other. As it was, there was usually no check, and Colonel Custis, [3] collector of Accomac, who had been removed by Nicholson, had entertained all ships, even pirates, which paid him his unreasonable fees. The district

---

[1] Cal. 1693–6, p. 325.
[2] Cal. 1689–92, p. 656;  Papers of Randolph, VII, 356.
[3] See Cal. 1689–92, p. 654.

was full of small inlets and required much watching, and
the new appointee, Colonel John Lear, a councillor, Randolph did not consider well qualified to do this work.
Colonel Charles Scarborough, Randolph thought, was the
man for collector in Accomac, for his house was so situated
that no vessel could reach Somerset county in Maryland
without passing it.   He also knew all the tricks of interlopers and had given Randolph information concerning
them.   Facts like these should have taught Randolph that
the difficulties of his problem could not be removed by the
mere substitution of royal for chartered colonies, but that
they were deeply rooted in geographical conditions and
human nature, and might baffle any system of administration which at that time could be devised.

But in Maryland he found conditions worse than in
Virginia.   Nehemiah Blakiston was collector at St. Mary's
and Randolph, learning that two New England vessels were
loading tobacco near Blakiston's house, hurried thither.
He tried to get access to Blakiston's books and papers,
but was unsuccessful.   Later, in the presence of Governor
Copley, he asked to see the bonds of the two New England vessels which were then loading, but Blakiston said
they were in the hands of the naval officer.   Randolph
then turned to Copley and asked that he refuse to allow
the ships to be cleared until he (Randolph) was satisfied
that they had given proper security.

Randolph then crossed over to Somerset county, on the
Eastern Shore, where many Scotch and Irish lived, and
went to Robert King, the naval officer.   There he found
the ship " Providence," of London, with forged certificates,
and the " Catherine," of Londonderry, with irregular papers,
both having on board goods of Scotch manufacture.   Randolph seized them both, though the local collector had signed
papers stating that he believed they were proceeding legally.
Randolph reported these seizures to Copley and a court was
called to try them.[1]   Meanwhile Blakiston had discharged
the two New England ships and, when charged with it, said

---

[1] See Cal. p. 683 (August).   No provision was made for a sloop to carry
Randolph from point to point on his travels and therefore disputes arose
over his efforts to procure conveyance, which further embittered relations.

that officials must accept what security the country offered or take none.

In the court which was called for the trial of the ships which Randolph had seized on the Eastern Shore the jury returned for the defendants in the face of all the evidence which he could produce. Randolph was again meeting with experiences similar to those which he had in New England, and deplored the encouragement which such cases gave to interlopers. Blakiston, Brown, who was one of the council, and King, Randolph claimed, were great supporters of the trade with the Scotch. Blakiston also told Randolph that he could render no account of the king's money which was in his hands, nor of large arrears alleged to be due since the time of James II; and Copley said that while the assembly was sitting Blakiston's time was wholly occupied with other public business, but that he would have both him and George Plater, who was collector at Patuxent and whose papers were found in much confusion, ready to account when Randolph should again visit St. Mary's.

There was also an intensely personal side to these transactions, as is shown by letters of Randolph to his friend Blathwayt and of Copley to the lords of trade. Randolph indulged in personalities concerning Copley, Blakiston, Plater and their associates in office beyond those which appear in his correspondence concerning any New Englanders except Dudley.[1] Copley was offended at Randolph's commission from Blathwayt as deputy auditor, declaring that he, as governor, was especially ordered to account to the king, and he would do nothing about Randolph's deputation until he had met the assembly. Randolph's deputation as surveyor general was accepted, but Copley, on the whole, gave him only a "faint reception." So Randolph described the above-mentioned officials as Copley's "tools," making some especially gross references to Plater. The attorney general and the members of the council generally he spoke

---

[1] Papers of Randolph, VII, 373. Of Blakiston he wrote, "He is a starched, formall fellow, as great a knave, but not so cunning, as Mr. Dudley. He is next in Councill to the Governor and carries a great Stroak amongst those sylly animals the Councill." Before he became collector, added Randolph, he was a poor attorney, not worth a barrel of tobacco, and would not be so now if his arrears to the crown were paid.

of with the utmost contempt, and of the judges he said they would do nothing until mellowed with wine and with a present of 40,000 pounds of tobacco.

Copley, in his letter, returned these compliments with interest,[1] stating to the lords of trade that Randolph treated all alike " with scurrilous, haughty deportment, under pretext of zeal for the king's service, to which really he is a great impediment, for he is busier to satisfy his private animosities than to work for the king." He had aspersed the judges in public and had abused the jurors in his trials as base and perjured rogues, and had declared that all which was done in the province, from the assembly down, had been done for narrow private interests or to suit the inclinations of the governor. His only associates, said Copley, were papists or men professedly disaffected toward the government, and the country was weary of him. This, and more, shows that Randolph had approached Maryland in his worst manner, though there is no reasonable doubt that he told some truths.[2]

But his inquiries on this first tour were extended further northward. He had heard of irregularities on the Delaware and proceeded thither and to Philadelphia. Among the customs officers along Delaware bay he found abundant evidence of looseness and neglect. Trading with Scotland and the continent was common, accounts were loosely kept or not kept at all, and collectors could not tell how much they were in arrears to the king. One collector was given to drink and kept a tavern where he did a great business with merchants and masters who resorted thither, while he himself left the king's business to any who would do it for him. This official and another, at Randolph's request, Lieutenant Governor Markham suspended.

The chief recommendation which Randolph made, as the result of his observations of the courts and other conditions

---

[1] Cal. 1689–92, pp. 679, 750.

[2] If Randolph's account of his reception at St. Mary's be true, one ceases to wonder at the temper he was in. He says that Copley, to oblige Blakiston and many of the council and burgesses, left him to lodge where he could, and he was forced finally into an old uninhabited house, from the windows of which the glass had been broken out, and which contained two old beds without pillows. There Randolph lodged. It must have been some comfort for him to know that at or about the same time Copley was living at a "nasty, stinking ordinary" at St. Mary's.

at this time, was that the crown should establish a court of exchequer in both Virginia and Maryland, with an able judge of royal appointment. " Otherwise," he added, " it would be useless to seize ships and put their bonds in suit." This suggestion was not to be followed, but it pointed in the direction of a needed reform and was ultimately to give rise to the admiralty courts in the colonies. Before the end of 1693 Governor Copley died and Nicholson was appointed as his successor. Under him Randolph expected support in bringing Plater and the other delinquent officials to an accounting. Plater wrote to Blathwayt in his own defence.

In the autumn of 1692 Randolph extended his travels to New England.[1] Four years had passed since the fall of Andros, and in Randolph's eyes they had been years of disaster. Heavy losses of life and heavier taxes had resulted from Phips' expedition against Quebec. The Indian war along the frontier had destroyed the settlers in Maine, where the best trees were; and in New Hampshire, which now must be relied on for the masts, fear kept people out of the woods. Jahleel Brenton, who was surveyor of the woods, had not once visited them, and five saw mills were running at Exeter alone. Brenton was also collector of the customs and met with the usual obstacles in that office. One of his men had been imprisoned in Massachusetts and the government there sought to centre in the hands of the naval officer full control of the entry and clearance of vessels, so that the collector might not have a sight of the bonds and certificates which were given.

Randolph waited on Governor Phips, who received him in his coach house. When Randolph stated that his business was to visit and assist the customs officers, Phips said that this was his business and that the commissioners of the customs had nothing to do in Massachusetts, as none of the enumerated commodities were produced there. Turning to the subject of naval officers, Phips said that Randolph should not examine the books of the naval office or see certificates or bonds which were taken there. Randolph then mentioned to him several instructions which he had concerning the duties of naval officers, and on a second visit

[1] Papers of Randolph, VII, 409.

gave him copies of those and told him of the evils which would follow if the collector was prevented from doing his duty. " He [Phips] threatened he would drubb me if I had not been under his Roofe; upon which I left him." In this we have another instance of the extremely undiplomatic temper of the doughty old sea captain and governor. But many in Massachusetts would think such treatment was good enough for their former enemy and persecutor.

When Randolph talked with members of the council he found that they would stand by the naval officer, since that office was created to avoid the extravagant fees of the customs officers and that masters might be obliged to appear only at one office. But in the opinion of the surveyor general the creation of this office opened the door to all sorts of illegal trade, made the harbors of New England ports whence trade in enumerated commodities was carried on freely to Newfoundland, Scotland and the continent. As to Brenton, Randolph found it impossible to get an accounting from him, as he did from the Maryland officials. Brenton did not meet him, as he promised, at Piscataqua and, apparently to avoid accounting at Boston, went suddenly to Rhode Island. Randolph concluded that his administration had been irregular and arbitrary, he neglecting seizures or prosecutions in some cases and proceeding with the help of men not properly sworn in others.

His passage through the Jerseys and New York on his way to New England furnished Randolph with an occasion for pouring out vials of his wrath on Joseph Dudley and Chidley Brooke,[1] and praising Ingoldsby, Graham and Van Cortlandt as the men who had maintained the peace in New York and prevented another lapse into anarchy like the days of Leisler. As Blathwayt's salary in New York had been suspended during the revolutionary troubles and was not yet restored, Randolph seems to have measured his denunciation of individuals largely by their supposed attitude toward its restoration.

On his return to Virginia Randolph was arrested by a justice of Accomac county under a warrant from Maryland,[2] with the intent that he should be carried into that province.

---

[1] Papers of Randolph, VII, 398–404.          [2] Ibid., VII, 441.

But he escaped across the bay to the mainland of Virginia
and the officials there refused to surrender him or to detain
him in prison, as no legal cause for his arrest was shown.
Also the justice who had arrested him was suspended from
office and put under bonds.　In view of these and other experiences, it is not strange that Randolph should praise both
Andros and Nicholson as faithful servants of the crown.
The latter, he said, had spent several hundred pounds a year
in visiting frontiers and organizing the militia in the remotest parts of the province.　The dissatisfaction with him
was due to his insisting that collectors and other officials
should be diligent in their duties and to his searching after
large tracts of land which had been engrossed by the chief
men of the province.　In general, to the mind of Randolph, it
seemed that Virginia was the only province which had peace
and, on the whole, good government.[1]　Elsewhere strife, confusion and all the evils of poor government prevailed.

Meantime in New England, Governor Phips had given another exhibition of his brutality.[2]　Collector Brenton had
seized a quantity of goods valued at £1000, on the charge that
they had been imported contrary to law, and when he heard
of it, Phips came with fifty men and violently took away part
of it from the king's storehouse, beating and maltreating
Brenton.　Phips also freed the goods from seizure and bought
some for himself and in other ways interfered with Brenton
in the discharge of his duty.　Phips had also discouraged
several masters of vessels arriving from England and other
parts from clearing with Brenton, declaring that the collector
had nothing to do with this, and ordering them to apply to
the naval officer of his own appointment.　All of this was reported by Brenton to the treasury board at the close of 1693
and the commissioners of the customs at once undertook an
investigation of the charge, it taking its place among a number of similar ones,[3] the result of which was that about a
year later the governor was summoned to England to answer
the complaints against him.

On the subject of direct trade between the colonies and

---

[1] *Ibid.*, 430, 433.　　[2] Bd. of T. Journal, Trade Papers, VII, 233.
[3] B. T. Journal, VIII, 11, 43.　The Massachusetts law for appointment of
naval officers was disallowed in June, 1695.

Scotland the facts and charges marshaled by Randolph were fully sustained by the complaints of English merchants.[1] At the close of 1692 the customs officials of Liverpool wrote to the commissioners of the customs that they heard many such complaints from merchants and masters who traded with the plantations. The king's revenue was much lessened, they said, and themselves greatly discouraged by the connivance of colonial revenue officers with vessels which were engaged in this trade. In the spring of 1694, on a complaint of merchants trading to Virginia and Maryland that they were greatly injured by the share which the Scotch had in the trade of those provinces and Pennsylvania, the commissioners of the customs urged that a vessel of suitable strength should be sent to cruise off that coast.[2] It was urged that the former commanders of the king's ships there had been unskillful and their vessels had been of too heavy draught. The board also asked that the books of the collectors in those provinces might be inspected and that letters be written on the subject to the government of Scotland.

The treasury board reported favorably on this, and the order in council which referred it to the lords of trade included a proposal that Nicholson, who was just going as governor to Maryland, be empowered to hire a vessel of forty tons, with a competent commander, for the service in question.[3] This was approved by the lords of trade and an order in council was issued to instruct Nicholson to hire one or more such vessels and that a similar instruction be sent to Governor Andros of Virginia. Penn was just being restored to his rights of government in Pennsylvania but formal orders could hardly be given him. The hand of Randolph appeared when, on August 13, he submitted a list of fourteen ships which had

---

[1] Cal. 1689–92, p. 752. This trade was facilitated by the settlement of Scotch in New Jersey and Carolina, and small numbers elsewhere, as in New Hampshire and in Somerset County, Maryland. Their exports included coarse cloth, linen stockings, hats, and beef. Imports included tobacco, sugar, furs and skins. Vessels came to the colonies from the Clyde, but also from Aberdeen and Leith. Some plantation vessels visited Scotland. The trade was openly encouraged in Scotland and tacitly so at many points in the colonies. Keith, Commercial Relations of England and Scotland, 1603–1707.

[2] Cal. 1693–96 p. 279.

[3] Ibid., 308, 320, 321. B. T. Journal, Trade Papers, VII, June 18 and Aug. 8, 1694.

been seized for illegal trading in Virginia and Maryland in 1693 and 1694.[1]

In the early summer of 1695 Governor Nicholson and Sir Thomas Lawrence wrote at length on trade relations on the Chesapeake, especially as they were affected by conditions in Pennsylvania.[2] They both insisted that trade with Scotland, Holland, Surinam and Curaçoa was very extensive in Pennsylvania, as much so as it ever was in New England. To the latter islands tobacco, they said, was smuggled as flour and bread. Traders contrived to reach there when the fleets from Europe arrived and so procured large supplies of European goods. With this trade piracy in the Red Sea and East Indies was connected, and many seamen deserted and many settlers migrated from neighboring colonies to Pennsylvania to take advantage of its free and loose conditions. Similar conditions in the Carolinas, it was alleged, were also attracting away settlers from Maryland and Virginia, where there was not so much unoccupied land and where conditions were harder. An alleged " bank," or accumulation of capital to the amount of £20,000, which existed in Pennsylvania, and in which German settlers were interested, also loomed large in Nicholson's imagination, for he thought it meant the encouragement of linen and woolen manufactures. Lawrence especially, and Nicholson to an extent, also dwelt on the danger that the production and manufacture of cotton might develop to the great damage of the tobacco industry and of English interests. In Virginia several of the councillors were great promoters of cotton. Cotton clothing also was made. In March 1692/3 Andros had approved an act to promote the building of fulling mills, thus giving an indication of a woolen industry.[3] In Maryland they had begun to imitate Virginia. On the plea that too much tobacco was planted, its assembly was going to take up proposals for the manufacture of hemp, flax and cotton, but were discouraged and stopped by Nicholson. In Dorchester and Somerset counties, where Scotch-Irish were most numerous, the inhabitants made enough linen and woolen almost to clothe themselves, and planted little tobacco. The need of more shipping was insisted on in order that ample

[1] Cal. 1693–6. p. 323;  Writings of Randolph, VII, 472.
[2] Cal. 1693–6, pp. 501, 518.          [3] Hening, III, 110.

supplies of clothing might be brought from Europe. More guardships and officials to prevent illegal trade were also needed, while some measures should be taken to regulate the trials of illegal traders in the king's interest. These all go to confirm the general agreement of Randolph's views with those of other officials, when allowance is made for the asperity with which he expressed them. Hence it was that, at the beginning of 1696, the committee of trade expressed approval of Randolph's great care and diligence in the discharge of his trust and recommended him for fitting encouragement.

With the year 1695 trading activities in Scotland, which caused Randolph and others so much anxiety, culminated in the incorporation, under an act of parliament, of the Company of Scotland trading to Africa and the Indies. This is ordinarily known, from the locality where it made its disastrous experiment in colonization, as the Darien Company, the design of William Paterson.[1] It was the result of a natural effort on the part of a poor, but proud, people to change the conditions of what they felt to be a ruinously unequal partnership. By the acts of trade a barrier had been thrown around the realm and the plantations and the Scotch had been left outside. Within lay the sure prospect of abundant and profitable trade, with wealth and the resultant economic development of which the northern kingdom stood so much in need. Such profits as could be made by illegal trade in tobacco and other enumerated commodities, or in the transport of European goods to the plantations, were not sufficient to bring to Scotland such development as its leaders and people were ambitious to gain. They also had been deeply involved with the Stuart cause and were made intensely sensitive by its wreck. These were the conditions and motives which led to the foundation of the Scotch Company.

Colonization was included among the activities of the company as planned, which it was hoped also to extend to the development of Scotch manufactures and commerce on a large scale. Of its original capital stock of £600,000, one-

[1] Macpherson, Annals of Commerce, II, 655; Burton, Hist. of Scotland, VIII; MacKinnon, Hist. of the Union; Keith *op. cit.*; Bingham in Scottish Hist. Rev., 1906; Darien Papers (Bonnetym Club).

half was subscribed in London. But if the trade between the plantations and Scotland, as already described, was arousing jealousy, it is easy to understand why a storm of angry opposition was provoked in England by so large a project as that of the Scotch Company. The jealousy of the two nations reached an almost frenzied expression in connection with this plan. Parliament entered at once into the fray, addressing the king on the peril with which English trade in both the East Indies and North America was threatened by this project. It compelled the withdrawal of all English subscriptions and tried to punish those who had been concerned in procuring them. Protests were made to foreign cities — Hamburg, for example — against the possibility of subscriptions by their citizens. From the first the Scotch plan of colonization was watched with absorbing intensity in the hope that the enterprise might be wrecked or with the intent of actually destroying it if any pretext for this could be found. The same exclusive and hostile spirit was thus manifested toward Scotland as toward Ireland, though it was to be followed by less disastrous consequences in the case of the northern kingdom.

At the same time the new board of trade had been established and the trade act of 7 and 8 William III was under consideration. Randolph, who was now in England, sent in another series of papers and appeared before the committee of trade and probably other boards.[1] He dwelt at length on the manner in which Scotchmen found their way into the colonies as supercargoes, masters of ships and merchants. He enlarged on the dangers involved in the new Scotch Company, venturing the opinion that it might purchase one of the Lower Counties on the Delaware for a settlement, or one or more islands near the continent, where they would set up a staple port such as existed in Curaçoa. His remedy for this was the abolition of all chartered colonies and the combining of the colonies as a whole into larger unions. Information from Randolph followed on the desertion of seamen who went to the colonies and the numbers of these who shipped on board privateers and so became illegal traders and were lost to the king's service.[2] About a hundred men, he said, ran away

---

[1] Cal. 1693–96, p. 625; N. C. Col. Recs. I, 440.   [2] Cal., p. 630.

during the last year from ships which were loading tobacco in Maryland and Pennsylvania. These conditions made it very difficult to man ships for the homeward voyages. He insisted on the need of severe laws in the colonies against the harboring of deserters, supported by orders from England and the imposition of fines on masters or owners of merchant vessels who, by offering high wages, enticed away men from the king's ships. Brenton also had told the commissioners of the customs that in the coasting trade about Boston more than one hundred small craft were employed, and they discharged the cargoes of many foreign ships.[1]

Soon after the beginning of 1696 action began to be taken in England against these evils, of the existence of which in general there could be no doubt.[2] An order in council was issued referring Randolph's memorial on Scotch trade and a presentment which the commissioners of the customs had made thereon to the treasury board, and that both the commissioners and Randolph should attend the council to report article by article on the said memorial. On January 17 the customs board reported that, on perusing the remedies suggested by Randolph they saw the necessity for the passage of a new act of parliament and the draft of it was already in the hands of the attorney general.[3] Here we see the genesis of the important trade act which was soon to be passed. But, continued the board, some of the remedies seemed to be within reach of the executive power. One was to order all proprietors and governors to grant no privileges to privateers unless they gave security in £1000 for good behavior. The erection of courts of exchequer in the colonies by executive authority was again mentioned as a possible remedy for the partiality of courts and juries. As to the proposal to merge the smaller chartered colonies with the larger provinces, the board thought that would effectively secure all rivers and headlands from the possibility of settlement by the Scotch. Proprietors should also be sworn to obey the acts of trade, and many new officers should be appointed who would not be dependent on proprietors for subsistence or in any other way. The commanders of the king's ships should also be ordered to aid the customs officers.

[1] *Ibid.*, p. 631.　　[2] *Ibid.*, p. 638.　　[3] *Ibid.*, p. 639.

Ten days later the lords of trade stated that the question of erecting courts of exchequer in the colonies had been referred to the attorney general.[1] As to privileges granted by governors to privateers, they were awaiting the answer of the judge of the admiralty, while they desired to know if the king desired them to examine the charters and confer with the proprietors concerning the execution of the acts of trade. They recommended that a circular letter be sent to all governors to observe strictly the orders given by the commissioners of the customs, and that commanders of the king's ships going to the plantations be ordered to aid customs officers. On February 13 a circular letter to the above general effect was sent by the lords of trade to the governors,[2] and with it went copies of the Scotch act and of the address of the lords and commons concerning the obstructions that would result from the course on which the Scots had entered. The advocate general of the admiralty reported[3] that privateers such as those referred to by Randolph, not being commissioned from any prince or state, might be proceeded against as pirates.

Presently letters arrived from Nicholson and Brenton showing that the same practices and difficulties continued.[4] In West Jersey the case of a brigantine was mentioned which had been seized and was tried by a Quaker judge and jurors who were not sworn. Brenton was appealing to the king in council from the judgment of a court in Boston on three seizures which he had made; he had been defeated and the Massachusetts court had refused to allow his appeal. As these cases had long been ready for a hearing before the privy council, the commissioners of the customs begged that they might be brought to trial. Nicholson wanted to know the process by which a jury could be attainted, as that appeared to be the only way in which to secure justice in cases of illegal trade, and he did not believe that any lawyer in the colonies could tell him how correctly to attaint.

A most important result of the general activity in matters of trade and the colonies, and in particular of the activity of Randolph, was the passage in 1696 of the act 7 and 8 William

[1] *Ibid.*, 641.          [2] *Ibid.*, 645.
[3] *Ibid.*, 644.          [4] *Ibid.*, 654, 670.

III, c. 22, for preventing frauds and regulating abuses in plantation [1] trade. This is to be regarded, along with the creation of the board of trade, as a landmark in the development of the imperial system of control over the colonies. It recited the acts of trade of Charles II and declared that " great abuses are daily committed to the prejudice of the English navigation and the loss of a great part of the plantation trade to this kingdom, by the artifice and cunning of ill-disposed persons."

The intention of the act was to extend and to make more precise the provisions of the earlier acts of trade, in order to meet the needs which had been revealed since their passage. It therefore provided that no goods should henceforth be exported from or imported into any of the colonies except in ships which were built in England, Ireland or the colonies, or in prize ships and — for the space of three years — in foreign ships used under contract by the navy for bringing in naval stores. Upon the prize ships used in colonial trade the master and three-fourths of the mariners must be English. As several of the acts of trade had been passed since the oath for obeying and enforcing them was prescribed to be taken by the governors in 1663, it was enacted that the governors, including those of the chartered colonies, should be sworn to enforce all of these acts thus far passed, on penalty of removal and a fine of £1000 for neglect to do so. Randolph's complaints against naval officers found a response in the clause which provided that they must give security to the commissioners of the customs for the performance of their duty or be removed; and until such security was given and approved, the governors should be held responsible for the neglects and offences of their appointees.

The next and most important provision of the statute was that extending to the plantations the provisions of 14 Car. II, c. 11, respecting visitation and seizure of ships and goods entering or leaving English ports. The act empowered customs officers to go on board any ship, whether of war or a

---

[1] The journals of parliament throw no special light on the history of this act except that Blathwayt was one of the two members appointed to draft it. See Journal of Commons, XI, 495, 501, 505, 539–540, 541, 555. Journal of Lords, XV, 711, 714, 716, 718, 719, 720, 722, 732, 733.

merchant vessel, and bring on shore all prohibited or un-customed goods, except jewels, if the ship be outward bound; and if the ship be inward bound, to seize all small parcels of fine goods found in cabins or secreted in any place so as to create suspicion of fraud. Uncustomed goods might also be seized after clearing. Clause 5 continued: "And it shall be lawful to or for any person or persons, authorized by writ of assistance under the seal of his majesty's Court of Ex-chequer, to take a constable, headborough or other public officer inhabiting near unto the place, and in day time to enter and go into any house, shop, cellar, warehouse or room or other place, and in case of resistance to break open doors, chests, trunks and other packages, there to seize and from thence to bring any kind of goods or merchandise whatsoever, prohibited or uncustomed, and to put and secure the same in his Majesty's storehouse, in the port next to the place where such seizure shall be made." The new statute expressly provided that any who should aid in concealment of said goods or hinder officers in the performance of their duty, should suffer the same penalties as were provided by the former acts; that the like assistance should be given to officers; that officers guilty of fraud, connivance or concealment of goods in vio-lation of laws should be liable to the same penalties as those imposed in England under the aforesaid act. If an officer were molested in the discharge of his duty, he might plead the general issue and give the acts in evidence.

In order to correct the evil of forged certificates or coquets, stating incorrectly that due security had been given in Eng-land of the plantations to land goods where required by law, it was provided that officers in the plantations where they had come to suspect fraud of this nature should cancel the secur-ity given in the plantations till the authenticity of the certifi-cate could be proven. The fine for forging certificates or making use of the same was £500.

For the better execution of the acts of trade the treasury board and commissioners of the customs were expressly authorized to appoint and station customs officers in any town, port or inlet within the plantations, and jurors serving on trials of revenue cases must be natives of England, Ireland or the plantations. The same must be true of all who would hold places of trust in the courts of law or in the business of the treasury in the plantations. Only men of known means and position within the plantations should be sureties on bonds, and bonds should be collectible after eighteen months unless certificates were presented within that time showing that the goods had been duly landed at the place of their destination, whether in the colonies or in the realm. The landing of any colonial products in Scotland or Ireland, unless they had first paid duties in the realm, was expressly forbidden.

Proprietors were forbidden to sell their provinces to any but subjects of England, and their governors were to be approved by the king and take oaths required by the acts of parliament from all governors. Provision was finally made for the registry of ships as English, Irish or plantation built, and that their origin should be sworn to before a governor or collector by one or more owners of the vessels in question. The names of the vessels should not then be altered without a renewal of the register.

Early in 1699 the board of trade submitted a report to the house of commons on the woolen industry,[1] in which among other things foreign prohibitive tariffs and alleged severe Irish and Swedish competition were discussed; it brought the colonies within the scope of its observations. Attributing its views to those who settled the colonies, it said that when they were planted it was the intent that the people there should be employed only upon such things as were not the products of England, except so much as was needed for their own maintenance and the supply of provisions for their neighbors. New England, however, and other northern colonies had applied themselves too much to the manufacture of woolens, which in proportion was as prejudicial to Great Britain as was the same form of industry in Ireland. Hence it was urged that " the like prohibition be made with relation to the Northern Colonies as to Ireland." A draft of a clause to be inserted in the bill which was then under consideration by the house accompanied this report and the desired action by parliament promptly followed.

The legislation of 1699 respecting wool and woolens in the plantations was embodied in one clause of a comprehensive

[1] C. O. 5/389, B. T. Papers.

act to encourage woolen manufactures in England and to prevent the exportation of wool from Ireland and England to foreign parts, 10 and 11 William III, c. 10. In the preamble of this statute it was stated as a fact that " great quantities " of woolen manufactures had of late been made in Ireland and in the English plantations in America and were exported thence to foreign markets, hitherto supplied by England, tending to reduce the value of land in the realm and to ruin its trade and manufactures. So far at least as the colonies were concerned, this was a very exaggerated statement, if not essentially false, but it is interesting as a revelation of the sensitiveness and prejudice of the merchants and officials at that time, a state of mind to which men like Randolph and Quary could appeal with almost the certainty of eliciting a prompt and favorable response.

The act in general provided, with heavy penalties for its violation, that no woolen goods should be exported from Ireland to any place but England and Wales. Certain ports in Ireland were specified as the only ones whence such goods could be shipped, and the customs officials were strictly required to report to the commissioners of the customs at London the amounts and character of the goods so exported. The clause relating to the colonies provided that, after December 1, 1699, no wool or woolen goods, produced or manufactured in the plantations, should be laden on any vehicle with intent to be conveyed out of the plantation or from one plantation to another, subject to the same penalties for violation thereof as were prescribed elsewhere in the act relating to the Irish trade. All officials concerned were required carefully to execute this provision of the law. Offenders might be prosecuted in the courts at Westminster.

The position occupied by this clause in the act might be taken to indicate that great stress was not at that time laid upon it and that it was introduced in order that effective means might be at hand for the suppression of plantation trade in wool and woolens if it should become dangerous. But the following year, with a view to discouraging homespun manufactures in the colonies, a heavy duty on woolens exported thither was taken off.[1] The course pursued in this

[1] 11 and 12 Wm. III, c. 20.

case was in general accord with England's policy toward the plantations. Though this act might, in certain cases, affect oppressively individuals or small groups of colonies, on the whole it was a stroke in the air. " In fact, the law as a whole accorded very well with some colonial legislation, the purpose of which was to prevent shipping out of the colony wool, iron, leather and other materials used in manufactures." [1]

At the close of the first intercolonial war Sir Charles Davenant, the ablest politico-economic writer of the time, outlined the situation affecting the colonies substantially as follows [2]: That a great increase of national wealth and strength had already come from foreign and plantation trade he was perfectly clear. Internal evidences of this, which were significant to the economist as well as to the general observer, abounded. But it appeared with special distinctness in the ability of England to maintain a powerful fleet and to bear the heavy cost of the war. Breaches had been made in some trades by neutral states, such as Denmark, Sweden, Portugal and Genoa. Corrupt governors in the colonies had winked at mischievous breaches of the acts of trade in the colonies. The island colonies had suffered from the French and the enemy had destroyed trading posts and defences in Africa. British neglect had forced the plantations to buy negroes of foreigners. Owing to war and piracy the East India trade had suffered, so that the capital of the company had been diminished. The Mediterranean trade had fallen off, and these losses had reduced the customs revenue. But the great burden was the land war, in which he thought England had engaged too deeply, as to maintain a navy and prosecute war at sea was enough for her.

But Davenant realized that the struggle with France had just begun, and he looked for territorial encroachments and the development of new activities and sources of strength on the part of the enemy in many directions. In order to meet these the North Sea and Atlantic fisheries should be developed, and administration throughout all departments of govern-

[1] Clark, Hist. of Manufactures in the U. S., 23.
[2] See Davenant's "Discourses on the Public Revenues and Trade of England," Part II.

ment should be invigorated, and backed by the authority of
the whole legislature. He therefore favored a council of trade
erected by act of parliament and with a membership appointed by parliament. " Such a council," he said, " can
watch that matters relating to our traffick be not neglected or
betrayed by our ministers abroad and that important points
be not lost for want of courage to assert the interest of England in foreign courts. They may be impowered to correspond with the king's ministers abroad and from time to time
to receive an account how the posture of our trade stands
and upon what foot we deal with the respective nations where
they reside." He would have this council given power to fix
the days of sailing of merchant fleets with convoys and com-
plements of men and at what ports cruising ships might be
stationed. An adequate number of frigates for convoys
should also be under its control. At every point the close
association of trade with politics was emphasized.

As to the plantations,[1] Davenant had no doubt of the great
advantages which came from them. Nearly one-half of the
increase in the wealth of Great Britain he attributed to profits
from the plantations. He held no special brief for the island
colonies, but admitted the value of the agricultural products
of the northern colonies which kept the islands going. The
existing course of trade he considered best for all, provided the
northern colonies did not develop any manufacturing. That
the northern and southern colonies were mutually supple-
mentary, he thought had been shown in the late war. But
he thought too many colonies had been allowed to develop
and therefore that some territory which it was difficult to
defend might well be abandoned and the whole brought into
closer relations with one another. Penn's plan of colonial
union he had seen and approved, and recommended certain
additions to it in the domain of trade. Of the sterling qualities of the northern colonists he was highly appreciative.
Their traditions of self-government he recognized and would
not have them lightly interfered with. He demanded that a
high class of governors should be appointed for them and that,
like the French governors, they should be paid from the royal

---

[1] Davenant's "Discourse on Plantation Trade" is at the beginning of vol.
I, of his Political and Commercial Works.

exchequer.  Such importance did he attribute to good and permanent laws in the colonies that Davenant advocated the revision of the whole body of them and that they should then be made permanent until repealed by parliament.  The growth of faction should be checked, a strong system of mixed governments should be built up and under these conditions the colonies might develop into great nations enjoying the liberties and constitution of Great Britain.

Davenant was not a party man and the breadth of his views, both economic and political, is in refreshing contrast to much that was being written on these subjects.  His superiority to almost any of the members of the board of trade is evident, and one may well deplore the fact that he was never given a seat within that body.

# CHAPTER VI

ADMINISTRATIVE CHANGES CONSEQUENT ON THE TRADE
ACT OF 1696.   POLICY TOWARD THE CHARTERED
COLONIES

With the part played by the chartered colonies and their founders in the early colonial system of Great Britain we are already familiar.   In connection with them the trend was started toward a relatively high degree of colonial independence.   Actual settlers began the processes of government largely according to methods which seemed to them convenient and under forms which were adapted to the immediate objects they had in view.   Great Britain was remote to them and its government at first interfered but little. Precedents were thus established which were favorable to individual and colonial rights and these were to have a strong and abiding influence.

But the imperialist ideal was also in existence from the first, and as we pass beyond the Restoration we shall see it appearing much more clearly.   It came then actively to control British policy and dominate the minds of her officials. According to it the colonists should not be allowed to choose their own separate course of development, to exist isolated from one another and practically independent of England. That would mean weakness and stagnation; England would derive no special strength from their existence and they would be in perpetual danger of conquest by some neighboring European power.   Instead of this, they should be bound together with the mother country in one whole, and according to certain well-defined principles should receive her protection and contribute to her well-being.   Her navy and army, her officials, the merchant vessels with their crews which brought colonial products to England and carried European goods to America should be the nerves and arteries of communication between the metropolis and her colonies.   We have seen how

185

this was, in the case of a single proprietary province.[1]  The old
British empire was a vast proprietary system, with the realm
at the head and the colonies as members.  In a certain sense
the colonists were an imperial estate, a source of revenue,
an object of exploitation.  They were not exclusively so,
but received benefits in return.  The form of colony which
lent itself best to this treatment was the royal province.  The
chartered colony could offer more obstacles and it lay to a
large extent outside the circle of imperial influence.  It was
therefore an object of dislike to all statesmen and officials
in whom the imperialistic ambition was strong.  The blows
which had been dealt at the chartered colonies before the
Revolution had been only partially successful.  Several were
left in existence after the changes of that time had passed.
Rhode Island and Connecticut survived as examples of the
corporate type of colony.  The Jerseys, Pennsylvania and the
Carolinas continued under the proprietary form.  War and
trade interests furnished sufficient motives for the continuance of a strong imperialistic policy.  To those who were
engaged in carrying this into execution, the chartered colonies,
or proprieties as they were called, were a constant source of
irritation.  The establishment of the board of trade and the
passage of the act 7 and 8 William III, c. 22, were the signals
for another forward movement for the purpose of regulating
if not eliminating them.  The measures which were made
necessary by the new act of trade or adopted on the strength
of Randolph's representations affected royal provinces and
proprieties alike.  But special use was made of these, and of
others in addition, to force the proprietors into line.

Previous to the passage of this act, though the desirability
and even necessity of doing so had been affirmed, the British
government had never attempted to control the appointment
of governors by proprietors or their election in the corporate
colonies.  There had been no provision of law for this.  But
the act of 1696 provided that all governors must receive the
approval of the king.  By this means it was intended to insure the appointment of able and loyal men and through them
to exert an influence which should be permanently felt in
every chartered jurisdiction.  In close connection with this

---

[1] Osgood, American Colonies in the 17th Century, I. 34 *et seq.*

was the other requirement of the act, that all governors should be put under oath faithfully to enforce the acts of trade, on penalty of a heavy fine if they should fail so to do. The appointment of attorneys general to act as prosecuting officers for the king in all the colonies and the erection of admiralty courts were other measures which Randolph and his supporters had long favored.

Randolph at once proposed to the customs board that in all the proprieties [1] the governors be duly qualified for the enforcement of the acts of trade, that fit persons be appointed as governors of Pennsylvania and Carolina to prevent illegal trade there, that commissioners be appointed to administer these oaths in all the plantations, that duly officered admiralty courts be established, and that all officers who had encouraged or connived at illegal trade be removed. The oath, prosecution and various penalties were the favorite means used by the imperialistic reformers to attain their ends.

The commissioners of the customs stated [2] that, owing to the remissness of the governors, the acts of trade were not enforced in the chartered colonies, and therefore they desired that men of reputation and estates, and otherwise qualified for their trusts, might be appointed to those places and subjected to the requirements imposed by the new law. This was referred by the treasury board to the board of trade for report, and Randolph was called before it. [3] He gave a list of all the governors who were then in the plantations and enlarged on the partisan attitude of the judges and juries in the common law courts of the colonies whenever cases involving illegal trade were on trial. [4] This he attributed to the fact, though he could have had no adequate proof of it, that most of these people were themselves interested in indirect methods of trade. His experiences before these courts now led him to urge that admiralty courts, each with judge, register and marshal, be established in the colonies, and also that attorneys general be appointed to prosecute cases in the king's name. They should all hold by royal appointment, and with

[1] Mss. of House of Lords, N. S. II, 419.
[2] Cal. St. P. Col. 1696–1697, p. 43.
[3] Plants. Gen. Journal of Board of Trade.
[4] He produced authentic copies of several of these trials.

their assistance appeals to the crown would be facilitated, especially in trade cases. He also stated that he had already submitted a memorial to the customs board concerning these matters, with a list of the names of men whom he thought fitted to serve in the new offices. The board of trade now asked Randolph to submit his " scheme " or memorial and list of names to them, which he did a few days later. He added that he had consulted the attorney general about commissions to be sent authorizing fit persons to administer the required oaths to governors of the chartered colonies, but nothing could be done until the board of trade " settled that business."

On July 17, 1696, the customs board submitted to the treasury board lists of nominees to act as commissioners in administering the oaths to governors and commanders-in-chief of the royal provinces as well, from New England to Barbadoes. In every case these were members of the councils of the respective provinces. The board also urged again that proprietary governors be similarly sworn and that admiralty courts be erected.[1]

As neither the recent statute nor any of the earlier acts of trade provided for the establishment of admiralty courts in the colonies, the crown was evidently intending to base its action upon the general right of the executive to establish courts in the dominions. The navigation act of 1660 [2] mentioned a court of admiralty before which foreign ships taken by the navy as prizes because they were trading to the colonies might be brought for trial, and this obscure expression was afterwards taken to mean admiralty courts in the plantations. Vague grants of vice-admiralty powers had been made in the colonial charters, and in the more important chartered colonies maritime cases had occasionally been tried before some common law tribunal. But in the royal provinces, beginning with the West Indies and as early as the Interregnum, admiralty courts had been erected. After the Restoration, because of the pressing need for such courts which was occasioned by the wars of the time and the acts of trade, the extension of admiralty jurisdiction in the colonies

---

[1] Mss. of House of Lords, N.S., II, 422.
[2] Beer, Old Colonial System, I, 292 *et seq.*

went on apace. The duke of York was then lord high admiral, and in February, 1662/3, his jurisdiction was extended to all the foreign possessions in Africa and America.[1] Special instructions or commissions for the exercise of these powers and for the holding of admiralty courts now began to be issued to the royal governors in the West Indies. The trial of prize cases constituted the chief business of these courts, though violations of the acts of trade, particularly those of vessels seized by men-of-war for violating the navigation act, were tried before these courts. Near the close of the period of the Restoration, admiralty courts were established in New Hampshire and the Dominion of New England, while the jurisdiction of the duke of York as admiral had existed in his province while he was its proprietor. In Virginia, however, no admiralty court was established prior to the English Revolution and cases involving illegal trade were tried in the common law courts. Such were the precedents, arising chiefly in the island colonies, for the policy which was now to be inaugurated.

Early in August, 1696, Randolph informed the board of trade that he had received an order from the customs board to attend the lords of the admiralty about deputations to be made by them for constituting courts of admiralty in the plantations; but he desired that the board of trade would first come to some resolution about the regulation of the proprietary plantations, as the two subjects were connected, and by the late act of parliament it was required that the governors of those plantations should take the prescribed oaths before the close of the following March.[2] From the privy council also came an inquiry as to what progress had been made in the matter of admiralty courts in the plantations and it desired that the reference concerning attorneys general in the colonies be expedited. Randolph also insisted that this be arranged before he sailed for America, which would be soon, for otherwise he should not be able to perform for the king the service which his office required. Thereupon it was

---

[1] Cal. St. P., Col. 1661–1668, p. 79.

[2] Randolph's view, as stated July 24, was that admiralty courts could not be established in the chartered colonies till their governments were regulated according to the terms of the new act of trade, Cal., 1696–7, pp. 53, 58–9.

resolved that a representation be sent to the lords justices, agreeing with that from the customs board presenting the names of Randolph's nominees for attorneys general and officials of the admiralty courts. The extent to which they relied upon him is evidenced by the statement of the board that, as surveyor general of the customs in America, he should know best. Randolph's lists included officials for the continental colonies and the Bahamas and Bermudas. A statement was also to be sent to the lords justices [1] that in the opinion of the board of trade commissioners should be appointed under the great seal to administer the oaths required by the late act for preventing frauds in the plantation trade. Randolph's specific recommendations which lay behind this last proposal were not only that the governors of the chartered colonies should be duly sworn,[2] but that persons properly qualified should be appointed as governors of Carolina and Pennsylvania to check illegal trade, and that collectors and others who by ignorance or connivance had encouraged illegal trade should be removed and honest men appointed to all vacancies in the service. In the list of governors which accompanied this were Randolph's comments on certain of them whom he deemed unfit, with a list of the vessels prosecuted by him in Virginia, Maryland and Pennsylvania in the years 1692–1695,[3] he losing his suit in every case. Shortly afterward Randolph submitted a statement relating to the encouragement of illegal trade in Virginia, Maryland and Pennsylvania, this being a revision and elaboration of the memorial which he had presented in December, 1695, and both of these went first before the customs board and then before the board of trade.

In connection with his representation on oaths for the governors, Randolph enlarged on what he regarded as the inferior characters and estates of those who were usually appointed to that office in the chartered colonies.[4] Their maintenance

---

[1] Cal. St. P. Col. 1696-7, pp. 68, 69, 74. Mss. of House of Lords, N. S. II, 426.

[2] At the close of 1694 Randolph had reported a list of 12 such vessels. Edward Randolph (Pubs. of Prince Soc.), VII, 472.

[3] Cal. St. P. Col. 1696-7, p. 71.

[4] See proceedings of Board of Trade relating to approval of Webb as governor of Bahamas on salary of £1,000 a year. House of Lords Mss. N. S. II, 429.

was inconsiderable, their status generally precarious. Their power also was slight, it being, in his opinion, equal only to that of magistrates of municipalities in England. The chief object, he continued, in granting these tracts to proprietors was to encourage settlement at the beginning, subject to English laws and for the benefit of the crown. But this last hope had been disappointed, for large numbers had settled in some of these colonies who had long been trying to break loose and set up for themselves, having no sort of regard for the acts of trade and discountenancing appeals to the king in council. This was in a sense true of Puritan Massachusetts, as Randolph had known it. As the Puritans always thought of Laud when a bishop was mentioned, so Massachusetts was the synonym in Randolph's mind for a chartered colony. What he said was not true of Pennsylvania, the colony which he now was chiefly attacking. Other facts were true of Pennsylvania, however, which almost equally interfered with Randolph's administrative plans.

As examples of governors against whom he objected, Randolph cited Trott of the Bahamas, Archdale of South Carolina, the appointee of Ludwell in North Carolina, Markham of Pennsylvania, and Caleb Carr, who was lately governor of Rhode Island. To Andrew Hamilton of the Jerseys his objection was that he was a Scotchman and that there were so many other Scotchmen in those provinces. Of Partridge and Allen in New Hampshire and of Maryland, he had nothing unfavorable to say, though on his and their own showing the acts of trade were no better observed in those provinces than elsewhere; but their governors were appointed by the king. Of Connecticut he said that its people were mostly husbandmen, but they were quite ready to carry prohibited goods to New York or Boston. As to Pennsylvania, Randolph asserted that nine or ten vessels had gone directly from thence to Scotland, several known pirates lived and traded there, trading chiefly to Curaçoa. Governor Markham had refused to grant Randolph a special court at Philadelphia for the trial of the " Dolphin," but called it at Chester where a verdict was rendered for the defendant and Randolph imprisoned on suit of the captain and assessed £46 in damages. Several details he also gave concerning the doings of pirates in South

Carolina and enlarged on the general freedom of trade to all places there and on the shipment of tobacco from North Carolina to New England.

Proceedings relating to these matters occupied Randolph and the boards during much of the summer of 1696. Early in September [1] the board of trade recommended to the lords justices that William Randolph of Virginia, George Plater of Maryland, David Lloyd of Pennsylvania and Anthony Checkly of Massachusetts, all attorneys general, be removed from their offices. The charge against Randolph of Virginia was that he was wholly unacquainted with the laws and practice of the courts in England, against Plater that he encouraged illegal trade, against Lloyd that he declared he served the province only and so refused to put certain bonds in suit. Checkly was said to be ignorant of the laws of England and had been an illegal trader. The board of trade accepted in full the opinions which Randolph gave them concerning the men to be removed and reproduced them in the report which it made to the lords justices. [2]

In the recommendations for new appointments the colonies were grouped into sections. A very large section was made of the colonies from North Carolina to New Jersey inclusive, and Edward Chilton of Virginia was recommended for its attorney general. East Jersey, New York and Connecticut were grouped together, and James Graham of New York was the candidate there. For Rhode Island, Massachusetts and New Hampshire Thomas Newton of Massachusetts was named for the place. On September 10, 1696, the subject of these appointments was referred to the attorney general of Great Britain.

The proprietors and agents of several of the colonies involved in the above plan — the Bahamas, Carolina, Pennsylvania, East and West Jersey and Connecticut — now petitioned the king that they might have a copy of the report of the attorney general and be given an opportunity to reply. On November 5 this was referred to the lords of trade. [3] Action in the attorney general's office was delayed and on

---

[1] Cal. St. P. Col. 1696–7, p. 94. Edward Randolph, VII, 493–4.
[2] Cal. St. P. Col. 1696–7, p. 98; Acts of P. C. Col. 1680–1720, p. 306.
[3] Cal. St. P. Col. 1696–7, p. 192.

November 12 [1] we are told that the question of the attorneys general in the colonies had been referred back to the lords of trade. On November 16 [2] the above proprietors and agents were present at a meeting of the board of trade and were told that the recent act was based on miscarriage in the colonies and it could not be thought unreasonable for the king to appoint officers to enforce the acts. The legal question had not yet been reported on, but would be very soon.

The question of the establishment of admiralty courts in the plantations now became involved with the others, and the chartered colonies, in particular, necessarily regarded the establishment of admiralty courts, in the way and with the jurisdiction proposed, as a serious encroachment. At the instance of the commissioners of the customs the admiralty reported that all governors might have commissions of admiralty if they applied for them, but from a list it appeared that several had no such commissions. This matter was therefore referred by an order in council to the lords of trade. On November 21 the attorney general was again asked if the king might establish admiralty courts and appoint officers for them in the colonies. On December 4, Penn, Colonel Winthrop and others,[3] interested in the chartered colonies, attended the board of trade and desired a copy of the representation concerning attorneys general in the colonies, or at least of the information on which it was based, that they might vindicate themselves against Randolph's calumnies. They were told that the point at issue was one of right and that nothing would be done till they were heard. On December 4 the attorney general, Sir Thomas Trevor,[4] after examining all the charters, reported that the king had the power to erect admiralty courts throughout the colonies and that he might direct the commissioners of admiralty to issue commissions for exercising the same. This opinion was read at a meeting of the board of trade three days later,[5] and the representatives of the chartered colonies desired to be heard by counsel against it, which was allowed. On December 14 Penn and the others attended [6] and desired more time to

---

[1] *Ibid.*, p. 210.                    [2] *Ibid.*, p. 215.
[3] Cal. St. P. Col., 1696–7, p. 234.
[4] *Ibid.*, p. 238.  Mss. of House of Lords, N. S. II, p. 428.
[5] Cal. St. P. Col., 1696–7, pp. 240, 241.        [6] *Ibid.*, p. 252.

prepare their case, though they then and there presented some arguments against the proposed policy. They desired a copy of the attorney general's opinion and promised a speedy answer. Two days later they submitted a memorial in which they claimed that in their charters were clauses containing grants of admiralty jurisdiction [1] and the power to erect admiralty courts. Such courts had not thus far been erected or officers appointed, because all suits upon breaches of the acts of trade might be tried in the common law courts, while the erection of admiralty courts would have involved great expense. They felt that there was no need for such courts except for the condemnation of prizes, few or none of which had been brought into their colonies during the war. But they were willing to erect such courts and appoint officers who would be careful of the king's interest and for the enforcement of the acts of trade. Because of these objections, it was now resolved by the board of trade to refer the whole matter to the king, and a letter was written accordingly.[2]

On December 31 an order in council was issued [3] that the proprietors should be heard in this matter. But nothing further appears until, on January 24, 1696/7, the proprietors petitioned the board of trade [4] that their governors might have commissions as vice admirals, like the governors of other plantations. On the 27th there was an order from the board, occasioned by a petition from the New Jersey proprietors, stating that the lord keeper desired them to consider the form of the oath required to be administered by the recent act for the regulation of trade, the manner of administering it and the commissioners who should administer it. Randolph attended and stated that this matter was now under consideration by the treasury. He gave the names of those appointed to administer the oath to the governor of the Jerseys.

On February 1 the board of trade wrote Governor Nicholson [5] that the design for the establishment of admiralty courts

[1] *Ibid.*, p. 256. Mss. of House of Lords, N. S. II, 439. In accordance with the statement of the admiralty board that all colonial governors had or might have commissions as vice admirals, a number of proprietors now petitioned that they might be granted such commissions with powers similar to those held by governors of royal provinces. See Randolph's list of proprietors which follows.

[2] Cal. St. P. Col. *ibid.*, p. 258.          [3] *Ibid.*, p. 288.

[4] *Ibid.*, p. 314.          [5] Cal. St. P. Col., 1696–7, p. 342.

in the colonies was still pursued, so that they supposed there would be no occasion for an exchequer court for attainting juries, as had been suggested in one of his letters.

The house of lords was interesting itself, for two of its committees asked for copies of the report of the board of trade relating to admiralty courts and to Fletcher's commission as governor of New York.[1] The board of trade called on the attorney general for the form of bond to be issued in this.[2] A few days later — February 24 — the board of trade, moved by Sir William Trumbull, secretary of state, wrote to the commissioners of customs desiring as speedily as possible a list of persons fitted to be employed in the admiralty courts in the colonies, and ordered Randolph to attend the commissioners if required. The next day the commissioners of customs wrote[3] that they had summoned Randolph and received from him a list which he laid before the admiralty, of persons fitted to be officers of the admiralty courts in the plantations.

On March 2 the board of trade wrote[4] that the list did not include Jamaica, Barbadoes or the Leeward Islands, nor any advocates, and desired a complete list. A reply was immediately received[5] that the above list was intended only to apply to those colonies which Randolph visited; but they would do their best to prepare a list for the other islands. They sent a list of persons selected by Randolph to be attorneys general and advocates in the continental colonies and the Bahamas. The colonies are here grouped as Randolph had suggested above, and the names proposed were the same as above. It was recommended by Randolph that the same persons in all cases be attorneys general in pleas of the crown and advocates in admiralty. Attorneys general were appointed under the great seal or privy seal, and advocates by warrant of the admiralty board to the judge of admiralty in England, who thereupon issued his deputations under the seal of his office. Fees should be allowed to the

[1] *Ibid.*, p. 367.

[2] *Ibid.*, 431, 439, 440, 441, 449. This bond was forwarded by the attorney general on April 9. It was sent to the Treasury Board for approval.

[3] *Ibid.*, p. 382.    [4] Cal. St. P. Col., 1696-7, p. 389.

[5] *Ibid.*, 390. Mein was surveyor general of Jamaica, Barbadoes and the Leeward Islands.

officers of admiralty on a scale laid down by the judge of admiralty in England.

An amended list of names for attorneys general and advocates was submitted by Randolph,[1] March 4, and the same day the full and amended list for judges, registers, marshals and advocates in admiralty for North America and the Bahamas was sent by the board of trade to the king. On March 17 a letter was received from the office of Secretary Trumbull that the above list had been laid before the king,[2] but Mr. Penn desired that the persons who were to serve Pennsylvania should also serve the three Lower Counties, being under the same government and on the same river and bay. The king thought this reasonable and so the list was returned to the board of trade, that Penn might be heard and his objections considered. Randolph had also meantime met Benjamin Lynde of the Inner Temple, a native of Massachusetts, and found him able and willing to serve, and now thought him preferable to Thomas Newton for advocate, especially as Newton was not a barrister[3] and it appeared that he had no intention of returning to Massachusetts. Therefore Lynde was appointed to take his place in both offices.

For a time after the establishment of these courts there was doubt as to the body in England before which appeals from them would go. In July, 1703, the board of trade reported to the committee of the council for hearing appeals from the plantations,[1] " that all appeals without distinction, as well in cases marine as others, did always lie before the king in council, as the most easy, expeditious and less expensive method for the inhabitants of the Plantations concerned in appeals." But two years later this view was corrected by an opinion of Sir Edward Northey, that from courts held under authority from the admiralty in England — as they were — appeals would go to the high court of admiralty.[5] Practice conformed with that opinion, and in 1720 Richard West, counsellor of the board of trade, wrote in reference to a party to a case in one of these courts, " to the king in council he cannot appeal, for that is irregular; from

---

[1] *Ibid.*, p. 391.      [2] *Ibid.*, p. 401.      [3] *Ibid.*, pp. 405, 411.
[4] Plants. Gen. E. B., July 7, 1703.      [5] Chalmers, Opinions, 532.

the sentence, therefore, of a court of vice admiralty abroad he must apply to the court of high admiralty at home." [1]

A committee of the house of lords, with the earl of Rochester in the chair, devoted several sessions in February and March, 1696/7, to inquiry into these matters. In addition to the papers submitted, oral testimony was taken, Randolph and William Penn being the chief witnesses, the one on behalf of the royal interests and the other for the proprietors. Other minor witnesses were called, while the clerks of the board of trade and customs board appeared with papers and statements from those bodies. One point brought into discussion was the right of Penn to the Lower Counties and proofs of this right were submitted. The chief point at issue was the enforcement in the proprieties of the common obligation to execute the acts of trade — the oath and bonds of governors, inspection of traders' bonds, and the like, trials of cases under these acts, — such being the points covered in the papers submitted. Near the close of the hearings the chairman expressed [2] to Penn the view of the committee, that proprietary governors should receive the same instructions from the king as the royal governors, and that proprietors were under obligation to see those instructions observed and were liable for the misconduct of their deputies; and, finally, that if there were further complaint against the proprietors the parliament might take another course which would be less pleasing to them.

The results of the inquiry were embodied in an address to the king,[3] which was sent in on March 22. In this the king was asked to write to all the royal governors and to the proprietors requiring a strict observance of the laws of trade as of great importance to England and its customs revenue, and that if he should be informed of any neglect in future, he would look upon it as a breach of trust, to be punished with removal from office and such other marks of displeasure as should be deemed proper. His Majesty was also asked to direct that all proprietors give security for their governors to obey all royal instructions, and that especial precautions in this matter be taken with Connecticut and Rhode Island

[1] *Ibid.*, 518.    [2] Mss. of Ho. of Lords, N. S. II, p. 414.
[3] Lords Jo. XVI, 126–8, 131.   Cal. St. P. Col. 1696–7, p. 402.

whose governors were annually elected. The king, on receiving this address, promised so to comply as to make it
effectual.

On April 1, 1697, as Randolph was about returning to
America,[1] the board of trade asked him from time to time to
give them accounts of whatever he judged proper for their
consideration, as they were sensible of his great knowledge
and experience in all matters relating to the plantations. It
was at this time also that Lord Bellomont was about to be
appointed to his governorship. On April 12 it considered [2]
the circular to the proprietors, and its secretary was ordered
to send a copy of the address of the house of lords, with
papers, to the treasury for its opinion. The papers referred
to included [3] a copy of the bond to be required of the proprietors of all colonies for the execution of acts of trade by their
governors.

On April 17 the board of trade sent to the duke of Shrewsbury [4] drafts of letters to the governors and proprietors pursuant to the late address of the house of lords. The circular
letter from the king to the proprietors and governors [5] of the
colonies was dated April 22 and was to the general effect that,
notwithstanding the laws for the prevention of frauds in
plantation trade, it was evident that great abuses continued
to be practised, which must needs arise from the insolvency
of persons admitted for security or from the remissness of
governors past and present who ought to take care that those
who gave bond should be prosecuted in case of non-perform-
ance. To Rhode Island, Connecticut and Pennsylvania the
statement was made that continued failure to observe the
laws by wilful fault or neglect would be looked upon as tending to the forfeiture of their charters. To the proprietors
of East and West Jersey marks of highest displeasure were
threatened; while to governors of the royal provinces the
penalty would be loss of place and such further punishment
as should be judged reasonable.

Early in March, 1696/7, William Penn submitted [6] to a
committee of the house of lords an elaborate draft of regula-

[1] *Ibid.*, p. 433.      [2] *Ibid.*, p. 445.      [3] *Ibid.*, p. 449.
[4] *Ibid.*, p. 453.           [5] *Ibid.*, p. 458.
[6] *Ibid.*, p. 471; Mss. of House of Lords, N. S. II, 490, 491.

tions intended to enforce upon commanders of vessels obedience to the law in the matter of entries, clearances, bonds
and certificates.  He also urged that no province should by
any custom or duty obstruct the passage through it of goods
from England destined for another province, and that trade
between colonies should be as free as it was in England from
county to county.  When asked what he meant by the first of
these references to intercolonial trade, he cited the case of
New York forcing vessels bound for East Jersey to land in
its own port and pay custom there, her customs laws having
been passed without the consent of the inhabitants of East
Jersey, as if New York had a representative of East Jersey
in her assembly.  Still more did it vex those of West Jersey,
which lay on a wholly different river and bay, to be subjected to this treatment by New York.  But more bitterly
than of these did Penn complain of the Maryland law which
imposed a 10% duty on all Pennsylvania goods which came
through Maryland — a great discouragement to trade and
injustice to Pennsylvania.  By means of it they were deprived of supplies and denied the benefit of the king's high-
ways.  Were the goods sold in Maryland the pretence would
be more allowable, but they were conveyed to Pennsylvania
without opening, and such an impost was without precedent
and indefensible by law.  Again, a duty of 4d. or 9d. per
gallon was laid on all liquors carried from Pennsylvania into
Maryland, and this was so rigorously executed that passengers
from England coming by way of Pennsylvania must pay for
what they brought for their passage only, and their chests
were rifled in search of drink, " things never heard of in
America, and a severity that cannot but breed bad blood between the people of those provinces."  If the people of Pennsylvania should, in retaliation, deny those of Maryland
requisite provisions for the ships bound home with tobacco,
the consequence would not be well.  The reason at bottom for
the conduct of Maryland was Pennsylvania making a law
against tobacco being brought from Maryland into Pennsylvania, " which we have been of late troubled much about in
England, but which it was both our interest and safety to
enact," and Penn believed it to be agreeable with the desire
of the commissioners of the customs.  Whatever was not

made to pay customs to the king by the acts of trade, Penn insisted should go free from colony to colony, be it of the growth of the provinces or English goods. Provisions had ever gone free from colony to colony, and so had English commodities, one province being sometimes better stored with them than another. In order to escape injury to trade and hostilities among subjects, let this be communicated to the board of trade and let the remedy be quickened.

To these observations of Penn the customs board replied,[1] showing that the points referred to by him had been anticipated and provided for in the acts of trade, though the student of these acts will hardly find in them the precision of language which appears in Penn's criticism or in the reply of the customs board to them. As to the 2% duty imposed by New York on New Jersey goods and the 10% Maryland duty [2] on goods in transit for Pennsylvania the customs board confessed they knew nothing. But they consulted Chidley Brooke, collector of New York, and his answer was a justification of the New York duty on the ground of the burden of defence which rested on that province. He also claimed that the New York authorities in levying the duty had the support of royal instruction of years' standing to the governors and collectors. No one offered any explanation or justification of the Maryland duty.

To Penn's suggestion that intercolonial trade should be as free as that between counties in England Brooke replied that the proposal would be reasonable if the colonies were united in their public expense, laws and interest as the English counties were; but where their constitutions, laws and interests all jarred, how, he queried, could free trade between them be expected? The merchants desired returns from England and it was the interest of each province to keep for the traders who dwelt there such part of its produce as might best supply them, and Brooke was not aware that any animosity was caused thereby. This statement measures well the degree of union which then existed among the colonies. Penn had given expression to the ideal to which they must attain before they could become a nation, while Brooke, like any official, was living in the present.

---

[1] Mss. of House of Lords, N. S. II, 492.    [2] *Ibid.*, pp. 500–504.

One of the most interesting sequels to the trade act of 1696 is to be found in the influence which it had on the appointment of governors of the chartered colonies. The British government now had some hold upon this by means of the security which must be given and the oaths taken by them to enforce the acts of trade. At the request of the board of trade a form of bond for the purpose was drawn by the attorney general and approved by the treasury. The customs board thought this should vary from £2000 to £5000 according to the trade of the colony, but £1000 or £2000 were the amounts usually specified. It was expected [1] that the names of candidates would be submitted and opportunity given for the submission of protests to the board of trade and treasury against their personal qualifications and the security offered. But when, in order to answer an inquiry from the privy council, the board of trade sent to Randolph in America for a list of the governors who had not been confirmed and he, replying in 1700, was able to report only on the case of the governor of the Bahamas, the attorney general was asked how proprietors could be more effectually obliged to present the names of their governors. His reply was to the effect that the language of the act of 1696 was not such as to compel them to present their governors, and that it had been the intention to provide for it in the act for punishing pirates which had passed the last session, but it had been omitted and therefore some new law for the purpose should be enacted. But such law was never passed. [2] As proprietors were usually resident in England and made their appointments there, the government found less difficulty in enforcing the requirements in their case. But in the case of the two corporate colonies, with their elective governors chosen for short terms, the problem was quite different. The neighboring royal governors of Massachusetts and New York, however, were to attend to this matter on behalf of the crown. An instruction to this effect was given to Bellomont but not thereafter, and proof is lacking that he acted upon it. [3] In

[1] Cal. St. P. Col., 1696–7, pp. 441, 449, 470. Root, Pa. and the British Government, 50.

[2] Plants. Gen., E. B. Cal. St. P. Col., 1700, p. 642.

[3] N. Y. Col. Docs., V, 600.

1698 and 1703 Winthrop took the oath before the assembly at Hartford, it being administered by members of the council [1]; but we hear nothing in this case of the filing of a bond. As late as 1722, when Dummer was agent for Connecticut, he informed them that Shute had been ordered to take a bond from their governor and the general court resolved that such an act would be inconsistent with their charter.[2] As to Rhode Island, we hear that Walter Clarke, who was a Quaker, refused to take the oath; Samuel Cranston, who succeeded him for a number of terms, seems to have gone through the formality of the oath. But in the case of both these colonies, it would be impossible to trace any effect upon their policy which resulted from the taking of the oath. If one were to judge from the letters of Quary such paper restraints proved utterly useless.[3]

The experience of Penn in this connection was more varied than that of any other proprietor on the continent. In an indirect way Markham was removed by him under pressure from the British government growing out of illegal trade. When Penn hastily returned to England in 1701, leaving Andrew Hamilton as governor, Quary charged that Hamilton had not been approved or given security. Penn replied that it was not done because of doubt concerning the issue of the bill for the recall of the charters. He also insisted that it was necessary to leave some one in charge and produced an opinion of Atwood, chief justice in New York, that the appointment of Hamilton was good until the royal approval could be secured. Penn now petitioned the crown to approve Hamilton, but Quary and Randolph opposed on the grounds — also urged against his appointment as the first royal governor of New Jersey — that he had connived at violations of the acts of trade, opposed the admiralty court and shown great favoritism to Quakers. On this evidence both the board of trade and privy council opposed the confirmation of Hamilton. Penn asked for his confirmation as a matter of necessity. The board of trade seized upon the occasion to fasten on Penn the conditions not only that security in £2000 be given,

[1] Conn. Recs., IV, 243, 258, 407.
[2] Ibid., V, 364.
[3] N. Y. Col. Docs., V, 30.

but that the royal confirmation should not prejudice the title of the crown to the soil and government of the Lower Counties. Penn conformed to both these requirements and Hamilton was approved.[1]　A *dedimus potestatem* for administering the oath was sent over, addressed to six members of the council, and was to be used regularly for successive governors. A dispute arose over the custody of this document between the council as a whole and the six who were named in it and this delayed the administration of the oath to Hamilton for about five months.　The oath was administered to the councillors for the interim between Hamilton's death and the arrival of Evans.　The board of trade inquired into the qualifications of Evans, Gookin and Keith, but under the young proprietors no evidence is forthcoming of inquiries of this kind.[2]

Proceedings in the case of appointments of the governors of the two Carolinas, so long as they remained proprietary provinces, followed the regular course.　On June 26, 1702, a letter from the proprietors was read before the board of trade that they had appointed Sir Nathaniel Johnson governor and desired for him the approval of the crown.　In due course this was given, his security being fixed at £2000.　In the case of Governor Tynte, appointed in 1708/9, the procedure can be followed in full detail.　So the routine can be followed through to the appointment of Robert Johnson for South Carolina and from Hyde, in 1711, to Everard, in 1725, for North Carolina.[3] It therefore appears that the proprietors obeyed the provisions of the law in reference to these matters with reasonable fidelity.　But in the two corporate colonies it was not so, and after about 1730 their failure in this respect was added to the list of reasons which were urged for the recall of their charters.

It appears that upon an address from the house of lords, the

---

[1] Root, *op. cit.*, 52 *et seq.* and references.　B. T. Journal, Nov. 3, 1702, *et seq.* Follow references also in Cal. St. P. Col.

[2] Pa. Col. Recs., II, 62, 69, 92, 94, 96, 116.　The action of the board of trade on the confirmation of these governors may be followed in its journal under the dates of their appointment, *e.g.* in case of Evans, July 7, 1703, *et seq.*

[3] B. T. Journal, June 26, 1702; Jan. 7, 1708/9; Apr. 13 and July 11, 1712; May 7 and June 4, 1713; March 13, 1723/4; March 2, 1724/5, and following dates.

king had ordered that proprietors should also be bound to give security for their governors; but this was clearly not provided for by law. An effort, however, was made to enforce compliance with it, but general objection to this was made by the proprietors.[1] The secretary of the Carolina proprietors wrote that, since the act of parliament had vested the approval of their governors in the king, it could not be expected that they should give security for persons so constituted, and they were not aware that it was required of them by act of parliament. Jeremiah Basse, when appointed governor of East Jersey, concealed his objections to taking the oath in a mist of words and departed for his province without conforming to either requirement.[2] He was proprietor as well as governor. On February 14, 1697/8, Penn wrote to the board of trade [3] that he thought it hard that proprietors should be required to give security for governors whom the king had already approved, for the two requirements seemed to amount to the same thing. If proprietors had the full right of appointment, they could not well refuse the required security. As it was, he urged that the deputies themselves be required to give the bond, as otherwise a proprietor who was absent and innocent might be ruined by the fault of his appointee. Such protests as these led the board of trade to ask Trevor, the attorney general, for an opinion. In June, 1701, he replied [4] that he could not find any law which required proprietors to give security for their deputy governors, but two acts had been passed the last session, one for the suppression of piracy and the other for the punishment of governors for crimes committed in the plantations, which in some measure might serve the purpose. These acts, it is plain, would not apply to the case in hand, for the proprietors were not governors, and therefore this part of the imperial policy it was found impossible to execute.

Meantime charges, accompanied with proof and reported at great length, continued that illegal trade and piracy were being carried on upon a large scale. Responsibility for these

---

[1] Cal. S. P. Col., 1696/7, pp. 441, 449, 458–9, 478, 490, 493, 589.
[2] N. J. Arch., II, 139, 141–2, 150, 153, 156, 161.
[3] Cal. St. P. Col., 1697–8, 105.
[4] Cal. St. P. Col. 1700, p. 350.

evils, as described by the royal governors and customs officials and echoed by the administrative boards at home,
rested chiefly on the shoulders of the chartered colonies.
This certainly was an exaggeration, for, as Bellomont's correspondence shows, complicity with piracy and smuggling
was nowhere greater than in the royal province of New York.
From Virginia and Maryland came charges of similar
offences. Conditions natural, social and administrative were
too much alike in all the colonies to justify distinctions so
sharp as were drawn by the royal officials.  They were, to
a large extent, the outgrowth of prejudice and official interest,
the result of the desire of all imperialists to get rid of the
chartered colonies.  They therefore were used as convenient
objects to which to attribute every evil, and there was truth
enough in the charges to give a certain weight to the conclusion which was drawn from them.

The legislation to which reference has just been made
was largely the outgrowth of this feeling and was directed at
least as much against the chartered colonies as against the
royal provinces.  In the report of the board of trade which
led to the passage of the act for the suppression of piracy
it was stated as notorious that too favorable encouragement
had been given to pirates in several of the colonies, " more
particularly in the Proprietaries and Charter Governments."
While this act was in its passage a clause was added providing that if governors in any of the chartered colonies, or any
persons in authority there, should refuse to yield obedience
to it, such refusal should work a forfeiture of their charters.
This was followed by the passage of an act for the punishment of governors of all colonies alike for malfeasance in
office, the cases to be tried in English courts.  No governor
of a continental colony, however, was prosecuted under this
act.[1]

---

[1] 11 and 12 William III, c. 12.  It provided that, if any governor, lieutenant
governor, deputy governor or commander in chief of any colony should, after
August 1, 1700, be guilty of oppressing any British subjects there, or of any other
crime or offence, contrary to the laws of the realm or those in force in their
respective colonies, such oppressions and crimes should be inquired into and
determined in the court of king's bench in England or before such commissioners and in such county of the realm as should be assigned by royal commission, and such punishments should be inflicted as were usually inflicted for
offences of like nature when committed in England.

The admiralty courts were duly established in the colonies grouped into districts, as Randolph had suggested, and were furnished with judges, registers and marshals of his nomination and from among his sympathizers. The proprietors had opposed their establishment and had claimed that the clause in their charters giving them power over land and sea was, in effect, a grant of admiralty powers. The corporate colonies claimed it under their right to choose judges. The new courts proceeded without juries and the bestowment upon them of jurisdiction over violations of the acts of trade was in excess of the powers which they possessed in the realm and might readily give them entrance into the counties themselves. For these reasons they were objects of intense dislike among the colonists from the first, and so, of course, were all their officials. As usual in such cases, the British government made no provision for salaries for the admiralty judges or other officials, and they were left to depend on fees and the rewards of informers, and these were too precarious to attract able men into the service. Their work was hampered by all the methods which were known to the patrons of illegal trade. They had an active rival jurisdiction in the common law courts to contend against and were often thwarted by writs of prohibition or other technical obstacles. They came generally to be attacked on the ground that their existence in the colonies was a violation and deprivation of the right of trial by jury, the ancient guaranty of the liberties of Englishmen wherever they lived. But, whatever the obstacles against which the new courts had to contend, they were the answer of Randolph and his like to the gross partiality of colonial judges and juries in the trials of cases involving violations of the acts of trade. Rival judicial bodies had now been established before which the customs officers in the colonies could bring their suits for trial and it remained to be seen how much could be accomplished through these in restraint of illegal trade.

Robert Quary, who was soon to fill the place of Randolph as surveyor general of the customs and chief agent of the British government in all matters of trade, was appointed judge of admiralty for the Pennsylvania district. There the contest began, and we are indebted to his correspondence for information as to the experience of an official of the new courts in a leading proprietary province. Piracy was rife and trade with Madagascar was added to trade with Scotland, with Curoçoa and other forms of illegal traffic.[1]

In 1698 an act was passed in Pennsylvania providing for the trial of breaches of the acts of trade in colonial courts with juries,[2] and persons who objected to taking an oath were permitted to affirm. In every respect the ordinary usage of Pennsylvania courts was to be followed. To men like Randolph and Quary this was an exceedingly offensive act, not only because it expressedly continued the jurisdiction of the common law court over trade cases, but because the presence of judges and jurors in court who had not been sworn was regarded by them as inconsistent with the very nature of a court. Quary wrote to Nicholson that by this act his commission was quite destroyed, for he could not allow trial by jury and they would not permit trial without it.[3] He must await further instructions from home. Randolph also, he said, had made some poor appointments. The man whom he had selected for register lived down the bay, one hundred miles from Philadelphia. His appointee as marshal was not then in the province, and the advocate never intended to come thither. Quary had asked John Moore, the only fit person in the province, to serve as advocate, and he was willing to serve provided the government at home would assure him a competent reward for the labor and risks of the office, which he knew were great.[4] Randolph, when he visited Pennsylvania to aid Quary in escaping from his difficulties, was arrested and held for a time in custody. Quary had to depend upon Governor Nicholson of Maryland for advice, as he was the nearest royal governor and, like others similarly situated, was given a certain right of superintendence in these matters over neighboring proprieties. Though Penn vetoed

[1] Board of Trade, Proprieties, C. O. 5/1288 *et seq.* Mss. of the House of Lords. N. S. IV, 318 *et seq.*

[2] Charter and Laws of Pennsylvania, p. 272. Randolph's comments are in Cal. St. P. Col. 1697–8, pp. 402, 403; Quary's on pp. 395, 398.

[3] Later Quary wrote that lawyers in the colonies declared that the admiralty courts must use the jury trial. Mss. of the House of Lords, N. S. IV, 326.

[4] See Moore's letter, Cal. St. P. Col. 1679–8, p. 395.

the obnoxious act before the end of 1698,[1] for a time it caused Quary considerable inconvenience. Justices seized goods from the marshal of the admiralty and the authority of the admiralty officials was treated with contempt by David Lloyd in open court. In the council also Lloyd declared that all those who set up a court of admiralty were greater enemies to the liberties and properties of the people than those who set up ship money in King Charles the First's time. The justices tried to persuade the grand jury to present the officers of the admiralty court as enemies of the people of the province. Quary's complaints, accompanied as they were by his statements about the encouragement of illegal trade which was occasioned by this state of affairs, led to an inquiry in England and Penn was ordered to remove Lloyd from the council, to displace Markham and to uphold the court of admiralty and the officers of the customs.[2] His departure for Pennsylvania was hastened in order that he might attend to these matters. The Pennsylvania trade act was also expressly disallowed by the crown, because the veto by Penn was not considered sufficient. In support of the admiralty courts and customs officials a circular letter was also addressed by the lords justices to the proprietors of Carolina and Pennsylvania, and to Connecticut and Rhode Island.

Penn, on his arrival in his province, did as he had been ordered. He removed Markham and Anthony Morris, the justice who had given offence to Quary. An offending sheriff was turned out, and pirates kept in close prison. Lloyd was also removed from the council, but when it came to the point of actually prosecuting him — for which Penn gave an opportunity — Quary weakened, on the ground that harmony would be better restored without it. The reason clearly was that Quary had no case against Lloyd which would stand examination in court. A proclamation against piracy was issued and two bills passed, one against piracy and the other — more acceptable than its predecessor — against illegal trade.[3] Penn, in writing to the secretary of state and board of trade

---

[1] *Ibid.*, pp. 483, 578. Cal. St. P. Col., 1699, p. 83.
[2] Cal. St. P. Col., 1699, pp. 118, 223, 247, 328, 382–384, 399, 418, 436.
[3] Cal. St. P. Col., 1700, pp. 84, 85, 105.

about these measures, expressed the hope that they would
" pass for an essay of our zeal and care to suppress and prevent those evil practices we have been taxed with." He
had been earnest to have them enacted and would be zealous
to see them executed. Quary was quite enthusiastic in his
first letter after the return of Penn, noting what he had done
with the admission that he had made a great change and that
he was zealous in promoting all that concerned the king's
interest.

But all was not to be smooth sailing and it soon appeared
that the situation had not been essentially changed.[1] Penn
presently wrote that the people thought themselves injured
in their reputation and unsafe in their interests, believing the
common law to be overruled by the admiralty office, that the
king was to give way to the admiralty which would swallow
up half the civil government. As a result of the extension
of the powers of the admiralty over cases of illegal trade,
it was now established at Philadelphia, one hundred and
fifty miles up the bay and river. Vessels were there taken
from their wharves and quays, property was judged away
without a jury and by those whom the people charged with
aggravating weakness into guilt and inadvertences into design,[2] an undiscriminating series of accusations. The county
courts and common law jurisdictions generally — as Penn
expressed it, the *corpus comitatus* — saw themselves threatened with extinction. Moreover, they charged that trials
before the admiralty courts were four times more costly than
those before the common law courts. They therefore believed that they were being enslaved by these new courts,
though " they came hither to have more and not less freedom than at home." Here, in the picturesque language of
the Quaker proprietor, was launched the first colonial indictment against the admiralty courts. It was not to be the
last, but it described an attitude which was natural and permanent and which all the protests and complaints of the
Quarys and Randolphs were powerless to change. It was

---

[1] *Ibid.*, p. 210.

[2] See the case of Lumby and his sloop, "Providence," in Mss. of House of
Lords, N. S. IV, 332, *et seq.* A few papers concerning this case and Quary's
experiences in general are also in Admiralty In Letters (Solicitors Letters),
March, 1700–February, 1703, No. 3667.

akin to the jealousy which Englishmen had always felt against the civil law jurisdiction, whether in the form of ecclesiastical courts or the chancery — foreign they had always considered them to be. To the colonists it promised some melioration of their lot that the men who were appointed admiralty judges among them were really as untrained in their calling, as unfitted for it by practice or study,[1] as were the colonial judges themselves, and that Quary himself had to admit and to send to England for guidance.

The situation was a perplexing one for Penn. He was between two fires, the demands of the home government and the pressure of his own people. " You cannot imagine the difficulties I lie under," he wrote, " what with the King's affairs, those of the Government, and my Proprietary ones. No King's Governor has had more care and vexation, though I receive nothing from the Crown to support me under it." He regarded the money taken from the pirates who had been arrested in Pennsylvania as a perquisite of his own, since in his grant nothing had been reserved by the king " save allegiance and quit rent, appeals and approbation of laws." The people were soured to see their accusers believed, and thought themselves both innocent and meritorious. They were therefore cool toward their proprietor and he felt that he really had to " pay the reckoning." He urged that the reactionary provision about oaths in the recent act of trade might be corrected by " a short clause that those called Quakers in the Plantations may register their vessels upon their customary attestation in other cases, as freely as if they took an oath." [2]

Quary soon had occasion to withdraw the favorable things he had said about Penn, and to raise the charge of insincerity. His theory of the alleged change was that the Quakers,[3] failing to drive Quary out of the province, had refused financial support to the government of the proprietor unless he would asume an active rôle against the admiralty court. Quary had become involved in doubts as to whether appeals from his

[1] Cal. St. P. Col., 1700, p. 652. Mss. of House of Lords, N. S. IV, 332, 337.

[2] See Cal. St. P. Col. 1700, p. 598, for important suggestions by Penn as to other matters of policy.

[3] *Ibid.*, p. 651 *et seq.*;   Mss. of House of Lords, N. S. IV, 331 *et seq.*, 341 *et seq.*

court lay to the high court of admiralty in England or to Westminister Hall.[1] Sir Charles Hedges, as judge of the high court, had asserted the jurisdiction of his tribunal; but practitioners of the common law in England had denied it on the ground that the high court could not assume jurisdiction over trade cases. The colonists took advantage of this to gain a point upon the unpopular court in Pennsylvania. Penn appointed water bailiffs[2] for the counties of the province, giving them authority over all writs and processes directed upon any persons, ships or goods from any court of record up and down the river so far as their respective counties extended. This would make the men virtually executive officers of the admiralty court and so would seriously invade its jurisdiction. So Quary told Penn, but he contended that it was within his right, as the admiralty court had not the jurisdiction on the river within the body of the counties; he was not interfering with the jurisdiction or rights of the court. Quary's inference from this was that, in order to exercise his jurisdiction, he must go down to the capes of the Delaware. All that he could do was to urge the admiralty in England to come to his support. In this way the controversy was reopened and was presently carried before the boards in England. Penn was soon obliged to return thither in order to oppose the passage of the bill of 1701 for the recall of all the proprietary charters. Quary followed and the two joined issue before the board of trade.

Although everywhere unpopular, the admiralty courts were established, after more or less delay, but without special opposition, in all the other chartered colonies except Rhode Island.[3] Of controversies relating to them which developed later, especially in Massachusetts, we shall hear in another connection. When, in 1698, Jahleel Brenton[4] came to Rhode Island with commissions for Peleg Sanford as judge and for the other officers of the court, and Sanford went to Walter Clarke, the governor, to be sworn, Clarke took the commission from him, carried it to the assembly, then in session, and told them that the creation of a court of admiralty in the colony would destroy their charter, by virtue of which they

---

[1] *Ibid.*, 332.    [2] *Ibid.*, 337.
[3] Kellogg, 264.    [4] R. I. Col. Recs., III, 339.

claimed to possess vice-admiralty powers. He refused both
to return the commission and to administer the oath to the
appointees. The colony also appointed a court to try pirates
and continued to issue commissions to privateers. As its
attitude toward an admiralty court was only one of the many
offences with which Rhode Island was charged, in December
the board of trade recommended[1] that a commission be sent
to the earl of Bellomont to make an inquiry into its affairs
and report. This accordingly was done and the Rhode Island
government was duly informed.[2] In response Governor
Cranston wrote[3] to the board of trade in a very humble tone
claiming to have erred through ignorance, the natural fault
of plain people, and not through malice, and promising careful obedience in the future. Piracy and illegal trade were
the most serious charges. But in a session of the assembly
in August, 1699, the governor urged[4] that the necessary
preparations be made for vindicating their just rights and
privileges, and declaring that nothing should be wanting on
his part to maintain them; they had better spend one half
their estates, he said, to maintain their privileges than to be
brought into such bondage as the people of other governments
suffered. This speech was not intended to be made public,
but it got abroad and increased the suspicions of the board
of trade toward the colony. The report of the commission
was very unfavorable to Rhode Island.[5] Its act for the erection of a separate admiralty court was disallowed by the
crown, and the condition of Rhode Island affairs, as now
revealed, contributed strongly to the bill of 1701.

William Atwood, when chief justice of New York, was also
appointed judge of admiralty for all New England, as well
as New York and the Jerseys. The new vice-admiralty
powers of Dudley included the three easternmost colonies
of New England, while those of Cornbury extended over
Connecticut, New York and the Jerseys.[6] Inasmuch as the
same man was now both chief justice and judge of admiralty
in New York and the Jerseys, had that arrangement long

---

[1] *Ibid.*, 353.    [2] R. I. Col. Recs., III, 363.    [3] *Ibid.*, 373.
[4] Kellogg, 266. The journal of this session is not in the Colonial Records.
[5] R. I. Col. Recs., III, 385, *et seq.*
[6] Cal. St. P. Col., 1701, pp. 110, 112, 320, 324, 587, 594, 596.

continued it must have checked conflicts between the two jurisdictions. Yet in New York, over the ship of one Wake, some difficulty of that nature arose.[1] In New England, however, Atwood met with serious obstacles. In Connecticut the governor and council thought the admiralty jurisdiction interfered with their charter, and though they would probably submit to it, Atwood thought that by compositions with offenders or in other ways the actual enforcement of the authority of the court would be prevented. At Boston Atwood was insulted by an attorney while he was giving sentence in admiralty and was treated with scant respect by the judges of the superior court. He was threatened with prohibitions and suspension of sentences and considered the prospect of enforcing his jurisdiction to be very slender. The case[2] which revealed this situation was one in which the deputy collector at Boston, for permitting a cargo of wine and brandy, said to have been imported by Samuel Vetch from Europe without trans-shipment in England and seized therefor, to be embezzled and disposed of into hands unknown. Against the sentence pronounced upon him in the admiralty court the collector petitioned the superior court and it suspended the execution of his sentence until further order. Thus early was a good illustration furnished of the legal obstacles set up by the common law courts against the admiralty jurisdiction, especially in New England.

Toward the introduction into parliament of the bill of 1701 for the recall of all charters the long series of tendencies we have been describing led the way — piracy, illegal trade, the trouble over admiralty courts — in short all the difficulties with which the home government found itself confronted in the administration of the colonies. In the writings of all her officials the chartered colonies had long been described as the ultimate source of trouble. Randolph had always harped upon this string. So had Nicholson, and now Quary had taken up the refrain. Personal ambition had also its share in the work. Bellomont had just died and Joseph Dudley was scheming for appointment as governor of Massachusetts, and desired to have Rhode Island and Connecticut included within his commission. Jeremiah Basse was

---

[1] Cal. St. P. Col., 1701, 588, 708, 710.      [2] *Ibid.*, 709–716.

in England, intriguing for the dissolution of the New Jersey proprietorship in order that he might secure appointment as royal governor there.

In 1700 Randolph returned for his last visit to England and there found the project launched for the introduction of a bill into parliament at its next session to reunite to the crown the governments of several colonies in America. The right to do this existed as the highest possible exercise of power by a sovereign legislature, but it had never yet been used. The possibility of resorting to so autocratic a measure had never before been much discussed. But it is suggestive that now, at the time when in the act of settlement the parliament was making its highest assertion of authority, a measure affecting the colonies to this extent should be brought forward. As on previous occasions, Randolph was now employed again in collecting evidence against the chartered colonies and formulating the charges. In February, 1700/1, he presented a paper to the board of trade [1] in which he made specific charges against all the chartered colonies which had been visited by him as surveyor general — in other words, from the Bahamas northward. This paper closed with the statement that the misdemeanors which had been noted arose chiefly from the neglect of the proprietors to provide an honorable maintenance for their governors, so that honest men would not go out to live on the spoil of the proprietors; that the chartered colonies had made no provision for defence, so that they all lay open to invasion by the French or Spanish. In order to check these evils, their governments should be vested in the crown, though their territorial rights should be reserved to them, a precedent for which already existed in the case of Maryland and nominally in that of New Hampshire.

After other papers had been submitted by Randolph, the board of trade, on March 26, submitted to the king [2] the authoritative indictment which the government, as the mouthpiece of mercantilism, now brought against the proprieties. The inquirer who is familiar with the history of the chartered

---

[1] C. O. 5/1288, E. B. Proprs. Feb. 19, 1700/1. One version of these charges is in N. J. Arch. II, 358.

[2] Cal. St. P. Col., 1701, p. 141. Kellogg, The Colonial Charter, p. 286.

colonies can judge of its bias and estimate the degree of prejudice by which it was inspired. The chartered colonies were charged with not having answered the chief design for which such large tracts of land and such privileges had been granted by the crown. They had not obeyed the acts of trade as royal provinces had done, had not presented their governors for royal approval or taken the required oaths. They had made laws repugnant to those of England and prejudicial to trade. Some had refused to send their laws to England and others had done this very imperfectly. Several of them had denied the right of appeal to the crown, thus depriving their inhabitants and others of such protection against the arbitrary and illegal proceedings of their courts as was enjoyed in the royal provinces. They were the refuge of pirates and illegal traders, the receptacle of smuggled goods and the source whence goods were illegally exported to foreign countries. They undermined trade and welfare by raising and lowering the value of their coins, exempting their inhabitants from customs duties to which other colonies were subject, harboring runaway servants and debtors. They were promoting the manufacture of woolens and other commodities instead of applying themselves to the production of such as were fit to be encouraged according to the true design of such settlements. They did not properly care for their own defence by building forts or providing their inhabitants with arms and ammunition, though the dangers they were in constantly increased. Many of them had not a regular militia and some were in a state of anarchy and confusion. These evils chiefly arose from the ill use they made of the powers given them in their charters and the independence to which they laid claim, each colony considering itself obliged to defend itself without regard to its neighbors or the general preservation of the whole. Because of these evils and the growing necessity of introducing such a form of administration and such a regulation of trade as would make the colonies more secure and more useful to England, the board deemed it expedient that all the charters should be recalled, a result which could be attained only by the exercise of the legislative power of the kingdom. In this representation the board summed up the results of its chief activities since its formation and the conclusions to which it had been brought by the evidence submitted to it. It is one of the board's most important confessions of faith. It had to do with one of the broadest questions which colonial administrators of that time had to face. Nearly every issue, as then understood, led to the question of the chartered colonies and their relations to the British system and was influenced by it.

The king in council accepted the advice of the board, and a bill was introduced into the house of lords, April 24, which provided that the powers of government which had been granted by charter to all the proprieties should be declared void, but that the territorial rights of the grantees should be left intact and the people of those colonies should continue to be governed in accordance with the laws then in force among them and those which should later be enacted by their assemblies.[1] On the same day the board of trade presented to the house of commons a full list of the irregularities and offences of the various chartered colonies, charging Rhode Island with her reception of Lord Bellomont's inquiry and pretending by her charter to be independent of England, Connecticut with her denial of the right of appeal in the Hallam case and the public declaration of Governor Winthrop that no appeals should be allowed, the Jerseys with their utter confusion and unlawful trade, Pennsylvania with opposition to the courts of admiralty and illegal trade, the Carolinas and Bahamas with the misconduct of their governors and harboring pirates. As to this class of colonies in general, their independence made it necessary, said the board, that they should be made more subservient and useful to Great Britain.[2]

This was a government measure. Randolph was engaged to lobby for the bill and provision was made by the treasury for meeting his expenses.[3] The house of lords called on the board of trade for such of its books and papers as might

[1] Mss. of the House of Lords, N. S., IV, 314. Journal of Lords, XVI, 659 *et seq.* This was the session when occurred the bitter struggles between the Tories and Whigs connected with the impeachment of Lord Somers for the blank papers he had sent the king in the matter of the partition treaty. This resulted in a partial victory for the Tories. With war approaching we can hardly expect that much attention would be given to American affairs.

[2] Cal. St. P. Col., 1701, p. 171. Kellogg, p. 288.

[3] *Ibid.*, pp. 179, 184. Toppan, Edward Randolph, V, 273. Kellogg, p. 288.

be useful in making out the allegations of the bill. Important correspondence from Quary and others was sent in by the admiralty. The younger William Penn, on behalf of his father who was still in America,[1] found that from this list some papers which were favorable to the proprietor had been omitted and on his petition the house had ordered them brought in.[2] On May 3 hearings began before the house of lords, counsel appearing for the bill and counsel and agents for some of the proprietors. Witnesses were heard, among them Randolph, though the counsel for Penn objected to his appearing. Popple, the secretary of the board of trade, was present with papers which he read. The petition of Penn was to the effect that the bill seemed to take away the estate of his father, which had been purchased from the crown for a valuable consideration; that of John, earl of Bath, on behalf of the proprietors of Carolina and the Bahamas, that the bill had been introduced in the absence and to the surprise of the proprietors, and that it tended to disinherit them and ruin the planters and that in an enterprise which had cost them much more than it had yielded. Sir Henry Ashurst, who had recently been appointed agent for Connecticut, in connection with the Hallam appeal case and its boundary disputes, took the lead in activity on behalf of the proprietors against the bill.[3] He had long been opposing the appointment of Dudley as governor of Massachusetts, and now he learned that Basse, Dudley, Randolph and others had contrived this bill, which was to do all the business at once. Ashurst immediately put in his petition to the lords to the effect that the bill, if enacted, would dissolve the government of Connecticut which was closely interwoven with property, and expose the colony to confusion and ruin. He claimed that Connecticut had never been accused of maladministration, piracy or illegal trade and that its case differed from that of the other plantations. He was a man of position and influence and was incessantly active on behalf of the colonies. Baltimore and the Carolina proprietors made

---

[1] Mss. of the House of Lords, N. S., IV, 315 *et seq.*; Cal. St. P. Col., 1701, p. 223.

[2] Journal of the House of Lords, XVI, 659, 660, 662, 666, 668, 670, 676, 678, 688, 700, 715.

[3] See Winthrop Papers, 6 Mass. Hist. Colls., III, 69, 75–77.

a languid defence, and the latter were probably not disinclined to an escape from an unprofitable investment. So on the fighting line Ashurst was pitted against Randolph who was now old and in declining health, though keeping up his usual show of activity. As the result of his energy long lists of papers against the proprietors were laid before the lords from the board of trade, the admiralty and the customs board.[1] Randolph asked and was granted the protection of the house on the plea that his enemies were threatening him with arrest. Hearings were pushed and every effort made to secure the early passage of the bill. Ashurst made use of " an interest " he had with some in the lords to stop the bill, a course of action which Gurdon Saltonstall thought, if it became known, might damage the cause of Connecticut.[2]

The bill passed the second reading on May 23. But the close of the session was now approaching and with it the usual pressure of business. Four times a date was set for the third reading and as many times it was postponed. It was not yet before the lower house, and on June 11 Randolph had to report to the board of trade[3] that there was no probability of the passage of the bill that session. It was, however, confidently expected that it would come up at the next session, but as Randolph could not then be present, he was directed by the board to take all affidavits which might be necessary before a master in chancery and lodge them with it.

During the recess the opponents of the chartered colonies continued their activity. On July 16 Basse proposed to the board of trade that a royal commission[4] be appointed to inquire into the complaints against that group of colonies, and stated several points to which it should give attention. The board thereupon ordered that letters be sent to Nicholson of Virginia and Blakiston of Maryland to collect and send over proofs of the misdemeanors of proprietary governors and governments in their neighborhood, and that Cornbury and Dudley, when they should be ready to depart for their provinces, should receive a similar instruction. Randolph

---

[1] Mss. of Ho. of Lords, N. S., IV, 318–355.
[2] Winthrop Papers, 6 Mass. Hist. Colls., III, 75, 82.
[3] Cal. St. P. Col., 1701, p. 296.
[4] Cal. St. P. Col., 1701, pp. 352, 353, 371–373.

should be ordered to do the same when he should reach America. With the letters to Virginia and Maryland went a summary of the board's charges against the chartered colonies which have already been given, that the governors might use it as a guide in their inquiries. Penn hastened back to England to meet the threatened peril,[1] and Ashurst wrote to Winthrop that they must expect another attempt upon the charters the following winter by act of parliament.[2] It was reported that the next attempt would be made through the commons. Penn interpreted the surrender of the Jerseys as a preface to what was to follow and raised a subscription among Quakers in Pennsylvania to be used in defence of their charter. The parliament was dissolved in November and in the new elections a large Whig majority was returned. But this signified little for the colonies, and the rapid approach of war, consequent upon the recognition by Louis XIV of the titular James III as king of Great Britain, seemed to tell against the proprietors. The board of trade continued to report their defenceless condition, and in February, 1701/2, one of the secretaries of state sent to it the heads of a new bill.[3] This contemplated simply the appointment of a commander-in-chief for the colonies, the reuniting to the crown of the military power by sea and land, and the provision that the commander should superintend the officials of the customs and admiralty, while other civil authority should remain where it was. The board was not satisfied with this, and replied that the plan was not adapted to the proprieties in general nor to Pennsylvania in particular. It did not go far enough, as it would not secure the enforcement of the trade system by turning the produce of the colonies to the benefit of England. While they were considering this bill, the king met with the accident which caused his death. England was already at war and attention was for some time diverted from colonial reforms.

We have now reached the time which was signalized by the appointment of Cornbury as governor of New York and

[1] Penn-Logan Corresp., January 4, 1702.

[2] 6 Mass. Hist. Coll., III, 86.

[3] B. T. Journal, Feb. 18 and 20, 1701/2. This was Charles, earl of Manchester, who for a brief time was secretary for the northern department.

of Dudley to a similar post in Massachusetts. The New Jersey proprietors were surrendering their rights of government and Cornbury was made governor of their province. Both he and Dudley were ardent imperialists and were eagerly watching for any chance to bring Connecticut and Rhode Island under their control. The plan of the imperialists in England was to try again, in 1702–3, to secure the passage of a law for the recall of the charters, but room was not found for it on the calendar. At the close of a report to the council, in April, 1703, on the salaries of governors,[1] the board, after charging that, not being appointed by the queen, they connived at unlawful trade and other irregularities not consistent with the interest of the kingdom, declared that it had nothing to recommend concerning them except that they be reduced to immediate dependence on the crown. The sack of the Bahama islands by the French and Spanish in 1703, though this was the weakest of all the proprieties, furnished an excellent example in point. Penn was well aware of the trend of things and had already felt the pressure in several ways. These considerations, added to his financial difficulties, induced him now to begin negotiations for a surrender of his province to the crown.

This was also the time when the Society for the Propagation of the Gospel was founded and the further extension of the English Church through the colonies was seriously undertaken. Both Cornbury and Dudley were supporters of this policy, though the latter had necessarily to be very quiet about it. The tendency of the movement was to promote loyalty and strengthen distinctly British influence in the colonies. Of this Penn and dissenters generally were fully aware, and the course taken by events will be fully traced in another connection. In New York, Pennsylvania, South Carolina and elsewhere the Anglican clergy cooperated with the officials and others who were active supporters of imperial control. In the last-named province, however, the doings of certain high-flying Anglican politicians, in 1704 and 1705, came little short of inducing action by the crown and parliament which would have ended the proprietary régime in the Carolinas. The house of lords passed vigorous resolutions

---

[1] Acts of P. C. Col., 1680–1720, p. 432. Kellogg, *op. cit.*, 292 *et seq.*

and in an address called on the queen " to use the most
effectual methods to deliver the said Province from the
arbitrary Oppressions under which it now lies and order the
Authors thereof to be prosecuted according to Law." Though
this event lay somewhat outside the direct line of proceedings
against the chartered colonies, it had an influence on the
general issue and should appear in its proper place in the
general stream of events.[1]

Connecticut was sensitive to influences which were now
coming in from New York. The board of trade favored not
only giving Dudley control over the militia of Rhode Island
but even his appointment as its governor. The years 1704 to
1706 witnessed the heaviest attacks upon these two colonies,
and their magistrates at home as well as Ashurst, the agent,
and others in England were kept busy in efforts for their
defence. A long series of complaints against Rhode Island
was made by Dudley and supported by Cornbury, and
Byfield, the judge of admiralty,[2] gave an account of his
experience there. Rhode Island had not yet renounced her
claim to separate admiralty jurisdiction and illegal trade was
rife there; the doings of her magistrates in that connection
were attracting a good deal of notice. The disallowance of the
law upon which Rhode Island based her claim to admiralty
jurisdiction was procured by Dudley. A law relating to
heretics, passed when the excitement against Quakers was at
its height a generation before, occupied a similar place among
the charges against Connecticut, and it was also disallowed.
In 1704 an order in council was issued, based on an opinion
of the attorney general, that upon an extraordinary exigency
happening through the neglect of a proprietor or his appointees, or their inability to protect their province in time
of war, the crown might appoint a governor to take charge
of both the civil and military affairs of such province, though
he should not alter any rules of property or of procedure in
civil causes which had been established pursuant to the
charters.[3] This was the rule upon which the crown had acted

[1] Journal of House of Lords, XVIII, 130, 134, 143, 144, 150, 152, 153;
Osgood, Am. Colonies in 17th Century, II, 326–330.

[2] R. I. Recs., III, 537, 543.

[3] B. T. Proprieties, C. O. 5/1291, Nov., 1704.

in the case of Maryland, for a brief time in that of Pennsylvania, and under which government existed for about ten years (1720–1729) in South Carolina; but elsewhere the crisis did not become sufficiently acute to lead to such action. The military delinquencies of Rhode Island, however, were a source of continual irritation in New England. The opposition of Connecticut to appeals in the Hallam and Winthrop-Lechmere cases — described elsewhere — gave rise to another serious charge against her.

The first step toward the introduction of another bill against the charters into parliament was the sending of a list of charges over to Dudley and Cornbury in order that proofs in support of them might be procured. They exerted themselves to secure evidence but were not very successful.[1] Among the proofs sent by Cornbury was a volume of the statutes of Connecticut, with several marked as repugnant to the laws of England. The laws of that colony respecting religion came in for special comment, and various statements were included expressive of the determination of its people to defend their charter at all hazards. But without waiting for these proofs, such as they were, the board of trade, after receiving a letter from Dudley complaining that the two colonies would contribute no assistance in the war, sent to the privy council a report that they continued disobedient. Upon this the council ordered it to enumerate their illegal proceedings. This was done in a detailed arraignment of the chartered colonies of New England, under date of January 10, 1705/6.[2]

In this it was declared that they had not conformed to the acts of trade by presenting their governors for royal approval, that they had passed laws repugnant to those of England, they had denied appeals, they were a refuge for pirates and illegal traders, they protected deserters, they encouraged woolen and other manufactures, they neglected defence and refused to furnish the quotas which were required of them, they refused to acknowledge the vice-admiralty jurisdiction of the crown, they disregarded the royal proclamation respecting the value at which coins should circulate in the planta-

---

[1] Kellogg, *op. cit.*, 300.

[2] R. I. Recs., IV, 12. A copy of this in manuscript is in C. O. 5/3.

tions. Special and additional charges also were made against Rhode Island respecting its admiralty court, while the case of the Mohegan Indians appeared among the special complaints against Connecticut. These charges were a repetition of earlier ones and bear the same partisan character as those which Randolph had been in the habit of presenting. Many of the practices which were condemned in them were also common in royal provinces, though the implication conveyed was that the chartered governments were the sole cause of the evils and their removal would effectually cure them. This was sent to Secretary Hedges for the queen's further pleasure. On February 14 leave was given in the commons to bring in a bill to regulate the chartered governments in America, Hedges and Blathwayt being designated to prepare the bill.[1] It provided that the government of these colonies should be taken into the queen's hands, but that property rights of persons and bodies corporate should be guarantied, as also the continuance of the laws then in force there which had been or should be approved by the crown. After being approved by the board of trade, it was introduced into the house by Blathwayt. Sir Henry Ashurst was still the agent on the ground who was chiefly active in opposition to it.[2] But probably more effective than his efforts was the the growing strength of the Tories and also the reports which were already circulating about Cornbury's misgovernment in New York and the charges against Dudley. The bill was rejected on its second reading by a vote of 50 to 34.

The recall of Cornbury and the difficulty into which Dudley was brought by the charge that he was involved in trade with the enemy in Nova Scotia removed the danger of further attack by them on the proprieties. In 1706 a new commission was issued to the board of trade, not only Blathwayt but Pollexfen, Prior and other members being dropped and new ones substituted. From this time until after the accession of George I changes in the personnel of the board were fre-

---

[1] Journal of H. of C., XV, 151, 168, 180, 181, 183. The bill is in C. O. 5/1291, under date of Feb. 20. A copy of the same, without date, is also in C. O. 5/3.

[2] 6 Mass. Hist. Colls., III, 384.

quent. At about this time parliament legislated on two other subjects of great importance, both of which affected the interests of the colonies as a whole and one bore directly on the issue as it was now framed with the chartered colonies. The first of these subjects was coinage. If the British government cherished the definite purpose of keeping the colonies in a primitive agricultural stage of development and of preventing them from becoming commercial and industrial rivals of the parent state, its failure to see that they were provided with an adequate circulating medium was certainly well calculated to secure that end. England not only remained totally indifferent to the appeals of the colonies on this subject, but frowned on their efforts to supply themselves with coin as a violation of the royal prerogative. Her commercial system also was so arranged as to intensify rather than relieve the natural tendencies which kept them in the chronic condition of debtor communities, with the result that such coin as came to them in the course of trade promptly flowed out again in the payment of unfavorable balances. The statesmanlike proceeding would have been to establish a mint for the colonies. But in the absence of any provision for their convenience they had to depend on a variety of foreign coins which came in the course of trade with the West Indies.

The confusion in colonial exchanges was due to the lack of a standard and to the existence of so many varieties of coins and currency, all of which were debased and depreciated to an extent which differed for almost every time and place. Differing rates for the pieces of eight existed in the various colonies and by artificial ratings on the part of certain colonies the complaint was made that coins were drawn from one centre or colony to another. It was in response to charges of this kind and with the purpose of establishing a standard, that the proclamation of 1704 was issued by the British government. In preparation for this Sir Isaac Newton, then master of the mint, was called before the board of trade and submitted computations of the value of various foreign coins which circulated in the colonies, in terms of sterling. The attorney general was also consulted and he told the board that, since the Massachusetts law of 1697 had been allowed to stand, the government was stopped from making any regulations about colonial currency which were inconsistent with this. Had it not been for this, if William Penn was rightly informed, "the English standard had been the measure of America at large."[1] The board of trade reported that a proclamation should be published in all the colonies forbidding the rating of Seville pieces of eight higher than 17½ pennyweight. This being worth 4s. 6d., sterling should be rated at 6s. in the colonies. All baser coins should be adjusted to this and their circulation should be by weight and fineness. A table prepared by Newton showing comparative weights and intrinsic values in terms of English coins, of all coins circulating in the colonies and the rate at which they should circulate there, was appended to the proclamation.[2]

The rating prescribed in the proclamation, however, did not correspond with any coin in existence or with the money of account, and therefore rather added to the confusion than checked it.[3] It was not obeyed or enforced and could not be. Much was said about conforming to the standard of "Proclamation money," and it was now a requirement of the crown that this should be done. Complaints of clipping and other abuses were as frequent as ever. Dudley tried in vain to induce the general court of Massachusetts to add the halfpenny required by the proclamation to the ordinary valuation of the piece of eight. In the other colonies the situation was as unfavorable as in Massachusetts. The same complaints continued as were uttered before the order was issued. Those from Lord Cornbury, especially against Connecticut, seem to have had the most direct influence in England, and royal governors generally found it convenient to lay the blame on the proprieties. In 1705 the board of trade asked the attorney general whether the proclamation should be revoked or reinforced.[4] His reply was that the evil could only be remedied, as it had been in England, by an act of parliament, and if the chartered colonies fixed

[1] Chalmers, History of Currency in the British Colonies, 12, *et seq.* Penn and Logan Correspondence, I, 248. Acts P. C. Col., II, 419, 441, 452.

[2] Brigham, Royal Proclamations, 161.

[3] Sumner, Yale Review, 1898, p. 407, and Am. Hist. Rev., 1897-8, p. 614.

[4] B. T. Plants. Gen. E. B.

higher rates upon coins than were prescribed in the proclamation, they would forfeit their charters or at least their law-making powers, but they could not be held responsible for the doings of individual colonists.

The board of trade and its supporters, in both America and England, naturally added this subject to their general indictment of the colonies. After the failure of the bill of 1706 the board, on complaints that coin was being drawn away from Barbadoes, requested of the queen and the house of lords that an act might be passed for enforcing the proclamation and also one for bringing the chartered colonies immediately under the government of the crown. All the papers connected as proofs with the bill of 1706 were laid before the lords, but no legislation against the proprieties followed. The act of 1708 (6 Anne, c. 30) for enforcing the proclamation by making it punishable with fine and imprisonment to accept foreign coins at higher than the rates which it prescribed, was passed. Proclamation money thus became nominally a standard for the colonies, but, owing to the fact that no effort was made to change the rating and that within a very few years nearly all the colonies went over to a paper money régime, this law proved as ineffective as the proclamation had been. The term " proclamation money " was used, especially by representatives of the crown, to mean a certain standard to which they desired the medium of exchange to conform, though in reality it never agreed with the ideal.

The other statute, which though it only indirectly mentioned the dominions yet affected them much more widely than did the law concerning coinage, was the act of union of 1707 with Scotland. By opening to the Scotch the advantages of the English trade system and the full right of office holding, it brought to an end some of the most serious complaints affecting the colonies. The charges of Randolph and Quary had chiefly concerned illegal trade with Scotland. With the disappearance of that question and also the decline of piracy, which became apparent within a few years after the treaty of Utrecht, complaints about violations of the acts of trade abated. As charges of this kind were always made an excuse for an attack on the chartered colonies, the change in the political relations with Scotland tended to their advantage.

In 1712 and 1713, however, after the Tories had become well installed in power they meditated some readjustment of colonial relations to accompany the conclusion of peace. Of this Jeremiah Dummer got information which, as agent for Connecticut, he conveyed to that colony. After consulting with Massachusetts and Rhode Island, £300 was raised and sent to Dummer to be used toward defeating the plan.[1] But the death of the queen and the overthrow of the Tories following a few months later, nothing more was heard of their designs. At the same time Dudley's career as colonial governor came to an end, Quary had died, Blathwayt was an old man and out of office, the first stage of the armed conflict with France had passed and with it much of the peril which had menaced the self-governing colonies. Though the surrender of Penn's powers of government was nearly consummated, in the end that project did not succeed. It could not be foreseen whether or not the proprieties would be drawn from their seclusion into the fuller stream of imperial relations, but peace certainly brought with it some hopes of a respite in their anxieties.

[1] Conn. Recs., V, 410, 414.

# CHAPTER VII

WAR, FACTION AND FINANCE IN NEW YORK UNDER
SLOUGHTER AND FLETCHER 1691-1697

APART from the perils of war, to which it was peculiarly
exposed as a frontier province, the special inheritance of
New York from the English Revolution was the Leisler
experiment and the intense factional conflict which resulted
therefrom. The province was divided between Leislerians
and anti-Leislerians. For half a generation after the Revolution New York society and politics were deeply influenced
by that controversy. Governors and other royal officials
became involved in it. Its bitterness was primarily due to
the imprisonments and other indignities which were inflicted
on Bayard, Van Cortlandt and other colony leaders by
Leisler and on the other side to the execution of Leisler and
Milborne. The feeling was strongest in New York City and
the southern part of the province. How far it extended northward and to what extent it faded out as one approached
Albany, it is hard to tell. It was intensified by the pride and
touchiness of a petty colonial aristocracy on the one hand
and on the other by the stubborn prejudice of the poorer class,
largely Dutch, to whom Leisler had appealed. The provincial councillors and the entire body of officials who were
left by Sloughter were declared enemies of the Leislerians.
Several of the latter were in prison, so that it was fair to
assume that the Leisler faction was under the ban of the
government. The official, merchant and landed aristocracy
of New York was again in the saddle. With this group
Benjamin Fletcher identified himself on his arrival as governor in 1693. He could hardly have been expected to act
otherwise, if he desired a quiet and successful administration.
But it did not follow that a governor should identify himself
with all the evil forces which were connected with the anti-
Leislerian faction.

228

In addition to the execution of Leisler and Milborne, certain other things were done during what remained of the brief administration of Sloughter and immediately thereafter which were to have important consequences in the future. One was the passage, as the first act of the new assembly, of a law for quieting disorders in the province and securing the present government against like disorders in the future. This contained a full acknowledgment of William and Mary and the provision at the close that whoever should, by force of arms or otherwise, attempt to disturb the peace and quiet of the government, as now established, should be deemed rebels and traitors and suffer such penalties as were provided therefor in the laws of England.[1] This was going far, certainly beyond the statute of 25 Ed. III. Was it not making possible an interpretation which should elevate a variety of minor trepasses and acts to the rank of treason, and so was it not forging an instrument which could be used for severe reprisals? Was it keeping within the limits of the common law, or was it by implication making acts treason which were not such by common law?[2] It was the outgrowth of very disturbed conditions and might easily be used for purposes of violent reprisal.

In the act for general pardon thirty Leislerians were expressly exempted from amnesty, on the ground that they had been guilty of treason or treasonable acts. As treason had certainly been as far as possible from the intent of Leisler and his adherents, though at the end they had been betrayed, or had blundered, into something which looked like it, this was an almost savage act, one well calculated to prolong strife rather than to assuage it.

To the same class belonged the act, passed at the second session (c. 16), for regulating compensation for the damages done in the time of the late disorders.[3] This created by name commissions in all the counties except Suffolk — and they were all anti-Leislerians — to assess damages, as they should appear to them. These assessments should be effectual in law and should be based on claims of the injured parties, which

[1] Col. Laws of N. Y., I, 223.
[2] Case of William Atwood, Esq., Colls. of N. Y. Hist. Soc., 1880, p. 244, et seq.          [3] Col. Laws, I, 262.

must be filed within forty days after the passage of the act. Cases of alleged error might be appealed to the governor and council — another body which for years was to be wholly anti-Leislerian — provided the value appealed for exceeded £100 and proper security was given.

Another measure in the list was the setting up of Ingoldsby, on the death of Sloughter, as commander-in-chief though he had no commission as such, and that contrary to the first of the above acts, which provided that no one should exercise power in New York except by authority under the broad seal of England. Yet Ingoldsby served without such appointment from August, 1691, to March, 1692, and he was the commander whose troops had suppressed the Leisler movement.[1]

In earlier discussions of the position of New York among the colonies and of the colonial wars in their general aspects enough has been said to indicate the strategic importance of that province. In the time of Leisler the conditions, territorial and military, under which the struggle, then beginning, must be carried on became clear. Leisler and his supporters understood them and, so far as they were able, tried to secure the cooperation of the colonies, east and south, in the defence of the frontier adjacent to Albany. The officials in England who were responsible for the appointment of Henry Sloughter as the first governor of New York under William and Mary were in a way conscious of the same thing. At the time of the appointment of Sloughter, Francis Nicholson returned to the colonies as lieutenant governor of Virginia under Lord Howard of Effingham, who now became the absentee governor. Nicholson, as we know, was acquainted with New York and its needs as viewed from the imperialist standpoint. Of his activities in that direction we shall find evidence when the provinces on the Chesapeake come up for consideration. Sloughter's career as a colonial governor was to be brief and ineffective except for evil. But he and Nicholson started out together at the head of two of the most important provinces on the continent and for a time, as we shall see, the Virginia executive carefully watched conditions in the north and, so far as his influence could

[1] For a discussion of this anomalous procedure, see Spencer, Phases of Royal Government in New York, 38–40.

go, the way was prepared for genuine cooperation in defence, if not in other activities.

Near the end of October, 1689, and before Sloughter's commission was drawn, a statement was presented by him — whoever may have been its originator — in which was outlined the policy that should be followed for the preservation of New York. It included the fortification of Schenectady and the enlargement of the defences of Albany, the building of defensive works at Sandy Hook, the Narrows and Hell Gate (this was the most comprehensive scheme for the defence of New York harbor which had yet been outlined), the renewal of alliance with the Five Nations, the sending over of arms, ammunition and equipment and of a military and naval force as well. In order to defray the cost of so much of this plan as could be devolved on the colonists, the plan of Dongan and Andros for the annexation of Connecticut, the Jerseys and Pennsylvania, including the whole of the Susquehanna valley, to New York, was revived.[1] It is possible that the program, as here outlined, was set down by Nicholson. It was a restatement of Stuart policy and comprised the objects, so far as New York was concerned, which were chiefly to be sought during the first half of the period of the colonial wars. In connection with it developed plans to secure the cooperation of the colonies from southern New England on the north to Virginia on the south. Those may be regarded as the limits, at that time, of the sphere of influence of New York. The efforts to secure joint action within that territory led not only to the oft-repeated exhortations of its governors and to the attempts to extend their control over the militia of its immediate neighbors, but to proposals for bringing commissioners together in consultation and the application of requisitions, with accompanying quotas, to the problem of defence. Massachusetts was the centre of a similar combination for eastern New England, extending to Nova Scotia and for occasional purposes even further, but this was not so central and vital for the security of the continental colonies as a whole as were the arrangements which centered within New York.[2]

[1] Cal. St. P. Col. 1689–1692, p. 169.
[2] Cal. St. P. Col. 1689–1692, pp. 399, 400.

As soon as Sloughter reached his government his letters were added to the chorus of complaint not only against the Leislerians in New York but against the revolutionary régime in New England and of gloomy forebodings of disaster if more vigorous control from England was not instituted and with it some semblance of colonial union. He had been well coached by Dudley, Nicholson and Randolph. New England, he wrote, was in great disorder for want of royal commands and loyal subjects were discontented and unwilling to submit to the arbitrary usurpations of power there. Before Sloughter had been in New York a week several persons had applied to him for relief. They had assured him that they were taxed beyond all precedent, were unhappy, and that the establishment of royal authority would be welcomed. They had apparently made him believe that this was true of all the people of Connecticut and that they were ready to receive royal orders as to government. So simple did it seem to him that he thought he could settle the affairs of Connecticut by its annexation to New York, without charge to the crown. He was counting on the annexation of the Jerseys to New York or that in some other way they should be acceptably disposed of. If this ideal of union under effective royal control could be attained, the teeming thousands of New England would be available for any service against the French which the king might order and New York would be rescued from its hardships and dangers.

In the midsummer of 1691 Sloughter had his first taste of the difficulties which lay in the way of cooperation. He wrote to the New England colonies for their assistance in a joint expedition for the conquest of Canada. Connecticut at first cautiously insisted that this could be arranged only after the deliberation of commissioners, and even then they feared that the summer was too far spent for operations that year. But the assembly would meet shortly and the governor and others would do their best to persuade them. The governor of Massachusetts wrote about the failure of their hope of peace with the Indians and the outbreak of hostilities again on the frontier. Their present concern was a vigorous prosecution of the war against their treacherous enemy, but the woods and rivers to the eastward greatly obstructed their operations. They were not only raising forces, but equipping two ships to cruise the coast, where trade had recently suffered from a French privateer, which Kidd and Walkington failed to capture. They were willing to help New York, wrote the amiable Bradstreet, but the vast cost of their own defence made it quite impossible. They would be glad to know, however, if New York contemplated establishing a garrison at Pemaquid or elsewhere in Cornwall. Rhode Island enlarged on the operations of the same privateer, especially at Block Island, and feared the attack of others.[1] The governor wished their power was commensurate with their good will, but owing to disloyal and discontented people in the colony they could not raise money. Thus every colony thought its energies fully occupied at home, and those of Massachusetts certainly were so.[2] Both Sloughter and his council — or the one hand who drafted both letters — wrote home that the New England colonies "flatly denied" their request for aid, alleging that there were no compelling reasons.[3]

On June 29 the council of New York, under the influence of a rumored French invasion, issued an order requesting that East Jersey raise and arm 50 men and send them to New York within ten days, and that West Jersey, Virginia, Maryland and Pennsylvania be called on to furnish 375 fully equipped men, the quotas being specified in the order.[4] On what positive authority these orders were based it is hard to see. The commission and instructions of Sloughter gave him no authority to raise quotas.

On July 11, after his return from a conference with the Indians at Albany, and afterward, as a result of the report of an intended French invasion, Sloughter had raised 100 men and sent Major Schuyler with a force of English and Indians into Canada to watch the French. He also sent a circular

---

[1] *Ibid.*, 477.

[2] *Ibid.*, 478. It is interesting to note that at this same time Phips, who was politically Sloughter's opponent, was urging on the English government preparations for another expedition for the conquest of Canada. New England would raise the necessary ships and men, if England would grant a third rate, three hundred cannon, four mortars with shells, one thousand barrels of powder and two hundred small arms.

[3] *Ibid.* .513, 514.                    [4] *Ibid.*, 478.

letter [1] to all the governors as far south as Virginia, not only asking them to send quotas of 150 men each, but suggesting, with the council of New York, that commissioners be appointed to meet and agree upon a general plan of defence and to raise a fund therefor. In this way, " by a hearty union among us," the French might be driven out of America. He insisted on the heavy expenditures of New York and on its limited size and resources. But a slur on the loyalty of the New England colonies, because of their help to the late usurper, was introduced, which of itself must be fatal to any application, especially to Connecticut. The governor and council of Connecticut in their reply, which was prompt, came to close quarters in argument with Sloughter.[2] " You tell us of your great charges," said they. " We could tell you of ours, but that would not make them less. You have a large trade; we have not. We live by hard labor at the earth, subject to blights and other accidents. We have had our boundaries narrowed, as well as you. We doubt not you can spare men from Long Island for Albany. We have borne heavy expenses, formerly at Albany, and for the past three years in the Connecticut valley. Yet we should give all the assistance in our power, in case of an actual invasion, but we cannot incur such expense on mere rumors. The peril is quite as great up the Connecticut river and to the eastward. Your plan of a conference is worthy of careful consideration, but it will cost money and we must lay it before the assembly. Moreover, you mention no time or place of meeting."

From Maryland and Virginia came equally discouraging replies.[3] In the case of both the assemblies would have to be called, and the council of Virginia declared at once that it would take too much time and cost too much to do this; and even if it were called it would probably do no more than to provide for its own frontiers. The transportation of soldiers so great a distance would also involve very great difficulties. As to a contribution in money, the quit rents could not be drawn upon, but Nicholson was requested by

[1] *Ibid.*, 503. N. Y. Col. Docs. III, 784–786, 791.

[2] Cal. St. P. Col. 1689–1692, p. 508. N. Y. Docs., III, 786.

[3] Cal. St. P. Col. 1689–1692, pp. 428, 503, 513, 515, 517. The Virginia assembly had been prorogued only two months before Nicholson wrote.

the council to send to New York the balance of the king's revenue to be expended on the Indians as Sloughter should think best.  Maryland was more inclined to submit the matter to its assembly and sent Blakiston to New York to consult and secure the best information he could to lay before the assembly.  The president of Pennsylvania,[1] Thomas Lloyd, wrote that they had no revenue, at least for the purpose indicated, and the expenses of government were being defrayed from private purses.

But before this letter was written, Sloughter had died.[2] An address from the council and another joint address from Ingoldsby, who was now commander-in-chief, and the council were sent to England, repeating the former pleas for the annexation to New York of neighboring territory; but a return to the union with Massachusetts was not desired because of the seditious and anti-monarchical principles which prevailed there.

In October, 1692, in consequence of an order in council, circular letters were sent by the British government requiring Virginia, Maryland, Pennsylvania and New England to aid New York, on application of its governor, in men and money, and that they should agree upon quotas for this purpose and report, in order that further instructions from England might be given.[3]  Again, in February, 1692/3,[4] an order in council was issued that £500 be paid from the quit rents of Virginia and £250 from the revenue of Maryland toward the defence of New York, while, as we shall see, urgent steps were taken in reference to Rhode Island and Connecticut. Before this order arrived Virginia had sent £600[5] and the auditor was now directed to reimburse himself from the quit rents.  Maryland appears to have sent her quota, though after some delay.[6]  Fletcher sent out invitations[7] for a conference to meet in October, 1693, but was unable to secure a meeting.  He at the same time sent to the lords of trade a list of quotas of men whom the colonies from Massachusetts to Virginia should contribute for the defence of New York,

[1] Cal. St. P. Col. 1689–1691, p. 525.        [2] Ibid., 513, 520.

[3] Acts of P. C. Col. II, 227; Cal. St. P. Col. 1689–1692, p. 717 et seq.; ibid. 1693–1696, p. 635.

[4] Cal. St. P. Col. 1693–1696, pp. 26, 36, 39, 41.  See full references in the Index, p. 712.    [5] Ibid., 89, 154.    [6] Ibid., 171, 236, 285, 296.    [7] Ibid., 171, et seq.

based on an estimate of their adult male population. In the following August (1694), on a representation from the lords of trade, these colonies were again ordered to furnish quotas.[1] New York was included in this list and was assessed 200 men; it was empowered to call on New Jersey for a number not to exceed 700, and the rest of the colonies named were to contribute a total of 998 men. This plan, however, entirely failed. Most of the colonies to which application was made neglected or refused to grant the requisition for troops,[2] though a few small sums of money were given by Virginia and Maryland. Such special reasons as were given for this action will appear in the accounts of the colonies especially concerned.[3] The despatch of troops would have required vessels and capacity for administrative activity which the southern colonies hardly possessed at that time, at least under the leadership which they then had. The general result was the failure of the policy of requisitions, as tried in the first colonial war. New York had to provide as best she might for her own defence.

Though, as we have seen, the English of New York experienced no direct attacks from the French after 1690, their frontier was frequently disturbed by alarms and these made perpetual garrisons there and the occasional outfit of expeditions necessary. This increased expenditures and brought questions of finance into prominence. That in turn quickened the activity of the general assembly and furnished occasions, as always, for the growth of its powers. New York had had little experience with an assembly and from 1691 on its functions had to be developed almost *de novo*, on a background, of course, of British and colonial tradition. Under the commission and instructions of Sloughter a legislature was brought into existence which was not that contemplated in the so-called Charter of Liberties, but practically the same as that authorized by the instructions of 1683 to Dongan.[4]

---

[1] *Ibid.*, 315, 336, 635.   The letter to New York, as printed in N. Y. Docs. IV, 111, made no mention of a quota from New Jersey.

[2] *Ibid.*, 382, 594.  See Index.

[3] A partial statement of the amounts these netted to New York is in Cal. St. P. Col. 1696–1697, p. 3.  From Maryland the amount was £700 and from Virginia £1560, New York money.

[4] See the comprehensive account of the New York legislature by C. W. Spencer, Phases of Royal Government in New York, 59–96.

Of its two houses the upper, which was also the executive council, was a very small and also a permanent body. Its quorum was five and often only that number were present. For many years after the time of which we are speaking the governor always presided, voted and took a full share in its proceedings. It was he too who, by his power of recommending to the king, practically decided who should be its members. He could suspend councillors and, by urgent request to the king, secure removals. It was chiefly in these ways and by death that the personnel of the council changed.

The members who were named in Sloughter's commission were Frederick Philipse, Stephen van Cortlandt, Nicholas Bayard, Willian Smith, Thomas Willett, Gabriel Minvielle, Chidley Brooke, William Nicoll, William Pinhorne. Joseph Dudley was also named, but was a non-resident and did not serve. These men were all prominent as lawyers, merchants and officials in the southern part of the province. The first three had been in office when Leisler usurped the government and had suffered at his hands. Nicoll had also been imprisoned by Leisler. They, like the other councillors, were strong anti-Leislerians and were active in bringing about the destruction of Leisler himself. Smith, though not specially trained, was regarded as the lawyer of the council and was soon to become chief justice. The others had been or were to be mayors, justices, secretaries, revenue officers, and agents. They were connected by marriage or descent with one another or with the other wealthy families of the province. Their own wealth as it accumulated was by preference invested in land, after the manner of the nobility of Europe. In 1693 the purchases of Philipse, the richest man in the province, were consolidated and erected into the manor of Philipsborough, with its centre at Yonkers. In 1697 the Cortlandt manor, lying in the Croton valley on the east side of the Hudson, was created. By such steps as these the manorial system, which had declined toward the close of Dutch rule, was revived in New York. Caleb Heathcote, a wealthy merchant and colonel of militia, who was later to become lord of the manor of Scarsdale, became a member of the council in 1692. The northern part of the province found representation there the same year in the person of

Peter Schuyler,[1] whom the Five Nations fondly called Quider — "the Indians' friend." His father had been the first mayor of Albany and had laid the foundation of the family's greatness, based on the profits of Indian trade and dealings in wild lands. In the course of the next twenty years Schuyler obtained leading shares in the great Saratoga Patent, in Schaghticoke, east of the Hudson, and in the Westenhook and Oriskany patents, to say nothing of many other grants. Already the rival of Schuyler in northern New York was Robert Livingston, the canny Scotchman who had married into the Schuyler family, and by his many activities and fortunate deals was able to turn everything into money and land. Bellomont appointed him to the council in 1698, and in 1715 his vast holdings, of more than 160,000 acres on the middle Hudson, were consolidated into Livingston Manor.[2] The Van Rensselaers, though the original patroons and the largest landlords in the province, were never so active in politics as the rest, and it was not until 1704 that a representative of that family appeared on the council. These, with the active supporters of the Leislerian faction, who were brought in by Bellomont, constituted the leading members of the council during the period of which we are now speaking.

The members of the assembly, or lower house, of the New York legislature were elected from the counties, of two of which — New York and Albany — cities were components. Later two boroughs — Westchester and Schenectady — were created, and three manors — Rensselaerswyck, Cortlandt and Livingston — and all these were given representation in the assembly. Of the cities and counties, New York sent four members and Albany three. The other counties were each represented by two members. The boroughs and manors sent one each. Orange county received representation in 1698. Dutchess and Ulster were at first represented together, but later were separated.[3] In early times the assembly contained about twenty members, increased to twenty-six in 1717. As yet there was no law in New York limiting the right of the governor to call, prorogue and dissolve the assembly. Elec-

[1] Schuyler, Colonial New York, I, 380.

[2] Schuyler, Colonial New York, I, 224, 243, et seq.

[3] For details see Spencer, 75, et seq., and Scharf, History of Westchester County, I, 124.

tions were held under authority of the governor's writ issued through the secretary's office to the sheriffs of the counties. The qualification of electors, who were British subjects, was the possession of land in freehold and unincumbered to the value of £40. In the cities all who had been admitted freemen could also vote. The elections were held according to the forms of the English hustings and were *viva voce* or by poll. Everything was public and therefore the vote of the elector was known to his social or political leaders. Violence occasionally occurred, but only when the leaders fell out. The great majority of the inhabitants of the province were leasehold tenants on the manors or other large estates, or did not possess the requisite freehold unincumbered. They were thus excluded from the arena of politics. The actual voting population, therefore, was small, even provided in any county at any election they all appeared at the poll. We hear that in a hotly contested election in Westchester as late as 1733, the appearance of 370 freeholders at the polls was unprecedented.[1] In the excited times just before the Revolution the number of votes cast at any election in New York City probably never reached two thousand. No attempt was made to approximate the representation of the different counties to their population, and therefore Long Island, which was most thickly populated, enjoyed less than its proportion of members.

In New York the influence of the executive was always powerful. The council was a stronghold of the provincial aristocracy. In the assembly also power was concentrated in the hands of the propertied and conservative class. So far, then, as colonial conditions would admit, society was aristocratic in type, led by great families which themselves were bound together by a network of intermarriages, blood relationships and common interests, so that something like a dynastic policy appeared. Bitter political conflicts occurred, but they were usually between rival factions of the leaders or were carried on by them against the governor. By this means restraints were imposed upon the executive and laws and precedents developed which were favorable to local or corporate liberty, but the process was analogous to that by

[1] Memorial History of City of New York, II, 233, from Zenger's Journal.

which the aristocracy of England won its triumphs over the crown.

The members of assembly who came from Albany, Schenectady, Ulster, Dutchess and Kings were almost wholly Dutch. Those from Queens, Suffolk and Westchester were English, while Richmond and New York sent delegations of mixed English, Dutch and French origin. From the Dutch counties members usually served for long series of terms, while among the English this was often true of those who belonged to leading families. Members from New York were more frequently changed than those from any other county. Taking the province as a whole, political life was sluggish, there were few changes and they were long in coming about. In addition to the ordinary hindrances to political and social movement in the colonies, it should be remembered that through the entire eighteenth century Dutch was the vernacular in all the northern parts of the province and among large bodies of people in other sections. The Dutch were unaccustomed to political activity and intercourse between them and the English was difficult. But political cleavages did not follow the lines of the nationalities, English and Dutch were found on both sides of all questions, during Leisler's rebellion as well as the conflicts which followed it.

In the common speech of the times the income of the province was known as " revenue " and " taxes." The former was regular and permanent and sufficient to meet expenditures in ordinary times. It was derived from export and import duties and duties on trade up the Hudson, an excise on retailed liquors, fees at the weigh-house, fines, forfeitures and quit rents.[1] Of these the customs, excise and weigh-house duties above depended on the vote of the assembly, the customs and excise yielding about 85% of the revenue.[2] They were granted together in successive acts of the legislature, and were administered by the collector and receiver general under the supervision of the governor and council. Although the customs duties were distinct from those levied under the acts of trade and constituted a separate provincial revenue, the two were subject to much the same liabilities to smug-

[1] N. Y. Col. Docs. IV., 173.
[2] Spencer, 105.

gling and other forms of fraud. In complaints respecting these irregularities the two forms of revenue were likely to be confused and indiscriminately grouped together. This was true in the case of all colonies which had a customs revenue of their own. The collection of the excise was farmed out by counties, a method inherited from England, wasteful, liable to corruption and testifying by its very nature to the weakness of the government. So comparatively unimportant were the other sources of " revenue " that for the purposes of the present discussion they can be omitted.

The " taxes " were direct levies upon property in general, and were resorted to when the " revenue " did not suffice to meet the expenses of the province. This was very regularly the condition during the war. They were voted in the form of a lump sum and distributed by quotas among the counties. The officials whose duty it was to assess and collect county rates — assessors, supervisors, constables and treasurers — were utilized for the general " taxes " also.[1] It was the duty of justices of the peace in counties and of mayors and aldermen in the cities to keep these officials up to their task, and considerable difficulty in this regard was experienced. During the first colonial war Albany county furnished quarters for the troops who were stationed there. On account of delays, which were inevitable in their collection, provision was often made for the advance by individuals on loan of a part of these levies, the same to be later repaid with interest. The wealthy men of the province were then called upon in emergencies to shoulder its burdens as creditors and wait for their pay. In this way, prior to the beginning of currency issues — which were regarded as anticipation of taxes — temporary debts were incurred. During the first war this frequently occurred, and led after 1692 to the laying of certain duties over and above the duties imposed by all other acts.

During the period of which we are speaking altogether the chief objects of expenditure were defence and presents to the Indians. The former included not merely the pay of soldiers but a multitude of special services connected with messengers,

---

[1] See Chaps. 6 and 8 of the acts of May, 1691. Colonial Laws of New York, I, 237, 239.

supplies and transportation. Because of inadequate provision by the home government, a part of the support of the royal troops or independent companies fell upon the province. A minor object of expenditure was the salaries of the governor, of the collector and receiver general, and of other minor officers who were entitled to them. The salaries of the governor and receiver general, to begin with, were fixed by the home government. The salary account varied, during the first two wars, from less than £2000 to about £3500 per year.[1]

Though New York had existed so long without an assembly, the principle of its Charter of Liberties, that the taxing power was lodged exclusively in the legislature, was henceforth fully obeyed. In the making of appropriations the assembly took the initiative, but for more than a decade the governor and council fully shared in this task. So far as large matters of defence were concerned, the governor made the general demands in his speeches to the legislature and it responded by appropriate legislation. In these acts the grants were made and the objects of expenditure were stated in general terms. According to his commission and instructions, it was left to the governor, with the advice of the council, to issue the warrants for all expenditures, and he was required to see that full accounts of receipts and payments were kept and periodically sent to the treasury and board of trade. But England was too far away and its officials too preoccupied or too loose in the conduct of their own affairs properly to control expenditures in the colonies and exclude extravagance and fraud. Particularly, too, in matters of defence the home government was likely to be far more liberal in its demands than suited the means or tastes of the colonists. Events in New York soon indicated that the governor and council alone, or under such pressure as came from Great Britain, could not be trusted to prevent these evils. This gave rise to a prolonged and most important struggle on the part of the lower house to limit expenditures, and as an incident of this to exclude the council from an equal share in making appropriations. The first step which was taken in this direction was to make appropriations specific. This was first done by adding the words " for no other intent

<hr />

[1] Spencer, 108.

whatsoever," after the clause which stated the general purpose of the appropriation. In later acts the appropriation was itemized and the purpose for which every component sum was to be used was specified. These specifications appeared first in resolutions of the lower house and were then incorporated in the acts.

From the beginning of the period the assembly made use of committees of accounts,[1] to inspect taxes and revenue and state the public debt. But for a time, through lack of experience, these were of little utility. In 1692 and 1696 a joint committee of the two houses corrected the collector's accounts and on the basis of that occasioned the passage of acts granting an additional duty for the payment of debts. From such bodies and from the house itself the executive might and did withhold muster rolls and accounts of expenditures to thwart the assembly.

But the fundamental reason why the devices to which the assembly resorted in the early years of the period were not effective was that the governor and other officials who had charge of expenditures were not responsible to the tax-granting body.[2] They held their appointments from the crown by a tenure which was not fundamentally affected by any policy as to supplies. Therefore it was impossible by means of specific appropriations or through committees of audit fully to control the action of the executive in expenditures. Alarms or threats of invasion often made prompt action necessary and a breach with the executive would be dangerous. When the house flatly refused a supply and the breach with the governor became complete, a dissolution would follow and after a new election the policy, whether modified or not, would be tried with another assembly. That was the process through which conflicts went in all the provinces, New York, partly because of the pressure of war, furnishing some of its best examples. As a result, in the domain of finance as well as in other lines, precedents valuable to the cause of liberty were slowly established and the powers of the colonial executives and of the British government were defined and limited.

During the brief administrations of Sloughter as governor

[1] Spencer, 116.  [2] Spencer, 114.

and Ingoldsby as commander-in-chief — from the spring of 1691 to the close of August, 1692 — the customary attention was paid to the defence of the northern frontier. Influenced by rumors of a French invasion, the assembly, in September, 1691, appropriated enough to maintain 150 fusileers at Albany during the winter.[1] These, as usual, were drafted from the militia of the counties.[2] These, together with an equal number who were already in service, constituted the garrisons of the northern frontier during the winter. Though alarms were frequent, no encounters occurred except between the French and Indians. To keep the troops, whose arms were poor, from deserting they were offered full pay at the end of their term of service and the right to take up land anywhere in the province. As spring approached strict orders were issued to keep the inhabitants from abandoning the frontier[3] and to prepare them for active service. The assembly in its May session, after an audit of accounts had been laid before it by the council,[4] granted an appropriation for sending 200 more fusileers to Albany to take the place of those whose term of service had expired. Thus, unless some event occurred to break the routine, provision was made for the defence of the frontier summer and winter. On this occasion the justices of several of the counties were called upon to explain delays in the collection of the revenue.[5] The poverty of the people was the most common excuse. Before the money could be collected, sums were needed for defence and to meet the expense of Ingoldsby's conference with the Indians, and merchants and members of the council had to be asked to advance money for immediate needs.

On his return Ingoldsby stated to the assembly, at its August session[6] in 1692, that he found Albany in great disorder, all the fortifications out of repair and the out-settlements forsaken, the people discontented and the Indians weary of the war. He had reinforced Schenectady with thirty

---

[1] Ass. J. I, 3 *et seq.*, Leg. Council J. I, 2, 8. Laws, I, 258–262. N. Y. Col. Docs., III, 812, 813.

[2] The measures adopted for this draft or "detachment" are in Minutes of Ex. Council, for October 22 and subsequent dates.

[3] Ex. C. Min., Cal. St. P. Col. 1689–1692, p. 628 *et seq.*

[4] C. J., I, 14, 15, 16, 17.

[5] Ex. C. Min., Apr. to June, 1692.          [6] C. J., I, 18.

men and garrisoned Half Moon with forty. He found it
necessary that there should be a garrison at Canastagione,[1]
but he could not supply it for lack of men. The 200 voted
for Albany were 50 short of a complement. So discouraged
were the Indians, who had borne all the recent attacks of the
French and had been reproved by Ingoldsby for not doing
more, that he had felt obliged to make additional presents to
them and this made the cost of the conference heavy. So
delinquent had the people been in paying their taxes, that
less than half of what was due the forces had been collected.
He believed that 300 more men would be needed for the
frontier and the debt must be paid. After these had been
provided for, Ingoldsby urged that the assembly take
measures to compel the payment of taxes. At this juncture
Fletcher, the new governor, arrived and after it had been
decided that the session might legally continue, an appropriation was made for raising the 300 men. It was also agreed
that the county justices be warned to secure the most prompt
collection of the revenue under threat of the utmost penalties
of the law.[2] If all arrears could be collected, all expenditures
would be met, and a surplus of £925 would be left for the
payment of the debt.

Benjamin Fletcher was a military man of some experience,
active and ambitious to make a reputation, as well as money.
He was on easy terms with Blathwayt and the earl of
Nottingham, secretary of state. He again rang the changes
on the interests which New York and the neighboring colonies
had in common and especially, as he had a commission to be
governor of Pennsylvania, he naturally emphasized the policy
of cooperation among the colonies. Under an order from the
king he released the imprisoned Leislerians.[3] Though he
understood the tendency of the French to boast, he found
them threatening the northern frontier, while New York was
in debt and its system of defense very imperfect.[4] An early
visit to Albany confirmed this impression. The conviction
was now established in his mind that New York was over-

---

[1] This was on the Mohawk just west of Cohoes, in Saratoga county.
[2] Ass. J. I, 24.  C. J. I, 23.  Col. Laws, I, 282 *et seq.*
[3] N. Y. Col. Docs., IV, 54, 83.  Cal. St. P. Col. 1693–96, pp 169, 170.
[4] N. Y. Col. Docs., III, 846 *et seq.*, 854.

burdened and that the assistance of the other colonies should be called in. This he never ceased to urge as long as he was governor, but with what lack of success in certain quarters has been explained in other connections.

It was necessary for Fletcher at once to dissolve the old assembly and order a new election. Like his predecessors, he identified himself with the anti-Leislerian group. But with the lapse of time and the release of their imprisoned leaders, the Leislerians now began to raise their heads and factional heats appeared in the election. Abraham Governeur soon went to Boston and gave Governor Phips a full account of New York affairs from the Leislerian standpoint.[1] It was very natural that a man of Phips' origin and history should sympathize with the course of Leisler and that he should go far beyond the limits of diplomatic propriety in expressing his views. Prevailing sentiment in Massachusetts might well be on the same side, especially as the surrender of Martha's Vineyard was being demanded by New York under the terms of the duke's charter. Governeur in a private letter reported some very personal and offensive remarks by Phips concerning Fletcher and the New York council. These came to the knowledge of Fletcher and drew from him a sharp letter of reproof, to which Phips replied with emphasis. As Governeur had not yet been fully pardoned and Phips was known to be furthering his departure for England to present there the cause of the Leislerians, an envoy was sent from New York to demand his return as a fugitive from justice.[2] In the interviews between Clarke, the envoy, and Phips, in the presence of councillors and of Usher and Rev. Joshua Moody, of New Hampshire fame, the Massachusetts governor denounced in unmeasured terms Fletcher and those who had put Leisler and Milborne to death, and refused to surrender Governeur. Clarke, after narrowly escaping a long imprisonment, was sent back to New York with several threats and choice bits of personal criticism to repeat to his superior. As it was now certain that Governeur was going to England, an address to the crown was sent by the council

---

[1] *Ibid.*, IV, 4. [Professor Osgood follows the spelling of the official journals in the name Governeur. D. R. F.]

[2] *Ibid.*, 8–12.

of New York complaining of Phips and asserting their claim to Martha's Vineyard.[1]

The younger Leisler was already in England and, as the result of petitions from him and Abraham Governeur, decisive action on behalf of the Leislerians was taken.[2] The estates of Leisler and Milborne were restored to their families as an act of mercy and a full pardon was issued to Governeur and his associates. Permission was also given to apply to parliament for a reversal of the attainders of Leisler and Milborne and, in May, 1695, an act providing for this was passed and received the royal assent.[3]

While the New York executive was occupied with these affairs, and with efforts to secure appropriations from the assembly for five years instead of two-year terms,[4] with the audit of accounts and the issue of circular letters to hasten the collection of arrears of taxes, word came from the north that a large body of French and Indians had captured one of the Mohawk castles and was near Schenectady. It was now midwinter of 1692/3.[5] In the then unprecedented time of three days Fletcher reached Albany, but he and the troops he brought found it useless to go further than Schenectady. Schuyler, starting from Albany, followed the retreating French as far as the upper Hudson and then left them to pursue their disastrous march homeward. Fletcher was complimented by the Indians and by civic bodies and in confident terms made a report of the defeat of the enemy by his prompt action. But the expedition was barren of results. Letters had been sent to the colonies to the southward for help and the only response had been a small sum of money from East Jersey and an expression of good wishes from Pennsylvania.[6] "Our neighbors to right and left," wrote Fletcher, "sit at their ease and govern by their own fancies." Connecticut was full of people but would not send a man nor a sixpence to the relief of New York. So Fletcher had to content himself with describing the fort at New York as

[1] Ex. C. Min., Feb. 10 and 14, 1692/3. Cal. St. P. Col. 1693–6, p. 27 et seq.
[2] Cal. St. P. Col. 1689–92, pp. 584, 612. Acts of Privy C. Col. II, 204, 205.
[3] Cal. St. P. Col. 1693–6, p. 470. Acts P. C. Col. II, 205.
[4] Ass. J. I, 27 et seq.: C. J. I, 31 et seq.
[5] N. Y. Col. Docs. IV, 14–24.
[6] Ibid., 31. Cal. St. P. Col. 1693–6, p. 45.

" dropping down for want of repair," and begging the goverment at home for two additional companies and arms for two troops of dragoons.

Every year, as the first of May approached, when the terms of service of the recruits expired, they must be reenlisted or others found to fill their places. Taxes were always in arrears; money therefore was lacking to pay off the levies or to pay Robert Livingston for subsisting them . As it was generally agreed that provision must be made for the frontiers before all other expenditures, the machinery for collecting the revenue was jogged, where possible, into greater activity, and accounts were more carefully audited. While, in conjunction with the council, this business was in progress, in the spring of 1693, Fletcher made his first visit to Pennsylvania. The history of his attempt to govern the Quaker province has been related elsewhere.[1] The aid which New York received as a result of the experiment was almost *nil*. When Fletcher returned from this visit, he wrote that he never yet had found " so much self-conceite. They will rather dye than resist with carnall weapons, nay they would perswade me their Province was in no danger of being lost from the Crown, though they have neither Arms nor Ammunition." [2] He told the council of New York that the people of Pennsylvania were fond of having their own way and he could prevail with them but little.

But the representation of the needs of New York which Sloughter, Ingoldsby and Fletcher had been making were having an effect in England. The previous February Blathwayt asked the attorney general to examine the charter of Connecticut and the grants to the Jersey proprietors and to report as to the king's powers therein. The report, which soon followed, was that the king might appoint governors with powers to raise men and furnish provisions for the necessary defence of subjects or of neighbor colonies as he saw fit.[3] The Jerseys could not be so completely separated from New York as not to be liable to contribute toward its defence.

---

[1] Osgood, American Colonies in the 17th Century, II, 269 *et seq.*

[2] N. Y. Col. Docs. IV, 31. The stubborn opposition of the Quaker interest was well expressed in two letters of Penn, one of which was written to Fletcher at the time of his appointment, Cal. St. P. Col. 1693–1696, p. 116.

[3] Cal. St. P. Col. 1693–1696, pp. 16, 19, 20, 26. N. Y. Col. Docs., IV, 29.

This report was followed by the despatch of letters to Connecticut and Rhode Island bidding them help New York if required, and later by the issue of the commission to Fletcher to command the Connecticut militia.

In the summer of 1693 Charles Lodwick was sent by the governor and council as an agent to England[1] to report to the lords of trade the position, services and burdens of New York and the failure of the other colonies to assist her. The remedy which he was to suggest was the annexation of the Jerseys, Pennsylvania and Connecticut to New York, as the only means through which military and financial relief could be secured, and the emigration of inhabitants of New York to other and less heavily taxed colonies could be checked. This policy Lodwick urged in a memorial which he presented in the autumn of 1693, adding the statement that the Five Nations were inclined to make peace with the French because they lacked the usual supplies and presents. This furnished the reason for a demand that a supply of military stores and a reinforcement of regular troops be sent to New York and that annually a sum of money be sent to pay for presents to the Indians. Contributions from all the continental colonies for the defence of Albany should also be required. This was the plea of New York in its broadest outlines. It was often repeated during the first two colonial wars, but after that date it was not frequently to be urged. It was invalid in so far as it was based on an overestimate of the strength of Canada and of the strength France was then ready to exert for the increase of her dominions in North America. It was also not accompanied by unusual efforts toward self-defence on the part of New York herself. And yet the policy was justifiable, when viewed from the standpoint of the British alone and judged according to the criteria of those times, for had it been thoroughly adopted, French Canada must soon have vanished from the map and the long conflicts which were to follow would have been avoided. The fact that it was so often urged and met with so little response furnishes additional and eloquent testimony, if such were needed, to the lack of the spirit of union among the English and their weakness from the standpoint of defence.

[1] N. Y. Col. Docs. IV, 32, 53.

Fletcher called a meeting of commissioners at New York in October to agree upon quotas from the different colonies for its defence.[1] But only Virginia and Connecticut sent delegates, and nothing could be done.[2] Those of " Pennsylvania," wrote he, " deny the carnall sword, nor will they dip their money in blood "; or, as he varied the language in a later communication, " Pennsylvania will neither kill [nor] contribute Aid to the Arm of flesh." In the following spring he reported that the crown had ordered £500 sterling paid out of its revenue in Virginia and £250 sterling from Maryland, but these sums had not yet been received.[3] The excuse of these provinces was that they had already given equivalent sums before they received the king's orders and these should be accepted as a full discharge. The New York government did not think so, and as to a Maryland bill drawn by Governor Copley for £362, it had been returned from London protested. A little later Governor Hamilton wrote [4] that an Independent minister of Elizabeth was leading an opposition to the raising of troops in East Jersey, while the Quakers everywhere were stubborn.

Near the close of 1693 Fletcher had some difficulty with the city of New York, which indicated another possible source of opposition.[5] A battery was then building on the point of rocks at the end of Manhattan island, and a discussion occurred between the governor and council and the authorities of the city relative to the obligation of the latter to bear the expense and furnish the stockade. The city tried to escape, not so much on the plea that defence was properly a province charge, as on the quibble that it had no power by charter to levy a tax. Fletcher told them that, if they could not levy for this, they must not impose a tax for any purpose; and yet they had a treasurer and common purse and had levied money for the repair of fortifications. In view of this argument and of the danger that it might lose its charter, the city abandoned its first plan of raising the fund by voluntary contributions and imposed a tax of 3d. in the pound for the purpose.

[1] Cal. St. P. Col., 1693–1696, pp. 157, 173.
[2] N. Y. Docs. IV, 56.    [3] Ibid., 37, 84.    [4] Ex. C. Min., Oct. 6, 1693.
[5] Ex. C. Min., Dec. 18, 1693, et seq.    Min. of Common Council of the City of New York, I, 338 et seq.

During the winter of 1693/4 and the summer which followed the New York authorities were harassed by the fear that the Five Nations were slipping away from their control. The influence of Frontenac, coupled with the pitiful showing made by the English, was telling upon them. Schuyler reported [1] that they were wavering in their adherence. A peace belt had been sent to them from Canada. Father Millet, the Jesuit missionary among them, was active. To prevent them from sending to Canada to conclude peace, a meeting with some of the chiefs was arranged at Albany. They were with difficulty induced not to meet Frontenac in council, but to send envoys to the Praying Indians of Canada with their excuses for declining the invitation.[2] At the same time arrangement was made for an interview of the governor with them the following summer. Before the date for that arrived, Massachusetts was alarmed by reports that the Five Nations had actually concluded peace with the French. Though this was soon disapproved,[3] it influenced both Massachusetts and Connecticut to send commissioners to attend the conference at Albany. Pynchon, Sewall and Penn Townsend [4] came from Massachusetts, Allyn and Caleb Stanley from Connecticut, and Governor Hamilton from New Jersey.

Shortly before Fletcher and his councillors left for Albany to attend the conference, Lodwick arrived with a supply of military stores and cannon from England and also the news that two additional companies of regulars were on their way. These, with the two companies which Ingoldsby had brought in 1691, formed the four independent or grenadier companies, of whose condition we hear so much during this and the next war.

When Fletcher reached Albany and found that the New England commissioners had brought presents, it was agreed that they be combined with those of New York into one common gift. Fletcher also insisted that only one treaty be concluded, for if a separate one for New England were agreed to, it would put a stigma upon other provinces for which he

[1] N. Y. Docs. IV, 59 et seq.
[2] Ibid.,74–83, 85–99.
[3] Ex. C. Min., July, 1694.
[4] 4 Mass. Hist. Coll. I, 102–110.

was equally concerned.  The Five Nations, however, should
be urged to send peace belts to the Eastern Indians.   The
Iroquois were brought to a resolve not to allow the French
to rebuild the fort at Cataraqui.  As this was a measure upon
which Frontenac had set his heart, if the Indians could be
committed to opposition to it, the immediate danger of
negotiations between them and the French would be removed,
and they would see the necessity of continuing their alliance
with the English.

While the commissioners were together they discussed what
was needed for the defence of the frontier, and it was agreed
that 500 men was the least number requisite.  It was also
the opinion that Half Moon, Canastagione, Schenectady and
The Flats — the last named being the site of the Schuyler
residence — should be newly fortified, as they contributed to
the security of New England and New Jersey, as well as
to that of New York.  With the aid from England the number
of cannon at Albany could be increased and more troops
could be stationed in the northern garrisons.[1]    Later, by
the council and assembly of New York the rate of pay of the
troops was discussed.  The king had ordered that the two
independent companies already in New York should be raised
to 100 men each to correspond with the establishment of those
which were soon to arrive.  Their daily pay was to be 8d.
New York money, of which 2d. sterling was to be stopped
in England for their clothing, and $5\frac{1}{2}$ d. New York money for
provisions was to be paid in New York.[2]  Because of the low
rate of pay, Fletcher feared that the soldiers would be disappointed and many would desert; therefore he desired that
the assembly would add four pence to their pay and propor-
tionably advance the wages of the subaltern officers.

Throughout the following winter alarms among the Indians
continued in view of what was known to be the determined
policy of the French governor concerning Fort Frontenac.

---

[1] We learn that by November the stockade at Albany had been completed,
twenty additional cannon placed there, and that the garrison then consisted
of 200 men, besides Ingoldsby's independent company or company of grena-
diers.  N. Y. Docs. IV, 113.

[2] Ex. C. Min., Sept. 4, 1694.  For the complicated system of paying British
regulars, with its disastrous results for the common soldier, see Fortescue, Hist.
of the British Army, I.

The rebuilding of that fort was a necessary step toward any advance movement against the Iroquois. The opposition to it came, as usual, from the intendant and he had persuaded the government at home to support him in this. But, in the summer of 1695, before the order prohibiting the measure arrived, the expedition had been sent out which rebuilt the fort and thus re-established the control of the French over Lake Ontario. During the many months of preparation for this and while it was regarded as almost certain, Fletcher was vainly trying to bring together a force, but only for the defensive. The two companies of regulars had not yet arrived. No one among the English seems to have thought of any aggressive action on their part, such as an expedition against Canada or the planting of a rival fort on the lake. And yet the move of the French was seen to be only a prelude to an attack on the Iroquois, which might force them to seek peace with the French.[1] The rebuilding of Fort Frontenac, followed the next year by a French attack on the Onondagas, futile though the matter was in its immediate effect, put the stamp of failure on the bustling activity of Fletcher, with its combination of boastfulness and persistent appeals for help.

But internal opposition against Fletcher was already developing, and evidences of dishonesty in the government of New York were beginning to appear which went far toward thwarting even the governor's best efforts, and in the end were to contribute to his recall. In the fall of 1693 Fletcher dissolved his first assembly. It was an anti-Leislerian body. On the whole it had been submissive to the lead of the executive, and in its last session it voted a revenue for five years.[2] Fletcher had been demanding appropriations for the life of the monarch, but the most that had previously been granted was an appropriation for two years. And yet, though the assembly had made this important concession, Fletcher received it with bad grace. He came to a more direct issue with the house over his right of collation to benefices and his bill for the establishment of the church, to which extended reference is made in another chapter. In his closing speech he took the assembly roundly to task and charged it with

---

[1] N. Y. Docs., IV, 118 *et seq.*          [2] Col. Laws, I, 325.

assuming too much power and with prolonging its costly sittings to little purpose.[1]

In the election which followed an entirely new set of members was chosen from New York City. Among the new members were two leading Leislerians, De la Noy, and Staats, while at least one other was of that group. Thus the relentless opponents of the governor and his party got their first foothold in the house. Though in this assembly, or the next, it is impossible to discover clear evidence of their activity, it is certain that their influence was steadily cast against the government. The assembly as a whole seems also to have become more alert. It at once took up the condition of the frontier and appointed committees not only to inspect accounts but to examine the muster rolls.[2] Chidley Brooke was collector, and they found difficulty in getting from him the accounts. Several of the muster rolls were missing and the names of absentees were found to be numerous on those which they did examine. The result was that the appropriation fell considerably short of the number of troops for which Fletcher had asked and their pay was reduced from one shilling to eight pence per day. The great subject of controversy during the next session, which was in the fall of 1694, was the rate of wages which the assembly had fixed for the troops and the number for whom provision had been made.[3] The governor enlarged on the evil of desertions and, with the approval of the council, asked that four pence per day be added to their wage, with fire, candles, transportation, hospital service and other incidentals. But the house could not be moved. Let the subject, it said, be postponed till next session, when the troops from England would have arrived. Under strong pressure they did provide pay for 100 — instead of 80 — men on the frontier during the coming winter. A joint committee was appointed to examine accounts, but the assembly's own committee reported that it was not satisfied with the accounts of the collector and of others, and that the collector had promised to submit next session a statement of the entire revenue down to the close

---

[1] J. of Leg. C., I. 48; Ass. J., I, 34.
[2] Ass. J. I, 36 et seq.
[3] Ass. J. I, 41 et seq. C. J. I, 59 et seq.

of 1694. Fletcher, too, had already begun to protest his own innocence.[1]

In the spring session of 1695 Fletcher and the council came to a complete breach with the assembly and it was dissolved. The house stated that, the previous September, it had been informed by the muster-master that the number of soldiers then at Albany was 48 short of the complement.[2] Since then there had been several desertions. It had now again asked for the muster rolls of the last two drafts, but Fletcher had said they were on the frontier and could not be produced, and the council had voted that the demand to see them was improper. The assembly had therefore inferred that, if the government was being honestly administered, considerable balances of the last two appropriations remained unexpended. It therefore refused to appropriate more than £1000, to be added to the unexpended balances — called surpluses — and insisted that that would be sufficient. In justification of this, they laid strong emphasis on the troops which were expected from England. Fletcher, on his part, declared that he desired to relieve the province [3] from the burden of detachments, but he could not do it without an adequate supply of money, for the honest expenditure of which the council, composed of men who had the largest interests at stake, were responsible. Being unable to bring the assembly to terms, and already recognizing that De la Noy was one of its leaders, he dissolved it on April 22, and ordered a new election.

It was the irregularities alleged to have been committed at this election in New York City which first brought Fletcher's conduct before the authorities in London. Considerable sums had become due to Robert Livingston for subsisting troops at Albany and, owing to the financial difficulties of the government, these had not been paid.[4] Some of these debts had accrued before the appointment of Sloughter, one being of a date as early as the administration of Dongan. The principal

---

[1] For Fletcher's view of the opposition which he was facing — from some of the leading Leislerians who had got into the assembly — see his letter of November 19, 1694, N. Y. Docs. IV, 113.

[2] Ass. J. I, 48, *et seq.* C. J. I, 68 *et seq.*     [3] C. J. I, 76.

[4] N. Y. Col. Docs. IV, 127–145. Cal. St. P. Col. 1693–1696, pp. 564, 598 *et seq.*

due aggregated £3719 and the interest about £635, though Livingston claimed £1503 as interest.[1]   He also demanded the restoration of ten barrels of powder which had been taken from him by Leisler at the time of the Revolution.   Another element in Livingston's claim was that two merchants, Merryweather and Harwood, in connection with procuring and discounting tallies to the amount of £1670, had presented charges amounting to £901.[2]   It was in order to procure a settlement of these claims, and also a salary for his services as Indian agent at Albany, and to state his many other duties there as well, that Livingston left his large and growing family and journeyed to London in 1695.   His case was submitted to the lords justices and thence to the committee of trade and hearings were held in August and September.   Livingston's charge, so far as it affected Fletcher, was that the payments due to himself and others were not and could not be made because the money raised was diverted to the defence of the frontiers.[3]   But in addition to testimony produced to prove this, Philip French, William Kidd and three others made depositions that the election of May, 1695, in New York City was carried by intimidation and fraud, the former by bringing soldiers and seamen from the man-of-war to the place of election and the latter by the admission just before the election of several of the lower officers to the right to vote.   It was also stated that Fletcher had openly threatened to shoot any one who should vote for Peter De la Noy.   These tactics, whatever they were, were successful in the defeat of the Leislerians who had been the members from New York in the previous assembly.   In their places James Graham, Brandt Schuyler, Lawrence Reade and Teunis De Key were returned.   New members were also elected in Westchester.

But the experiment was to cost Fletcher dear, for not only were these facts presented at the Livingston hearings, but De la Noy retaliated by sending a long and virulent letter

---

[1] *Ibid.*, 600.

[2] *Ibid.*, 598, furnishes a good example of the items contained in these accounts.

[3] This probably refers to what is elsewhere mentioned as suspending the act of March, 1692/3, for paying the debts of the government, Docs. IV, 202, 205.

against Fletcher to England,[1] which was delivered to the committee of trade by William Penn. In this he enlarged in effective terms not only on the above charge, but on the state which the governor assumed, his overbearing manners, the greed and peculation which were alleged to accompany all he did and above all his corrupt relations with pirates. Charges which were to be urged again and again in the years to come make their first appearance in this letter. It was well and effectively written. It closed with an indictment of the clique system under which it was alleged that everything was then done in New York. " In short, nobody lives tolerably under him except those who submit to be his creatures, such as the judges and other officers dependent on him. His accounts were indeed passed by the council, but for such jobs only his own creatures are summoned, who dare not oppose him." And then follows a reference to the ostentatious piety of Fletcher: — " You will wonder to hear after this that this man's bell rings twice a day for prayers and that he shews great affectation of piety, but this makes him only more ridiculous, not even respected." De la Noy closed with the expression of a desire that New England, New York and the Jerseys might be put under one general governor, but with the preservation of their distinct assemblies, courts and laws. The elements of the entire case were thus placed before the lords of trade.

Livingston was also very successful in the prosecution of his own claims in England. Under an order in council the matter was referred to the lords of the treasury.[2] They reported that he be paid interest to the amount of £668 — New York money at 30% discount — in England and that the interest on the other sums be paid out of the revenue in New York, under an order to the governor. In view of the financial difficulties of New York, Livingston had agreed, for the time at least, to be satisfied with this, though New York would still be liable for the payment of the principal. He was also to be allowed a salary of £100 per year as Indian

---

[1] Docs. IV, 221; Cal. St. P. Col., 503 *et seq.*
[2] Cal. St. P. Col., 617, 635, 639; Docs. IV, 140; Acts of Privy Council Col., II, 290.

agent for life and to be confirmed in all his offices.[1]  This
was approved by the king in council and orders duly issued
at the middle of January, 1695/6.  But owing to the fact
that the presentation of Livingston's case in England had
been accompanied with the raising of serious charges against
Fletcher, it was almost certain that obstacles would be thrown
in the way of the thrifty Scotchman in New York.

From his new assembly Fletcher experienced no opposition.[2]
The two houses now acted together in perfect harmony.  With
its appropriations the governor expressed satisfaction.  A
joint committee was appointed to examine accounts since
the appointment of Sloughter and report at the next session.
That session opened at the beginning of October, 1695.  On
September 26th the committee held its first session and then
received from a Mr. Wood two statements, one of the taxes
as they stood September 20th and the other an account of
payments by public warrants out of taxes.  After such a
tame procedure as that, it was hardly necessary for Fletcher
to urge members, as he did at the close of the session, to
procure evidence of oppression or maladministration in order
that they might be remedied by reform measures.  Of course
none were reported.

Upon receiving news that Fort Frontenac was rebuilt, the
governor and legislature at once resolved that agents should
be sent to England to guard the interests of New York and
correct the unfavorable reports which might be made by the
agents of other colonies.  William Nicoll and Chidley Brooke,
both members of the council, were appointed and £1000 was
appropriated for their support, though only Nicoll was
mentioned in the act.  Their instructions related to matters
of defence, the Indians and the attitude of other colonies;
but they were also empowered to take action according to
their discretion upon any other matter which affected the
interests of the province.[3]  The Leislerians understood that
these agents were appointed in part to oppose them and
therefore tried from the first to discredit them.

[1] These were collector of the excise, receiver of quit rents in city and county
of Albany, clerk of the peace and of common pleas there also.  Docs. 203.
[2] Ass. J. I, 56 et seq.
[3] C. J. I, 88.  Cal. St. P. Col. 1699, p. 177.  N. Y. Docs. IV, 322.

On the voyage to Europe Brooke and Nicoll were captured by the French. By September, 1696, however, they had reached England, whither new instructions and documents were sent them to take the place of those lost in the capture. They laid before the board of trade — and this was among the earliest business which came before it — a summary statement of advantages which would follow from the conquest of Canada; but if that project seemed impracticable, they urged that £1000 be annually expended in presents for the Indians, that during the war 1000 men be kept in garrisons on the frontiers, that a stone fort be built at Albany and fortifications at Schenectady, Canastagione, the Half Moon, the Flats and other points; that annual recruits of men and stores be sent from England to make good the number and supply the needs of the forces in New York; that a few English youth be sent to live among the Indians and learn their language and customs and that English missionaries be sent among them. At the close appeared also one of the early suggestions that a good strong fort and settlement be established at some convenient place near Lake Ontario.[1]

On September 12, at a meeting of the board,[2] which was attended by the earl of Tankerville, Locke and Pollexfen, the above mentioned memorial was read; Brooke and Nicoll were heard in explanation of it. Some general estimates of the strength of the militia of the northern tier of colonies were given as a basis for judgment concerning the plan of an attack on Canada, while in reference to the defence of the New York frontier itself they admitted that the present number of 400 men would be sufficient if it were not necessary to make an impression on the Indians. The agents were not provided with definite information as to the number of troops whom death and desertions left in the garrisons of New York, nor as to the amount of military supplies which were then in that province. As to Canada and its strength, they mentioned John Nelson as one who had long been a prisoner there and was able to give the board full information. Before many days had passed Nelson had submitted a comprehensive memorial on Canada, the substance of which has appeared in its relation to the northern colonies in general,

[1] Docs. IV, 183, 231.          [2] Docs. IV, 185.

a subject which, under order from the lords justices, the
board was considering when the agents from New York appeared.

As the war approached its close New York was more
agitated by alarms than it had been at any time since its
very beginning. This was the consequence of the rebuilding
of Fort Frontenac, which was followed in 1696 by an expedition in force against the middle section of the Iroquois territory. At the same time the approach of a large French force
from Europe was also reported, but it never appeared. During the previous winter a rumor was circulated that a large
force would soon attack Albany.[1] This furnished the occasion in the following spring for another strong appeal to the
assembly,[2] to which it responded with an appropriation act,
the language of which was more specific and restrictive than
that of any previous grant. The governor was offended by
its language, which prohibited further detachments, but
finally had to accept it. Another consequence of the alarm
was this, that it led Fletcher to make one more appeal to
Connecticut for help.[3] He asked her to send 60 men to
Albany for a year, where they should be furnished with the
king's pay, arms and other supplies. They should also serve
under New York officers. After considerable delay Connecticut, mindful of the man with whom she was dealing,
agreed to send the men to remain six months, unless in the
meantime their help should be needed at home. She also
requested that their arms and other supplies should be sent
to a designated place in Connecticut itself, where the soldiers
might receive them and thence march to Albany. They would
also prefer to serve under their own officers. To this fastidi-
ous stickling for colonial rights, so characteristic of Connecticut, the governor and council of New York replied, that
it was an evasion, that they were trifling with an affair which
concerned his majesty's interest and their own welfare.
Connecticut denied the charge and declared it to be reasonable that the arms should be conveyed to some convenient
place, so that the men might have them to carry through

---

[1] Ex. C. Min., Dec., 1695.
[2] Ass. J. I, 65 *et seq.* C. J. I, 89 *et seq.* Col. Laws, I, 365.
[3] N. Y. Col. Docs. IV, 152 *et seq.*

the woods for their own defence. The result was that no men were sent. To an application for her quota of 48 men, Rhode Island made the stereotyped reply, through Clarke, her Quaker governor, that her long and exposed coast line was defenceless and, though her loyalty was unimpaired, the king could not expect impossibilities. With renewed meditations on the favors which were enjoyed by the colonies which were free from war and its burdens, Fletcher fell back for protection on the 400 regular troops whom, with the recruiting of the old companies and the arrival of the new, he now had in the province.

But, as was always the case with the war in New York, it was chiefly a continuation of the ancient feud between the French and the Iroquois, and the Indians bore the brunt of the attacks. When, in the midst of their fears, they sent appeals to the English for help, and Fletcher proposed to go with a force to the frontier, the council told him that more men could not be taken from the harvest and that he should write encouragingly to them, suggest presents and tell them to be watchful.[1] When it became known that the French were on the march, all that could be done was to find a few men, if possible, near the frontier who were ready to enlist. Some of the councillors again pledged their credit and Fletcher again hurried northward. When he reached the frontier, the French were already on their homeward march. All that could be done was to condole with the fugitive Indians and supply them with corn and presents for the winter. Little permanent damage had been done them. The following winter Fletcher spent in Albany, but it passed without incident, and with it both the war and Fletcher's administration approached a close.

It was in the summer of 1696 that Livingston returned from England and resubmitted his claims, so far as they were not already adjusted, to the governor and council.[2] They amounted to about £1150. In submitting vouchers Livingston stated that the committee of trade had reported that they should be paid from the revenue accruing under the act of 1692 for paying the creditors who had advanced money

---

[1] Ex. C. Min., July and August, 1696.
[2] N. Y. Col. Docs., IV, 201–206.

in the service of the province.[1]  But Livingston states that,
under the plea of extraordinary necessity, the revenue under
this act had all been diverted to the war and other immediate
purposes.  Fletcher, of course, was very angry at Livingston
because of the many charges and disclosures which he had
made to the governor's harm in England.  Therefore Livingston, on his return, was at once suspended from all his offices,
and Fletcher tried to induce the council to address the king
against him, charging that he had invented the office of Indian
agent and had surreptitiously obtained the commission for
it.  Though this was not done, the council in a report to
Fletcher expressed a very low opinion of the value of Livingston's services in Indian affairs, while Livingston, on his
part, paid his respects to Honan and other special appointees
of the governor, whose salaries were a burden on the province
treasury.  In his characterizations of Livingston and his
thrift, Fletcher duly exhibited his ability in the use of billings-
gate.  Livingston fell back upon his official and personal
record of 22 years in New York and upon his status as one
of the Scotch *post nati* as justifying his position quite as much
at least as would be possible in the case of the men of
French and Dutch birth who were prominent among the
governor's supporters.  Of course no further progress in this
case was made in Fletcher's administration and it became
one of the many legacies which were passed over to his
successor.

It was during this and the succeeding administration that
the question of the so-called " bolting act," involving, as it
did, one of the most valued privileges of the city of New
York, was a prominent issue in the politics of the province.
Basing its claim on its exclusive rights as a staple port and
market for the province in Dutch times, which rights had
been confirmed by Nicolls and Dongan, the city now insisted
that it had the exclusive right of bolting flour and baking
bread and biscuit for export.  In 1684 the city had received
a confirmation of this privilege from Governor Dongan.  It
therefore continued to claim that this industry was one of the
chief supports of its inhabitants and that by means of it alone
could the quality of the product be guaranteed and trade

---

[1] Col. Laws, I, 312.  Docs., IV, 252.

with the West Indies and other regions maintained.  While Long Island lived by husbandry and whaling, they said, Esopus by tillage and Albany by the Indian trade, to New York should be left the manufacture of flour and bread.  In this connection they also called attention to the advantage which came to New York from its having only one port and that a first-class one, over colonies like Virginia which had many landing places or nominal ports but no real one.  With this condition, in the opinion of New Yorkers, went certain monopolistic rights, this being a survival of the policy by which the cities of continental Europe, as well as of England, had risen to power and wealth.  It was a characteristic mercantile idea of the time and in it the sectional interest of Manhattan Island, the soil of which was too poor to yield a decent crop, found expression.  In Fletcher's time and later James Graham, recorder of the city and the foremost lawyer of the province, formulated with great ability the arguments of the merchants and stood in the forefront as a defender of the right which they claimed.

The rural communities throughout the province opposed these claims and insisted that they had as good a right as the city to bolt flour and manufacture bread for export.  As early as 1691 Jacob Rutsen, of Ulster county, with William Nicoll as his attorney, brought suit before the supreme court against the city on this issue and was beaten.  Then Nicoll turned to Fletcher and the assembly for the purpose of securing the passage of a law which should destroy the monopoly.  Money and gifts from both sides passed and Fletcher may have profited from both, while the usual pressure in the form of a refusal to vote taxes was brought to bear.  In the spring of 1694 the act desired by the rural interest was passed, under the title, " against unlawful by-laws and unreasonable forfeitures."[1]  It declared null and void all the ordinances and other measures by which the city had enforced this monopoly and its claim to an exclusive market to be null and void and the whole policy to be pernicious.  Due provision was made for the execution of the act.  Its effect, as viewed by the merchants and city fathers, was to destroy the prosperity of the town and to make " Every

[1] Col. Laws, I, 326.

Planter's hutt throughout this Province a Markett for wheate, for wheat Flour and Biskett, whereby the Principalls of Trade are Reduced to Confusion."

But the act was approved by the crown in 1697, Nicoll presumably contributing to this result while he was agent. Before the year had ended the mayor and common council asked Recorder Graham to "Recollect himself & bring the best Arguments he Could Conceive for yᵉ Defence of the Right of yᵉ Said Citty." This he did in the form of an address of the entire city magistracy to the king, asking that the injurious act might be repealed and their privilege restored. Later Graham supported the claim of the city in a detailed and eloquent argument. When the earl of Bellomont arrived as governor an address on the subject was delivered to him. Money was also raised to be used by Weaver as agent to aid the cause of the city in England. As Graham stated its argument, the only way to prevent forestalling and regrating was to have a fixed market in only one place. Under the lead of the merchants of New York, organized in a single city controlling trade and its related industries, the quality of goods had been maintained and the entire province had prospered. The beneficial effect of having only one trade centre had also been shown by avoiding the too rapid extension of settlements. But under the recent act, for the sake of thirty bolters in Kings, Queens and Ulster counties, among a population of less than 500 families, the livelihood of two-thirds of the 8000 inhabitants of the city was taken away. The city paid from one-fifth to one-third of the taxes for defence. But now not only was the livelihood of the inhabitants of the city endangered, but as the result of this "Anarchy" and "Libertisme of Trade," adulteration of flour had been carried to such a degree that there was danger that the trade of New York in this commodity would be lost. In 1700, on the advice of the recorder, the city passed an ordinance levying an imposition on flour brought into the city from the country. This so enraged the country members that they refused to pass a money bill till the ordinance was repealed. In order to get money for the fort at Onondaga, on which he had set his heart, Bellomont removed Graham in order to secure the repeal of the ordinance.

With this the struggle between town and country over this question ceased with the abandonment by the former of its efforts to maintain its monopoly.[1]

[1] The sources for the history of this question are in Minutes of the Common Council of the City of New York, 1675–1776, Vols. I and II, — see Index; in N. Y. Col. Docs., IV, and in Cal. St. P. Col., 1697–8, p. 284.   C. W. Spencer in Pol. Sci. Quarterly, Sept., 1915, has discussed the episode in connection with sectionalism in New York politics.

It is interesting to note that in 1694, while discussing contributions toward defence, Fletcher wrote, "The people of Nassau Island value themselves upon their situation and grow hard hearted toward their brethren up the Hudson, saying that if Albany be destroyed they will be able to shift better than Maryland, Virginia and Connecticut. They bear great sway in our Assembly and I doubt not will throw great difficulties in the way of furnishing a supply for next year's reinforcement."   Cal. St. P. Col. 1693–1696, p. 236.

# CHAPTER VIII

COLONIAL UNION: THE ADMINISTRATION OF THE EARL OF
BELLOMONT IN NEW YORK AND NEW ENGLAND
1697–1701

COLONIAL officials of the reigns of William and Anne,
whether in Great Britain or America, lived and moved largely
within the Stuart tradition. Though they were forced to
tolerate colonial assemblies and the narrow local spirit of
the chartered colonies, they regarded them as perplexing
obstacles which they would be glad to see removed out of
their path. The Dominion of New England never lost its influence on them as an ideal. The wars kept it very much
alive. The efforts which were made to bring the militia of
Rhode Island and Connecticut under the control of the
near-by royal governors, and the repeated attempts to legis-
late the charters out of existence, were experiments in the line
of Stuart policy, but without its thorough-going effectiveness.
We come now to another effort in the same direction, an
ineffective attempt to bring the colonies of the northern
frontier together again under a single executive, that by its
means the imperial policy in matters of trade and defence
might be more successfully carried out. As it happened to
have been made during an interval of peace, it had no influence upon the system of defence. It was also cut short
by the death of the governor before he had been in office long
enough really to test the merits of the plan. Therefore,
interesting and suggestive though it was, the administration
of the earl of Bellomont passed without any very permanent
results.

As early as 1695 the earl had been decided upon as the
successor of Phips in Massachusetts.[1] His commission and
instructions were then drafted. Samuel Allen and the agents
of Massachusetts were at that time contending over the ques-

[1] Cal. St. P. Col. 1693–1696, pp. 506, 520, 534, 541, 594.

266

tion, whether or not New Hampshire should be annexed to the larger colony. It was finally decided that Bellomont should be its governor and have command of its militia, the period of nominal and ineffective separation which was provided for in the Massachusetts Charter of 1691 being brought to an end. Bellomont was also empowered to take command of a quota of troops from Rhode Island — if he could get them. Now that a stranger to Massachusetts was to be appointed governor, the question of his salary was a difficult and important one. In that colony, except during the hated Andros régime, salaries had been voted annually and their amounts had been fixed wholly by the legislature. Bellomont foresaw trouble on this score, and the lords of trade were strongly in favor of specifying the governor's salary in advance.

As we have seen, the need of closer union and better cooperation between the colonies was constantly being forced on the attention of officials at home and in the colonies. At the close of 1696, Stoughton, the lieutenant governor of Massachusetts, and its council addressed the king in favor of some plan of cooperation in prosecuting the war and bearing its losses.[1] Two frigates were already stationed on the New England coast, but they desired one or two more and a supply of military stores. As vessels went regularly to the West Indies for salt for the fishery — which was a staple industry — they desired to have such a naval force on the coast and such a supply of seamen that one frigate could be regularly spared to convoy these vessels. But particularly they desired that ways and means might be considered for the reduction of Canada, " the unhappy fountain from which issue all our miseries." Like New York, Massachusetts was beginning to complain of the removal of some of her inhabitants to less heavily taxed colonies.

When it became clear that Fletcher should be recalled, the opportunity was believed to have come for dealing broadly with the situation. On January 25, 1696/7, at a meeting of the board of trade the agents for New England urged the immediate consideration of the memorials which were before it. Afterwards Harrison of Virginia and Coxe

[1] Cal. St. P. Col. 1696–1697, p. 245.

of New Jersey, in the name of all, moved that New England and New York might be united under one government, and that their governor might have military command also over the Jerseys and the adjacent chartered colonies. They also recommended Lord Bellomont for the position, to whose support Coxe rashly said the colonies would be willing to contribute. The New England agents intimated the same thing, with the restriction that the support should be voluntary.[1] At the beginning of February Harrison again presented the arguments in favor of this policy as the only means of securing support for the governor and effective cooperation against the French. As it was, declared other memorialists, the English had to an extent lost their fishing, furs, mast, timber and peltry trade along the entire coast from Newfoundland to New York, so that, unless the further progress of the enemy was checked, it would end in the subversion of the colonies. Union in some form was their only salvation. The confusion which had arisen from the establishment of the Dominion of New England should not be attributed to union itself, but to the extreme and illegal commissions which were then granted and the oppressive manner in which they were executed. If a person of worth and honor were appointed, with proper instructions, all would go well.

It was at this time also that the idealist, William Penn,[2] suggested in outline what might have developed into a colonial federation, and thus in thought he far outstripped both colonists and officials. He proposed that annually or oftener, in some central place, probably New York, a congress should meet. It should consist of two commissioners from each of the continental colonies and be presided over by a royal commissioner. The business of the congress should be to hear and adjust all complaints or controversies between colonies over escaped debtors, fugitives from justice, injuries done to trade, and to consider means for supporting the union and protecting the provinces against public enemies. In such a congress, said Penn with truth, quotas of men and money could be much more easily and equitably determined than in England, for the colonists knew their own condition better,

---

[1] *Ibid.*, 318, 338, 339.
[2] *Ibid.*, 354; N. Y. Col. Docs. IV, 296.

could debate with freedom and better adjust their affairs. Not only colonial union but, through it, colonial independence were written large in this plan. As an advance upon the colonial congress of 1690 and especially upon the policy of requisitions which had just been vainly tried, this plan opened a way toward a real understanding and cooperation. But in spirit it was far ahead of the times, and there was no chance of its receiving consideration on either side of the water.

The utterances of some of the colonial agents in these very conferences showed how strong the opposition was to effective colonial union. Samuel Allen, of course, was striving to keep New Hampshire in its existing condition in order that he might, if possible, realize something from the Mason claims. John Winthrop voiced the consistent opposition of Connecticut to the surrender of its militia to outside control. If they must submit to a general, they asked, as was provided in the new Massachusetts charter, that he might not be empowered to march their levies out of the colony without the consent of its general court.[1] Brooke and Nicoll, though admitting the advantages of union, objected to the placing of New York and Massachusetts under the same governor because of their distance apart and of the difference in their policies. They inferred that, as under Andros, Boston would be the governor's residence, and hence that New York would suffer, in trade and in all other ways. What they favored was the appointment, under act of parliament, of a commander-in-chief for all the forces of the continent, but not a half-way measure such as the one now proposed. Sir Henry Ashurst and Edmund Harrison presented a joint memorial,[1] directed against the arguments of the agents of New York and contending for the single governor of New York, Massachusetts and New Hampshire. They were strongly opposed to a union of all the colonies under authority of parliament.

On February 25th[3] the board of trade reported to the king in favor of the appointment of a fit person as governor of the three above mentioned colonies, with authority also as captain general of the forces of Rhode Island, Connecticut

---

[1] Cal. St. P. Col. 1696–1697, 351–353.
[2] Ibid., 355–358.          [3] Ibid., 384–5.

and the Jerseys, and that his chief residence during war should be at New York. This was as near to the appointment of a captain general over all the forces of the colonies as they felt it was possible to go at that time. The same day orders in council were issued approving of this representation and that the attorney general inspect again the charters of Rhode Island and Connecticut. The earl of Bellomont was at once selected for the new appointment and the work of preparing new commissions and instructions for him proceeded through the spring of 1697. He made a few suggestions, especially with reference to the salaries of himself and his lieutenant governors and to the despatch of stores of war and of men enough to fill the ranks of the independent companies in New York.

The project of colonial union which took form in the appointment of Bellomont was in line with what Fletcher had been advocating during his entire administration. He therefore should have welcomed it. But really it was the least desirable event which could have happened to him. In the first place, it made necessary his own recall. But, had this been all, it might have ended quietly in his transfer to another government, and nothing more would have been made of it. Looking at his correspondence alone and the statement of his friends, one would infer that such would have been the result. Considering those as sources, one would see simply an active and bustling administration, a governor who was loud in protests and exhortations but who accomplished little. Of dishonesty and oppression only a faint suggestion would appear.

But, as we have seen, toward the close of the administration, Fletcher's opponents by representations in England had begun to reveal other aspects of the case. These affected both Fletcher and the anti-Leislerian leaders, who were in the council or other positions of influence. They threw a sinister light on social and political conditions in New York. Governeur and Leisler, to say nothing of the charges of persecution which they brought against Sloughter and Ingoldsby,[1] gave several instances of reprisals against the Leislerians which had occurred after Fletcher took charge of the gov-

[1] N. Y. Col. Docs. IV, 215 *et seq.*

ernment. A number of those who had been Leisler's councillors, it was said, had been punished by fine or imprisonment for their support of the crown under Leisler. The arms which, on the arrival of Sloughter, the Leislerians had left in the fort had never been returned, though a promise had been made that their owners should have them again. The Leislerians had been politically proscribed, while members of the present council and Dutch ministers, like Dellius, who would not pray for William and Mary but only for the crown, or who even opposed the Revolution, were admitted to favor. Since 1694 the freedom of elections had been seriously interfered with in New York county and several other counties as well. Leislerians had been insulted and intimidated in various ways when they attempted to vote.

At a meeting of the board of trade in December, 1696,[1] William Penn, after speaking on several other points affecting Fletcher, placed in the hands of the board a letter to himself, with its signature erased, containing several complaints against the governor. In conversation Penn suggested similar complaints against Nicholson. Secretary Popple at once wrote to Penn and Fitz-John Winthrop requesting them to state in writing such charges as they could make good against both those officials, as such information would be very acceptable to the board.

Early in 1696/7 the board, in speaking of the great prevalence of piracy, warned Fletcher that in the trial of some of Avery's crew [2] New York had been mentioned as a place where such villians were protected and reference had been made to the favors which the governor in particular had shown to Captain Tew. Fletcher's reply to this was to the general effect that Tew and others had appeared to him only in the guise of privateers and had received commissions to attack the French on the Gulf of St. Lawrence and elsewhere. Kidd was the only one who had gone from New York about whom Fletcher seemed to have a suspicion that he would turn pirate. He had also been rather encouraged to pursue this tolerant attitude by the bill against piracy which he had brought over and, under orders, had enacted in New York, for by it pardon

---

[1] Cal. St. P. Col. 1696–1697, pp. 241, 251.
[2] N. Y. Col. Docs. IV, 255, 274.

was offered to all pirates who within a specified time should come into the province, give bond for good behavior and not leave it without license.

Bellomont, a member of the Irish peerage, was a man of ardent temperament, honest, indefatigable in what he undertook. In politics he was a thorough-going Whig, a supporter of the Revolution and of all it implied. Viewed comprehensively, Bellomont was appointed for the purpose of promoting all the objects which the British government had in view at that time. These he interpreted as his policy — to suppress piracy in the northern colonies, to check illegal trade and promote the production of naval stores, to expose and check corruption wherever it was found, to promote colonial union, improve colonial defence, encourage friendly relations with the Indians, to secure appropriation for long periods, to enforce efficiency among officials and to strengthen in all legitimate ways orderly connection with Great Britain. Then all had their bearing, of course, on the colonies which Bellomont was appointed to govern, and especially on New York. It was suggested by the lords justices that he should go first to New York, because it was a frontier province and there he was to supersede the governor.[1] It was to that province that he was to devote his chief time and energy. Before he left England he had been informed in a general way of the charges against Fletcher and of the crookedness which existed in New York politics. As soon as he arrived there — in April, 1698 — he began to follow up these clues and they proved so important that the first months of his administration were devoted to the exposure of corruption and misgovernment under Fletcher. For the time the broader lines of policy to which he was committed seemed to converge on New York, and the best service which he could render seemed to be in straightening out relations there. This process began before Fletcher had left the province, followed him to England and led to a prolonged hearing there from which he escaped, it is true, without criminal prosecution, but also without any chance of again holding a colonial appointment. In his letters to the board of trade and treasury Bellomont poured in accusation after accusation and pursued his victim with relentless partisan zeal. Taken

[1] Cal. St. P. Col. 1696–1697, p. 587.

together they furnished a most detailed exposure of corrupt political methods as they existed at that time.

We can see from his early letters how Bellomont's wrath was stirred — somewhat as Leisler's was before him — by the frigid reception which was given him by the council and by the reports of their meetings at Fletcher's lodgings [1] for the purpose of thwarting his measures and making him uneasy in office. They had heard that he came as a reformer and proposed to hamper him all they could. In league with them were the merchants who were interested in the various forms of illegal trade. Bellomont's first open collision was with the collector, Chidley Brooke, who was unwilling to make a seizure when ordered to do so by the governor — perhaps because he and Fletcher were interested in the vessel. The first few seizures which were made under Bellomont's orders threw the merchants into a panic and they talked about openly opposing the government. The customs officers were found to be careless and corrupt, and the sheriffs incompetent and wholly unreliable when it came to making election returns.

In the council the encounter began in earnest. Bellomont found it subservient to Fletcher. Several of its members were financially interested with him. It would not cooperate with Bellomont's policy of reform and purification. Hence the opposing members had to go. Nicoll, Pinhorne and Brooke were the first to feel the blow. Later, in September, 1698, Bellomont suspended Bayard, Willett, Minvielle, Townley and Lawrence. Philipse resigned. Townley was a resident of New Jersey and had not attended at all. The others had dissented when Bellomont proposed that four ships which were bound for Madagascar should give bonds not to trade with pirates.[2] Bellomont also states that they were restive and perverse in reference to everything which he did and outside the council were always intriguing against him. A long list of special reasons were assigned for the removal of

[1] N. Y. Col. Docs. IV, 303–384. See Treasury Cal. and N. Y. Docs. IV, 354, for seizure of goods at Van Sweeter's house. Cal. Treas. Papers, Letters of Bellomont, Dec. 15, 1698. On Jan. 1, 1698/9, the commissioners of the customs made a comprehensive report on conditions in New York, Cal. of Treas. Papers. This was based on Bellomont's letters to the treasury.

[2] N. Y. Col. Docs. IV, 398. Smith, History of New York, ed. of 1829, I, 130 et seq.

Bayard, connecting him with several of the most corrupt doings of Fletcher — illegal trade, encouragement of pirates, embezzlement of public moneys and overawing elections.[1] To those charges Bayard replied at length, flatly denying some and explaining away the most serious of the others.[2] The prominent Leislerians, De Peyster, Staats and Walters, were named to fill a part of the vacancies.[3] David Jameson, who was clerk of council and deputy secretary, Bellomont also removed, and in one of his letters [4] made a savage attack on Jameson's character. Early in his administration Bellomont had appointed a hearing in the case of Livingston, but no one had appeared against him. A decision favorable to Livingston was therefore reached, and reported to the board of trade — that Livingston should be continued in his offices and receive full payment of his claims.[5] His services as a victualler of the forces at Albany were acknowledged by all as indispensable. Had it not been for him they could not have been subsisted. The other victuallers had become discouraged and by the fall of 1698 almost £4000 was due on that account. In reward for these services Livingston was soon appointed to the council.

Against Thomas Weaver the hostility of the anti-Leislerians became especially bitter. Being a lawyer, Bellomont had selected him to act as king's counsel against the opposing faction in the hearings before the council. There he had inveighed smartly against the merchants for unlawful trade and factious behavior. He also repulsed their efforts to bribe him and through him, to bribe Bellomont also. Weaver charged Ebenezer Willson with false swearing as returning officer for New York city and county in the assembly election of 1698.[6] Willson brought suit against him for this statement and the jury found against Weaver with damages at £500. Bellomont says that, with the help of one Clarke, the coroner, who empanelled it, the jury was packed, but that

---

[1] Cal. St. P. Col. 1697-8, p. 494; Docs. IV, 427-8. Bellomont asked Bayard to join with and support him in the government, but he refused to do so.

[2] Smith, I, 131.

[3] Docs. IV, 411. They were confirmed by order in council, Oct. 25, 1698.

[4] Docs. IV, 400.

[5] Docs. IV, 331, 399. The adjustment of some of Livingston's later claims may be traced in Blathwayt's Journal.    [6] Docs. p. 400

the attorney general and others had given such weighty reasons in arrest of judgment that it was believed the suit would be carried no further.

As we have seen, parliament had passed an act for reversing the attainder and for the restoration to their heirs of the estates of Leisler and Milborne. But Fletcher had neglected or refused to execute it. Partly because of this and to show special respect for the law, as well as from a feeling of compassion, Bellomont in the early fall of 1698 ordered the bodies of the two men removed from the place of their interment near the gallows and their Christian burial in the Dutch Church. A throng of people attended this ceremony, but without disorder. Though this was an act of justice to Leisler and his supporters, nothing could have been more irritating to the prejudices of the aristocrats. The governor had now become fully identified with the Leislerians and, whether he desired it or not, a partisan color was given to his whole administration. Party strife and hate again became intensified.[1] Bellomont's letters abound with accounts of efforts and intrigues against him. One of the schemes of his opponents was to secure the passage of a so-called indemnity act for the payment of damages extorted under oppressive suits and decrees at law, which act should apply only to deeds committed before the arrival of Fletcher in New York. Bellomont charged that a sum had been raised to procure influence at home by which the governor should be ordered to pass this. Other efforts were naturally directed toward discrediting Bellomont in England and securing his recall. These never had a chance of success, but they illustrate the political methods of those days.

Instead of the earl being disturbed in his office, the board of trade in England was forced to hold a special inquiry into the doings of Fletcher, a rare thing in the case of colonial governers. In his letters Bellomont described one abuse after another — piracy and illegal trade, exorbitant grants of land, official corruption and embezzlement of public money, interference with elections, false muster rolls and neglect of the troops. Thomas Weaver was sent as agent to England to urge more strongly the case against Fletcher.[2] The whole

---

[1] Docs. 416.    [2] Ibid., 384 et seq.

body of evidence was then brought together into one elaborate report by the board of trade. In this they urged that Bellomont receive the full support of the government, that Bayard and the councillors whom he had suspended be removed, that De Peyster, Graham, Staats and Livingston be appointed in their places, that the pirates be prosecuted and the exorbitant grants of land be annulled.[1]

Fletcher had meantime reached England, and on November 28, 1698, the charges, formulated under eighteen heads, were delivered to him at the board of trade. He presented written replies to them and two formal hearings were held.[2] Weaver also replied to Fletcher's written answers.[3] Bayard and Brooke, as well as Fletcher, testified, Fletcher being accompanied by counsel. Weaver and the attorney general appeared on the other side. A variety of depositions which had been taken by Bellomont were submitted. Though the evidence was somewhat loose and inconclusive, it could leave no doubt that the governor and council had extended protection to pirates and had profited thereby. In these and all other shady transactions Daniel Honan, the governor's private secretary, bore a prominent share. Members of the ring and their favorites had been magnificently rewarded at the expense of the Indians and of other inhabitants of the province by land grants, some of which would make respectable principalities. A muster roll of Fletcher's company was exhibited showing 100 effectives when only 49 were actually in service. Though Bayard sought to discredit this, Fletcher admitted receiving a certain allowance for more from the king's forces. But this was a small matter, when compared with the protection of pirates and the colossal land grants. There is no doubt that favors had been widely and corruptly granted during Fletcher's administration and that private fortunes had been made or enhanced thereby. In the prevalent looseness of the times New York shared more fully than did any other colony, because it reflected European conditions. At the close of the hearing Fletcher's counsel read the letter of recall from the duke of Shrewsbury, in which he said that the king was not dissatisfied with him, but would employ him in some other way. At the close of the hearing, as was usual,

---

[1] *Ibid.*, 395, 396.        [2] *Ibid.*, 443, 466.        [3] *Ibid.*, 456.

the board of trade summed up the evidence in a report to the king.[1] This, so far as recommendations for action were concerned, was non-committal, and with it Fletcher and the immediate subject of his misdeeds dropped out of sight.

Among the leading episodes in the conflict, as it continued in New York, were naturally the elections to the assembly. The first one under Bellomont occurred in 1698 and the anti-Leislerians were successful. Bellomont complained that the sheriffs, who were the election officers of the counties, were " the scum of the people, Taylors and other scandalous persons." [2] He charged them with making false and corrupt returns of members, so that of the nineteen members of this assembly the returns of eleven were disputed. They threatened to invalidate the elections in the counties of New York, Kings, Queens, Westchester and one seat in Richmond.[3] These questions were carried into the assembly and the contest was especially violent over New York county, where De Peyster, Staats, Lewis and Governeur sought to invalidate the return made by Ebenezer Willson, the sheriff.[4] The men returned by Willson were finally seated. This was the result in the other counties, except in the case of John Teunisen of Richmond county. The anti-Leislerians were thus able to force an organization of the house, with Philip French as speaker. But it was carried amid great disorder, and nine remonstrated to the house, but their remonstrance was rejected. Six of the remonstrants then withdrew, protesting against these acts, and petitioned the governor and council.[5] They were Ryer Schermerhorn and Jan Jansen Bleecker, of Albany, Thomas Morgan of Richmond, Cornelius Sebring, Cornelius Van Brunt and Thomas Woglom of Kings.

At the opening of the session Bellomont had urged peace and reconciliation, that the needed reforms might be made. A bill aiming at conciliation or indemnity was passed by the house and sent to the council. Bellomont states that he had not interfered with elections, as his predecessor had done, but being convinced of the corrupt methods of this assembly

[1] N. Y. Col. Docs. IV, 479.
[2] Docs. IV, 322.      [3] Ass. J. I, 86 *et seq.*
[4] See Bellomont's account of this case, Docs. IV, 322-3. It was a novelty, for New York and Orange counties combined and not a freeholder of Orange was permitted to vote.      [5] Ass. J. I, 90.

and of the " villanous tricks " which it resorted to, to justify
the false returns of the sheriffs, he dissolved it before any
piece of legislation had been passed.  " I shall forthwith," he
says, " appoint better men Sheriffs in the several counties
and call another assembly."  He would restore the blessing
of an English government by a free and fair election, though
it cost much time and trouble.[1]

Naturally only a brief time was allowed to pass before
the holding of a new election.   The conflict had become so
bitter that nothing short of a complete triumph would satisfy
Bellomont and the Leislerians.[2]  Writs were therefore issued
and the election was held in the winter of 1698/9.  " There
was the greatest struggle at the elections," wrote Bellomont,[3]
" that ever was known in this Province, and in some places
fighting and broken heads.  Mr. Nicholls, late of the Council
and Jameson, clerk of the Council under Colonell Fletcher,
were the greatest incendiaries, especially Nicholls, who rode
night and day about the country with indefatigable pains and
all the flattering insinuations. . . ."  Letters from Fletcher
were circulated stating that he was certain of his ability to
"baffle all the accusations " sent home against him.  On the
receipt of these letters, as Bellomont received none by the
same ship, his foes were greatly exalted with the hope of his
recall and their own triumph.  The anti-Leislerians attempted
to rouse the English against the Dutch, but that failed, though
in Queens county many of the English were so dissatisfied
that they opposed taking the oath to the king.

Another issue which the anti-Leislerians forced into great
prominence was that of the abolition of the " revenue " or
customs duties.  Nicoll, Jameson and Bayard's son circulated
a paper on this subject and a general effort was made to
convince the people that now was the time to get rid entirely
of customs duties, which were a badge of slavery, and to
put themselves on the same footing with neighboring colonies
which did not have that form of taxation.  It was charged
that one of Bellomont's purposes was to secure a permanent
revenue, and the expression " now or never " became the

---

[1] Docs, 322; Ass. J. I, 91.
[2] Ex. C. Min., Jan. 19, 1698/9.
[3] N. Y. Col. Docs. IV, 507 *et seq.*

watchword of his opponents.[1]  This policy appealed strongly
to the merchants, and a club of about thirty of them was
formed in New York City to support it.  Jacobus Van Cortlandt was brought before the council, severely reproved by the
governor and threatened with prosecution [2] for using seditious language on this subject to influence voters.[3]  In this
election the Leislerians won a decisive victory.  Of the
twenty-one seats in the assembly they won sixteen.

When Bellomont met this assembly, near the close of March,
1699,[4] he reproved suggestions which were abroad that the
colonists were independent of England and that therefore the
limitations which were put upon their trade were an injury
to them.  This was closely connected with an exhortation to
abandon internal strife, and with the submission to the assembly of a proposal that they continue the " revenue " for such
a period as they thought fit.  He had found the province
considerably in debt, an estimate of which, with the usual
statement of accounts, would be submitted.  A reference was
finally made to his late successful conference with the Indians.

Apparently through the influence in part of the governor,
James Graham was elected speaker, though according to
Bellomont's own statement he was generally unpopular.[5]
After about a month the feeling of aversion became so strong
that the house came almost to the point of expelling Graham.
A remonstrance containing a condemnation of all the proceedings against Leisler and Milborne was drawn up by
Governeur with the intent of forcing Graham to appear with
the house and read it before the governor.[6]  Graham came
to Bellomont and told him he would sooner be torn in pieces
than do this.  Fortunately an order had been received from
the lords justices some months before to swear in Graham as
a member of the council, and taking advantage of this, Bellomont informed the assembly of this command and admitted
Graham to the council.  Governeur was then chosen speaker
of the house.

[1] Bellomont denied this and said he should leave it to the assembly to fix the
term of years for which it would appropriate the revenue.  That customs duties
could not be abolished he showed by reference to the heavy cost of defence.

[2] N. Y. Col. Docs. IV, 508; Ex. C. Min., Feb. 6, 1698/9.

[3] Cal. St. P. Col. 1699, p. 174.          [4] Ass. J. I, 94; C. J. I, 119.

[5] N. Y. Col. Docs. IV, 511.

[6] The remonstrance is in Cal. St. P. Col. 1699, p. 178.

As Governeur was the most prominent and certainly one of the most intensely partisan of all the Leislerians, this offered little prospect of domestic peace. Already a number of contested election cases had come before the house and under his lead they had been summarily decided in favor of the dominant party. As an incident of these contests, the defeated New York candidates petitioned [1] that Governeur might be removed from the house on the ground that he was not a natural-born or naturalized English subject. Governeur acknowledged that he was foreign born, but produced a sealed and sworn certificate that he was in New York when the act of 1683 was passed naturalizing all foreigners who were then residents of the province.[2] The revival of the charges of murder and treason for the purpose of unseating him was, of course, easily disposed of by a reference to the royal pardon and to the act of parliament reversing the convictions of the Leislerians. The minority, therefore, had to tolerate Governeur till the opportunity of defeating him might come in some future election.

In its legislative work this assembly began with certain acts which were intended to remove the remaining disabilities of the Leislerians.[3] Indemnity was granted to all supporters of Leisler who had been excluded from pardon in the act of 1691. All writs, prosecutions and judgments by reason of what had happened in New York during the late revolution were declared to be stopped, in order that the people's minds might be fully quieted. The estate of Jacob Milborne was settled on his sons and widow, and an act of 1691 providing for the assessing by a commission of damages arising in the late disorders was repealed, because it had proved grievous and had not answered the design of such an act. All acts and decrees under it were declared null and void. This was a very direct slap at the anti-Leislerians. The act of indemnity and the one for preventing vexatious suits passed without serious opposition.[4]

Under the circumstances it was inevitable that the public

----

[1] Ass. J. I, 95.    [2] Col. Laws, I, 123.    [3] *Ibid.*, 384, 386, 393, 395.

[4] N. Y. Docs. IV, 524, 821; C. O. 5/1044, In 28, O. P. N. Y. Mr. Montague, who opposed the ratification of these acts in England, claimed to act for several hundred inhabitants of New York who opposed these, but Bellomont had never heard of such opposition.

accounts should receive much attention from this assembly. The usual committee was appointed, but its business proceeded slowly.[1] For a time the tax book was not produced. Then they found that the muster rolls for 1697 were lacking and vouchers not to be had. Ten days later they stated that the accounts were so extensive and intricate that they thought it would be necessary to have a standing committee appointed to report next session. Nicoll was called sharply to account for the money expended when he was agent. The governor and council found that for several years the excise had been negligently farmed, and therefore its farmers on Long Island had been ordered to present the best accounts they could of the sums for which they had let the collection of the tax. But Samuel Burt and Ebenezer Willson, prominent anti-Leislerians, had stubbornly refused to comply and were committed to custody.[2] After conferences and considerable amendment by both houses, an elaborate act was passed granting a revenue for six years.[3] A salary of £1500 was provided for Bellomont and of £500 for Lieutenant Governor Nanfan.[4] An attempt was made to fix the rates of fees by law, but after Bellomont had shown them his instruction reserving this power to himself, the measure was dropped.[5] As Bellomont later stated, the revenue would not have been granted except in consideration of the earlier laws of the session which were favorable to the Leislerians.[6]

From the consideration of revenue and Indian relations the assembly passed naturally to the subject of the excessively large grants which had been made by Fletcher to certain of his favorites during the last year of his administration.[7] Prior to that time he had made many grants, and in one instance several in succession to the same person, but they had not been unusually large. As soon, however, as he learned of Bellomont's appointment, several vast tracts were granted in total disregard of the rights of the Indians and of the interests of would-be settlers. The absurdly small payments which were required of the grantees promised to deprive

[1] Ass. J. I, 97, 98, 102.          [2] Col. Laws, I, 392.

[3] Ass. J. I, 144; C. J. I, 134; Col. Laws, I, 419.

[4] Col. Laws, I, 397.          [5] C. J. I, 138.

[6] N. Y. Col. Docs., IV, 821.

[7] Ass. J. I, 94, 96 et seq.; Cal. St. P. Col. 1697–1698, pp. 303–306.

the king even of the moderate quit rents which were legally his due.  The grants were made hastily, with scarcely an attempt at surveys or the accurate fixing of bounds, and with the knowledge only of the small governing clique in the council.  Of course, in the provincial system, territorial affairs lay almost wholly within the sphere of the executive and the legislature had less to do with them than with any other department of public business.  In New York, at the time of which we are now speaking, the tendency toward the accumulation of large manorial estates in the hands of a few great families was again uppermost.  Like their European contemporaries and predecessors, the leading merchants of the times invested their surplus wealth in land, adding estate to estate till finally they were bound together in one comprehensive manorial grant.  The Livingston, Van Cortlandt and Philipse families were passing through this transition and taking their position beside the Van Rensselaers.  Several others in a smaller way were moving in the same direction.  The times favored it, and it was in this connection that privilege, favoritism and monopoly furnished some of their choicest exhibitions in New York of the eighteenth century.  Had Fletcher's grants stood, the process of subjecting New York to a landed aristocracy would have been quickened and intensified.

The grants which now fell under Bellomont's special criticism were five in number.[1]  One of these was to the Rev. Godfrey Dellius, then Dutch clergyman of Albany, prominent worker among the Indians and member of the board of Indian commissioners.  This grant lay on the east side of the Hudson and extended from Batten Kill seventy miles northward to Otter Creek, near Vergennes in the present state of Vermont.  Its breadth was twelve miles, more or less, eastward from the Hudson river.  It was estimated to contain 620,000 acres.  The second grant extended fifty miles along the lower and middle course of the Mohawk river and two miles back from the river on both sides.[2]  The grantees in

---

[1] Col. Laws I, 412.  Act of May 16, 1699; Schuyler, Colonial New York II, 135 et seq.; N. Y. Col. Docs. IV, 391; Doc. Hist., of N. Y. I, 380.

[2] It is supposed to have extended from Amsterdam, in Montgomery County to Little Falls or West Canada Creek in Herkimer.  N. Y. Col. Docs. IV, 381.

this case were Schuyler, Dellius, Wessels and Bancker, and, on a demand from the council, Pinhorne was included. When it became known great opposition was made to this grant in Albany, and under the influence of it Schuyler and Wessels withdrew. The other grantees were not moved by such consideration for the Indian or for public interests and resolved to stick. The third grant was made to Nicholas Bayard and was located on Schoharie Creek being on the south side of the Mohawk, about twenty-four miles above Schenectady. It extended on both sides of the creek from Fort Hunter to Middleburg, in Schoharie county.[1] This is said to have been nearly thirty miles in length. The fourth grant was to Captain John Evans, of the royal guardship Richmond. It consisted of a number of tracts on the west side of the Hudson, extending forty miles in length and twenty miles in breadth, including the southern tier of towns in Ulster county, two-thirds of Orange and part of Haverstraw in Rockland county. To Evans a small grant was also made on Manhattan Island. Lastly, to Caleb Heathcote was granted a lot about fifty feet long and forty feet broad, which had been a part of the King's Farm, while the King's Farm itself had been leased for seven years to Trinity Church.

In the previous November (1698), under the influence of Bellomont's continual representations and of the statements which were made in connection with the hearings in Fletcher's case,[2] the lords justices issued an instruction that he should pursue all legal methods for annulling exorbitant grants and should grant no more land with a lower quit rent than 2s. 6d. per hundred acres. The result was the passage by this assembly of an act[3] vacating the grants to Dellius and his associates, to Bayard, Evans and Heathcote and the lease of the King's Farm to Trinity Church.[4] The last two grants

[1] Cal. St. P. Col. 1697–1698, p. 306; Laws of New York, Van Schaack's ed., p. 32.  [2] N. Y. Col. Docs. IV, 425.

[3] Col. Laws, I, 412; N. Y. Docs. IV, 510, 529, 535, 622, etc.

[4] Some rather loose statements concerning the King's Farm are given in Blathwayt's Journal. A monograph by Stephen P. Nash, entitled "Anneke Jans Bogardus, Her Farm and how it became the Property of Trinity Church," gives the facts concerning it with painstaking accuracy. A map showing its location is in Stokes, Iconography of Manhattan Island, vol. I. The farm contained 62 acres and was leased to Trinity Church for an annual rent of 60 bushels of wheat.

were obnoxious not so much because of the size as because they took away a part of the governor's support and were apparently intended to harass Bellomont. On this bill the council was equally divided and it required the governor's casting vote to carry it. In the house it passed without difficulty, and a rider was there added suspending Dellius from his living in Albany. Bellomont could well write, " The getting this Bill passed has drawn upon me the implacable hatred of all parties concerned, and the rest of Fletcher's Palatines, those I mean that have unmeasurable grants, fancie I shall push at them the next time, so that they are equally angry with the others. As for the King's Farm granted to the Church, the whole faction, I understand, are resolved to bring on my head the anathemas of London and the Clergy. . . ." [1] Dellius soon left the province to seek redress both in England and in Holland. The Rev. William Vesey, rector of Trinity Church, ceased to pray for the governor, but prayed instead for Dellius by name, that he might have a prosperous voyage and be saved from the violence of his enemies.[2] Bellomont, who was in Boston at the time, expressed the opinion that, if this should continue, he could no longer attend church on his return and filled his letters with racy comments on the two clergymen and their relatives and friends.

Bellomont was now eager for the passage of another act which should vacate the large grants held by Schuyler, Livingston, Van Rensselaer, Beekman, Van Cortlandt and William Smith. He descanted upon the great size of these,[3] especially on the estate of Smith on Long Island, which he said was fifty miles in length, a large part of which he was reported to have procured from the town of Southampton for a paltry ten pounds. It contained five forests valuable for pitch, tar and rosin, and long beaches on which drift whales were often found. If such estates as these could not be broken up, Bellomont thought that the approval by the

[1] *Ibid.*, 510. Cal. St. P. Col. 1699, p. 257.

[2] N. Y. Col. Docs. IV, 489, 580.

[3] *Ibid.*, 535, 822 *et seq.* In the last-mentioned reference Bellomont stated his belief that 7,000,000 acres had been granted away in 13 patents, and all except the Van Rensselaer manor were almost without inhabitants. They also paid almost no quit rent.

crown of the act which he was now sending would be
an injustice and he would prefer to have it rejected. But
if he was to sweep away all the large estates, he needed a
peremptory command from England to nerve the assembly
to the task. That did not come, and before the privy
council passed upon the act Bellomont died. It continued to
lie unnoticed in England until after the appointment of Lord
Cornbury as governor, and then, under the influence of a
reaction against the Leislerians, it was repealed by the
legislature of New York.[1] The subject was again held in
suspense until June, 1708, when by an order in council the
repealing act was disallowed and the original act of 1699
was confirmed. Owing to the long delay and to the imperfect character of the act itself, it is pretty clear that the
results of this policy were not commensurate with the amount
of irritation which it produced. It was Bellomont's complaint that he could get no adequate legal advice in this
matter and in reference to violations of the acts of trade,
which results led to the appointment in England of Atwood
as chief justice and Broughton as attorney general of New
York.[2]

A little later this became connected in idea with that other
important phase of Bellomont's policy, the encouragement
of the production of naval stores.[3] He proposed that the
Pinhorne-Dellius grant be divided up, for that purpose, into
small farms among ex-soldiers. He would require the full
amount of quit rent and limit estates to 1000 acres each.
If this were made general — and for it an act of parliament
would be necessary — " it would mightily reduce our Palatines,[4] Smith, Livingston and the Phillipses, father and son,
and six or seven more."

The attention of the assembly, during its session of July,
1700, was much occupied with Indian affairs and the proposal to build a fort in the Onondaga country.[5] The act by
which an appropriation of £1000 was made for this purpose
imposed certain additional duties for one year on the importa-

[1] Col. Laws, I, 524 (Nov., 1702); Acts of P. C. Colonial, II, 553.
[2] Cal. St. P. Col. 1699, pp. 257, 493; Acts P. C. Col. II, 363.
[3] Cal. St. P. Col. 1699, p. 405; N. Y. Col. Docs. IV, 553.
[4] This was a term which Bellomont applied to the large landholders.
[5] C. J. I, 145 et seq.; N. Y. Col. Docs. IV, 712; Col. Laws, I, 432.

tion of European goods.  Three commissioners were named in
the bill to superintend the building of the fort.  Though
Bellomont accepted the bill, he was dissatisfied with ,the
method specified for raising the revenue and especially with
the encroachment on the executive which appeared in the
appointment of the commissioners.  The merchants complained of the act as injurious to trade, and that, added to
the influence of Bellomont, procured its repeal the following
October and the substitution of a direct levy by quotas on
the counties for the same purpose.  The new act also contained no provision for commissioners to superintend the
building of the fort.[1]  As the event proved, this was the last
session of the New York assembly which Bellomont ever
met.  Before it came together again he was dead.  The
measure for which, in the face of considerable opposition,
he had induced it to provide was never carried into execution, and nearly a generation was to pass before anything
like it was again attempted.

As a result of his struggles against the aristocrats of New
York, Bellomont became conversant with its politics and,
so to speak, thoroughly at home there.  The political fer-
ment, however, into which he was plunged in New York,
had no bearing on intercolonial relations or on that cooperative action among the colonies, for the furtherance of which
he had been appointed.  Instead, by one of the ironies of fate
Bellomont had been led to exhaust his energies very largely
in a struggle than which none could be more local or have
less interest for colonies outside of New York.  In the matters of piracy and illegal trade, it is true that Bellomont
touched interests which were broader in scope and left an
impress upon them.  They, too, reacted upon his career in
New York and helped greatly to increase the bitter feeling
with which he was regarded.  But it is from his struggle
with the anti-Leislerians, to which all lines of his policy
contributed, that Bellomont's administration chiefly derived
its character.

In New England his career was very different.  In Massachusetts internal quiet prevailed.  The people were recovering from the exhaustion of the war.  In Stoughton, a Massa-

[1] Col. Laws, I, 444;  N. Y. Col. Docs. IV. 821.

chusetts man, they had a lieutenant governor who fully understood and shared their spirit. In character and aim the people were virtually a unit, and under the charter of 1691 the only political conflict which ordinarily could occur would be with the royally appointed governor. Their pride was gratified by the appointment of a peer to that office, and when Bellomont landed at New York they had sent three of their leading citizens to welcome him. They were Elisha Cooke, Wait Winthrop and Penn Townsend. These men were among the opponents of Dudley, and with them Bellomont, by his friendship for Leislerians in New York, had natural affiliations. In New England affairs he continued to be identified with the men who had supported Phips and were not favorable to the return of Dudley to office there. During his residence in New York Bellomont had some correspondence with Stoughton, but naturally it did not bring him into real touch with Massachusetts affairs.[1] Engrossing cares kept him from visiting Boston until May, 1699. He remained there about fourteen months, returning to New York in July, 1700.

A great variety of business engaged his attention during that interval and through it all he moved with a certain lofty integrity and impartiality which won general approval. His conciliatory attitude was shown by his regularly attending the Thursday lectures in Boston. In the matter of the charter of Harvard College he wrote, and presumably spoke, in a tone above that of either the ordinary Anglican or Puritan [2]; on the right of visitation, which had long been in dispute between the English government and the college authorities, he favored its lodgement with the governor and council [3] rather than with the governor alone. What the college asked he pronounced reasonable and consistent with the toleration act, while he expressed the eighteenth century view that it was better to cramp the colonists in their trade than to disturb their consciences. He also urged the grant of a proper support for the clergy and especially for the French ministers in Boston as a testimony in recognition of

---

[1] Cal. St. P. Col. 1699, pp. 257, 268, 291, 412 *et seq.*
[2] C. O. 5/909. fol. 207. E. B. N. Eng.
[3] Palfrey, IV, 194.

their sufferings at the hands of Louis XIV. No controversies of note marred the quiet of his administration, and though he was not satisfied with the salary which was granted him — £1000 Massachusetts currency or about £750 sterling — or with its bestowment as an annual present, the subject was not made an issue.

The assembly, during the session which immediately followed, under Bellomont's advice passed a judiciary act which brought to an end the efforts of Massachusetts to preserve in some measure that freedom from appeals which had always been asserted in its corporate period.[1] Since 1692 three acts for the establishment of courts had been passed, all of which had been disallowed in England, and two of them because of some fault in the provision on this subject. In the first act the right of appeal had been restricted to personal actions, later it had been confined to cases of pecuniary importance, and, finally, in the third act the right of trial by jury had been granted in all cases, irrespective of the fact that the admiralty court, so important for the enforcement of the acts of trade, proceeded without a jury. On Bellomont's advice all reference to the controverted subjects was omitted from the fourth bill. This act was allowed to stand and with it Massachusetts secured a permanent judicial system.

The building and repair of fortifications throughout eastern New England naturally received much attention. The engineer, Romer, was then in New England and Bellomont sent him eastward as far as St. Georges to survey the coast and report on the condition of defences and the need of new ones. The fortification of Boston harbor was also a subject of anxious consideration. All this was natural in view of the fact that the French were claiming the territory as far west as the Kennebec river and were attempting to exclude the English[2] from trade and fishing along the coast of Acadia as well. The Indians, under Jesuit lead, had also established themselves at Norridgewock, on the middle course of the Kennebec river. The board of trade, on the other hand, repeated to Bellomont its determination to insist on

---

[1] Palfrey, IV, 172 et seq.; Cal. St. P. Col. 1699, p. 412.
Hutchinson (1795) II, 104 et seq.

the St. Croix as the true boundary, though the ministry was absorbed in more important affairs and the provisions in the treaty of Ryswick on this subject were resulting in nothing. Massachusetts continued indifferent to the rebuilding of Pemaquid or the addition of other forts along the eastern coast. Bellomont at once saw that, so long as they neglected properly to fortify Boston harbor, they would not willingly bear the expense of remoter defences,[1] though he considered the province wealthy enough to do so. Therefore he urged the board of trade to stir them up on the subject. Some attention was also given to guardships and convoys for vessels which went annually to the West Indies for salt.[2] Bellomont had brought orders to send two ships on this errand, and there was still as much need of a convoy in those seas as in time of war. With his eye upon pirates and illegal traders, he was still of the opinion that a fourth rate at Boston and a fifth rate at New York could be made to protect the coast as far south as Florida, but the governors must be honest.

The subject which occupied Bellomont's attention more than any other while he was in Massachusetts was the arrest of William Kidd and the collection of evidence against him and his associates pending their transport to England and trial there. The governor's activity against pirates in general was as great in Boston as elsewhere. It occupied an especially large place in his dealings with Rhode Island.[3] But Kidd's arrest, in view of his early connection with Bellomont and other English noblemen, was the most dramatic episode in the history of piracy along the northern coast. Its treatment, however, belongs under another head.

The production of naval stores [4] was another subject of general interest to which Bellomont gave much attention both in New York and New England. On his visit to New Hampshire and in his talks with parties concerned, he found, as all others had done, that timber was being destroyed in large quantities in the woods, and that the production of

[1] Cal. St. P. Col. 1699, p. 412.
[2] Cal. St. P. Col. 1699, p. 486.
[3] Ibid., p. 488.
[4] Ibid., pp. 427, 470, 495-6 et seq.

naval stores in New England was slow and costly. This was due, he found, to the few hands that were available for the work — there being not above 700 families in New Hampshire — and the high wage of 3s. per day which had to be paid for labor. The men who had contracted to furnish ship timber for the navy he found were spending much more than their product was worth and charging it up to the king. From Bridger he was unable to secure an accounting, because he insisted that he was responsible directly to the navy board. With Partridge he had a violent controversy over his right, under the acts of trade, to export lumber direct to the continent of Europe. His observations only confirmed his opinion that soldiers should be employed in this industry and that New York offered better facilities for the work than did New England. He went back to New York and, in excess of his instructions, contracted for the delivery on ship-board of twenty-four masts, they being cut in the forests of the lower Mohawk and floated down the Hudson.[1] His death left this uncompleted, the masts may have reached the British ship yards, and bills to the amount of several hundred pounds added to the complexities of New York accounts for some time after.

New Hampshire was visited by the earl in the summer of 1699 and a session of the assembly was held.[2] Two years before, on Bellomont's appointment, the brief nominal governorship of Allen had been terminated, and William Partridge had taken the place of John Usher as lieutenant governor.[3] For a time thereafter Usher had continued his interminable fussy letters to the lords justices and the board of trade,[4] bemoaning the lack of respect which was shown to himself, the disorders which prevailed and the alleged guilty opposition of his enemies to the king himself. Owing to the lack of any one who had authority to swear him in, Partridge had assumed the government without taking the customary oaths. This Usher had interpreted as evidence of disloyalty. When Bellomont arrived, Usher presented

---

[1] Cal. St. P. Col., 1701, p. 147.
[2] Cal. St. P. Col. 1699, p. 425 *et seq.* 452; N. H. Prov. Papers, II, 313–358.
[3] N. H. Prov. Papers, II, 259, 266 *et seq.*
[4] Cal. St. P. Col., 1697–1698, pp. 63, 72, 91, 147, 216, 275.

to him his oft-repeated charges against members of the
council and declined to take his seat in that body.[1] The
charges were in form very serious, but the governor made
the best inquiry he could and came to the conclusion that
they were due more to " Mr. Usher's unhappy choleric
temper " than to any other cause.

Usher was trying to fight the battles of his father-in-law,
Samuel Allen, the proprietor, against the united opposition
of the colonists. Allen was in the province endeavoring to
realize upon the shadowy claims of Mason to the soil, which
Bellomont says Allen had taken in payment of a debt of
£300. If he could collect an annual quit rent of 3d. per acre
upon the land of New Hampshire, Allen absurdly estimated
that his income from that source would be £22,000 per year,
a profit sufficient to dazzle the eyes of any man in that
age. In various ways, including bribery and offers of inter-
marriage between the families, Allen tried to secure the
earl's support.[2] But it was in vain. It was clear to Bellomont that Allen belonged to the same class of land speculators as those of New York whom he was trying to dis-
possess. Allen's claim was coming to trial before the New
Hampshire superior court. In preparation for this Allen
and Usher had made one Joseph Smith chief justice. He
was a man of almost no visible estate and Bellomont found
him occupying not only the office of chief justice, but those
of councillor, treasurer, naval officer and colonel of militia.
In response to addresses and petitions from the assembly
and outside, Bellomont made a clean sweep of Allen's appointees on the bench, retaining only the justices of the peace
and constables. Other officers were also turned out. He
listened to reports of attempts on the part of Allen to brow-
beat counsel for the people in previous trials of his suit, and
told the would-be proprietor that he was pursuing just the
course to lose his support. His claim was the occasion of
chronic disturbance in the province and frightened settlers
away. The people were opposed to him almost to a man,
and a trial which should have an issue satisfactory to Allen

[1] Cal. St. P. Col., 1699, 424, et seq.
[2] C. O. 5/909. E. B. N. Eng., Bellomont to B. T. June 22, 1700. Bellomont
was offered £10,000, or a share of New Hampshire.

was an impossibility. And yet Bellomont pitied Allen, for he was deeply in debt and necessitous, and therefore he desired that the home government would assume jurisdiction in the case and effect an equitable settlement. But he could remain in New Hampshire at most for only a few weeks, and therefore had to leave Allen and the rough and determined frontiersmen of its town to fight out their quarrel much as they had been doing in the past.

The trial, in August, 1700, went against Allen, and for the third time the Mason claim was carried on appeal before the king in council. It was heard in December, 1702, and the judgment of the lower court affirmed.[1] But as that judgment was not final, the appellant was given liberty to bring a new action of ejectment, and, if any doubt in law should arise, the jury should be directed to render a special verdict showing what the parties had severally made out and the point in law being reserved to the court. Doubts about evidence should also be taken down in writing. The object of these precautions was that, in case another appeal should be taken, the crown might be fully informed and so the case brought to a final determination. But before further decisive steps were taken Samuel Allen died. In 1705 his son, Thomas, asked the privy council to revive the former appeal, which had been abated by his father's death. This petition was granted and the appeal brought. In December, 1708, it was finally dismissed and the judgments of the New Hampshire courts affirmed. By that act, after three-quarters of a century, the Mason claim was laid to rest. The last doubt that the king was proprietor as well as sovereign of New Hampshire was removed.

Though Bellomont had accomplished something against piracy and illegal trade, and had discussed in a suggestive way the question of naval stores, no appreciable progress had been made during his administration toward effective colonial union. What might have been accomplished had he lived through a part or all of the second colonial war can never be known. But, as it was, the colonies entered upon that struggle quite as destitute of the spirit and means of united action as they were in 1690.

[1] N. H. Prov. Papers, II, 341; Acts of Privy Council Colonial, II, 365–367.

# CHAPTER IX

## MASSACHUSETTS AT THE BEGINNING OF THE
## COLONIAL WARS

MATHER and Phips returned to Boston in May, 1692, and there government under the new provincial charter was inaugurated. Just six years had passed since Sewall, after witnessing the ceremony which made Dudley president of New England had expressed the belief that the very foundations of the Puritan Commonwealth had been destroyed. When Phips was inaugurated no words of despair were entered in his famous diary, but, instead, the cheerful statement that ten companies of militia guarded Sir William and his councillors to the Town House, where the commissions were read and the oaths taken, and that on the same or the following evening, as he was journeying toward Ipswich the justice saw a rainbow, which seemed to him a special augury of good fortune.[1] Under the provisions of the new charter Massachusetts at any rate had enlarged her borders and the two original Puritan colonies were now one. With the exception of the executive the institutions of the colony had passed unchanged through the transition. That the spirit of self-government in her people was as strong as ever there could be no doubt, though with its royal appointees and the loyalist interests surrounding them, the colony could never again present the united front which had always been maintained in the past. Henceforth the conflict was to be carried on chiefly within the colony itself, the will of the people finding expression through the assembly and the press, while the home government received its impressions regularly through letters from its appointees in the colony and sought the enforcement of its policy in the ways which were common in all royal provinces. In New Hampshire the situation was essentially the same and a half-century was to

---

[1] Sewall, Diary, I, 360.

pass before it secured its official independence of Massachusetts. In Rhode Island and Connecticut the old conditions of the corporate colony continued, with such modifications as the wars, colonial expansion and the development of the system of imperial control brought in their wake.

In England Increase Mather had done what he could to save the Puritan commonwealth intact, but when he found this impossible he yielded to the demands of the home government and thereby incurred the enmity of extremists, like Cooke, throughout the province. But the Mather interest did what was possible to soften the transition by securing the appointment of Phips as the first royal governor. In New England the Mathers and their friends supported the Puritan tradition in the most conservative form. In order fully to understand the meaning of this statement it will be necessary to refer to the history of the dissensions over the so-called half-way covenant and the consociation of churches. As we know, the former of these subjects had been a prominent one among all the Congregational churches of New England since the middle of the seventeenth century, and the latter, growing out of the need of a stronger union in a system which in its origin and theory gave great liberty to the local or individual church, had assumed a more pressing importance as the social and political dangers which threatened Puritanism became more serious toward the end of the century and the civil power became less inclined to afford protection and relief.

The Puritan founders of New England had broken very completely with the parish system of Europe, by excluding from membership in the churches all who could not claim a definite religious experience and accept the church covenant.[1] From this fact and from the spirit to which it owed its origin arose, too, a fundamental distinction between the ecclesiastical system of New England and those which existed in the other colonies. After the first generation, however, a difficulty appeared, for the covenant, like that made by God with Israel, was held to include the children as well as the adults of the family. Gradually there arose a class of the children of the first and later generations who had

---

[1] W. Walker, The Creeds and Platforms of Congregationalism, 244 *et seq.*

been baptized and then reared in the Christian faith, but who had not experienced what is known as conversion and been admitted to full membership in the churches through participation in the Lord's Supper.  The Presbyterians, who in 1646 had put forth the Child Memorial, had raised in Massachusetts the question, what should be done with people of this class.  Their solution of the problem, as well as that which would have been at once proposed by Episcopalians, would be to admit to the communion all who were moral in life and were familiar with the truths of the gospel.  That would have been to confound the church with society and reintroduce the European parish system.  The purism of the fathers marked the other extreme, the result of which would have been to exclude from the church and its discipline all who could not testify to a definite religious experience, thus as time went on making the churches include an even smaller minority of the community than during the first generation.  Toward a result analogous to this gravitated also the views of the Baptists, who limited baptism to adult believers.

The compromise which opened a way of escape from this dilemma and which was widely adopted after much controversy was the so-called half-way or partial covenant. According to this those who had been baptized in infancy but who had remained unregenerate were regarded as church members, but could not themselves partake of the communion.  On assuming the covenant, as the expression went, or assenting to the main truths of the gospel and promising fidelity and submission to the discipline of the church, they were entitled to have their children baptized.  To the strict Puritan or religionist the effects of this compromise seemed evil, for it lowered the tone of church membership and formed a half-way home where a multitude of simply moral people could rest and enjoy the name Christian without its visions and enthusiasms.  An assembly, consisting of thirteen ministers from Massachusetts and four from Connecticut, which met at Boston in 1657, and a larger body of seventy members, exclusively from the Massachusetts clergy, which met at the same place in 1662, and which was called a synod, pronounced in favor of the half-

way covenant. Of the last-named body the young Increase
Mather was a member and joined with President Chauncy,
of Harvard, in opposition to the majority. The colony of
New Haven, under the lead of John Davenport, also stood
firmly against the innovation, but Connecticut, led by its
general court, went strongly in favor of the half-way covenant. The minority fought vigorously against the change
and the press teemed with pamphlets. The policy which was
adopted, though it by no means abolished religious tests,
was favorable to a somewhat less rigid interpretation of
them. It thus fell in with the enforced abandonment of
the religious test as a requirement for active citizenship
which came to be general in New England in the last half
of the seventeenth century. It was in harmony also with
the growing mercantile spirit and the religious indifferentism
that accompanied it, both of which were indicative of the
spirit which during the eighteenth century was destined to
act slowly as a solvent even of the granite of New England
Puritanism. An evidence of its power appears in the later
conversion of Mather to the support of the half-way
covenant, though it was powerless to break down his innate
and highly trained conservatism. In Connecticut and
western Massachusetts even the extreme views of the Rev.
Solomon Stoddard, of Northampton, found wide acceptance,
that it was the duty of those who had been reared under
Christian influences but who were not consciously regenerate,
to attend the Lord's Supper.

In 1679 and 1680, under the lead of Increase Mather and
with the approval of a large body of the Massachusetts
clergy and the general court, the so-called Reforming Synod
was held at Boston, and its findings were recommended to
the people by the general court. These involved no important departure from the Westminster Confession or the
Platform adopted by the New England churches in 1648.[1]
But in the light of these as fixed standards and with full
approval of the spirit of the founders of New England, this
body set forth its diagnosis of the moral and spiritual decline from which it conceived the country to be suffering.
While indications were cited of a positive decline of morality,

[1] Walker, *ibid.*, 426.

the burden of the indictment was that there was " a great and visible decay of the power of Godliness amongst many Professors in the Churches." "Inordinate affection to the world" was taking the place of the heavenly mindedness and scrupulous observance of religious practices which had prevailed during the first generation. This meant that the hold of the clergy, which had been due to the narrow and exceptional conditions of the past, was slowly weakening, and a cry of distress was raised in recognition of that fact. The clergy, as professional interpreters of the divine will, declared that God had a controversy with his people in New England and because of their spiritual declension was bringing upon them the calamities of Indian war, followed by the overthrow of the charter and the tyranny of Andros. This was the clerical interpretation of the crisis, as stated by this synod and in later utterances of its members and sympathizers. It found eloquent expression, in the combined imagery of the Bible and the early Puritans, in the preface which Mather wrote for the findings of the Synod. Among its recommendations for reform the most positive was the insistence that none should be admitted to the Lord's Supper without making a public profession of faith and repentance. It deplored the disappearance of ruling elders from the churches, insisted upon a general renewal of the covenants and greater care on the part of the civil power for the support of the clergy. But respecting the development of associations and closer unions among the clergy or churches it said nothing. Political conditions in Massachusetts at that time were too uncertain to make it safe to enter upon a very positive program of reaction. The creed or confession of faith which was put forth by the synod was that which was issued by the Savoy Conference in 1658 in England. This was a repetition of the Westminster Confession with certain modifications which were particularly acceptable to the Congregationalists.

In 1691, while Increase Mather was in England as agent for Massachusetts, he took a leading part in a meeting of Congregationalist and Presbyterian divines, the purpose of which was to bring about a union of the two sects. The Heads of Agreement were issued as a result of these con-

ferences and for a time indications seemed to point toward
a merging of the two bodies. In the end, however, the movement was abandoned and came to nothing in Great
Britain. But in New England the Heads of Agreement
were published and warmly praised by the Mathers as their
own product and a highly workable program for Congregationalism. Of the three men who had prepared it — Mead,
Howe and Mather — two were Congregationalists and the
third, Howe, had been reared as one but had later become
a liberal Presbyterian. It therefore naturally followed that
the Heads of Agreement, in its statements concerning church
polity, should be more favorable toward the Congregational
than the Presbyterian system. There was nothing in it
which expressly favored church courts, synods or general
assemblies, though it was aristocratic to the extent that it
lodged the administration of church affairs wholly in the
clergy and elders and reserved to the brethren only the
right of consent. The emphasis was laid upon the local
church and its independence, but it was also urged that the
pastors should frequently meet for advice and encouragement, especially in weighty and difficult cases. This suited
with the tendencies which were operative in New England,
and therefore the Heads of Agreement were to have a distinct influence on Congregational polity there in the eighteenth century.

The idea which was coming to be known, especially in
Connecticut, as the " consociation of churches " was abroad.
This implied the development of associations of the clergy,
or of clergy and laity combined, inclusive of larger or smaller
areas as convenience might indicate, for purposes of conference on any or all subjects of common ecclesiastical
interest, and implying, of course, the possibility that by
means of these a coercive influence of indefinite extent might
be exerted over opinion, and consequently over action.
Meetings of the clergy had been not uncommon in Massachusetts in the early years, but possibly from the fear of
Presbyterian tendencies which lurked in them, they later
fell into disuse. The revival of the practice is said to have
been due to the influence of Rev. Charles Morton, who
came to New England in 1686 and became pastor at Charles-

town.[1]  His views agreed with those of the Mathers and
such was his reputation that he was considered an available
candidate for the presidency of Harvard.[2]  It was through
his influence, and in imitation of an earlier model in England, that the first district association was organized in
Massachusetts in 1690.  It included most of the ministers in
the vicinity of Boston and held many of its meetings at
the college.  Its declared purposes were to discuss matters
of common interest and to consider cases presumably involving advice and action.  The account of this body, given
by Cotton Mather,[3] shows that it considered a great variety
of subjects, theoretical and practical.  Similar bodies were
organized in Essex and Bristol counties, and by the leaders
the development of them into synods, whose action should
be decisive to an indefinite extent, was contemplated as
desirable.  The evident purpose was to strengthen Congregationalism by adding to it certain features of Presbyterian
church polity.  By this means the conservative spirit would
be strengthened, by a return to the spirit and practice of the
first generation of New England Puritans, and an equivalent might be gained for the loss which had been suffered
from the withdrawal to an extent of the support of the
civil power.

   This point had been reached by the Mathers and their
sympathizers at the time when our history opens.  They
stood at the head of the college and of the leading churches
of the province.  Both Increase and Cotton Mather were
able preachers, the former being the leading pulpit orator
of his generation.  Both were indefatigable workers and most
prolific writers.  Increase Mather in particular was a skill-
ful politician, and both made use to the utmost of their wide
family and social connections in America and England in
the interest of every cause which met with their approval.
They shared fully in the prejudices and superstitions of the
times, and with their continuous fasts, prayers, and exhortations to a holy life were combined not a little of personal
rancor toward adversaries and of the ambitions and arts

----

[1] Walker, *op. cit.*, 470.
[2] Quincy, History of Harvard, I, 69.
[3] Magnalia, II, 237–269.

of political life.  They represented New England Puritanism in the last stage of its undisputed supremacy.  The
younger Mather constituted himself its historian and in his
own career exhibited many of its qualities in the exaggerated
form characteristic of a system already going to decay.
The glories which the Mathers admired lay in the past;
about the future they were habitually pessimistic.  The
degeneracy of the times, the inroads of worldliness, the
lamentable falling away from the path of the fathers into the
half-way covenant and other beliefs and practices which
savored of deism formed the burden of much that they wrote
and spoke.  Many a private and public fast was held by
them or at their instance, as a means of strengthening the
faith and keeping back the flood of worldliness and indifference.  But a new and secular age was upon them and the
bulwarks they threw up were too weak to prevent its advance.  In communities, however, which were so isolated as
those of New England and whose culture was so meagre
except in the Bible and Puritan theology, progress must necessarily be slow.  For a long period to come views like those
of the Mathers were accepted without question in the country
towns and the middle of the eighteenth century had passed
before the grip of the Puritan clergy on the beliefs of the
people began appreciably to weaken.

With William Phips as governor the Mathers and their
sympathizers might believe that they could control affairs
in Massachusetts.  To the connection between him and them
in church relations and afterwards in England reference has
already been made.  In social and civil relations Phips was
inexperienced, not to say uncouth, and for that reason might
be expected readily to submit to the guidance of the more
polished and practical leaders who lived in and about Boston.
They claimed to have made him governor and his success
in that office might well depend to a large degree on their
support.  The list of councillors named in the charter for the
first year was made up in England and did not contain the
names of Cooke and Oakes, with whom Mather had differed
in the later stages of his negotiations; but the well known
leaders of Massachusetts politics were fully represented.  At
their head stood William Stoughton as lieutenant governor,

himself trained in earlier life to be a clergyman, but turning to secular pursuits, he was sent as an agent to England and later accepted a place in the council under Andros, but now for the better part of a decade was given the opportunity to redeem himself, by useful service to the province.  By agreement between the council and representatives a method was adopted for the election of councillors which was continued throughout the provincial period.[1]  In the two houses voting separately a double number of candidates from each of the sections of the enlarged province were nominated, and from these by a second ballot, taken in joint session, the correct number of councillors were selected.  They were eighteen from the old colony of Massachusetts, four from Plymouth, three from Maine and one from the territory between Sagadahoc and Nova Scotia.  Upon the names of all who were thus selected the governor had the right of veto.  Taking the period as a whole this right was used with discretion, though in times of conflict the executive did not hesitate to employ it.

The councillors who were selected from year to year were typical Puritan laymen, who showed to the full the characteristics of their time and place.  But in their practice from the outset a departure in one most important respect from the course of the magistrates under the first charter should be noted.  They did not call the clergy into conferences and submit questions to them for advice or decision, as had been the custom until the establishment of the Dominion of New England.  Now that Massachusetts had been brought into line with the provincial system this practice had become impossible, and its abandonment was also in harmony with the spirit of the eighteenth century which slowly made itself felt even in Massachusetts.  With the cessation of conferences, or better, of caucuses between magistrates and the clergy, and the abandonment of the religious test, disappeared the theocratic feature in the Massachusetts government.  This proved fatal to any ambitions which the Mathers, or any others of the clerical body, might have cherished directly to control the politics of the province.  Such influence as they possessed must now be exerted from outside and under

[1] Acts and Res. VII, 15.

conditions similar to those which existed in other provinces
and in Europe. Though the connection between church and
state and a rigid orthodoxy, with strict censorship of the
press, were long maintained, no one could henceforth doubt
that the control of affairs was in the hands of laymen. Government in the leading Puritan province had at last become
unmistakably secular. In Connecticut also, though the
corporate system continued, the trend in the same direction
was steady and decisive.

The representatives who met on June 8, 1692, were the first
to be elected in Massachusetts under a property qualification.
Their bills were now for the first time subject to the governor's veto, and must also be sent to England. By means of
appeals and the transmission of the acts and journals of both
houses, the legislative and judicial processes of Massachusetts were now subject to review by the home government.
Forms of legislation which agreed better with those of parliament had to be adopted, and the house presented its
speaker for the governor's approval. Though Massachusetts
was still classed by the crown as a chartered colony, it was
more truly a chartered province and British officials had
become a permanent part of its system. Phips, however, was
not the man to throw many obstacles in the way of the free
action of the houses. Besides having the predispositions of
a New Englander, he was careless and inexperienced in affairs
of this kind. Overlooking the power vested in the governor
by the charter to appoint civil officers, Phips allowed them
to be designated by the council, and this was not corrected
until after the close of his administration.[1] In fact, owing
to the brevity of Bellomont's residence in New England, a
decade passed before Massachusetts, upon the arrival of
Dudley, was brought under the rule of a governor whose
spirit and policy corresponded in full with the intent of the
British government. And it was not until even a later time,
when external peace on the whole was restored, that the
antagonisms inherent in Massachusetts as a province were
clearly revealed. Connecticut and Rhode Island by retaining
the corporate form of government escaped many of the
obligations to England which had now become customary

[1] Palfrey, IV, 138.

and continued undisturbed under conditions which were essentially those of the late seventeenth century.

In order to provide for the new necessities and to perpetuate in the province as much as was possible of the available legislation of an earlier time, considerable activity in lawmaking was necessary for some years in Massachusetts. At first a number of acts were passed which were disallowed at Westminster, but after about a decade the governor and assembly became sufficiently accustomed to the routine to avoid this result. A variety of revenue acts had first to be passed, providing not only for new levies but for the collection of arrears of the old ones and for continuing bills of credit. Such local laws of Massachusetts and Plymouth as were not repugnant to those of England or to the new charter were to continue temporarily in force. An act for the erecting of a naval office, one for holding courts of justice and one for incorporating the college were passed, but all these were disallowed by the crown. Naval offices and their incumbents were wholly under imperial jurisdiction; as the charter provided for the justices' courts an attempt was made by the statute in question to enact into law a provision of the charter; the law incorporating the college was found to be defective, as power was not given the crown to appoint visitors. The governor was authorized, if needful, to march the militia into any New England colony or New York, an enactment the repetition of which was necessary as long as wars continued.

During its fall session this assembly passed a number of still more important acts. The first of these set forth general privileges, somewhat after the manner of the so-called " charter of liberties " enacted by the first New York assembly under Dongan. This, of course, was disallowed, the part selected upon which to base the rejection being, not the one which affirmed that the exclusive power of taxation within the province was in the general court, but that which provided that lands should be free from year and day, waste, escheat and forfeiture except in cases of high treason, and that bail should be taken in all cases except treason and felony, both of which were inconsistent with the somewhat antiquated law of England. Another act specifying the term of five years' quiet possession as the requisite for acquiring permanent title to land, and directed against such a policy as was attempted under Andros, was rejected because it did not contain a clause saving the right of the crown. A similar omission led to the disallowance of an act making lands liable for the payment of debts and of an act for the distribution of insolvent estates. The important general act for the continuance and readjustment of the judicial system was disallowed because the provision concerning appeals to England did not conform with that in the charter and seemed to exclude appeals in real actions. The act for better securing the liberty of the subject and preventing illegal imprisonment was disallowed because it required that the writ of habeas corpus should be granted as by the law of Charles II in England, though that privilege had not been extended to the plantations. The act for continuing in force the local laws of Massachusetts and Plymouth was rejected because it did not specify the particular statutes to be continued. An act against witchcraft was disallowed because it did not agree with the statute of James I, by which dower was saved to the widows and their inheritance to the heirs of those who were convicted. Much important legislation, however, was passed in 1692 which did not meet with this reception, as a law specifying judicial fees and those of the secretary; another regulating towns, the choice of town officers and their powers; others providing for the keeping of the Lord's day and for the orderly celebration of marriage, including civil marriages.[1] Legal provision for registering births and deaths came also as a result of the establishment of control by the British government.

The council carried on with regularity the executive business of the province on the lines and with the methods customary on the part of such bodies, while a multitude of matters of detail were adjusted by resolutions of the two houses, approved by the governor. The adjustment of accounts occupied the usual prominent place in business of this

[1] The history in part of action on these laws, with references to the law officers which it involved, may be followed in B. T. Journal VIII, C. O. 391/8. This is the last volume of the Journal of the Lords of Trade. The final action, as notified by letter from the privy council, is given under the respective laws in Acts and Res. of Mass. I, 35 *et seq.*

character, and earlier practice had given the assembly a control in these matters and necessitated a precision which was not abandoned when Massachusetts became a province. Two sets of accounts, those of Andros, the governor, and of John Usher, the treasurer, of the Dominion of New England, were inherited from an earlier period. The claims of the governor were not persistently urged and soon disappeared from view, but Usher kept his claim for about £800 before the authorities of Massachusetts and made it the burden of much of his correspondence with England for nearly fifteen years, until a final adverse decision was reached from which further appeal could not be taken.

When Phips arrived in Boston and while government under the new charter was being established in the calm and regular fashion which has just been indicated, the superstitious fears of the people were being roused to the highest pitch by the alleged revelations of witchcraft at Salem village and other neighboring towns.[1] Occasionally in earlier times an unfortunate in Massachusetts or Connecticut had suffered the death penalty under this horrible charge. Four years before in Boston the Goodwin children had been afflicted and Goody Glover was executed as a guilty agent of the evil one and responsible for their sufferings. Cotton Mather had taken a special interest in this case and in 1689, under the title of "Memorable Providences," had published a detailed account of his observations in connection with it. Some notable protests against this delusion had been published in Europe,[2] even in recent years, but they seem hardly to have found their way into the library of the Mathers, at least not into their active consciousness, while the writings of Joseph Glanvil and other defenders of witchcraft had been accepted with full approval. In the Christian world at that time the belief in witchcraft was universal except in the minds of a few highly enlightened and humane individuals. In countries where superstition and religious enthusiasm, particularly of the Calvinistic type, existed, the persecution of witches

[1] Cotton Mather's Life of Phips, in his Magnalia, gives a contemporary account of the governor's connection with this episode. Correct this by reference to Palfrey, Hist. of New Eng. IV, and to Wendell, Life of Cotton Mather.

[2] See Notestein's History of Witchcraft in England, 1558–1713, published among the prize essays of the Amer. Hist. Assoc.

reached the greatest excess.    On a reduced scale these
beliefs and tendencies were reflected in the colonies and
especially in New England.    Late in the history of witchcraft, New England had its one and only experience of that
evil.

The special conditions which occasioned the outbreak at
that time and place have been found in a variety of neighborhood and parish feuds,[1] some of which were of old standing, and in the conjuring tricks of a number of girls and
young persons who were more or less closely connected with
the family of Mr. Parris, the local clergyman.    Two servants,
of mixed Indian and negro blood, were also involved in the
business.    What had begun as a game passed into hysteria
and hallucination, which the village doctor and neighbors
soon pronounced to be the possession by evil spirits.    Clergymen and leading men from the near-by villages and towns
were next called in and they concluded that the afflictions
were preternatural, " and feared the hand of Satan was in
them."    Prayer and private fasts were resorted to, and then
public fasts, extending finally to the whole province, for
the purpose of seeking that the Lord " would rebuke Satan."
Every step that was taken proceeded on the supposition that
these were cases of witchcraft, advertised their existence and
nature 'more widely and thus spread the sympathetic contagion.    Soon the people of large parts of the province were
terrorized and under the influence of the mob spirit were
ready on the merest rumor to take the lives of multitudes
of worthy people.

The intellectual and social conditions which made this
possible are not difficult to understand.    One of these was the
emphasis which was laid in the religion of the time on the
unseen world, its inhabitants and the fate of souls when they
entered that realm.    Hell and the demons who inhabited it
were even more prominent in their consciousness than were
heaven and its angelic hosts.    This attitude of mind and
belief had been inherited from mediaeval Europe, but was
emphasized in many quarters at the time of the Reformation,
especially in countries, like Scotland and New England,
where the Calvinistic faith was accepted in its narrowest

[1] See C. W. Upham's exhaustive and standard work on Salem Witchcraft.

and most intense form. Theirs was a religion not merely of time but of eternity and, in the absence of other elements of culture, this idea was kept constantly before the minds of the people of every community. The Puritans were also certain that they were the elect of God and that their career was not merely natural and historical but providential. As the century progressed the morbid excess to which these views were carried had increased in certain influential quarters. The faith of Bradford, Winthrop, Cotton and their contemporaries had been robust, for theirs was the period of militant and triumphant Puritanism. But with every successive decade after 1660 the prospect of its conquering the world grew fainter and the inroads of secularism became more serious. As a stimulant to waning faith and a source of strength in times of growing discouragement, the clergy, and especially the Mathers, turned more to the unseen world and sought miraculous evidences in the past history of Puritanism which would justify belief in its ultimate success — if not in this world at least in another.

Because of their prominence and their manifold and prolonged activities, the Mathers must be taken as representative of declining Puritanism in New England. Their writings fill altogether the chief place in a period of literature, the authorship of which was almost exclusively clerical, between the annals of the founders of New England and the political discussions of the eighteenth century which indicated the approach of the Revolution. They emphasized the divine mission of New England as scarcely any one had done before them, and dwelt with endless repetition on the supreme importance of the unseen world. Moved originally by a suggestion from England, which struck a responsive chord in their own minds, the Mathers devoted much attention for years to the collection of instances of the intervention of Providence in recent human affairs. Increase Mather started an organized effort to this end among the New England clergy and in 1684 published, under the title of " An Essay for the Recording of Illustrious Providences," the classified results of his investigation. The inquiry was continued for many years afterwards and the subject was given a prominent place in Cotton Mather's " Magnalia Christi Americana," that entire work being indeed an exposition of the peculiar favor which God had shown for New England and its churches.

But the argument proceeded a step further than this. Not only in the " Magnalia," but with the utmost explicitness in other writings of the Mathers and of their contemporaries, America before the advent of the English was represented as the territory of the devil. Here over the degraded native tribes he had ruled for ages, and the first assault upon his dominion had been made by the invasion of the Puritans. " The New Englanders are a People of God settled in those which were once the Devil's Territories," wrote Cotton Mather in his " Wonders of the Invisible World," " and it may easily be supposed that the Devil was exceedingly disturbed when he perceived such a People here accomplishing the Promise of old made unto our Blessed Jesus, That He should have the Utmost parts of the Earth for his Possession. There was not a greater Uproar among the Ephesians when the Gospel was first brought among them than there was among the Powers of the Air when first the Silver Trumpets of the Gospel here made the Joyful Sound. The Devil thus Irritated tryed all sorts of Methods to overturn this poor Plantation, . . . . I believe that never were more Satanical Devices used for the Unsettling of any People under the Sun, than what have been Employed for the Extirpation of the Vine which God has here Planted." Thus, in the imaginations of these divines and their hearers, the great conflict between good and evil which had begun in the courts of heaven and had resulted in the expulsion thence of Lucifer and his angels, was continued on earth and had centered at last in New England, where it was being waged with a peculiar ferocity. This was their epic, the realm in which the Puritan imagination found its only natural atmosphere. Upon images of this nature and origin it had fed for generations. The mythology of the middle age, with its hierarchies of angels and demons, its witches and magical arts, had been accepted as literal, and of the continuous intercourse between spirits, good and evil, and men there was no doubt in the minds of the people in general.

It is also to be remembered that the decades which preceded and followed 1690 were times of unusual stress and excitement in New England and especially in Massachusetts. Political and social changes of the greatest import followed one another in rapid succession. Of the events of the time those which most deeply impressed the general consciousness were the Indian wars. Since 1675 the people of New England had lived under the shadow of these conflicts. They had now broken out afresh and with added peril which came from the fact that the savages were supported by the French. To the Puritans of that time aboriginal America was the kingdom of Satan and the Indians were his subjects. To them the gloomy wilderness, stretching back interminably toward the north and west, was literally the abode of fiends in human form. To the mediæval pictures of the devil and his victims in the inferno were now added the actual experiences of Indian massacres, perpetrated by painted and screeching furies and rivalling in horror the darkest imaginings to which the doctrine of hell and eternal punishment had given rise. In the colonies outside of New England Indian atrocities, until the last intercolonial war, were rare and left no vivid impression on the popular mind; but in New England for more than a generation they were not only frequent but of a nature so horrible as to strike all sensitive minds with immeasurable fear. To the New Englander the dread which was occasioned by these events became a permanent fact of consciousness, peculiar and abnormal in its effects, but one which could disappear only with the cause to which its origin was due.

That belief in witchcraft would be universal in communities whose environment and religious training were like those of New England goes without saying. Both external nature and their gloomy and severe theology combined to banish elves, fairies and all the brighter forms of popular mythology from the imagination and to substitute the dark and sinister forms which had followed in the wake of mediæval Christianity. Against the obsession of the unseen and mysterious, under the influence of which they lived, science had not yet erected any effective barriers. Medicine was in an utterly rudimentary stage, a combination of guesses and superstitions. Of abnormal psychology, the subject which would have furnished the key to most of the phenomena involved, no one was to have any adequate conception for two centuries to come. The law was as brutal and as abstruse as the theology of the time, and there were no guaranties in legal procedure which could be relied upon to protect the accused from the destructive effects of popular clamor. The only reliance against the spread of popular frenzy on the subject of witches, or on any subject which touched closely the moral and religious susceptibilities of such a people must be upon what we loosely term common sense, that is upon the mental and moral balance of the community. New Englanders have always possessed a moderate share of the qualities in which this consists. But they alone were not sufficient to insure in all localities, especially at such times as we are discussing, immunity from an emotional craze or epidemic of superstitious terror. Their religion strongly predisposed them to such experiences.

Returning to the course of events at Salem: after the views of the physician, the clergyman and the average layman had been secured, the next and fatal step was to consult the oracles of the law. Hathorne and Corwin, two local magistrates, began hearings in the village. The afflicted girls had already " cried out upon " a number of persons in the neighborhood — mostly women — and the accused had been arrested and now were examined according to the methods accredited in treatises on witchcraft and used in the English courts. The girls were brought into court to testify and point out those who were tormenting them, and by this publicity their hysterical fits were intensified. Not improbably the danger and horror of the business in which they presently found themselves engaged drove them in self-defence, and to an extent consciously, from one excess of falsehood and deception to another. Many of the most respectable people in the town were accused. The contagion spread to other towns. Even George Burroughs, a reputable clergyman in Maine, was caught in the network of suspicion and accusation. Under the excitement which was now abroad innocent women of nervous temperament began to confess themselves to be witches and all sorts of diabolical stories of covenants and meetings with the devil and the employment of infernal arts were invented and spread through the country.

The frenzy had reached such a height when Phips arrived from England as governor that, without waiting for the action of the general court, he issued a special commission of oyer and terminer to seven magistrates, with Lieutenant Governor Stoughton at their head, to act upon all cases of felony and other crimes in the three original counties of the province. The sessions of this body continued until the following October, and in Essex county its business was the trial of the victims who were accused of witchcraft. The procedure in these trials revealed again the defects of those which years before had resulted in the condemnation of Antinomians and Quakers. The accused had no counsel. The proceedings were accompanied with continued disorder occasioned by the crazy pranks of the accusers.[1] Leading questions were asked by the court and no attempt was made to sift the testimony or ascertain the credibility of witnesses. Prejudice and credulity were given free rein and before their power no reputation was safe. Parris himself took a prominent part in the proceedings. Under the pressure and the influence of excitement many of the accused soon began to confess. Confessions rapidly multiplied and might easily surpass the extravagant imaginings of the so-called victims. Stoughton was a firm believer in spectral evidence in its most rigid form, and in this he carried the court with him. This insured the acceptance as valid not only of the declarations of the afflicted but of the " spectral evidence," on the ground that the persons whose spectres the devil employed to afflict others must be in league with Satan and could not be wholly innocent persons made use of without their knowledge and consent. When the craze was at its height a number of the leading clergy were consulted by the governor and council. Their reply was written by Cotton Mather, and while it expressed some doubt concerning spectral evidence, it urged the speedy and vigorous prosecution of the accused in accordance with the laws of God

---

[1] Samuel Sewall was one of the judges in these trials and the entry in his diary respecting them was: "Went to Salem, where, in the Meeting-house the persons accused of Witchcraft were examined; was a very great Assembly; 'twas awfull to see how the afflicted persons were agitated. Mr. Noyes prayed at the beginning, and Mr. Higginson concluded." In the margin, presumably at a later time, Sewall had entered the words "Vae, vae, vae, Witchcraft." Diary, I, 358.

and of Great Britain. Increase Mather attended some of the meetings and Cotton Mather had an abridgment made of the proceedings for his special use. The latter professed a strong belief in the gospel method of casting out devils by prayer and fasting, but he at no time opposed the proceedings at Salem. A number of clergy, however, did protest against them when they realized the awfulness of the tragedy

At last, after twenty persons had been executed and the prisons of Essex county were filled with the condemned, or those awaiting trial, the Rev. Samuel Willard, pastor of the South Church in Boston, and even the wife of the governor were accused. This revealed the fact that no persons, however remote or however high their social position, were safe. Fortunately, in August the special court adjourned for two months. Before it met again Phips returned from a visit to the eastern parts of the province and the general court came together for its fall session. At the instance of the governor, as well as by the judiciary act above referred to, the special commission was superseded and when proceedings were resumed it was before the superior court of the province. In spite of the fact that Stoughton, as chief justice, again presided, spectral evidence was now rejected. Only three persons were convicted by this court and they were pardoned. Proceedings against the rest were stopped and the jails were speedily cleared of accused witches. The community soon returned to its senses and with that change came the end of witchcraft tragedies in New England or elsewhere in the colonies. That there were individuals, even in Massachusetts, who at the time or soon after were able effectively to criticize the phenomenon is proven by the writings of Thomas Brattle and Robert Calef. Both of these men belonged to the mercantile class of Boston, the latter being a somewhat recent immigrant from England and the former a native of the colony, a graduate of Harvard, a man who also had studied abroad and had won such distinction in mathematics and astronomy as to be made a member of the Royal Society of London. Brattle was for many years treasurer of Harvard, while his brother, William, was one of its most honored tutors and also pastor of the church in Cambridge. In a letter [1] to a member of the Royal Society, written in October, 1692, Thomas Brattle subjected the proceedings of the court at Salem to such keen analysis as to discredit its procedure and effectually destroy the validity of spectral evidence. He denied that the look and touch of the accused produced the effects claimed and declared that the use they were making of these was nothing less than sorcery. As to the confessors, many of whom he had heard, he affirmed that they were deluded and imposed upon, " and therefore unfit to be evidences either against themselves or anyone else." He also showed the absurdity of accepting both spectral and human testimony; if the former was valid, what need was there of resorting to the latter? It also did not escape his observation that most or all of the human testimony was irrelevant. So trenchant was this criticism that, had it been printed at that time, it is not unlikely that it would have provoked a violent controversy, in which not only the believers in witchcraft but the defenders of the judicial procedure of the time would have become involved.

Robert Calef's book, " More Wonders of the Invisible World," was completed in 1697 and printed in London in 1700.[1] From the standpoints of both literature and argument it is inferior. It is made up of a number of ill-compacted fragments, the most important of which was the story of the afflictions of Margaret Rule, contributed by Cotton Mather. An account of the trials at Salem was also included. But the chief purpose of the book was to bring the average common sense to bear upon the problem, especially in such a way as to puncture the conceit of the Mathers. Their conduct in connection with the case of Margaret Rule was described by Calef in such a way as to make them appear ridiculous. Ironical thrusts at them appear repeatedly in the book. The blind following of precedent and authority on their part was indicated as the cause of Cotton Mather's failure to condemn spectral evidence and of the ambiguous position which he had

---

[1] Printed in 1 Mass. Hist. Colls. V, and reprinted in Burr's Narratives of the Witchcraft Cases.

[2] It has been reprinted with notes by S. G. Drake in 1866, and by Burr in his Narratives of the Witchcraft Cases.

assumed throughout the crisis. Though he had professed to
have the healing of the community at heart, and this was
the chief burden of his pen and of his innumerable prayers,
so rooted was his belief in the mythology of the inferno that
the result of his activity had been to deepen rather than to
relieve the tragedy. Calef's book set this forth in such pun-
gent form as to make it intensely offensive to the Mathers.
President Mather is said to have ordered a copy of it burned
in the college yard. They brought suit against Calef for
slander, but later abandoned it. Cotton Mather made a
severe entry concerning it in his diary, while a number of the
parishioners of the North Church affixed their names to a
published reply. In connection with other issues it disturbed
the equanimity of the Mathers for a considerable time and
affords one of the first faint signs of the approach in New
England of a kindlier and more enlightened day. Finally,
in 1696, official indication was given that Massachusetts
had awakened to a sense that at best a terrible mistake had
been made by the holding of a fast, the principal object of
which was to seek divine forgiveness for " the late Tragedie
raised amongst us by Satan and his Instruments, through the
awful Judgement of God." On that day Samuel Sewall stood
up in the presence of the congregation in the South Church
while the pastor read from the pulpit a confession, written
by the judge himself, of his sorrow for the share he had borne
as one of the magistrates on the special commission at
Salem, as involving the heaviest burden of personal guilt of
which his soul was conscious.[1] Stoughton declared that he
had nothing to repent of in this connection, while the Mathers
never publicly expressed sorrow for the part they had borne
in the deplorable event.[2]

The most commendable act of Phips' public career was that
by which he brought the prosecutions at Salem to an end.
It of course met with approval of the home government,

---

[1] Sewall's Diary, I, 440, 445.

[2] The bibliography of Salem Witchcraft can be found adequately discussed
in Winsor's Literature of Witchcraft in New England, in Proc. of Amer. Antiq.
Soc., 1895. Since its publication Professor Burr's Narratives of the Witchcraft
Cases has been issued. It brings together the most available body of original
sources on the subject. Valuable discussions by Kittredge and Burr may be
found in Proc. of Amer. Antiq. Soc., 1907 and 1911.

though in the history of imperial policy the witchcraft delusion was an event of very minor significance.  Of far greater importance in this connection were the relations which developed between Phips and the other imperial officials both within Massachusetts and outside.  Reference has already been made to his absurd and blustering conduct toward Governor Fletcher, of New York, and toward Randolph, the surveyor general of the customs.  Accounts of this found their way to the government offices at Westminster.  But of still greater seriousness were his brutal encounters with Captain Richard Short of the guardship " Nonesuch," and Jahleel Brenton, the collector of the imperial customs for the New England district.

Friction between governors and the commanders of royal guardships stationed at ports along the coast were not uncommon, and this was one of the earliest and most conspicuous instances of that class.  Though Phips was later eulogized as a hero by Cotton Mather, he was really little more than a typical sea captain of the period, generous it may be in his impulses but the victim of outbursts of passion during which his language and conduct reached the lowest depths of brutality.  As was usual when in port, a number of Short's men deserted and he resorted to impressment without the governor's warrant.  Though at so early a date as this in New England the proper relations in this matter may not have been understood, this was an encroachment on the governor's right. The quarrel reached its culmination in misunderstandings and impossible orders in reference to the defence of Pemaquid and to cruising off that coast.  Captain Fairfax, of the " Conception Prize," was associated with Short and in the main agreed with him in his conduct on this occasion.  The two captains understood that Phips intended to keep them on the Maine coast all winter and this they believed would almost surely result in the loss of the vessels.  Therefore, in November, 1692, they returned to Boston, this according to Phips' view being a desertion of the post and a violation of orders.  It also seems that Short afterwards refused to send certain of his men to Pemaquid.  This was the last straw and was followed by a personal encounter in which the governor, because the captain's right hand was disabled, succeeded in

knocking him down and probably beating him into insensibil-
ity. Short was then imprisoned for séveral months, during
which time he presumably recovered from his wounds, after
which he was put on board a merchant vessel to be taken as
a prisoner to England. But the captain of this vessel went
first to Portsmouth, New Hampshire, where Phips suspected
that he was adding to his crew some of the men who had
deserted from the " Nonesuch " and who had been harbored in
that province. Usher, the lieutenant governor, partly as an
incident of his jealousy of Phips, now espoused the side
of Short. Citing as his authority his commission as vice-
admiral, Phips went to Piscataqua, boarded the vessel and
carried off or rifled a trunk and chest which belonged to Short.
This Usher and his friends denounced as a gross violation of
the rights of New Hampshire. Short, however, had escaped
and the following summer sailed for England with the squadron of Sir Francis Wheeler. There in due time his complaint
against Phips was submitted to the lords of trade and to the
privy council.[1]

Toward the close of 1693 there came through the customs
board other complaints from Brenton to the effect that, when
he had seized a vessel for illegal trading, Phips had come with
a body of men, and, after grossly insulting Brenton, had forced
him to give up the vessel and its cargo. Other irregularities
in connection with the seizure and condemnation of vessels for
illegal trading, as well as his own personal concern in that
trade were charged against Phips. Admiralty courts had not
yet been established in the colonies and Phips, under the
authority of his commission as vice-admiral, had presumed to
hold court and sit in person as judge for the condemnation
of prizes. In one or more of these cases it was also charged
that he had failed to account for the king's share of the
prize, as well as that of the ship's company which made the
capture.

Some of these offences were serious and prolonged inquiry
concerning them was made in England, Benjamin Jackson
appearing as counsel for Phips and Joseph Dudley, who was

[1] Cal. St. P. Col., 1693–6, pp. 24, 33, 58, 64, 67, 68, 74, 77, 91, 121,
217, 234; C.O. 5/858. N. H. Prov. Papers, II, 101. Hutchinson, Hist. of
Mass. II.

on the spot, bringing all the influence he could to bear against him. After considerable evidence had been collected, it was decided that Phips should be summoned to England, and that previous to his coming inquiry also should be made in the colonies concerning his conduct. Orders were accordingly issued that all who were concerned should collect authentic copies of records and depositions and that all the evidence should be sent to England. This was done and Phips was also ordered home to answer in person.[1]

Meantime signs were not lacking which indicated that Phips had failed to win the respect of the people of his province. From the standpoint of the Mathers he may have been the most — or even the only — available candidate for the governorship, but he was totally unfitted for an office of that character. His neighbors in and about Boston, who knew him best, realized this fact and opposition to him began to develop in the house of representatives. Phips had vetoed the election of Elisha Cooke to the council because he was an irreconcilable opponent to the new charter. To all those whose hearts had been finally set on the restoration of the old charter Phips could never be specially acceptable. As a crude product of the frontier, he was naturally unacceptable to the leading families of the coast towns and to all sympathizers with England. His hold upon the office was therefore weak. It was a broken reed upon which the Mathers had chosen to lean. Before the close of 1693 it was evident that Phips had lost control of the house. Its speaker, Nathaniel Byfield, was one of his active opponents and a dispute arose between the two over the question of adjournment.[2] On one or two occasions also the governor and council offended the representatives by ordering the payment of money for purposes not designated in the appropriation acts. This led to a number of protests on the part of the house and in 1695 the passage of a bill in which they secured the rights of the house of commons in such matters.

But the most interesting result which followed the friction between Phips and the lower house was the passage by a small

[1] Cal. St. P. Col. 1693–6, pp. 224–5, 227, 232, 234, 241, 246, 250.

[2] Goodell, Acts and Res. of Mass. VII, 390–394; Sewall's Diary, I, 380, 386; Hutchinson, op. cit. II, 78.

majority of an act requiring representatives to be residents
and freeholders in the towns from which they were elected.
This measure was introduced to prevent such men as Byfield,
Foxcroft, Brenton and others, inhabitants of Boston and
vicinity and opponents of Phips, from appearing as representatives of outlying towns and thus packing the assembly
against him.  It was a measure in the interest of the executive and vigorous, though futile, protests were made against
it.  When the assembly of 1694 met six non-residents had been
returned.  The governor insisted that they should not be
sworn, and on Byfield telling him that the house was a proper
judge of its own members Phips commanded silence.  After
vainly making a second protest they returned from the
council and Legge declared that they would not go out until
rejected by the house.  " The Governor, hearing of this,"
writes Byfield in a letter to Dudley, " came down to the
Representatives in fury, without his hat [and] said that he
had heard that a member, against whom he had objected, had
refused to leave the House unless the House put him out, and
that he wished he knew who it was.  Legge at once came
forward, and the Governor said he had nothing against him
and wished he had been returned from Boston . . ., but as
to the others, if the House did not turn them out he would
turn them out himself." [1]  This was decisive and writs were
issued for filling the vacant seats.

It was near the close of 1694 when the collection of evidence
in support of the charges against Phips was completed and he
was finally able to depart for England.  He arrived there
early in the following year, but was seized with an acute
malady of which he died before his case could come to a
final hearing.[2]  Had he survived, a precedent from the New
England colonies would doubtless have been established for
such a hearing as occurred two years later in the case of
Governor Fletcher of New York.

With the exception of a few months during which Lord
Bellomont was resident in New England, William Stoughton

[1] Cal. St. P. Col., 1693–6, p. 294.
[2] Ibid., pp. 309, 345, 354, 390, 397–8, 429, 498;  Mather, Magnalia,
Bk. II.  In Sewall's Diary, I, 393, is an account of Phips' departure from
Boston.

and the council administered the affairs of Massachusetts from the departure of Phips until the arrival of Joseph Dudley as governor, a period of about seven years. It was during that time that the French and Indians destroyed Pemaquid, completed their reoccupation of Nova Scotia, took possession of parts of Newfoundland and in connection with these gains reasserted their claim to the territory as far west as the Kennebec river and prohibited the continuance of fishing by the English along the Acadian coast. Massachusetts, with little aid from the other colonies, had found the burden of defending Maine to be heavy and emerged from the war in a state of depression and financial exhaustion which the few years of peace were all too short to remedy. Stoughton and the council fully realized this situation and repeatedly gave expression to it in their letters to the home government. They urged that the interests of Great Britain, as well as those of New England, demanded the permanent occupation of Nova Scotia, because the establishment of posts on the St. Croix and eastward would influence the Indians much more than the mere occupation of Pemaquid. In this way also the question of boundaries and of the fishery would be forever settled in harmony with English claims, and the resources of the New England forests in naval stores would be much better secured. But a half-century was to pass before arguments of this nature met with a response at Westminster.

In New England politics Phips was an accident, but Stoughton fell in with the normal course of development. Though from the modern point of view Phips made a better showing in the affair of Salem Witchcraft, Stoughton's attitude was more that of the average New Englander. Stoughton was an educated gentleman of the Boston type, regular and orthodox in all his doings and connections. As an official he had been connected with Andros, and he continued to live in friendly relations with John Usher and Samuel Allen. He expressed belief in both the correctness and the justice of Usher's claim for remuneration for his services as treasurer of the Dominion of New England. In the trial of prizes and distribution of the proceeds there was no charge of irregularities or dishonesty against Stoughton. No quarrels with other officials or attempts to thwart the plans of Bellomont, his superior, marred the quiet of Stoughton's administration. Though he was a genuine Massachusetts man, there could be no doubt of his loyalty to the British government and its policy. In many respects, therefore, the similarity between him and Dudley, who was to be his successor, was apparent, though Stoughton did not incur the dislike or have to bear the charges of treason toward the colony which conservatives and people of the Mather type succeeded in fixing upon Dudley. Stoughton's administration accustomed the people to the peaceful working of government under the new charter and fitted much better the needs of a time of transition than could any achievement of a man like Phips. Of the thorough loyalty of Stoughton both to Massachusetts and to Great Britain there can be no doubt.[1]

Throughout the decade which we are now considering, the question of the charter of Harvard College and of the disposition of its presidency was under discussion, and it was not without a bearing on the religious and political situation of the time.[2] The college had thus far existed under an act of incorporation passed by the general court in 1650, one of the notable instances in which that body had exceeded its jurisdiction. It was therefore felt that its so-called charter had fallen with the charter of the colony.[3] Though Increase Mather was criticized for his work in securing the new charter for the province, his influence immediately after his return was sufficient to enable him, in opposition to the general prejudice against corporations, to secure the passage of an act incorporating the college, of which he was president, with very independent powers. Though this act was subject to the royal veto, under the lead of President Mather the new corporation organized, granted degrees and transacted other business. But among the first acts of Massachusetts to be negatived by the crown was the one incorporating Harvard

---

[1] Proofs of these statements may be found in Cal. St. P. Col., 1693–6, pp. 34, 35, 350–1; *ibid.*, 1696–7, pp. 141, 143, 245, 624; *ibid.*, 1697–8, pp. 94, 500, 544.

[2] Quincy, Hist. of Harvard University, I. Palfrey, Hist. of New England, IV. Goodell, Acts and Res. of Mass. VII, 608.

[3] See the letter of Increase Mather to Joseph Dudley, 1707–8. 1 Mass. Hist. Col. III, 126. "The cow was dead and the calf in her belly."

College, the reason being that no provision was made for the exercise of the power of visitation. At the time of his return with the province charter Mather had contemplated the possibility that popular dissatisfaction with the result of his work as agent would soon compel him to return permanently to England. Owing to the flattering reception which he met with in many quarters, this result would not have been unwelcome to him. The idea was now revived in a still more attractive form, namely that he should return on a second agency for the purpose of securing a suitable charter for the college. Under the guise of supernatural influences and suggestions, this subject was now kept prominently before the minds of Mather and his son for several years and found a lodging place in their diaries.

The method adopted by the general court was to submit to the crown the heads of a charter in the form of a bill, while Mather, had he secured appointment as agent, hoped to procure a grant, like the province charter, from the king. In this way he hoped to perpetuate his own influence and that of his supporters in control of the college, though doubtless the crown would have insisted that the right of visitation should be vested in the governor, and that the way should be kept open for the Anglicans at some future time to obtain a share in the management of the college. In 1696 Mather succeeded in promoting the passage of a bill for a charter which contained several obnoxious provisions. In the following year a bill with provisions which were somewhat more favorable to Mather was allowed to pass, but the arrival of Lord Bellomont in America and the strong hope that he might still go as agent, increased Mather's confidence that this would also be rejected in England.

Ostensibly the point at issue between Mather and the general court was the place of residence of the president: should he be allowed to continue his residence in Boston and his pastorate of the leading church of the province, or should he be compelled to remove to Cambridge and to reside at the college? This latter alternative Mather opposed and in this course he was supported by his church and by most of the religious conservatives of the province. Over the choice of officials who should exercise the power of visitation Mather naturally desired much influence, and it may be that he would have preferred to see it lodged in the governor alone rather than in the governor and the council, as was insisted by the general court.

But the real issue, which gave significance to the diplomatic sparring that long continued over these minor questions, was a religious one. It was nothing less than the control, through the college and the churches, over religious tendencies which were operative in Massachusetts and more widely through New England. As had been the case for the past thirty years, the issues were being drawn and the conflict waged over the practices involved in the so-called half-way covenant. For two decades these had been thrown into the background by the struggle over the charters and the Andros régime. But the institution of government under the new Massachusetts charter, with the changed conditions which it had brought, opened the way for many changes which might imperil what remained of New England Puritanism. It behooved the conservatives to be alert, and at the head of the most rigid of this type stood the Mathers. In 1697 they sounded the alarm by the publication of Cotton Mather's "Life of the Rev. Jonathan Mitchell," a former pastor of the church in Cambridge, to which was prefixed an " epistle dedicatory," from the pen of the elder Mather.[1] Mitchell had been a protagonist of the Cambridge Platform and as such he was now eulogized by his biographers. Upon that platform the Mathers took their stand, both for defence and for offence, and opposed every deviation therefrom. Hitherto discussion had chiefly concerned the sacrament of baptism, but now it centered in the Lord's Supper. In either case the object of the framers and defenders of the platform, the founders of New England Congregationalism, was to exclude the unfit, to keep the membership of the churches pure. To this end a rigid insistence upon personal confession of faith before the church and upon evidence of a true religious life and spirit had been made a prerequisite for admission to baptism and the Lord's Supper. But owing to complications which had arisen among the second generation of colonists from the baptism of infants,

[1] These were afterwards included in Cotton Mather's Magnalia, Book III, and may be most conveniently found there.

concessions had been made in Connecticut and elsewhere in the administration of that sacrament. But the conservatives now made all the firmer stand in their requirements for admission to the Lord's table. It was upon this that Mitchell had laid emphasis and it was as its advocate that he was now selected for eulogy. And Mather made the application personal, at the same time implying that he himself was the patriarch and chief apostle of conservatism, by dwelling upon the importance of keeping Harvard, the nursery, the fountain of the faith, the school of the prophets, true to the ancient principles.

This homily was not delivered into the air, but was intended by its author as an attack upon John Leverett and William Brattle, both of whom had long been the leading tutors in the college, but who were known to have departed from the strict views of the fathers respecting public confession and admission to the Lord's Supper. Brattle had just been chosen minister of the church in Cambridge and had given evidence of his " looseness " in that church. With him sympathized his brother, Thomas, the able Boston merchant and treasurer of the college, who had differed so radically from the Mathers on the witchcraft question. Ebenezer Pemberton and Benjamin Colman, talented young ministers, were understood to be on the same side. All of these were graduates of the college and all except Colman had been connected with its government since Mather had been president. As the tendency which they represented was in harmony with the spirit of the times, it was hard to tell how far the evil had spread; and that it would prevail unless a firm stand was made against it was altogether likely. Therefore the Mathers devoted their energies to the task of excluding Leverett and Brattle from the corporation of Harvard College, and the opposition which this aroused was felt in the council and house of representatives and in the end defeated the plan of Increase Mather to go as agent to England to secure a new college charter. The struggle over these matters lasted during 1697 and 1698, and was at its height when the earl of Bellomont reached Boston for his term of residence in New England. Projects for a new college charter were permanently before the general court and President Mather was skilfully parrying the demands that he should remove to Cambridge or resign his office.[1]

On Bellomont's arrival he made it clear that the British government would not assent to the inclusion of the elective council as a part of the board of visitors. But in his letters home he finally expressed himself as in favor of this concession to the colonists,[2] while meantime, as a compromise measure, the general court voted to include a part of the council among the corporation of the college. But Bellomont vetoed the draft of 1699 because of the inclusion by the conservatives of a test clause providing that no person should be chosen president, vice-president or fellow who should not declare and continue his adherence to the principles of reformation which were expressed by those who first settled Massachusetts and founded the college and which had hitherto been the practice of the generality of the churches in New England. Now it was proposed that application should be made to the king direct for the grant of a charter, but it was arranged that Bellomont and not Mather should act as agent. This plan, however, was defeated by the sudden death of the governor. Though Mather succeeded in excluding his opponents for a time from the corporation, his course aroused so many enemies that, in 1701, he himself was dropped from the presidency by a resolution of the general court.[3] No charter was obtained from the crown, but in the next administration, at the suggestion of Governor Dudley, the so-called charter of 1650, though doubtless illegal, was revived as part of a resolution of the two houses for the payment of the president's salary. It was not necessary that such an act should be submitted to the privy council, and so the affairs of Harvard continued to be administered on this extra-legal basis until after the Revolution.[4]

[1] The course of these events may be traced in Increase Mather's Diary and in Sewall's Diary, I, extracts from both of which are printed in the App. to Quincy, Hist. of Harvard. The recently published Diary of Cotton Mather gives his searchings of heart on the subject.

[2] Cal. St. P. Col., 1700, p. 416; Mass. Arch. Ms., Letter Books, 1658–1779, Bellomont to Stoughton, May 31, 1698.

[3] This was done by an invitation to Rev. Samuel Willard to perform as vice-president the duties which President Mather had declared his inability to perform by declining to remove to Cambridge.

[4] Quincy, I, 159, 611.

Not only did the Mathers fail in this effort to retain control of the college, but as a direct result of the controversy in which they had engaged at the close of 1699 the Brattle Street Church was founded in Boston and Benjamin Colman was called home from England to be its pastor.[1]  The prime mover in this enterprise was the merchant, Thomas Brattle, and he was supported by the clergymen who were opposed to the Mathers, and other men of liberal tendencies who had become dissatisfied with some of the practices followed in the other three churches of the town.  As the founders of the new church accepted the Westminster Confession of Faith, no question of doctrine was at issue.  But in the public service of the other churches the Bible was not read or the Lord's Prayer used.  Candidates for the Lord's Supper were required to recount in public their religious experiences.  The controlling spirit of the churches, as already indicated, was one of stiff opposition to change, worship of the past, strict adherence to the principles of the founders of Massachusetts in matters of church polity as well as doctrine.  Soon after the founding of the Brattle Street Church it put forth a manifesto containing the reasons for the step which had been taken.  In this they professed to be following the usages common among the sect in England, to insist upon the reading of some selections from the Bible in the public service, to ascertain the qualifications of members, to leave more discretion in the hands of the minister and officers of the church and rely less on public narratives of religious experience, and, in choosing a minister, to admit the votes of all adult baptized persons who contributed to his maintenance.  In matters of faith they were in full agreement with the churches and desired communion with them.  In their type of culture they differed in no essential respect from the more intelligent men by whom they were surrounded, though Colman had lived for four years in England, where he received Presbyterian ordination, and had been broadened by that experience.  The changes, therefore, which were in-

---

[1] Turell, Life and Character of Benjamin Colman, Boston, 1749; Lothrop, History of the Church in Brattle Street, 1851; J. G. Palfrey, Sermons preached to the Church in Brattle Square, 1825; MS. Records of Church in Brattle Square, Mass. Hist. Soc.; Quincy, History of Harvard, I.

volved in the experiment were slight, but its leaders were young men and were recruited from the most cultured laymen of the community. It is interesting to find that John Nelson was a friend and supporter of Colman.

Slight as was their divergence from the standards, the establishment of the new church implied change and an independent spirit. As such it met with sharp reproof from Higginson and Noyes, of the Salem Church, and with the determined opposition of the Mathers and their followers. Cotton Mather confided to his diary the fact that " a company of the headstrong men of the town, the chief of whom are full of malignity to the holy ways of our churches, have built in the town another meetinghouse." They had proceeded without the knowledge of the neighboring ministers and had issued a manifesto, certain articles of which would " subvert our churches " and " throw all into confusion." They were " innovators," " ignorant, arrogant, obstinate, and full of malice and slander, and they fill the land with lies, in the misrepresentations whereof I am a very singular sufferer." The " infection " of their example was greatly to be feared.[1] But such was the influence of Stoughton, Willard, the able pastor of the South Church, Justice Sewall and others, that the Mathers were compelled at least to share in the services at the dedication of the new church.[2] Their feeling of hostility, however, was not allayed and for years it continued to find expression in the writings of both father and son. In 1700 Increase Mather, under the title, " The Order of the Gospel preffered and Practiced by the Churches of New England Justified . . .," expounded in a controversial spirit the principles of the fathers upon a variety of points in dispute. This drew from Colman and his supporters a reply, " The Gospel Orders Revived," to which was prefixed a note to the reader which stated that the press in Boston was so much under the sway of the reverend author whom they were answering, that it was necessary to have their pamphlet printed in New York. The third brochure of this series was entitled, " A Collection of some of the many Offensive Matters in a Pamphlet entitled, ' The Order of the Gospel

---

[1] Diary of Cotton Mather, I, 325–6, 329–330, 332.
[2] Sewall's Diary, Jan. 1699–1700.

Revived.'" This was signed by Increase Mather, but was written by his son, and, as its title indicated, was not an argument but an accumulation of personal attacks and reproaches because, in violation of the commandments and of the rights of superiors, a group of young men had ventured to criticize the venerable president of the college. In this important fashion the controversy ended for the time, to reappear in other forms and relations at a later period. But to the Mathers and men of their views times of degeneracy had set in and New England was seen to be steadily drifting away from the ideals of the fathers.

# CHAPTER X

### VIRGINIA DURING THE FIRST INTERCOLONIAL WAR

VIRGINIA had a homogeneous population. It was as purely English as was New England and therefore did not have to face the problems of divergent nationalities which existed in colonies to the north of her. She also as yet had no religious disputes. She had no perplexing boundary controversy, though the partial alienation of the Northern Neck raised issues which bore some resemblance to a question of that sort. As the French had not yet completed their occupation of the Mississippi valley, her frontier was not imperilled or disturbed otherwise than by bands of Iroquois on their raids against their foes further to the south. And yet the remembrance of the Indian outrages which ushered in Bacon's Rebellion survived and must have given wings to the minor alarms which still occasionally agitated the frontier. Population had reached the falls of the rivers, but the necessity of keeping up water communication with the coast was destined to stop their progress at these points for some time to come.[1] The remotest inland settlements did not differ as yet in faith or nationality from the population of the tidewater.

From this it follows that, during the early eighteenth century, relations in Virginia were stable, its development quiet and uneventful, as compared with most of the other colonies. Among royal officials it had the reputation of being better governed than other colonies and, whatever may be said on that point, to the English mind it certainly better fulfilled the conditions of what a province should be. After the English Revolution as before, its most important public questions centered in trade and tobacco culture, the attempt to establish ports, coast defence, frontier defence, finance and the clergy. In close connection with the church arose now the

[1] Bruce, Institutional History of Virginia, II, 297.

new question of the college. For some time such controversies as the governors and council became involved in centered largely in James Blair, the man to whose energy the college owed its beginnings and who was the steady champion of the clergy.

In none of the colonies were the tendencies of the later Stuart policy reflected more clearly than in Virginia under Lord Howard of Effingham, though they did not go so far as to make it the centre of a vast southern dominion.[1] The strength of its aristocracy, as centered in the council, has already been emphasized as the leading characteristic of Virginia society and government. Berkeley's strength had been due to his identification with this system. It had received a blow at the time of Bacon's Rebellion and the tendency of Lord Howard's policy had been to transfer the lead to the governor. The enlargement of executive discretion was his watchword. Following the lead of Berkeley and Culpeper, he insisted on the right of the governor and council alone to impose a tax to meet an emergency,[2] while his claim of the right to appoint their clerk was bound greatly to restrict the independence of the burgesses. But this tendency, as well as the temptation to appoint Catholics to office, was checked by the Revolution. After that event Virginia affairs returned again to their natural channel and the county families were continued in their position of leadership and were not again imperilled by popular insurrection or serious encroachments by any governor. The employment of slave labor kept steadily increasing, while the introduction of indented servants and the speculative use of head rights maintained the system of large estates and the plantation type of society.[3]

On the return of Lord Howard to England, the council was left in charge of affairs. At its head as senior councillor was Nathaniel Bacon, Sr., now an old man and soon to be retired at his own request from public life.[4] Ralph and Christo-

---

[1] See the chapter on Virginia at the Close of the Stuart Régime in Osgood American Colonies in the 17th Century III. [2] Bruce, *op.cit.*, II, 527.

[3] Hartwell, Blair and Chilton, State of Virginia, 1 Mass. Hist. Soc. V, 132. This valuable pamphlet is abstracted in Cal. St. P. Col., 1696–1697, pp. 641–666.

[4] A few changes in membership were made when the new commission was issued to Lord Howard, in October, 1690. Cal. St. P. Col. 1689–92, p. 326.

pher Wormeley, Richard Lee, John Custis, John Page, William Byrd and Isaac Allerton were among its other members. Nicholas Spencer, the secretary, who had long been one of the most active members of the council and who had recently led in the suppression of certain disturbances in the northern section of the province which were a reflection of those that were agitating Maryland,[1] died in September, 1698. A month later the council wrote to the lords of trade that they would do their best to put the country in a position of defence, though neither of the station ships was then in a condition fit for service.[2] As usual, ammunition was scarce and a new supply was greatly needed. As previously reported by Lord Howard, the effective military force of Virginia was 3000 foot and 1300 horse,[3] but he admitted later that, because he found Virginia in debt and without an adequate revenue, he had been unable to repair the carriages and platforms of the cannon.[4] A report made at the beginning of 1691 shows that this was too true and that the harbor and river defences of Virginia could be considered negligible.

At the beginning of May, 1690, in consequence of news of Indian depredations in New York, the council ordered the commanders of the counties to their posts, that the frontier settlements be instructed to be on their guard and in case of alarm that the militia be called out. A month later Francis Nicholson arrived and was sworn in as lieutenant governor[5] and the commission of the bishop of London to James Blair as commissary was read. Nicholson was now definitely entering on a long and varied career as a colonial official, which was to bring him into connection with many colonies and many sides of colonial life. In it all he was to be a staunch upholder of crown and church and was also to win a certain vague military prestige. He showed a marked capacity for grasping colonial relations as a whole, so far as they were related to the interests of the home government. He became

[1] *Ibid.*, pp. 32, 162.

[2] The "Deptford" had capsized in a squall and proved a total loss. In April, 1691, the "Dumbarton" was ordered broken up, as she was no longer serviceable. *Ibid.*, 163, 224, 335, 383, 411.

[3] *Ibid.*, p. 44. A decade later Beverley estimated the total population liable to military service at nearly 18,000 men. Hist. of Va., 218.,

[4] *Ibid.*, 422, 983.          [5] *Ibid.*, 277.

interested in so many general enterprises, secular and ecclesiastical, that as colonial governor he was always likely to keep in touch with events far and wide. But in New York he had failed conspicuously at an important crisis and at no point in his later career did he show special executive ability. He travelled much but he never roused any province which he governed to special activity.

After an administration of less than a year and a half, Nicholson was superseded by Sir Edmund Andros, who was continued at the head of the government of Virginia until after the close of the war. This, as well as his earlier appointment in the line of succession to the Maryland government, shows the undiminished confidence of the home government in his serviceableness as an official. The fact also that he was received without a breath of protest in Virginia shows how intensely sectional New England was and how different were the conditions and sentiments which existed in Virginia. In Virginia and Maryland Andros fell in at once with the routine of government and his administration there passed quietly and with an average degree of success. In passing from Nicholson to Andros one misses the abundant correspondence of the former. Andros probably did not travel through the province and he did not watch so carefully events in other colonies. His natural stolidity was increased by advancing years and by impaired health during the latter part of this, his last administration. Virginia was consistently Anglican and loyal, and so long as this was true of any province, Andros would not disturb the regular course of its life. We shall find that the aid which it gave to New York, though small, was chiefly bestowed during this administration, though, as was expected, nothing effective was done to improve the defences of Virginia itself. Even during Nicholson's administration there were indications of a possible breach between the governor and Blair, and it came under Andros in the form of the suspension of the commissary from the council, followed by certain sweeping indictments of the governor's policy and of Virginia life and society in general.

Nicholson at once began writing in a pessimistic strain concerning the condition of the northern colonies and the danger from French and Indians. But the most interesting episode in connection with Nicholson's efforts in this line was the journey of his agent, Cuthbert Potter, through New York to Boston and Salem in Massachusetts for the purpose of ascertaining what was the condition of the northern colonies and reporting it to the Virginia governor. It was not often that such a step as this was taken by a royal official and it shows a certain breadth of view on the part of Nicholson to take it. He was a man of some wealth, as is shown by not a few gifts of money which at critical times he made for causes in which he was interested. So far as we know, he bore the expense of Potter's mission. Potter bore letters to trusted parties in the colonies whither he went, but the severity of Leisler toward strangers was so great that he did not dare to bring them on show in New York.[1] He passed through New England to Boston at the time when Winthrop was on his Albany expedition and when Phips' expedition against Canada was being fitted out. As his purposes were understood to be hostile to the existing government in Massachusetts, the magistrates searched Potter before he left and took from him some of his papers. This, they said, was done under an order to examine all strangers because so many attacks were being made on the government. In consequence doubtless of the reports which Potter brought, Nicholson wrote more letters home which were highly critical of conditions in New York and New England. These added to the volume of testimony which was coming from adherents of Andros and opponents of Leisler. In the letter of protest which Nicholson and the council of Virginia wrote to Massachusetts concerning Potter's arrest, they said they were informed that illegal trade there was rife and that there was no collector at Boston; hence they had ordered that ships bringing to Virginia English goods from New England must produce coquets from England or be prosecuted.

By their zeal for the English Church Nicholson and Blair seemed well qualified for cooperation and the immediate effect of their arrival was to infuse greater activity into Virginia affairs. Nicholson ordered a survey of guns and military stores and that a return should be made of the officers

---

[1] *Ibid.*, 334, 340 *et seq.* Potter's Journal is printed by Mereness, Travels in the American Colonies, 1690–1783.

and privates in the militia. Interpreters were sent to the friendly Indians to dissuade them from listening to foreign Indians who were trying to tempt them away.[1] On the suggestion of Nicholson, it was agreed by the council that it would be well for him to visit the heads of the rivers in person. Thus originated the series of tours through the province, which constituted an important feature of Nicholson's activities at this time. He also kept up correspondence with various persons in the northern colonies [2] and this, together with his tours and the mission of Cuthbert Potter, had for its object the securing information for himself and the British government respecting conditions at or near the seat of war. One of his correspondents was Robert Livingston, who wrote in a tone extremely hostile to Leisler and confirmed Nicholson's opinions to the effect that affairs could not well be in a worse state than actually existed along the entire northern frontier.

Maryland, and now and then Carolina, also demanded a share of Nicholson's attention as likely sources of disturbance. Virginia authorities, backed by the home government, always assumed a sort of guardianship over these provinces, and in the case of Maryland this now seemed the more necessary because the royal governor had not yet arrived and because John Coode charged certain Virginians with giving aid and comfort to the supporters of Lord Baltimore and for that reason with harboring treasonable sentiments toward William and Mary.[3] In addition to affairs of this nature, Nicholson and the council were active in enforcing the requirement of the home government that the Virginia and Maryland fleet should sail only under convoy and, therefore, at a time fixed in advance. This also necessitated correspondence with the province on the Chesapeake,[4] as well as with the places along the rivers of Virginia where ships regularly took on their cargoes of tobacco.

Early in the summer of 1692 Nicholson, in the course of

---

[1] As to the source whence peril from Indians came to the Virginia frontier, see Osgood, *op. cit.*, II, 422, III, 258 *et seq.*

[2] Cal. St. P. Col. 1689–1692, 280, 308.

[3] *Ibid.*, 267, 309.

[4] *Ibid.*, 300, 302.

one of his tours,[1] spent two days with Governor Copley in Maryland, and met certain members of its legislature. In consequence of what was told him there of the appearance of strange Indians on the upper Potomac, he also visited that region and joined with the people there, as elsewhere, in the expression of the hope that the two provinces, now both under royal government, might cooperate on all occasions. This was suggestive of local alignments which were sure to arise as the colonies were growing into one system, but from the nature of the case these must be free and consequently fluctuating. On his return to Jamestown, Nicholson attended to the dispatch of the fleet, using his influence also to promote tobacco culture and check the tendency toward manufactures.

The Pamunkey lands and the Northern Neck also received attention. The Pamunkey Indians had become so few that it was felt that their former territory should be opened for settlement, while the partial alienation of the Northern Neck from Virginia rankled in the minds of all. This question was now forced again upon the public attention by the return of Philip Ludwell from England as agent for Lord Culpeper's heirs,[2] and his setting up various offices there and asserting territorial claims to the great alarm and disturbance of settlers. This led the governor and council to restrain his activities as they were able, but especially to send another appeal to the home government that the Northern Neck might be fully reunited with Virginia. When, early in August, Nicholson wrote his first letter to the lords of trade,[3] accompanied with its inclosures of proofs so characteristic of his correspondence, he reviewed these activities and gave the impressions which resulted therefrom. He found the militia, because of their poverty, not so well armed or disciplined as present circumstances required. He had seen some of the places called forts but did not think they deserved the name,

---

[1] Cal. St. P. Col. 1689–1693, p. 674. The position which Nicholson held as a trustee of William and Mary College continued later to give him occasions for visiting Virginia and of thus keeping up a connection with its affairs. Cal. St. P. Col. 1696–1697, p. 466.

[2] Ibid., 335, 421. The fact that Ludwell had also been appointed governor of Carolina gives added proof of the success of his visit to England, which was made for the purpose of submitting charges against Lord Howard of Effingham.

Ibid., 308.

and as to the frontier settlements, they were not defensible and he wished that the forming of others might be forbidden, — an opinion which many British officials shared, thus placing themselves in opposition to the naturally adventurous spirit of the prospector and squatter. Judging from all he heard, there was no prospect of concerted action among the colonies along the northern frontier against the French and Indians, while New York was in great disorder. He stood ready to aid them, if Virginia could be induced to do it, and desired orders from England as to whether this should take the form of men or money. Under the circumstances it was natural that he should express a desire for the establishment of a post route between Virginia and New England, so that some improvement might be made on the tedious and costly service of special messengers.[1] Andrew Hamilton's deputation as postmaster was recorded, and a proclamation was issued giving Neale the right to establish ferries on all waters in Virginia where the power to do so had not already been granted away. In the spring of 1692/3 the Virginia assembly passed an act for the encouragement of a post office in that province, specifying rates of postage and making other regulations. In the end also the regulation of ferries remained in the hands of the assembly and did not pass to the postmaster.

Nicholson regarded the settlement of Maryland affairs as especially desirable, because the customs were almost surely being defrauded there and because of the need of united action against the common enemy. As to Virginia itself, he begged that a further supply of arms and ammunition might be sent from England. For the protection of the shipping he repeated the futile suggestion that there should be a good fort or two on each of the four rivers, but he realized that Virginia was not financially able to build them. Frigates and a fire-ship — a poor reliance — must therefore be depended on for the immediate defence of both Virginia and Maryland.

During the autumn and winter of 1690/1 the governor and council continued their activity along these lines. In order to secure a clearer understanding of conditions on the northern

---

[1] A response favorable to the same came in the issue of the patent to Thomas Neale, and the appointment of a deputy postmaster of Virginia. Cal. St. P. Col. 1693–1696, pp. 4, 109, 637.

frontier, depositions of various masters of vessels who had visited it were taken, and these set forth the dangers to which it was exposed since the failure of Phips' expedition. The commanders of the forces which were now kept near the limits of settlement on the four great rivers [1] and who had been in active service at least since Cuthbert Potter's return, were ordered to appoint an officer and eleven whites and two Indians to range from river to river once a week till further order. Provision was also made for the rapid spread of alarms from county to county in case of an Indian attack. Orders were issued for watching the coast in Lower Norfolk county and on the Eastern Shore. Copies of these orders concerning ranging were sent to North Carolina and Maryland. Nicholson was anxiously looking for the dispatch of a royal governor to Pennsylvania, for he suspected, though quite incorrectly, that they might be in correspondence with the French.[2]

In all important matters the governor had to act in cooperation with the council and, as we know, that body was a very important factor in Virginia government. In aristocratic character and permanence of tenure it was similar to the council of New York. Three generations of the Byrd family occupied seats in the council, and held other offices, from 1670 to 1775. Generation after generation the leading families of the council intermarried, and from every point of view they formed a powerful and well compacted clique. Good behavior, which generally meant life, was the limit of tenure of councillors. The body usually numbered twelve. They drew handsome salaries, not only as councillors, but as members of the general court and for attendance on courts of oyer and terminer. Many other sources of income, connected with government, were also available for them. The facility with which members of the council could be gotten together was a serious question, especially in time of war. If it was necessary to summon them in winter, not more than

---

[1] Cal. St. P. Col. 1689–92, pp. 255, 300, 334, 379. In July, 1690, the militia act of 1684 was ordered to be strictly enforced. See Hening, III, 47, 83.

[2] Here we have a suggestion of the prevalent opinion that Quakers were Jacobites, because they would not take the oath. See Cal. p. 390, for vigorous orders of Nicholson and the council as to trade, desertion of seamen and conduct of Carolina officials. Also p. 394, after arrival of Lord Howard's commission and instructions.

three or four could meet. They lived on different necks and often in winter eight or ten days might pass before the rivers would be passable. Colonels Lee and Allerton lived nearly 100 miles away. Custis was on the Eastern Shore. Nearly all of the others had at least one river to cross in order to reach Jamestown. It was desirable that councillors should come from all sections of the province, but Nicholson urged that a sufficient number to make a quorum should be appointed from among the residents on the same neck with the capital; especially should this be the case in time of war. Soon after this Edward Hill and Henry Whiting were sworn in as councillors, their appointment having accompanied the issue of a new commission to Lord Howard as non-resident governor.[1]

Five years had now elapsed since the meeting of a legislature in Virginia which had passed any laws. As the last acts providing for a public levy had been passed in 1686 and the impost duty on liquors of that year was to continue only to 1689, it is hard to see what, except the quit rents, the province could for some time have relied on for meeting the public charges.[2] And yet the minutes of the council record the fact that government was regularly carried on and new expenditures for defence and other objects were met as they arose. This shows how large was still the discretion of the Virginia executive. Although among the standing committees of the house of burgesses was a committee of claims, upon whose reports the supply bills were based, it does not appear that the control of the governor and the council over expenditure was as yet strictly limited. The fiscal system of Virginia was substantially as undeveloped as it had been before Bacon's rebellion.[3] The poll tax, or levy by tithables, was still the chief source of revenue from which parish, county and provincial expenditures were met. At the time of which we are now speaking the indirect taxes were an export duty of

---

[1] *Ibid.*, 394. See p. 434 for Lord Howard's views on important questions.

[2] And yet the committee, in the assembly of 1691, for the examination of the duty on liquors of 3d. per gal., reported the balance on hand from that source to be £789 and the balance due £950. *Ibid.*, 420.

[3] Osgood, *op. cit.*, III, 90, and later references; Bruce, *op. cit.*, II, 534 *et seq.*; Cal. St. P. Col. 1689–1693, pp. 575, 671 *et seq.*; Hartwell, Chilton and Blair, State of Virginia, 1 Massachusetts Historical Colls. V, 154 *et seq.*

two shillings per hogshead on tobacco and an import duty on liquors made necessary by the war as a rather permanent source of revenue. The quit rents — with the exception of those from the Northern Neck — and the small amount of revenue collected under the trade act of 1673 should have gone into the imperial exchequer, but the king had already granted that the quit rents should be used for provincial purposes. Payment of these was required to be made in money, and was collected in that form so far as possible. It was from accumulations in the treasury derived from quit rents, if from any source, that advances must be made for aiding the northern colonies in the war or for other similar purposes. With a view to the possibility of such action, it was fortunate that the governor and council had complete control over the revenue from quit rents and, subject to the approval of the crown, could use it as they chose. It amounted to about £800 a year. The revenue from other sources was subject to appropriation by the assembly and its amount was fixed with a view to meeting the ordinary expenditures of the province in time of peace or such measures of defence as were strictly Virginian.

In April, 1691, Nicholson met his assembly in its first session.[1] The appointment of the clerk of burgesses was still in the hands of the governor, though the demand continued to be made that it be restored to the house as one of its ancient privileges. But in this the house was not successful and the appointment of its clerk remained in the hands of the governor and council throughout the colonial period.[2] The burgesses consisted of two representatives from each county and one from Jamestown.[3] Much of the business of the house was done through standing committees, of which the most important at this time were those on claims, elections, and grievances. Other committees at later times were concerned

[1] Cal. St. P. Col. 1689–1693, p. 411 *et seq.;* State of Virginia, *op. cit.,* 147; Bruce, *op. cit.,* II, 478.

[2] Cal. St. P. Col. 1693–1696, pp. 38, 44; J. of Burgesses, 1660–1693, pp. 333, 416 *et seq.;* Miller, The Legislature of Virginia, C. U. Studies, 83, 84; Flippen, *op. cit.*

[3] In or about 1705 William and Mary College received separate representation, as did Williamsburg and Norfolk at later dates. After the removal of the capital to Williamsburg, Jamestown became a "rotten borough," most of the island being owned by two families. Miller, *op. cit.,* 44.

with courts of justice, trade, religion and morals and private causes. The committee on claims was, in a way, a survival of the effort of the house to draw judicial appeals to itself and thus become the supreme court of the province. This practice had been brought to an end by an order of the king in 1683.[1] Local and popular complaints found utterance on the floor of the house through the committee on propositions and grievances and from it proceeded very many of the bills which originated in the house itself. According to a contemporary authority, " To know the pressures, business, common talk and designs of the people of that country, perhaps there is no better way than to peruse the journals of the house of burgesses and of the committee of grievances and propositions." During the session of which we are now speaking this committee introduced half a dozen bills or more relating to various local and purely provincial matters. As agreed on in the council the only important measures recommended in the governor's speech were the laying of an import duty on liquors and the regulation of the Indian trade. The object of the former of these was to relieve the inhabitants to an extent from the levy by poll tax and again slightly diversify the fiscal system. This course of policy had been urged since Bacon's rebellion, and the questions which now appear were an inheritance from the previous period.

The assembly was in session more than a month and many important subjects were discussed. Conference committees were freely appointed and the council amended money bills [2] and, as we have seen, initiated them. Twenty statutes were passed.[3] Among these one for an impost on liquors and an elaborate act for the establishment of ports and for better securing the customs occasioned the passage of still a third law, by which the office of treasurer was made elective by the general assembly and Colonel Edward Hill was designated as its first incumbent. He was to receive and keep the revenues arising under the above acts, until he was required by warrant to pay it out for purposes specified by law.[4] As the book

[1] Miller, *op. cit.*, 170.

[2] Cal. St. P. Col. 1689–1693, p. 451.

[3] *Ibid.*, 455; Hening, III, 42–97.

[4] *Ibid.*, 93, 197, 476, 495; Blair, Hartwell and Chilton, Present State of Virginia.

of claims, consisting of specific sums due from the province,
formed the basis of supply bills, had this office been permanent, it would have secured for the burgesses a pretty effective control over expenditures. But the office was temporary
and limited in its scope and, though occasionally brought
into existence again by later enactments, it never became a
permanent part of the fiscal system of Virginia. The discretion of the executive in the matter of expenditures therefore remained large in the province.

As to Indian trade, Nicholson had been asking for instructions from England and had expressed an opinion[1] in favor
of the formation of a company, through which a fund might
be raised to carry on the trade and check incursions. But
this met with no response and the assembly passed a brief
act declaring the Indian trade open to all and at all times
and places and repealing former restraints upon the trade.
But this sweeping concession to the spirit of the frontier was
qualified by a provision that none should go on remote hunting excursions without a license. The governor's plan for the
employment of bodies of rangers between the upper courses
of the rivers was embodied in law.

The views of this assembly and of Virginia at the time on
important questions were set forth in several addresses to the
British government, which were supported by the representations of the agents, Jeffrey Jeffreys and James Blair.[2] These
related to the need of abolishing the special jurisdiction in the
Northern Neck and at the same time of getting rid of the disorders which existed in the office of surveyor general. A
confirmation of all existing privileges of the province, as embodied partly in the charters to the London Company and
also in the grant of 1675, was requested by both council and
burgesses. The general desire was that the crown should
make no more grants of land in the province without definite
knowledge that they would not be prejudicial to it. The
burgesses also insisted that the sole right of the general assembly to vote taxes should be confirmed, also the former
method of allowing appeals from the general court to the

[1] Cal. St. P. Col. 1689–1692, p. 381;  Hening, III, 69, 82.
[2] Cal. St. P. Col. 1689–1692, pp. 421, 452, 454, 576;  J. of B., *ibid.*, 371, 373, 375.

general assembly.[1] Blair went fully instructed as to the charter and contributions which were desired for the college, while Jeffreys, somewhat later, presented a memorial setting forth how the low price of tobacco reduced the meagre support of the Virginia clergy and caused good men to leave the province and others to refuse to come.

In transmitting the proceedings of the assembly, Nicholson [2] dwelt most at length on the act to revive a law of 1682, for the encouragement of manufactures in Virginia for three years, for it seemed to threaten the supremacy of tobacco culture and to indicate that the manufacture of cloth might grow to a dangerous extent. The passage of the act was due to the failure of a supply of European goods which was adequate to the needs of the province, and this of course was caused by the partial suspension of trade on account of the war. Nicholson estimated that at least thirty ships ought to trade to and from Virginia during the coming year to keep up the spirits of the people. He feared disturbances and a development of the mob spirit if their comfort and prosperity were not secured and if the examples of misgovernment in neighboring colonies were not removed. As winter approached, the governor wrote again that the people felt the need of clothing and hoped that a strong fleet would bring a supply and take away their tobacco.

As soon as the port act and the act concerning hemp reached England, they were sent to the treasury and in March, 1691/2, the customs board reported adversely on both of them.[3] To the port act they objected, as had been done before, that it required the landing of goods and loading of vessels at places where for a long time there could be no conveniences for the purpose. The act also included unrelated provisions for specific export duties on hides and furs, which it was believed amounted to 20% of their value. This the board believed was three times as high as the trade would bear. But as the object of this feature was stated to be to secure a perma-

---

[1] Cal. St. P. Col. 1689–1692, pp. 551, 611.

[2] Cal. St. P. Col. 1689–1692, pp. 473, 569. Hening, III, 50. This was an act for the encouragement of the production of flax and hemp, the term manufacture being used to cover production of that kind.

[3] See Hartwell, etc., Present State of Virginia (1 Mass. Hist. Soc. Colls. V, 139, 150).

nent support for the ministry, the board suggested that 7½% should be fixed as the rate of duty. The act, however, should be repealed, another passed and the new governor should be instructed to have wharves and quays built. In the other act the board objected to a provision that debts might be paid partly in products of the country other than tobacco and also to clauses which unduly favored debtors and were in the nature of a stay law which they thought would ruin the credit of Virginians with British merchants and so injuriously affect British trade itself. The lords of trade recommended that both of the acts be referred back to Virginia for amendment.[1] Early in 1693 the port act was indefinitely suspended by the legislature itself, and more than a decade passed before another law on that subject was enacted. As the act concerning manufactures was temporary, nothing further relating to it seems to have been done, except the passage in 1693 of a temporary measure to encourage the production of linen cloth.

The custom of biennial sessions of the assembly was now being gradually established in Virginia, though in practice there were always many exceptions to the rule. Sometimes the governors still prorogued the assembly beyond the biennial period, and again the house met much oftener than once in two years. In the autumn of 1693 an election was held for a new assembly, while at about the same time it became necessary for Andros, according to his commission, to visit Maryland in order to regulate the government and maintain order there after the death of Governor Copley. When the new assembly met,[2] the subjects which had received attention in the previous session again came up for consideration, but no change of policy in regard to them is noticeable. A site was selected for the college and the surveying and open-

---

[1] Cal. St. P. Col., 1689–1692, p. 661; Hening, III, 108, 121, 404.

[2] *Ibid.*, 1693–1696, p. 184 *et seq.*; J. of B., *ibid.*, 449 *et seq.* For the conditions of suffrage at this time and later, see Miller, *op. cit.*, 62; also McKinley, Suffrage Franchise in the Colonies, Pubs. of U. of Pa. In the monographs of Miller and Flippen, with Bruce's Institutional History of Virginia, will be found all the facts about the organization and procedure of the burgesses in the eighteenth century which will ordinarily be needed. Details may be greatly multiplied by the use of the excellent introductions to the published volumes of the Journals of the Burgesses, the final resort, of course, being the text of the Journal itself.

ing of its lands to settlement were brought under discussion. A committee on revision of the laws was appointed and many statutes were passed in review. In Virginia, as in some of the other colonies, this was done periodically, not so much on the initiative of the colonists themselves, as under the stress of a royal instruction to their governors to send to England a complete body of their laws with opinions as to the action which ought to be taken on them. In common with them, and owing to the scarcity of able lawyers, Virginia statutes were often imperfectly drawn and later were patched up and mended by subsequent laws. " By this means the body of their laws is now become not only long and confused, but it is a very hard matter to know what laws are in force and what not." [1] " Their laws want revisal, not only to bring them into a good order and method, but in order to the paring away several of them that seem inconsistent with law and equity." [2] " For remedy whereof several of their General Assemblies have entered upon an useful design of the revisal of their laws; but that work is so great, and their other avocations so many, that they could never yet bring it to any perfection; and till this work is finished most of their laws are like to remain without applying for the royal assent." In this quotation the status of the laws and their revision as it was at the close of 1697 is described, and the condition was to remain the same for many a year to come.

The next assembly met in the spring of 1695. Many subjects of importance were considered, to which reference elsewhere has been made — the Northern Neck, ports, manufactures, the size of tobacco hogsheads and the export of tobacco in bulk, revenue, the sending of aid to New York, the continuance of the rangers at the heads of the rivers, salaries of the clergy, besides many purely local subjects, as the dividing of counties, roads, pounds and the restraint of hogs in James City. Conference committees frequently met; addresses and replies were drawn. But, notwithstanding the discussion,

[1] Hartwell, Blair and Chilton, *op. cit.*, 148. Cal. St. P. Col., 1696–1697, p. 595. An instruction on this subject relating to Virginia had first been given to Lord Howard of Effingham.

[2] These were chiefly stay laws and legislation in general that was favorable to debtors. An act belonging to this class was cited by the authors as an example.

only a few laws, and those mostly of a routine nature, were passed.[1] In the preparation of the bill for the continuance of the rangers at the heads of the rivers the council desired that the appropriation be taken out of the impost on liquors, but the burgesses carried the point against them and it was provided for in the levy by poll.[2] It was not till after this decision was reached that the amount of the impost on liquors was fixed and that bill was passed.

In view of the many important questions which were under consideration, the burgesses urged Andros and the council to join with them in an address [3] to the crown which should so describe the state of Virginia as to secure a favorable consideration of their proceedings. On May 16 an address to the crown was read in the house setting forth the poverty of Virginia, the cost of defending the frontiers, its readiness, if possible, to obey requisitions, but praying that they be not imposed on the province in the future. This was approved and sent to the council for concurrence. Complaints from the inhabitants of the Northern Neck occasioned also the drafting of an address to the king for a new charter while in another address the history of this grant was reviewed and the evils of divergent practices as to land in different parts of the province were explained. The council now urged that the three addresses be combined in one, with a memorial for each grievance, but to this the burgesses objected, and what was finally done, except the dispatch of letters by the governor and secretary, does not appear.[4]

The spring session of 1696 resulted in no legislation, while the most important act of the fall session of that year, as will appear later, was one increasing the allowance to the clergy.

Beginning in November, 1690, and continuing during a large part of every year thereafter as long as the war lasted,[5] a small guard of men — usually one officer and eleven privates — was kept on the upper waters of each of the four large rivers of Virginia. This was a continuation of the mode

[1] Hening, III, 126 et seq.
[2] Cal. St. P. Col. 1693–1696, p. 480. Hening, III, 129, 135. J. of B., 1695–1702, p. 37.
[3] Ibid., pp. 466, 467, 472, 480.
[4] Ibid., 496, 499.          [5] Cal. St. P. Col. 1689–1692, p. 334.

of defence against Indian raids which had been in vogue in
the past. Its cost, even when added to what was spent upon
the militia at large and on the repair of the small defences
along the coast and lower courses of the rivers, was very
light as compared with the sums which the war cost the
northern colonies that were directly concerned. To this, however, should be added the loss which the trade of the tobacco
colonies suffered from embargoes and other causes connected
with the war in Europe. But the controlling fact, overbalan-
cing all the disadvantages of the time, was this, that Virginia,
Maryland and the colonies on the Delaware remained at
peace throughout the early and middle stages of the struggle
with the French. Yet, when, in 1693, the demand came from
New York for aid, backed by a requisition from England,
the burgesses pleaded as excuses for their refusal the cost of
defending the heads of the rivers and the claim that New York
was not a protection to Virginia and could never hinder the
enemy from attacking her.[2]  On the coast Virginia was quite
as much exposed as was New York and it was claimed that it
would not do to reduce her supply of men for possible action
in that quarter. The governor and council, however, directed
the auditor to furnish £600 to New York.

When, in the spring of 1695, the question was again brought
up the burgesses took the same ground, insisting that Virginia
had always borne its own charges without assistance from outside and preferred now to be its own defence. But the council
took the opposite ground, stating that the expenses of Virginia for inland defence were inconsiderable when compared
with the sums spent by New York and New England. They
also insisted upon the binding force of a royal requisition and
upon the moral obligations of the colonies to assist [2] one another. This, they insisted, was a national war, and all the
provinces stood mutually obligated to defence and protection,
as would the counties of England in a similar crisis. The
fact that this reasoning produced so little effect proves that
the analogy was true only in name and not in fact. At an
earlier meeting of the council in executive session it had resolved that, if a quota was applied for, vessels, provisions and

---

[1] *Ibid.*, 1693–1696, pp. 203, 224, 227.
[2] *Ibid.*, 436, 466–467.

necessities should be sent with the men. In legislative session it recommended that a levy be raised by poll or by a duty on liquors to meet the expense. Though the burgesses still repeated their arguments, and asked that such orders be not repeated, they appropriated £500 for New York and the bill was duly passed.[1] But in notifying the lords of the grant the secretary of Virginia repeated the statements of the burgesses, declaring that the revenue of the province was not sufficient to pay its contingent charges, much less to render assistance outside. About a month later on further application from New York,[2] the council ordered that 250 men be sent thither and the governor wrote promising that the quota should be sent by the first of the next May. But before the time came when military operations might begin a letter came from the king directing that money might be paid instead of dispatching men.[3] Thereupon £1000, New York money, was sent, that being in excess of the £500 which had been appropriated by the assembly. The burgesses, however, persisted in the opinion that Virginia could not afford this expenditure. But the governor and council were able to order it because they had the royal quit rents to fall back upon, and it was to the account of the quit rents that all, or nearly all, of these expenditures were finally charged. The requirement for quotas of money, though not of men, in aid of New York was continued until the close of the war,[4] but it does not appear that any more appropriations were made for this purpose by the assembly.

The question of the founding of a college, which was so strongly urged by Blair, and to the support of which the assembly committed itself in 1691,[5] had a financial bearing which was not without importance. As agent to England on

[1] Hening, III, 132. Cal. St. P. Col. 1693–1696, pp. 466–7, 482, 495, 496, 499.
[2] Ibid., 546, 561.
[3] Ibid., 635, 636, 672–675 Cal. St. P. Col. 1696–7, pp. 1, 26. This amounted to £769/4/6 sterling. According to a statement sent by Fletcher from New York, the amount which Virginia had sent to her assistance from 1691 to 1694 was £1560. See Cal. St. P. Col. 1693–1696, p. 293, for a memorandum on the revenue of Virginia as it stood in June, 1694.
[4] Ibid., 464.
[5] Cal. St. P. Col. 1689–1692, pp. 452, 575, 671; ibid., 1693–1696, p. 154; Hartwell, Chilton and Blair, op cit., 164 et seq. A fuller account of provision for the support of the college will be found in a later chapter.

behalf of this enterprise Blair was instructed to secure a charter for its incorporation and leave to collect donations for it. This memorial was also accompanied by another in which, owing to the fall in price of tobacco, an increase in salaries of the Virginia clergy was requested. Blathwayt, the auditor general, and the commissioners of the customs reported. Though adverse reports were made on several important points relating to the proposals for the support of the college, a charter which embodied most of them, was granted. With the support thus obtained, added to such subscriptions as could be procured, efforts were made to proceed with the actual work of building the college at Middle Plantation. But Andros did not prove so active in its support as was Nicholson and after a time Blair and his friends began to complain that he was hindering the payment of subscriptions and obstructing the surveys of the tract of land which had been granted to the college.

The clergy also had been for some time complaining of the inadequacy of their support. This was one among several grievances which, as we shall see, were chronic with them in both Maryland and Virginia. The low price of tobacco at the time gave special emphasis to their complaints, for they were paid in fixed amounts annually. They also said that the price at which the tobacco was rated for them was much higher than the market prices.[1] It was due to irritation caused by these grievances combined with the stubborn assertiveness of Blair and the equally obstinate reserve of Andros, that the quarrel developed. Andros had the support of the council, for it believed with him that the clergy were in comfortable circumstances and would rank well with the planters who each possessed a dozen servants. In the fall session of 1696 the long discussion was ended for the time by the passage of an act which increased the salary of the clergy to 16,000 lbs. of tobacco each and made special provision for its collection, as well as for the purchase of glebes in the parishes.

But before this was done occurred the break between the governor and the commissary. At the close of Nicholson's

---

[1] Cal. St. P. Col., 1693–1696, p. 466; *Ibid.*, 1696–1697, pp. 461 *et seq.;* Hartwell, Chilton and Blair, *op cit.*, 163; Hening, III, 151.

administration Blair seems to have taken some credit for his transfer to Maryland.[1] The process of founding the college and of administering church affairs in general under Andros led in the spring of 1695 [2] to an open quarrel between the commissary and that governor. It came to an outbreak when Andros, on application of the church wardens, designated a minister to preach in the church at Jamestown during Blair's illness and, it was said, with his consent. But for some reason the commissary had made such severe reflections on the government that the case was brought before the council, of which he was a member. Blair asserted that neither the governor nor the king had the right to appoint a minister to preach, that it was sufficient if ministers produced their orders before him and not before the governor, and that he found Andros so cautious or reserved that he knew not how to discourse him. The governor declared that he bore with Blair's restless conduct until the council voted unanimously that he ought not to sit longer at the board and he was accordingly suspended. Before the close of the year, however, the king ordered Blair's restoration to the council until it should appear that he had justly forfeited the good opinion of the monarch, but he did not resume his place till nearly a year later.[3]

No sooner had Blair taken his seat again than the friction between him and the governor reappeared.[4] Blair proposed a bill to facilitate donations to the college, which was found irregular. A paper by him relating to the college was read, which later he withdrew by permission. The governor, a few days later, read a letter in council from the bishop of London in which it was stated or implied that the clergy of Virginia were oppressed, that the bill for increasing their allowance had been dropped in the council, and the assembly, which had seemed favorable to it, had been dissolved. Andros complained, in language which Blair described as unwarrantably harsh, that he had been misrepresented in England. In this he had the full support of the council, though in the

---

[1] Cal. St. P. Col. 1693–1696, p. 69.
[2] Ibid., pp. 465, 497, 499, 616.
[3] Ibid., 1696–1697, pp. 68, 145.
[4] Ibid.; see Index under Blair, p. 682.

opinion of the commissary both governor and council were indifferent to the welfare of the clergy. This was in October, 1696, and affairs now drifted on until the following February.

When the act of trade of 1696 arrived Blair desired the opinion of the council on the question whether, as a native of Scotland, he was now disabled from sitting as a judge in the general court. Their opinion was that he came within the prohibitive terms of the act.[1] This only furnished him with an additional reason for going to England, in order to present the alleged grievances of the clergy and friends of the college against the governor. In anticipation of the charges Andros and the council wrote in defence of their policy and the governor expressed the hope that he would not be blamed unheard. In August, 1697, Blair had arrived in London and gave testimony before the board of trade in reference to the price of tobacco as bearing on quit rents, and the pay of the clergy in Virginia. Henry Hartwell was also in London, but was prevented by illness from appearing at that time before the board. Queries, however, were sent to him which drew out answers on a great variety of matters relating to Virginia,[2] while a letter was sent by the board to Andros complaining that the information he had sent them and the replies he had given to their queries had been inadequate.[3] Presently also Edward Chilton attended the board and gave information concerning the engrossing of land in Virginia and other matters.[4] Three men were now available in England and through them information could be obtained concerning Virginia which would not bear the distinctive stamp of the governor and council. The result was that, at its request, their views were soon to be laid before the board in elaborated form.[5] This was the origin of the well known pamphlet which was later issued by the three authors jointly under the title of " The Present State of Virginia."

If one compares this pamphlet and the replies which preceded it, by means of which the board of trade sought to penetrate further behind the scene in Virginia, with the color-

---

[1] *Ibid.*, 454, 461, 466.  [2] *Ibid.*, 594, 602, 606–610.
[3] The replies of Andros to queries of the board are in *ibid.*, 455–458.
[4] *Ibid.*, 615.  [5] *Ibid.*, 628, 641–666.

less and official statements of the governor and council, important differences will appear. Though it is impossible to tell what were the shares borne by the three authors in their joint production one would infer from Hartwell's replies to the queries of the board of trade and from the known character and ability of Blair that they bore the chief share in the writing of the pamphlet. The view of Virginia which they presented was to the general effect that the exclusive devotion of its planters and people to tobacco culture and the resulting system of large plantations was an evil, as a result of which it was very imperfectly settled, crude and unkempt, and its great natural advantages for varied forms of agriculture and for mining were being allowed to go to waste. A most important social result of this was the inability of the province to develop towns with their markets and other facilities for local and general trade. The people lived in isolation, did not know what towns were and were averse to cohabitation. Those who hitherto had sought by legislation to encourage the development of towns had overshot the mark by attempting to create too many of them. Maryland had suggested the better plan by seeking to found only one town on either shore. In Virginia two or three towns, in the opinion of the writers, would be enough at first. In the development of this feature so much needed in Virginia life the king, supported by a strong governor, must lead, for little was to be expected from the people.

Another great obstacle to the proper growth of the colony was the want of money, and the consequent use of tobacco as a medium of exchange. The governor was charged with encouraging this, for he received much of his salary in bills of exchange payable in England, and for what he wanted to expend in Virginia he could buy cheaper for quit rent tobacco than for money. This was followed by an argument in favor of the establishment of a common standard of value in the plantations, a suggestion which before many years was to be followed by legislation concerning the so-called proclamation money.

Unjustifiable speculation in head-rights was also dwelt upon as another potent cause of the system of large estates and, what was worse, of the tying up of land so as to keep it indefinitely out of the hands of actual settlers. To this evil the ignorance and knavery of surveyors had contributed, supported by the selfish interests of the masters and seamen of vessels which brought in immigrants, the provincial government conniving at the whole on the pretense that in this way the king's land was being thrown open to the people. But really a meagre revenue from the quit rents from unsettled lands was the only return, where otherwise ample income from the staple product might be enjoyed.

Coming to the political system, the account which the writers gave was to the effect that the governor was an autocrat; the members of the council simply heard his policies and opinions, and directly or through them as local justices and members of the general court, or in other capacities, he was able to control the entire government of the province. This was facilitated by the relatively few provincial offices, by the wide jurisdiction of the general court, and by the general mingling or confusion of functions among officials.[1] Through his right of appointing its clerk, his other well known powers over it, and the fact that the council constituted the upper house, the governor could make such an interest among the burgesses as at least to prevent effective opposition. There were also many offices in the governor's gift, for the holding of which burgesses or their relatives were ambitious, and in that way, too, pressure could be brought to bear. Men who complained to the king against the governor, if office holders, were likely to lose their places. Various influences were also used to prevent petitions from being heard or acted on. The house, moreover, did not have the complete control over either revenue or expenditure which — they might have said — under the influence of war it was gaining in other provinces. This passage which certainly overlooks many facts may reflect Blair's prejudice against Andros.

Coming, finally, to the affairs of the church, the evils which resulted from the insecure tenure of the ministers and from the general failure to provide them with glebes or to keep in repair their residences received due comment, and to the many restrictions of these and other kinds which lay

---

[1] Benjamin Harrison well expressed this aspect of the situation in a memorial to the board of trade in 1698. Cal. St. P. Col. 1697–1698, p. 330.

upon them was attributed the fact that Virginia was so poorly supplied with clergy.

The few remaining months of Andros' administration in Virginia passed without important incident or change. In May, 1698, his resignation was received by the crown and steps were taken to appoint Nicholson in his place. Peace meantime was concluded in Europe and duly proclaimed. No steps were taken by British authorities to profit by the criticisms of Blair and his associates and Virginia passed into another century with her social and political system practically unchanged. With the beginning of 1699 Andros closed his official career in Virginia and with it his active life.

# CHAPTER XI

UNLIKE Virginia, Maryland had just passed through a revolution which had resulted in the withdrawal of powers of government from the Calvert family, though they retained their customary rights over the land and territorial revenue of the province. Maryland consequently was in a state of more or less agitation. Disturbances of the peace within its borders were looked for by its southern neighbor, and though little of that nature occurred, a few of the old revolutionists caused some additional trouble before many years had passed. Because of the number and variety of its dissenters religious issues had always been prominent in Maryland. The overthrow of the Calverts was a severe blow to the Catholics and was to place the Anglicans, officially at least, in the lead in the province. But the Quakers were numerous and active and Puritans were intrenched in Ann Arundel county, though as a sect they appear no more distinctly in the events of the succeeding period than did the Presbyterians and Independents at the same time in England. In accordance with the ideas of the time, the establishment of the English Church, which is elsewhere described, was considered to be a necessary means of maintaining its lead and of supporting the royal government in a province where there were so many dissenters. The extension of royal power and of Anglicanism in the colonies went hand in hand at this period, as in modern times it had always done in England, and in a province with a population like that of Maryland this would necessarily keep religious issues and controversies somewhat to the front. Like New Jersey and Connecticut, Maryland was relatively protected both on the frontier and toward the sea, and did not need the attention to defence which was imperative in other colonies.

Maryland now became one of those half-way royal provinces, like New Jersey a decade later, in which the territorial jurisdiction of the proprietor survived — the crown did not possess control over the quit rents — and one-half of the export duty on tobacco went to the proprietor. For all fiscal purposes, therefore, and especially for the prosecution of war, the royal government was restricted to an important degree. It was not able to command the resources of the province even to the extent which was possible in Virginia. Moreover, when laws were passed or acts of government performed which affected land and the proprietary revenue in any form, the Calverts would be stirred to activity, more often to criticize and obstruct than to further the policy of the government. Immigration into the province and the extension of settlement also closely affected them and was in turn influenced by their attitude. Indian relations were involved with these lines of policy and were affected by everything which determined the course of surveys and land purchases. All of these considerations show how unique was the position of Maryland, even when compared with Virginia, with which in its location and economic system it had so much in common.

Early in 1691 Lionel Copley [1] was selected in England, as a loyal and active supporter of William and Mary, to be the governor of Maryland. His commission and instructions were issued during the summer of that year.[2] Francis Nicholson, already lieutenant governor of Virginia, had been appointed the previous February to the same office in Maryland, with full authority to exercise the powers of Copley's commission and instructions in case of the latter's death. In March of the same year Sir Edmund Andros was also given authority to act as commander-in-chief in Maryland, in case of the death of Nicholson and absence of Copley.[3] These precautions indicate the solicitude of the home government lest Maryland should be left without a royal governor and the policy also that a neighboring royal province should exercise supervision over a chartered colony, especially if it had been recently the scene of disturbances and unrest.

---

[1] One Thomas Copley had been a prominent and wealthy inhabitant of Maryland in the days of Giles Brent. Md. Hist. Mag. I, 125, 135.
[2] Md. Arch. Council, 1688–1693, pp. 204, 263–271.    [3] Ibid., 300.

The informality and possibly the temporary character of the transfer of government to the crown — it being partly a war measure — was indicated in the preamble to Copley's commission. In the instructions the articles which were made necessary by special conditions in Maryland provided that the half of the revenue accruing to the government from the export duty of 2s. per hogshead, which since 1679 had been levied on tobacco, should be taken in part by the governor toward his salary and in part used for keeping the province stocked with arms and ammunition. The other moiety of this impost, together with the revenue from the tonnage duty on vessels trading to Maryland, Lord Baltimore should be permitted to collect for his own use. The revenue arising from the export duty on tobacco during the period between the meeting of the late Convention and Copley's arrival was reported to the lords of trade and the treasury board and, from this, £600 was ordered paid to Copley and a part was spent for arms and ammunition.[1]

Governor Copley entered upon office in Maryland early in April, 1691. In England by careful inquiry a list of councillors had been prepared which contained the names of substantial property holders of whose fidelity to the cause of the Revolution there was thought to be no reasonable doubt. Among its members[2] Blakiston, Jowles, Greenberry and Coates were taken from among the supporters of the uprising in Maryland. Brooke and Frisby were taken from a list submitted by Lord Baltimore, and the latter at a subsequent time made trouble for the government. The governor, with nearly all whose names appeared in the list of councillors, constituted the provincial court. One of the first matters which came before the governor and council was the disposition which should be made of Nicholas Sewall and the two prisoners who were held on the charge of complicity in the murder of John Payne, the customs collector. Sewall was a virtual exile in Virginia and the other two were under sentence of death. Sewall was allowed to go free under a bond

---

[1] Cal. St. P. Col. 1689–1693, p. 563; Md. Arch. Council, 1688–1693. pp. 281, 285–292.

[2] Cal. St. P. Col. 1689–1693, pp. 527, 543–4, 669; Md. Arch. Council, 1688–1693, p. 282 *et seq.*

of £500 and was never thereafter molested. The other two
were kept in prison until 1694, when their case was carefully considered by the assembly, with the advice of lawyers,
and they were released under heavy bail and were finally pardoned by the king.[1]

Henry Darnall was appointed by Lord Baltimore as his
agent and the receiver of his dues, as he had been for several
years before the Revolution.[2] A royal letter was issued on
his behalf and later an order of council that liberty should
be given for the collection of the revenue which belonged to
his lordship. But the proprietor now complained that, owing
to various obstacles, the agent and his deputies had been
prevented from acting. In response to another appeal from
the proprietor, the king, in November, 1691, issued another
letter commanding that all hindrances to the proposed object should be removed, and as soon as royal government was
established this was read in council and entered on its minutes.
But when the assembly met in its first session under Copley,
Darnall, in a memorial to the governor, again brought forward the claims of Lord Baltimore. According to statements
which he had laid before the lords of trade and the king in
England,[3] shipmasters in various ways were avoiding the payment of his tonnage duty and during 1689 and 1690 he had
naturally not received a shilling of income from either of the
imposts, though by royal order he was entitled to them.
When Darnall's memorial came before the assembly, it proceeded to dicker with him by offering to confirm the impost
of 12d. per hogshead provided the proprietor would grant the
same conditions of plantation which had existed before the
late Revolution, or the same which had been granted in Virginia. As to the tonnage duty, the house declared that its

[1] Md. Arch. Council, 1688–1693, pp. 309, 311, 314; Ibid., Ass. 1693, pp. 89,
99, 433.

[2] Md. Arch. Council, 1688–1693, pp. 313, 563. The office of agent of the
proprietor was continued from this time until the close, or nearly so, of the
colonial period. The succession of agents, with many of the instructions to
them and of their doings, may be traced in the Calvert Papers which are still in
manuscript.

[3] Cal. St. P. Col. 1689–1693, pp. 573, 574, 579; Md. Arch. Ass. 1684–1692,
p. 311 et seq. As late as August, 1695, Darnall was petitioning in reference to
this duty, for then the council ordered the strict collection of the shipping dues
belonging to Lord Baltimore. Cal. St. P. Col. 1693–1696, p. 560.

original purpose was to provide money for the defence of the province and that the revenue from it ought now to be vested in the crown, as it was unreasonable that it should now have to provide for defence while Lord Baltimore enjoyed revenue which was granted for that purpose. An act was passed providing that the tonnage duty should go into the province treasury, but it was disallowed in England and expressly ordered by the crown that Baltimore should collect the same for his own use.[1] As to legal fines and amercements, the assembly claimed that those accruing after the Revolution should also go to the crown. The disposition of escheats also needed regulation, but did not receive it. The demand for waifs and strays the assembly regarded as involving a franchise which was not consistent with new plantations, because the country was largely uncleared and private estates were so large that it was impossible to fence them. Therefore all the cattle and other stock of the country ran promiscuously — sometimes twenty miles away — and were distinguished only by their marks which were entered upon record. Under such a regulation, therefore, as Baltimore demanded he might engross all the stock of the province. The title to unmarked cattle, which had been vested in Baltimore, should now be vested in the crown, and documentary evidence of titles to land should be lodged in the office of the secretary of the province. It does not appear that the question of waifs and strays was officially decided.

In its further assertion of claims to fixed rights on behalf of the new government the assembly called upon Darnall, who had been a naval officer before the Revolution, to produce the books of entries of vessels [1]; but he replied that he could not comply, as the books belonged to Lord Baltimore, of whom he was only a servant, and his lordship would probably look upon it as a breach of trust if he parted with them. Therefore the house committed Darnall under a charge of contempt and he petitioned the council on the matter, but they referred him back to the assembly as it had full jurisdiction in the premises. The principle on which the house proceeded was that it was the duty of all officials to attend it with their

[1] Cal. St. P. Col. 1693–1696, p. 31.
[2] Md. Arch. *Ibid.*, 321, 392 *et seq.*, 395, 412.

books, from which it could be ascertained what revenues belonged to the crown for the support of the province and that a refusal to do this was a violation of its rights and a contempt. For a time Darnall was kept closely confined, but before the end of the session, and on his promise to obtain Lord Baltimore's answer on the point in dispute and then give satisfaction, he was released.

Respecting this special point no further direct evidence appears. But the hostile attitude of both houses at this time toward the late proprietary government was evidenced not only by these discussions but by a joint address of theirs to the king and queen at the close of the session.[1] This, indeed, was to be expected, for Cheseldyne was the speaker of the lower house and the entire body was filled with supporters of the late revolution. In the address, with partisan zeal, they declared that, by serious inquiry, they had found all the articles of impeachment prepared by the agents of the province against Baltimore and his deputies to be true, and they stood ready to prove them so before any royal commission, and also several offences of which his agents had since been guilty and which were aimed at the subversion of royal government. They claimed to have found also that the revenue from the export duty on tobacco had been misapplied and that Baltimore was very heavily in debt to the province. Of this his agent had peremptorily refused to give account or to produce his books, and they asked for a royal inquiry into the matter.

On this particular point no further evidence appears, but a law was passed giving to the secretary of the province the fees which accrued from the land office. In accordance with an opinion of the solicitor general that the records of the land office were public in character, they were placed in the custody of this same secretary, Sir Thomas Lawrence. He also raised the question of his right to take fees from Darnall and his clerks for consulting the records in making up the rent roll or for other purposes. Darnall was heard and after much discussion between the houses it was decided that, until his majesty's pleasure was further known, the payment of fees as between the two jurisdictions should be suspended but a

[1] *Ibid.*, 343, 344.

record of services rendered should be kept pending a future settlement.[1] It was also stated at that time that, if Baltimore surveyors would qualify themselves according to law, they might be recognized as officers of the province. In January, 1695/6, Trevor, the attorney general, rendered an opinion in favor of the claim of the secretary of the province to be custodian of land records and that by all parties who used them the fees required by law should be paid, except for copies taken by servants of the proprietor for making up his rent roll. The substance of this was embodied in an order of council, which in due time was issued as a proclamation in Maryland. When, a year later, Darnall was going to England, a formal request was sent to the board of trade for an order which should fully define relations between the two jurisdictions, but apparently this was not considered necessary.

Inquiry also had to be made into the attitude of a number of officials in various counties toward the newly established royal government and several removals and new appointments followed.[2] In Talbot county the feeling in favor of the proprietor was unusually strong and there it found expression in words and acts well-nigh verging on treason. In Cecil county Frisby, the councillor, was prominent in encouraging disturbance, but fortunately withdrew to England before it was necessary to take decisive action against him. No outbreak anywhere occurred.

As Quakers were more numerous in Maryland than in Virginia, a larger proportion of those who were returned as members of the lower house in 1692 were of that persuasion, and they objected to taking the oaths. In Virginia those who assumed this attitude, though not necessarily because they were Quakers, were dismissed and others were ordered to be chosen in their places.[3] Copley was required by his commission to see that the same course was pursued in Maryland, and

[1] Md. Arch. XIX, 55–58, 94; XX, 435, 531; XXIII, 34. For a good summary statement of the territorial questions at issue, see Kilty, Landholder's Assistant, 162. For the extent to which the territorial administration, at least in form, went on throughout the royal period, see Baltimore's orders and instructions to his agents, 1695 and 1712, Kilty, 127–133.

[2] Md. Arch. Ass. 1684–1692, pp. 266 et seq., 258, 287 et seq., 318, 398.

[3] See cases of Arthur Allen and James Bray in 1691.

in his opening speech [1] he warned the house not to admit any to seats except such as took the oaths and were qualified by law.  But the house, considering that the assistance of all was needed in the weighty matters before them, consulted the governor and council on the subject.  In their reply the council fell back upon the laws and practice of England and the governor's commission.  To this the assembly yielded and new writs of election were issued to fill the seats of the Quakers who had been returned as members.  Among them was John Edmundson, of Talbot county.  It was in this way that Quakers were made for the first time to suffer from religious disabilities in Maryland.[2]

The question of fees also came before this assembly.  During the proprietary period much progress had been made toward the regulation of fees by statute, but not all had been brought under this form of limitation.[3]  Copley, like all royal governors, was instructed to determine their amount, with the advice of the council.  When an act for the enrollment of conveyances was now under consideration, the council claimed it to be their duty and that of the governor to fix the amount of the fees provided for in this and other similar laws.  To this the house, referring to Magna Carta and several statutes of England and the general practice of parliament, asserted that it was their right to fix the amount of all fees, on the principle that it was the privilege of the freemen that no fees should be imposed but by their own consent in assembly.  As the governor interpreted his instruction on the subject to empower him only to lessen or moderate fees, no objection was made to the specification in this act of the sums which might be taken for the services it required.  Two comprehensive acts for the limitation of officers' fees were passed, it being their declared object to bring to an end the extortion which officials had hitherto committed in the province by the

[1] Md. Arch. Council, 1688–1693, p. 265;  *Ibid.* Ass. 1684–92, pp. 252, 254, 257, 267 *et seq.*

[2] For an instance of the continuance of this policy see Md. Arch. Ass. 1693–1697, pp. 29, 155, 185.  Quakers complained of being taxed without representation, but no relief was given.

[3] Mereness, Maryland as a Proprietary Province, p. 374;  Osgood, Am. Colonies in 17th Century, II, 363;  Md. Arch. Ass., 1684–1692, pp. 382, 474, 506.

abuse of this power.  Though this legislation was temporary,
it was revived at intervals and continued with little change
until 1719.

No less than eighty-five acts were passed at this first session of the assembly under royal government and accepted
by the governor.[1]  Many of them were of great importance
and related to the chief matters of interest in which the people
of Maryland were concerned, from the establishment of the
church to the regulation of the militia.  The enactment of a
body of laws like this was necessary as the province passed
under the new régime, and they were now sent to England for
action by the privy council, a treatment to which Maryland
laws had never before been subjected.

The subject of fees leads by a natural transition to an account of the famous case of Sir Thomas Lawrence, the
secretary of Maryland, which lent some spice and variety to
the later months of Copley's administration.  Lawrence was
an Englishman, a thorough spoilsman of the period, bent on
exploiting the fees and perquisites of his office to their full
extent.  For this a number of valuable precedents were at
hand from the period of Maryland history which had just
closed, when its government had been a family perquisite.  At
the time of Copley's appointment he was made secretary and
also a member of the council.  Before he left England [2] he
obtained from the lords of trade an opinion that, as in the
previous period, the appointment of the clerks of the ten
county courts in Maryland belonged to the secretary and that
these offices should not be sold.  As the secretary was to give
security for the good behavior of the clerks he should be allowed a fee, on their appointment, of one tenth of one year's
value of each clerkship, the value or income to be estimated
by the governor and council when vacancies occurred.  After
his arrival in the province Lawrence contended that all these
clerkships were held subject to his absolute right of appointment and removal.  He acted on this principle in at least
two instances and defended his course before the council.
From depositions it was also shown that he not only collected

[1] *Ibid.*, 421 *et seq.*
[2] Md. Arch. Council, 1688–1693, pp. 289 *et seq.*, 385, 398, 409, 454;  Cal.
St. P. Col. 1689–1693, pp. 569–578.

the tenth of the profits of the offices on appointments to them, but exacted from incumbents as a condition of their retaining their places as much as one-half the profits. Another phase of the business was the removal of experienced officials to make way for inexperienced men. Sir Thomas' remedy for this was to allow the new incumbents to employ substitutes to officiate for them and to instruct them until they were able to perform the duties of the offices. One of the clerkships thus made vacant Sir Thomas bestowed on his son, who was under age, and it was to be managed for him by a deputy whom the secretary had brought with him for that purpose. Another clerkship was given to a second imported favorite who was at present capable only of acting through a deputy; and a third it was reported would be granted to a person who would use it for Sir Thomas' own personal benefit. When the council tried to separate from the whole body of fees those which properly belonged to the secretary and proposed to submit the question to the assembly, Sir Thomas flew into a passion and showed that he valued his bare right to dispose of the ten clerkships at a thousand a year.

But even this did not satisfy Sir Thomas. He complained that by a recent act the right to issue licenses for ordinaries had been taken from the secretary and a new office had been created in the chancery, which he feared would absorb the fees from that source. Still earlier the creation of the naval office had taken from the secretary the fees for entering and clearing vessels. But at the same time he had been in the province for a year and had neglected or been unable to give the bond which was necessary to qualify him to receive the records of the provincial court and land office. The council told him he must qualify before he could receive these records and that a bond for £2000 would be accepted in his case. Its members, however, declined to be his bondsmen and he then declared that what they required was an impossibility for him, a stranger in the province.

After inquiring into this case of eighteenth-century patronage mongering, Copley wrote to the lords of trade asking that the arrogant pretensions of Sir Thomas might be checked. Sir Thomas himself wrote to the king stating his alleged

grievances and asking for redress.[1]  In presenting the case
the lords of trade, proceeding on the theory that office is a
a form of private property, passed over what to a modern
mind appears to be the grosser instances of graft, and discussed the question whether the acts creating new offices and
transferring to them fees which previously had belonged to
the secretary should be repealed, so that his former fees
might be restored and his security limited to £1000.  The
lords reported that the act regulating ordinaries should be
disallowed and the order of the Maryland council transferring the fees and routine business of the chancery office to the
chancellor should be set aside and the same restored to the
secretary; but the act concerning the naval office should not
be disallowed.  The legal basis for this ruling was the fact
that in the commission of Sir Thomas it was provided that
he should have the perquisites which had customarily belonged
to his office in Maryland.  As usual, this report was at once
approved by an order in council and Sir Thomas seemed for
the time to have won his case.

But while this settlement was being made in England, the
dispute reached a serious personal stage in Maryland.[2]  On
March 27, 1692, the governor suspended Sir Thomas from the
council, from his place as a justice of the provincial court
and from all his official duties and cited him personally to
appear.  It was about the same time that Edward Randolph,
as we have seen, was ordered under arrest, though he was
not then in the province.  Both these officials had savagely
criticised the Maryland government and denounced its officials, and partly as a result of that both were charged with
being Jacobites.  But in the case of Sir Thomas the charges
arose chiefly from his maladministration of the secretary's
office, as above described, to which was added the complaint
that he associated with none but papists and enemies of the
government.  Sir Thomas appeared before the council and
listened to the charges, with their accompanying proofs.  He
was then ordered under arrest and was told that an appeal
would be taken against him to England.[3]  Peter Sayer and

---

[1] Md. Arch. Council, 1688–1693, p. 450 *et seq.*
[2] *Ibid.*, 482, 484, 489.
[3] *Ibid.*, 497, 500, 503, 560, 565.

Thomas Smith were ordered under arrest at the same time as suspected Catholic sympathizers, Talbot county being the centre of Stuart propaganda. Another French and Indian scare was started at the same time, though it by no means reached the proportions of that of four years before. As soon as the news of his arrest reached England an order was issued that Lawrence should be released and his offices restored and he be permitted to make full answer to the charges against him. Copley meanwhile had died and the order was fully executed, Sir Thomas being restored to the council in May, 1694. Blathwayt then wrote to Sir Thomas that he was glad he was out of the trouble which the governor had brought upon him.[1]

Lionel Copley died September 12, 1693, and the later troubles in which Lawrence became involved were the outcome in part of fears that an effort might be made at the time of the change of government to restore the proprietary system. Reports reached England of the danger of such an outbreak,[2] but they were doubtless much exaggerated. Such agitation as there was, the prompt arrival of Sir Edmund Andros from Virginia checked. Though the very reverse of the conditions under which he had been ordered to take charge of affairs in Maryland existed at this time, Andros at once assumed the government *ad interim*, dissolved the assembly, which was in session, and issued an order continuing all persons in their offices.[3] On his return to Virginia a proclamation was issued empowering Nicholas Greenbury, who was then senior member of the council, to preside there till the commander-in-chief should return.[4] This arrangement continued until the next May, when Andros made another brief visit to St. Mary's.[5] Sir Thomas Lawrence, having now been restored to the council, was proclaimed its president and left in charge. He continued to officiate at the head of the gov-

[1] *Ibid.*, Council, 1693–1696/7, pp. 18, 53, 55, 117, 272.

[2] *Ibid.*, 121 *et seq.*     [3] *Ibid.*, 9 *et seq.*, 127.

[4] Blakiston was then fatally ill and had been dropped from the council. Lawrence had not been reinstated. *Ibid.*, 27, 40, 53, 59.

[5] It was then that he took, with the consent of the council, £500 on account of his salary and directed £150 to be paid to Greenberry. Most of this they had later to restore. Cal. St. P. Col. 1697–8, pp. 242, 509; Md. Arch. *ibid.*, 140, 147–8, 156–159. The board of trade thought the government should have directly devolved on the council.

ernment until July 26, when Colonel Nicholson arrived and his commission as governor was published.

In connection with the brief session of the assembly which was brought to an end by Andros, further light was thrown on alleged arbitrary methods which the Copley government had used against Lawrence and also against Colonel Jowles.[1] This assembly was favorable to both of these men, and its committee of grievances reported that Jowles had been put under very heavy bonds to keep the peace for expressing sympathy with Lawrence, the cause of which no one seemed to know, and for commenting on the " tyranny " of the government. After Copley's death the council had tried to send Jowles to prison, and all this without alleging any crime. This report, severely arraigning the policy of Copley and the council, was unanimously accepted by the house. In view of the strong Protestant and loyal feeling of that body, this action effectually disposes of the charge that Lawrence was concerned in a plot for the restoration of Catholic and proprietary government in Maryland.

With the advent of Nicholson as governor, in 1694, the personal quarrels of Copley's administration disappeared and the trend of affairs toward Anglicanism and that type of morals and orthodoxy which accompanied an established church and loyalty to the crown was emphasized in every possible way.[2] As part of a general inquiry into the condition of the province, which Nicholson instituted, there appeared a detailed statement showing the state of the parishes as to church buildings and ministers. Under the influence, apparently of impressions received during his late visit to England, Nicholson struck a note of intense orthodoxy in his speech to his first assembly,[3] and it would seem as if the strong religious tone so noticeable in his later correspondence dates from this time. A fast was ordered, while the instructions which were sent to the house related chiefly to the conversion of negroes and Indians, treatment of slaves, the table of marriages, public morals and the need of work-

---

[1] Md. Arch. Assembly, 1693–1697, pp. 8, 12, 13, 15, 18, 19, 90.

[2] Md. Arch. Council, 1693–1697, p. 105 et seq.

[3] Md. Arch. Ass. 1693–1697, p. 31 et seq. The pious ejaculations with which his letters abound make their appearance at this time.

houses. The upper house took up at once the inspection of the laws, making extended comments on the act for the establishment of the church in Maryland, to the end of showing what additions and changes should be made. In this connection the governor and Sir Thomas Lawrence offered to give 1000 pounds of tobacco toward the cost of every house which should be erected in the province for a clergyman and to bear the cost of surveying the land for every glebe which should be laid out. It was also insisted that Maryland must follow the example of Virginia to the extent of establishing a free public school and that project was now brought before the general assembly. Nicholson offered £50 toward building the school and £25 a year during his term toward its support, while Lawrence made similar offers expressed in terms of tobacco.[1] Individual members of both houses also made contributions, though no appropriation was made. Other proposals favorable to the church were made and the burgesses declared that a suffragan bishop or commissary for the regulation of the churches in Maryland ought[2] to be appointed, though they were not ready to provide for his support.

One of the most important consequences of royal and Protestant ascendancy was the resolve to move the capital from Catholic St. Mary's, which lay at the southern extremity of the province, to Protestant and more central Annapolis.[3] When this proposal was broached, the mayor and other magistrates, along with the citizens, of St. Mary's, addressed the governor against it. They used a long series of arguments in favor of the claim of the old capital to continue as the seat of government; that it was the original settlement with a good climate and a good harbor accessible for ships and the despatch of mail; that it had been incorporated and public buildings had been erected there with the view to its continuing as the capital; that on the strength of assurances from Lord Baltimore to this effect some persons

---

[1] This is one of the conspicuous instances of Nicholson's generosity on behalf of the Church. But later he offered to pay the expenses of John Povey as agent for Maryland, if no resources were at hand, and the offer was accepted by the assembly. It is also probable that he made some payment to Blathwayt. *Ibid.*, 165.

[2] *Ibid.*, 92. One Payne was even then claiming the office of commissary.

[3] *Ibid.*, 71–78, 110, 119; Osgood, Am. Colonies, II, 53 *et seq.*

had invested there. They even offered to provide a coach and saddle horses to carry people, especially during sessions of courts and assemblies, between Patuxent river and St. Mary's. The answer of the house was decisive and even insulting in its tone and was so framed as to express the view that removal was already decided upon and that all arguments against it were false or absurd. Precedents and implications derived from the proprietary régime were rejected with scorn and the interests of the province, together with the superior wealth and location of Annapolis, were emphasized as decisive beyond appeal. An act was passed this session erecting Ann Arundel into a port town, the system of government for which was perfected two years later. The assembly, at its session of February and March, 1694/5,[1] met there, and under the name of Annapolis it became the permanent capital of Maryland.

The peculiar concentration of power in the executive which was so characteristic of Maryland during the later years of proprietary rule disappeared with the Revolution of 1689. The relations thereafter approximated to those which obtained generally in royal provinces. But it would have been strange if executive discretion had not survived in some marked degree, especially in view of the example of Virginia and the fact that financial pressure was not so great in Maryland as to furnish a decisive leverage for the lower house. The fact that Nicholson had been governor in Virginia must have had some influence. At the opening of his first assembly [2] Nicholson raised the question of the tenure by which the office of clerk of the burgesses was held. On being advised that there was once a contest over this and that it ended in the proprietor making the appointment, he asked the council to inform him of a fit person and on the afternoon of the same day he made an appointment, to continue during pleasure. But on the resignation of this appointee in the following spring the house presented a nominee for his successor and he was approved by the governor.[3] When, in October, 1698, it became necessary to choose another clerk

---

[1] Md. Arch. Ass. 1693–1697, p. 211. The name of the town of Oxford, which was created at the same time on the Eastern Shore, was changed to William Stadt.    [2] Ibid., 25, 26, 29.    [3] Ibid., 172.

the process was again reversed and the governor commissioned the appointee and he was accepted by the house.[1] Thus the Virginia method of appointment was in part adhered to and it must have given the executive a certain freedom of access to the doings of the house and a means of influencing it which did not exist in all the colonies.

The governors of Maryland regularly presided in the council when it was in legislative session, as they did when it was in executive form, and shared fully in its business. This resulted, in the case of Nicholson, in his leadership of the council and the almost perfect agreement between them. Between the two houses there were no disagreements of any account during his administration. The governor dealt very freely with them, not in the form of speeches or messages, but by laying before the lower house, with at least the implied approval of the council, many and varied proposals for discussion and legislation.[2] This practice became especially prominent in the spring session of 1696, and it furnishes added proof of Nicholson's active mind and reforming zeal. These proposals related to a great variety of subjects, local and general, from the building of a bridewell or a school house to transmit duties on Pennsylvania goods, commissions in chancery, and general revision of the laws. Taken in connection with his correspondence, his tours and his widespread activity in the service of the church and education, these proposals furnish indisputable evidence of the ability and serviceableness of Nicholson as governor in a province where political and social life was sluggish and where conditions were favorable to autocratic rule. The great majority of his proposals received some attention from the lower house and found their way into the statute book. Many gave rise to administrative measures.

All this throws light on the part taken by the executive in initiating legislation and government action at this time in Maryland. It was undoubtedly large and in Nicholson's time it was directed toward many beneficial objects both in the internal affairs of the province and in its relations with imperial interests at large. Its tendency was to quicken and

[1] *Ibid.*, XXII, 209.
[2] *Ibid.*, XIX, 288, 360, 511, 515.

regulate the indifferent burgesses and their constituents in lines germane to normal British development.

In common with Virginia, Maryland suffered from the interruptions in the tobacco trade which were caused by war. In addition to that the Revolution, followed by the rather inefficient rule of Copley, left the province in debt and affairs in some confusion.[1]  Under Nicholson the administration became more honest and systematic.  As was his custom in Virginia, he made tours through the province.  He many times urged upon the burgesses the need of a new and more effective militia law, which should bring it up more to the English model.[2]  The council supported him in this and did something by the exercise of the ordinance power.  But owing to the plea of the lower house that the province was too poor to bear the expense, no new militia law was passed or extensive changes made.[3]  In June, 1695, Nicholson wrote to the board of trade that the militia was very badly officered, was comparatively undisciplined and many members were too poor to provide themselves with arms.  In 1696 various suggestions for improvement were considered by a committee of the lower house, but it was not thought best to put them into effect at that time, and in this the people concurred.  The old law remained in force with little change until the close of the colonial period.[4]  It is not probable that there had been much improvement by the time Nicholson's administration closed.  Maryland had no fort nor any guardship, although the governor urged the assembly to take steps to have a small vessel sent for the purpose from England.[5]  Such supply of arms and ammunition as the province possessed was bought with threepence out of the twelvepence duty on tobacco, but after Copley's death it was charged that he had taken the whole for himself and an effort was made by the council and burgesses to recover it,[6] but without result.

---

[1] Cal. St. P. Col. 1696–1697, p. 419.

[2] The existing law had been passed in 1661 and amended in 1678.  Mereness, Maryland as a Proprietary Province, 283.

[3] Md. Arch. XIX, 39, 86, 162, 301–303, 451, 461, 508, 534, 543, 546; XX, 58, 133, 152, 245, 474, 585.

[4] Mereness, op. cit., 283 et seq.

[5] Md. Arch., XIX, 451, 512, 517, 519; XX, 240, 262, 263.

[6] Cal. St. P. Col. 1696–1697, p. 34.

The Indians of Maryland had become so insignificant that their doings aroused little anxiety [1] and no disturbances of consequence were made by Indians from outside the colony. The usual legislation for regulating intercourse with the natives was passed. For protection against possible raids by them two small bodies of rangers were maintained, each relieving the other weekly.[2] The expenditures for these purposes were certainly slight, but they figured prominently among the excuses for refusal to aid New York.

Indirect taxes occupied a larger place in the fiscal system of Maryland than was common among the colonies. There was the export duty of 2s. per hogshead on tobacco, one shilling going to the proprietor and one shilling for the support of government. Usually an additional duty of threepence was imposed for the governor or for some other special purpose.[3] With the accession of Seymour, in 1704, this grant came to be expressly made for the governor's term. An import duty was often imposed on liquors, and an export duty on furs, beef, bacon and other domestic products. A tonnage duty was also a permanent form of levy. These left a minor place for the ordinary direct levies, in the form of an occasional poll tax for the church and clergy or a special tax on servants and slaves for general purposes. County taxes were levied for local purposes, as the payment of burgesses, and the support of the rangers, of the county justices and their courts.

As was the case in New York, one of the forms which was taken by complaints over heavy taxation was the charge that it occasioned the removal of many settlers into other provinces, especially into Pennsylvania and the Lower Counties or even as far south as North Carolina.[4] Of the extent of this emigration we have no definite account, and it is not probable that it was large. Heavy taxation could hardly have been its cause, for the simple reason that taxation was not heavy, while in October, 1696, the assembly acknowledged that the province was out of debt. The over-

---

[1] See the removal of the Piscattaways in 1697, Md. Arch. XIX, 508, 556, 566, 570; XXIII, 146, 216, 219, 232, 238, 323; XXII, 108, 127.

[2] *Ibid.*, XIX, 227, 244; XX, 487, 523; XXIII, 111, 214.

[3] Md. Arch. XXII, 496; XXIV, 416; XXIX, 442.

[4] *Ibid.*, XIX, 225, 238, 250, 344, 464. Cal. St. P. Col., 1696–1697, pp. 420, 546.

production of tobacco and its low price, with the irregular marketing of the product which was due to war, was an effective cause, as in Virginia, of such economic distress as existed. In addition to that some were attracted by the freer conditions as to trade which existed in Pennsylvania and North Carolina. The use of money in the first-named province as a medium of exchange was said, with reason, to have attracted others. Seamen who frequently deserted in large numbers from the tobacco fleets are said to have fled largely to Pennsylvania. But both Nicholson and the two houses believed that the cry of heavy taxes, when used in this connection, was a manufactured one, and in 1695 a proclamation was issued against those who should entice people away by statements of the superior attractions and lighter burdens of other colonies. They should be punished as divulgers of false news.[1] It was said, however, that the support of families who had been deserted by the men, the bread-winners, who had gone into other colonies, imposed an appreciable burden upon the counties.

The legislature of Maryland, of course, had always claimed and enjoyed the right of voting supplies, but, as we have seen, some of the indirect taxes were permanent, that is, they were levied continuously under laws of long standing. Out of revenue of this character the salary of the governor and of others and a part of the general support of government were paid. This prevented the rise of a salary question. Conditions which were generally peaceful, together with a reasonably well ordered government, kept expenditures down to a low level and long obviated a necessity for the issue of paper currency. Owing to these causes, the pressure did not arise which elsewhere relegated the council to a decidedly inferior place in the voting of supplies. It is true that a well developed system of specific appropriations by the lower house was inherited from the proprietary period,[2] though precedents from that time were treated loosely and were seriously affected by royal instructions and other influences. It is also true

---

[1] The issuing of an ordinance, or possibly the passage of an act on this subject, was under discussion in 1698. The governor and council then favored such action. Md. Arch. (Ass.) XXII, 44, 47.

[2] Osgood, American Colonies, II, 371.

that before the royal period had been long in continuance
four standing committees appeared in the lower house: on
privileges and elections, on laws, on grievances — from which
proceeded not a little of general legislation — and on accounts.
Fragmentary minutes of this last committee have been preserved, and they show that its work was to hear and adjust
claims for specific services rendered to the province by individuals and report the same to the burgesses.[1]  On this
apparently was based the public levy or supply bill for the
year, this being prepared by a committee of the lower house
on the public levy.[2]  When the governor and council asked
that they might join this, the lower house prayed that they
would not press a matter which trenched so much on their
right not only to consent to the raising of money but to the
levy of it when raised.  On the same day the house presented
the governor with a bill for the public levy which he refused
to pass on the ground that it did not particularize any allowances, and he asked that this defect be remedied or that the
house would appoint such of its members as were justices
of the provincial court to be joined with the governor and
council to impose the levy.  But the house was unanimous in
the resolution not to recede, contending that it plainly appeared in the bill that the tobacco to be raised by the bill
was to be applied to defraying the necessary charges of the
province, as had formerly been the usage.  Later in the year
suspicion was aroused in the minds of some that public funds
had been misused by the governor, but neither house found
anything to confirm this and expressed sorrow that such an
idea had been entertained.[3]

Money bills did not originate in the upper house, but they
were amended there.[4]  No money could be expended except
upon the governor's warrant and some discretion was allowed
the governor and council in determining the purpose for which
it should be used.  In September, 1693, the governor and
council decided that the money arising from the duty might
be applied " to any of the uses in the said Act prescribed,"
and some of it was applied to the payment of soldiers.[5]  The

---

[1] Md. Arch. XIX, 193–208, 258–275.
[2] Ibid., 322 et seq., for 1696.          [4] Ibid., 231, 235.
[3] Ibid., 462–467.                        [5] Md. Arch. XX, 21.

houses acted jointly in the election of the treasurers, one for the Eastern and the other for the Western Shore.[1] Accounts of collectors and of the receiver general were submitted to both houses[2] or to a joint committee of the houses. It thus appears that the exclusive supremacy of the lower house in matters of finance was not fully established. This was due to the lack of financial activity and pressure. That the executive had not wholly lost its discretion in these matters would have been of importance in war, for it was from the governor and council that the pressure came for cooperation in larger schemes of an imperial nature. The burgesses were usually the inert mass, which had to be moved if activity were attained.

In view of the general similarity between the position of Maryland and that of Virginia, it was to be expected that their attitude toward the defence of New York would be much the same. Appeals for aid were sent by Ingoldsby and Fletcher to Maryland as often as they were to Virginia and in practically the same terms. These were supported by specific orders from the home government to the colonies to furnish quotas. When, in 1691, the demand was made from Virginia and Maryland for 150 men each, the latter complained that "you equalize us with Virginia which has four times our wealth and population."[3] No grant was then made. Early in 1693 the king ordered Governor Copley to pay £250 out of the public revenue toward the defence of New York.[4] A bill for £362 seems to have been sent by Copley before he knew of this order. This he did without the knowledge of the burgesses and no reference to it was entered on the council journal. The bill was protested and never paid.[5] But finally, in April, 1694, bills for the £250 st. which had been ordered by the king a year before were sent to New York by a special messenger.[6]

In March and again in May, 1694, Fletcher wrote asking for further aid, to which the council of Maryland replied men-

---

[1] *Ibid.*, XIX, 234.          [2] *Ibid.*, 54, 229, 251.

[3] Cal. St. P. Col. 1689–1693, pp. 515, 669.

[4] *Ibid.*, 1693–1696, pp. 26, 36, 171, 224; Md. Arch. XIX, 53, 142; XX, 234 *et seq.*

[5] The account, including cost of protest, was £453.

[6] Md. Arch. XX, 48, 71.

tioning " present indigency and want of a bank," but promising that the matter should be laid before the assembly when the new governor arrived. Nicholson, however, was now more impressed with the significance to the middle and southern colonies of the plan of the French to settle on the lower Mississippi than with their doings on the northern frontier.[1] In September Fletcher made another appeal, sending a copy of his treaty with the Five Nations and dwelling on the interest which the colonies to the south had in keeping the Indians steadfast to the English interest. He also sent his scheme of joint operations, with details as to cost, which apparently had been worked out in New York.[2] But to these appeals the council and burgesses replied that the great and prolonged charges occasioned by the late Revolution and the large sums expended by the agents of the province in England, the necessity of keeping troops to guard the frontier and other debts and charges made it impossible for them at that time to contribute anything toward the defence of the New York frontier. At the same time they petitioned the king that they might be excused from further calls of this kind.

But already, in a letter from the queen, Maryland was commanded[3] to furnish 160 men whenever New York should call for them, or a number proportional to the quotas sent by the other colonies. To the governor the burgesses made a non-committal statement to the effect that what they did would depend on the cost of their own frontier defence — the same attitude which Virginia was taking. Governor Nicholson, however, proposed that by laying a duty on the importation of negroes and servants, upon earthen ware and wood, and upon sugar and molasses brought in by foreigners, a bank of money might be accumulated, from which advances could be made to New York, an agent being appointed to see that it was well expended.[4] At the same time Thomas Tasker, of the burgesses, offered to lend the province £200. This offer was accepted and Tasker was sent to New York to deliver

[1] Cal. St. P. Col. 1693–1696, p. 518.
[2] Ibid., 215; XIX, 97; Cal. St. P. Col. 1693–1696, p. 383.
[3] Md. Arch. XX, 213; XIX, 142.
[4] Ibid., 149, 181, 186.

the money, provided Fletcher did not expect the men.[1]   It was accepted, but Fletcher at once wrote that it bore no proportion to what was required by the royal order.   When, somewhat earlier, Fletcher had demanded the full number of men, Nicholson had replied that Maryland was not bound to furnish a larger proportion of its quota than the other colonies had sent and asked if he had called for their entire quotas.   Again the matter was brought before the burgesses, and they resolved that, if the governor would advance £133, being the amount which was necessary to raise Maryland's grant to a sum proportionable to that of Virginia, they would refund the same out of the first available public revenue.[2]   To this he agreed and the sum was sent.   Early in 1696 the king wrote to Governor Fletcher directing him to accept the sums of £500 and £200 respectively from Virginia and Maryland in lieu of the quotas of men which they had declared themselves unable to furnish.[3]

Fletcher continued to appeal for money, but in May, 1696, the burgesses, after recounting the ills of the province, real or imaginary — great mortality of cattle, scarcity of provisions, heavy debt and the like — resolved that no further supply be granted to New York nor any further answer given to that government on the subject of defence until his majesty's pleasure should be signified.[4]   The governor of New York, they said with truth, had not taken care to make the absolute necessity of such assistance apparent to the house. Two months later Nicholson offered to loan some money if the house would vote additional aid to New York, but they declined the offer and again addressed[5] the king on their incapacity for further contributions.   But early in 1697 the board of trade again[6] insisted that the quota of men previously specified should be sent to New York, in reply to which the burgesses sent another address praying for relief from this requisition.   Still again in the autumn the board

[1] *Ibid.*, XX, 274; XIX, 221; XX, 331; Cal. St. P. Col. 1693–1696, pp. 560, 581.

[2] Md. Arch. XIX, 222, 247; XX, 333.   The exact sum was £133  8s. 7d.

[3] *Ibid.*, 342; Cal. St. P. Col., 1693–1696, pp. 610, 636.

[4] Md. Arch, XIX, 244, 313.

[5] *Ibid.*, 388.   Cal. St. P. Col., 1696–1697, p. 33.

[6] *Ibid.*, 342, 527, 596.

renewed its demand, but without result, so far as this war was concerned. The assistance actually given by Maryland consisted of £450 in 1694 and £133 in 1695.

At the close of the spring session of 1698 there was some sharp discussion between the two houses, and especially between the governor and the lower house.[1] This arose in part out of a disagreement over Indian affairs and the ranges, the governor attributing greater importance to the withdrawal of the Piscattaways into Virginia than did the burgesses and desiring that they might be induced to return.[2] The suspension of an attorney named Crawford from his right to practice, and that on the opinion of three law officers of the province without submitting the case to a jury, was also a subject of complaint by the lower house because it seemed to them wrongfully to deprive a man of his freehold and source of livelihood.[3] Though the governor cited cases from English procedure in justification of this course of action, the affair doubtless had helped to provoke a more general discussion. It was even proposed to refer this matter to the board of trade. A complaint was also raised by the lower house that county justices and vestrymen were being compelled by strict and unusual means to appear at Annapolis and there were called to account as offenders, to their great damage and for slight causes.[4] The governor replied that he hoped they did not consider such officers to be above the law and he was afraid some of them had tolerated disorder and brawling, so that they had been abused and affronted in open court without punishing the offenders. Some had also taken tobacco from the public levy for their own use. Those who had been summoned were presumably delinquents in some form or other.[5]

But the main issue at this time was over a proposal to revive certain laws which were to expire at the close of the

---

[1] Md. Arch. XXII, 64 *et seq.*, 127 *et seq.*

[2] It appears that Nicholson called a number of men to consult with him and the council on this subject, and this aroused the jealousy of the burgesses. *Ibid.*, 66 *et seq.*

[3] *Ibid.*, 20, 34, 54, 106, 107, 139. Crawford was soon restored to his right to practice.    [4] *Ibid.*, 35, 56.

[5] It was also charged that Nicholson, by sitting in the provincial court, "struck an awful fear upon Attorneys, Jurors and Suitors." *Ibid.*, 109, 141.

session and among them one carrying the public levy.[1] The governor and council desired to have it continued three years longer and cited the royal instructions against the passage of temporary laws and laws impairing the royal revenue without special leave from the crown. The lower house objected to enacting perpetual laws. The upper house insisted at this time that certain of its members should be admitted to sit with the committee of the burgesses for apportioning the levy. To this, following a precedent of the previous session, the lower house seems in one resolution to have yielded, but no evidence appears that any councillors actually sat with the committee or that the revenue act was extended over the three later years as the governor desired.

By the attitude which he took against the former revolutionist, John Coode, in the fall session of 1696,[2] Nicholson became involved in a bitter controversy which lasted through the rest of his administration. The trouble began the previous July, when the governor and council ordered Cheseldyne and Coode to be prosecuted for the recovery of a sum of money which they were alleged to have taken wrongfully at the time of the Revolution. On many occasions also Coode had shown himself to be a profane scoffer, particularly at the doctrine of the Trinity.[3] Nicholson's rigid orthodoxy had been grievously offended by the alleged coarse and profane language of Coode, and when he was returned to the assembly he refused to let him in. To support himself in this position he took advantage of the technicality that Coode was a clergyman and therefore, according to the laws of England, could not sit in such a legislative assembly. The house claimed that this fact would not exclude him, and also cited the instances of his membership in assemblies and holding secular offices in the proprietary period. They also said that these had in effect unfrocked him. But Nicholson would not admit that the irregular doings of a proprietary province should serve as precedents in such a case. After the house had sent several messages, Nicholson closed the discussion with the

---

[1] *Ibid.*, 129–146.

[2] Arch. XIX, 435 *et seq.*; XX, 453, 489–493, 515.

[3] One statement which Coode is reported to have made, namely, that "all Religion lyes in Tullies Offices," indicates that in some respects he was an ultramodern man.

statement, "I do acquaint you that I shall not swear that person notwithstanding your vote."

Presently Coode and his son-in-law, Gerard Sly, both of whom were residents of St. Mary's county, began to make trouble for the governor.[1] A charge of blasphemy was raised against Coode and he fled to Virginia, whither several letters were sent for his arrest and rendition to Maryland, but Andros was indifferent and nothing was done.

In July, 1697, Philip Clarke, one of the judges of the provincial court, was charged with libelling the governor, alleging in his charge that Nicholson was prejudiced against him because he refused to grant a judgment against Coode.[2] A few months later, the governor and council, having been told that Robert Mason, treasurer of the Western Shore, was corresponding with Coode, issued a warrant for the seizure of his papers.[3] Sly then published charges of misgovernment against Nicholson, and claimed to have made representations in England which would lead to his recall. These complaints were submitted to the council and provincial court, and testimony was given which tended to show that Coode and his friends designed to overthrow the government. Clarke and Sly were arrested and examined before the governor. A proclamation against the ill affected was issued.[4] In a subsequent letter to the board of trade Nicholson stated — probably with exaggeration — that he thought there had been an attempt at rebellion, that Catholics and Jacobites had joined with the malcontents and some had cherished hopes that Lord Baltimore would receive the government again. Coode he considered a diminutive Ferguson in point of government and a Hobbist or worse in religion. Sly finally acknowledged from prison that he had wronged the governor and begged his pardon.

Philip Clarke, who was among those arrested under order of the governor and council, was a member of the lower house. This brought up the question of privilege and the house even proposed to have its clerk sworn to secrecy and the speaker

[1] Arch. XXIII, 293, 375, 412, 441, 443, 447, 519, 521, 525 *et seq.* See many other references in index of this volume.
[2] *Ibid.*, 178–180.     [3] *Ibid.*, 266, 332 *et seq.*
[4] *Ibid.*, 375, 412, 436, 441, 443, 447, 448, 451, 470 *et seq.*

to keep the journal.[1] But the clerk was sworn before the council with the usual oath. Among the rules of procedure which were adopted by the house was one to the effect that neither the clerk nor any member should reveal what was said or done in any of their proceedings on penalty of fine. An address was presented to the governor praying for Clarke's release. Nicholson replied by stating the cause of his imprisonment and declaring that whoever should take him out of prison would be a rebel. So high was the language which he used toward the house that it appointed a committee to draft an expression of its resentment at his implying that they were guilty of sedition. In their address they claimed the same privilege in the premises as the house of commons, a thing which Lord Baltimore had never denied. But their feeling of uncertainty was indicated by their submitting the question finally to the governor and council and agreeing to acquiesce in their opinion. The council declined to give an immediate answer to so important a question and the attention of the house was for the time diverted to routine business.

After inquiry the council ordered the prosecution of Robert Mason for holding secret correspondence with Coode.[2] Mason was then called upon for his accounts, and as this was the last of many futile demands, the council thought he ought to be remanded. But the house took issue; Mason submitted a report, but after the close of the session he was removed from the office of sheriff of St. Mary's county and finally was tried and sentenced to imprisonment along with Clarke. On finding that the governor was preventing Mason from accounting to it, the house addressed to him a memorial of protest. This had been preceded by a report of the committee of grievances,[3] which was embodied in another address which dealt comprehensively with the privilege of freedom of speech in the assembly. They asked that the governor would not overawe or deter any member from freely debating matters and that no member should be declared a malignant, or summoned before the council or summoned by writ of *venire* for free

---

[1] Arch. XXII, 208, 211, 214 *et seq.*

[2] *Ibid.*, 241; XXIII, 266, 333, 345, 508; Cal. Col. 1697–8, pp. 86, 144–6, 158, 215, 220, 299, 420, and under corresponding dates in the Md. Arch.

[3] Md. Arch. XXII, 237, 243.

speaking in the house; that so long as they bore themselves loyally toward the king they should not be troubled by false reports of what was done in the house; that he would cease calling clerks of committees on oath to reveal what was done in their meetings; that justices of the peace and other local officers might be under his protection and not troubled by obsolete laws, nor should juries be intimidated so as not to give verdicts according to their consciences.

To this the governor gave a brief and non-committal answer, to the general effect that the assembly was not above the law, that it should welcome as much publicity as the house of commons, which published its votes; that all officials must account and were liable to punishment for offences against the laws. As Clarke was prominently referred to in the address of the house, the governor stated to it the reason for his imprisonment, which was not only that he had delayed accounting but that he had overcharged the province fifty pounds.[1]  All rebellions, he added, coming closer to the real reason for the prosecution of Clarke, were begun by scandalizing and making odious the persons in authority, as was the case of Bacon's rebellion in Virginia.  The governor and council together expressed great surprise at the apparent claim of the lower house to be equal with the house of commons.  The entire government of Maryland they took to be dependent on the crown.  Though they were councillors, they were far from pretending to be a house of lords, and though they did not wish to abridge the burgesses of their privileges, they desired them to be tempered with greater justice and modesty.  The council also demanded that the house would leave its insinuations and dark sayings about clerks who copied their journals and the governor overawing the house and the like, and " speak plaine and show when, where and how and in what his Excellency hath so dealt with any members of your house; otherwise you seem afraid of Invisible nothings and are not capable of a Remedy." If any one desired freedom of debate at random, and without regard to dignity of king or government, and under pretence of privilege arraigned prerogative, they must expect the governor to check such practices.  That they should desire the

[1] *Ibid.*, 246, 248, 251, 254, 274.

governor to refrain from questioning their clerks was enough to cause suspicion that some members cherished designs against the government.   Their implicit claim that justices and juries might do as they pleased meant the placing of the king's government under the guidance of the house.   But the king's government the governor and council were sworn to uphold.   Some jurors were now held under suspicion of perjury and should be tried.   In all these points the governor had done well.   The assembly and his opponents having thus been trounced like school boys, the controversy ended and at the close of the session council, house and provincial court joined in a complimentary address to Nicholson on his satisfactory administration.   One of his last acts was to release Clarke from prison on security for good behavior.

# CHAPTER XII

## THE SURRENDER OF PROPRIETARY GOVERNMENT
### IN NEW JERSEY, 1702

THE fatal defect which existed in the claim of the New Jersey proprietors to rights of government has already been explained, as have also the difficulties which they met with in their efforts to establish and carry on government. The towns of the Elizabeth and Monmouth Patents persistently refused to acknowledge the claims of the proprietors either to rights of government or to land, and took their stand on the superior validity of the grant made to them by Governor Nicolls before information had been received of the grant made by the duke of York to Berkeley and Carteret. Their opposition was quieted for a time only to break out again as soon as the proprietors met with opposition from other quarters. The concession by the duke of York in 1680 of what appeared to be full rights of government quieted internal opposition for the time, but even this could not stand searching criticism because it did not receive proper legal confirmation by the king. When the sway of Andros and his Dominion of New England was extended over New Jersey in 1688 it was not necessary to take legal action against the proprietors. They felt themselves too weak to resist and at once made submission. The rule of Andros lasted but two months and carried little real authority with it.[1] No effort was made to uphold it at the end and it fell without regret. But its existence, even for so brief a period, still further weakened the hold of the proprietors on the province and opened the way for renewed outbreaks in the future. For some three years after the fall of Andros no general government existed in New Jersey. How far the localities were then active it is impossible to tell, for almost no records of the time have survived. Two men, John Tatham and Joseph Dudley,[2] were

[1] See N. J. Arch. II, 433, a statement from Dockwra against Hamilton (1701), which throws some additional light on this time.

[2] N. J. Arch. II, 349.

appointed governors of East Jersey in the course of that period, but the people scrupled to obey them and they never assumed office.

The weakness of government in the Jerseys was increased by the large number of proprietors. For East Jersey the number was twenty-four, in West Jersey the whole body of freeholders were proprietors. In the case of East Jersey most of the proprietors were non-resident. It was practically impossible to secure united action among them. Factions developed, with resulting intrigues and working at cross purposes. Some of the proprietors played into the hands of the opposition in the province and thus increased the confusion and general inefficiency which existed. In West Jersey quiet and order were better maintained, but there the predominance of Quakers largely unfitted the province for the performance of its duties in time of war. In both provinces jealousies and conflicts due to the struggles of hostile religious sects added to the confusion especially after the English church won a foothold during the last decade of the seventeenth century.

Under these conditions New York could hardly fail to be a menace to the independence of the two Jerseys, to their continued existence as distinct provinces. New York was now a royal province and was situated at the strategic centre of the northern frontier. As the struggle with the French developed, we have seen how imperative and repeated were its calls upon the neighboring colonies for aid and how these always had the support of the British government. We have also seen how, with the support of Great Britain and under the plea of military necessity, the governor of New York tried to take the militia of Connecticut under his command. This was not attempted in the case of New Jersey, but the argument, urged so often by Governor Dongan before the Revolution, that the territory which had formerly been included in the province of New Netherland should be re-united with New York, was still used and received much additional strength from the existence of war. The demand for the suppression of piracy and illicit trade, both of which were promoted by the war, suggested a remedy of the same nature.

As early as 1687 the form which trade relations between

New York and the Jerseys was to take was suggested by Dongan's seizure of a vessel at Perth Amboy. Against this the proprietors petitioned the king and the question was referred to the committee of trade. In June, 1687, in a representation to the king, the proprietors called attention to the loss which they had suffered through the seizure of the vessel, and advanced the claim that the right to levy a colony duty was a mere matter of property, not revertible to the king.[1] Though they were not subject to New York customs, they would consent to levy them at the same rates. In December the king instructed Plowman, the collector at New York, to permit vessels to enter directly at Perth Amboy, provided a collector should be appointed for that port by the governor of New York or if Plowman himself should live there.[2] Negotiations for a surrender of their rights of government by the proprietors were then in progress and this reveals the intention of including the two provinces within the same customs system. This, of course, was done when Andros assumed control. But for seven years after the Revolution probably no duties were collected by the Jersey governments and the question of their commercial relations with New York had to be taken up anew.

Proprietary government was reestablished in East and West Jersey in 1692 by the appointment of Andrew Hamilton as governor.[3] An Edinburgh merchant, he had come to New Jersey with Lord Neill Campbell and had served for a brief time as governor of East Jersey before its submission to Andros. With the establishment of a post office in the colonies under the patent of Thomas Neale, Hamilton, as we have seen, was appointed postmaster for the continental colonies. Both in this capacity and as governor he showed himself to be a man of honesty and ability. In West Jersey, after the fall of the Andros government, Dr. Daniel Coxe, disappointed in his plans of establishing a sole proprietorship there, sold out his chief interests to the West Jersey Society,[4] which now held the right of government over that province. Of this

---

[1] N. J. Arch. I, 533, 535.    [2] *Ibid.*, 543.

[3] N. J. Archives, II, 84, 87; Whitehead, East Jersey under Propr. Govts., 188.

[4] Tanner, The Province of New Jersey, 121.

body Coxe was a member, but Sir Thomas Lane was its head. It appointed Hamilton as governor.

Hamilton's administration in both the Jerseys was quiet and successful until 1697. In West Jersey it passed without any event of note. In East Jersey sessions of the assembly were regularly held and the usual legislation passed. This related in part to contributions of men and appropriations for the assistance of New York.[1] This was an agreement with the opinion of the attorney general, Sir Thomas Trevor, that the duke of York, by his grant to Berkeley and Carteret, could not "absolutely sever" New Jersey from New York, but that it still remained dependent and liable to contribute toward the defence of New York. In 1692 and again the following year appropriations were made for this purpose.[2] But in 1696 there was general opposition, and Hamilton was able to secure a grant only on condition that the troops should not march except in case of an actual invasion of New York and should be at liberty to return when the action was over and the enemy had retreated. This was probably occasioned in part by distrust of Fletcher and of the alarms which he was instrumental in circulating.

Trouble for the proprietors and their governor began again in 1697, partly as the result of the passage of the act of trade of the previous year. It required that none but natural-born subjects of England should serve in any public post of trust or profit in the realm or dominions. Hamilton was a Scotchman, and, like Livingston in New York and Blair in Virginia, doubt arose as to whether he could receive the royal approval. This furnished Jeremiah Basse with his opportunity to come forward and secure appointment in Hamilton's place.[3] Basse had been a Baptist preacher. The first we hear of him in connection with New Jersey was his appointment in 1692 as resident agent in the colony for the West Jersey Society, to take up lands there, superintend the buying and selling of the goods of the society and attending to its interests in general.[4] At some time between that date and the period of which we are now speaking he had returned to England and had made the acquaintance of a number of the opponents of

[1] N. J. Archives, II, 89–91, 100.    [2] Whitehead, 189 et seq.
[3] N. J. Archives II, 143, 149.    [4] Ibid., 91, 97.

proprietary government. The proprietors of both Jerseys, in their anxiety to avoid offending the crown, appointed this man, who was soon to prove a thorn in their side, in the place of their faithful servant Hamilton, and presented him to the crown for approval.[1] This was granted, though, as we have seen, he went to America without giving the security which was required in connection therewith. From the first Basse sought to recommend himself to the British authorities by a show of zeal against piracy. He wrote at length to the secretary of the board of trade on that subject[2] and later as governor was somewhat active in the arrest of pirates. In his letter he reflected pretty strongly on the conduct of the middle colonies in this matter and in that of illegal trade, but his information was not specific enough for the board and it desired him to collect more concerning the colonies in general and transmit it to them after he had assumed the duties of his office. This was intended to commit him to lines of activity similar to those for which Bellomont was then being appointed and in which Randolph was engaged.

Basse came over with Lord Bellomont, reaching his province in the spring of 1698.[3] In his first letter home, to his friend Secretary Popple, he said that he had been in consultation with Randolph and had just come to believe that the only effectual means of regulating affairs in the colonies would be to " bring all to a level by an Act of Parliament." What his relations were to be with the Quakers of New Jersey was indicated at once by the fact that none of them, on his arrival, even paid him the civility of a visit at his lodgings. This was a strange position for a proprietary governor to be in and it shows that the train was already laid for the intrigues which were to follow between Basse and the Anglicans, and for his alignment with the foes of chartered colonies, whether inside or outside his province.

The arrival of Bellomont and his vigorous assertion of the claims of New York again brought to the front the question of the port at Perth Amboy. Among his instructions was one that he should not allow the inhabitants to trade separately with the Indians and all goods that went up the Hudson

---

[1] *Ibid.*, 150, 176, 409.　　　　[2] *Ibid.*, 150–163.
[3] Cal. St. P. Col. 1697–1698, p. 186; N. J. Archives, II, 208.

should pay duties at New York as previously.[1]  During and
after the preparation of his instructions, the question of the
right of the Jerseys to ports of their own was under consideration by the proprietors and in the British administrative
offices.  An opinion favorable to the claim of the proprietors
was obtained from Sir Creswell Levinz.[2]  He said that the
separation of the two colonies had been so complete that the
people of the Jerseys could no longer be compelled to land
their goods and pay duties at New York.  The commissioners
of the customs meanwhile, in pursuance of their plan of uniform imperial customs administration, established two ports,
one at Perth Amboy for East Jersey and the other at Burlington for West Jersey.[3]  The officials thus provided for were
to collect the sums accruing under the trade act of 1673 —
which at the best would be very small — and inspect the
enumerated commodities which should be exported and the
European goods which should be imported and see that the
provision of the acts of parliament relating to this trade were
obeyed.  They had nothing to do with the administration of
customs provided for by New York law, though the customs
board expressed sympathy with the claim of New Jersey to
ports of its own.  This latter subject, however, was the one
chiefly in dispute between the New Jersey proprietors and the
New York authorities.  On the other hand, the fact that the
customs board had established two ports in the Jerseys told
in favor of their contention against New York, for they
now had the ports and vessels might be entered and cleared
there.  There lay the ambiguity of the situation.  For the law
officers of the crown, Trevor and Hawles, on October 18,
1697, gave an opinion apparently opposed to that of Levinz,
to the effect that the duke of York never possessed the power
to establish ports such as were provided for by the act of 1673
and over which the treasury and customs boards had exclusive authority.  Therefore he could not transfer such
power to the New Jersey proprietors and they did not now
possess it.  This was true of ports such as the attorney and
solicitor general had in mind.  But the board of trade, in a

---

[1] N. Y. Col. Docs., IV, 289.           [2] N. J. Arch. II, 136.
[3] *Ibid.*, 163–173, 177, 179.  See report of customs board to board of trade,
Feb. 21, 1698/9.  Cal. Treas. Papers.

representation to the lords justices on this opinion, extended
its meaning to include the claim that the proprietors had no
authority to establish ports of any kind, and that all the trade
of East Jersey at least should pass through New York and
pay duties there.[1] In the interest of its imperialist policy,
that is, the board of trade adopted in full the New York view.

Of course, if the New Jersey proprietors had no powers of
government whatever, they had no authority to establish
and maintain ports. But they had actually exercised powers
of government for a generation and the validity of the concession of the duke in their favor in 1680 had never been
authoritatively denied. If they were in actual and rightful
possession of powers of government, the fact that the duke
of York, as proprietor, had established the port of New York
afforded glaring proof that the present contention of the board
of trade was wrong. The right to establish ports for purposes
of local trade and customs had been granted in all the royal
charters and exercised by all proprietors and corporations
under them. It was closely connected with their territorial
powers. If the Jersey grantees were proprietors in the full
sense of the term, there could be no doubt of their right to
establish ports. But, as we know, there was ground for denying that they possessed rights of government, and the board
was now ready to take advantage of this in order, by adopt-
ing the contention of New York, to reap the full advantage
for its imperialist policy. On November 25, 1697, an order
in council was issued approving the representation received
from the board and commanding that Bellomont's instruction
concerning trade and the payment of duties in Hudson's river
should be enforced.[2] The order was sent to Bellomont, with
a direction that, as the proprietors of the Jerseys had no right
to erect ports, he should take care that the privileges of New
York were not infringed.

Bellomont was naturally inclined to the enforcement of
this order, for he shared the views which Dongan and Fletcher
had expressed concerning the interests of New York and of the
crown in the matter.[3] As soon as the order in council arrived
he issued a proclamation forbidding, on penalty of seizure
and prosecution, any vessel to land at any port in East

[1] *Ibid.*, 180 *et seq.*    [2] *Ibid.*, 200.    [3] *Ibid.*, 216–222.

Jersey with goods on which duties arose by virtue of the laws of England or of New York without first entering them and paying duties at the New York custom house. In this proclamation nothing was said about West Jersey. Bellomont also forbade the printing at New York of the proclamation of the proprietors that ports had been established in their provinces. Of what he had done he immediately informed both the board of trade and the treasury.[1] Basse, under the authority of the order of the customs board, proclaimed Perth Amboy to be a port, and referred to a letter of instructions which they had sent to Randolph requiring him to cause all merchants and others to load and unload at this port. Thus the issue was joined between executive officials on this question. After some correspondence Basse visited New York and Bellomont thought he had so far convinced him that he would no longer dispute the king's orders.[2] But when they came to be executed, it was seen that they necessitated submission on the part of Jerseymen to the jurisdiction of the admiralty court of New York. To the trial of a ship there which Randolph had seized in New Jersey no objection was made, but when a demand came from the admiralty court for the surrender of two pirates of Avery's crew who had been captured in the Jerseys, Basse called his council and it unanimously resolved not to deliver them until the commission under which the admiralty court was held was published and recorded in the Jerseys. Bellomont, with the advice of his council, then sent a command which Basse did not dare to refuse and the two pirates were given up. As an incident of this, James Graham, attorney general of New York, gave an opinion in support of the claim of his province in the question of ports.

About the end of July, 1698, on a report that a ship had demanded clearings at New York for Perth Amboy, in order to unload goods there without paying duty, but with a bond to answer all charges at Westminster Hall, Bellomont, who was then absent in Albany, had Basse and Willocks, the agent of the East Jersey proprietors, appear before Lieutenant Governor Nanfan and the New York council, where his proclamation was shown them.[3] The skill of Basse was shown by the

---

[1] *Ibid.*, 221.     [2] *Ibid.*, 235, 236, 242.     [3] *Ibid.*, 237 *et seq.*, 242.

fact that he did not attempt to justify the existence of a
port at Perth Amboy on the ground that the proprietors had
the right to establish one there, but on the fact that one
had been erected there under an order of the customs board
and the authority of the act of 1673. He submitted the
commission of the collector already installed there and other
documentary proofs that he was acting directly under royal
authority. He thought he was able to show that the royal
authority was in conflict with itself.

Bellomont, on his return from Albany, sent Hungerford, the
New York collector, to Perth Amboy to seize a sloop which
was unloading there,[1] but he and his posse were met by a
crowd of inhabitants who by force prevented the seizure and
compelled the New Yorkers to returned baffled. Encouraged
by this, in the following December, Basse loaded the ship
"Hester" at Perth Amboy with barrel staves for Madeira
and was about to send her away, when Bellomont again sent
Hungerford, this time with forty soldiers, and seized the
vessel.[2] He later offered to restore her, if Basse would promise
to have her tried at New York. But he refused, claiming that
he had received positive command from the proprietors not to
yield to any of Bellomont's orders. Bellomont now had the
ship tried and condemned at New York.[3]

But meantime the board of trade had learned on inquiry
that the action of the customs board, under authority not
only of the act of 1673 but of that of 1696, was valid, though
it was not intended to exempt the inhabitants of New Jersey
from the payment of any duties they were previously under
obligation to pay to New York.[4] The two obligations, they
said, were wholly different, and the collector at Perth Amboy
was not charged with the enforcement of the claims of New
York. The difficulty in this situation was that goods liable to
New York customs and to imperial customs might be found on
the same vessel. The East Jersey proprietors at once petitioned the king against the proceedings of Bellomont, asserting
their inherent right to establish ports and carry on trade, as
well as sheltering themselves to an extent under what the com-

[1] *Ibid.*, 238.          [2] *Ibid.*, 246, 341–2.
[3] N. Y. Col. Docs. IV, 439, 605; Whitehead, 205; N. J. Arch. II, 312.
[4] N. J. Arch. II, 244, 247, 251–254.

missioners of the customs had done.[1]  The board of trade had
contended that, as East Jersey and New York were on the
same river, they therefore should not be separated in
jurisdiction any more than would be two towns on the Thames.
But the proprietors cited Virginia and Maryland as examples
of customs jurisdictions both adjacent to Chesapeake bay.
They also offered as a concession that they would have a
law passed laying rates of duty at Perth Amboy equivalent to
those imposed at New York.  But this presented an opportunity for an assertion of the right of appeal too favorable to
be neglected and therefore the board of trade decided that the
case of the " Hester " should be combined with that of the
claim of the proprietors to governmental rights and the two
should be tried before the court of king's bench.[2]  Though
the proprietors had made the original suggestion that the case
of the " Hester " should be tried in Westminster Hall, they
objected to making their claim to government a part of the
case.  The trial of the " Hester " and of the claim of the
proprietors to ports was held in England, though no record of
it is extant, and the proprietors won.[3]  Their right and that
of the Jerseys to ports was confirmed, and damages were
awarded to Basse.

But though the New Jersey governor in this case won a
victory over Bellomont which must have been rather mortify-
ing to the earl, in the purely domestic affairs of the Jerseys
Basse was already in great difficulty.[4]  By the Quakers and
many others he was regarded an an adventurer who had no
right to the government.  Especially was this true when it
became known that the Scotch descent of Hamilton presented no legal barrier to his holding the office of governor.
The proprietors of East Jersey were strong in support of
Hamilton, while those of West Jersey proved more friendly to
Basse.  In the spring of 1698 the young Lewis Morris, who
for half a century was to wield a very large influence in
Jersey affairs, openly denied the right of the Basse faction

[1] *Ibid.*, 254–269.  In these papers will be found the fullest statement of the
New Jersey case.

[2] *Ibid.*, 268, 269.

[3] *Ibid.*, 404; Whitehead, 206; Proceedings of N. J. His. Soc. X, 139–146.

[4] Whitehead, 197 *et seq.*; Tanner, 76 *et seq.*, 94.  The commission of Basse
had not been signed by the requisite sixteen proprietors.

to hold court and was imprisoned therefor. Under these
circumstances Basse identified himself with the anti-pro-
prietary faction in East Jersey. This had been recently
strengthened by the favorable decision they obtained in England on an appeal in the case of Jones vs. Fullerton, February,
1696/7. This case involved a dispute between Jones, one of
the original associates to whom the Elizabethtown tract was
granted by Governor Nicolls, and Fullerton, the holder of
a proprietary interest. Jones had ejected Fullerton and judgment had been given against the former in the court of common pleas at Perth Amboy in 1695. Jones appealed to the
privy council and employed William Nicoll, agent of New
York, as counsel. Thomas Gordon was sent as agent to
England by the proprietors. The record of the proceedings
is not extant, and so it is not known whether the judgment
was rendered on the merits of the case, as claimed by Nicolls,
or because of an error in the procedure of the provincial court,
as claimed by the proprietors. But it had a far-reaching
effect, for the Elizabethtown associates at once petitioned
the king to be annexed to New York, as they were not under
a legal government. In view of the rising opposition the East
Jersey proprietors sent over George Willocks to dispose of
their quit rents and collect arrears.[1]   It was into this tangle
that Governor Basse now ventured.

He delayed calling an assembly for several months. Finally,
in February, 1698/9, one was called. Though in this assembly the governor and his supporters stood with the proprietors
in common opposition to the encroachments of New York, an
act was passed prohibiting the election as deputy or representative of any person who was either proxy or agent for
any proprietor.[2] This was aimed at Willocks, who had
arrived a few months before and had been returned as a
member from Perth Amboy. He protested against the bill,
but he was unseated and the bill was passed. No more
serious blow could have been struck at the influence of the
proprietors in East Jersey.

Basse now found it convenient to visit West Jersey for a
time, and Andrew Bowne, president of the council and one
of his friends, was left in charge. At once, under the lead

[1] N. J. Arch. II, 189.                    [2] Whitehead, 200.

of Morris and Willocks, opposition began.  Riots occurred.
Sessions of the courts were broken up and the peace of the
province was seriously disturbed by the excesses of both
parties.[1]  The authority both of the proprietors and of Basse
was openly defied.  It was under these conditions that the
majority of the proprietors in England secured the assent
of the government to the return of Hamilton as governor for
a limited term, while negotiations were actively begun for
the surrender of their governmental rights.  The West Jersey
Society appointed him as their agent and governor.  At the
close of 1699 Basse left for England, that he might the better
advance his own interests when the inevitable change should
come.[2]

The conditions proposed by the East Jersey proprietors as
those which would make the surrender of their rights of
government tolerable were these: — That their rights in and
control over the lands and quit rents of the province might
be confirmed to them; that they should continue as lords of
the soil, hold courts and appoint all officers whose duties
related to land; that they should grant markets and fairs;
that all mines, wrecks, estrays, treasure trove, goods of felons
and traitors should belong to the proprietors as amply as by
the grant of March, 1681/2; that upon the annexation of the
government to New York — already quite probable — Perth
Amboy should be a port where rates of duty equivalent to
those of New York should be paid; that the province should
have liberty of trade with the Indians and the proprietors
have the sole privilege of buying from the Indians such lands
within East Jersey as were still unpurchased; that courts
like those of New York be continued in the province and the
inhabitants be not required to go to New York for the trial
of cases which should arise in East Jersey or be compelled
to serve on juries or in any ministerial office in New York;
that all wills and letters of administration of persons dying
and estates lying within East Jersey be made and granted
by its chief judge, who should reside at Perth Amboy, and the
register be kept there; that the records of the province should
not be removed and that the proprietors should have the right

[1] N. J. Arch. II, 315 *et seq.*, 440.
[2] N. J. Arch. II, 276, 294, 299, 301, 303, 321.

of appointing the secretary, register and surveyor general; that the existing counties in East Jersey be continued and that they be increased in proportion to any increase in the number of New York counties and that the representation from the East Jersey counties be kept equal to that from those of New York; that a proportionable number of the inhabitants of East Jersey be appointed to the governor's council and have votes in the upper house; that no person be molested or deprived of any civil right or be made incapable of holding office on account of religion.[1]  The two-fold object of these conditions was to retain in the hands of the proprietors their existing estates and the control of all ungranted land in the province, and to guarantee East Jersey, as far as possible, from the danger of absorption into New York.  It is noticeable that nothing was said about the militia, this indicating that the proprietors were indifferent to it or accepted the principle, already so often declared, that the regulation of that for general purposes should be in the hands of the crown.  In a separate memorial[2] the proprietors stated that the main inducement which led them to consent to the surrender of their government was that through it they might obtain a port at Perth Amboy.  Their investment in the province had been a losing one — at least not a gain — and the existence of a separate port in it, with facilities for trade, was about the only thing that could make the province of value to them and give them the opportunity to recover their purchase money and what they had expended on improvements.

In a later statement, drawn in 1701,[3] the West Jersey proprietors were included.  This, together with the maturer views which in the meantime had been reached, led to some modification of the terms of surrender.  It was now specified that East and West Jersey should be erected into one distinct province and should have one general assembly, sitting alternately at Perth Amboy and Burlington, with an equal membership in both houses from the two original provinces; that there should be one supreme court for the province, meeting alternately at Perth Amboy and Burlington, and that all

[1] A later statement of the proprietors makes it certain that they would have excluded Catholics.  N. J. Arch. II, 407.
[2] N. J. Arch. II, 308.          [3] Ibid., 404 et seq.

necessary offices and courts should be established in each division.  The exclusive right of the proprietors to purchase land from the Indians and their right to grant all patents for land to settlers and to collect quit rents from them received increased emphasis.  This was due to the fact that in the interval, as a result of the renewed opposition of the Elizabethtown and Monmouth patentees, supported by squatters, frontiersmen and the dissatisfied generally, Roger Williams' theory concerning the origin of land titles in the colonies had again come to the surface.[1]  It was asserted that the king's right to those parts of America which were discovered by English subjects " was only Notionall and Arbitrary and that the Indian Natives are the Absolute Independent Owners and have the sole disposall of them."  Those who held this view — and they were to become more and more numerous in New Jersey — would, if possible, make purchases from the Indians without license, neglect the procuring of patents and refuse to pay quit rents.  This was a natural form of protest against proprietary monopoly of the land, a monopoly also which was not accompanied with firm and efficient government.  It was inferred, if this went far, that it would lead to a denial of the right of the crown to both soil and government.

The delay of the home government in bringing proprietary rule to an end in the Jerseys, after it had virtually collapsed, furnished the occasion for the continuance of outbreaks.  Basse reappeared in the province and openly contested the right to the governorship with Hamilton.  The fiery Lewis Morris, who was made a justice and a member of Hamilton's council, threatened bloodshed and in the Monmouth patent armed men were called out to arrest Salter and Bray, antiproprietary leaders.  These were met by mobs of the other party, who called for assistance from their friends in Essex and Middlesex counties.[2]  In May, 1700, the East Jersey assembly refused to raise any money, on the plea of uncertainty as to Hamilton's right to the government.  He charged them with really intending to bring the government of the proprietors into disrepute and thereby to rid themselves of it.  He explained to them fully how the approval of the crown came to be withheld from him and that it did not imply a denial

[1] *Ibid.*, 346.    [2] N. J. Arch. II, 327–339, 362–373, 398, 437–442.

of the right of the proprietors to carry on government prior
to the decision of the case against them in England. But
as they declined to do anything, he dissolved the assembly,
and the wheels of government came nearly to a full stop.

Under these conditions, by 1701 all parties agreed that a
surrender of government to the king was desirable and necessary. Basse had been waiting for it all the time. The
proprietors, especially those who lived in the provinces, had
repeatedly proposed it and some had specified terms on which
it should be made. The special concession which they now
urged was that Hamilton should be appointed governor.
Finally, in October, 1701, the board of trade reported on the
condition of the Jerseys, taking the ground that the proprietors
had never legally possessed rights of government and that,
owing to the strife of factions, affairs had now fallen hopelessly into confusion.[1] The proprietors, realizing this, had
proposed to surrender the government provided they could
secure their rights of property. Meantime, though no determination of the question of right had been reached at Westminster Hall, there was danger in the general confusion that
on the outbreak of war New Jersey would be lost to England.
Therefore the board recommended that the king assume the
government. This was agreed to by the lords justices and
the board set about drawing a commission and instructions
for the royal governor. Not until January, 1701/2, were these
transmitted to the king, accompanied with the suggestion that
the appointee should be a person wholly unconnected with the
factions of the province.[2] This was likely to prove decisive
against Hamilton's chances of being the first royal governor
of New Jersey. On April 15 the formal surrender of the
government, signed by the proprietors of both provinces, was
made, and it was duly enrolled in the court of chancery.[3]
But so deliberate was the home government that considerable
time was still allowed during which the proprietary factions
continued to urge and oppose the claims of Hamilton.[4] In
June Quary and Randolph added their testimony to that of
the opponents of Hamilton, Quary pronouncing him a man
of good sense and parts, but so deeply involved with the New

---

[1] N. J. Arch. II, 420 *et seq.*       [2] *Ibid.*, 448.
[3] *Ibid.*, 452.                        [4] *Ibid.*, 468–479.

Jersey factions as to be a most unfit person for governor. Randolph charged him with favoring illegal trade with Scotland and other countries. The board of trade, after listening to all that could be presented for and against Hamilton, repeated its advice that a wholly neutral man be appointed.[1] Lord Cornbury was already governor of New York, and had visited New Jersey for the purpose of proclaiming the queen there. He was a near relative of Anne, an Englishman and at the head of a province which, in the war that was just beginning, would again need the aid of all the neighboring provinces. During the previous war several attempts had been made to place the militia of Connecticut and New Jersey under its control, while its executive had for a time been made governor of Pennsylvania. It was most natural, and in harmony with the persistent, though ineffective, efforts toward colonial union that the crown should take advantage of the surrender by the Jersey proprietors to place that province under the charge of the New York executive. A commission and instructions were accordingly made out to Lord Cornbury to be governor of New Jersey, December, 1702, in which were incorporated the chief guaranties on which the proprietors had insisted in their submission.[2]

Cornbury was instructed[3] to secure the passage of an act confirming the lands of the province to the proprietors and to those who had purchased under them. Their quit rents also were to be secured and all the other territorial rights which had been granted them by the duke of York. All private lands properly held were to be confirmed, under such conditions as should tend to their most speedy improvement; but Cornbury was not to consent to the levy of any tax on unprofitable land. None but the proprietors were to buy lands of the Indians and Cornbury was to permit their surveyors to carry on their work and assist their agents to collect the quit rents, provided they took the customary oaths and gave security. He must also see that all lands purchased were cultivated.

A list of the names of twelve councillors was inserted in

[1] *Ibid.*, 484.    [2] *Ibid.*, 489–500, 506–536.
[3] N. J. Arch. II, 517; Tanner, 755.

the instructions, which, after much contest, had been unanimously agreed upon by the proprietors of both divisions.[1] Basse and Coxe were not included, though their names had been strongly urged, for the nominal reason that they had little or no estate in the province.

The regulations concerning the assembly were such as the proprietors had desired, and various important commands were laid upon the new governor in reference to acts which he should have passed. He should secure the passage of a law for the support of the government, and that, if possible, for an unlimited time[2]; an act securing the lands to the proprietors and to those who had received grants from them; another safeguarding the proprietors' quit rents and other privileges; an act securing to the Quakers, as in England, the right of making the solemn declaration in place of the oath. He was to obtain contributions for the defence of New York and secure the passage of an act for disciplining the New Jersey militia. Acts were also to be passed insuring to creditors in England the payment of debts due from persons having estates in New Jersey, and restraining all inhuman severity towards servants and slaves. But of none of these measures did Cornbury secure the passage.

A comparison of these requirements with the provisions of the routine instructions which by this time were being issued to the royal governors generally will show that little change was needed to adapt them to the purposes which the proprietors wished to attain in New Jersey. In view of this fact and of the character which Cornbury was already revealing, the question now was whether by his appointment the nonpartisan administration to which the board of trade referred had really been insured.

[1] N. J. Arch. II, 503, 507.
[2] Tanner, 223; Arch. II, 513–532.

# CHAPTER XIII

## THE SECOND INTERCOLONIAL WAR, 1702–1713

ONE of the greatest triumphs of French policy was won by De Callières, the successor of Frontenac, when in September, 1700, he concluded a treaty of peace and neutrality with the Iroquois, the terms of the agreement being extended so as to include also the relations between the Iroquois and all the western tribes. Negotiations looking toward such a treaty had been begun by Frontenac as soon as news came that peace had been decided upon at Ryswick.[1] They were continued and brought to a successful termination by his successor.

This event could not fail to have an important influence on New York, for its position and policy depended largely on the Five Nations. We have seen that in the previous war the share actually borne by New York in the conflict was slight. But the peace which they had now concluded with the Indians was so utilized by the French, with the connivance of New York authority, as wholly to exempt that province from attack during the first two-thirds of the war which was to follow. During that period New York was in position of practical neutrality. The French desired to avoid encounters with her, lest they might provoke the Iroquois to a renewal of hostilities, while New York was willing that her frontiers should remain unmolested, especially if they were to be left without Iroquois protection.[2] During the early years of the war the British government made a few efforts to procure quotas for the defence of New York or for improving its defences, but they proved even less successful than they were in the first war.[3]

[1] N. Y. Col. Docs. IX, 670.
[2] *Ibid.*, 743, 745.
[3] The details of these are given in the chapters on Virginia and Maryland.

New England, therefore, had to bear the full force of the French attack. That this should be so, appeared to be distinctly a part of the French purpose. For, when war again became certain, the plan of the last years of the previous war was revived—that New England should be laid waste or conquered by a fleet and a Canadian land force, which should form a junction at Penobscot bay.[1] After Boston had been captured, the fall of New York was considered to be inevitable. Le Moyne d'Iberville, who had a hand in formulating such schemes, considered it possible to march a force southward from Canada, by the way of the Chaudière and the Kennebec rivers. He desired also to send out parties to lay waste the country to the gates of New York and make the place a desert. Expeditions on this scale however, were not attempted, but, instead, small predatory raids, like those of the previous war, were continued, and with much the same results. As before, the Abenakis were roused to activity by their priests, and, in imitation of the settlement of praying Mohawks at Caughnawaga, successful efforts were made to collect them in considerable numbers into a permanent defensible post at St. Francis, and thence to launch them against the English settlements, Norridgewock on the Kennebec river was also settled, and became for many years an important centre of Jesuit and Indian activity.

Another event which modified the situation in this war, as compared with its predecessor, was the transfer of Spain from the British to the French alliance. This was the result of the seating of a Bourbon on its throne, an act which gave rise to the question of the Spanish Succession, the issue which gave a name to the war as carried on in Europe. Though this event affected the struggle in the West Indies, and brought forces into relations which they were to hold for a half-century to come, it did not as yet seriously affect the course of the war in the continental colonies. An order even was sent to the governors of the colonies in general, in February, 1703/4, that trade should be continued with the Spanish in all commodities except stores of war and such goods as were prohibited by law to be carried to any foreign country. This policy had been suggested by the States

[1] *Ibid.*, 725, 729, 735.

General of the Netherlands and was to be continued during the war.[1]

When the conflict between France and Great Britain was reopening in Europe, Joseph Dudley was appointed governor of Massachusetts. He remained in that office throughout the war. Like the earl of Bellomont, Dudley was made governor of New Hampshire and had the support, such as it was, of its lieutenant governor. As in the previous war, the peril to which the New Hampshire settlements were continually exposed, made them submissive to Dudley's leadership. He was also given the same undefined rights of command over the militia of Connecticut and Rhode Island as had been bestowed on Phips and Fletcher. Thus, so far as the home government was able, the administrative conditions of the previous war were renewed, but with royal control somewhat strengthened. In the person of Dudley a much abler and more successful man now held the governorship than were any of its incumbents during the previous war. He was not a soldier or seaman, he did not lead expeditions against Canada or Acadia, but he was an able and experienced lawyer and administrator as well as a skilful politician, who knew both England and New England better than any officials who had previously been selected for that section.

One of the first tasks which the war imposed upon Dudley as governor in New England was that of raising a body of troops for service in Jamaica. So far as appears, Massachusetts was the only continental colony to which this requisition was directed, and it is suggested that it was imposed as a sort of compensation, in view of the fact that the northern colones were not so serviceable to the crown in trade and customs as were the islands. It was without earlier precedent, though such a measure was resorted to on a larger scale nearly forty years later. It was required that the men be raised as volunteers and be furnished with supplies and transportation in guardships or otherwise to the West Indies. No instructions were sent as to the establishment upon which to put the men. There was no province law specifying the cost of subsistence in quarters, but Dudley was told that twelve pence per day was usual, besides

---

[1] C. O. 5/209.  Plants. Gen. Letter Book of Secy. of State.

allowance for rum. There was no law for punishing desertion. Though war was declared, no assembly had sat and
there were no soldiers in the province till several months
later. But Dudley ordered Captains Larrimore and Walton,
the former well known in Boston and the latter from New
Hampshire, to take charge of the enlistment of the troops.
They divided the two provinces between them. Two companies were raised, Larrimore getting off first in the "Gosport,"
and Walton's forty-nine men sailing in a vessel hired for
the purpose, in January, 1702/3. Dudley had to visit New
Hampshire to attend to the dispatch of Walton's men. For
about three weeks they were billeted upon the inhabitants,
to the great dissatisfaction of the latter. It was a new experience in New England, and there was much aversion to
going or to sending men to the West Indies at all. The
men had to be assured that they should be kept together and
under their own officers. The hope of plunder from the
Spanish, of a special grant from the crown and a bounty
from the assembly of Jamaica was also held out as an
inducement. But in all these the men were disappointed.
They were also put on the lowest British establishment. If
the men had stayed at home, they could have received the
New England pay of five shillings weekly for garrison service
or six to seven shillings for marching service, and run no
risk from the sea or tropical diseases. But they served for
several months, and were brought back by the fleet to Newfoundland, where they almost perished from cold and lack
of food, and many of them came home sick. There they
were disbanded, with the word of approval from Admiral
Benbow that they had served well. This service Dudley
managed with great diligence, making up all the accounts
and muster rolls and duly returning them to the offices in
England.[1]

In September, 1702,[2] Dudley visited Newport and informed
Governor Cranston and his council that by a clause in his
commission under the great seal, he had been appointed

---

[1] C. O. 5/751, Dudley to Sec. of State, Aug. 8, 1705. Extract also from a
letter of his to the B. T., Nov. 10, 1702. Various references to this expedition
also appear in Dudley's letters to B. T. and Sec. of State, in N. Eng. O. P. and
E. B., 1702.

[2] R. I. Col. Recs., III, 458 et seq.

commander of all the forces and places of strength within the colony of Rhode Island, and also vice admiral. At this the Quakers " raged indecently, saying that they were ensnared and injured." Governor Cranston, however, administered the oaths which would enable Dudley to act in Rhode Island; but a formal statement was then made in the council that the power of the militia had been granted in the royal charter and nothing could be done in pursuance of Dudley's commission until the assembly should act. Dudley, attempting to ignore most of earlier Rhode Island history, replied that he had nothing to do with the assembly, but only with the governor and council. The major of the regiment at Newport also declined to call out his force under a warrant from the Massachusetts governor.[1] Like others before him, Dudley was forced to abandon his quest and content himself with writing to the board of trade that the government of Rhode Island, in its present hands, was a scandal to the crown. Its two thousand men, fit for military service, could not be utilized, he said, because Quakers so controlled the government and left out all men of estates, ability and loyality. Rhode Island, on its part, chose Joseph Sheffield as agent and sent him to England to look after its interests in this matter, and also in reference to the interminable boundary controversies in which the colony was engaged.[2]

The right of Connecticut to control her militia had already been so effectually settled that Dudley did not attempt to assert the full power of his commission there. The fact that such power was given him, was probably due to official routine. In the case of that colony, he had to contend not only against its natural jealousy of outside interference, but against a personal dislike of himself which had been inherited from the Andros régime and was strongly felt by the whole Winthrop interest. How successful he was in procuring aid from Connecticut, will appear as the history of the war progresses. One thing was clear, that in spite of all the efforts of the home government to the contrary, the colonies were entering on this stage of the conflict in an even more divided condition than had existed a decade before. In New

[1] C. O. 5/910, E. B. N. Eng., Sept. 17, 1702.
[2] R. I. Recs. III, 464.

England the situation in this regard had not improved, while the inopportune death of Bellomont, taken in connection with the peace between the French and the Iroquois, gave New York an opportunity to drop out of the struggle for a number of years. Of this chance, under the degenerate Cornbury, she was only too willing to avail herself.

Another subject on which the home government persisted in its former instructions, was that of the rebuilding of Pemaquid. In the course of the first summer after his arrival in New England, Dudley visited the ruins of the fort and reported to the board of trade that the cost of rebuilding it would be too great for the resources of Massachusetts, and that the expense of maintaining it, with men and ordnance, would be £5000 a year. Still, he would urge the measure upon the assembly, though a supply of cannon for it and for other forts should be sent from England. Skilled workmen also were needed. Dudley brought the subject before the legislature in the fall session of 1702. A committee of the council reported that, as the foundations were in place, the trench still open, and a supply of lime accessible, the walls might be rebuilt. But it was impossible to get the assembly to consent, though Dudley was urgent in pressing it upon their attention. He had to report failure to the board of trade and it in turn to the queen. This drew out a letter under an order in council to Dudley, to inform the Massachusetts assembly of the queen's sense of their neglect in this matter, and to press them again most urgently to undertake it, and also to furnish their other forts with stores and to contribute toward the cost of the fort on the Piscataqua.[1]

During 1700 — the last year of Bellomont's administration — many rumors were afloat that the Indians intended a general uprising.[2] In Connecticut the Mohegans circulated sinister reports. To the assembly at Boston, in its early spring session of 1700, Bellomont used those reports as an argument for putting Massachusetts in a thorough state of defence and seeking the cooperation of other colonies.

---

[1] Original Papers, New Eng. C. O. 5/863. Various entries in Entry Bk. New Eng. C. O. 5/910. Cal. St. P. Col. 1702.

[2] Cal. St. P. Col. 1700, pp. 90, 123 *et seq.*, 400, 424, 469, 523, see index.

Attempts, he said, to avert the blow by treaties or promises were in vain. It was said on the other hand that the Indians were provoked to their activity by rumors, which originated among the French, to the effect that the English were preparing a great expedition for their total destruction. The legislature ordered that some efforts should be made to undeceive the natives and keep them quiet, but the feeling on both sides was such as naturally presaged the war which was soon to break out. One object of the visit of Governor Dudley to Pemaquid in the fall of 1702, to which reference has just been made, was to hold a conference with the eastern sachems and to confirm the peace. In this he was outwardly successful. But later the peace was broken on two occasions, in one case a Massachusetts privateer being the offender and in the other the Indians themselves. The threatening reports as the following summer approached led the governor to visit Casco in June, 1703, where a much more largely attended conference was held and the usual words of reconciliation spoken and ceremonies performed.[1] But it was all to no purpose. The Indians were faithless and the influence of the French over them was too strong.

The war which was now about beginning falls naturally into two periods. The former, which lasted from 1703 to 1707, consisted wholly of local assaults and raids. During the second period, from 1707 to 1713, the same form of warfare continued, but it was thrown into the background and attention was centred on a succession of ambitious efforts by the English against Acadia and Canada. Plans to secure the joint action of the colonies on a considerable scale were then resumed, and in these the British government took some share.

In order to keep the Abenaki Indians faithful and destroy the effect of their dealings with the English, De Vaudreuil, who, on the death of Callières, had succeeded to the governorship of Canada, in August, 1703, sent Sieur de Baubassin, with a force of more than five hundred French and Indians, against the Maine border.[2] Wells, Cape Porpoise, Winter

---

[1] Goodell, Mass. Resolves, 1703, chap. 31 and notes.
[2] N. Y. Col. Docs. IX, 756. Charlevoix, trans. by Shea, V, 160. Penhallow, Wars of New England with the Eastern Indians.

Harbor, Saco, Spurwink, Scarborough and Fort Casco were in a brief interval attacked. Some of these places were entirely ruined and all suffered many losses. About 150 persons were slain, with the usual barbarities, and there was the customary proportion of captives.[1] Major March, most of whose estate was destroyed in the raid, distinguished himself by personal prowess in the defence of Fort Casco; but it was only the fortunate appearance of Captain Southack,[2] with the province galley, which saved March and his post from total destruction. Black Point, Berwick, York, Hampton in New Hampshire, and Haverhill in Massachusetts later suffered to some extent. The French governor could write that the Abenakis had "brilliantly broken with the English by this last expedition."

For a short time before the blow fell Dudley had had intimations that a force was being dispatched from Canada.[3] An Indian chief had also brought a report that a French ship had arrived at Mount Desert and that some Cape Sable Indians were with the French in that region. A shallop was ordered thither to reconnoitre, and men from Essex and Middlesex counties were dispatched into the woods on the northern frontier. Letters were sent to Rhode Island and to Connecticut asking for aid. From the former came the stereotyped reply "that they could not spare any," and the request was not repeated. But in Connecticut more hopeful conditions seemed to exist. These precautions, however, were without effect in averting the attack.

After the French and Indians had delivered their blow Dudley showed himself to possess energy and resource equal to those of the best officials of the time. As reports came in quick succession of the disasters on the frontiers, they were communicated to the council and defensive measures adopted. On the first report of the attack on Wells, Povey, the lieutenant governor, was ordered to go to Piscataqua and with the advice of the New Hampshire government improve the forces at Wells, Berwick and other places, and repel the

[1] Williamson, in his History of Maine, says more than 155; Pike says 73 killed and 95 captured, but may not have intended to be exhaustive.

[2] Mass. Res., 1703–4, c. 69 and notes by Goodell; Willis, Hist. of Portland, 315.

[3] Goodell, Res. 1703–4, C. 53, note.

enemy. A levy of 150 men from the southern regiments of Massachusetts was at once ordered. A company of dragoons and 100 men were ordered to Wells and the province galley was sent out on the cruise which proved the salvation of Fort Casco. Volunteers were also called for in Middlesex and Essex and a levy was ordered from the companies of Hingham and Weymouth. After the report came of the attack on Saco and Winter Harbor an order was sent that the women and children from the whole region should be sent off and the men retained under pay for service. On August 18 war was declared by Massachusetts against the various tribes of Eastern Indians with whom her magistrates had so recently been engaged in what appeared to be friendly conferences. This was immediately followed by orders to the commissary general to provide for the forces raised 500 hatchets, powder horns, belts and knapsacks; also 500 pairs of shoes and stockings, and to deposit the same with the several commissions to be distributed among the soldiers as occasion should require. Six or eight shoemakers were ordered impressed to make shoes for the soldiers. Arms were to be sent to the garrisons at Kittery and Casco in exchange for their defective ones, which should be repaired. The house on Fort Hill, Boston, was ordered fitted up as a depot for arms and ammunition, while Pepperell's Garrison in Kittery was to be used as a magazine at the other end of the route. Colonel Converse was put in immediate command of all the forces. At the close of August Dudley had 900 men, besides officers, in pay, and yet, because so many were needed for garrison duty on the extended frontier, not much more than half of the entire number could be kept on the march. He estimated the cost of this force at £36,000 per annum. At the close of the first two weeks in September he stated that he had 1100 in pay, and was hoping to march one-half that number to the headquarters of the enemy.[1]

In New Hampshire, meantime, the measures of Massachusetts were to an extent imitated.[2] On August 23 sixty men from its towns were ordered by the council to be detached for service against the enemy. But the condition of unpre-

[1] 6. Mass. Hist. Colls. III, 150, 152.
[2] N. H. Prov. Papers, II, 403 *et seq.*

paredness in that province is indicated by entries showing that the work which had long been in progress under Romer on the fort at Great Island was not yet completed; that it had a garrison of two men, which was now increased to six, but the additional four were engaged for only a month; that at the same fort there was no paper for cartridges, its boat lacked a grappling iron and six oars and that no wood or oil for lights had been provided for the fort. Steps had to be taken to supply these, now that war had burst on the country. Selectmen and militia officers in the towns were given power to bring all grain and corn into garrisons for its preservation.

The efforts in the two provinces resulted, in the fall of 1703, in the dispatch of two expeditions to search for the rendezvous of the Indians.[1] They consisted of about 400 men each and pushed their way through the wilderness to Pegwasket, which was far inland near what later became the boundary between New Hampshire and Maine; but the lairs of the Indians were not found and little execution was done. It was said that the undergrowth was so thick that the unused trail was lost. The province galley and two sloops were meantime kept cruising along the coast as far as the river St. Croix.

As the first winter approached a measure was adopted by Dudley which was in advance of the practice of the previous war. This was the sending out of winter expeditions in imitation of the French, so as to keep the attention of the enemy continually occupied. As the assembly considered this service too hard for the regularly drafted soldiers, who had been on duty at least a part of the summer, it was resolved to rely on volunteers and to encourage them by a special bounty on scalps.[2] The bounty which was regularly offered to the drafted troops was quadrupled and made £40 Massachusetts currency for each scalp, and the offer was extended to New Hampshire men as well. During the winter of 1703/4 three such parties were sent out on snowshoes and were out about three weeks each. Though they met few Indians and did little execution, their presence probably made it more dangerous for the enemy to approach the frontier, and for

[1] Mass. Recs. 1703–4, c. 66 and Notes.
[2] *Ibid.*, c. 66 and c. 85, and Notes.

this reason the same policy was continued the following winter.

During the previous war the Connecticut valley had been comparatively unmolested. But because of the neutrality of the Iroquois and the passive attitude of New York, operations there were safer for the French than they had been a decade before. At the same time the Indians were being hard pressed in eastern New England. Vaudreuil was conscious of all this and therefore directed his war parties well toward the valley. The trails which had led thither from Canada passed from Lake Champlain up the Winooski, French or Onion river, across the Green Mountains and down one of the western tributaries of the Connecticut. By this route it was easier to reach the valley towns from Canada than it was the settlements of Maine and New Hampshire. The drifting of war into this region inevitably occasioned negotiations between Massachusetts and Connecticut and furnished Dudley with an opportunity to use such powers or influence as he had.

As soon as the disasters of 1703 began, Dudley asked Connecticut for 60 men and a small number of Indians for service in New Hampshire and Maine.[1] This was the first of several such requests, and on this occasion Dudley offered to transport the men by sea and furnish their subsistence. Winthrop referred the request to the council and it was declined on the plea that the strength of the colony was only equal to the defence of the valley, which was its own frontier.[2] In his letter home Dudley coupled Connecticut with Rhode Island in his complaint that no troops were obtained. This in due time drew statements from Connecticut in defence of her conduct, the purpose of which was to show that it was the same as it had been in the earlier wars. Connecticut declared that she was active, as she had been in Philip's War, but in her own immediate defence, a statement which could not be truthfully made of Rhode Island. But, after all that was possible had been said in her defence, the futility of the policy which she followed for the protection of the Connecticut valley was clearly shown by the fall of Deerfield.

[1] 6 Mass. Hist. Colls. III, 139–159. Kimball, Career of Dudley, 143.
[2] Connecticut did offer a small body of Indians.

This was the advanced post in the valley, exposed to almost certain attack if the French should make a descent in that region. It was remote from the other towns, and in addition to its stockade and its own inhabitants should have had a permanent and efficient garrison. There had been repeated alarms about it. In August, 1703, Captain Partridge of Hadley — who in this war occupied the place of leadership which had formerly been held by Pynchon — sent an appeal to Connecticut for aid. The officers of the board of war in Hartford county hastened to muster 50 or 60 men to meet the need. With reasonable promptness they marched to Deerfield and vicinity. According to arrangements they stayed there but two days while scouts searched the woods for a distance of thirty miles. Finding no trace of the enemy, the men returned to Hartford after having been out about a week. The inference of Captain Chester, of the Hartford board of war, from this experience was, that it seemed difficult " to do them any real good except by keeping garrisons among them; the going where mischief is done proves ineffectual, the enemies by that time they get thither are far enough out of their reach." [1]

The same Chester (then a major) described the difficulties which he met in raising this small force in terms which deserve quoting, because they evidently refer to a condition that was typical.[2] " I find it very difficult " he says, " to have men well fixt; the country paying so meanly, no man cares to trust anything on the public account; and this method of warning of men to be in readiness when called is not so effectual as the former (they being impressed by the constable, and in pay for the time of their being impressed, were incorridjed, [encouraged?]) and we find that of those ordered some were sick, some gone out of the precincts and no penalty if they neglect; which forced me to issue forth warrants to the constables to supply such want. We have not one line in the law to give rule or direction in these affairs, nor to empower officers to punish delinquency. The laws of the neighbouring province are ample and full in every particular, which is a great help to facilitate the work; ours being silent, I have no way but to turn the neglectory and

---

[1] 6 Mass. Hist. Colls. III, 147.    [2] Ibid., 141.

delinquents to your Honor to be proceeded with as you shall see meet. No troops are out of the way of serviss save the taking of their salleries or any advantage the law allows you. I find such difficulties in these things and the law being so deficient, there being no rule to proceed by, that I am desirous not to meddle for the future." As the people of Connecticut construed their charter strictly and held that the obligation of defence should not take them out of the colony without the consent of the general court, Major Chester renewed his request that some adequate law should be passed for the raising of soldiers and sending them into other colonies. Nothing, however, was done.

When, at the beginning of winter, Dudley was planning to send out his snowshoemen,[1] Connecticut was asked to send 100 Mohegans to be quartered for six months or more on the east side of the Lake Winnipisaukee on condition that they should be supported by Massachusetts and receive rewards for scalps at its rates. The Indians were inclined to go, but more definite information was desired about the country where they were to camp. When this was furnished, without reason they raised their demand to twelve pence per day in advance of the Massachusetts allowance. New Haven and Fairfield counties were also reported to be opposed to the whole scheme, and it was stated that the last assembly was not in favor of sending any men to the east the present winter. The governor and council favored paying what the Indians demanded, but there was so much opposition that it was referred to the assembly at its March session. It approved of the expedition and the Indians were sent, but during the delays the winter had passed, and we do not hear that the Indians, though they remained there till the next summer, accomplished anything against the enemy.

In February, 1703/4, came the long feared attack on Deerfield and yet, as was to be expected, it was a complete surprise. It is famed in literature and history and all the events connected with it can be studied in the greatest detail. But in its general character it did not differ from a score of other similar disasters during the border wars. It left the towns in the valley in an agony of fear, which found

[1] *Ibid.*, 163, 166, 172, 174, 181–190; Conn. Recs., IV, 456.

expression in an appeal [1] of Partridge to Connecticut for help. " Our people are so terrified with the late stroak," he wrote, " that I can hardly pacify them without men to garrison our towns."

In May their terror was increased by an attack on a settlement just south of Northampton,[2] while the establishment of a body of hostile Indians at Cowassic on the Connecticut, near the mouth of Wells river, was a constant menace to the towns below. Deerfield was now garrisoned and thus the integrity of the frontier was preserved. In response to appeals before the middle of June, Connecticut had 560 men in pay and most of them were in the upper valley. Some of them were making long, exhausting, and futile marches through the wilderness in search of the enemy, and others were doing garrison duty. Major Whiting was their commander. As the Connecticut men were all or nearly all volunteers, they could not be kept out indefinitely without their own consent. While scouting was regarded as necessary, it was exhausting and offered little prospect of destroying the enemy. The only achievement of the summer in that region was the destruction of the hostile post at Cowassic. Partridge and the inhabitants of the imperilled towns desired the soldiers to go into garrison among them, and some discussion followed as to the relative advantages of scouting and garrison service.

The Connecticut officers felt uneasy because they were required to serve under Massachusetts commissions.[3] Dudley sent blank commissions of his own to be filled out by Partridge, but he found that the Connecticut officers objected to receiving them. They contended that in the past it had been customary for Connecticut commissions to be issued, and such had already been made out, though those who received them were ordered to obey the Massachusetts governor while they were in his province. Dudley asked Winthrop to direct the men to receive his commissions, as Connecticut was not to be permitted to exercise authority in the royal province of Massachusetts. Winthrop in reply stated what orders had been

---

[1] 6 Mass. Hist. Colls. III, 182. For all details of the massacre see Sheldon, Hist. of Deerfield, I, 288 et seq.

[2] 6 Mass. Hist. Colls. III, 200.

[3] Ibid., 216.

given, and referred to the point which Dudley had raised as a nice one, but expressed no inclination to yield to his demand. Though the Connecticut men were eager to return home, owing to the succession of alarms and the pleas of Colonel Partridge and others, the numbers of those out seem to have been pretty well kept up during the summer.[1]  The French succeeded in making no more effective raids that year, though one was attempted under Baucouer.

While Connecticut and western Massachusetts were thus occupied, Dudley was busy organizing a raid against Acadia, the last and most extended of those led by Colonel Church. Its object was to destroy property and stop trade between the Indians and the French.  The plan was submitted by Church and the necessary appropriations were made by the general court.[2]  Church was instructed to rendezvous at Piscataqua, sail thence to Matinicus, there embark his forces in whale boats and proceed along the coast to Passamaquoddy bay; thence they were to sail to Mines and Chignecto and from there to Port Royal.  On his way Church was to burn and destroy the buildings of the enemy, break down the dams of their corn grounds, inflict all the damage he could and bring away the prisoners.  This, together with a call at Penobscot on the way back, he was expected to accomplish in six weeks.  After that he was to consider whether he could proceed to Norridgewock, and thus keep the expedition together until the middle of August.  Though an effort was made to procure volunteers from New Hampshire, the peril to which its towns were then exposed almost entirely prevented response.  The captains made return that scouting along the frontier was the preferable course, and orders for this service were issued.  But a general command was issued that at least sixty men be raised in New Hampshire for Church's expedition, even if it had to be done by impressment.  Winthrop Hilton was most useful in raising this detachment and he later went on the expedition.  Church himself, after embarking his Massachusetts contingent at Nantasket for Piscataqua, went overland in person to raise recruits.  His

---

[1] Goodell, Mass. Res. VIII, 398, 401.  6 Mass. Hist. Colls. III, 245 *et seq.*
[2] Church, Expeditions, etc., 36,141.  Goodell, Mass. Res. 1703-4, Chaps. 100, 112 and Notes.

force, when collected, consisted of 550 men.[1]  The transports
and small craft which carried the force were followed by two
ships, these being ordered to join the expedition in time to
share in its doings in Acadia.

In three months Church, so far as possible, carried out
his instructions to the letter.  He plundered all settlements
he could find on the coast from Matinicus to Passamaquoddy
and then, while the war vessels went to Port Royal, with
small craft he plundered the farms and towns of the Acadians
in the region of Mines and Chignecto, capturing many prisoners.  It was not thought safe to attack Port Royal, though
Church had with him 400 men.  The force returned by way
of Penobscot, but it did not attempt the expedition up the
Kennebec river.  It was a marauding enterprise, modelled
after those of the French, and, like them, inflicted its heaviest
damage on non-combatants.  Church did not escape the charge
of cruelty, but, at its worst, this was of slight importance
when compared with acts in the guilt of which the French
must share through their incitement of the Indians.

Meantime Dudley showed himself by no means satisfied
with the efforts which Rhode Island and Connecticut had thus
far put forth.  His letters to England were filled with complaints against them.  At the beginning of December, 1704,
he wrote to Governor Winthrop that on the advice of the
Council of Massachusetts, he had sent a committee, with
Wait Winthrop and Nathaniel Byfield at its head,[2] to Connecticut and the same to Rhode Island to lay before them the
necessity of a grant of money and men for the common
defence.  He stated plainly that he thought Connecticut
should bear one-third of the burden and cost of the war, and
that it should be shown by the quotas she contributed.
These might be employed in Hampshire county, but they must
be paid and subsisted by Connecticut.  Dudley had apparently concluded that the marching of Connecticut men to
the east and of eastern men to the Connecticut valley was
too laborious to be further continued except at crises.  In

---

[1] Williamson, Hist. of Maine;  Goodell, Mass. Res. 1703–4, p. 338, where
a full list is given.
[2] 6 Mass. Hist. Colls. III, 273 *et seq.*;   Mass. Res. 1704–5, chaps. 81, 97,
106, 112 and Notes.

making these demands Dudley was also expressly acting in harmony with the plans of the crown.

But it is to be remembered that the Massachusetts governor was at this time an object of keen suspicion to Connecticut leaders. The correspondence of Sir Henry Ashurst, agent of Connecticut, shows that he was now and had long been using his influence in England to procure the recall of Connecticut's patent as well as all other charters. This subject was soon to be brought before parliament again and there was great anxiety in Connecticut and elsewhere about it. Dudley was also concerned in the complaints of the Mohegan Indians of Connecticut to the privy council respecting their lands. He was considered as an arch enemy of corporate liberties, and this must be remembered as one reads the polite phrases in Winthrop's letters of reply.

Winthrop after deliberation with his council replied that the quota of men and money which was required by Dudley was so unreasonable that he had not thought it fit to enter on any long debate of it with the commissioners; but the Connecticut government had concluded to raise 200 men for defence of Hampshire County, provided Massachusetts would subsist them and furnish 100 men with ammunition; the Connecticut men should also serve under commissioners issued by their own colony, but be under Dudley's direction while in Massachusetts, as had been the custom in the former war.[1] Winthrop expressed surprise that Dudley should have represented Connecticut as a delinquent in view of the detachments of dragoons she had often sent to the frontiers, the forces sent to the eastward and the fact that she had kept 400 men in Hampshire county all summer, besides sending added forces at times of alarm. Dudley replied that a force of 200 men was far below the proportion which Connecticut should contribute and that she was expected to subsist her own troops, as well as furnish them with ammunition; Massachusetts left 600 men on the frontiers and 350 preparing for winter marches. To this Winthrop replied that Massachusetts, being rich, thought all the world so too; so many troops could not be longer supported without starving the people of Connecticut. He thought that the means of escaping this

[1] Kimball, Career of Dudley, 151 *et seq.*, 279, 281.

was to arouse the Iroquois to action, they having said that their hatchets were ready when Curler [1] should give them orders. The situation might be reversed and the English be able to send out flying parties which would bring in scalps.

Such efforts and suffering as those of the New England colonies drew attention to the neutrality of the Iroquois and the consequent peaceful situation in New York. In the spring of 1704 John Schuyler, in a letter to Governor Winthrop of Connecticut, had suggested that they hold a conference with the Iroquois. About two months later Winthrop sent Captain Nathan Gold to Cornbury to ask that New York contribute a quota of men for service on the New England frontier. At the same time Deputy Governor Treat called attention to the probable failure of the policy of defence in which New England was engaged, and suggested that something should be done to disturb the quietness of the Canadians at home, recommending a land expedition in which he thought the Iroquois, by proper treatment, could be induced to cooperate. It was his opinion that Cornbury should be approached on the subject. Four days later Treat, who was consulting members of the committees of war of Hartford and New Haven counties, suggested that Cornbury be asked to cooperate in a treaty with the Five Nations.[2]

Already the government of Massachusetts had resolved to negotiate with them and had appointed commissioners and provided a present of £200. Connecticut was now invited to join in this and it agreed to do so.[3] In the autumn, as soon as the condition of the frontier would permit, Penn Townsend and John Leverett were appointed envoys to go by the way of Connecticut and New York to Albany. John Livingston — son of Robert and son-in-law of Governor Winthrop — and Captain Gold accompanied them as the commissioners of Connecticut, taking along a small present for the Indians. As was necessary, the consent of the government of New

---

[1] Cadwallader Colden writes thus of the amiable Dutch Indian trader and agent, Arendt van Corlaer (or Curler), who for a time managed Rensselaerswyck: "It is from him, and in remembrance of his merit, that all governors of New York are called Corlaer by the Indians to this day, though he himself never was governor." — D. R. F.

[2] 6 Mass. Hist. Colls. III, 222, 223, 225, 231.

[3] Mass. Res., 1704–5, c. 5, c. 8, c. 35, c. 101, and Notes.

York to this conference was obtained, and the envoys were well treated at Albany. But the Indians for a considerable time delayed appearing, and then contented themselves merely with a renewal of assurances of friendship. They could not be induced to take up the hatchet. This the New Englanders attributed to the unwillingness of Cornbury and his advisers to sacrifice in any measure the profitable trade which they were enjoying with the French and Indians. The commissioners returned in November.[1]

Owing in part to the exhaustion of the combatants, hostilities were to an extent suspended during 1705, and there was some talk of a total cessation of the war. During that year the Massachusetts government in particular was occupied with negotiations for a general exchange of prisoners.[2] Of these the French held a large number, since Church's expedition there had been more in Boston than the jail could hold. Before that event Dudley had written to Vaudreuil protesting against the barbarities of the Indian allies of the French, and stating how well the English had always treated the prisoners in their hands. After Church's expedition he wrote again proposing an exchange, in the belief that the failure of Baucour's expedition would make the French governor more inclined to this policy. John Sheldon and John Wells of Deerfield, both of whom now had relatives in Canada, volunteered to carry the message by the way of Albany and were entrusted with the task, John Livingston being sent with them.[3]

In reply to the charges of barbarity Vaudreuil cited the murder of Gourdault and his companions by Church after they had surrendered as surpassing anything that the French had done.[4] He also called attention to the fact that the French rescued nearly all their prisoners, on their arrival in Canada, from the hands of the Indians and treated them

---

[1] "The Narrative of the Treaty and Negotiations," which was the report of the Massachusetts commissioners, does not appear among the archives at Boston, and hence the details of the negotiations are not known.

[2] Mass. Res., 1705–6, chaps. 13, 15, 36, 51, 83, 85; 1704–5, c. 25; 1705–6, c. 54, 56, 57, 62 and Notes.

[3] The conditions of exchange which Dudley sent have not been preserved.

[4] This was the chief offence charged against Church on his recent expedition to Acadia.

well.  Vaudreuil was not averse to a general exchange, provided it might include Jean Baptiste,[1] a French naval officer,
who had been held since the previous war as a prisoner at
Boston, charged with murder and piracy.  This was due to
the fact that he had attacked Englishmen after, as it was
alleged, he had taken the oath of allegiance and had become
an English subject.  His release, however, was now insisted
on by Vaudreuil as indispensable.  In June, 1705, after a
preliminary message had been sent from Canada by Samuel
Hill, who had been captured at Wells, Livingston and his
associates were sent back accompanied by Sieur de Courtemanche, who was commissioned to negotiate on behalf of the
Canadian government.  The pressure of the relatives of
prisoners in Canada now became strong for exchange.  The
envoys advised the governor secretly to insist on the exclusion of Baptiste from exchange, but if it was found impossible otherwise to obtain it, then to consent to his release.[2]
Courtemanche, acting probably on instructions, consented to
sign the articles offered by Dudley, Baptiste excepted, provided Chafours, brother of Vaudreuil's wife, might go back
to Canada with him on parole, pledging his honor to return
if the governor general should not accept the articles.  This
was approved by the general court, through a number of
merchants presented an unavailing protest against it.  Courtemanche and his companion, accompanied by Samuel Vetch
and William Dudley, the governor's son, returned to Quebec
by sea.  Four months passed and nothing was heard from
them at Boston, when the brigantine which had carried
Courtemanche came back bringing Vetch and Dudley with a
draft of a treaty from Vaudreuil for the governor's acceptance,
November 21, 1705.[3]  This provided for a truce and cessation of hostilities, on the part of the Indians as well as the
English, pending the exchange of prisoners; also for a return
of all prisoners, without exception, by both parties.  The
document, in addition, required the assent of the governor
of New York as necessary to its enforcement and included
Acadia in the French territory to which it should apply.

[1] Mass. Res., *ibid.*, p. 511.
[2] *Ibid.*, 1705–6, c. 13.
[3] *Ibid.*, Chaps. 15, 51, 83, and Notes.

Because of the last-mentioned feature, the house at once advised Dudley not to accept the terms, and the assent of Cornbury was never given, though a letter to him on the subject was prepared and approved. But though the exchange in this form failed and hostilities began again in the spring of 1706, negotiations were resumed in that year. The form now taken was this: the English sent their prisoners to Port Royal and notified the Canadian authorities of the fact. They also sent Samuel Appleton, as agent, with a vessel to Canada to demand in return the surrender of the English prisoners which were held by the French. This, after some delay, was agreed to. The Rev. John Williams, the well known Deerfield pastor, arrived in Boston near the close of 1706, and the rest who were willing to come were restored during the next year.[1] In this way some of the deepest wounds which had been inflicted by the war were healed.

During the interval of comparative quiet in 1705 the question of rebuilding Pemaquid was again taken up. The home government had continued to urge it. But now an address to the queen was prepared by the two houses, thanking her for a recent gift of cannon and stating at length that the general court was not only unable to rebuild the fort but did not believe in its utility. They also declined again to contribute toward the support of the fort at Piscataqua. It was said that the war had cost Massachusetts more than £80,000,[2] a very great part of which was now a debt on the province. Such an argument as that could not be otherwise than decisive, while, if the British government desired the maintenance of Pemaquid as a support for her claim on Acadia, in fairness she should have contributed to the cost of its maintenance. In the same session the work which Redknap, the engineer, had begun on the fort at Winter Harbor, was ordered to be suspended; but the next year £100 was added to a grant of £200 made in 1704, for that fort as a substitute for the fort at Saco.[3]

[1] Mass. Res. 1706–7, c. 54–62, 88, 107, 125, and Notes.

[2] In a petition to the treasury, early in 1705, it was stated that the war was costing Massachusetts £20,000 per annum and that during the previous summer every tenth man in the province was constantly under arms and more than 140 sail of ships had been lost. Col. Treas. Papers, March 15, 1704/5.

[3] Mass. Res. 1705–6, c. 57; *ibid.*, 1706–7, c. 76.

In the early summer of 1706 outrages were renewed by the French and Indians at many places along the frontier, while it was expected that D'Iberville with vessels from the West Indies would make a descent on the coast.[1] Colonel Hilton, on the eastern frontier, and Partridge in the Connecticut valley were in actual charge of the garrisons, scouting parties and raids, while the operations as a whole were under the general direction of Dudley. After a few weeks the attacks almost ceased and by fall quiet was restored. In the course of the following winter Hilton was sent up the Kennebec toward Norridgewock and later along the coast region about the mouth of the river, but only a few of the enemy were found. These events gave further indications that the activity of the Abenakis was declining.

While popular rage against the enemy was being formed anew by the outrages of 1706, the fact was revealed that traffic of some sort was being carried on by certain Boston parties with the French of Acadia. Under the irregular relations and with the keen desire for profit which existed, it is reasonably certain that trade, the accompaniment of fishing in that quarter, had never wholly ceased. But the instances of traffic with the enemy which now became known, had their origin in the negotiations of the previous year for the exchange of prisoners. During the late peace Samuel Vetch had traded with Canada and had a considerable sum due him there when the war began.[2] In the hope of collecting it, he agreed with the Massachusetts government to go back to Quebec with Courtmanche in 1705 and there to help complete the negotiations for the exchange of prisoners. According to Vetch's statement, he agreed to do this without reward and was permitted, in return, to bring back the value of his debt in beaver.[3] It was quite in accord with the mixture of private and public motives and activities which characterized government as then conducted that such an arrangement as this

---

[1] Penhallow, op. cit.; Goodell, Mass. Resolves, VIII, 668, 700.

[2] Vetch had been charged in New York with illegal trade with Canada, and a vessel of his had been condemned in the Admiralty Court there, some time before June, 1702; Ex. C. Miss., June 11, 1702; the case of Wm. Atwood, Colls. of New York Hist. Soc. Fund Series, 1880, p. 295.

[3] See the case of Vetch, as presented before the privy council in Eng. C. O. 5/912, fol. 235, E. B. N. Eng.

should be made. Dudley was certainly not above entering upon it. But owing to the stiffening up of the rules Vetch found it impossible to export his beaver from Canada. Then his debtor promised to meet him the next spring at Canseau and pay the bill. With the consent of Dudley Vetch hired a sloop and went to Canseau, but no merchant appeared. On his way back, being forced by the weather to put in at several points on the Acadian coast, a little traffic was carried on with the Indians, the proceeds of which Vetch brought back to Boston.

Other parties became involved in dealings with the Acadians as a result of their being sent direct to Port Royal to co-operate in the exchange of prisoners. They stated that in order to redeem certain English vessels which had been taken by the French, with the consent of the Massachusetts authorities they took some goods to Port Royal for exchange. It was also said that the retention of Port Royal by the French had such advantages for the New England merchants that Church was forbidden to recapture it, though on his last raid he had a force which was vastly superior to the French.

In the early summer of 1706 reports of these transactions and of others like them got abroad. They were exaggerated and perverted, as would naturally be the case. Vetch was the first to be implicated, and he increased the impression of his guilt by landing his goods at Plymouth and elsewhere on Cape Cod. The general court was in session, and the county members in the lower house were smarting under the attacks upon their homes and the loss of relatives and friends.[1] The master of Vetch's sloop was brought before the general court and testified that the sloop had gone to Acadia loaded with arms, ammunition and provisions, to trade with the enemy, thus putting into their hands the very means of slaughtering the wives and children of the English.[2] A letter from Vaudreuil to Dudley was also shown in which the French governor said that it was not strange that Indians committed many murders when English vessels came privately and sold implements of war to the savages. Excitement ran high in

[1] Mass. Res., 1706–7, chaps. 11, 14, 16, 20, 38, 45, 58, 68, 73, and notes. Journals of Council and Reps. for 1706.

[2] 6 Mass. Hist. Colls. III, 334.

Boston and Dudley had to fall in with the current. One of the members of the house was sent to seize the vessel, and that, with another to which its cargo was being removed, was brought to Boston. John Borland and William Rouse of Charlestown, it was learned, had been concerned in the trade; and it was stated that others were still on such voyages. Therefore the province galley and a tender were fitted out to go for their arrest, and the governor issued a proclamation calling upon all persons to make public such information as they possessed. The result was that, in addition to Vetch, Borland and Rouse, Roger Lawson, Ebenezer Coffin and John Philips, Jr., were imprisoned upon the charge of illicitly trading with the enemy.

Under the influence of popular clamor and resentment the general court now resorted to a measure which in its arbitrariness reminds one of the trials of the Antinomians under the first charter. Instead of sending the accused before a court of justice according to the ordinary forms of procedure, it imprisoned them without bail until the next session in August.[1] Then the attorney general exhibited articles of impeachment against them before the houses in joint session and the accused were heard at the bar. Their condemnation was as much a foregone conclusion as was that of the Antinomians before the same tribunal in 1637. After summary hearings bills were prepared, agreed to in conference and promptly passed imposing heavy fines on all the accused and declaring them hereafter incapable of holding any public office. They were all to stand committed till their fines were paid.

By this measure a blow was aimed at what was undoubtedly a serious evil, one, too, which kept recurring throughout the colonial wars. But it was done in such arbitrary fashion that the act was sure to be reversed in England. Dudley, in transmitting the acts, expressed the opinion that the fines were too heavy and hoped they might be remitted.[2] Queries relating to the procedure in this case were presented in due time to Attorney General Northey, and he replied that the charter conferred on the general court only the power of

---

[1] Journal of Council, session of August, 1706.
[2] C. O. 5/912, E. B. N. Eng.; Dudley to B. T., Oct. 8, 1706.

legislation, that to confirm the acts would be to establish a precedent most dangerous to liberty and that they should be disallowed and the offenders tried according to the regular process of law.[1] This was done by an order in council, September 24, 1707, and it was directed that the fines should be restored, and that the trials should be held in Massachusetts. These occurred in Suffolk county, in November, 1708. Coffin, of Nantucket, was found guilty. Because of sickness Lawson was unable to appear. Vetch was not tried, because he had gone to England and had not yet returned.[2] The others were found not guilty or escaped on technicalities. Charges were afterwards presented in England by some of Dudley's enemies that he was concerned in trade with the enemy, but no action against him followed.

With 1707 began the second period of the war, and with it plans for an expedition against Port Royal. Subercase had recently arrived there as governor in the place of Brouillan and it was expected that greater activity against the English would be shown in that province. Subercase did indeed urge upon the Canadian government the making of Acadia a leading centre of Indian trade and control.[3] At its March session Dudley laid a proposal for an expedition before the general court.[4] The house at once voted in its favor, provided means requisite for it could be obtained. The council resolved that a committee be appointed to consider the practicability of the enterprise and, if practicable, what forces, ships, transports and supplies would be necessary; and also if the province was in condition to undertake the expedition. To this the house agreed and a joint committee was appointed, with a request to hasten its labors.

Already Dudley had applied to Rhode Island and Connecticut for aid.[5] From the former he received a more favorable reply than was usual. Its assembly voted that an armed

---

[1] *Ibid.*, March 28, 1707; Acts P. C. Col., II, 516.

[2] C. O. 5/865, O. P. N. Eng.; Dudley to B. T., March 1, 1708/9, inclosures. Dudley wrote at the close of 1710 that he had received an instruction against illegal trading with the enemy under flags of truce, but he was confident that nothing of that nature had happened in Massachusetts.

[3] Docs. rel. a l'Histoire de la Nouvelle France, II, 460.

[4] Resolves of Mass. 1706–7, c. 131, and p. 665.

[5] *Ibid.*, c. 142 and p. 679 *et seq.*

vessel of not more than 80 tons be impressed, and volunteers
to the number of 70 or 80 be raised; 48 men also might be
impressed. Governor Winthrop, of Connecticut, dwelt in his
reply on the probable ease with which Port Royal could be
taken and the likelihood that, at the close of the war, it would
be given back to the French, a result which would be offensive
to the "very stout" but "very thoughtful and cautious"
inhabitants of Connecticut after they had lavished their blood
and treasure upon the enterprise. A later appeal, which Winthrop laid before the assembly, was also rejected and Connecticut bore no share in this expedition.[1] Acadia, if conquered, could not become a part of her territory, while her
interest in the fishing along that coast was not great. As
usual, she considered her energies sufficiently occupied with
the protection of her immediate northern frontier.

The report of the committee of the two houses of the Massachusetts general court was duly presented and after some
discussion was accepted and made a joint resolution.[2] It
empowered the governor to take suitable action in reference
to all measures which were necessary for the outfit of the expedition, such as the procuring of transports and armed
vessels, military supplies and provisions of all sorts, the payment of the force and the distribution of plunder, and the
procuring of aid from outside the colony. The rates of wages
for officers and men were, of course, fixed by the general
court. The force was to consist, so far as possible, of volunteers, and impressment should be resorted to only in case
the full number of 1000 could not otherwise be raised. In the
course of preparations Dudley visited New Hampshire and
almost commanded it to furnish a quota, and this it did,
to the extent of one company under Hilton, who was also
made colonel of one of the two regiments of which the expedition consisted.[3]

In organizing the expedition the commissary was brought
into large and constant requisition, while the council of war
exercised general supervision. The methods employed were
much the same in New Hampshire and Massachusetts: com-

[1] *Ibid.*, 685.
[2] *Ibid.*, 681, and c. 142.
[3] N. H. Prov. Papers, II, 497, and III, 339.

mittees and subordinate officials were made use of in the work of selecting the transports and other vessels and appraising them, but the council of war finally determined what ones should be selected. Under orders of the council clothing, colors, intrenching tools and other equipments were provided. Colonel John March, of Newbury, who had commanded at the defence of Fort Casco in the first year of the war, was appointed commander, and Francis Wainwright, of Ipswich, second in command. The force consisted of two regiments and numbered about 1150 men, including 100 of Church's Indians. Of the regiments Wainwright and Hilton had immediate command. Redknap went as engineer and commander of the ordnance. The fleet gathered at Nantasket and the land forces mustered at Hull. The former consisted of the station ship " Deptford," the province galley, 15 transports and 8 open sloops carrying 36 whale boats. The transports varied in size from sloops to ships. The force sailed on May 13, but because of bad winds, did not reach the vicinity of Port Royal until the 26th of that month.

This expedition resulted in the greatest fiasco of which there is any record in the annals of colonial warfare. The English force equalled two-thirds of the total population of Acadia, while the actual defenders of Port Royal, inclusive of sixty Canadians who had just arrived, numbered about three hundred.[1] But Subercase, the governor, who had just come from Placentia, was a man of resource and bravery comparable with the best partisan leaders who had already inflicted stinging blows upon the English. The French also enjoyed the protection of a stone and earth fort which was favorably situated and well supplied with the small artillery of the time.[2] For the capture of forts by assault colonial levies were exceedingly unfitted, and of siege operations no one among them, except the engineer, Redknap, had any knowledge. The landing was made by the English within Port Royal basin, but at a distance of seven or eight miles from the fort.[3] March, with 750 men, landed on the south shore and Appleton, with 320 men, on the north shore of the Basin.

[1] Rameau, Une Colonie Feodale, I, 331.

[2] Mass. Min. of Ex. Council, June 14, 1707; Report of Redknap; Goodell, *op. cit.*, 727.                [3] *Ibid.*, p. 725.

The arrival of the fleet took the French by surprise, but during the interval before the English approached the fort Subercase had time to collect provisions, repair a breach in the walls and otherwise prepare for defence.

The ground over which the English had to march in their advance toward the fort was broken, swampy, and covered in parts with fallen and tangled trees.[1] The English also fell into ambushes of the enemy, though they were dispersed from these without serious loss to the invaders. But discipline was not maintained and no care was taken by March or other officers for the comfort of the men. Exaggerated reports of the strength of the French were circulated. There was delay in bringing up the artillery and opening fire on the fort. Hence, although the men possessed the usual New England energy, they very soon became despondent and lost confidence in their leaders. The incompetence of the officers justified this opinion, and amid general demoralization it was resolved in a council of war to embark and return home.

A messenger was sent to Boston to announce the news in advance. Since the departure of the expedition strong confidence had been felt in its success and that the removal thus of the nest of corsairs who had preyed on New England trade and obstructed its fishing would at last be effected. The chagrin was correspondingly great when the people awoke to the fact that it was a failure. The forces landed at Casco Bay and there awaited orders. Appleton, Redknap and Holmes were sent to Boston to report and to receive further instructions; but there, so intense was the popular anger, that they were grossly insulted in the streets.[2] Dudley however, though he saw the failure of the plan by the success of which he had hoped to silence his enemies, soon recovered himself sufficiently to resolve that the expedition should return, though not under March as the sole commander. Instead the futile plan was adopted of appointing a commission of civilians to exercise a general supervision over the force, and Elisha Hutchinson, Penn Townsend, and John Leverett, the last named being president of Harvard, were selected for this duty. They held this place without any change in the relative

[1] See Autobiography of Rev. John Barnard, 3 Mass. Hist. Colls. V, 191.
[2] Winthrop Papers, V, 387. Goodell, op. cit., 727, etc.

positions of March and Wainwright until the return voyage to Port Royal had been partly completed, when March fell ill and Wainwright was appointed by them to the chief military command. Officers and men were very discontented and many deserted to escape the second expedition.[1] In this way numbers were reduced to a little over 700 and these were so dispirited that they were estimated to be worth no more than 300 good men. Connecticut again declined to aid, but a further interchange of cordial letters occurred between Dudley and Cranston of Rhode Island, and that colony continued to assist the enterprise.

Before the return of the enemy Subercase had collected a fresh stock of provisions and had secured the aid of a frigate under Bonadventure. The English again reached the vicinity of Port Royal on August 10, and the French were now posted in sufficient strength on the south side of the Basin to prevent their landing nearer than some two miles from the fort and that on the opposite, or northern, side of the bay.

This, wrote Wainwright, was " a mighty advantage to the enemy," as it enabled them to stretch the line of their defences so as to cover the most accessible approaches to the fort. The result was that such efforts as the English made to cross the water and actually approach the fort were repelled. Such as came under fire bore it reasonably well, but by the end of ten days so many had been disabled by sickness that the enterprise was abandoned and the fleet started again for home. As soon as possible after the return of the troops to New England a court martial, consisting of fifteen officers and civilians, was organized to hear and punish offences; but it found no one in particular to be guilty.[2] Its report was to the effect that March, in ordering the first retreat, had acted within his instructions and upon the advice of a council of war; the failure of the second expedition was attributed to the badness of the weather and the " unpersuadable temper of the men," which was a convenient phrase in which to express

[1] Goodell, 734, 735. Hutchinson, Hist. of Mass. II, 154, speaks of a round robin having been signed by a large number of the officers refusing to go to Port Royal; but they were brought into submission.

[2] Goodell, 748, 749. Redknap's opinion was that they did all that was possible with militia and without cannon superior to those of the French. C. O. 5/864; O. P. N. Eng., Feb. 20, 1707/8.

the lack of discipline among them, and of capacity for command among the officers.[1] The expedition cost Massachusetts about £22,000, and in the annals of the time it occupies a place between the exploits of Phips in 1690 and the famous achievement at Louisburg in 1745, as an example of what the unaided efforts of the colonists in enterprises of this kind were like.

While the attacks on Port Royal were in progress the French were sending their allies, the Indians, against many points on the New England frontier. Assaults and consequent alarms continued during the present year and the summer of 1708.[2] These drew from the council and assembly of Massachusetts a memorial to the queen in which they insisted that the best way to subdue the Indians was through men of their own race, meaning the Iroquois, who, as a friendly people, should before this have been enlisted actively in the war on the English side.[3] New York was remaining at peace while New England, as its barrier, was forced to meet the assaults of the enemy alone. As peace would be impossible for it so long as Port Royal remained in the hands of the French, they appealed to the crown for aid in an expedition which should insure its conquest. Merchants were interested in support of the same proposal because of the relief which it would give to the fishery and by prospects of returns from the coal deposits and forests of Nova Scotia.[4] With the close of Cornbury's administration and the arrival of Lord Lovelace, as governor of New York, a serious obstacle to the enlistment of the Iroquois in the war was removed, and to this fact Dudley called the attention of the general court of Massachusetts in his speech of February 16, 1708/9.[5]

After his condemnation by the general court of Massachu-

---

[1] Dudley wrote to the treasury that, owing to the great lack of officers, he could do nothing against Port Royal or Quebec, but with a force from England they could easily be captured. Cal. Treas. Papers, June 20, 1708.

[2] Palfrey, IV, 274. Goodell, op. cit., 750, 758, 769.

[3] C. O. 5/912, E. B. N. Eng. 20. In N. Y. Col. Docs., V, 42, is another paper from Mass., under date of 1708, protesting against the neutrality of New York, and the Five Nations, by means of which New England was forced to bear the brunt of the war.

[4] C. O. 5/865, 21. Letter from Col. John Higginson, received through Sir Stephen Evans.

[5] Journal of Upper House.

setts Samuel Vetch visited England and Scotland. There
is no evidence, however, that he actively urged the disallowance of the measure by which he had been condemned. But
in July, 1708, he presented before the board of trade an
elaborate paper, entitled " Canada Surveyed," in which he
argued in favor of the immediate expulsion of the French
from North America. He called attention to the fact that
the French, though few, were surrounding the English, and
planning to drive them from the continent. Maine, a valuable source of several stores, was already nearly lost. He
also dwelt upon the heavy losses to the English trade which
were occasioned by the presence of the French, and to the
still heavier losses inflicted upon communities directly by
the war. His proposal was a revival of the plan of 1690 for
a joint attack upon Canada by land from New York and
by sea from New England, and that levies from all the
colonies north of Virginia be called out. He proposed that
in addition two full regiments — 1600 men — be sent from
England.[1] Vetch was examined before the board of trade
and his memorial was approved in a report to the queen.
This was in line with the desires of Dudley and the Massachusetts government, though an enlargement upon them.

The assent of the crown to the plan in general was at
once obtained and in March, 1709, Vetch was instructed to
sail for New York and acquaint the governor there with
what would be expected of him.[2] The plan, as formed, was
that a squadron should be sent from England with five
regiments of regular troops. The colonies were expected
to contribute quotas — New York 800 men, including its
four independent companies; Connecticut 350, New Jersey
200, Pennsylvania 150, these to form a land expedition the
total strength of which should be 1500 men. The quotas
were to be ready by the middle of May and they were to be
furnished with arms and ammunition from the magazine at
New York, and provisions for three months should be collected at Wood Creek. Large boats for transporting men

[1] For a short sketch of the career of Samuel Vetch, with references to his
connection and that of his brother William with the Darien colony, see Reports
of Nova Scotia Hist. Soc. IV, and an article by Wilson in International Review,
Nov. 1881.

[2] Newcastle Papers, B. M. Addtl. Mss. 32696a; Pa. Col. Recs., II, 449.

and provisions up the Hudson were to be provided and a store-house built at Wood Creek. The Five Nations were to be pledged for the enterprise and as many canoes were to be procured from them as were needed.

Dudley was separately informed of the expedition and was told that the armament might be expected at Boston by the middle of May and thence they would proceed by sea against Quebec. Vetch was instructed to deliver letters to the governors of Massachusetts and Rhode Island requiring those colonies to provide 1200 men, with three months' provisions and a sufficient number of transports and able pilots. Arms and ammunition for the colonies on this expedition were sent from England with Vetch. Contracts were to be made for the building of ten or more large flat-bottomed boats, to carry sixty men each, for landing troops. It was expected that all would be ready to start from Boston by the middle of May, so that the two expeditions might move at the same time.[1] Dudley was ordered to collect what information he could of the condition of St. John and Placentia in Newfoundland and to put them at the service of the commander when he should arrive; he should also send to the governor of Rhode Island to meet him at Boston and concert measures for executing the queen's orders.

Colonel Nicholson, who since the close of his stormy administration in Virginia had returned to England, offered himself as a volunteer in this expedition, and Vetch was ordered to communicate his instructions to him and to admit him when private consultations were held with the governors. Vetch and Nicholson landed at Boston on April 28th. They conferred at once with Governor Dudley, and expresses were sent the same night to Rhode Island and Connecticut, New York, and the Jerseys and Pennsylvania, with the substance of the instructions from the crown to the governor of each of these colonies. The next morning the royal instructions were read before the council and were dutifully received. A few days later an embargo was laid on all shipping except coasters in order to prevent the French from securing intelli-

---

[1] According to James Logan, it was estimated that the expedition would cost the colonies concerned at least £70,000 or £80,000. Logan to William Penn, Aug. 21, 1709. P. L. II, 358.

gence and also to prevent the exportation of provisions until enough had been secured for the expedition. Such an embargo was laid on all the colonies concerned. Also scouts were placed along the northern frontiers of Massachusetts to prevent information being carried that way. Colonel Wanton, instead of the governor, responded to the summons to Rhode Island and stated that the assembly, which was soon to meet, would be induced, if possible, to levy a tax for the support of 200 men for at least four months, their transports, pilots, surgeons and all supplies save arms and ammunition.

Arrangements were now made by Vetch and Nicholson in consultation with the Massachusetts authorities for the division of 1000 of the Massachusetts men into two regiments, Sir Charles Hobby to be colonel of one and William Tailer of the other; a third regiment to be formed of the Rhode Island and New Hampshire men and to be commanded by Colonel Walton, it being hoped that this would contain about 400 men. Besides its regular officers each regiment was to have one physician, with a surgeon and assistant, one chaplain, a commissary and his assistants for " their victualling transports." The expedition was to be supplied with hospital ships and medicines, and with pilots for the transports and the men-of-war. Contracts were made for the flat-bottomed boats at £23 each. So far as possible all the men who had been prisoners in Canada were to be procured for the service on the expedition. A plan was also formed for sending expresses between Albany and Boston. Barracks and wooden houses were ordered to be built on Noddles Island in Boston harbor for the use of the men who might be landed from the British fleet. A proclamation was issued to satisfy the colony troops that they would not be left in garrison in Canada and acquainting them that an additional bounty would be paid.

These preparations having been made, the departure of the commissioners for New York was hastened by news of the death of Governor Lovelace and the fear that that would hinder their project. Eleven carts were hired to transport the provisions from Massachusetts (which were intended for the expedition up the Hudson) to Bristol, Rhode Island, where they were loaded for New York. Vetch and Nicholson found that the Rhode Island government had taken care to provide their soldiers, transports, provisions, and all other necessities, and their assembly had made due provision for the payment of the same as their address to the queen, " herewith transmitted doth make appear." In Rhode Island Vetch and Nicholson met Colonel Church, who had been employed by Dudley to raise about 200 Indians. Church convinced them of the great value of whale boats on the St. Lawrence, " being far nimbler than any pinnace, able to carry 15 men, each being about 36 feet long, yet so light that two men can easily carry one of them." Thirty-five of them were ordered, which would carry 500 men " upon any sudden or secret design "; Massachusetts was to pay for fifteen of them, and the crown for twenty. The price was £6 per boat, New England currency.

On their way to New York the commissioners called at New Haven to see Governor Saltonstall; they found that he was in attendance on a session of the assembly at Hartford, but that preparations were in active progress in Connecticut and that the governor would in two or three days repair to New York.

On May 18 Vetch and Nicholson arrived at New York. Colonel Ingoldsby, who was then at the head of the government, summoned the council the next day, by which it was stated that Van Rensselaer and Robert Livingston had been sent to Albany to despatch the spies according to instructions. Then the lower house was called in, and both Vetch and Nicholson addressed them, setting forth the plans and needs of the expedition, enlarging on the care of the queen in sparing troops and money for it, when they were so needed for the greater affairs of Europe. The instructions of the queen to Vetch were laid before the house, as also an abstract of what had been done by the other colonies. A joint committee was appointed to wait on Vetch and Nicholson and concert measures. The sum of £6000 was appropriated and immediate provision was made for it by an issue of £5000 in bills of credit, the first issue of this kind made by New York. A quota of 487 men was voted. The money was to be paid out for the use of the expedition and nothing else, and that by the cooperation of the treasurer and four commissioners appointed by the house to procure provisions and military supplies. A committee of three at Albany was to receive them, and send them north. Accounts should be kept by the treasurer and submitted to the two houses, accounting to be at the next session in the fall.[1]

Lieutenant Governor Gookin of Pennsylvania had come to New York to meet Vetch and Nicholson and they took him with them to the meetings of the joint committee, that " he might see the methods of our proceedings with them and be able to inform his council and assembly of the same, whither time would not allow us to go." Three days later Governor Saltonstall arrived and regularly attended these meetings, " and showed a hearty zeal for obeying every part of Her Majesty's commands with relation to his own government." The governors of the colonies which were to be concerned being present, they undertook the arrangement of the forces. Vetch presented a memorial showing that, as Lovelace had died, the governors should jointly appoint a commander. This led them, with the council and assembly of New York, unanimously to ask Colonel Nicholson to command the land expedition. To this, because of the difficulty of the task, Nicholson showed much aversion. When he came to New York he said he had no thought but to return with Vetch and go on the expedition by sea; yet he would go as a volunteer by land and give all the advice and assistance he could. But on Vetch urging that, unless he took command, the expedition must fail, and on the refusal of Colonel Peter Schuyler, who had been selected as second in command, to go unless Nicholson took the chief command, Nicholson accepted the honor. Schuyler was then formally appointed second in command, to succeed in case Nicholson died or was disabled.

It was then decided to reorganize the troops into four battalions, but as the independent companies were found not to be as full as was expected and as there was only one captain who was able to go, it was resolved to depart from the instructions, and form the four regular companies into a battalion by themselves to be commanded by one of their own officers according to their rank and seniority, and the rest into three battalions according to the establishment. The five small field pieces, the coehorns, mortars, arquebuses, swivels and

[1] See Journals of C. & Ass. for what it did.

blunderbusses, which were to be sent along with the expedition, were to be under the charge of Colonel Redknap, who should take as assistants one of the bombardiers whom Vetch had brought from the Tower, and twelve gunners whom Vetch, by virtue of instructions from the ordnance board, was to procure at New York.[1]

The wages paid to soldiers in the colonies were found to be at least 18d. per day and this, with the payments in advance and the bounties, rested as a heavy burden on the colonists. Hence a special effort was made to call out as many of the Indians as possible, and Vetch and Nicholson planned to draw on the British government for a small reward for them — either a gun for each, or about three yards of strouds and duffels, enough for a suit for an Indian. The arms in the magazine at New York were found to be very much out of order, "having been entirely neglected for want of a proper storekeeper and an armourer, as by report of the committee of the council appears." There was no money in the treasury of New York to pay for mending and cleaning these arms and therefore the sums due to the gunsmiths, hired to do this, had to be charged to the crown. These preparations being completed, about May 24, 400 regulars and colonial troops of New York and Connecticut, with about 200 Indians, carpenters and other workmen, were sent to Wood Creek to make a strong stockade fort and build canoes. In this way, under the lead of the British government, New York abandoned her attitude of neutrality and was again committed to the policy of war.

Vetch and Nicholson now visited Perth Amboy, where the New Jersey assembly was in session and considering the proposed expedition. This was the utmost southern limit of their journey, though Pennsylvania was included among the colonies required to provide quotas. The attitude of the Quakers, who held a decisive majority in the assembly of Pennsylvania and were strong in the lower house of New Jersey, toward the requisition was the same in both provinces. They refused to appropriate money expressly for the war, and in Pennsylvania they plead, in addition to their

[1] It had ordered him to raise 80 of these, the rest of whom were to be procured at Boston.

principles, the weak excuse of colonies further south that they must provide for their Indians. In New Jersey, as we shall see, a political conflict was in progress and this obscured to an extent the clearness of the result. In Pennsylvania the governor and the majority of the council, supported by the demand of the Lower Counties for adequate protection, insisted that the command of the queen should be obeyed. The assembly, with many misgivings, at first voted £500 as a present to the queen, but after persistent proddings increased the amount to £2000,[1] but this was not embodied in an appropriation act. In New Jersey the house voted not to resort to the draft, but to support the expedition only by voluntary enlistment,[2] and it decided to raise £3000 for this purpose. By means of an intrigue of Ingoldsby and his supporters, the object of which was to throw blame upon the Quakers, the passage of the necessary act was delayed and almost prevented. But the insistence of Vetch and Nicholson led to an extra session, in which the legislation was put through and means were provided for the payment of volunteers. In Pennsylvania volunteering also occurred and enlistments were made among indented servants, respecting which and payment for the loss of their services more or less complaint was made.

The preparations for this expedition have been described at length, because they so well illustrate such schemes when they were initiated by the home government. In this case an unusually large number of colonies was brought within the scope of the plan of cooperation. Preparations were all made with system and efficiency and had the expedition itself been timely and as well managed, the result could hardly have been doubtful. But in this instance a disaster in Spain, wholly unconnected with affairs in the colonies, prevented the dispatch of the force from England. Before the middle of June this decision was provisionally reached in London and it became a finality before the close of August. In balancing the elements of efficiency as between the colonies and the mother country, this fiasco might well be taken as offsetting the one of two years before at Port Royal.

[1] Pa. Col. Recs. II, 460 *et seq.* Pa. Votes, II, 34, 36, 98. Penn–Logan Correspondence, II, 349, 351. N. J. Arch., III, 461, 470.
[2] Tanner, Province of N. J. (C. U. Studies, 30.), p. 402.

Notwithstanding the disappointment which was caused by this failure, Massachusetts again took up the enterprise of 1707, the conquest of Acadia. In repeated letters to the British government it offered to besiege Port Royal in 1710 if four of the queen's frigates and five hundred of her soldiers might be in Boston by the end of March. Nicholson, who was returning to England, was asked to aid in this. In the futile preparations of the year just passed Massachusetts, in conjunction with New Hampshire and Rhode Island, had spent more than £46,000, but she was ready for another effort to secure relief from Indian attacks and freedom for her fisheries. The application for help was successful, but it was not sent in March; indeed, it was past the middle of that month before Nicholson received his commission and instructions as commander of the expedition.[1] They were in many points the same as those given to Vetch the previous year. The quotas were the same as were then required, though now they were limited to the New England colonies. Provisions were required in the same fashion, while a quantity of military stores were sent with Nicholson.

The British force did not arrive at Boston until the middle of July. For some time previously the Massachusetts government had been preparing in the customary way for the expedition.[2] Andrew Belcher comes prominently into view as commissary general on this occasion. For weeks he was the centre of manifold activities which had as their object the procuring of provisions, clothing and miscellaneous supplies from Massachusetts itself and the neighboring colonies. The general court met and a joint committee of the two houses was appointed to inquire into the public store of provisions and report what further quantities were needed. They relied largely upon Belcher's statements and, having so reported, orders were accordingly issued by the houses for the purchases.

When Nicholson came, bringing four hundred instead of five hundred marines, they were lodged on Castle Island until the expedition should be ready. This in itself was a notable

---

[1] Reports of Nova Scotia Hist. Soc. I, 59 et seq.
[2] Mass. Arch., (Ms.) 71, fol. 620 et seq.

event, for these troops were the first reinforcement from England which had been sent directly to the northern colonies and had reached them in condition for service. They are not to be classed with the independent companies of New York, except as far as they were later detailed for permanent garrison service in America, but were sent for only a single expedition. They came as forerunners of a larger body which was to appear the next year. Taken in connection with what had preceded and what was to follow, they serve clearly to differentiate the last years of this war from any which had preceded, so far as the northern frontier is concerned. Now that the great victories of Marlborough had been won, and France was evidently in a state of exhaustion, the way was open for a serious attempt to conquer Acadia and Canada. The frequent appeals on this subject were at last to find a hearing, and this was to be facilitated by the rising Tory spirit in England and the accession of that party to power in the later years of Anne. Attention was to be diverted somewhat from the Caribbean to the Gulf of St. Lawrence, and thus we have for a short period an anticipation of what was to occur with decisive results a half-century later. For the time the petty local raids of the wars thus far were lost sight of in preparations for larger operations which were conceived on an imperial scale. These for the moment brought the northern colonies together in cooperation for a common purpose and thus promoted the slow trend toward union.

On learning that as large a body of militia as was raised the year before was expected, the general court at once voted it, and that for three months of service instead of the two which Nicholson suggested. In the general orders it was provided that one commissioned officer sent by the crown should be appointed to each company of the colonial levy to aid in the work of discipline. A source of anxiety to the militia was removed by the provision that they should be allowed to return after the fall of Port Royal, except such as should volunteer to remain in the garrison. Special inducements were issued to volunteers, while at the same time a draft was ordered, those who volunteered being accounted part of the quotas from the towns whence they came, the colonies in their returns distinguishing the names of the volunteers from the drafted men. A small body of Indians was also enlisted. In general superintendence of preparations, such as procuring ordnance, military supplies, and transports and preparing a hospital ship, a council of war was active.[1]   Similar measures of preparation were adopted in New Hampshire, Rhode Island and Connecticut. The colonial force, as thus gathered, numbered about 1500 men, of whom Massachusetts contributed 900, Connecticut 300 and New Hampshire and Rhode Island together about 300. They were organized in four regiments. The naval force from England consisted of three fourth rates, two fifth rates and a bomb ketch, while the colonists contributed the province galley of Massachusetts, one or more hospital ships, several sloops and a part of the transports.[2] The size of the force and the extent of preparation were due to the belief of Nicholson that the fort at Port Royal had been reinforced and strengthened since the last attack.

But really the post was weaker than it had been two years previously. Its garrison consisted of less than 300 men and they were suffering from a dearth of provisions. Possibly because of his inability to support them, Subercase had declined a reinforcement offered him from Canada. Just after the siege began he wrote to Pontchartrain,[3] " I have not a *sou* and our credit is exhausted. I am engaged for considerable sums. I have found means by my industry to borrow wherewithal to subsist the garrison for these two years. I have paid what I could by selling all my movables. I will give even to my last shirt, but I fear that after all my plans will prove useless if we are not secured during the month of March or early in April [1711], supposing the enemy should let us rest this winter."

But Nicholson's force was already within the Basin and his troops were landed, as those of March had been, on the two shores. In the face of slight resistance they advanced their positions and planted their cannon within easy range of the fort. But before the bombardment was begun, a parley

---

[1] Some of its orders are to be found in the Mass. Archives.

[2] The fifth rates were the "Lowestoffe" and "Faversham," which were guardships ordered from New York.

[3] Murdock, Hist. of Nova Scotia, I, 312.

was opened by the French which ended in their capitulation, the articles being signed on the second of October.[1] In this way they escaped from a hopeless situation without the shedding of blood. The articles provided that the garrison should be sent to France, with their arms and other effects, and that the inhabitants within cannon shot of the fort might within two years leave the colony, or at their option remain, provided they took the oath of allegiance to Great Britain. In the fort, whose name was changed to Annapolis, a garrison was left of 200 marines and 250 colonial troops who volunteered to remain. These were left under the command of Vetch, who had participated in the expedition and already had been appointed governor of Nova Scotia.

Twice before had Port Royal been occupied by New England men, once by Sedgwick in 1654 and again by Phips in 1690, and in each case it had been restored to France by treaty.[2] Now it was to be retained by the English and therefore this petty operation figures in history as the conquest of Acadia. So small were the other settlements about the Bay of Fundy that the surrender of Port Royal was necessarily followed by the submission of the rest. But the government at Quebec and the priests, with the Indians whom they controlled, did not abandon the hope that it might yet be regained. During the long period of peace and inactivity in these matters on which Great Britain soon entered, no steps were taken to fill Nova Scotia with English settlers or to strengthen it in a military sense. The weak garrison at Port Royal and the few English who drifted into the province, therefore, had to contend, as best they could, against the French *habitants* who, as time passed, avoided taking the oath of allegiance and with growing self-consciousness and outside support preferred to free themselves from English rule.

In the autumn of 1710 Nicholson returned to England. There he renewed application for a combined effort the next year for the conquest of Canada. The province, as shown by a statement sent by Vaudreuil to the minister two years

---

[1] Report of N. S. Hist. Soc. I, 64–88; William Douglass, Summary Historical and Political.

[2] Parkman, Half Century of Conflict, I, 149.

before, had only the following forces with which to resist
such an attack [1] : —

1200 men between ages of 15 and 70 in Government of
Montreal.

400 men between ages of 15 and 70 in Government of Three
Rivers.

2200 men available for service in district of Quebec.

The total was 3800. Exclusive of the detachment at
Detroit, there were but 350 regular troops in the country, of
which 250 were at Quebec. There were about 500 sailors in
the colony. The total available force, after deducting sick
and those left to protect women and children, was 3350 men.
Of these 1000 would have to be left to defend Montreal.
Only 2350, therefore, would be available to repel an attack
on Quebec.

In England, owing to the accession of the Tories to power,
and to the desire particularly of Bolingbroke to emulate the
triumphs of Marlborough, the persuasions of Dudley, Vetch,
Nicholson and Dummer were now to bear fruit in an enterprise on a larger scale than any previously attempted by
England for defence of the colonies. French observers of
what the English government was now doing, and had been
doing for two years past in this line, interpreted it as a
design on its part to impose the yoke of parliament on the
northern colonies.[2] La Ronde Denys suggested the idea to
M. de Costibelle, governor of Placentia, who suggested to
Pontchartrain that Denys should be sent to Boston to inform
the governor and council there of this as the true purpose
of British policy and to be on their guard against it. The
minister approving of this, La Ronde Denys was sent to the
" Bastonnais," instructed to negotiate with them as with an
independent people and to promise them exemption from
French hostility if they would promise to give no more aid
to Old England in ships or men; if he found unwilling
listeners, he was to pass the whole thing off as a pleasantry.
When he reached Boston, he was detained because preparations were on foot for an attack on Canada, and when he tried

[1] N. Y. Col. Docs. IX, 833, quoted by Kingsford, History of Canada, II,
450.

[2] Parkman, Half Century of Conflict, I, 150 et seq.

to escape his vessel was seized and moored under the guns of the town. In spite of the truth which underlay the view the Frenchman took of the situation, his mission proved of course a failure.

The selection of Jack Hill as commander of the land force on this expedition was an incident of the ascendancy of his sister, Abigail Hill, now Lady Masham, over the mind of the queen as the favorite who had taken the place of Sarah, duchess of Marlborough. The promotions which he had already received in the army had been wholly the result of court or official favoritism and his military record was anything but distinguished. Hovenden Walker, who was now knighted, made rear admiral and appointed to command the naval contingent, had had a long and varied service as a captain and commodore in the navy and, so far as appears, it had been an honorable one.[1] The expedition, as organized in England, consisted of 15 ships of war and some 40 transports and store ships. They carried seven regiments of the line, five of which were Marlborough's veterans: — a total of 5000 men, with artillery and marines. A joint land and sea expedition was planned as in 1709.

Colonel Nicholson was sent in advance with two men-of-war and two transports, the supplies in which were to be delivered at New York for the use of the forces which were to proceed overland. On June 8, Nicholson arrived at Boston and gave the magistrates and people there the first detailed information they had received of the plans of the home government. Instead of sending his transports to New York, he left them in Boston harbor while he accompanied Dudley to the conference of governors of Massachusetts, Connecticut, New York and Rhode Island, which met at New London on the 21st of June.[2]

There the general instructions from the crown were read and it appeared that the quotas required for the land expedition were 600 from New York, 300 from Connecticut, 200 from New Jersey and 240 from Pennsylvania. Governor Cranston reported that Rhode Island would raise 60 men. Colonel Vetch was to be summoned from Port Royal to

[1] See article by J. K. Laughton in Dict. of Nat. Biography.
[2] N. Y. Col. Docs. V, 257.

accompany the sea expedition and provision was made that Sir Charles Hobby should act as deputy governor there during his absence. Redknap, the engineer, was to serve with the land expeditions. The conference was chiefly concerned with measures to secure provisions and other supplies for the forces and their transportation to Boston or Albany or the various colonies where they were procurable. Steps were to be taken to secure the cooperation of the Iroquois, and in August Governor Hunter held a conference with them at Albany for that purpose.[1]  Arrangement was made that Hunter — who held the leading place in the conference — Dudley and Nicholson should draw out what money was needed for the expedition from the offices of receipt of the several colonies, warrants, therefore, being given by the governor of each colony jointly with Nicholson. It was recommended that all the colonies concerned issue the same orders against the assisting of deserters which Massachusetts had made. Provisions were finally made for later meetings of the conference, or a part of its members, if such should appear necessary, which of course, was not the case. All were requested by Nicholson to inform Colonel Hill as soon as he should arrive, of the proceedings of their assemblies in the premises and that Hunter would give him an account of what had been done by way of preparation at Wood Creek and elsewhere. Dudley also was to lay before Hill the proceedings of this conference.

The general court of Massachusetts, at its session in May, 1711, had voted that 900 effective men, besides commissioned officers, be raised, and of these 100 or more should be Indians; the Massachusetts levies were to serve under their own officers. Wages of privates were fixed at 8 shillings per week; of seamen at 40 shillings per month; the officers to have proportionately higher wages. Transports carrying between 50 and 100 tons were to be paid at the rate of 7 shillings per ton per month, the owners fitting them up. Provisions for 126 days were to be procured for the troops and sailors of Massachusetts. Prices of provisions and liquors for the expedition were not to be increased above the ordinary market rates at the time of the arrival of the royal fleet, and an authorized list of prices of the more important commodities

[1] *Ibid.*, 265 *et seq.*

was published. The commissary was ordered to impress all kinds of provisions necessary for the expedition; also to impress bakers, brewers, and all artificers and laborers who were necessary. A committee was appointed to equip transports, and another to provide physicians and surgeons, and surgeon's stores, if any should be necessary besides those sent from England. A committee was also to consider the credit necessary for the expedition, and it reported that £40,000 in bills of credit should be issued. The necessary steps for issuing these were taken. Hill states that just before the expedition started an additional sum of £10,000 was voted to be used in case more than the £40,000 should be needed. An act was also passed against desertion. From this it will be seen that Massachusetts took promptly the steps, so far as the legislature was concerned, which were necessary and which she was accustomed to take on such occasions. The result will show that she followed them up with reasonable diligence.

In its July session the assembly of New York, after some grumbling, appropriated £10,000 for the support of its quota.[1] But in raising the troops assigned to them they included 150 Long Island Indians and 100 Palatines, thus leaving only 350 to be drawn from the permanent white population of the province. Hunter was able to raise all of these except 100 of the Indians, but for that deficiency he made up in part by 40 Indians from Connecticut. He employed 100 more Palatines to fill the depleted ranks of the independent companies. The " Faversham " was also sent from New York, loaded with provisions for Walker's expedition, but was lost at sea before overtaking it. Nearly the full quota of New Jersey Hunter obtained in the form of volunteers, with an appropriation of £5000. Connecticut sent 360 men to Albany. Early in August, after considerable delay, £2000 were appropriated by Pennsylvania for the queen's use.[2] When, toward the middle of September, Hunter had succeeded in collecting a force of 1500 whites and 800 Indians at Albany and had heard news of the progress of the fleet by sea, he wrote to his friend, Secretary St. John, " This is the present state of this glorious enterprise which God Prosper."

[1] N. Y. Docs. V, 253 et seq.; N. Y. Ass. J. I, 289 et seq.
[2] Pa. Col. Recs. II, 534–538.

Walker's squadron, the destination of which great effort had been made in England to conceal, arrived at Nantasket on June 24, only two weeks after Nicholson had brought the first definite information of its approach. Dudley was then at New London. New England, of course, was Whig and was surprised, though not exactly suspicious, that such an effort should be made by Tories. This was the largest royal armament which had ever visited the North American coast, and New England was called upon at once to supply it with provisions. In view of the size of the force, the season of the year, when provisions had mostly been sold or consumed and the crop of the present year not yet harvested, in view also of the exertions of recent years, the task naturally seemed formidable to the New Englanders. On the other hand, Walker, Hill, and their subordinates exhibited all the superciliousness of courtiers and military men toward the colonists and their methods. However corrupt and inefficient might be the commissary department at home, promptness and wholly satisfactory results were instantly expected at Boston. When, as was necessarily the case, these failed to appear, the British officers, in conversation, letters and in their journals, vented their wrath and contempt, and drew sweeping conclusions as to the need of asserting royal authority and making changes in systems of polity. As one now reads the journals of Walker, Hill and King, one can see the outcropping of this feeling of aversion, provoked by the delays in procuring supplies, raising the colonial contingent and preparing what was necessary for the voyage to Quebec.[1]

Dudley was at heart a Tory, was in sympathy with the objects, immediate and remote, which were sought by the British government. Under his lead, as soon as he returned, the administrative machinery of Massachusetts was set in motion. The power of the government was used to the utmost,

---

[1] Among the sources for the history of this expedition, a prominent place belongs to the journals of Walker, Hill, Vetch and King. Walker's Journal, as noted below, is separately published. The journal of Vetch is in Colls. of N. S. Hist. Soc. IV. The Journals of Hill and King are still in manuscript in the Public Record Offices. Jeremiah Dummer's "Letter to a Noble Lord concerning a late Expedition to Canada," 1712, gives suggestive observations not only on this expedition, but on the relation of the proposed conquest of Canada to British interests in general in North America.

indeed beyond what was customary in some directions, to meet the demands of British officers; and commendable progress was made. But Walker and his associates insisted that a plot existed to defeat the expedition by delay — a characteristic excuse for incompetency on their own part. One can see here the natural antipathy between the British courtier-soldier and the provincial, which appears as an underlying and controlling fact throughout our colonial history.

And yet outward courtesy was maintained. The morning after the fleet landed deputies came from the council — in absence of the governor — to congratulate the admiral and general on their fortunate voyage. They informed Walker and his officers how Nicholson had left his transports in Boston harbor, and it was found a little later that they were careened there so that they could not be sent to New York for at least three days. This irritated the commanders, because it was alleged to imply neglect on Nicholson's part. Not only were the supplies needed at once in New York, but the transports and their convoy should be there in order to bring provisions thence to Boston. On the colonies to the west the expedition must chiefly depend for its supply of flour and peas. When Nicholson returned he was questioned about this. Hill states that Nicholson said he had no control over the captains of the ships-of-war and they got permission from the governor and council to clean the vessels at Boston. Walker said he would inquire about this from the captains when they returned from Nova Scotia, but nothing more appears.

Vetch had been sent for from Annapolis, in Nova Scotia, before the arrival of the fleet, for he had been appointed to command the colonial contingent on the expedition by sea. He arrived at Boston at about the same time as Nicholson. Vetch was ordered to bring with him such men and artillery as could be spared from Annapolis. These he did not bring, but stated that 100 marines with stores could be spared. Sir Charles Hobby, who was appointed Vetch's successor as deputy governor, however, wrote that he could not spare the marines designated, and said nothing about sending stores. Hence Captain Southack, with the province galley and a brigantine, was dispatched for the troops and stores, and as soon as he had put them on board he should follow the fleet.

The "Sapphire" was also sent as convoy, and a body of New England troops was despatched to take the place of the marines at Annapolis. On June 27, the British troops were landed from the fleet and encamped on Noddle's Island, now East Boston, where there was abundant ground, good water and air, and there they were to remain till preparations were completed. One of the serious problems was, how to procure sufficient fresh provisions, especially meat, for these men. It was difficult to procure so much, and to slaughter and preserve it in mid-summer, and there was not much butter or cheese then for sale. But for the health of the soldiers and to save the salt provisions for the voyage, it was necessary to procure fresh meat, if possible. The difficulty was somewhat relieved by delivering fresh provisions every other day after the 20th of July. As soon as the fleet landed, Hill and Walker began to call for fresh provisions. Hobby asked some merchants to advance ready money for this purpose, but he says he found them so unreasonable that he applied to the government as soon as Dudley returned. The governor and council appropriated £3000 for the relief of troops until the assembly could make definite provision. Hill later informed the governor and council that he had been told that merchants in Boston were concealing provisions. Two merchants, William and Francis Clarke, were then designated by the governor to accompany such officers as Hill should send to search for provisions. Major Allen and Mr. Nutmaker, the commissary of stores for the British force, were sent by Hill. They found a quantity of provisions in storehouses and on board vessels from other colonies which they secured for the use of troops.[1] Lists of these were kept and prices for them fixed by the governor and council in Massachusetts currency at 4% below sterling. Some dissatisfaction was expressed by the townspeople at this rate, but there was no outbreak against it. Andrew Belcher is said by Walker to have refused, on the arrival of the fleet, to supply provisions for the men-of-war, stating that the time

---

[1] Walker, Journal, p. 85, states amount found as 132 bbls. beef; 1155 bbls. pork; 692 bbls. of flour; 1333 bush. peas; 560 bbls. rye; 30 firkins butter; 1331 C. of bread; 2800 cwt. cheese; 392 bbls. rum; 175 wine; Indian corn; 18882 bush. wheat.

for which he contracted was past and the prices paid were too low. Walker told him he should receive bills on the victualling board in England attested by Walker himself, but he could not be persuaded. Walker began to fear that the fleet would be distressed for provisions, for no one could furnish them so well as Belcher, and some of the captains declared that Belcher was going to buy up all the provisions of the province and hold them for high prices. Peter Faneuil then offered to supply the fleet, though apparently Walker did not engage him, but instead, he appointed two pursers as agent victuallers to contract for three months' provisions for both land and sea forces, their bills for payment to be drawn on the commissioners for victualling the navy in England. Hill, fearing that provisions would not come from New York and through the other colonial channels, purchased, at an expense of £4872, three vessels lying in the harbor, with their cargoes of wheat, rye, Indian corn, and flour. Some packers and others, who were at work at these provisions, were ordered to work on Sunday, but refused until warrants were procured from a justice of the peace for their arrest, when they yielded to this gross violation of one of the strictest rules of Puritan discipline. But, on July 26th, the province galley arrived from New York and in her convoy six transports loaded with provisions, which were transferred to the vessels of the fleet.

But to Walker and Hill things seemed going heavily. Their officers frequently complained that the colonists would not obey them; for example that lightermen refused to bring ballast. The agent victuallers complained that Belcher, who was commissary for the colonial troops, had employed all the bakers and they could get no bread baked for the fleet. But Belcher, on being consulted, assured them that he had employed only two bakers, and then the agent victuallers went away to hire the rest.

Walker had much difficulty, too, in procuring pilots. He could find none who wanted to go, especially on the men-of-war, or who said that their knowledge of the St. Lawrence was sufficient to fit them for the duty. Impressment had to be resorted to at Marblehead and other places, to get enough pilots. Vetch with difficulty induced Captain Bonner, an elderly man, to accompany him, while Walker,[1] perhaps to his ultimate destruction, placed chief confidence in a captain, named Paradis, who was captured with a French prize by cruisers in the Gulf of St. Lawrence and put on board the fleet after it sailed. He took a bribe of 500 pistoles to pilot the fleet up the St. Lawrence. As an accompaniment of this task, he filled the imaginations of both Walker and Hill with accounts of the severity of the Canadian winters, and the perils of navigating the St. Lawrence. He said that no ship ever wintered at Quebec, that the water of the river froze to the bottom, that between the mouth of the river and Quebec there was no harbor where ships could be in tolerable security, that the water was very deep, shores very steep, currents swift and unknown, fogs and storms frequent. Walker concluded from this that, if he was compelled to stay at Quebec all winter, he would have to take all his ships out of water to prevent their being crushed by ice, and store them in frames on land. For his troops, he saw visions of famine and cold, with the accompanying horrors of cannibalism. That Walker's mind was prepared for accepting such ideas as these, and that they largely explain the collapse of the enterprise, is shown by entries in Walker's journal before he left Boston. On June 28 Walker writes, " By all that appeared to me, every day producing something unexpected, I began to think this expedition would prove difficult and hazardous; not only with respect to the danger of the Bay and the River of St. Lawrence, but the several Impediments we met with as to the provisions and other necessaries we hoped to have had there." July 11 we find him writing that things were going so heavily, in view of the general and admiral, that they would have gone against Placentia instead of Quebec, if their instructions had not positively enjoined the expedition against Quebec as the first move.

On July 24, the Massachusetts troops embarked, though their transports were not yet ready to receive them, no sailors were on board and beds and other necessaries were not fully supplied. This was interpreted by King as showing perverse and wicked intentions, any one who had seen the country knowing that it could fit out twice the number of vessels they

[1] Walker, Journal, p. 119, *etc.*

were to furnish and in much less time. King could not imagine what the colonists could intend by delays, unless to keep the expedition at Boston until the approach of cold weather should defeat it. He drew as an inevitable inference from his supposition, that the queen and even those who profited by these disorderly conditions would now see the necessity of changing them and of putting all the northern colonies under one form of government.

The same day as that on which the Massachusetts troops embarked a ship arrived with the Rhode Island contingent. They were clothed and had muskets, but lacked bayonets, swords and cartouche boxes. None had been provided for them in the stores sent from England, because Rhode Island was either not mentioned or thought to be a distinct government, when the expedition was planned. But the Rhode Island men were taken on board and accompanied the expedition. On July 30, having forces victualled for three months and the New England transports manned, the fleet sailed from Nantasket. The same day Nicholson set out for New York and Albany, to take command of the forces which Hunter had raised and provisioned there for the land expedition. On August 6 the fleet passed Cape Sable. Off Cape Breton the " Sapphire," one of the ships sent to Annapolis for artillery and other equipment, joined the expedition and brought an account that Annapolis was still blockaded by French and Indians. Hobby had made an unsuccessful sortie on them, but was unable to get the marines and guns which were wanted out of the place.

Amid considerable fog, but without storms, the fleet proceeded on its way to the Gulf of St. Lawrence. Vetch, who probably had as much knowledge of the coast and waters as any one else on board, was for a time sent ahead with three of the small vessels to indicate the course; but that was discontinued before they entered the Gulf.[1] From that time Walker relied on the advice of Paddon, the captain of his flagship " Edgar," and on the dismal accounts given by Paradis. On the night of the 22nd of August the disaster came, one of the greatest which a British fleet ever suffered.

[1] See Vetch's Journal of the voyage. Reports of N. S. Hist. Soc. IV, 150 et seq.

It occurred at the Isle aux Oeufs (Egg Island) near the north shore of the Gulf, where it was some seventy miles wide. The wind was strong from the east and the weather foggy. For more than twenty-four hours no land had been in sight and the fleet was more than fifty miles to the north of what its pilots and commanders supposed to be its true position. They supposed it to be near the south shore, but it was really approaching the north shore and its true position was revealed late in the evening by the noise of the breakers just to leeward.[1]  Eight of the British transports, one storeship and one sutler's sloop were destroyed, but all of the warships escaped.  A total of 705 officers and sailors were lost though at the time it was believed that the loss amounted to nearly 900.  This, however, was not sufficient to incapacitate the force for capturing Quebec.  If well commanded it was still far more than adequate for that purpose, and the season was not too advanced.

But the commanders were incapable and their lack of courage and resource was now clearly shown.  Vetch reminded Walker that ships had reached Quebec in October, and that without a man on board who had been up the river before.  But in a council of war, which was now held for the first time during the expedition, after examining the pilots it was unanimously resolved that, " By Reason of the Ignorance of the said Pilots, it is wholly Impracticable to go up the River St. Lawrence with the Men of War and Transports so far as Quebec, as also the uncertainty and Rapidity of the Currents, as by fatal experience we have found."  To this conclusion the commanders at once acceded and word was hastened to Nicholson to abandon his part of the expedition.  The fleet returned to Spanish River on Cape Breton, Walker for a time cherishing the idea that he ought not to return to England without at least capturing Placentia.  But soon Hill persuaded him that even this was not necessary and that he could with good assurance take his 4000 survivors directly back to England.  As it was found that provisions could not be easily obtained from New England for an expedition against Newfoundland, all further operations were abandoned and the fleet sailed for home.

[1] Walker, Journal;  King, Journal;  Vetch, Journal.

Thus, to the chagrin of all concerned, whether British or colonials, ended the serious operations of the Second Intercolonial War. An armament such as Walker commanded, especially when supported by the force which was on its way from New York, should have easily conquered Canada, which was ill prepared to meet them. But the chance of its conquest was now indefinitely postponed. In England no inquiry was made into the causes of the failure by the Tory government. Hill was protected by court influence, and in fact had not had an opportunity to do anything on land which could be made the subject of an inquiry. The blowing up of the flagship " Edgar," soon after she reached England, involved the destruction of all of Walker's papers, so that in case of an inquiry documentary evidence would have been sadly lacking. Instead of this, Walker was immediately sent off in command of a convoy of merchant ships to the West Indies. After the accession of George I, Walker was called to account, not, it is supposed, because of his failure to reach Quebec but on suspicion of Jacobitism. His name was stricken from the list of admirals and his half-pay as a retired officer was withheld. Finding life uncomfortable in England, Walker removed to South Carolina, whence he returned in 1720 for the publication of his " Journal or Full Account of the late Expedition to Canada." The rest of his life was spent abroad.

So far as military operations in America were concerned, this war was as indecisive as its predecessor had been. In the raids along the northern frontier the French had continued their offensive, but with no decisive result. Had the capture of Port Royal by the British been followed up by the settlement and proper care for the defence of Nova Scotia, an important gain would have accrued to that belligerent; but this was not done. The offensive operations of the British took the form chiefly of the attempted expeditions of 1709 and 1711. But both of these were total failures and, taking the war as a whole, it reveals little, if any, advance in the art of securing joint action on the part of the British colonies. Neither side advanced its frontier by military operations to any important extent. Roads were not opened anywhere for the passage of troops, new forts or outposts of appreciable strength were not built. At the close of this war the British and Canadians had approached scarcely nearer to one another than they were in 1690. The advance of settlement which, now that France had excluded the Huguenots from America and was coming to put so low an estimate upon the value of Canada, offered to the British the surest path toward success had in certain ways been hindered by the war. Conditions at its close were still primitive among them, whether they are considered from the standpoint of available financial resources, of military operations or of administrative methods in general.

But the war in Europe had told in favor of the British and their allies. In the Low Countries, which was the section of the European continent of most critical importance to the Sea Powers, the plans of Louis XIV had been defeated. On this theatre Marlborough, continuing the strategy of William III, but with a military genius far superior to that which the king exhibited, had won a succession of victories. These, with Blenheim, had set a limit to the advance of French power on the continent during the age of Louis XIV. Efforts on the part of France to conquer the Low Countries had for the time to be abandoned. The border fortresses of the Netherlands were restored to the control of the allies and the territory which had been the Spanish Netherlands was transferred to Austria. This placed them in the hands of a power which had no fleet, and so long as that arrangement continued they could not be dangerous to Great Britain. The fortifications of Dunkirk were to be destroyed by the French. The Scheldt remained closed, and a later effort on the part of the Emperor Charles VI to develop a trade centre at Ostend came to nothing. The power of the Dutch Republic was steadily declining and the time was long passed when it could be considered a commercial rival of the Island Kingdom. Therefore the ascendancy of Great Britain on the North Sea was secured. Louis XIV had also been forced to agree that the two crowns of France and Spain should never be united, while Austria was given important possessions in southern, as well as northern, Italy. The cession of Gibraltar and Minorca to Great Britain and the relations which that power had entered into with Portugal, were also severe blows to French and Spanish prestige in the Mediterranean. By the transfer of the privileges of the Asiento contract from a French to a British trading company a new way was opened during thirty years to come for the importation of slaves and incidentally of British goods into Spanish America.

The growing superiority of the British navy also brought results of equal importance in the North Atlantic. The cession of Newfoundland, Acadia and the territory about Hudson Bay gave Great Britain control over the entrance to the Gulf of St. Lawrence and a leading interest in whatever might be developed through the whale fishery and the fur trade in the Arctic regions beyond. Its hold also upon the fisheries of the entire North Atlantic was greatly strengthened by these cessions. In view of these facts the group of treaties which go by the name of Utrecht, registering the results of a quarter of century of warfare, appears as one of the most important landmarks in the history of the nations which surrounded the Atlantic Ocean. But the changes signified little for the elevation of humanity or its progress in any higher sense. It involved a wholesale readjustment of boundaries and relations, arrived at through war and diplomacy, manipulated by aristocratic and official cliques, peoples being shuffled about like cards in a pack, and all intensely characteristic of the old régime.

Though the negotiators of these treaties tried to get a somewhat permanent adjustment of relations, no attempt was made to fix boundaries in America, not even the much disputed boundaries of Acadia. These matters were reserved for further adjustment, a futile effort to reach which was made a few years later.[1] Provision was made that the inhabitants of the ceded territories should have the liberty in the course of a year to remove to another place, taking their movable goods with them; but those who desired to remain should enjoy the free exercise of their religion according to the usage of the Church of Rome, so far as was compatible with the laws of Great Britain. In an obscure and ambiguous clause provision was made that the French inhabitants of Canada should not molest the Five Nations subject to the dominion of Great Britain, nor the other native Americans

[1] C. O. 5/4, A. W. I.; Plants. Gen. Undated draft of a commission to Martin Bladen to act as an appointee for this purpose.

who were in alliance with them.  In like manner the British
colonists should behave peaceably toward the Americans
who were subjects or friends of the French, and on both sides
they should enjoy full liberty of resort for trade.  Also all
Indian nations should resort with equal freedom to British
and French colonies for trade without molestation or hindrance.  But what Indian tribes were to be accounted subjects or friends respectively of Great Britain or France was
left to be determined by the course of later events, a seed
plot of future wars.

# CHAPTER XIV

## INDIAN RELATIONS DURING THE EARLY EIGHTEENTH CENTURY. DEVELOPMENT OF THE WESTERN FRONTIER

EXTENDED reference has already been made to the significance of the frontier in American history and especially to that part of it which marked the western limits of British settlement and stretched from the Great Lakes on the north to Florida on the south. The location of the various Indian peoples along the Allegheny watershed has been indicated. The discoveries of the French in the region of the Great Lakes and Mississippi Valley have also been noted and the fact that already before 1690 their plan to occupy that region was foreshadowed. Of this and what it implied only a very few English were even dimly conscious. For a considerable time to come attention was to be chiefly centered on Canada and Florida, the terminals of this vast frontier line, and especially on the conflict which was in progress in New England. Indian relations in that section, which were almost continuously hostile, have been sufficiently described in connection with the history of the first two wars. In the Carolinas also, during the period of which we are now speaking, occurred two great local conflicts, those with the Tuscaroras and the Yemassees, but adequate attention to them is given elsewhere in dealing with the history of the colonies immediately concerned. The effect of these conflicts in the Carolinas was to clear the more accessible and settled parts of those provinces of savages, leaving the English to face directly the Creeks and Cherokees of the interior and through them the remoter tribes of the southwest which acted more directly under French influence. The task which must now be undertaken is to trace the development of relations with Indian peoples along the western frontier as a whole. This subject, of course, is closely connected with that of immigration, with the filling of unoccupied areas and the advance of settlement, like the ranks of an invading army, toward the mountains. Military operations and the needs of defence also have a direct bearing on the problem. But the process in its essential nature will be fully understood only when viewed from the standpoint of Indian relations. Until toward the middle of the eighteenth century the French lay far in the western and northern background, and though the desirability of checking their advance or expelling them from the continent was perceived, this had to be viewed as essentially a military problem to be met by expeditions, attacks and counter attacks delivered at particular points, rather than as pressure steadily exerted along the frontier as a whole.

The Indians, however, lived on the frontier, or, more correctly, the frontier extended through their territory. To the eastward or southward of that slowly changing section which we call the frontier, a region which had no exact bounds, lived Indians who were no longer independent. Only yesterday the land on which they still had a foothold had been in their possession, but now it had passed to the whites, of whom they had become the helpless wards. To the west and north of the frontier lived the free tribes of the forest who as yet had not felt the white man's sway; and yet even here there were signs that the red men might still be hemmed in and subdued, for the French were beginning to appear in their midst or in their rear; English and Dutch traders were pushing forward from the east and there was danger that the Indians might be encircled and crushed between the two peoples from Europe. Within the narrow frontier section itself the Indians and the English were in continuous and direct contact and the process of absorbing or eliminating the weaker party was in full swing. The English under the forms of purchase were steadily appropriating land within this section. Trade was going on with the natives. Attempts were being made to conclude treaties and alliances with them. Intercourse was maintained with them in many less formal ways. And also, every now and then, Indian raiders would pass through the section on their way to attack other native tribes, or some colonist would be slain. Again with a more general attack an Indian war would break out and a larger or smaller section of the frontier would be the witness of its horrors. Within the frontier, as a protection against such calamities as this, rude forts were erected and small garrisons established, and to the maintenance of these a large part of the attention of the colonial militia was directed. White and Indian guides, interpreters, commissioners and officials of all sorts who were engaged in the subtleties of forest war and diplomacy were especially familiar with this region and might often be seen there. And, finally, it was always of great interest to geographers and map makers, because upon its location hinged boundary questions and disputes of every description. It is with the continuous relation between the English and the representatives of primitive man along this section known as the frontier country that we are now concerned.

During the period covered by the first two colonial wars events of the greatest significance occurred in the region of New York. This was due to the existence there of the Five Nations, to the peculiar three-cornered relation between them and the French and English — which has already been described — and to the state of war on the northern frontier. War greatly magnified to both parties the importance of their Indian allies, because upon them they depended in this early time for something like decisive assistance. The French began the struggle largely in retaliation for the descent of the Iroquois upon La Chine. Against the Iroquois their attacks were chiefly and almost exclusively directed throughout the first war and so far as it was waged within the territory south and southwest of Montreal. Toward the Dutch and English colonists this league served therefore as a buffer state, protecting them from blows which otherwise might have fallen directly upon themselves. To the British it became an object of far more pressing importance than ever before to maintain their alliance with the Iroquois and continue the hostile relations which existed between them and the French. So keen was the Indians' consciousness of independence of both parties that this friendship had to be bought. Frontenac was ready to pay for peace if the English would not secure it for themselves by similar means. In this way the wars perpetuated the system of Indian presents and fully committed both the home government and the colonies to that policy. It was followed as long as the colonial wars lasted and was resorted to by all frontier provinces, though by none on the scale or with the regularity which appears in New York.

Conferences with the tribesmen at Albany now came to be held yearly and sometimes oftener. The Indian commissioners who were resident there found their office increasingly burdensome, and for many years to come there was no similar body elsewhere which was comparable with them in importance. In 1696 Governor Fletcher issued a new commission to the board, empowering them, or any two of them, " to treat, confer and consult with the Five Indian Nations, . . . to hold correspondence with them, pursuant to such instructions as you shall from time to time receive from me, so as by your endeavours they may be confirmed in their fidelity and allegiance."[1] It is probable that at least since Dongan's time the magistrates of Albany had served in this capacity. The provision of Fletcher's commission that its mayor should be *ex officio* a member involved a perpetuation of that idea. But the other members were made such by the commission, and those first named were Peter Schuyler, Rev. Godfrey Dellius, Evert Bancker and Dirck Wessels. Schuyler, under the familiar name of " Quider," the Iroquois recognized as the man who understood them best and who most commanded their confidence. The strategic importance which attached to the Hudson valley extended also, so far as the wider expanses of the interior of the continent were concerned, to the territory of the Five Nations.

They occupied the Mohawk valley, which lay between the Catskills and the Adirondack mountains and was thus a very important northern gateway to the interior. It opened more directly toward the prairies of the west than did the French waterway through the St. Lawrence and the Great Lakes. Owing to the victories which the Iroquois had won over adjacent Indian peoples about the middle of the seventeenth century their influence extended far beyond their immediate confines, even to the Mississippi on the west and the Caro-

---

[1] N. Y. Col. Docs. IV, 177. This commission was granted immediately after Frontenac's raid into the Iroquois Country.

linas on the south.  As the French extended their discoveries and claims westward, they therefore found the Iroquois and their dependent peoples projecting like a wedge into the territory which they were ambitious to occupy.  In the wake of the Iroquois came Dutch and English traders, who in this way gained access to the remote Indians of the Huron and Michigan region and the upper Mississippi valley.  On the economic side the fur trade played a very important part in this entire process.  Land, men and commodities were the elements involved.

To Frontenac, the *coureurs de bois* and the party of expansionists in Canada, this was a serious menace.  Canada depended for its staple industry, the fur trade, on obtaining a steady and large supply from the far Indians, who were reached through the Ottawa river and the Great Lakes.  Those tribes depended in return upon the French for arms, ammunition and other supplies to which they had become accustomed. In 1696 a Pottawottamie chief told Frontenac to his face that that was the last time they would come to talk with him if the French should cease to visit them as they seemed inclined to do, and bring the accustomed supplies.  " Father, since we want powder and iron and every other necessity which you were formerly in the habit of sending us, what do you expect us to do? "  " The speech of the Indian," writes the reporter of the interview, " and the boldness with which he spoke closed every one's lips, and the strongest opponents of the Beaver, the sole staple of this country, were unable to cover their astonishment. . . . The entire loss of the trade is not the sole evil we have to apprehend.  The garrisons which might be stationed in the respective parts in the Upper Country will run daily risks of being slaughtered by these brutal Tribes, who are so difficult of management; it will be impossible for them to live there; the Commandants will be without authority, having no means to enforce it as formerly by the occasional muster of the Voyageurs, who, conjoined with the Regular troops, would impress the Indians with fear and respect; the enemy will take advantage of the coolness of our allies, who, in consequence of this abandonment, will lose all the confidence they once reposed in us; the latter will not fail to go over to the English; they will soon become friends and those same Indians who were the main stay of Canada will be seen coming hither to procure scalps and to compass its destruction." [1]

These were the sentiments of the expansionists among the French colonists. The *coureurs de bois*, the traders, explorers and officials who were in sympathy with them continued to urge this point of view. Though it was opposed by the clergy and not expressly supported by the crown, it was the most vital force among the French on the continent of America and led to their occupation of the Mississippi valley. Frontenac was leader of this party in his time and it was his influence which helped greatly to keep the colony true to this policy, in the interest of the fur trade and of unlimited dominion over the interior of the continent. After the beginning of the colonial wars the feeling of rivalry with the English became a stronger force in helping forward the movement. The foothold which was gained by the English on Hudson's Bay threatened an invasion by them of the Indian and fur-bearing country from the northeast, while the appearance of English traders in the Ohio region and along the Great Lakes was viewed as the beginnings of an inroad from the southeast. It was a task of the utmost difficulty to keep the many fickle and warring tribes of the interior even nominally attached to the French interest, and in the mazes of their diplomacy Frontenac and his subordinates were deeply involved. This task was inherited by the generations which followed, and it became all the more serious when half a century later the aid of these people was needed for the defence of Canada against the English. In 1697 very important, though temporary, successes were won by the Le Moyne brothers — Iberville, Bienville and Serigny — in the complete occupation of Newfoundland and the capture of Fort Nelson on Hudson's Bay. A blow was thus struck at the interest of England in the fisheries, while the advance of the English from the northeast for the time was checked. But the condition which more than anything else was favoring the ambitions of the French was the indifference of the British government and of the body of the English colonists toward the interior of the continent. To them, until they

[1] N. Y. Docs. IX, 586, 673.

were forced to contend for their very existence in North America, the frontier along the eastern slope of the Allegheny watershed was a boundary line beyond which they did not seek to penetrate.  To such an extent were they absorbed with their local and personal concerns and with trade to the West Indies that they were content to leave the magnificent inheritance of the Mississippi valley to such sparse settlements as the French and Spanish were able to found there. It was with a spirit so divergent as this that the French and English approached the problem of the frontier.

The establishment of the post at Cataraqui (Kingston), on the shore of Lake Ontario, was regarded by Frontenac as one of the notable achievements of his first governorship, and it bore his name.  The significance of it lay in its connection with the westward movement of the French and its convenient location as a base from which to attack the Iroquois.  When this fort was destroyed by order of Denonville, just as Frontenac had returned for his second term, this act was regarded as one of the clearest signs of the decline of the colony and its possible ruin.  Among the measures which the heroic governor resolved to execute in order to restore confidence and inspire the colonists with what he believed to be their true mission was the rebuilding of this fort.  It was accomplished in 1696 and was at once followed by his attack on the western cantons of the Iroquois.

This move was the culmination of a long series of hostile acts and reprisals, interspersed with efforts at negotiation between these parties, which began with the opening of the first intercolonial war.  Even while the Convention was in control at Albany the French began to bid against their rivals for control over the Iroquois.[1]  Preliminary to this the French urged upon the Indians the conclusion of a peace that should bring to an end the feud which had lasted almost since the founding of Canada.  In the course of events which followed, the Praying Indians of the Mohawk tribe, who as captives had accepted the Catholic faith and were settled at Caughnawaga on the St. Lawrence above Montreal, bore an important part.  The influence of the Jesuits and of other French agents among the Iroquois, especially in the western cantons, also

[1] Doc. Hist. of N. Y. II, 137 *et seq.*; Brodhead, Hist. of N. Y., II, 582 *et seq.*

attracted some attention among the Dutch and English and was not without significance. Notwithstanding the intense hostility that prevailed, Jesuit missionaries at intervals had worked and suffered in this field since 1645. As the mission had originated with the capture of Father Jogues, so now its representative was Father Millet, who had been taken by the Iroquois at Fort Frontenac but later adopted and made an Oneida sachem, an apt example of the partially secularized spirit and work of the Jesuits in the later history of New France. His hand appears, though obscurely, in the transactions which follow.

Negotiations on the subject of peace occurred at Quebec and Montreal in Canada and at Albany and Onondaga, the meeting place of the Iroquois Confederacy. The question of the mutual return of prisoners held by the two parties occupied a prominent place in all the negotiations. Demands for such restoration regularly appeared as conditions requisite for the successful presentation of the treaty, and they were as often avoided or refused by each party. Frontenac brought back with him certain Iroquois prisoners from France and at once sent three of them as envoys to Onondaga to solicit a meeting at Fort Frontenac.[1] Immediately the Convention at Albany was informed by the Mohawks of this move, and Arnold Viele, the interpreter, was sent, with Robert Sanders, to Onondaga to warn the Indians not to listen to the French proposals. In accordance with principles already recognized, the chief lines of policy which were to be followed throughout the future were indicated in the correspondence which now passed between the parties. The Dutch and English insisted that no dealings with the French should be had except at Albany, and to prevent their yielding to solicitations to visit Canada envoys were sent to the council fire at Onondaga. The French made exactly the opposite demand and insisted that there should be no negotiations outside the Indian country except at Montreal or Quebec. Both the French and the English insisted that the Iroquois were their subjects, or at least in a state of dependence upon them. So totally inconsistent were these positions that no progress toward an understanding could be made between the two European parties.

---

[1] N. Y. Docs. IX, 464 *et seq.*: Brodhead, II, **604.**

The initial move toward negotiation and an exchange of prisoners was very soon cut short by the destruction of Schenectady, followed by the active participation of the Mohawks in the pursuit of the French and their share in the military preparations of the following summer.  As this was followed by the raid of the French in the winter of 1693 and minor encounters later, the weight of which fell chiefly on the Mohawks, and little effective aid came from the English, the eastern cantons in particular began to show signs of weakness and discouragement.  Frontenac's raid into the country of the Onondagas in 1696, though it resulted in few fatalities among the Indians, destroyed many of their villages and cornfields and correspondingly strengthened the peace party in their councils.  All the cantons except the two westernmost, the Cayugas and Senecas, had now felt the weight of the enemy's attacks.  Instead of ravaging the St. Lawrence valley, as they had been accustomed to do, the Iroquois themselves were now being placed on the defensive.  The western cantons had never been so fully under English influence as the eastern, and the former began steadily to incline toward a neutral attitude or even to an alliance with the French.  As a result of their losses, especially in the form of prisoners who had settled permanently in Canada, the Mohawks, the especial friends of the English, in succeeding decades threw a diminishing weight into the councils of the confederacy.  As the wars progressed the influence of the confederacy diminished and, as interpreted by the fears of the English, it often seemed to be gravitating toward the French. The so-called River Indians, or Algonkin peoples who still dwelt along the Hudson,[1] received some attention, but they were too weak to be longer a peril either to the Dutch settlers or to the French.

In June, 1693, shortly before Governor Fletcher held a general conference at Albany to assure the Iroquois of the care of the British for their protection, and to receive due words of friendship and submission from them,[2] Father Millet had been instrumental in sending an Oneida chief to Quebec with proposals for peace.  Onontio (Frontenac) received

[1] N. Y. Docs., IV, 38.
[2] *Ibid.*, 41–45, 47–51; IX, 565, 572.

him graciously and sent him back with the assurance that, if the other cantons shared in the desire for peace which the Oneidas seemed to entertain, he would be ready to listen provided they immediately sent two of the most influential chiefs of each nation, among whom should be his old acquaintance Decanissora, who should express their sincere regret for their past faults. Schuyler at Albany presently learned, through Indians whom he had sent to Onondaga, and also from Rev. Godfrey Dellius, of this project. He at once informed Governor Fletcher, who had now returned to New York,· and he wrote a strong letter of protest to all the sachems of the Five Nations. He reminded them of the solemn treaty they had lately made at Albany, where they renewed the ancient covenant chain and promised to keep it bright and clean as long as the sun should shine. After all this they should not have defiled their hands by touching a belt of peace from the governor of Canada, but should have sent it, with the packet of letters, to himself and should at the same time have surrendered the priest, Millet, according to their promise. "If the governor had first proposed peace to me, I should have sent for you to the wonted place of treaty at Albany and made you acquainted therewith, and unlesse I doe advise you thereof you are not to hearken to the Governor of Canada or any other and are not to hold any correspondence without my knowledge and consent, if you observe the covenant chaine."[1]

Dirck Wessels, of the board of Indian commissioners, was at once sent to Onondaga to prevent the holding of a council there in the interest of peace with the French and to urge the Indians to deliver up Millet to the English. He found all the cantons assembled, to the number of eighty sachems. It was the desire of Wessels to prevent a general council and to deal with the chiefs of each canton separately. This he found impossible, though his presence kept Father Millet away and Wessels was sure from the first of the support of the Mohawks. The Indians gave inflated reports of military forces which were coming from France to crush them, all of which the Dutch envoy surpassed by his accounts of the vast armies which the king of Great Britain was hurling

[1] N. Y. Docs., IV, 59.

against the French in Europe. After long consultation the Indians decided not to give up the French priest. But the chief sachem of the Onondagas, with whom Wessels had a private conference, while admitting that Fletcher had done well for a newcomer, wondered where the other English colonies were whose assistance he had promised, and added that he was utterly uncertain in mind because no decisive action had been taken against the French. Still at the final council this chief gave his voice for a continuance of the war and of the alliance with the English, and so the decision was finally declared. But while the orator expressed in graphic language this decision still to acknowledge the English as their masters and to put all their force under their command and negotiate with the French only at Albany, he warned Fletcher that as he was reputed to be a soldier they wanted to see some proof of this in order that the enemy might be overcome.

This might be considered a diplomatic triumph for Wessels, but the uncertain value of it was indicated in the following spring, when Decanissora, with two of the most influential chiefs of each Iroquois nation, appeared at Quebec and laid down ten belts, each with its appropriate message of peace. Frontenac received them graciously and told them to return in eighty days and bring with them Father Millet, or some one else, who should be accompanied by all the French prisoners who were held in their villages. " As to the Dutch and English," he continued, " the war we have with them does not concern you. Your relations with us are direct and you can come here safely, as can our foes from Albany if they come properly authorized and in pursuit of peace." But the eighty days passed without the hoped-for response, sporadic hostilities continued between the French Indians and the Iroquois, and though an Indian with a pretended message now and then appeared in Canada, the conclusion was that the Confederacy was keeping faith with the English.[1] Hence it was that Frontenac rebuilt Cataraqui and led his raid into the Iroquois country in 1696.

As we know, the subjects of defence and colonial union were then under consideration in England, especially by the newly

[1] N. Y. Docs. IV, 121 *et seq.*; 175 *et seq.*

created board of trade.[1]  Brooke and Nicoll, the agents from New York, reported that the Five Nations numbered scarcely 2500 men, but owing to their league they were of consequence in war and their friendship was highly important to the English.  John Nelson, from personal knowledge obtained during his long residence in Canada, described the policy by which the French extended their influence so widely among the Indians and held them so faithfully to their alliance.  He urged that this policy should be imitated by bringing Indian chiefs from time to time on visits to England that they might be impressed with its power, by continuing the regular bestowment of presents, by establishing Protestant missionaries among the Indians, and especially by encouraging English and Dutch hunters and traders to penetrate more into the Indian country, accompany the Indians on their expeditions, and identify themselves, as the French did, with their life and interests.  Nelson was greatly impressed with the value of the fur trade to the French and with the close connection between it and their Indian policy.  Those who were masters of the Indians would, in his opinion, prevail.  These views were echoed by the board of trade in a report to the lords justices and a proper place was assigned them in the general plan for united colonial action which was then formulated in connection with the appointment of Lord Bellomont to be governor of New York, Massachusetts and New Hampshire. When Fletcher met the Five Nations for his last conference with them, in October, 1696,[2] he found them cast down by their recent defeat but insistent that aid should be procured from England by the time " the trees grow green " the next spring and the cooperation of the colonies should be secured in a general assault on Canada which should result in the overthrow of the French power there.

After spending the winter at Albany, Fletcher wrote to the board of trade of the pains he had taken to " join the hearts of the Heathen."  He had entertained their chief sachems at his table, and some of them, on coming to New

[1] Ibid., 181, 206, 227.

[2] Ibid., 235, 249, 254, 257.  For a joint attempt on the part of the four western cantons to propitiate Frontenac at the close of 1696, see N. Y. Docs. IX, 678 et seq.

York City to pay him a visit, he treated with every kindness
and courtesy. " I ordered them on board the greatest ships
we have and the guns to be fired the king's birth day happening at that time, I ordered them to be by when all the guns
were fired. I caused some of them to be loaded with ball, to
show how far they would carry upon the River. I caused
Granada shells to be fired before them and let them see the
armory. I ordered six horses to be put into my coach and
my coachman to drive them round the City and into the
Country to take the air, by which they were extremely obliged,
and dismissed them with considerable presents, at which they
did express great satisfaction." [1] Nothing could better indicate the difference between the spirit and policy shown by
the two nations toward the Indians than the contrast between
this and the pictures of the redoubtable Frontenac dancing the
war dance with his allies at Quebec and the long procession
of canoes which annually come down the St. Lawrence loaded
with furs.

With the arrival of Bellomont came the announcement of
the conclusion of peace in Europe and the report that commissioners would be appointed preparatory to an adjustment
of boundaries in America.[2] Of this project nothing came.
But correspondence could now be resumed between the governors at New York and Quebec, and so long as Count
Frontenac lived it was carried on in much the same spirit
which had been shown more than a decade before by Dongan
and Denonville.[3] Both governors proudly and frankly stated
their claims in extreme form and referred to their governments
in Europe for support. John Schuyler and Dellius carried to
Quebec a demand from the earl for the return to Albany of
all the prisoners who were in the hands of the French preparatory to a general exchange. English prisoners Frontenac was
ready to return, but not the Indians, and of the English
nearly all preferred to remain in Canada. As to the Indians,
he denied that the English had any concern with them, as they
were disobedient subjects of the French and were not included
in the peace. Hostilities against them were actually continued

---

[1] N. Y. Docs. IV, 275.
[2] N. Y. Docs. IX, 682 *et seq.*
[3] Osgood, Am. Colonies, III.

by the Indian allies of the French.[1] The Five Nations sent Decanissora to New York to complain to Bellomont, who informed Frontenac that he had ordered the Indians to make reprisals against their assailants and they would be supported by the power of the province and Great Britain. As to the Jesuits who were among the Five Nations, if they fell into his hands he would execute upon them the penalties provided for such as they in English law. Wessels was again sent to Onondaga and the lieutenant governor to Albany to watch developments. The indications were that necessity would force the Iroquois to maintain close relations with the English.

But the extravagant land grants made near the close of Fletcher's administration Bellomont found were operating directly against this. The growth of the Rensselaer manor gave its lord the advantage over the traders of Albany by enabling him to intercept the Indians when they came down with their beaver and secure the best bargains. The excessive and fraudulent grant to Dellius in particular drew complaints from the Mohawks and the scandal was made worse by the fact that the offender was an Indian commissioner. Dellius, however, was soon forced to leave the province and Bellomont sought, though probably in vain, to make the Indian commissioners less a private clique by admitting to the board all the magistrates of Albany.

De Callières, the successor of Frontenac in the governorship of Canada, proved more conciliatory toward the Iroquois, and by the spring of 1699 the danger seemed imminent that a full understanding would be reached between them and the French and prisoners would be mutually restored. Therefore a delegation was sent by the English to a great council at Onondaga, the legislature deeming it so important as to instruct Schuyler and Bleecker specially for the purpose.[2] Bellomont was also actively interested in promoting trade with the far Indians and was corresponding with the governors of Virginia and Maryland on this subject. Of this the board of trade approved, provided it did not interfere with the

---

[1] N. Y. Docs. IX, 691; *ibid.*, IV, 367–364, 402, 404, 435. "How can the Five Nations be the subjects of the king of England? "asked Frontenac. " A father (Onontio) is nearer of kin than a brother. Shall not a father chastise his children when he sees fit? " he asked.

[2] N. Y. Docs. IV, 488, 491–501, 632.

tobacco industry. Robert Livingston also, who was very active as secretary of the Indian commission, thought that a considerable body of British traders, woodsmen and Iroquois should be sent to the region of the later Detroit to establish a post, and that in connection with this project the exhausting attacks on the Iroquois should be stopped by the conclusion of a peace with the Ottawas and other hostile tribes of the west. At the close of the council at Onondaga the orator, Decanissora, delivered the resolution of the sachems that they would refrain from coming to terms with the French, but it was couched in such terms of sarcasm and impatience as to leave the final outcome quite uncertain. A few weeks later a conference was held at Albany, as a result of which special envoys were sent to Canada to arrange, if possible, a final exchange of all prisoners.[1] But as hostilities continued between the Indians, the situation continued unsatisfactory. In the spring it was made acute for a time by a rumor, thought to have originated with the French, that the English were preparing to disarm and massacre the Iroquois, and Bellomont, who was then residing in Boston, had to take special pains to allay the panic thus caused.[2] On the other hand there were fears of a general Indian uprising in combination with the French against the English, and the governor had to face the probability that, if such a movement should occur, the colonies would be lost.

It was under these conditions, in addition to a larger military force and more valuable presents to the Indians, that Bellomont proposed the building of an earth fort in the Onondaga country and the stationing there of one or more missionaries.[3] Commissioners were sent to Onondaga to negotiate concerning the location of the fort. At a largely attended conference, held in August, 1700, the Indians seemed to agree to this plan, and Romer, the engineer, was sent to select a site. He found the Indians surly and met with little success. Their minds were filled with rumors that the French

---

[1] *Ibid.*, 567 *et seq.*

[2] *Ibid.*, 636, 638, 639, 654.

[3] *Ibid.*, 717, 766, 769, 1074, 1077. Smith and Moore were thought well qualified for such missionary work. Livingston had thought out very fully the question of the missionaries as well as the fort at Onondaga, as is shown by his report of his journey thither. Docs. IV, 649.

were also going to build forts in their country. Though the plan of a fort received the full support of the British government, Bellomont died before it could be carried into execution.[1]

But the controlling fact was that the English, both during and after the war, failed to protect the Iroquois. The French influence therefore steadily grew among them. Trade at Albany was poor, the war had caused the settlers on the frontier to diminish, while since 1689 the confederacy was said to have lost one half of its warriors.[2] After the death of Frontenac Father Bruyas became active as a negotiator and, with Maricourt and Joncaire, steadily increased French influence among all the cantons. The result was that, in September, 1700, Bruyas brought a delegation of Iroquois to Canada, with whom De Callières concluded peace. The dilemma in which they had found themselves, between the assertions of both the English and the French that there was a general peace, and the continued attacks of the far Indians, had brought them to listen to the persuasions of the French agents when they appeared. De Callières told them that it was their long delay in coming to him, together with their attack on the Miamis a year before, which had caused their sufferings. But now without delay a deep trench was figuratively dug and the war hatchets thrown into it, a large rock placed over it and a river turned over that, so that they might never use them again against each other. The treaty was informal and without specific terms, but as it closed a feud which had lasted well nigh a century and one in which all the Indian allies of the French had also been concerned,

---

[1] *Ibid.*, 654, 717, 727 *et seq.*, 769, 782. Bellomont thought that a clique of four or five men at Albany who were opposed to him — probably in part because of the question of land grants — and who had several sachems as their followers, had caused many of the Five Nations to be averse to the building of a fort in the Onondaga country.

[2] Livingston stated that the Mohawks had been much lessened by the late war, but more since the peace by the French daily drawing them to Canada, so that nearly two-thirds of the nation were already there with their families, where they were kindly received, clothed, secured in a fort and had priests to instruct them. The principal causes of this he considered to be fear of the French, who were destroying their cattle, the fact that the English were not able to protect them, and the neglect of the English to send clergymen among them. Livingston thought that the English should purchase land and induce the Oneidas and Onondagas, and especially the Mohawks, to move nearer to Albany.

it was fit that, the following year, it should be solemnly ratified in the presence of those allies. Among them were Sacs, Foxes, Pottawottamies, Hurons, Kickapoos, Mascoutins, Ottawas, Nipissings, Abenakis, Indians of the Sault and Mountain, as well as the chief contracting parties. Representing thus the sphere of influence of the French, these painted tribesmen came from a territory which was bounded by the Mississippi on the west and Nova Scotia on the east, the Ohio on the south and Hudson's Bay on the north. It was one of those great and weird assemblages, a source of infinite pride but also of the greatest perplexity, which gathered from time to time on the banks of the St. Lawrence as an expression of the spirit of French dominion. On this occasion Iroquois prisoners were delivered up by most of the tribes who responded to De Callières' summons, their hatchets were all thrown into the deep trench and they smoked together the calumet of peace. The sky was pronounced to be clear, and if one trusted their words one might believe that a vast league of peace had been formed at Montreal under the aegis of France, which would extend over half a continent.[1]

But meantime plans were forming in the fertile brain of Lord Bellomont which, if carried out, might in a few years have transferred the seat of potential empire from Quebec to New York. In a letter which he wrote to the lords of trade,[2] on January 16, 1701/2, Bellomont, in addition to mentioning his plan for the production of naval stores on a large scale, referred to a second design which was nothing less than to induce the Abenakis or Eastern Indians to remove and settle at Schaghticoke on the Hudson opposite Albany and enter into a firm alliance with the English. A third design was to engage in trade the Ottawas, Twightwees, Tobacco Nation and " all those numerous nations," " which the French by their

---

[1] The words of De Callières in the conference which ended in the conclusion of the peace were: — "In order that this Peace which I grant you in the King's name may be stable, should any difference occur or any blow be struck on one side or the other, he who may be aggrieved shall not seek vengeance either by himself or his nation; but he shall come to me that I may have satisfaction done him," and he would ask the governor of the English to join, if necessary, in making the aggressor who should refuse to give satisfaction yield or to chastise him.

[2] N. Y. Docs. IV, 833.

missionaries have at present monopolized." "I hope in a
year's time," he continued, "to give your Lordships a good
account of those nations, if I may be allowed to use my own
methods and that I be well supported by your Lordships. If
I can bring things to bear according to my expectation and
hopes, I fancie I may within a year tell your Lordships you
may set the French at defiance and laugh at all their projects
to circumvent us, their new settlement at Mechisipi [Mis-
sissippi] and Canada and Nova Scotia put together." In
order to support this plan he thought that the beaver trade
ought to be encouraged by parliament, that all duties upon
it and other skins should be taken off both in the colonies
and in England. He had recently learned that the French
government had ordered all hatters to mix a certain quantity
of beaver's fur in their hats, and he wished parliament would
do the same to help the consumption of beaver, which had
gone almost out of fashion in England. When these proposals
are taken in connection with Bellomont's efforts to enlist the
colonies along the whole frontier as far as the Carolinas in
a joint participation in Indian trade, to be accompanied with
the pushing of British settlers into the Indian country, it
appears that in imagination and breadth of conception they
compare well with the exalted dreams of empire which were
cherished in the minds of French leaders.

Bellomont's estimate of the importance of the Iroquois
alliance and of the extent of their influence was expressed as
follows: [1]  "For all their security from South Carolina
to the easternmost point of this province [Massachusetts] —
which ought to be the river St. Croix — is bound up in the
preservation of the Five Nations of Indians in amity with us,
and trying to rescue and retrieve the eastern Indians from the
French, which I believe I could yet accomplish, as late as it
is, and notwithstanding the opportunities and advantages we
have given the French of gaining the Indians to the eastward
by our want of care and indeed of justice and kindness to
them." By evidence which was laid before the queen in 1709 [2]
it appears that Bellomont had sent to the board of trade a
memorial by Nicholas Bayard, the purpose of which was to

[1] N. Y. Docs. V, 74–77.
[2] N. Y. Docs. V, 74–77.

show that the Five Nations had been dependent on New Netherland and New York ever since the settlement by the Dutch. The board also had one prepared in 1697, for use by the commissioners who, it was intended, should be appointed under the treaty of Ryswick to adjust boundaries. This document recited the official record of the dealings of Dutch and English with the Confederacy from 1609 to the summer of 1698. In order to leave nothing further to dispute about, it was claimed in this document that the conquering raids of the Iroquois had extended to the Pacific Ocean and Northwest Passage on the west and northwest and to the Cape of Florida on the south. All of Canada was also included among their conquests. On the historic deduction in the paper was based a claim of sovereignty over the Iroquois, carrying with it sovereignty also over all the peoples whom they had conquered or made dependent. A claim of this extent left no room for the French in North America and little for the Spanish.

Lord Bellomont died in less than a year after he committed to paper his interesting scheme for checkmating the French. Had he lived a decade longer and been properly supported by a British government, which at all times was too preoccupied with European interests and too indifferent toward those of America to appreciate such plans, and had his energies not been diverted by war, the project of the French to occupy the Mississippi Valley might then have been thwarted. The decision was to be postponed for half a century and then reached in a far different way.

But the struggle between the French and British for the control of the fur trade and of the interior of the continent was now begun in earnest. The next move centered in Detroit, the most important of the western passes, which commanded the approach to Lake Huron and to the vast fur-bearing regions in that neighborhood and beyond. Before 1690 Denonville had attempted the erection of a fort at that spot. In a report of April, 1700, to Bellomont, Robert Livingston had declared that the best way in which the British could establish trade with the far Indians would be by establishing a post at Detroit, " the most pleasant and plentiful inland place in America." [1] In imagination he saw Indian tribes coming

---

[1] N. Y. Docs. IV, 650.

there to trade from the borders of the Carolinas on the south
to the utmost regions of the Ottawas on the north. " This
would not only produce vast trade, but raise a great many
Bushlopers to be ready to serve the king on all occasions
and in a short time defray the charge his Majesty would be
at in settling it." If the boundary line were then run between
the French and the English, Livingston felt confident that
most of these nations would fall to the share of the latter and
it would be easy to destroy the small huts of bark which the
French might have built in those regions and called forts.

But the problem proved to be not quite so simple as
Livingston imagined. The attention of La Mothe Cadillac
had long been fixed upon this same spot, and while he was
commander at Michilimackinac he had started a vigorous
propaganda for the purpose of convincing the Canadian
authorities and the French government that a settlement
should be established. So strong was the opposition of the
Jesuits and the intendant that La Mothe had to carry his
cause to Paris before he succeeded. He returned with authority to carry out his plan and in 1701 Detroit was founded.
Though for some time it did not flourish as was expected, the
British were not in a position to oust the French, and the
settlement was at once recognized as a capital stroke in the
game which was being played for the control of the
continent.[1]

But the Dutch and English of New York were not to be
entirely outdone, and one must bear in mind the ideas already
expressed by Livingston, as well as the settlement of Detroit,
upon which the French were now engaged, in order to explain a
somewhat remarkable transaction which occurred at the conference which Lieutenant Governor Nanfan held with the Five
Nations at Albany in July, 1701.[2] In the speech of the
sachems on the fourth day of the conference appears a passage
in which Robert Livingston was desired to go to England
and inform the king how the French encroached on their
lands by building a fort at Niagara. For the moment they
were mistaken as to the place where the French intended

[1] Margry, V; Parkman, Half Century of Conflict, I.

[2] N. Y. Docs. IV, 905, 908; V, 543, 545; Severance, Pubs. of Buffalo
Hist. Soc. IX, 123, 125; Parkman, op. cit.

next to settle; but the important point is that the Indian
commissioner, whom we have just found expressing such ambitious views concerning the west, is now mentioned by the
sachems as the one whom they would select as agent to
present their case before the crown.  Continuing, they said
that they would give up to the king in return for his protection all the hunting grounds which they had conquered,
and they desired that Livingston would draft an instrument
for this purpose, which they would sign and seal.  The instrument follows, drawn in regular English style, and conveying
to the king the entire territory between Lakes Ontario, Erie
and Huron and extending southwest to near the modern
Chicago, a region said to be eight hundred miles long and four
hundred miles broad.  It was claimed by the Iroquois as
their hunting grounds, by virtue of their conquests of the
Hurons and Eries.  In the record the deed appears signed and
sealed by twenty sachems, coming about equally from all
the cantons, and by John Nanfan, Livingston and James
Weems.  The magistrates of Albany to the number of ten,
together with two members of the council and two interpreters,
were present as witnesses.  The fact that a year later, in their
first conference with Cornbury, the Five Nations complained
that their deed of the year before had been slighted and
" thrown into some hole," would indicate that to them it had
some meaning.[1]  They again insisted that Livingston should
be sent to England to complete the transaction and further
inform the new queen of their condition.

The inference would seem to be that in a mood of discouragement and perhaps of panic, from which they were
by no means free, the sachems yielded to the persuasions of
Livingston and his colleagues and allowed him to draft for
them this remarkable paper.  Or again it may have been the
work of the British faction within the Confederacy and may
have been meant by them as a counter stroke against the
peace which about a month later was ratified at Montreal.
In any case the document must be regarded as genuine and
the transaction as a real one, but one which was almost
immediately obscured by the partisan conflict which then
raged in New York and by the indifference of Cornbury to

[1] The deed was also referred to at a later time.

questions of this kind.   In 1703 Livingston went to England, but in the correspondence which has survived concerning his visit no reference appears to the deed of 1701.   Though his errand related chiefly to his claims and restoration to the offices from which Fletcher had removed him, Livingston did bring prominently before the board of trade and the authorities of the Church of England the desirability of establishing a number of Anglican missionaries in the Iroquois country to counteract the influence of French priests.[1]   The need also for more and better forts along the frontier and of more troops he also urged, and of securing much more effective cooperation on the part of the colonies in defence of the frontier.   The English Church found it possible to furnish two missionaries, but their work was of short duration and followed by no results of importance.

The important effect which the peace of 1701 between the French and the Iroquois had upon the course of the second colonial war along the northern frontier has already been noted.   Since, by means of the neutrality, New York, thus insured, was freed from the pressure of war for about seven years, it would have been all the easier for her to advance British influence among the Indians.   But in this respect, as in all others, Cornbury was the opposite of Bellomont. Though it was now more desirable than ever that Albany should be the centre for dealings between the Five Nations and Europeans, Cornbury held very few conferences there, and at those which were held no business of special importance was done.   In 1708 he wrote that no presents had been bestowed on them since the first year of his administration.[2]   During these years therefore the tendency was to transfer the centre of negotiations to Onondaga, next to Montreal or Quebec, the place that was most favorable to the French.   In Albany the management of Indian affairs fell almost wholly under the control of the commissioners.[3]   They sent the usual envoys to Onondaga and received the sachems when they came to Albany and such Indians from farther west as came there

[1] N. Y. Col. Docs. IV, 1063, 1067, 1074.

[2] N. Y. Docs. V, 65.

[3] For the best record of what occurred see the Abstract of the Minutes of the Indian Commissioners, by Peter Wraxall.

to trade. All the members of this board were traders and as time passed the greed for profit in its lowest form took possession of them, and it stayed with them during the half-century which followed. Their chief interest in Indian relations was in the profit which came from them. In connection with British producers and traders in general, they sought to furnish goods more cheaply than the French and they succeeded. With this bait they sought to lure the far Indians, allies of the French, to Albany. But the long overland carriage for beaver, and especially for buffalo, elk and other heavier skins, proved an obstacle which it was very difficult to overcome. The French had a great natural advantage in their waterway. The Albanians also cultivated trade relations with the Caughnawagas in Canada, hoping thereby to attract them back to their Mohawk kinsmen. But no such result followed, and this enterprise developed into a large direct trade with the French of Canada. The enemies of England in war and their persistent rivals in peace profited from the cheapness of British goods, and by furnishing them to the Indians of the west were able to thwart to an extent that very direct trade westward which the Albanians were seeking to build up. The culmination of this we shall see later, but its beginnings belong to the time of which we are now speaking.

The spirit of almost incredible baseness in which this trade with the Indians was to a large extent carried on is illustrated by a statement made at Albany in May, 1709, by sachems of the Messasagas, a nation of the Far Indians. On their arrival, they said, they were taken into the traders' houses and the furs they brought were taken from them. " We are not masters of our own things," they continued, and " pray we may have our furs and go and trade where we can find the best market." The reply which was made to this was not entered in the journal, and Wraxall's comment was that most of the offenders were probably members of the commission, and that down to his day the common practice, when Indians were expected in Albany, was to lay hold of them as customs officers would of smugglers, carry them into their houses, make them drunk and then cheat them. " The traders are as jealous of each other and mortally hate one another,

when their interest is concerned, as the greatest enemies can
do; but all join in cheating." In spite of frequent protests
from the sachems of the Five Nations, the drink traffic continued unabated and was one of the fundamental causes of
the disappearance of the red man. On one occasion the
sachems declared that they were not to blame for the traffic.
" They had so often desired that rum might not be sold to
the Indians that the beavers they had given to enforce that
request, if laid on a heap, would reach to the clouds. " We
must think you sell it with no other design than to
destroy us." [1]

At not infrequent intervals during Cornbury's administration messengers from one or another of the Five Nations
warned the English of French activities among them, and of
the likelihood that they would have to transfer their support
to the French if they were not supplied with what they needed
from Albany. Reports were brought of direct dealings between themselves and the French government, to offset which
Schuyler or others were occasionally sent to Onondaga. The
despatch of more French missionaries, especially among the
western cantons, was duly reported. The pressure which
came from occasional raids of Indians allied with the French
was continued and also duly noted; so also were efforts of the
French to divert the remoter tribes from direct trade with Albany. The sachems kept repeating at Albany requests for a
capable interpreter to be sent to live permanently among them,
also for a gunsmith with proper tools and equipment, and for
an adequate supply of ammunition at moderate prices. It does
not appear that a gunsmith was furnished, and as to ammunition there was apparently much delay and a very inadequate
supply. Andrew Montour, a French half-breed, came to
reside among them in the English interest, but he was later
slain by the Indians at the instance of the French.[2] On their
own side the French secured the permanent services of de
Longueil and Joncaire, two of the most effective agents of the
middle period of French rule. Joncaire was adopted into

[1] Wraxall, *op. cit.*, May, 1709, May, 1710.

[2] See the monograph of F. H. Severance, The Story of Joncaire, Pubs. of
Buffalo Hist. Soc. IX, p. 105; N. Y. Docs. V, 65; Wraxall, May 8 and May 31,
1709.

the tribe of the Senecas and it was among them and the other westerns cantons that his influence was chiefly felt.[1]  So quiescent were the British throughout those years that the French were easily able to confirm and extend their colonies, though the superior cheapness of British goods was an attraction which it was not safe to ignore.  It was this, together with rum, which in the end kept the Iroquois in the main true to the British alliance and offset the superiority of the French as negotiators with the Indians.[2]

In the spring of 1708 Lawrence Claessen, a Dutch interpreter, brought to Albany the report that the French were going to rebuild the fort at Niagara, which had been abandoned since 1688.[3]  Though the establishment of the post at Detroit had to an extent lowered the importance of Niagara, it still must be regarded as a valuable link in the chain of western forts.  Joncaire at this time became greatly interested.  In the fall of 1708 an agent whom the French minister, Pontchartrain, had sent to report on Detroit, met Joncaire at Niagara and listened to his statement of the advantages which would follow from the establishment of a fort there.  The Iroquois were also worried lest the post might be established and their hunting grounds encroached on and in the end they would be subjugated by the French.  But the agent, d'Aigremont, reported adversely to Niagara unless at the same time a settlement was made at La Galette, near the present Ogdensburg, New York, where alone he thought there was fertile soil enough for the production of the foodstuffs needed to support a garrison at Niagara.  He also suspected that Joncaire was personally interested in the fur trade at Niagara and therefore that his advocacy of that place was not honest.  This report was approved by the French minister and, together with the immediate necessity which soon arose of defending Canada against the formidable attacks that were planned against it in the later years of the war, diverted attention from Niagara for a decade or more.[4]  With the resumption of military operations along the line of the

[1] Severance, The
Doc  IX  81  S

Hudson efforts to secure the active cooperation of the Five Nations were renewed by the British. To offset these at the beginning the French not only [1] made careful preparations for defence, but caused a report to be circulated among the Indians that the British were preparing to destroy them root and branch and that a great force was coming from England for the purpose. Another form which the rumor took was that the French and English were going to unite for the destruction of the Indians and the division of their country. These were some of the imaginings which the growing dread of white encroachment kindled in the minds of the savages. Their effect was to paralyze the Five Nations with doubt, to divide them into a pro-English and a pro-Gallic faction, and in their counsels to drive them now in this direction, now in that. The Senecas [2] in particular excused their leaning toward the French by the pressure upon them which came from that nation and fear that if they did otherwise their country would be seized. The Onondagas and others now expressed a willingness to have the English build forts and garrison them in their country, while one or more smiths were sent to live among them in response to their more emphatic demands. A move was also made against the French priests, their chapel and house at Onondaga being destroyed and one priest returning to Canada and the other being taken to Albany. Meantime, with the disappearance of Cornbury and advent of Hunter, conference were again resumed at Albany.[3] As the Praying Indians of Canada were prominent among the assailants of New England, an effort was made by Governor Dudley, in connection with the conference of 1710, to induce the Five Nations to interpose for checking these savages. But, they, of course, could be induced to do nothing effective, and even said that as the result of French influence they frequently suffered from similar visitations at the hands of the far Indians. The removal of the Palatines into the

[1] *Ibid.*, 829 *et seq.*
...... the Se........ ....... a conference, "It is reported to us
...... ...u have us do? If we
...... ...es us his instruments
...... ...not get." Wraxall,

Schoharie region also gave rise to discussion with the Mohawks over their interest in the lands there.[1] They were not averse to granting the lands desired, but insisted that it should be done in public and not in the clandestine manner of earlier times. But at the close of the conference they finally went away without signing the deed.

In connection with the expedition of 1711 against Canada, Vaudreuil, the governor general of Canada, strove to keep the Iroquois neutral and to impress them with a sense of the unanimity with which the other Indian peoples supported the French.[2] On the other hand, special efforts were made by the British to secure their cooperation, though it was in violation of their treaty with the French and of many warnings from that quarter. Longueil and Joncaire had already built a small blockhouse in the Senecas' country, but Hunter sent Schuyler and others thither to insist that it should be torn down, the French dismissed and their covenants with the English performed. The house was destroyed. In August a force of nearly seven hundred Iroquois gathered at Albany to follow the troops who had already started northward. In the leisurely conference which Hunter, Nicholson, Saltonstall and the Indian commissioners held with them before their departure, Decanissora found occasion, among other things, to tell the English that they were now demanding for the last time that they should sell goods, and especially powder, more cheaply; if this were not done, the sachems would no longer be able to restrain their young men and they would have to leave th᠎ castles and the confederacy woul᠎ be broken up.[3] But ᠎ ᠎ ᠎ absence on this futile er᠎

After the expediti᠎
᠎sistently than ᠎
᠎tended᠎

᠎᠎ By
᠎ the Tuscarora War, ᠎, 3, V.
᠎, Oct. 18, 1711; N. Y. Docs.᠎
᠎, Maryland disturbed
᠎nia, actually disturbed
᠎lish, old
᠎ rear

᠎23.

᠎21 ᠎90᠎
III, 556; Wraxall, op. cit., May 28, 1708; N. Y. Docs᠎
IX, 821, 826.
Story of Joncaire, Pubs. of Buffalo Hist. Soc.᠎

effect of it overcome.  Neither the French nor the English
desired to provoke the Five Nations again to war.  In June,
1712, Pontchartrain wrote to Vaudreuil, " His Majesty is
persuaded, like you, that you ought not to embroil yourself
with the Iroquois by reason of the cruel war which would be
the consequence in the colony."  Immediately after the return
of the force in 1711, Governor Hunter asked the executive
council of New York whether it was advisable to break
neutrality between the Five Nations and the French and
engage them in actual war, observing at the same time that
he wished to prevent incursions of the French and their Indians into Connecticut and Massachusetts.  The opinion of
the council was that the Five Nations should not be engaged
in actual war, because of the destructive consequences which
would follow on the frontier of New York and other frontiers,
unless such a force was kept constantly in pay, as their
province was not in a condition to support.[1]  These considerations were decisive, and the English devoted themselves to
the building of Fort Hunter in the Mohawk country near the
Schoharie district and in establishing a missionary there,
who now came over partly as a result of the visit of Schuyler
and the Mohawk chiefs to England.

By the treaty of Utrecht, the parties to which agreed to
respect the tribes allied with each, rivalry between the French
and English for control over the Indians was again brought
back to trade as a basis and there it was to remain for a
generation.  But while this treaty was being negotiated the
great Tuscarora War was in progress in North Carolina.
This tribe was allied by blood to the Five Nations and after
the war its union as the sixth nation with that Confederacy
was effected.  For some time before this struggle the French
had been fanning the feud between the Iroquois and the
Catawbas and Cherokees on the Carolina frontier, this bei
a part of their policy so to occupy the attention of th
enemies that they would be unable to aid the E
these hostile raids the peace of the Pennsylv
and Virginia frontiers was imperilled o
This evil was considerably increased

[1] N. Y. Docs. IX, 862; Min. of Ex
384.

while the southern provinces also felt the reaction of the later Yemassee War as a disturbing factor.  Hitherto, with slight exception, outside of New England, each colony had dealt separately with the Indians who lived within its borders or closely adjacent thereto.  There had therefore been as many centres of Indian administration and policy as there were colonies, though all exhibited the same general characteristics.[1]  But circumstances were now arising which directed attention to the need of joint action in this matter by all the colonies along the western frontier, an attitude to which the Puritan colonies of New England had been responsive in the seventeenth century but which later, as danger was removed from their very midst, they seemed to be forgetting.

The agitation and fears aroused among the savages by the wars in the south were kept alive by the rumors, already referred to, that one or both of the European nations involved were planning their immediate destruction.  The founding of Louisiana at this time suggested to the Indian commissioners at Albany, as it did to others, that the French from that centre might be provoking Indian wars in the south.  As the chain of French posts was perfected through the Mississippi valley and the connection between Canada and Louisiana established, the possibility of a reaction from that quarter upon all the Indian peoples along the frontier became evident.  In 1712 and 1713 much evidence came before the governor and council of New York of restlessness among the Indians who lived along the waters of the Delaware and Susquehanna rivers. This involved the tribes of Pennsylvania and Maryland.  The Delawares and Shawnees, whose home was in Pennsylvania and thence westward on the upper Ohio, had been partially subjugated by the Iroquois in the previous century.  The Susquehannas of Maryland, as well as the Tuscaroras, were of Iroquois blood, and the disturbances attendant on the war in North Carolina could not fail to affect all these tribes.  In May, 1714, the New York authorities received information of a secret meeting to be held at Onondaga and attended by representatives of all the tribes as far south as Carolina, and though death had been threatened against any who should

[1] See the chapter on Indian Relations in the author's work on the Am. Colonies in the 17th Century.

divulge what passed there, the Albany commissioners engaged
the Mohawk Hendrick to report to them what transpired.[1]
Though all that he reported related to keeping a general
peace with Canada, there appeared for a moment a possibility
of a great Indian confederation facing both the French and
the English and extending along the entire western frontier.

Virginia in particular soon experienced the disturbing effects
of the feud between the Five Nations and Catawbas and
Cherokees and of the raids which as a consequence were made
along the western frontier. The Valley of Virginia was the
path through which these bands of marauders went. During
the Tuscarora War a caravan of Virginia traders bound for
the villages of the southern Indians was attacked, it was
alleged, by a force of Iroquois, their horses and some of their
men killed and all their goods seized. It was in the hope
of checking such raids that Governor Spotswood, as has been
noticed in the account of his administration, established the
post at Christanna. In April, 1717, while he was conferring
there with some Catawbas and members of other southern
tribes, a band — also known to be Iroquois — killed several
of the Indians who were then present and carried off some
prisoners. This second outrage led Spotswood to write to
Governor Hunter and also to send Captain Christopher Smith
to New York to expostulate. Hunter's explanation of the
event was that it was occasioned by his urging the Five Nations to interpose in the war in South Carolina for the relief
of the whites, and that in the course of a raid started with
that in view some Iroquois had come in contact with Catawbas
who three years before treacherously murdered certain Iroquois envoys. Not knowing that the Catawbas were under
English protection, they had taken summary vengeance on
them.[2] At the conference of June, 1717, at which Smith was
present, this was given by the Indians as their excuse, and the
sachems who were there repeated the ineffective promise that
they would do what they could to prevent raids in that
direction in the future. But to the proposal which Spotswood
also made, that they should send deputies to Virginia to

---

[1] E. C. Min., May 25, 1714; Wraxall, *op. cit.*, May 20, 1714.

[2] N. Y. Docs. V, 483, 490–493; Pa. Col. Recs. III, 21, 82–89; Min. of Ex. C.
of Va. Aug. 13, 1717; Spots. Letters, II, 257, 261.

treat and adjust all matters with him, the Five Nations objected. They declared, undoubtedly under New York influence, that Albany was the original and established place of council, to which Lord Howard of Effingham had come more than thirty years before and where he had concluded a lasting peace and buried the hatchet. They therefore proposed that the next summer agents of Virginia and of its tributary Indians meet them there for a general conference and treaty. This was the message which Smith took back to Virginia. But in little more than two months after the conference ended a large body of young Iroquois warriors started on a raid southward from which it was impossible to divert them and which ended in another bloody reprisal on the Catawbas. This showed anew how vain it was to trust to Indian promises.

Pennsylvania was now drawn into this chain of relations, for the arrogant spirit shown by the Five Nations toward their subjects, the Delawares and others, and toward Pennsylvania because of conflicting claims to lands on the Susquehanna river necessitated some action.[1] Smith, on his return from New York, had the Shawnees called into conference at Conestoga for the purpose of ascertaining whether or not the charge was true that they had shared in the attack on the Catawbas at Fort Christanna. They admitted that some of their tribe were near by, but denied that they took any part. Smith, in accordance with his instructions, then asked Governor Keith for leave to treat with the Shawnees in order to conclude a league with them on behalf of Virginia. But now the spirit of colonial separatism in this relation appeared in clear relief. Keith told him that it would not be useful for persons to treat with the Indians other than those of the colony to which the tribes in question belonged; however, if Governor Spotswood, for whom he had a great regard, would frame such propositions as he desired, he (Keith) would try to procure an acceptable treaty. He then told the Indians who were present that all the colonies from New England to South Carolina, though they had different governors, were subject to the same king, so that when one of these governments made a friendly treaty with the Indians, the latter

[1] Pa. Arch. I, 360–365.

must enter into the same bond of friendship with all the rest of the English, " by which means all the Indian nations who are in League and friendship with any English government must also be friends to each other." Conversely, an injury committed against Indians who were in friendship with any English government would break the league with Pennsylvania, the terms of which had been inviolably observed on its part.

The return of Smith to Virginia drew from the governor and council there a declaration that the recent conduct of the Five Nations was a breach of the peace of 1685 and that Virginia could feel secure only if those Indians were restrained from passing to the south of the Potomac river and to the east of the mountains. The demand also that Albany should be the only place of treaty with them was pronounced dishonorable to the other colonies. It was also the opinion that a representation on these subjects should be sent to the home government. A proposal was actually made and approved that a fort should be built at the lately discovered pass across the Great Mountains and that this fort and Albany should be alternately the places for the delivery of his majesty's presents and for renewing alliances with the Indians.[1] Spotswood also made a journey to New York, taking Keith with him from Philadelphia, in order to talk over the situation with Hunter,[2] and to present the two conditions of peace just mentioned. But the end of Hunter's administration was now approaching and though Spotswood doubtless freed his mind in no ambiguous terms, he failed to get a satisfactory reply from either the New Yorkers or the Indians. Hunter told Spotswood that he must not insist on punctilios with the Indians, as they were strangers to our refined notions of honor and justice and would not bear reasoning upon their conduct. Hunter could certainly speak from experience on this point, for he had once sought to break the force of their reiterated demands that the English should sell their goods more cheaply by reasoning with them upon the law of supply and demand as the determining cause of price.

[1] Min. of Ex. C. of Va., Aug. 13, 1717.
[2] *Ibid.*, Pa. Col. Recs. III, 30, 87, 88; N. Y. Docs. V, 548–9.

Spotswood bore with the repeated breaches of the peace on his frontier and continued vain efforts to bring about a negotiation in Virginia until the spring of 1720, when in a long letter to Schuyler, who then, as president of the council, was in charge of the government of New York, he poured out not only his denunciation of the Indians but his criticism of what he regarded as the narrow spirit in which New York insisted that Albany must be the sole place at which to hold conferences.    He charged New York, and especially the commissioners, with lowering the English in the eyes of the Indians by allowing them to insist on their haughty demand.    They must not stir a foot, but we must run a thousand miles to treat with them!   The reply of Virginia to this was the calling out of the militia of her frontier counties and preparation to meet the Indians with force.    This letter roused Schuyler to correspondence with Pennsylvania and Virginia on the subject.    It was also sent to England and Hunter was questioned there by the board of trade in reference to its charges.    In 1720 an agreement was reached between the Indians of Virginia and Pennsylvania in harmony with the terms which Spotswood had proposed and in July of the same year James Logan at Conestoga delivered to the Pennsylvania Indians a talk which for the idyllic beauty of its language and sentiment should be a classic in what might be called the literature of the league or covenant between the whites and the American Indians.    Schuyler also, in a conference at Albany with the Five Nations, renewed the convenant chain with them in the name of all the English colonies and the agreement was in words accepted by them in this sense.[1]

The arrival of Burnet as governor of New York augured well for a broad and rather idealistic policy in reference to all matters connected with the frontier.    In his first conference with the Five Nations, held in September, 1721,[2] he sought to explain to them the reasons for the hostility between the English and the French, briefly sketching for that purpose the overthrow of James II and the wars which followed under William III and Anne (being careful in good Whig fashion to condemn the Tory ministers for recalling Marlborough and

[1] Pa. Col. Recs. III, 93 et seq., 205;  N. Y. Docs. V, 565, 567.
[2] N. Y. Docs. V, 635 et seq.

concluding the treaty of Utrecht; but, he added, the accession of the Hanoverians in England and the policy of the regent in France were helping to improve relations, though there was still much in the conduct of the French, especially in America, to prove them untrustworthy. It is safe to say that no governor except the son of the famous bishop of Salisbury ever gave the sons of the forest in America such a lecture on history as was this. He also presented to the sachems the proposals, which he had received from Spotswood, that both the Five Nations and the Indians of Virginia should henceforth confine themselves to their respective sides of the Potomac river and the great ridge of mountains which formed the western boundary of Virginia and should not cross them without leave from the governor of that province. The reply of the sachems who were present was that they would do the best they could to enforce this policy, but they warned the governor that the authority which they had over their people was not equal to that of officers in European armies.

In 1722 Spotswood yielded to the necessity of visiting Albany and there meeting the Five Nations. After correspondence it was arranged that both he and Keith, accompanied also by members of their respective councils, should go. This course was fully assented to by the legislature of the two provinces and the necessary appropriations made for presents to the Indians and travelling expenses. In recognition of the fact that they were entering a province which chiefly controlled relations with the Five Nations, they asked and received permission from its governor and council to attend the conference and negotiate. Burnet tried to make the spirit of this conference still broader by calling the attention of the Indians to Râle's War, which was then in progress in New England, and asking that they would send deputies thither and urge the conclusion of peace. Canada and the Far Indians also came in for their usual share of attention, giving to this conference, on the whole, a breadth of outlook on the English side which had not previously been attained. The covenant chain was again renewed, this time in the presence of three governors and on behalf of all the English colonies of North America, the Indians speaking only in the name of the Six Nations, though later, stung probably by the proud language of Spotswood, they added the names of the Tuscaroras, Shawnees and of a few other minor tribes.

The governors of Virginia and Pennsylvania each held one separate session with the Indians, and it is certain that no Englishman before his time had ever assumed at Albany the tone of lofty command and authority with which Spotswood so cowed the sachems that the reply of their orator seemed humble and beseeching in comparison. Not only did they at once assent to his demand in reference to crossing the specified boundary line, but also that they would not seek to treat with any Indians of Virginia except through the government of that province, and that they would at once return all runaway negroes who might fall into their hands. As to a demand which they made for reprisal for four Indians who, they alleged, had been poisoned in Virginia, he compelled them to acknowledge that the complaint was wholly unfounded. He also accused them directly of being guilty of many acts of hostility, robbery and treaty breaking and warned them of what might be expected from Virginians if this conduct on the part of their foolish young warriors was not abandoned. A weak acknowledgment of guilt and of thanks for forgiveness was the only reply which the Indians could make to this charge. "Above six hundred miles have we from Virginia come hither to treat with you," continued Spotswood. "Nine days after the appointed time of our meeting did we wait before I could have an opportunity of speaking with you, and nine days longer before you answered my first Proposition. So that serving a Treaty at Albany occasions so much trouble and expence, you must not expect that the Government of Virginia will again agree to the renewing of it after this manner, in this place." This was his final answer to the claim of New York and of the Five Nations that Albany must be the only place of conference with them, and his warning also that, if they did not thereafter keep the peace, Virginia would maintain it with armed force. To the Iroquois orator who was compelled to reply to these imperious utterances, it may have seemed a small compensation that at the close he received a golden horse shoe to be worn on his breast and to be carried with them when any of his people should seek to pass the mountains

and enter Virginia. Had Spotswood been continued twenty
years longer at the head of the government of Virginia, some
of the results which were foreshadowed in his speeches might
possibly have come to pass, but under the mild and correct
Nott, Drysdale and Gooch, who soon succeeded him, an
aggressive attitude like the one indicated was impossible.
The speech of Governor Keith was mild, as became the relations which thus far had developed between white and red men
in Penn's province, and neither it nor the reply implied any
essential changes. With this the conference ended. On his
return Spotswood desired to hold a conference with the Pennsylvania Indians, so as to bring them into the agreement with
Virginia, but owing to the objection of some of the council
of that province he was forced to abandon the project.

In Indian relations as in other affairs Virginia lay on the
border between the north and the remote south. She was
being drawn more into connection with affairs on the northern
frontiers, while an old-standing controversy existed between
her and South Carolina over the rights of Virginia traders
who passed through a corner of Carolina territory on their
way to and from the Cherokee country. But in the period
before us the relations between Virginia and the colonies to
the south of her, so far as Indian trade was concerned, went
scarcely beyond this. In Indian relations the Carolinas, with
the addition of Georgia at a later time, while subject in general
to conditions like those of their northern neighbors, formed
a distinct group by themselves. The Cherokee and Maskoki
peoples of the south were their savage neighbors, the Spanish
of Florida and French of Louisiana their European rivals,
and in matters of defence they gravitated about the Caribbean
rather than the St. Lawrence centre. The country of the
Creeks, or Maskoki proper, lay to the south and west of the
Savannah river and extended to the region of the Alabama
river, northeast of Mobile. Of kindred origin with them were
the Yemassees, the remnants of whom now lived with related
peoples in Florida and continued at times to disturb the
southern border. The Catawbas, now reduced in strength by
their feud with the Iroquois, lay on the western half of the
boundary between the two Carolinias. West of them, extending far to the north and westward beyond the mountains, was

the land of the Cherokees, the most powerful of the group of tribes which were reckoned as allies of the English.  The territory occupied collectively by these peoples extended along the mountain barrier, and some distance to the east and west of it, from the latitude of southwestern Virginia on the north to Florida on the south.  Collectively they were more numerous than the Iroquois — being able to muster perhaps 5000 warriors — but they were not united into a single confederacy and hence were sometimes at war with one another.  They had not made widely extended conquests, as had the Iroquois, and an alliance with them did not imply such territorial claims as resulted from connection with the Five Nations.  Their territorial claims could not be greatly utilized to strengthen the pretensions of the English.

At the time of which we are speaking the French were just beginning to secure a foothold at Mobile and on the lower Mississippi.  It was in 1702 that permanent settlement was begun at Mobile, while New Orleans was not founded until 1720, when it became the capital of the province under John Law's Company of the Indies.  After the grant was made to Crozat, in 1714, a French post named Fort Toulouse was established far above Mobile, where the Coosa and Tallapoosa rivers join to form the Alabama.  This was in the region of the "Alibamons," a Maskoki people, and was intended to control the approaches to the English colonies.  This fort was an occasion of considerable anxiety to the English and is referred to in the records of Carolina whenever French encroachments are mentioned.  Daniel Coxe, in his "Carolina," dates from the founding of this fort the decline of English influence among the Indians of the entire south.  It was certainly an event of the greatest importance in the series of those which made the two European peoples conscious of each other's presence in the south and of the rivalries and hostility which were sure to result from this fort.  Hostilities between English and French traders and Indians in fact occurred soon after the founding of Fort Toulouse.  Fort Rosalie, on the Mississippi in the country of the Natchez, had already been occupied by the French, and at a later time a second post, Fort Tombigbee, was established in the Alabama region.  By means of these and the posts further up, in the Illinois country, the French secured complete control of the Mississippi and such influence over the Indians of that region as naturally resulted from that fact. On their maps Louisiana was made to extend, though without exact bounds, to the Appalachians on the east. Through the Illinois country connection was opened between Louisiana and Canada, the occupation of Detroit in 1701 helping to complete the line of posts. An outlet for the French fur trade was opened down the Mississippi, as well as down the St. Lawrence, and the fertile prairies of the Illinois region were secured as a source of food supply for the weak and hardly self-supporting forts and towns in Louisiana proper.

The Indian tribes upon whose support the French of Louisiana chiefly reckoned were the Choctaws and Chickasaws. The former of these are said to have been the most powerful Indian nation of the south. They lived adjacent to New Orleans on the lower Mississippi, while the country of the Chickasaws lay nearly two hundred miles to the northeast. They were divided in their allegiance and could not be depended upon for faithful support by either of the European rivals. For an early period British traders penetrated into the country of both these tribes. Efforts were made to establish permanent relations with them and to win them away from the French. Similar efforts were of course being made by the French among the Creeks and Cherokees, but in neither case were they specially successful. Presents were bestowed by both nations, and rarely Indians from the valley of the Mississippi appeared in the Carolina settlements, while corresponding visits were made by Creeks and Cherokees to the settlements of the French. When known, these always awakened fears that the Indian allies, whichever they might be, would be lost and efforts would be made through presents, conferences, the appointment of new agents or commissioners, the correction of abuses, and new legislation for any or all these purposes to offset the unwelcome tendency.

It is of details such as these that the Indian records of the southern provinces largely consist. Until the founding of Georgia, Carolina, and finally South Carolina, controlled Indian relations in general, so far as they concerned the English, throughout the south. Since a time early in her proprietary period, as we know, she had administered these affairs with system.[1] For some two years after 1716, the Indian trade was vested in the public and money was appropriated by the assembly to carry it on. But the waste which resulted from this led in 1717 to the throwing of the trade open to those who under license would adventure upon it. Factors were kept among the leading tribes and the province garrisoned the frontier settlements as a protection to traders as well as the colonists.[2] This was continued until after the Revolution of 1719. By a statute of 1721 a board of three commissioners, with William Bull at its head, was created and empowered to visit twice a year Fort Moore and the other forts on the frontier. On these visits they were to hear Indian complaints and award damages and also examine into the condition of the forts and garrisons and give directions for improvement therein. No Indians were to be allowed to come into the settlements unless they were sent for. Trade therefore with them must be carried on chiefly in their own country. Hence the important function of traders and packmen, and of the system of licenses which was established for their regulation and as a source of revenue in South Carolina. After a year's trial this board of commissioners was abolished as unsatisfactory and their powers were vested in the governor and any three members of the council. A year's experience of this arrangement led to the conclusion that the burden was too great for the governor and council, and by an act of 1723 John Moore was created sole commissioner, with the aid of a secretary designated by himself. Some more systematic regulations concerning traders and their licenses were made in the act. It remained in force until 1731 and the single commissioner instead of a board was the arrangement adhered to permanently after that time.[3] Tobias Fitch and William Drake in succession filled the place which had first been held by Moore. But conferences with the Indians in the south never reached the importance which they had early attained at Albany, neither did any individual gain the influence among the natives which was long enjoyed by the Schuylers.

[1] Osgood, Am. Colonies in 17th Century, II.
[2] C. O. 5/433, L. H. J., May 21, 1734.
[3] S. C. Stats. III, 141, 184, 229, 327.

In the south the French were much more remote, established themselves later and were much weaker than in the north. Until late in the colonial period the competition for control over the Indians was therefore less keen in the south and the institutions for maintaining it were less fully developed there than in New York. Intercourse with the tribesmen was kept up more through traders and special agents sent occasionally among them than by periodical and largely attended conferences. The specific Indian records of the south have been far less fully preserved than those of the north and therefore such generalizations as the above must be qualified by the statement that were the extant records fuller, events which are now obscure might be shown to have occurred on a much larger scale.[1]

In view of what has been narrated, it may be said that, by the close of the first quarter of the eighteenth century, the need of a comprehensive Indian policy for the entire frontier had presented itself to leading minds and some vague proposals had been made and events had occurred which suggested joint action; but the spirit and precedents which were opposed to this were evidently too strong to justify sanguine hopes for the future.

[1] A book of Indian records is often referred to as having existed among the archives of South Carolina, though it seems to have been kept at dates later than 1730.

# CHAPTER XV

## THE POLICY OF THE BRITISH GOVERNMENT IN REFERENCE TO THE PRODUCTION OF NAVAL STORES

THE term naval stores includes masts and ship timber, tar, pitch, rosin, hemp, and also iron in certain of its relations and utilities. These were the products of the extractive industries in America or elsewhere which entered into the construction of the merchant vessels and ships of the royal navy of the seventeenth and eighteenth centuries. With the exception of masts and ship timber the utilities of all the commodities mentioned extended to many other industries than that of ship building. Especially was this true of iron, which is a product of the widest and most fundamental uses in the whole field of industry.

Previous to the beginning of the eighteenth century England had procured her naval stores from the Eastland countries. Russia had furnished most of the hemp, Sweden the tar and pitch, while the northern countries had all yielded ship timber. The most extensive trade had been with Sweden, and as England exported thither much less than she imported from thence the balance of trade was unfavorable to her and that to the extent of more than £200,000 yearly. This was a situation from which an escape at any time would have been most desirable, but especially so in an age when policy was wholly guided by the principles of mercantilism.

At the beginning of the eighteenth century two events occurred which greatly increased the importance to England of a supply of naval stores and correspondingly increased the difficulty of procuring it from Sweden. One of these was the war with France and her allies, which made it necessary that the British fleet should attain the best possible condition as to size and equipment. The other was the formation of the Stockholm Tar Company, for monopolizing trade in pitch and tar.[1] This company insisted not only on selling to Eng-

---

[1] Eleanor Lord, Some Industrial Experiments in the British Colonies of North America, J. H. U. Studies, Extra Vol. XVII, p. 56 *et seq.*

land all she needed and at prices fixed at high rates, but on delivering it at English ports and thereby monopolizing the freights which accrued from the trade. This was done on the eve of the War of the Spanish Succession, when England's demand for naval stores was at the highest degree of intensity. A correspondence between the secretary of state and the British envoy at Stockholm on the possibility of procuring from that quarter an adequate supply at reasonable prices revealed a prospect so hopeless that the envoy suggested the development of the resources of the colonies in these commodities, even though it might cost a third more to bring them across the ocean. This was in harmony with the principles of mercantilism and had its influence in determining the course which policy should take.

By this time the British government had become partially informed as to the resources of America in naval stores. The early explorers of the seventeenth century had dwelt upon this at great length, though in general terms, in their letters and relations. Captain John Smith, for example, had been very explicit, especially concerning the resources of New England which would be valuable for the British shipbuilder. But the information which directly influenced British officials in such a way as to lead to action upon the subject came at a much later period and from a different source. The letters of Edward Randolph subsequent to 1691 contained accounts of timber lands which he had observed or surveyed in northern New England while he was there during the Andros régime. Now that he had become surveyor general of the customs, he asked for permission, as he travelled through the colonies, to mark trees that were fit for the navy.[1] His later letters referred to the resources of the colonies in general in pitch, tar, rosin and hemp, as well as in timber for ships. As soon as the first intercolonial war was well under way comparisons began to be sought by the treasury board and others between the probable cost of naval stores from the plantations and the supply which was obtained from the continent of Europe.[2] It was in this connection that references were made to the

[1] Cal. St. P. Col., 1689–1692, p. 553.
[2] See many entries in the indexes of Cal. St. P. Col., 1693–1696, and later volumes.

colonies in general, to the great resources of the Carolinas for pitch and tar and to the excellence of the timber in many of the colonies.

In 1690 or the following year Jahleel Brenton, of Rhode Island, was appointed surveyor of the woods in New England. His application for that office was apparently connected with the memorials of Randolph on the subject of naval stores and was favorably reported on by Blathwayt as auditor general.[1] According to a variety of statements made a few years later, Brenton was very negligent in the performance of the duties of this office and scarcely developed the possibilities of it at all.

Beginning about 1687, the growing interest in the subject was evidenced by the efforts of a number of merchants to secure charters of incorporation for the production of naval stores, and of individuals or associations of merchants who wished to undertake their importation into England under contract with the government. The first proposal of this kind came from Sir Matthew Dudley and about a hundred notable merchants and gentlemen of London, as his associates. Their first application was made just before the English Revolution and was for the exclusive right to work mines in New England.[2] Powers so extensive were desired, over land, servants and employees of the company, extending even to the exercise of judicial powers, as well might raise a strong prejudice against the plan in any colony where it might be established. The attorney general reported that they were too great except for an uninhabited country, and regarding New England in this light a patent was ordered to be drawn. But the Revolution put a stop to further proceedings.

As the demand for naval stores became strong in England with the outbreak of the colonial wars, an offer to procure these was added when Dudley after the Revolution applied for the grant of a charter. Mining soon dropped out of sight and the question became solely one of chartering a company to exploit the resources of New England in naval stores.[3] In 1691 favorable action was obtained from the privy council.

---

[1] Blathwayt's Journal (Ms).
[2] Lord 6, 15 *et seq.*
[3] Cal. St. P. Col., 1693–1696, references in the index under Dudley.

In September, 1693, the attorney general reported favorably on a petition from Dudley. But when the plan was submitted to the treasury it suggested that, before further action was taken, the plan be referred to the New England governments.

By this time a number of other parties had begun to petition for similar privileges, while one John Taylor was bringing in ship timber under a contract with the admiralty of three years' standing. Sir Stephen Evans, Samuel Allen and Sir Henry Ashurst now began to oppose Dudley's plan and undertook, though in an ineffective way, to import naval stores themselves. But their decisive work against Dudley was done by causing delays in the grant of his charter and by inducing the general court of Massachusetts to protest against it as a monopoly. This it did in June, 1694, and Ashurst was instructed to prevent the issue of the charter.[1]

The business was now delayed until the creation of the board of trade, in 1696. Both Randolph and Brenton then presented memorials to the board on the resources of the colonies in naval stores. A very suggestive paper was also submitted by Colonel Charles Lidget, a New England merchant, on the advantage of encouraging the export of naval stores from New England as a valuable staple product and means by which to improve the market for English manufactures. Lidget also drafted a charter for a company, an almost identical copy of which was sent by the board of trade to the privy council. This contained a provision against stock jobbing which was intended to remove one strong objection against companies of this kind. The petitioners protested, as was of course the case, that stock jobbing was not their intent but rather the production of naval stores, and that they were willing to submit to all reasonable restrictions. They even cited an instance of a monopolistic grant which Massachusetts had earlier made. But Ashurst, in his bustling and partisan fashion, kept up the fight through 1696, presenting to the board of trade no less than nine reasons against the grant. The result was that Dudley's project was shelved for the time and it was resolved to ascertain, if possible, what actually were the resources of the northern colonies in naval stores.

---

[1] Cal. St. P. Col., 1693–1696, p. 297; *ibid.*, 1696–1697, pp. 53, 59, 60. Lord, 19.

To this end a commission of four men was appointed, two selected by the navy board and two by the agents of Massachusetts. The two former were John Bridger and Benjamin Furzer, the other two being William Partridge and Robert Lamb. Bridger was an English shipbuilder. Partridge, the lieutenant governor of New Hampshire, was engaged in the lumber trade and, though possessed of local knowledge, was thought to have prejudices which would largely unfit him for usefulness as an administrator. Of the qualifications of the other men nothing is known, and it matters little for Furzer died on the way over and Lamb's place was taken by one Jackson before the commission left England. Owing to delays the two English appointees did not reach the scene of their labors until May, 1698.

Bridger and his associates were instructed to report as to both the quantity and quality of naval stores in New England, to learn the best methods of producing them, to teach these to the New Englanders and correct the faults in their methods, especially in the production of tar. They were to examine the woods reserved to the king and investigate facilities for water-carriage and shipping. Strict accounts and a journal were to be kept and specimens were to be shipped to England for examination.[1] The problem was a complex one, for the conditions affecting the production of hemp differed wholly from those which related to pitch and tar, while masts and ship timber lay within the realm of forestry and were subject to its conditions. Both the soil and climate of New England were unfitted for the production of hemp, while the colonists must be instructed in the methods of producing tar which were in vogue in Finland. The yield of ship timber was determined by the resources of the king's forests and these varied not only with their extent and excellence but according to the care with which they were being preserved. All the ungranted land in the colonies was royal domain, and, so far as pine trees were concerned, the Massachusetts charter of 1691 provided that all such trees which were twenty-four inches through at one foot from the ground should be reserved for the king's use. This charter was in force in Massachusetts and Maine, and by general custom was held to

[1] Lord, 10.

apply in New Hampshire also, but there was no law to that effect. New Hampshire, however, possessed much of the best ship timber in New England and its forests were conveniently accessible to the coast and to settled regions. But in those forests a vigorous lumbering industry had long been in existence which, among other things, was the basis of ship building in New England. Lumber was also being exported to the south of Europe, and this all was due in part to the stimulating effect of the navigation act on shipbuilding in the colonies. Saw mills were operating in considerable numbers, and the New England lumbermen would not be slow to meet a royal agent with rough usage who sought to enforce restrictions which interfered with the freest use of the forests. Other obstacles of great importance had their origin in the wars which were desolating that region and making all activities on the frontier at times very dangerous. Such was the problem, not easy of solution, which faced Bridger and his associates.

The commissioners, too, were not very well qualified for their task. Bridger, who remained in New England until 1702, does not appear to have cooperated much with the others. During the first summer he spent a considerable part of his time in southeastern New England, where he found no resources in naval stores which it was ever thought worth while to exploit. At the same time he asked the general assembly for assistance in viewing the woods of New Hampshire and was granted sixty men from its militia; but what use was made of so large a force as this, or whether it was ever called out, does not appear. The assembly was also induced to urge the inhabitants to sow hemp as a test of the capacity of their soil to yield that product, but no success attended the experiment.[1] The three commissioners inspected the woods to a certain extent and experimented in the Finnish method of making tar. Bridger was sanguine enough to assert that he could supply the demand of England for these commodities from that section, but Partridge called attention to the scarcity and high wages of labor as serious obstacles to the enterprise.[2] The inspection of the forests to the eastward

---

[1] N. H. Prov. Papers, III, 62, 63; Cal. St. P. Col., 1699, p. 9.
[2] Cal. St. P. Col., 1699, pp. 428, 449; ibid., 1700, p. 72.

as far as the French possessions, where much of the best timber was to be found, had to be postponed because no sloop was available for the use of the commissioners. The accounts of all agree that the lumbermen of New Hampshire were making great inroads upon the forests and that this evil should somehow be checked. But Partridge meanwhile was exporting lumber to Portugal and by his large profits was stimulating the people of the country to similar ventures.

As Lord Bellomont was then in office and the production of naval stores was one of the objects in which he became greatly interested, he watched the doings of the commissioners, especially during the year or more when he was resident in New England, and reported upon them in his letters home. His opinion of Partridge as a commissioner was expressed in these words: " He is a millwright by trade, which is a sort of carpenter, and to set a carpenter to preserve woods is like setting a wolf to keep sheep. I see plainly that he has so found the secret of building ships that he will not be broke of it. He is of the country and the interest of England is not in his head nor his heart, like the generality of people in these Plantations. . . ." [1] But Bellomont was unduly prejudiced against Partridge because of his exportation of lumber to Portugal, and in a long controversy tried to prove that the New Hampshire governor was violating the acts of trade. In doing so Bellomont was virtually trying by executive action to put lumber on the list of enumerated commodities. That had not yet been done and therefore the enterprise of Partridge was legal and Bellomont was not sustained by the home government.[2]

Bellomont also watched the proceedings of Bridger in sending specimens of naval stores to England for inspection, and insisted on seeing Bridger's accounts which would show the use he made of the money drawn from the English treasury for his expenditures. Bridger refused to submit the details, but Bellomont ascertained that nearly £2500 had been ex-

[1] Bellomont's uneasiness on this subject is further illustrated by the incident of his rebuking Sir Henry Ashurst for procuring the appointment of Partridge as governor and telling him he had a strange bias for carpenter governors, as it was he and Mather who had secured the appointment of William Phips. Cal. St. P. Col., 1700, p. 682.

[2] Cal. St. P. Col., 1700, pp. 177, 191, 197, 364, 557, 581, 681, 706.

pended,[1] which he considered a rather extravagant sum. When the specimens reached England and were inspected by the officials of the dockyards the plank they pronounced inferior, but of the tar they desired to make trial; in general the stores they thought inferior to those which had been in common use.[2] This was typical of the attitude which the navy office, and especially the officers of the dockyards, maintained toward colonial products. Their interest appeared to be to secure excellence of quality, but it was clearly the opinion of the board of trade and of Lord Bellomont that official routine and prejudice against products which came from a new source had much to do with it.[3] Their criticisms of the quality and crude methods of production of naval stores which came from the colonies continued to be severe and their attitude on the whole was unfavorable to the policy of encouraging their importation. On this occasion the advice of the navy board was that the commissioners should be recalled. After some discussion this course was followed and, because Bridger was unable to produce proper vouchers for many of his expenditures, two years passed before he received his salary of £250 a year for five years and three months of service.[4] This was granted on the recommendation of the board of trade.

Lord Bellomont had been dwelling in his letters on the resources of the colonies in general, in timber and other materials for naval stores.[5] He was more interested in their production than any other governor, with the possible exception of Spotswood of Virginia. He entered upon elaborate estimates of their cost and of the conditions under which they might be produced and transported to England. Throughout his correspondence he insisted specially upon the resources of New York, though the Mohawk valley, from which mast timber must be procured, if at all, was remote from the coast. Bellomont's zeal for the production of naval stores furnished an added reason for his aversion to the extravagant land grants of Fletcher and sharpened his re-

[1] Cal. St. P. Col., 1699, p. 496.    [3] Ibid., 566, 682.
[2] Cal. St. P. Col., 1700, p. 66.    [4] Lord, op, cit., 14.
[5] These letters are in Cal. St. P. Col., for 1698 to 1701, and in N. Y. Col. Docs. IV. See especially the last named volume, pp. 501, 587, 707, and context.

solve to vacate them. The largest of them comprised the very regions whence these products might be expected to come and if allowed to continue would defeat this valuable stroke of imperialist policy.

Bellomont was aware that, if possible, naval stores from the colonies must be delivered at the English market at cheaper rates than those for which they could be procured from northern Europe. The two great obstacles in the way of this were wages — at least 3s. per day — in the colonies, and the cost of land carriage and freight across the ocean. The question of wages, so far as New York was concerned, Bellomont proposed to solve by employing the soldiers of the independent companies, increased to one thousand men, in the work of producing naval stores in that province. Their regular pay was 8d. per day, to which he proposed to add 4d. to meet the additional wear and tear of clothing and their need of more food. He also proposed that, after seven years of this service, land be granted to the officers and soldiers in lots of forty acres, and meantime that money should be withheld from their pay to enable them to build houses and stock their farms. If the plan succeeded the soldiers would be provided for in their old age and as discharged veterans settled along the frontier would be added protection to the province.[1] Bellomont also thought that cost of transportation could be reduced by floating ship timber down the Mohawk and Hudson and, along with other stores, freighting vessels which brought cargoes to New York and, if it were not for this, would have to return almost empty. He states that he had known vessels to wait at New York five months for a return cargo and then go back half laden; they rarely waited less than three months. His plan, when it should be regularly working, would furnish them a staple, like tobacco, and masters had told him that they would carry naval stores under these conditions at much less than the regular rates.

The British state papers show that Bellomont's letters aroused among officials general interest in the subject of naval stores.[2] Between the offices there was more exchange

---

[1] The resemblance between this plan and that which gave rise to the Roman *coloni* is clear.

[2] See entries in the Journal of the Board of Trade and in the Calendars of Colonial Papers and of Treasury Papers for 1700 and two or three years thereafter.

of views on this subject during the few years which followed 1700 than at any other period, and it included many references to the letters of the New York governor. At that time other and very powerful forces were of course working in the same direction and Bellomont's efforts were one of the consequences of their activity. These were the prospects that war would soon reopen with France and her allies, and the adoption by Sweden of the extremely monopolistic policy regarding naval stores to which reference has already been made. These forced English administrators at least to consider what relief might be afforded by the colonies, and Bellomont's letters contained the largest and best digested body of information which was then available on that subject. So far as extant records go, it far surpassed the information which was derived from the commissioners. It is true that they sent over samples and that Bridger afterwards offered to contract with the government for supplying naval stores. But Bellomont sent over one cargo of masts and at his death left others ready to be brought down the Hudson preparatory for shipment to England. Moreover, in October, 1700, the board of trade sent to the lords justices one of its ablest and most comprehensive reports on the subject of naval stores in the plantations and the material for it may have been drawn almost wholly from Bellomont's letters.[1] In this they dwelt not only upon conditions in New York, but upon the vast resources of northern New England, extending as far east as the St. Croix river, and the waste of the woods in New Hampshire. In their letters to Bellomont the board had shown themselves decidedly hospitable to his ideas, though in their report no reference was made to his plan for the employment of the regular troops as laborers in the forests.

After Bellomont's premature death, which roughly coincided with the recall of Bridger to England and the outbreak of the second war, Dudley and a part of his former associates renewed their efforts to secure a charter and, being again opposed by Ashurst and the Massachusetts interest, the controversy was continued for some time.[2] The draft of a charter was submitted to the board of trade and

[1] Cal. St. P. Col., 1700, p. 563 et seq.

[2] Lord, 24 et seq.

after it had been amended so as to limit the amount of capital to be invested and land to be held, and the power to transfer stock, it was laid before the queen. By an order in council it was then referred to the attorney general and lord high admiral for their criticism. The latter insisted that the petitioners must furnish masts of the largest size and also certain quantities of pitch and tar, all at current prices. Upon the clause about stock jobbing the petitioners and the government failed to reach an agreement, and with 1704 the project was abandoned.

In 1700 one Richard Haynes, with whom Thomas Byfield and others were associated, had been negotiating with the English government in reference to the importation of naval stores.[1]  In 1703 Byfield and associates, who for some time had been engaged as a joint stock company in general trade with Pennsylvania, petitioned for a charter to enable them to import naval stores from the Carolinas. It was already known that large quantities of pitch and tar were procurable from that region. They offered to deliver in one year to the agents of the queen in Carolina two hundred barrels of pitch and four hundred barrels of tar at specified prices, or at those prices plus the freight if the government preferred delivery in England. They would double the quantity the second year and increase from year to year. If reports proved true that Carolina could furnish better masts than England, they would undertake to procure them at reasonable rates. But the risks of the business were so great that they felt that they could not proceed without a charter. When this proposal came before the law officers and the customs board, they suggested restrictions which placed the petitioners unduly at the mercy of the government. Among other conditions was one, that they should submit to dissolution by the government at any time when it should decide that they were not useful for the purpose intended. But on the other hand, as other parties were offering more favorable terms to the government and that without charters, the way was open for what was certainly a superior line of action. At the close of 1704 the privy council decided that the charter desired by Byfield was a matter for parliament to consider. This sealed the fate

---

[1] B. T. Plants. Gen., E. B. 35; O. P. 5; Lord, *op. cit.* 30.

of all such proposals as those of Dudley and Byfield and opened the way for a comprehensive treatment of the question of naval stores and one which was in harmony with the principles of mercantilism.

During the later months of 1703, under orders from Hedges, the secretary of state, the board of trade was much occupied with the consideration of the prices at which naval stores could be imported from America and the amount which could be procured.[1] They secured terms from Bridger and Haynes and a general discussion from other merchants of the dangers involved in all such contracts. The board reached the conclusion, and so stated in reports to the privy council, that the plantations could not furnish all that was needed and therefore that the government should in part offset the high freights by offering a bounty. This course of action was adopted, the Commons giving permission for the introduction of a bill, which was drafted by the board under orders from Secretary Hedges. The bill was passed with slight change and put into force in 1705 (3 and 4 Anne, c. 10). It provided for bounties on the importation of naval stores into England at the following rates: £4 per ton of tar and pitch, £3 per ton of rosin and turpentine, £6 per ton of hemp and £1 per ton of masts, yards and bowsprits. Eight barrels of tar were to constitute the ton, and the ton of ship timber was to be estimated by allowing forty feet girth measure according to the customary way of measuring round bodies. Importers were required to bring sworn statements under the hands of the governor, collector or naval officer of the colony whence the naval stores came that they were the product of that plantation, and then the premium would be paid by the commissioners of the navy. The destruction of small pine trees which were fit for the production of pitch and tar, in the New England colonies, New York and New Jersey, was forbidden. In the preamble of the act the reasons for its passage were given and its connection with the British commercial system in general was indicated by the statement, that the vast supplies of naval stores which existed in the colonies should properly be imported in exchange for the woolen and other manufactures of the mother country. It was by this act also

---

[1] Plants. Gen., E. B. 37. Lord, 60 *et seq.*

that naval stores were enumerated, for it was a necessary consequence of the policy now adopted that none of the commodities which it affected should be allowed to go to foreign countries. The act was to continue in force for nine years. By the statute 12 Anne, c. 9 (1713) it was continued for eleven years longer, that is until 1725, the rates of bounty being kept the same but provision being made for bringing naval stores from Scotland. The legislation was modified somewhat in 1722 (8 Geo. I, c. 12), while by act of 1719 (5 Geo. I, c. 11) it was provided that, before the premiums were paid, the customs officers should open enough barrels of pitch and tar in any cargo to make a test which should prove that it was free from dirt, dross and water.

Reports from New England continued to agree upon the fact that Brenton was almost totally neglectful of the duties of his office as surveyor general of the woods. Bridger testified to that effect. So did contractors who were getting out ship timber for the navy. The accounts given by Bellomont were to the same effect. There was no doubt that many saw mills, with gang saws were operating in the woods of New Hampshire, but the government both of that province and of Massachusetts asserted in excuse of their neglect to check the waste that they had received no complaints of the evil. Plaisted, one of Brenton's deputies, was an owner of saw mills and therefore was of no use as an official.[1] Of Brenton's activity as collector of the customs we hear much, but nothing of his work as surveyor general of the woods. For this reason, when at the close of 1705 Bridger applied for the office, he was appointed, with the special duty of enforcing the new act of parliament. He was instructed, with the aid of the local governments, to prevent waste in the woods and to instruct the inhabitants in the best methods of producing pitch, tar and hemp.[2] His yearly salary, as before, was to be £200 sterling and no provision was made for his travelling expenses and such assistance as he would need. When Bridger had fulfilled his mission in New England he was to pursue the same policy in other colonies; but his duties in

[1] Lord, 87.
[2] B. T. New England, 41, Dec., 1705. The commission was issued in Feb., 1705/6.

the first named section proved more than enough to tax his resources.

As was usual, the crown, and especially the treasury and admiralty, failed to understand the difficulties against which Bridger would have to contend and gave him neither the means nor later the support which were necessary to carry him through to success.  He remained in New England for nearly ten years — until 1715 — almost continuously engaged in a series of bitter conflicts[1] with lumbermen, contractors for the royal navy, and the people and legislatures of both New Hampshire and Massachusetts.  Joseph Dudley supported him throughout, furnishing him guards against the enemy and writing frequently home in his defence.[2]  Bridger seems to have been on the whole a good official, but one who, like so many others, was forced to contend against overwhelming odds.  At one time he suggested that, if he could be made lieutenant governor of New Hampshire and have sixty soldiers under him as captain of the fort, he would set two-thirds of them at work a part of the time in the woods and in that way produce a good quantity of tar.  In this one may see a hint of Bellomont's plan, though, unlike Bellomont, Bridger considered himself in need of a body guard to protect him against possible death at the hands of the lumbermen.

So far as the production of naval stores was concerned, Bridger was fairly successful.  During the first year under the new act there were imported from New England 6194 barrels of tar, 647 of pitch, 1145 of turpentine and 90 of rosin.[3]  At the beginning of 1707 Governor Dudley expressed his great interest in the results of the act and said that more tar and turpentine had been sent on the last fleet than for some years.  Though the quality of the product was not equal to that which came from northern Europe, the result was encouraging, especially since it was attained in time of war. The board of trade was naturally anxious for statistics, both of imports and of sums paid out in premiums.  Reports were accordingly made and, as we have seen, they were sufficiently encouraging to cause the renewal of the act in 1714.  From

[1] These are admirably outlined by Miss Lord, *op. cit.*, 91, 109.
[2] See Col. of Treasury Papers.
[3] Bridger to B. T., Oct. 24, 1706; Lord, 66 *et seq.*

statistics collated for the years up to 1718 it appears that, so far as tar and pitch were concerned, production from the colonies as compared with importation from Europe quite considerably increased, though the amount which came from America did not exceed 9358 barrels annually until after the close of the second colonial war. Then it leaped upward to 82,000 barrels in 1718, while importation from Sweden and the rest of Europe correspondingly declined. Wars between the northern crowns and between Sweden and Great Britain in 1718 account in part for this result. Toward the close of the period production from the southern colonies affected the result. But on the whole this result was considered to have justified the policy and the considerable expenditure which it entailed.[1] The largest importation of masts in any year between 1705 and 1715 was 261, while nearly 2000 were brought from Sweden and the rest of Europe. The efforts to encourage the production of hemp were a failure, notwithstanding the high premiums which were offered for it and the cooperation of many of the colonies by offering bounties on its production and passing laws for the promotion of its culture. The reason for this was that the difficulties of the hemp culture were too great for the colonists at that time to overcome. A rich soil and moderate climate were required, and both of these were lacking in New England. The seed which was sent from Europe often arrived in condition unfit for use. The care which was necessary for successfully raising and curing the crop it was usually beyond the ability of the colonist to give. Hence it was that, though the climate and soil of Virginia were suitable, and much encouragement in the form of legislation was given by that colony, no evidence appears of a favorable result.

But when one has described the economic results of the policy of which Bridger was the exponent in New England, one has far from exhausted the history of the surveyor general's career in that section. His experiences there as a royal official were to a certain extent a repetition of those of Randolph, though personally Bridger was less offensive to the colonists and at the same time less dangerous. But the spirit of the

[1] By 1717 about £90,000 had been paid by the British government in premiums on pitch and tar.

New Englanders had not changed and they were still able by methods to which they were well accustomed to hamper or thwart any royal commissioner. The township system presented one of the most perplexing obstacles in Bridger's path. In any New England colony towns could be created by acts of the legislature in any number and with any extent in square miles, and when they were created the claim might be made and perhaps sustained that the land comprised within their borders had been taken from the king's domain and placed in private hands, that is in those of the corporation which constituted the town. It was for the interest of all who were in the lumber business and their sympathizers to reduce the extent of the king's woods and to bring them as rapidly as possible under private control, the control either of individuals or of townships. In the forests boundaries at best were uncertain and they might be almost indefinitely extended. In carrying out this policy use was made of the clause in the Massachusetts charter which limited the restriction on trees which might be cut for use as masts in the royal navy to lands " not heretofore granted to any private persons." The word " heretofore " was ignored and the phrase " private persons " was so interpreted as to include townships as well as individuals. Both Governor Dudley and the board of trade supported Bridger in the contention that the charter should protect trees of proper size which did not stand on the land of private individuals.

In his efforts to maintain the king's rights Bridger became involved in specially bitter controversies with agents of Taylor and Collins, both of whom were getting out masts under contracts with the crown. He accused them of cutting many more trees than were called for in their contract, and of being engaged in the illegal export of these and other timber. They tried to bribe him and then sought to procure his recall. Like Randolph, Bridger found it impossible to secure convictions of offenders against whom he brought suits before New Hampshire courts. The legal question at issue was referred to the attorney general in England, and his opinion was to the effect that trees of the size mentioned in the charter would be protected against the king by town grants issued prior to 1691, but not by those subsequent to that date.

In 1708 New Hampshire passed an act for the better preservation of mast trees, but it seems to have been of little avail,
while it was found impossible to secure the passage even
of such a law in Massachusetts.[1]  And so the quarrel went
merrily on, with occasional seizures or destruction of timber
on both sides.  George Vaughan, who had succeeded Partridge as governor, was also interested in the lumber business,
and practically the entire population, from the governor
down, was opposed to Bridger.  In 1711 an act was passed
by parliament (9 Anne, c. 17), which extended to the colonies
north of the Delaware river, and fixed a penalty of £100 for
the destruction of white pine trees of the dimensions stated
in the Massachusetts charter, provided these did not stand on
the property of a private individual.  The object of this act
was to prevent the cutting of masts on the ungranted lands
of towns as well as outside.  But under a law of this character it was impossible to protect the woods, as it had been
under the Massachusetts charter, for the lumbermen continued freely to cut trees which were smaller than the prescribed dimension and which in a few years would become the
trees which the statute was intended to preserve.  The
extremists also claimed that the king had no right to woods
in New England and they would cut where and what they
pleased.  Against such even the king's arrow was no protection.  The large and growing trade in lumber with the
West Indies, added to that with southern Europe and to the
consumption in the colonies themselves, kept stimulating the
waste of New England forests beyond the power of any royal
official to control.

While the surveyor general of the woods was occupied with
his task in New England in the manner which has just been
described, another notable effort to produce naval stores on
a large scale was made in New York.  The production of
mast timber was not its object, but of tar and its kindred
products, while the plan of Bellomont was not followed.  Instead, this experiment connects itself with immigration into
the colonies, one of the great movements which did much to
change the face of American history toward the middle of
the eighteenth century.  This is not the place in which to

[1] N. H. Prov. Papers, III, 366, 577.

discuss the advent of the Palatines in New York as it stands related to immigration, but solely in its connection with efforts to add naval stores to the staples which England desired to procure from the colonies.  It was resolved that a part of the throng of Palatines who flocked to England in 1709 should be sent to New York, there to be utilized for frontier defence and the production of naval stores.[1]  The cost of their passage — about £4 per head — and of subsistence in New York for a year until they could support themselves — estimated at £5 per capita — should be advanced by the government and they, as indentured servants, should repay these amounts by labor and in some place suitable for the purpose indicated.

It was recommended that they be settled on one or more tracts of land, where they should clear the ground, build huts and there devote themselves to the production of tar, pitch, turpentine and rosin.  As events proved, such an experiment as this should have been made in North Carolina, to which De Graffenried's body of Palatines were removing at this very time.  But New York was a royal province, to which Bellomont's letters had directed attention, and it lay in the north where the production of useful staples was specially desired.  It was believed that, if there were six hundred men among them, they could produce seven thousand tons a year, and that possibly would more than supply the English demand and lead to an export trade.  The board of trade also recommended the appointment of officials to manage the enterprise — supervisors to live among the Palatines and have the oversight of their work, a storekeeper or commissary — to take charge of their products in New York City, keep accounts and attend to their shipment, an agent or factor to receive them in England and remit them funds necessary for the support of the Palatines.  The assistance of Bridger would also be required to instruct them in the art of producing tar and the other commodities.  Such of the stores as were found to be fit for its use should be delivered to the navy board and the rest sold to merchants and the money used for the repayment of the sums expended on the Palatines.  After each immigrant had paid in labor the cost of his transport and

[1] N. Y. Col. Docs., V, 44, 87, 112, 117 et seq.; Kapp, Die Deutschen im Staate New York; Cobb, Story of the Palatines.

supplies, he should receive a grant of forty acres of land. Governor Hunter, who just then was receiving his appointment, was especially instructed to execute this plan. It was a government enterprise, furnishing an example of state-aided and -controlled emigration in the eighteenth century.

About three thousand Palatines, according to the methods of the time, were packed into ten ships and, in January, 1709/10, started on their voyage across the Atlantic. The voyage was unusually stormy and prolonged and the summer was already well advanced before they reached New York. Nearly one fourth of the passengers had died on the way. Weary and sorrowful, the survivors were landed on Nutten (now Governor's) Island to recover and await the time when a place should be chosen for their settlement and they be removed thither. Five months passed before these questions were decided and a removal up the river became possible. As the act for vacating Fletcher's extravagant grants of land had recently been confirmed in England, some location near the Mohawk river, perhaps in the Schoharie region which had been the site of Bayard's grant, had been suggested by the board of trade as a possible place for the settlement. But upon inquiry it was decided that this region was too remote and — probably after the exercise of personal influence by the owner — it was decided to purchase from Robert Livingston six thousand acres on the east side of the Hudson, just north of Roeloff Jansen's Kill, and also to make use for the purpose of a tract of the queen's land on the opposite side of the river near Sawyer's Creek, and the modern town of Saugerties. These tracts were in or adjacent to the Livingston Manor, which was then in process of formation, and they were believed to contain an ample supply of pine trees of the quality which was needed for the object in view.

Late in the fall of 1710 the Palatines were removed thither. As two years must pass after the trees were first barked before they were ready for the kiln, that period of time must elapse before the yield of tar would actually begin. Bridger came at first, but considered his salary insufficient to meet travelling expenses. When, after a return to Boston, Hunter requested him to pay another visit to New York, he replied that he would come if his expenses were paid. This led to a breach

between him and the governor, and one Sackett was procured
in Bridger's place, and his services proved satisfactory.[1] But
though in their contract the Palatines had agreed to settle
in the place selected for them, they soon became discontented
where they were.[2] As they had for the most part been husbandmen and vine dressers, the work to which they were set
was new and probably distasteful. They were worked in
gangs under rigid supervision. Many of the children, especially of those who had died on the outward voyage, were
separated from their remaining relatives and apprenticed in
remote parts of New York or in other colonies. The food
supplies, which were furnished by Livingston, were to an
extent of inferior amount and quality. In those days this
was almost sure to be the case with provision contracts. The
winters were long and cold and the time when satisfactory
returns for their labor would be possible seemed remote. The
Palatines, and especially certain ambitious leaders among
them, were not minded to spend their lives or a large part of
them, as indented servants. Moreover, the locality in which
they were placed was not favorable for the production of naval
stores. Finally, though the British government at the outset
had appropriated £15,000 toward the expense of the under-
taking, it had not continued its support. Hunter soon paid out
the sum he brought with him, drew bills on the treasury for
more and then began to draw on his own credit.[3] Livingston,
of course, was demanding payment for the subsistence he
furnished, in order that he might repay the farmers of the
neighborhood for the supplies they had sold him. As months
passed, this kept pinching the supplies of food and clothing
which were doled out to the Palatines. To crown the whole,
the Schoharie region became known to them, originally from
Indians and later from whites, as a more desirable country,
and they began to long for removal thither.

At the close of the first winter discontent began to show
itself, with threats of removal. John Conrad Weiser, the
father of the man who afterwards became Pennsylvania's

[1] N. Y. Col. Docs. V, 211, 263, 264.

[2] Special light is thrown on the motives and conduct of the Palatines by
the material in the Doc. Hist. of N. Y, quarto ed., III, 658–660, 669–714.

[3] N. Y. Col. Docs. V, 189.

famous Indian interpreter and negotiator, was one of the spokesmen of this discontent and a leader in the further migration which was to follow. As the Palatines were armed, revolt soon became imminent. The governor summoned a detachment of sixty men from Albany and boldly facing the discontented prevented open resistance. All were disarmed. In the autumn, however, three hundred of the men were sent on Nicholson's expedition toward Canada, but on their return their arms were again taken away. During the succeeding winter and summer quiet was maintained and the work of preparing trees went steadily on. According to a report later made by the board of trade, by the fall of 1713 more than 100,000 trees, capable of producing 30,000 barrels of tar, had been prepared by the Palatines for the last stages in the process of production.[1] But meantime Hunter had received no statement that the bills he had drawn for the subsistence of the Palatines had been paid. Repeatedly he wrote about this, but no reply came. The Tory reaction in England probably furnishes the explanation. Finally, in October, 1712, Hunter was forced to tell the Palatines that his means were exhausted and that they must provide for themselves during the coming winter, but must return to work in the spring.[2] " The trees," wrote Hunter, " have received their last preparation, the staves prepared for the barrells, the magazine almost finished, and the road between it and the pine woods almost completed." But at this point the enterprise stopped and ended in failure. The Palatines were filled with consternation at the prospect opened by Hunter's announcement, and early in the winter a part of them started, through the snow along a path of their own making, for Schoharie. There, amid the greatest obstacles, they effected a settlement and were joined by others, so that in 1718, 680 were reported to be living there. Though the majority remained on the Hudson, by 1714, because Hunter had been informed that none of his bills would be paid, all thought of continuing the production of naval stores was abandoned. The Palatines became permanent inhabitants of the region, but as farmers or in other

---

[1] See the report of the board in 1721. N. Y. Col. Docs. V, 601. This tar would have sold in New York at 8s. per barrel, bringing a sum of £12,000.

[2] N. Y. Col. Docs. V, 342, 347, 364, 452, 515; Doc. Hist. of N. Y. III, 711.

callings, and not in that for which they had been brought into the country. With this experiment all efforts on any scale to produce naval stores in New York ceased.

In 1715 Bridger was recalled to England to answer charges.[1] Among them was one to the effect that he had refused to aid Hunter in the affair of the Palatines. But those which were really significant had their origin in New England and were to the general effect that he had not been diligent in his office, but particularly in the matter of granting licenses and taking fees he had been unfair and dishonest. It was even said that he had contributed to the waste by selling to favorites permits to cut trees. But Dudley supported him and a number of merchants testified in his favor. Bridger, in short, was able to show to the satisfaction of the board of trade that the charges against him, especially those of corruption, were false. An effort, however, was made to discontinue his office, or at least to cut off its salary. The admiralty board even joined in the opposition. In 1716 the commissioners of the navy denounced the policy of giving bounties on naval stores from the plantations, as no benefit but rather a hindrance. But this view did not prevail. Bridger was sent back to New England and the policy which had been entered upon in 1705 was continued.

The opposition in New England of course did not abate. The waste of the woods continued as great as ever and all the efforts which Bridger could make did not avail to check it. He no longer had the able support of Dudley, and though Shute, the governor of Massachusetts, and Wentworth, the governor of New Hampshire, upheld him, it was of little avail. Jeremiah Dummer was now agent of Massachusetts in England and through him the concentrated opposition to Bridger in New England was brought to bear. Hunter had made representations against him, and on general grounds the admiralty favored the abolition of his office. The board of trade, however, defended the policy which had been inaugurated and succeeded in continuing the office.[2] But, in 1718, one Charles Burmiston was appointed as Bridger's successor. The new appointee did not visit New England and Robert

[1] B. T. N. Eng., vols. 43 and 44.
[2] Col. of Treas. Papers, Jan. and Feb., 1716.

Armstrong, his deputy, also long delayed his appearance. Therefore Bridger continued to perform the duties of the office until late in 1720, when he finally returned to England carrying with him important testimonials of approval.[1]

According to all accounts Armstrong, who was also collector of customs at Portsmouth, was less attentive to his duties in the woods than Bridger had been.[2] His letters show that he met with quite as much opposition as did Bridger and accomplished little against it. His appointment at the outset was regarded as a poor one, in part because the duties of the two offices which he held were too many and difficult for one man to perform. In or about 1724 Armstrong returned to England under charges, to which he made a fairly satisfactory reply. He was allowed to return to New England, where he continued in the discharge of his duties until 1728.

During the years immediately before and after 1720 the production of naval stores was unusually prominent as a subject of discussion before the board of trade.[3] By that date we know that large quantities, especially of tar and pitch, were being produced in the Carolinas and imported from those colonies into Great Britain. Spotswood was also preparing for their production, as well as that of iron, on the large estates he was securing in Virginia. The forests of the Carolinas, however, without any of the supervision which attracted so much attention in New England, were yielding enough tar, it was said, in 1718, to supply the demand of England. A considerable fleet of vessels was kept employed in transporting naval stores from those colonies, and the production there continued steadily to increase until the close of the colonial period. So large had the yield from the plantations now become that the payment of premiums was a perceptible drain upon the British exchequer. In 1718 as much as £50,000 was paid out in this form. The treasury and admiralty were sceptical or decidedly opposed to the expenditure, and sympathized with the Eastland merchants in their preference for the products of northern Europe. The board of trade

[1] Lord, *op. cit.* 97.
[2] See letters of Armstrong, especially in Cal. of Treas. Papers, beginning about 1720.
[3] B. T. Plants., Gen. Entry Bk. and Original Papers.

on the other hand, though somewhat staggered by the expenditure, was not ready to abandon the policy it had originally supported without a thorough inquiry.[1] The board devoted many sessions to the subject of naval stores and prepared a number of representations, culminating in its summary of the results thus far, which was incorporated in the general report of 1721 on the state of the colonies.

The hearings were largely attended by British merchants and manufacturers — those who were interested in the Eastland trade as well as that of the plantations — who were called to give evidence and their opinions on results and the policy which should be pursued in the future. Joshua Gee and Micajah Perry appeared, the former presenting two important memorials in which he claimed that the naval stores produced in the colonies were of good quality and that their competition had lowered prices. He desired that bounties equal to the duty on naval stores might be continued for a generation longer and then he thought that they both might be dropped.

Ropemakers and shipbuilders were examined as to the comparative qualities of plantation and Eastland products. Among the colonial agents Dummer was especially prominent in his advocacy of New England products, and was supported by Thomas Coram, who had built a ship there and testified in particular about the excellence of New England iron. Bridger also testified, for the hearings began before he returned for his last sojourn in America. Boone and Beresford, who were in England to advocate specially the cause of the people of South Carolina against the proprietors, also spoke at length about the great resources of the Carolinas in naval stores. William Byrd delivered a memorial in praise of the fitness of Virginia for hemp and other naval stores. The plantation merchants insisted that the quality of their tar was as good as that from the north of Europe. But this was denied by the Eastland merchants, they claiming that it had a burning quality which was destructive to cordage. Some of the later hearings were attended by members of the customs board, the secretary of the treasury and the surveyor of the

[1] See Journal of B. T. and B. T. Plants., Gen. Entry Book and Original Papers; N. Y. Col. Docs. V, 591 *et seq.*

navy. So high did feeling run that one of the merchants who opposed the colonies complained of having been insulted by Dummer at the Royal Exchange. The subject was at the same time coming to be considered in parliament. The board of trade finally resolved not to recommend any change in the rates of bounty, but stricter inspection. A clause providing for this was incorporated in a bill against frauds in the customs which was then pending in parliament and became law in 1719 (5 Geo. I, c. 11). This, as has been stated, required the customs officers to ascertain the quality of tar and other products before paying the bounty.

The optimistic view of the situation was set forth by the board of trade in its report of 1721. " We have already had a very successful proof," it said, " of what due encouragements produce in the particulars of pitch and tar, which at present are made in as great perfection in your Majesty's plantations as in any other part of the world, and in such plenty as will enable us to supply foreign parts, since it both reduced the common price of those commodities one-third of their former cost within the space of a very few years, whereby the importation of pitch and tar from the Baltic is greatly decreased and much money saved in the balance of our trade." The statement concerning quality at last seems to have been exaggerated, for two years later the navy board stated that tar imported from the plantations, even under the act of 5 Geo. I, was inferior to that which came from the continent.

After more long hearings on the whole subject of foreign and plantation trade and manufactures, in 1722 the act 8 Geo. I, c. 12, continuing encouragement for the importation of naval stores was passed. The bounty on water-rotted hemp, provided for by the act of 1705, was continued for sixteen years and the duty on its importation into Great Britain was removed. The right of preemption was granted to the navy board for twenty days after landing. A duty on lumber from America was also taken off, a measure which greatly promoted the export of timber from the colonies. In order further to guarantee the quality of tar, a provision was introduced that none should be made except from trees prepared by removing the bark a year beforehand, thereby making it possible to decide whether or not the tree was fit for use. As to white pine trees in the colonies north of the Delaware river, the felling of those which stood outside of townships was prohibited, and provision was made that the penalties for the violation of this clause should be recovered in the admiralty court of the colony where the offence was committed. The arguments in support of this measure were very largely furnished by Joshua Gee.

The clause of the statute which related to the cutting of trees was at once nullified by the New Englanders, who interpreted it as permitting them to cut any trees which grew within townships. The issue of township grants, especially in New Hampshire, was therefore stimulated, in order that as much territory as possible might be under what they regarded as the permissive clause.[1] This necessitated in 1729 another step in the process of legislation, in the form of the act 2 Geo. II, c. 35. This prohibited the cutting of white pine trees on any land except that which belonged to private individuals, even though the land in question was located in townships. This, of course, did not obviate the quibble of earlier years, that all land in towns was private property and an opinion from the attorney general in England did not change the attitude of the colonists.

But the more important considerations which led to this statute were those affecting the amounts of the bounties that were given or whether the policy of bestowing them at all should be continued. The improved method of producing tar, for which provision had been made in the law of 1722, had not been enforced in the colonies. It was said by many that its enforcement was impossible and that the considerable production under the old rules proved their superiority for the colonies. The growth of shipbuilding, the carrying trade and woolen manufactures were making New Englanders independent of the production of all naval stores except masts and ship timber. Importations, however, had become so large that bounty money, amounting to some £50,000 a year, was an

---

[1] In 1726 Fane, the counsel of the board of trade, declared that the New Englanders were attempting to pervert the meaning of the act, so as to make it serve a purpose which was not at all intended. The prohibition of cutting trees outside townships did not imply that they might be freely cut within townships. Chalmers, Opinions.

appreciable burden on the treasury. The debt arising from the navy was large and the navy board was opposed at least to such high bounties. But on the other hand, Sweden had secured Finland and was evidently preparing to recover the trade in naval stores which she had lost. As the provision for bounties on plantation products expired in 1725, the navy board proposed reducing their rate, though not their complete abandonment. It was on this principle that the provision of the law of 1729 affecting bounties was formulated.[1]

The struggle over the preservation of the woods continued during the administration of David Dunbar, who was appointed surveyor general in 1728 and continued to hold that office for twenty years. By the time Dunbar took office contractors and others had begun to exploit the forests of Maine, where the supplies of naval stores far exceeded those of New Hampshire. The English were now reaching forward into the entire territory west of the St. Croix river. The time even was approaching when Nova Scotia itself was really to be brought under English control and to take her place among the British provinces. Her resources in naval stores were similar to those of Maine, and Dunbar long cherished a plan for reserving large tracts in each of those provinces for the exclusive supply of the royal navy. This in fact was suggested in his instructions and was repeatedly referred to in his later correspondence, though never carried into effect.

For a decade and more Dunbar fought vigorously for the preservation of the king's woods in northern New England. He tried to enforce the acts of parliament which referred to that problem, to secure the aid of local authorities and to fulfill the requirements of his instructions in general. At the beginning he had the assistance of salaried deputies, but here again the means furnished were inadequate, for Dunbar had to traverse much longer distances and guard the king's interests over a region far larger than any which his predecessors had visited. One of the deputies proved untrustworthy and had to be discharged. He was brought into direct relations — and they were decidedly hostile — with the government of Massachusetts, with consequences which royal officials usually suffered from such encounters. It is true

[1] Lord, 82.

that he could now claim the support of the admiralty court in many of the suits which he brought, but this was rendered ineffective by the rules of evidence which were enforced by Nathaniel Byfield, the aged New England official who was its judge. Dunbar was a man of greater assertiveness than Bridger, but he was even less successful in his efforts to solve the task before him, because he was totally lacking in tact. His protestations and complaints were continued for many years and fill hundreds of pages in the records of the time; but they were unavailing. The exploitation of the forests, by contractors, and by the inhabitants in general went on unabated. Dunbar and his men were insulted and defied by the loggers. On one occasion a riot occurred at Exeter, New Hampshire,[1] in which his men were severely handled, but so strong was the sympathy with the rioters that none was punished. The assignees of the parties who, early in the seventeenth century, had received large grants of land about the mouth of the Kennebec river and to the eastward of it claimed that those were all private property and therefore the king's surveyors had no right there. Some — perhaps many — even went so far as to assert that all of Maine, inasmuch as it was originally granted to Sir Ferdinando Gorges, and his rights had later been bought by Massachusetts, was a private estate and that the king had no territorial rights within its boundaries. There indeed was no limit to which logic might not carry wits which had been sharpened by generations of theological and political controversy, when their self-interest was thoroughly enlisted. Against such combatants Dunbar launched his invectives in vain.

In 1731, on the death of John Wentworth, Dunbar was made lieutenant governor of New Hampshire.[2] This, under some conditions, might have strengthened his position as surveyor general. But it rather had the opposite effect. For there were many political elements involved in his New England career and these had much to do with determining his fate. He was concerned in an effort to found a new province between the Kennebec river and Nova Scotia, and this helped to bring down upon him the intense hostility of Jonathan Belcher,

---

[1] N. H. Prov. Papers, IV, 678, 841–845.
[2] *Ibid.*, 600.

who was then governor of Massachusetts. This hostility followed Dunbar throughout his term as lieutenant governor of New Hampshire and helped greatly to defeat all his efforts both as governor and as surveyor general. In the midst of this characteristic New England feud the final effort to regulate the production of naval stores in that section and in accordance with the policy which had been inaugurated by the board of trade came to an end.

Meantime the production, especially of pitch and tar, in the Carolinas continued large. The reports which appear in the original papers of South Carolina show annual exportations, after about 1720, of many thousand barrels. For example, between the close of May and the end of September, 1721, 2690 barrels of pitch and 777 barrels of tar were sent to Great Britain and 677 and 332 of each product respectively to the other plantations. During the three years from May, 1721, to May, 1724, 40,830 barrels of pitch and 37,914 barrels of tar were exported from South Carolina. The production of these commodities was also going on at a rapid rate in North Carolina. The resources of both these colonies in ship timber were also large, though they were not utilized to any great extent during the colonial period. In November, 1734, Governor Robert Johnson wrote at length about the capabilities of South Carolina in all these respects.[1] Tar and pitch, he wrote, had hitherto been the staple products of this colony, by which many families had been supported. The large premiums at first offered had proved decidedly helpful, so that the soft pine near the rivers had now been exhausted and the cost of production was therefore higher. Of turpentine and rosin, though not much was produced at present, probably South Carolina could yield enough entirely to supply the British market.

Many statements prove that the production of pitch and tar in North Carolina throughout the period was large. In November, 1720, Boone and Barnwell wrote that of late, in

---

[1] B. T., S. C., O. P. An idea of the exports from South Carolina may be gathered from a description written by Purry, the Swiss, in 1731. He states that, between March, 1730, and March, 1731, 207 ships sailed, mostly for England, which carried, among other goods, 41,957 barrels of rice, 10,754 barrels of pitch, 2,063 of tar, 1,159 of turpentine, and 300 casks of deer skins. Carroll, Hist. Colls., II, 121; McCrady, 125.

North Carolina, they had made about 6000 barrels of pitch and tar, which sloops from New England had carried thither and thence to Great Britain.[1]  The export trade in these commodities from the Carolinas to New England was continuous. Thomas Lowndes wrote, in 1729, that New England got a large quantity of the best pitch and tar from North Carolina in barter for rum, molasses and other goods.[2]  The board of trade expressed itself to the same effect.  In 1734 Gabriel Johnston wrote to the board of trade that there was more pitch and tar made in the two Carolinas than in all the other provinces on the continent, and rather more in North than in South Carolina.[3]  The extent of their production in North Carolina is also proven by the fact that, like tobacco in Virginia, they were used as a common medium of exchange. So rapid was the destruction of pines by boxing them for turpentine and burning the light wood for pitch and tar, and so freely did the settlers make use of ungranted land for these purposes without the formality of patents or the paying of rents, that in 1735 Johnston issued a proclamation against it.[4]  In both the Carolinas the soil was favorable for the raising of hemp.  Various measures were taken to encourage this industry, and before the close of the colonial period rather important results in the production of this commodity were attained in both the Carolinas.

The ease with which the large production, especially of tar and pitch, was attained in the Carolinas proves that the British erred in judgment in bestowing so much attention upon efforts to stimulate this industry in New England. The only natural superiority of that section lay in its supplies of mast trees and ship timber.  But the political motive undoubtedly had much to do with the experiment in New England, because naval stores were the only staple which in that region could be set up to counterbalance the many natural tendencies toward manufacturing and therefore toward independence.

[1] N. C. Recs., II, 396.
[2] O. P., S. C.; N. C. Recs., III, 50.
[3] *Ibid.*, IV, 5.
[4] *Ibid.*, 41–42.

# CHAPTER XVI

### PIRACY DURING THE EARLY COLONIAL WARS

It is impossible thoroughly to treat the subject either of trade or defence along the American coast during the period we are now considering without some reference to piracy. The phenomenon itself is as old as history and still continues in some of the seas of the orient. During the early centuries of the modern era wars were so frequent by sea and land and the policing of the oceans was so undeveloped that piracy flourished. In the seventeenth and eighteenth centuries its two chief centres were the Caribbean Sea and the Indian Ocean. In both centres it was connected with the generally accepted belief in the existence of great wealth in the hands of a power which was not strong enough to guard it. In the one case this power was Spain, in the other the Mogul Empire. By the beginning of the eighteenth century the Spanish power had begun to decline, while India and its commerce lay open to the spoiler on every side. From the Caribbean, pirates extended their voyages along the North American coasts, while in the Indian Ocean Madagascar became their great place of rendezvous.

During the century and more that followed the reign of Elizabeth the conflict which had then begun with Spain was perpetuated in America largely by privateering and piracy; and these two forms of activity were closely connected, as they both were with smuggling and illegal trade in all its forms. Since Spanish conquerors and colonists had been attracted to the mainland by the wealth of Mexico and Peru, their islands were held by a weak connection. French, Dutch, Danes and English gradually occupied a part of the islands. The Spaniards were quite unable to enforce the law which was intended rigidly to exclude foreigners from trade with her possessions. As Spain was not an industrial state, it was impossible for her directly to supply the demand of

525

her colonists for European goods, and therefore traders from the north of Europe of necessity secured a share in the commerce of her dominions. Lax and corrupt methods of government encouraged freebooters and they made the Spanish treasure fleets their prey. Attacks on them by the English were a leading feature of war at the close of the sixteenth century and this policy was continued on a large scale by the Dutch West India Company in the seventeenth century. With the advent of Cromwell and the Protectorate the spirit of hostility against the Spaniard was revived and of this the conquest of Jamaica was the chief result. That island then became the centre in that region for all naval and military operations in which England was concerned. The slave trade, and the asiento contract under which it was carried on, also gave privileges to the French and afterward to the English.

Among the interlopers who established themselves, as a result of these tendencies, on the islands and coasts of Spanish America, the bucaneers held a prominent place. They were men, crews of wrecked vessels, deserters, marooners and the like, who had originally been attracted to Hispaniola, Jamaica and Porto Rico, and specially to the first of these islands, by the herds of wild cattle and swine found roaming there. These had sprung from the domestic cattle first brought from Europe by the Spaniards, but abandoned in the later sudden rush to the rich silver mines found on the mainland. The cattle were killed in large numbers by the interlopers, their hides sold and their flesh cured by a special process learned from the natives and sold to the crews of vessels which visited the coasts. In this way a large and profitable trade developed, in which many engaged, especially on the north coast of Hispaniola and on Tortuga.[1] *Bucan* was the name given to the apparatus, or the place, for thus curing flesh, and from this originated the name bucaneers. These brutal, often desperate, men developed an organized society and rulers for their calling. Under leaders they made raids on adjacent islands and coasts and added to the number of corsairs, filibusters and pirates with whom the West Indian seas were infested.

[1] Haring, The Buccaneers in the West Indies in the Seventeenth Century, 67 *et seq.*

After the conquest of Jamaica the operations of the bucaneers and of other assailants of the Spaniards were encouraged by some of the English governors and winked at by others.  The inhabitants of the British West Indies very generally favored them, because they brought in supplies of money and plunder in all forms which they had seized from Spanish towns and plantations.  During the reign of Charles II much the same attitude was maintained toward the operations of the bucaneers against the Spanish which Elizabeth had shown toward the exploits of Hawkins and Drake.  This is indicated by the fact that Sir Henry Morgan, the greatest of the leaders of the bucaneers, was for a long time lieutenant governor of Jamaica.  The Spaniards inflicted severe punishments on the English whom they captured, whether in Europe or America, in retaliation for the outrages committed against them in the West Indies.  Much suffering was caused, accompanied by frequent complaints, but these were not followed by a declaration of war.  Even in the midst of this period — in 1670 — the treaty of Madrid was concluded, by which the right of both Spain and England to the territories and colonies which they then possessed in America was mutually recognized.

During the last half of the seventeenth century several notable military exploits were performed by the bucaneers.  They captured Carthagena, Porto Bello and the city of Panama, and won victories in Nicaragua.  These amounted to the waging of war on a considerable scale, and the commander of the bucaneers at this time was Sir Henry Morgan.  In 1670 Sir Thomas Lynch was appointed governor of Jamaica for the purpose of suppressing the bucaneers and stopping their piratical attacks on Spanish territory; but he was also instructed to offer pardon to such as would come in and submit within a reasonable time.  Only a minority, however, availed themselves of this offer, while the sentiments of the people of the British islands were so favorable to privateering and piracy as to make the suppression of the bucaneers impossible.  The Bahama islands soon became a central place of resort for pirates and continued to be such until well into the eighteenth century.  Though they were under English rule, pirates resorted thither with great freedom.  Many commissions for privateering were also issued by the French of Hispaniola, and these were freely extended to protect indiscriminate plunder. The French islands in general harbored many pirates, and there was no essential difference between the attitude of their inhabitants toward the evil and that of the English.

For several years after 1680 Lieutenant Governor Molesworth of Jamaica was very actively engaged against the pirates. His correspondence abounds in details of their operations and of the efforts he made, with the help of the station ships, to hunt them down and bring them to justice.[1] A long list of well known pirates, as Banister, Davies and others, figure in these raids, many of them operating in the southern Atlantic and Pacific oceans, as well as among the islands of the West Indies. They formed more or less permanent settlements near the isthmus of Panama and at times blocked the route to and from the Peruvian mines. Trade under the asiento was made very difficult and at times seemed on the verge of ruin. The pirates also extended their operations northward, and about 1680 appeared in larger numbers than before off the North Atlantic coast.[2] Since in these colonies, as well as in the West Indies, they often found refuge, markets and protection from the inhabitants, in 1684 a royal proclamation was issued against the practice of entertaining them and the governors were ordered to enforce it.[3] At the same time the colonies were ordered to pass the act which was in force in Jamaica against the evil. This provided[4] that any who should help or hold any correspondence whatever with privateers or pirates should be prosecuted as confederates, and that the trials should be held in the admiralty courts under royal commissions, the judge being aided by special commissioners, as was provided for in England by the act 28 Henry VIII. By the Jamaica act military officers were also empowered to levy as many armed men as they thought necessary to aid in the capture of pirates found to be in the neighborhood,

[1] Cal. St. P. Col., 1685–88, index under "privateers."

[2] Cal. St. P. Col., 1681–85, pp. 514, 592, 617, 618. R. I. Col. Recs., III, 494. N. Y. Col. Docs., III, 387, 551, 571, 582. N. C. Recs., I, 348, 354. Hughson, in J. H. U. Studies, XII.

[3] Cal. St. P. Col., *ibid.*, 678, 685.

[4] R. I. Recs., III, 156; N. J. Arch., II, 280.

and persons who forcibly resisted were to be slain. In a few
of the colonies this act was passed, but at best was very
imperfectly executed.[1]

As the evil continued unabated, in 1687 James II commissioned Sir Robert Holmes to go with a squadron to the
West Indies and suppress the outlaws.[2] For the purposes of
this expedition Holmes for the time being superseded the
governors, he confining his activities to pirates who were
English or who at least were serving under English captains.
But the obstacles in the way of success were so many and
great that nothing very decisive was accomplished. Sympathy with pirates in Jamaica and in all the colonies went
far toward paralyzing effort,[3] and Holmes himself even wrote
home asking for power to assure all pirates of their pardon.
Lynch, the agent of Holmes, though offensive in some of
his doings, complained that in Jamaica warrants of arrest
had been issued against him by pirates in jail and he was
imprisoned. The practice also had arisen of bringing accused
pirates to trial before the evidence against them was ready
and using other evasions to secure acquittals. The treaty
of neutrality with France and the close relations then existing
between the two crowns also proved a hindrance in the way
of dealing with French privateers. With the outbreak of
war in 1689 the enterprise of Holmes was definitely ended,
and the need of experienced seamen led to a strong demand
that liberal offers of pardon be extended to pirates who would
surrender themselves and enter the navy  In this way it
was hoped that the evil of piracy would be abated and the
strength of the colonies increased.[4]

Of these pirates, crews with a single vessel, or rarely more,
appeared from time to time off the North American coast.
We hear of them off Carolina or Virginia or Long Island, or
further north on the New England coast. Among them was
Edward Davies and his crew.[5] In a petition of Micajah
Perry in their behalf it was stated that, after committing

---

[1] In imperfect form in New York in 1692. But it was given its original
strength or more in 1699. N. Y. Col. Laws, I, 279, 389.
[2] Cal. St. P. Col., 1685–1688, pp. 361, 377, 453, 488.
[3] *Ibid.*, 562–3, 581, 622.
[4] Cal. St. P. Col., 1689–1692, pp. 203–5, 208.
[5] Cal. St. P. Col., 1689–1692, pp. 12, 19, 77, 346.

some minor offences in the South Seas, they had returned
and in Maryland in 1688 had surrendered, as they supposed
under the terms of the proclamation of pardon, to the captain
of the royal ship " Quaker."  But they afterward went to sea
and were taken by the " Dumbarton " and committed to jail
in Virginia on the charge of piracy.  They petitioned for the
benefit of the amnesty and finally, on giving security, were
released by order of the council of Virginia and allowed to
go to England.  They, however, remained in Virginia until
after the arrival of Nicholson as governor in 1690.  Under
orders from the British government he sent them to England,
and with them depositions tending to show that their doings
in the South Seas had been far more serious and brutal than
had previously been supposed.  It was the opinion of Sir
Robert Holmes, of Lord Howard of Effingham and others,
that they were notorious pirates and ought already to have
been hanged.  Their papers were referred to the treasury and,
in spite of the advice of Holmes, it reported that, as they had
abandoned their ship in the first instance and surrendered
in good faith,[1] though not in full compliance with the forms,
their goods should be restored to them.  Much correspondence
followed, with the usual delays, but in the end, though they
are always called " pirates," the property of Davies and his
crew seems to have been restored, at least in part.[2]

Soon after 1690 complaints began to be urged that privateers
and pirates were committing outrages in the East Indies.
Sir William Beeston, governor of Jamaica, wrote that pirates
who had operated in the east were returning with great
treasures to the northern colonies, where they were permitted
quietly to enjoy their ill-gotten riches.[3]  Encouraged by
pardons which had been granted, seamen were running away
to join these freebooters and vessels were being bought and
fitted out to go on the same design.  Impressment and the rush
for the East Indies were drawing off or frightening away all
the sailors from Jamaica, so that Beeston did not know where
to find enough to man his station ships, unless they were sent
on merchant vessels from England.  All kinds of rogues

[1] *Ibid.*, 390.

[2] *Ibid.*, 431, 512, 521, 579, 610.  Cal. St. P. Col., 1693–96, p. 205.

[3] Cal. St. P. Col., 1693–96, 114, 134–5.

flocked to the pirates who had been pardoned and were fitting out anew. Such was the next phase in the development of piracy, and New York, along with Governor Fletcher, was brought prominently into connection with the movement.

In June, 1695, Peter De la Noy, among the charges which he presented in England against Fletcher, said, " We have a parcel of pirates, called the Red Sea men, in these parts, who get a great booty of Arabian gold. The Governor encourages them, since they make due acknowledgment." [1]  A little later Sir Thomas Lawrence wrote from Maryland, that the year before about sixty pirates came from the Red Sea to New England, New York and Pennsylvania and showed from £1000 to £1500 a man. They often landed first in the Bahamas, or South Carolina, where they left or disposed of their ships, and thence passed northward in several vessels. Others came directly to the northern ports and from those places fitted out again for the Red Sea. Their large shares of plunder tempted colonists and sailors to go along with them, and trade was greatly hindered by the many desertions of men from merchant vessels to go on these ventures. Pirates were becoming so numerous that it was feared they would soon be able to run away with armed ships. Nicholson wrote to much the same effect, and enlarged especially upon the resort of pirates from the Red Sea to Pennsylvania.[2]

According to evidence which was later presented against him in England, Governor Fletcher of New York was at this time granting commissions to persons who were known to be pirates bound for the East Indies, and letters of protection [3] to those who were returning which enabled them to land and dispose of their goods. The bonds also which were given by the recipients of commissions, that they would obey the laws of trade, were not signed by sufficient securities. The pirates with whom Fletcher was reported to have dealings were Coates, Tew, Glover, Hoare and Moston. With Tew in particular Fletcher publicly consorted in New York, so that it became a subject of public comment. In reference to the

---

[1] *Ibid.*, 505, 519.

[2] *Ibid.*, 511.

[3] Letters of protection were legal in the case of privateers, but not in that of pirates.

protection of pirates Fletcher wrote to Bayard that he would make no bargains, but he was ready to receive presents. As a practical instance of this, evidence was given that when Coates returned with his ship to Long Island, £700 was offered for a protection which would enable him to land at New York. An agreement was reached and the cargo was landed and, in lieu of the £700, the ship was given to Fletcher and a sum of money to Nicoll. The ship was sold to Colonel Heathcote for a sum larger than what was offered for the protection. It was also stated that £100 per man was an amount often collected for the issue of protections. Members of the council and Evans, the captain of the station ship " Richmond," were reported to have been involved as well as the governor, but the money and goods which the pirates brought promoted trade and therefore the traffic was connived at and encouraged.[1]

Before the British government had become aware of the doings of Fletcher its attention had been forcibly directed to the subject of piracy by complaints of the East India Company concerning the ravages of pirates in the East, the evils which came from their establishment at Madagascar and the illegal traffic between the East Indies and America through Madagascar as an intermediate station. As the navy was fully employed in the war, none of the king's ships were then available for service against pirates in the east. Hence, in accordance with many early precedents, the idea was suggested of equipping a privateer for that purpose. A prospect of profit — perhaps large — was always likely to be associated with such enterprises. Robert Livingston and William Kidd, both from New York, were then in London. Lord Bellomont was a prime mover in the plan of sending an armed privateer to the East, and Livingston it doubtless was who first suggested Kidd as one who was likely to prove a good captain for such a ship, and that he might pick up his crew in England or America.

In October, 1695, an agreement was drawn between Bellomont, Livingston and Kidd, in which Bellomont agreed to procure from the king or admiralty board one or more commissions for Kidd as a privateer, with express power to act

---

[1] N. Y. Col. Docs., IV, 385, 387, 446, 466, 481; R. I. Recs., III, 341.

against pirates.[1]   Within five months after Kidd's departure from England upon this expedition Bellomont agreed to procure from the king a grant, in the name of some indifferent and trusty person, of the goods and treasure which he should take from pirates.  The agreement also specified the proportions which the parties should respectively bear in the outfit of the vessel and receive from the spoil.  As it had already been decided that Bellomont should be appointed governor of Massachusetts,[2] it was provided that Kidd should carry his prizes direct to Boston without breaking bulk and deliver them into the hands of the governor.  Though the original idea seems to have been that Bellomont should be an investor in this enterprise, this was abandoned and toward the £6000 or thereabouts which the outfit cost he did not contribute a penny.  He procured, instead, from four noblemen, all of whom were high in office, a subscription of all the money which was needed, except what Livingston and Kidd subscribed.  The noblemen were Lord Chancellor Somers, the earl of Orford, who was first lord of the admiralty, Lords Romney and Shrewsbury, who were secretaries of state.  Their names, however, were not allowed to appear in the commission. The vessel which was fitted out for the expedition was named the "Adventure Galley," and some of the pirates against whom Kidd was expected to operate were mentioned, one of them being Tew, the man whom Fletcher had so ostentatiously entertained in New York.

Two commissions were granted to Kidd in the name of the king, one being a letter of marque in ordinary form, empowering him to capture French ships, and the other a special commission authorizing him to seize certain designated pirates.[3] At the time of his arrest Kidd claimed that he had kept a journal of his voyage as required, but that it had been seized along with many of his other effects when a part of his crew deserted him at Madagascar; after his return, however, he wrote up the account again from memory.[4]  In this it was

---

[1] N. Y. Col. Docs., IV, 128–9, 144, 762;  Cal. St. P. Col., 1700, p. 608.

[2] Cal. St. P. Col., 1693–1696, p. 506.

[3] Both are in Howell's State Trials, XIV, 170 *et seq.*, being part of the record of Kidd's trial.

[4] Galton, The True William Kidd, 255 *et seq.*  This is a rather ably written defence of the notorious privateer, though it suffers from the weakness of all special pleas.

stated that at the Nore, when he was starting on his voyage, his crew was pressed for the navy.  This necessitated a delay of three weeks, while he was collecting enough men to take him across the Atlantic.  If this statement be true, it will explain why he departed from his original instructions, by going first to New York and there filling up his crew and sailing from that port in September, 1696, for the east.  Such was the origin of this privateering enterprise, insignificant in itself, but destined to become famous, because of the reputation of the men who were concerned in it and of its tragic ending.  It admirably illustrates the way in which piracy developed and also the methods which in those days were resorted to in combating it.

Kidd's adventures, as well as the agitation of the subject of piracy which was then developing, help to explain the origin of Lord Bellomont's connection with efforts to suppress the evil and the emphasis which was laid upon this line of policy in his appointment as governor of New York, Massachusetts and New Hampshire and in his administration of that office.  It was his zeal and activity which laid bare the dealings of Fletcher with pirates.[1]  Though this did not result in the punishment of the ex-governor, it was doubtless the chief cause which prevented his appointment to any other post.  Throughout his administration the subject of general importance to which Bellomont devoted most of his energies was the suppression of piracy and illegal trade, especially in New York.  He always insisted that the extent to which his activities in this line thwarted the interests and reduced the profits of certain prominent members of the council and their friends, had much to do with the anti-Leislerian opposition to him.  It was Bellomont's seizure of Coates' vessel which brought out the most serious testimony against Fletcher.  All his early moves against Fletcher's friends in the council — who were anti-Leislerians — had as one of their motives the desire to make dealings with pirates and illicit trade impossible in New York.  The passage of the Jamaica act in 1699 was a

---

[1] For a dramatic account of the beginning of this campaign, and especially of proceedings in the executive council, see Ex. C. Min., May 8, 1698, and Bellomont's first letter home on piracy.  N. Y. Col. Docs., IV, 306; Cal. St. P. Col., 1697–1698, pp. 203, 224 *et seq.*

part of this policy. In the correspondence of the time evidence appears of the connection of the Phillips family and of the De Lanceys[1] with pirates who were operating between the East Indies and the North American coast. One Giles Shelley was prominent in this trade, and sloops sent out from the shores of New York and New Jersey met vessels like his, took on board parts of their cargoes and brought them safely into port.

Through the admiralty court and in other ways Bellomont made his influence felt in New Jersey and other colonies. His unfavorable reports, together with those of Randolph, about Rhode Island, directed the attention of the board of trade to that colony.[2] The name of Henry Avery was mentioned in this connection. In 1696 the East India Company reported that he had turned pirate and had plundered several ships in the seas of India and Persia. A royal proclamation for the capture of him and his crew was issued, copies of which were sent, with letters, to the colonial governors in America.[3] In the letters it was stated that several pirates had lately returned from the East Indies and were dispersed through the colonies. The governors were ordered to take all necessary steps for their seizure and the keeping of them and their goods in strict custody until his majesty's pleasure concerning them was signified. Special complaint was made of the conduct of the chartered colonies in this regard and a message of warning was ordered to be sent to their proprietors.

Early in 1697 Bellomont wrote to Rhode Island that, in recent trials of some of Avery's men who had been captured, mention had repeatedly been made of that colony as a place where pirates were too kindly entertained. In Governor Cranston's reply the admission was made that Mace,[4] or Mayes, one of Avery's men, had a clearance from their custom house and a privateer's commission against the French, but they believed that Avery had forced him into piracy. A few days later Randolph reported that Rhode Island had allowed

---

[1] N. Y. Col. Docs., IV, 413, 512, 544 *et seq.*; Cal. St. P. Col., 1699, p. 281.
[2] R. I. Recs., III, 336 *et seq.*
[3] Acts of P. C. Col., II, 300 *et seq.*
[4] Cal. St. P. Col., 1697–1698, pp. 204, 508.

some pirates who landed from Fisher's Island to escape with much treasure to Boston; also that three or four vessels had been fitted out there for the Red Sea and that John Greene, the deputy governor, had granted a commission to one without taking any security whatever.  In reply of the board of trade to Cranston's letter, they desired to see all the commissions for privateering which they had granted during the war and also the bonds given by privateers and all their proceedings relating to the two pirates who had recently been seized.  An important reason for this was that, though recently a commission to be judge of admiralty had been sent to Peleg Sanford, Governor Clarke had refused to administer to him the oath of office on the ground that the establishment of an admiralty court was an infringement of the colony charter. As no admiralty court legally existed in Rhode Island, doubt was thrown on all proceedings against pirates or concerning violations of the acts of trade.  The governors of Rhode Island also had not taken the oath to obey the acts of trade.

Without waiting for a reply to these demands the board of trade reported the facts to the crown and recommended that a commission of inquiry be issued to Lord Bellomont empowering him to examine persons on the place or elsewhere and report preparatory to *quo warranto,* or other proceedings, for the removal of the evils complained of.[1]  The commission was sent, with a list of interrogations.  In September, 1699, Bellomont, as we have seen in another connection, visited Rhode Island, met the council at Governor Cranston's house in several sessions and examined leading men, in office and out, concerning the affairs of the colony.  His report was confirmatory of the views of the board.  In the letter which Cranston sent in reply to the above communication from the board the admission was made that the commissions for privateering, from which the acts of piracy originated, had been granted by the deputy governor contrary to the judgment of the governor, and that bonds had not been taken because they were not aware of the precautions required in such cases.  The reply of the board to this was, that so ignorant a person should not have been put into such an office and that the colony was expected thoroughly to reform these abuses or

[1] *Ibid.,* 582.

they would be made sensible of their miscarriages when it was too late.[1] And yet no positive action was taken by Rhode Island, or by the home government, with a view to the punishment of that particular colony or its officials.

Delaware Bay and its neighborhood was another natural resort of pirates, there being no adequate provision for its defence and affording, as it did, convenient access to New York and Philadelphia. In 1697 Jeremiah Basse, of New Jersey, stated to the board of trade many details about the doings of pirates in that region and throughout the middle colonies.[2] The conduct of Governor Markham of Pennsylvania then became the subject of conflicting representations from Quary and Robert Snead on the one side and Penn and the governor himself on the other. Snead had recently removed from Jamaica to Pennsylvania and had been made a magistrate there. He was active in efforts to detect and arrest pirates who were living in Philadelphia. Certain members of Avery's crew, against whom the lords justices had issued a proclamation, were the chief objects of his search. One of them is said to have married the daughter of Governor Markham, and others were on friendly terms with the governor and other leading Philadelphians. Markham admitted that they had been civil to him, but they brought in money, he said, which was an advantage to the country. Snead's persistence and plain speech occasioned some sharp passages between him and the governor, and he found it impossible to effect unaided the arrest of the pirates. Governor Nicholson, who at the time was in Maryland, actively cooperated against Markham and the Quakers. On one occasion he even sent a body of men from Maryland into the Lower Counties in pursuit of an alleged pirate named Day, though Quary alleged that this all originated in a mistake. In the fall of 1698 several vessels were captured by pirates near the mouth of Delaware Bay, and a body of the marauders plundered the town of Lewes. The justices of Sussex county appealed to the governor and council for aid, but nothing was done.

All of these facts found their way before the board of trade and Penn was called up from Bristol to meet the charges

[1] R. I. Recs., III, pp. 339, 341, 351, 363, 374, 376, 385, 389.
[2] Cal. St. P. Col., 1696–1697, pp. 557, 561, 563, 568, 573.

and state what could be done. The delays of the board kept
him waiting till he expressed his impatience in a forcible letter
to Secretary Popple. When at last he attended, several depositions were read to him, to which he made some exceptions,
but said that he was ready to remove Markham if required.[1]
On August 4, 1699, the board, in a report to the lords justices,
summarized the charges against Markham and the attitude
of Pennsylvania generally, not only toward pirates but toward
the admiralty court and in the matter of illegal trade. In
reference to the entertainment of pirates it confirmed the
statements made by Snead and Quary and insisted that
Markham should be removed, and also David Lloyd from the
office of attorney general and Anthony Morris from the commission of the peace. A few days later, summing up further
testimony from letters of Bellomont, Basse and Quary, the
board urged that all pirates seized in Pennsylvania and West
Jersey be sent to England for trial. The lords justices accordingly ordered that all these matters be effectively urged upon
Penn and that pirates and their effects taken not only in
Pennsylvania and the two Jerseys be sent to England, but
from the New England colonies and New York as well.[2] The
return of Penn at this time to his province had the effect of
superseding Markham and of strengthening the attitude of
that province somewhat against all the evils with which it
was charged. Markham made several statements to show
that the complaints of his opponents had been exaggerated.
In December, 1699, Penn invited Quary to the council and
told him it was their intention to discourage and punish piracy
and illegal trade by all lawful means. He asked Quary's
advice as to ways and means, that officials of the province
and the crown might cooperate harmoniously. Quary replied
that that required thought and after consideration he would
propose what seemed most effectual. No entry in the records
shows that this was done. Complaints did not cease nor
apparently did the spirit of cooperation greatly develop. The
assembly of January, 1700, was called because of letters from

---

[1] Cal. St. P. Col., 1696–1697, pp. 613, 615, 616, 623, 636; *ibid.*, 1697–1698,
pp. 6, 17, 43–51, 181, 212, 444; N. Y. Col. Docs., IV, 378; Pa. Col. Recs., I,
539 *et seq.*

[2] Cal. St. P. Col., 1699, pp. 382, 387, 418.

the authorities in England, and in May it passed an act against pirates and one against frauds and abuses in trade.[1]

Penn, in writing very frankly both to Secretary Vernon and the board of trade about this assembly and the general situation, said: " I leave to those who have been so elaborate and elegant in representing the weakness of the Province of Pennsylvania to give you an account of mine since my arrival; who, if they will do me justice, will have less to say to my disadvantage." He spoke of his promptness in calling an assembly and its diligence in meeting at an unusual season and passing the laws referred to above; also to an address which they presented to him in which they expressed their abhorrence of pirates and denied that the inhabitants in general were concerned in illegal trade. " I shall say little in favour of our good intentions," wrote the proprietor, " and less of our abilities in composing of these laws, but I hope they may pass for an essay of our zeal and care to suppress and prevent those evil practices we have been taxed with." At that time Penn held two pirates as prisoners, one of whom had been connected with Kidd and the other with Avery, whom he was about to send to England for trial. Markham also sent to the board of trade a long letter in defence of himself.[2] In reference to pirates he declared that he had caused the arrest of all who to his knowledge had come into the province since he became its governor. It may help to reconcile this statement with the essential truth in the statements of his critics to quote also Penn's words concerning Markham, that " he is very weak and at best but a cripple and prisoner to the gout." Penn had earlier disclaimed full responsibility for the appointment of him, stating that out of submission to the wishes of Queen Mary he had continued him in the office in which he found him at the close of Fletcher's administration of the province.[3] The thriftiness of Penn is also shown in his correspondence at this time with the secretary of state, he insisting upon his right as lord of the soil to a share of the pirates' treasure which had been

[1] Pa. Col. Recs., I, 566, 574, 594.

[2] Cal. St. P. Col., 1700, pp. 83, 85, 101.

[3] In his earlier years Markham had served long and faithfully in the British army.

found in Pennsylvania. " I confess I think my interest in
these cases ought not wholly to be overlooked, who as Lord
of the Soil, erected into a Seigneury, must needs have a
royalty, and share in such seizures, else I am in much meaner
circumstances than many Lords of Manors upon the sea-
coasts of England, Ireland and Scotland. I think my grant
very much superior and quite of another nature and privilege.
And considering the province is equally beneficial to the crown
as if it were under a temporary Governor appointed by the
King, and that the King is at no charge to maintain one, it
looks with some hardship that casual profits and advantages
should not be allowed me.[1] . . . I do not write this to dispute
any right with the King, resolving to obey his commands and
submit myself to his further consideration." No utterance
of the period expresses better than this the feudal spirit which
lay obscured in the proprietorship, and it is noteworthy that
the Quaker proprietor should have voiced it so well, especially
at a time when, owing to his gross carelessness in other directions, he was becoming hopelessly involved in debt.

In June, 1699, Kidd reappeared off the coast of Long Island,
having been absent on his eastern cruise about two years.
As the story of his doings gradually became known the futility
of sending out a petty privateering craft like his to contend
against a foe so formidable, and yet elusive, as the pirates of
the Indian Ocean became fully evident. On his way out,
near the Cape of Good Hope, he had fallen in with Captain
Thomas Warren, who was returning with a convoy of East
Indiamen,[2] and then Kidd incurred the suspicion of intended
piracy. From such evidence as is at hand it would not be
safe to affirm that Kidd was guilty of more than a very few
minor offences against neutral craft. The two large vessels
which he captured, he affirmed, were sailing under French
passes and therefore were prizes covered by his letter of
marque. So far as he was guilty of offences against the law of
nations, he may have been forced into them by the clamor of
his crew. The act of assault by which he killed one of his men
would hardly be accounted more serious than manslaughter.
But in the reports of piracies which for months had been com-

---

[1] *Ibid.*, 83.
[2] Cal. St. P. Col., 1697–1698, p. 364.

ing in from the east, Kidd's name had frequently appeared with the rest, so that he and his crew, on the complaint of the East India Company, had been proclaimed pirates and a general search for them had been ordered. The order for their arrest, if found, was sent to Lord Bellomont, along with the other governors. When Kidd returned to the West Indies in a ship other than the one in which he had sailed and also having on board a considerable treasure, it was certain what the general inference would be.

Lord Bellomont was now in the midst of his campaign against pirates, and others whom he had denounced, if not arrested, had come in under circumstances much like those of Kidd. His vessel, the " Quetta Merchant," [1] Kidd had left in the West Indies and had come north in a sloop, hoping to make his peace with the authorities, and then bring the ship into some North American port and dispose of her cargo. But instead of receiving protection from his original employer — who was now in Boston — he was rigorously examined by both the governor and the council and was said to have involved himself in many contradictions and lies. His arrest followed and in due time his transportation to England [2] for trial. Among his papers, which were seized at the time of his arrest, were said to have been the French passes of the two vessels which he had captured in the East, in one of which he had returned to the West Indies. His papers were all sent to the British admiralty, but when, at his trial, at the Old Bailey, Kidd repeatedly asked that they be produced as the evidence which was absolutely essential to his case, he met with no response. The judge in his charge to the jury referred to the passes and stated that, if the vessels had really been prizes, they should have been treated by Kidd as such and brought to trial, but he had done nothing of the kind. He had suffered the deserters among his crew to take possession of one and had treated the other just as a pirate would have done his plunder.[3] When Kidd was tried for piracy he had already been convicted of murder, and that for an offence

---

[1] This spelling is given in Marsden, Law and Custom of the Sea, II.

[2] Cal. St. P. Col., 1699, pp. 274, 280, 366 *et seq.*, 566.

[3] Howell, State Trials, XIV. Galton, The True Captain Kidd, where an analysis of the proceedings at the trial is given.

which was probably only manslaughter. And in either case, so great was the prejudice against all who were situated as this man was, and so weighted against the accused was the judicial procedure of the time in England that, as to the essential justice of the result that was reached, judgment may be suspended.

The Tories sought to make political capital out of the Kidd affair, by charging that those who subscribed to the equipment of the " Adventure " had fitted out a notorious pirate. Lord Somers, because of his prominence among the Whigs and of the fact that he was not only a subscriber but had affixed the great seal to Kidd's commission, had to bear the brunt of this attack. A resolution that the letters patent were dishonorable to the king, inconsistent with the law of nations, contrary to the statutes of the realm and destructive of property and trade, was debated at length and with great heat in the house of commons, but was defeated by a substantial majority.[1]

By the close of 1697 complaints from the East India Company of outrages committed by pirates, and consequent losses inflicted upon their trade, had become so serious that the government was forced to consider action of some kind. Natives of India and other countries were also suffering and were apt to charge that the Company were in league with the pirates and shared their spoil. Interlopers, who were trying to break down the monopoly of the East India Company, were said to be associated with the pirates, and that there was danger that the towns and coast districts of India would be plundered. In view of the general insecurity the Company was put to heavy outlays for convoys. In the rapidly accumulating mass of testimony a prominent place was held by statements which tended to show that many of the pirates were fitted out in the North American colonies, and particularly in New York.[2]

Early in 1698 the board of trade recommended to Secretary Vernon that a squadron of three vessels be sent to the east, one half the cost of the expedition to be met by the East India Company.[3] It was also in view of their respon-

[1] Macaulay, Hist. of Eng. V.
[2] Cal. St. P. Col., 1697–1698, pp. 68, 97–98, 106, 109.    [3] *Ibid.*, 88, 121.

sibility in part for piracy in the East Indies that the board was so insistent that the chartered colonies should present their governors for approval and give security, as required by law, and urged that unless they conformed in this regard there should be another appeal to parliament. The passage of the Jamaica act by all the colonies was also recommended, and an order to this effect was issued. On February 28, Secretary Vernon wrote that the king had ordered the admiralty to designate two fourth rates and a sixth rate to go to the East Indies against pirates. After correspondence with the officials of the East India Company, the course to be followed by the expedition, the furnishing of equipment and supplies was arranged.[1] Captain Thomas Warren, who had lately returned from the east, was designated as its commander. A delay of several months then followed, during which it was decided to send three commissioners with the squadron, whose duty among other things it should be to publish a royal proclamation, stating that it was the object of the expedition to extirpate the pirates in those seas unless they immediately surrendered, and to call upon them to surrender, in which case they should receive pardon for piracies committed before they received notice of the proclamation.[2] Any pirates who would not submit must be pursued and destroyed, along with their forts and places of refuge. Among the names of those designated as commissioners, besides the name of Warren, the commander, appears that of Peter De la Noy, formerly of New York. The expedition apparently did not sail until near the close of 1698.

Piracy had now become a question of such moment that special attention had to be given to the law and procedure which bore on the subject. Piracy was felony only by the civil law,[3] which was administered in the admiralty courts. But its rules of procedure, which required that no one should be condemned to death unless he confessed or was convicted by witnesses who saw him commit the crime, had occasioned the escape from punishment of so many offenders that the

---

[1] *Ibid.*, 122, 126, 139, 148, 160, 342, 445, 472, 474.

[2] *Ibid.*, 411, 416, 445, 454, 470, 473.

[3] Opinion of West, in Chalmers, Colonial Opinions, 511; Marsden, Law and Custom of the Sea, II, 252.

act of 28 Henry VIII, c. 15, had been passed, which provided
that piracies should be tried within the counties of England
before commissioners specially named for the purpose, as if
the offence had been committed on land.  Though the commissioners acted under the direct authority of the admiralty,
common law procedure was used.  In this way convictions
were secured, but it was necessary in all cases that the accused should be sent to England for trial, and also all the
evidence which bore upon the cases.  This, in most instances,
was very difficult if not impossible, and led to the general
ignoring of the law and the holding of trials from time to
time in the colonies.

It was in order to remove the necessity of sending persons
who were guilty of piracy or other felonies beyond the seas
home for trial that parliament, early in 1700, passed the act
11 & 12 William III, c. 7.  It provided that piracy, or any
other offences mentioned in the law, when committed on the
sea or where the admiral had jurisdiction, might be tried by
a commission appointed under the great seal or the seal of
the British admiralty and directed to admirals, commanders
of royal ships of war or other persons designated by name
in the colonies.  These commissioners, or a quorum of seven
from among themselves or of persons designated by them,
were authorized to constitute a court of admiralty for the
purpose in any plantation.  Of the members of this court,
other than the royal commissioners, the governor, lieutenant
governor or a member of the council or the commander of
one of the royal ships of war must always be one, and none
should be summoned as members who were not known merchants, factors or planters or designated officers on a ship
of the royal navy or some English ship.  A court so constituted should have full power to try, determine and award
execution in any case of piracy or felony, according to the
civil law and the rules of the admiralty and the penalties
should be the same as if the accused had been convicted under
the statute of Henry VIII.  The act was to be fully in force
in the chartered colonies, as well as in the royal provinces,
and if the governors or any who were in authority in such
should refuse to yield obedience to it, such refusal should
be deemed to work the forfeiture of the charter of the colony

in question. This, taken in connection with the other act of parliament, 11 & 12 William III, c. 12, passed the same session, which provided that governors of any colony should be liable to punishment in England for offences against the laws of the realm, may be regarded as having notably strengthened the legal hold of the crown over the chartered colonies.[1] The weak point in the measure was the clause which left trials of those who aided or concealed pirates, or were accessories to piracy, to be held in England under the authority of the act of Henry VIII. Thus a most common offence in this connection was left under the previous difficult and ineffective provision as to place of trial. The act was to be in force for seven years and was made permanent by 6 Geo. I, c. 19.

The usual delays occurred in the drafting of commissions under the new law and none were sent to the American colonies until 1701. Then one George Larkin was appointed to carry over the commissions and, in connection with the governors to whom they were directed, " to settle such rules and forms of proceedings " as ought to be observed in the courts before which pirates were to be tried.[2] Several letters of Larkin have been preserved which contain his observations on conditions as he viewed them while journeying through the colonies from Newfoundland to Virginia, and also on his later experiences in Bermuda.[3] They show that his prejudices against the colonists were as extreme as those of Randolph, while his character and abilities were apparently inferior to those of the surveyor general. From Newfoundland he was able to throw light on the direct trade which the fishermen from New England kept up there with the French and also how, partly by the lure of rum, British seamen there were continually being drawn away into the New England service. When he came to New England he found nothing to approve and everything to criticise, from its courts and means of defence to Harvard College. Like Randolph, he evidently listened only to the disgruntled, and therefore reported that the New Englanders abhorred the very thought of the laws of

[1] Cal. St. P. Col., 1700, p. 350.
[2] Cal. St. P. Col., 1701, pp. 157, 165, 170, 430, 576, 568, 672, 719.
[3] *Ibid.*, 1701, pp. 430, 576, 658, 692.

England and that the only way to deal with them was for parliament to take away their charters and send judges from England. Nearly all merchants were engaged in illegal trade and the courts encouraged them in it, while the admiralty jurisdiction was not in half the esteem there which the least court baron was in England. Most of the people of Rhode Island and Connecticut, he stated, were wholly devoted to the manufacture of woolens and evaded the recent law by driving their sheep across the colonial boundaries, where they were shorn and then driven home again, leaving their fleeces behind them. In the colonies generally, especially those with charters, he found pirates entertained and caressed, even by the church people, and no money but Arabian gold was to be seen. In Pennsylvania Larkin found everybody avoiding him and glad to see him preparing to be gone. The recall of all the charters seemed to him the only remedy for conditions, as they were represented to him during the brief visits which he made. In Virginia he found the governor absent, and by that time Larkin had evidently become aware that the information he was getting about plantation affairs was not worth much, for he was not able to remain long enough, and he found very few, though they were old residents, who could give a tolerable account of public affairs. When, finally, Larkin reached Bermuda, he became involved in a bitter quarrel with the governor and others, was charged with scandalous conduct and imprisoned, and so his mission came to an inglorious end.[1]

After the treaty of Utrecht the island of Providence, in the Bahamas, became a notorious resort of pirates. By 1718 more than two thousand were estimated to be gathered there. Among them Charles Vane and Edward Thatch, or Teach, were leaders. They were made up of men who had been active as privateers or pirates during the previous war and who now refused to recognize the peace. They continued to prey upon the Spaniards, who in their turn attacked the English logwood cutters in the bays of Campeche and Honduras.[2] None of the adjacent coasts and no nationality was safe from the attacks of the pirates, and there was a revival of this evil

[1] *Ibid.*, p. 154 *et seq.*
[2] Charles Johnson, History of the Pyrates.

in the west similar to that which had occurred before the
outbreak of the colonial wars.  The East Indies, however,
do not figure so prominently at this time as they did at
earlier dates.  But the shores of North America, especially
those of the Carolinas, were subject to more serious
visitations.

The concentration of the pirates in the Bahama Islands
was made possible by the failure of their proprietors to develop a stable government there.  In the absence of any
force to resist them, and the islands lying, as they did, adjacent to the Florida Passage and convenient for operations to
the northward or southward, the pirates took possession and
became a peril to all American commerce.  In 1718 the situation was taken in hand by Captain Woodes Rogers, who had
rented the islands from the proprietors for 21 years.  Rogers
had recently returned from a successful circumnavigation of
the globe and was a man of great decision and experience.
A royal commission was now given him to be governor of
the island of Providence, and two men of war were ordered to
attend him.  The guard ships of all the continental, as well
as the island, colonies were commanded to join in the suppression of the pirates.  A royal proclamation was sent in
advance, offering pardon to those who would promptly surrender, but none took advantage of it.  Rogers in the end
received no aid from the royal frigates, but, with his own
privateersmen and some aid from the inhabitants of Nassau,
partially subdued or dispersed the pirates and hanged several
of them.  At the same time he had to bear up against threats
of attack by the Spanish, on the ground that he had no right
to the islands.  In the end, though it took some years, Rogers
triumphed, and an orderly government was established in the
islands.

It was during the revival of piracy that hundreds of craft
of that kind frequented the American coast as far north as
Newfoundland.  The Carolinas suffered most, not only because
they lay adjacent to the centre of the evil, but because their
governments — especially that of North Carolina — were
weak and disturbed and their coast line was extensive and
offered many safe places of retreat.  Thatch and Stede Bonnet,
with their crews, were two leading pirates who operated

in those waters and there met their fate.[1]   Thatch terrorized Charlestown, South Carolina, for a time, but he made the coast of the northern province near Ocracoke inlet, his chief place of resort.   To that long stretch of uninhabited coast he could bring his prizes, there he could lie and refit and thence he could sail with a minimum of peril.   He found the people and officials of North Carolina ready to profit by his calling, and to permit himself and his men to live openly among them.   The government, just recovering from civil strife and the struggle with the Tuscaroras, was too weak to expel the pirates, even if it had so desired.   On his voyages north Thatch was sometimes kindly received at Philadelphia.

The last exploit of Thatch, after he had once made surrender, was the capture and entry of a French vessel, with its cargo of sugar and merchandise, as a prize, and its acceptance as such by Tobias Knight, secretary and collector, sitting as judge of vice admiralty in North Carolina.   Thatch and his men made affidavit that they had found this vessel abandoned at sea, and even so incredible a statement as this was accepted by the court.   But the pirates themselves did not dare to let the vessel remain as the evidence of their villainy, and after her cargo had been removed they burned her.   This event was noised abroad and, added to other evidence that the authorities were conniving at piracy, roused Governor Spotswood of Virginia to action.   A reward for the arrest of Thatch had already been offered, but it had resulted in nothing, and Spotswood now resolved to send an expedition, though it was to the coast of another colony, and destroy the pirate crew.   In November, 1718, two sloops were secretly fitted out and filled with armed men under Captain Brend and Lieutenant Maynard of the station ships which were then at Hampton Roads.   This force surprised Thatch and his men near Ocracoke Inlet, and in a brief but desperate engagement totally defeated them.   Thatch and more than half of his crew were killed; the survivors were taken to Virginia and hanged.   The loss on the side of the Virginians was 12 men [2] killed and 22 wounded.   Goods also, to the value of more than

---

[1] Hughson, The Carolina Pirates, J. H. U. Studies, XII.   Also Johnson, op. cit., and N. C. Recs., II.

[2] N. C. Col. Recs. II, 318, 325 et seq., 334–340.

£2000, were seized and condemned in the vice admiralty court of Virginia and sold. Some controversy followed over the right of Spotswood to proceed as he did in another province, without showing an express commission therefor from the king. A plea was also entered against the jurisdiction of the admiralty court of Virginia, and it was said that the seizure of the goods amounted to a trespass on the lands of the proprietors. This caused Spotswood to state fully his view of the case to the board of trade and to Lord Carteret, and this prevented appeal or agitation of the subject in England. Tobias Knight and Governor Eden also found themselves sufficiently occupied in meeting the charge of protecting pirates and profiting by regular dealings with them, a charge which came home with crushing weight against Knight.

While the coast of North Carolina was being cleared by a force from Virginia, the people of Charlestown and vicinity were engaged in an even more determined conflict with Stede Bonnet and his men. Bonnet, during his early and middle life, had been a respected inhabitant of Barbadoes, and then, though without special knowledge of seamanship, had " gone a-pyrating." Being a man of property, he procured a vessel and manned it with a crew and started for the capes of Virginia and the adjacent coasts. During much of 1717 and 1718 Bonnet cruised along the coast from South Carolina to New England, capturing many vessels and inflicting much damage on commerce. For a time he was associated with Thatch, but as that pirate, who was an experienced seaman, deposed Bonnet from the command of his vessel, the two separated and, if they had met later, would probably have fought to the finish.

In September, 1718, while Bonnet was lying near the mouth of the Cape Fear river, an expedition was fitted out against him from South Carolina. Like the Virginia force, it consisted of two colony sloops, carrying a few small guns and 130 armed men. The commander was Colonel William Rhett, the receiver general and, as the result was to prove, a determined fighter. On this occasion the pirates were not taken so completely by surprise as were Thatch's men. The contest therefore was longer and for a time was indecisive. It was also quite as fierce and bloody as that in which the Virginians were engaged. In the end the pirates were worsted and the survivors surrendered. Bonnet and more than thirty men were taken to Charlestown. The assembly, which was in session, passed a special act for the trial of pirates and preparation was made for a session of the admiralty court for the purpose. But so great was the sympathy of some with these men, that Bonnet and one other were permitted to escape. But they only reached Sullivan's island, when Rhett and his men, who were sent in pursuit, forced Bonnet to surrender and shot his companion. Meantime the survivors, except Bonnet and his companion, were tried before a special commission of the admiralty in accordance with the statute of 1701 and the recent colony act, Chief Justice Trott presiding. They were condemned and duly executed. Bonnet, who by this time was reduced to a state of abject fear, was then tried and executed, though he attempted at the last moment to avert his fate by a pathetic appeal to Governor Johnson. After these events piracy abated and never again seriously disturbed the North American coast.

An account of piracy in modern times, even though it be limited to its effects upon the American colonies, would be incomplete without some reference to the Barbary pirates.[1] Their operations were a consequence, in the first place, of the expulsion of the Moors from Spain and later of the operations of Turkish admirals in the Mediterranean, followed, after the defeat of the Turkish navy at Lepanto, by the ravages of small bodies of corsairs who operated chiefly under the Dey and Divan of Algiers and to a large extent independently of the Sultan at Constantinople. Tunis and Tripoli occupied similar positions, so far as the eastern Mediterranean was concerned, though they were not so aggressive. From the latter part of the sixteenth century until the nineteenth these bold sea raiders infested the Mediterranean and the eastern Atlantic, from the English Channel on the north to the Western Islands and the sea routes of the Spanish galleons on the south. They insolently defied every European power, and were able to do this for centuries because of the perpetual rivalries and conflicts by which those powers were

[1] See Playfair, The Scourge of Christendom; Stanley Lane-Poole, Story of the Barbary Corsairs, and the literature referred to by the latter.

divided, at sea and in trade as well as on land and by arms. It was no uncommon thing for even the foremost European powers to encourage the operations of the corsairs against their enemies, in some cases even to employ them for such purposes. This enabled a few thousand freebooters, of the most brutal and faithless type and possessed of a ridiculously weak naval force, for centuries to defy Christendom, while they murdered and plundered and enslaved on all the adjacent seas. No merchantman, though armed, was safe on the Mediterranean or on the seas adjacent to southern Europe or Western Africa. When vessels without convoy started southward or westward from any British or Irish port they always ran the risk of capture by pirates from Algiers. In such cases all on board were usually held as slaves and subjected to the hardest labor and most cruel treatment. This was a chief source of Christian slavery. Raids also were occasionally made on land and booty and slaves increased in this way.

Trade and navigation to and from the American colonies were of course subject to the usual perils from this source. During the period of the Restoration references to it begin to multiply. The two best known instances of residents of the continental colonies who were captured by the Algerines and who for a time experienced their tender treatment were William Harris, of Providence, Rhode Island, and Seth Sothell, the proprietor-governor of Carolina. Since the beginning of the seventeenth century the English government, in the ineffective way characteristic of the time and especially of the Stuarts, had been trying to check the operations of the Barbary corsairs and to rescue enslaved subjects. Many expeditions were sent either for the purpose of negotiation or to punish the offenders. Consuls were sent to Algiers. A long succession of treaties was concluded. Occasionally the exhibition of power was such as to intimidate the pirates for a time. But the effect was only temporary. Treaties were renewed only to be broken after brief intervals, the radical mistake being that this nest of pirates was recognized and dealt with as a state.

As early as 1662 provision was made in a treaty with Algiers [1] that English ships, either furnished with admiralty

---

[1] About the same time treaties were concluded with Tunis and Tripoli.

passes or the major part of whose crew was English, should not be molested. A few years later evidence begins to appear that colonial merchants were demanding such passes as a protection, and a specification concerning them seems to have been included in a treaty of 1682.[1]   Early in 1698 orders were issued that passes should be granted for all ships that were on trading voyages or were remaining in any of the plantations, and that they should be used for ships built in the plantations as well as for those which were built in Scotland or Ireland.   Delay, however, followed in furnishing officials in the colonies with passes, and during 1699 and 1700 there was considerable discussion of the subject, both among the official boards in England and with the Dey of Algiers. The board of trade finally proposed that blank passes to be filled out should be entrusted only to such governors as were appointed or allowed by his majesty and had duly qualified according to the trade act of 1696.[2]   At the suggestion of the admiralty, on May 30, 1700, an order of council was issued requiring that owners and masters of all ships trading between Great Britain or Ireland and the plantations, or between one plantation and another, should take out passes for their security.   Elaborate regulations were proposed by the board of trade for the distribution of these passes, the collectors of customs to have charge of them in chartered colonies which did not have properly qualified governors.   In order to secure adequate time for distributing the passes, the Dey was induced to postpone for a year the date when his commanders at sea would begin to demand that they should be shown as a protection against seizure.   On the accession of George I a proclamation was issued continuing the arrangement.[3]   It was under this humiliating condition, not to mention many others which were inflicted on consuls and others, and all notwithstanding the British fleet, that trade was carried on throughout the century.

[1] Cal. St. P. Col., 1700, p. 355. Acts P. C. Col., II, 318.
[2] See entries in Cal. St. P. Col., 1699 and 1700; especially 1700, pp. 295, 298 and 664.
[3] Acts of P. C. Col., II, 682.